BAKER's Biographical Dictionary of
POPULAR MUSICIANS SINCE 1990

BAKER's Biographical Dictionary *of*
POPULAR MUSICIANS SINCE 1990

INTRODUCTION BY
David Freeland

SCHIRMER
REFERENCE ™

THOMSON
™
GALE

New York • Detroit • San Diego • San Francisco • Cleveland • New Haven, Conn. • Waterville, Maine • London • Munich

Baker's Biographical Dictionary of Popular Musicians Since 1990

This compilation copyright © 2004 by Schirmer Reference, an imprint of the Gale Group, a division of Thomson Learning, Inc.

Gale and Design™ and Thomson Learning™ are trademarks used herein under license.

For more information, contact
Schirmer Reference
300 Park Avenue South
New York, NY 10010
Or visit our Internet site at
http://www.gale.com/schirmer

For permission to use material from this product, submit your request via Web at http://www.gale-edit.com/permissions, or you may download our Permissions Request form and submit your request by fax or mail to:

Permissions Department
The Gale Group, Inc.
27500 Drake Rd.
Farmington Hills, MI 48331-3535

Permissions Hotline:
248–699–8006 or 800–762–4058

LIBRARY OF CONGRESS CATALOGING-IN-PUBLICATION DATA

Baker's biographical dictionary of popular musicians since 1990.
    p. cm.
    Includes bibliographical references, discographies, and indexes.
    ISBN 0-02-865799-3 (set : alk. paper) -- ISBN 0-02-865800-0 (v. 1) -- ISBN 0-02-865801-9 (v. 2)
    1. Popular music--Bio-bibliography--Dictionaries. 2. Musicians--Biography--Dictionaries.
ML102.P66 B35 2003
781.64'092'2--dc21

2003013956

Printed in the United States of America
10 9 8 7 6 5 4 3 2

Contents

M.C. HAMMER

Born: Stanley Kirk Burrell; Oakland, California, 30 March 1962

Genre: Hip-Hop

Best-selling album since 1990: *Please Hammer, Don't Hurt 'Em* (1990)

Hit songs since 1990: "U Can't Touch This," "Pray," "2 Legit 2 Quit"

M.C. Hammer is one of the most divisive figures in the history of hip-hop. The quantum leap the Oakland, California, native took from regional sensation to global superstar was a reflection of mainstream pop music's embrace of hip-hop. His major label debut, *Let's Get It Started* (1988), went double platinum thanks to his club-friendly funk samples, amicable raps, and sing-along choruses, but it was only the beginning of his career. Released two years later, the crossover hit *Please Hammer, Don't Hurt 'Em* (1990) sold 10 million copies, earned the singer two Grammy Awards (Best R&B Song, Best Solo Rap Performance), and charted three Top 10 singles. Unfortunately, it also won him the ire of his fellow rappers, many of whom accused Hammer of diluting hip-hop's hardcore aesthetic in favor of a softer, clownish style. Within two years, pop's changing winds—as well as the singer's financial mismanagement—had dethroned the once-ubiquitous rapper. Far from celebrated, Hammer's stint in the spotlight was as brief as his signature parachute pants were wide.

Stanley Kirk Burrell owes both his nickname and sense of enterprise to an after-school job as batboy for the Oakland Athletics. The team nicknamed the teen "Hammer" after his resemblance to all-time home-run leader "Hammerin'" Hank Aaron. More importantly, he won the affections of the team's flamboyant owner, Charles Finley, who taught the young Burrell the value of showmanship and hard work. Dedicating himself to hip-hop, the diligent Hammer recorded his debut, *Feel My Power (Bust It)* (1987), and spent the year driving throughout California promoting it himself. Hammer's diligence paid off. He signed with Capitol Records and his first release with the label, *Let's Get It Started*, went double platinum, thanks largely to its polished funk vibe and Parliament-sampling dance hit, "Turn This Mutha Out."

Hammer's second album for Capitol exceeded all possible expectations. Its lead single, "U Can't Touch This," may have borrowed wholesale from Rick James's funk hit "Super Freak" (1981), but its catchy chorus and a flashy video featuring Hammer's soon-famous parachute pants made him a national sensation. It would have been the first hip-hop single to top the charts but it was only released as a 12-inch single. His next two singles, "Pray" and "Have You Seen Her," also charted well and pushed his sales to heights previously unthinkable for a hip-hop album. Hammer capitalized on his icon status with endless commercial endorsements, a line of dolls, and a cartoon. Hip-hop purists like 3rd Bass attacked Hammer for his biteless raps, flashy costumes, and glossy excess.

Though Hammer's next album, *Too Legit to Quit* (1991), sold 3 million copies, his moment was over and the album's tour was cancelled halfway through when it failed to recoup the costs of its extravagant stage show.

He had by this time dropped the "M.C." from his name, referring to himself as Hammer; he would reattach the "M.C." to his name with the release of *V Inside Out* (1995). His last notable hit was "Addams Groove" (1991) off the *The Addams Family* soundtrack, but poor accounting, lavish living, and Hammer's good-hearted attempt to hire many of his neighborhood friends as dancers had done him in. Financially struggling, Hammer retired for three years before reemerging with the harder-edged and surprisingly aggressive *The Funky Headhunter* (1994). The hardcore act was unsuccessful, though Hammer was courted out of novelty by gangsta rap label Death Row. In 1996 Hammer declared bankruptcy and renounced luxury in favor of the hyper-positive, spiritually driven approach found on later albums *Family Affair* (1998) and the patriotic *Active Duty* (2001).

SELECTIVE DISCOGRAPHY: *Feel My Power (Bust It)* (Bustin', 1987); *Let's Get It Started* (Capitol, 1988); *Please Hammer, Don't Hurt 'Em* (Capitol, 1990); *Too Legit to Quit* (Capitol/EMI, 1991); *The Funky Headhunter* (Giant, 1994); *V Inside Out* (Giant, 1995); *Family Affair* (Oaktown 3.5.7., 1998); *Active Duty* (World Hit, 2001). **Soundtrack:** *The Addams Family* (Capitol, 1991).

HUA HSU

YO-YO MA

Born: Paris, France, 7 October 1955
Genre: Classical

One of the great cellists of the twentieth century, Yo-Yo Ma mastered the standard cello repertoire early in his career and then proceeded to engage in a series of dialogues with other art forms, cultures, and technologies. He uses his cello as a kind of admission ticket to a world of other cultures and collaborators. Although these explorations might seem the ramblings of a dilettante in the hands of a lesser artist, Ma's projects always ring with integrity and a spirit of discovery.

Born in Paris to Chinese parents, Ma began studying the cello at the age of four. At five he gave his first public recital, and at age nine moved to New York with his family and began lessons at the Juilliard School, where he studied with Leonard Rose. At the age of fifteen, Ma was featured in a concert by conductor Leonard Bernstein at the Kennedy Center in Washington, D.C. Instead of going to college to study music, Ma enrolled at Harvard College to study the humanities, spending summers at the Marlboro Music festival in Vermont. After graduating from Harvard in 1976, he became a full-time cellist, winning the prestigious Avery Fisher Prize in 1978.

Ma became a popular concerto soloist, performing with the world's great orchestras. He is also an accomplished chamber musician who has performed frequently with pianist Emmanuel Ax and violinists Isaac Stern and Jaime Laredo. Ax became Ma's regular partner, and the two toured and recorded extensively, collaborating on albums of the complete cello sonatas of Beethoven and Brahms.

A champion of contemporary music, Ma has premiered dozens of new works by composers such as John Corigliano, Stephen Albert, John Harbison, Leon Kirchner, William Bolcom, Tod Machover, Christopher Rouse, and John Williams.

In the 1990s Ma pushed beyond traditional classical music, teaming up with jazz singer Bobby McFerrin for an album of duets called *Hush,* which sold more than 1 million copies. He got together with bassist/composer Edgar Meyer and fiddler Mark O'Connor for two recordings of Appalachian country music. He recorded an album of Argentine tangos. And he recorded a children's album, *Lulie the Iceberg,* which tells a story about the environment.

Ma has worked with composer/inventor Tod Machover, a specialist in exploring and building virtual electronic instruments at MIT. Wiring up Ma while he played, Machover studied the cellist's subtle movements to understand how to build his own electronic instruments.

Ma also recorded the Bach solo cello suites. But instead of merely making a recording of music that many consider the ultimate cello pieces, Ma collaborated with a number of artists in multimedia interpretations. For the first suite he worked with a garden designer; the second suite explored the idea of great architecture and the work of the architect Piranesi; the third was a collaboration with choreographer Mark Morris; the fourth examined music's relationship with society; the fifth was an exploration of Kabuki; and the sixth was a collaboration with the ice dancers Torvill and Dean. The series was broadcast on public television.

At the turn of the twenty-first century, Ma embarked on his next major project—the Silk Road Project, an organization he founded to explore music and cross-cultural pollination along the route of the ancient Central Asian trade routes. Drawing on performers from many countries East and West, playing traditional and classical instruments, the group commissions work by composers from the region. The Silk Road company has toured extensively throughout America and Asia.

These various projects do not mean that Ma has abandoned the cello's traditional repertoire. He is in constant demand in the classical world and continues to perform traditional material. But his explorations into other music genres enrich all the music he performs.

Yo-Yo Ma's "Duet" with the Hypercello

Yo-Yo Ma has made a career of expanding what he can do on the cello. So he was the right artist to participate in an early 1990s experiment with the "Hypercello," a creation of MIT composer/inventor Tod Machover. Ma was hooked up with censors on his wrist and fingers and on his bow. The motions were fed into a computer, where they were measured, analyzed, and then fed back in the form of musical responses to what Ma was playing. The Hypercello responded to all of Ma's movements, no matter how slight, sometimes transforming the sound he produced into something else. Or it would accompany what Ma was playing or create new musical lines and sounds, creating a kind of spontaneous, evolving duet. While the instrument was interacting with him, Ma could also respond to what his Hypercello was performing, looping the interactivity of music-making back on itself—a kind of improvisation wrapped inside an improvisation. The human/machine interaction yielded a sense of musical direction. Ma would begin a riff, hear the instrument add a bass accompaniment, and then adjust his line to continue the section. With his electronic instruments, Machover tries to develop ways of extending the musician's technique and interpretive gifts in a manner that sounds as "human" as possible. Ma, always looking for ways of expanding the possibilities for music-making on the cello, was an ideal human collaborator.

In part, Ma's celebrity as a concert cellist helps make his musical excursions possible. He has been a guest on *Sesame Street*, has appeared in ads for Apple Computer and American Express, has been a regular performer on public television, and with his personable manner, has attained a crossover appeal in the popular culture.

Ma has made more than fifty recordings and has won fourteen Grammys. Among his many awards are an honorary doctorate in music from Harvard University and the National Medal of Freedom (2001). His cello playing is as warm, engaging, and natural as his personality; listeners are drawn to his music because of its sincerity and directness. Each new idiom he explores seems somehow an extension of a personal musical journey.

SELECTIVE DISCOGRAPHY: *Bach: The Cello Suites Inspired by Bach, from the Six-Part Film Series* (Sony, 1998); *Yo-Yo Ma & Bobby McFerrin: Hush* (Sony, 1992). **With Emmanual Ax:** *Prokofiev/Rachmaninov: Sonatas for Cello & Piano* (Sony 1991). **With Edgar Meyer and Mark O'Connor:** *Appalachia Waltz* (Sony, 1996).

BIBLIOGRAPHY: J. Attanas, *Yo-Yo Ma: A Life in Music* (Evanston, IL, 2003).

DOUGLAS MCLENNAN

MADONNA

Born: Madonna Louise Veronica Ciccone; Rochester, Michigan, 16 August 1958

Genre: Rock, Pop

Best-selling album since 1990: *Ray of Light* (1999)

Hit songs since 1990: "Justify My Love," "Vogue," "Beautiful Stranger"

In the 1990s Madonna consolidated her skills as a performer, producer, and songwriter, and emerged as the most commercially successful female pop artist of all time. Her position in the pop industry owes much to her ability to continually reinvent not only her image but also her musical style, thus remaining fresh and innovative.

At high school and the colleges she briefly attended in Michigan and North Carolina, Madonna did very well in subjects such as drama and dance. The start of her career stretches back to 1977, when she moved from Michigan to New York with aspirations of becoming a professional dancer. While studying with the choreographer Alvin Ailey, she also took up modeling to support herself. By 1979 she had become part of the Patrick Hernandez Revue, which she joined on a tour to Paris. There she met Dan Gilroy, with whom she formed the pop-dance group the Breakfast Club. In 1980 she formed the group Emmy with another former boyfriend and drummer, Stephen Bray. They soon started working on more dance-oriented material and sent a demo tape to the New York DJ/producer Mark Kamins, who forwarded the tape to Sire Records, which signed Madonna in 1982. Her first single, "Everybody," was released at the end of 1982 and became an instant club hit. This single launched what has been a phenomenal career, lasting well over twenty years.

Access into the Music Industry

Madonna's rise to fame is connected to the popularity of new dance trends, and it was by grasping these new

Madonna [PAUL NATKIN/PHOTO RESERVE]

technologies of production that her role as singer and producer provided her access into the music industry. Debbie Harry, the lead singer of the group Blondie, had a profound influence on Madonna at the beginning of her career. With a peroxide-blonde, trashy image, Harry marketed pop with a thrift-store appeal that was arty and sophisticated.

At the end of 1984, Madonna's second album, *Like a Virgin*, was released, and the title hit single became an international success. This record was marketed around a sexy Boy Toy image that catapulted Madonna into global stardom. The music consisted of dance styles of the day set to catchy melodies and glossy production work by Nile Rodgers. In 1986 she started working with Patrick Leonard, a collaboration that led to numerous number one hits. Selling over 5 million records in the United States alone, her third album, *True Blue*, sustained her commercial momentum.

The same cannot be said for her attempts at dramatic acting. Although she did score a critical success in the title role of a charming independent film directed by Susan Seidelman, *Desperately Seeking Susan* (1985), which featured her single "Into the Groove," the commercial movie comedy that followed, *Shanghai Surprise* (1986), co-starring her husband actor Sean Penn, was a disaster. It received nothing but poor reviews. On stage on Broadway in 1988 in *Speed the Plow* by David Mamet she appeared uncomfortable opposite veteran theater actors.

Superstardom

In 1989 one of her most successful albums, *Like a Prayer*, appeared with several number one hits: "Cherish," "Like a Prayer," and "Keep It Together." In all these hits Madonna delivers a playful, sexy, and polished performance in well-crafted songs. At the end of the year, she released a greatest hits album, *The Immaculate Collection*, which consisted of a few new songs, including the raunchy hit "Justify My Love," which ignited many debates about her sexually explicit representation in the promo/video. This controversy was compounded in 1992, when she published her book *Sex*, a glossy, platinum-bound production that featured soft-core pornographic photographs of herself with celebrities like Isabella Rossellini, Naomi Campbell, Big Daddy Kane, and Vanilla Ice.

Although the book was slammed by the critics, it did not detract from her success as a pop star. Her next album, *Erotica*, was stylish and outrageous in its sexual innuendo, with beautifully written songs such as the two big hits, "Deeper and Deeper" and "Rain." In a more elegant vein, the album *Bedtime Stories*, released in 1994, perpetuated Madonna's preoccupation with sex in a collection of songs that feature grinding rhythms and groove-based riffs. The production work on this album stands out as a breakthrough in Madonna's musical development, the fruit of her collaboration with a string of established musical producers and artists, such as the Icelandic icon Björk, who co-wrote the hit single "Bedtime Stories."

In 1996 Madonna's ambition to make it in the film industry was realized when her role as Evita Peron in *Evita* won her the Golden Globe for Best Actress. Before this she released another album, *Something to Remember*, which was her second greatest hits collection. It mainly features ballads intended to target the same type of audience as *Evita*. Her performance on all the songs results in a truly mature and professional vocal style with arrangements that are superbly put together. A track that stands out is "I Want You," a cover of Marvin Gaye's song, recorded together in trip-hop style with Massive Attack. In 1998 her album, *Ray of Light*, produced with William Orbit, was hailed by many music critics as her best album or at least on a par with her top album from the 1980s, *Like a Prayer*. *Ray of Light* stands out as another landmark in Madonna's ability to experiment with contemporary styles.

Madonna's keen interest in techno and electronic pop continued into her next album, *Music* (2000), which involved co-production work with Orbit, Mirwais, and Mark "Spike" Stent. *Music* is as innovative as *Ray of Light*, with Madonna turning to the vocoder on the title track. The song relies heavily on an electro-beat funk groove, underpinned by a simple organ and bass riff, all of which transport Madonna's vocal line amid a flurry of synthesized atmospherics. The track winds toward a conclusion that is intense and humorous with Madonna asking the listener, "Would you like to?" over and over again. Co-written with the French producer Mirwais, "Music" brings the entire album alive with its sparkle and freewheeling sensuality.

Throughout her career Madonna's live acts and music videos have been characterized by camped-up, ironic performances. Yet her controversial, ever-shifting image has often overshadowed her music. Only in the late 1990s did the media begin to afford more recognition to her musical output. Madonna's sound draws on a wealth of styles

Spot Light | Madonna's Videos

The power of Madonna's image in her videos has unquestionably contributed to her success. Two of her most famous monochrome videos, "Vogue" and "Justify My Love," both released in 1990, exemplify Madonna's venturesome sensibility and all the playful gestures that accompany it. Rich in its spectacle, the "Vogue" video positions her in line with other iconic female stars such as Greta Garbo, Marilyn Monroe, Bette Davis, and Rita Hayworth. In a form of masquerade known as vogueing, Madonna confronts and parodies the artificiality of gender constructions and the showbiz world.

In "Justify My Love," directed by Jean-Baptiste Mondino, Madonna's sexuality is on display at its most explicit. Filmed in black and white, this video explores a range of sexualities and panders to the voyeur. Madonna's seductive look plays on notions of exhibitionism as she lures the viewer into her world of erotic fantasy. Sexual pleasuring is inextricably tied up into the musical sound. The brilliant balancing between sight and sound in this video pushes forward the notions of desire as autoeroticism becomes a political goal. Rhythmically, the groove of this song transports the main musical impulse, while the sparse harmonies in parallel fifths enhance the tension of sensuality. Breathy sounds are mixed into this track as Madonna plays around with various sex scenes through imaginative camera angles.

that include disco, hip-hop, house, acid jazz, rock, synth pop, and soul. Spanning more than two decades, her musical expression is traceable through dance trends as much as through the development of digitized musical instruments. In the album *American Life* (2003), there is further evidence of Madonna's passion for dance-based tracks in the techno-driven, state-of-the-art mixes and song arrangements. Notably, the music video for the title track was withdrawn by Madonna just prior to its release on the grounds that it could have been construed as politically insensitive. In the video Madonna appears in military uniform ironically mugging as a superhero.

With a career that has spanned three decades and that has produced more than fifty Top 10 hits, Madonna stands as the most commercially successful female artist in the history of pop music. Through her videos, songs, PR stunts, and commercials, Madonna has become a controversial political figure while filling the role of the greatest pop diva of all time.

SELECTIVE DISCOGRAPHY: *Madonna* (Sire, 1983); *Like a Virgin* (Sire, 1984); *True Blue* (Sire, 1986); *Who's That Girl* (Sire, 1987); *You Can Dance* (Sire, 1987); *Like a Prayer* (Sire, 1989); *Erotica* (Sire, 1992); *Bedtime Stories* (Maverick, 1994); *Something to Remember* (Maverick, 1995); *Ray of Light* (Maverick, 1998); *Music* (Warner Bros., 2000).

SELECTIVE FILMOGRAPHY: *Desperately Seeking Susan* (1985); *Shanghai Surprise* (1986); *Dick Tracy* (1990); *Madonna: Truth or Dare* (1991); *A League of Their Own* (1992); *Evita* (1996); *The Next Best Thing* (2000).

STAN HAWKINS

CHEB MAMI

Born: Mohamed Khelifati; Saida, southwest Algeria, 11 July 1966

Genre: World

Best-selling album since 1990: *Saida* (1994)

Hit songs since 1990: "Desert Rose"

Cheb Mami, also known as "the kid" or "the mourner" (nicknames earned during his early professional experience), hid in his mother's robes during village rituals to hear the percussion music and secret songs of the Bedouin "meddahates" (traditional women's orchestras). Twice stymied in his attempt to break Algerian "rai" in the West, Mami has tried to popularize rai by bridging cultures, as in his collaboration with the singer Sting on the hit song "Desert Rose."

Mami was one of nine children, and from the age of twelve he earned money by adding his falsetto to the chorus of praise singers common at male banquets. In his teens, Mami would travel each weekend to Oran, the capital, to sing lewd and officially discouraged "rai" (truth), a partly improvised cabaret music.

Impressed by earlier modernizing Oran rai singers, Mami determined to rejuvenate the genre by applying Western instrumental arrangements to traditional Algerian scales and rhythms. He also wanted to create a "family rai" that would transcend the confines of its association with male decadence to find a broader respectability and acceptance.

In 1982, the sixteen-year-old Mami finished second in a singing competition organized by Radio Television Algerienne. That accolade brought him to the attention of Boualem, the producer of the Oran label Disco Maghreb. From 1982 to 1985, Mami recorded ten album-length cassettes for the label. Each release typically sold 100,000 to 200,000 units, with the singer earning only a very small cut.

In 1985, having severed ties with Maghreb, Mami made his first official public appearance at the First Oran Rai Festival. On a trip to France later that year, Mami found his music had preceded him and won him a significant audience. Invitations to the Bobigny and La Villette festivals and meetings with the manager Michel Levy convinced him to remain in Paris, where he recorded "Douni El Bladi" ("Take Me Back Home") and "Ouach Tsalini" ("I Don't Owe You a Thing").

Mami suspended his career from 1987 to 1989 to serve in the Algerian army, but upon his discharge he was welcomed back to Paris as the "Prince of Rai." He performed at the New Morning club and toured France, New York, Canada, Italy, Holland, West Germany, and England, making a notable stop at Peter Gabriel's WOMAD festival, which introduced rai's keening vocals and North African disco rhythms to British tastemakers.

Mami recorded *Prince of Rai* (1989) in the United States, but the first Gulf War foiled his attempt to establish an Arab music in America, and his album was banned on all French radio stations. Caught between Western anti-Islamic sentiments and fanatical elements in his homeland, Mami reached out to second-generation French Arabs with his trancelike songs "Haoulou" and "Douha Allia."

Virgin Records provided international distribution of Mami's third album, *Saida* (Happy) (1994), a tribute to his hometown. *Saida* attempted to give rai a high-tech sound appealing to Western audiences. It was produced in Los Angeles by Neneh Cherry and Paula Abdul, sold 100,000 copies in France, and won Double Golden Disc and Golden Disc Awards in Algeria and Morocco, respectively.

Mami raised his profile with a concert at the Zenith Auditorium coinciding with Ramadan in February 1996. He toured Japan, Brazil, and Scandinavia during the months he was onscreen with his rival Cheb Khaled in the musical comedy *100% Arabica*, directed by Mahmoud Zemmouri. Sponsored by the French government, he sang at Bastille Day celebrations that year in both New York and Los Angeles. He appeared at the Zenith again during Ramadan two years later to introduce his rai-rap-techno-ska-funk-reggae-gypsy fusion sound from *Meli Meli* (1998) with guest artists Idir of Kabyle, Imhotep, and the rapper K.mel.

Rai singers in Algeria have faced death threats and assassination. Mami has declined to perform at home, but returned on July 5, 1999, for a concert of symbolic and political importance at the foot of the "Sanctuaire des Martyrs", drawing some 100,000 listeners. Soon after Mami was invited by Sting to record a song for his new album and perform at New York City concerts in December; Mami was also co-billed with the disco star Gloria Gaynor at a New Year's Eve concert at an oasis in the Tunisian desert and performed with Sting and Burundi diva Khadja Nin in January 2000 at Bercy Stadium in Paris.

Following a Middle East concert tour with Sting, Mami released *Dellali* (2001), produced by Nile Rodgers of the band Chic and featuring the French singer Charles Aznavour, reggae's Ziggy Marley, and the American guitarist Chet Atkins, among other crossover artists. Mami's pure, bright voice and injection of Mediterranean and modern influences into rai remain to be discovered by broader audiences.

SELECTIVE DISCOGRAPHY: *Prince of Rai* (Shanachie, 1989); *Saida* (Blue Silver, 1994); *Cheb Mami MeliMmeli* (Mondo Melodia, 1999); *Dellali* (Mondo Melodia, 2001). **With Sting:** *Brand New Day* (Universal/A&M, 1999); *Desert Roses & Arabian Rhythms* (Mondo Melodia, 2001).

HOWARD MANDEL

MANÁ

Formed: 1986, Guadalajara, Jalisco, Mexico

Members: Fernando "Fher" Olvera, vocals (born Tlaxcala, Puebla, Mexico, 8 December 1959); Sergio Vallin, guitar (born Aguascalientes, Mexico, 26 May 1972); Alex Gonzalez, congas/drums (born Miami, Florida, 24 February 1969); Juan Calleros, bass (born Guadalajara, Mexico, 19 April 1961).

Genre: Latin, Rock

Best-selling album since 1990: *Dónde Jugarán Los Niños?* (1993)

Hit songs since 1990: "Vivir Sin Aire," "Me Vale," "Clavado en un Bar"

With intimate, acoustic-framed love songs, Maná rose to become the most popular purveyor of rock-en-Español from the mid-1990s onward. Rock in Spanish has been around almost as long as rock in English, but it took much longer to bloom into an autonomous genre. In its early decades it often suffered from political repression and creative apathy, with many groups simply translating hits from English or aping British and American acts. But Maná helped rock-en-Español mature, fusing the primal rock beat with Latin percussion and poetic lyrical imagery.

Their music took on a timeless quality thanks to simple arrangements and avoidance of synthesizer, and was easy for thousands of cover bands to disseminate in nooks and crannies all over Latin America.

The nucleus of the group was formed in 1984 as Sombrero Verde. Juan Calleros's brother Ulises managed the fledgling band and continued to do so for the next two decades. During a 1985 trip to Mexico City, Fher Olvera met Alex Gonzalez. Renaming itself Maná, the group released its self-titled debut in 1987. While Olvera's raspy tenor and Sergio Vallin's twangy guitar drew comparisons to the Police, Maná carved out a Latin identity with Gonzalez's Afro-Latin backbeats and Olvera's sentimental lyrics.

Their major-label debut, *Falta Amor* (1992), was solid, producing the hit "Rayando el Sol," a catchy, sing-along tune about unrequited love, a common Maná theme. Alex Lora, the leader of seminal Mexican rock band El Tri, cowrote the title track with Olvera in a symbolic baton-passing, though few then imagined Maná would become as popular as El Tri had been.

It was the album *Dónde Jugarán los Niños?* (1993) that vaulted Maná to A-list status with hits "Oye Mi Amor," "Cómo Te Deseo," "Me Vale," "La Chula," and, most importantly, the group's signature ballad, "Vivir Sin Aire." The follow-up album, *Cuando los Ángeles Lloran* (1995), did not match their previous CD's success but it features the stately tear-jerker "El Reloj Cucú," dedicated to a father who died young and the family that misses him. *Sueños Líquidos* (1997) was a return to form, featuring the urgent "Clavado en un Bar" and the poetic ballad "Como Dueles en los Labios." It sold more than 1 million copies in the United States.

At the time Mexico's political climate was evolving. The country's "perfect dictatorship" was beginning to fray at the edges. In Guanajuato a charismatic opposition-party candidate named Vicente Fox had become governor. He was elected president of Mexico in 2000, becoming the first opposition-party candidate to win Mexico's presidency after seventy years of uninterrupted rule by the country's infamous institutional revolutionary party. As Mexicans sensed that the government's grip on media access was slipping, a new generation of hip-hop and punk-influenced rockers derided Maná's lyrically tame approach. In 1997 the rap-metal group Molotov sold 400,000 copies of its explicitly antigovernment debut album, *Dónde Jugarán Las Niñas?*, whose title parodied Maná's 1993 release.

Maná played it cool, choosing not to strike a punk pose at this late date. Instead they released an MTV *Unplugged* effort in 1999 that featured covers of regional Mexican classics like "Te Solté la Rienda" and "Se Me Olvidó Otra Vez." Fans were dismayed by reports in December 2000 that creative differences between González

Spot Light | *Dónde Jugarán Los Niños?*

The album *Dónde Jugarán Los Niños?* (1993) helped reignite the rock-en-Español movement with its fusion of folk, rock, and Latin elements. With songs that were informal enough for a hole-in-the-wall acoustic jam, Maná hit on a formula that had it playing to packed arenas by the following year. The up-tempo "Oye Mi Amor," which combined a Roy Orbison beat with a sensual Andean pan flute riff, captured relationship angst perfectly: "I could even give you my eyes / But you have another / a cold, boring guy," Fher Olvera laments. The percussive "Como Te Deseo," the most Afro-Latin track, pulses with the promise of seduction. Olvera gets about as rebellious as early 1990s mainstream Mexican standards allow on "Me Vale." In a defensive song aimed at anyone feeling henpecked, he roars, "Whatever anyone thinks of me / I don't care." But the album's massive hit was acoustic ballad "Vivir Sin Aire," better known by its haunting "como quisiera . . ." melodic riff. The musical version of candles and red wine, the romantic song tells a partner that life without her would be like trying to live without air or water. The album sold more than 1.2 million copies in the United States and many more in Mexico, making Maná the most popular and influential group in rock-en-Español.

tar) and a bass. Santana returned the favor from *Supernatural* by contributing some blazing licks to "Justicia, Tierra y Libertad."

By fusing rock with Latin elements, Maná made rock-en-Español socially acceptable among people worried about Anglo-American "cultural imperialism" and showed the way for many other musicians who were proud of their roots but could not resist the power of the backbeat.

SELECTIVE DISCOGRAPHY: *Dónde Jugarán Los Niños?* (WEA Latina, 1993); *Cuando los Ángeles Lloran* (WEA Latina, 1995); *Sueños Líquidos* (WEA Latina, 1997); *Revolución de Amor* (Warner Music Latina, 2002).

RAMIRO BURR

BARRY MANILOW

Born: Barry Alan Pincus; Brooklyn, New York, 17 June 1943

Genre: Rock

Best-selling album since 1990: *Because It's Christmas* (1990)

Hit songs since 1990: "Turn the Radio Up"

Barry Manilow surged to a brief spell of superstardom in the 1970s, commanding a large audience enthralled by his slickly packaged bathos. Alternately lionized as an earnest songwriter and derided as a purveyor of soft rock melodrama, Manilow ebbed from his peak popularity in subsequent decades. He retained a substantial if narrowed audience for his later forays into jazz, American standards, and musical theater.

Barry Alan Pincus is the son of Harold Pincus, a chauffeur and factory worker, and Edna Manilow, a stenographer. Harold Pincus left the family when Barry was two years old, and Edna subsequently remarried. At the time of his bar mitzvah, Barry was given the surname Manilow. Edna encouraged Manilow's musical education and bought him an accordion and, later, a piano. Manilow was an average student at Brooklyn's East District High School but excelled in music. After graduation Manilow studied briefly at the New York College of Music and the Juilliard School. Working at the CBS mailroom, Manilow made important contacts and was asked to write the music for an off-Broadway play *The Drunkard*. Soon he was working as a freelance accompanist, jingle writer, conductor, and arranger for Ed Sullivan Productions.

Manilow performed with the singer Jeanne Lucas at the Upstairs at the Downstairs club in Manhattan, earning a reputation as a solid accompanist. In 1972 he was asked to replace the pianist at the Continental Baths, a

and Olvera had caused Maná to split. Fortunately, the principals set aside their differences and went on to reap a fruitful 2001 in Europe. "Muelle de San Blas," from *Sueños Líquidos*, became a surprise hit in Italy, and "Corazón Espinado," a Latin Grammy-winning duet with Carlos Santana on his *Supernatural* CD, gave Maná a foothold in Germany. Maná toured Germany, Italy, and Scandinavia in late 2001.

Revolución de Amor (2002), the band's first studio album in five years, debuted at an impressive number twenty-two on the *Billboard* 200 chart. The single "Ángel de Amor," a protective missive to an abused woman, shot to number six on Hot Latin Tracks. Another standout is "Mariposa Traicionera," a cantina-rock tune recorded Mexican bolero style, with two guitars, a *requinto* (small gui-

well-known center of gay culture, and subsequently accompanied the young singer Bette Midler. While their personalities clashed at times, the two complemented each other musically, and Manilow became her arranger and pianist. After successful appearances on *The Tonight Show* and a sold-out performance at Carnegie Hall, Midler signed with Atlantic Records and Manilow co-produced her debut album, *The Divine Miss M* (1972). During this time Manilow slowly embarked on a solo career despite misgivings about his singing voice and age. He signed with Bell Records, recorded his eponymous debut album, and surreptitiously nudged his year of birth forward to 1946.

During the recording of Manilow's second album, Clive Davis became the new president of Bell Records, subsequently Arista Records. Davis persuaded Manilow to record the upbeat song "Brandy," a minor success in the United Kingdom for singer Scott English. Despite some artistic misgivings, Manilow recorded the song, transforming it into a ballad and changing the name to "Mandy." The song soared to number one on the *Billboard* singles chart, and the album, *Barry Manilow II* (1974), went platinum.

Manilow followed up with a string of hits: "It's a Miracle" (number twelve), "Could It Be Magic" (number six), "Tryin' to Get the Feeling Again" (number ten), and "I Write the Songs" (number one). The adventurous "Could It Be Magic" begins with the opening strains of Chopin's Prelude in C minor, op. 28, and segues into a melodic ballad. The song inexorably builds with the gradual addition of strings, backing vocals, and the rhythm section, and concludes with a return to the Chopin material.

Manilow's biggest success came with "I Write the Songs," a paean to music written by Bruce Johnston of the Beach Boys. As before, Davis adroitly recommended this song and Manilow reluctantly acquiesced. The ballad opens with a melodic phrase shared by the orchestra and piano. The Beatles-influenced bridge introduces an ornamental pocket trumpet and pulsating strings, broadening with the return of the chorus. The choral and orchestral sounds expand as Manilow declares, "I am music and I write the songs."

With his next album, *This One's for You* (1976), Manilow scored with the singles "Looks Like We Made It" (number one) and "Weekend in New England" (number ten). The album *Even Now* (1978) introduced the hits "Can't Smile without You" (number three), "Copacabana" (number eight), and "Somewhere in the Night" (number nine). Manilow received an Emmy Award for his 1977 television special and garnered a Tony Award for his two-week run at the Uris Theater. Manilow created and starred in the televised movie *Copacabana* (1985), based on the lyrics of that song.

With *2:00 A.M. Paradise Café* (1984) and *Swing Street* (1987), Manilow underscored his jazz background in col-laborations with Sarah Vaughan, Mel Torme, and Gerry Mulligan. Manilow produced Nancy Wilson's album *With My Lover Beside Me* (1991), which includes new songs composed by Manilow with lyrics by the late Johnny Mercer. In the 1990s Manilow recorded a successful Christmas album and Broadway album, and continued his jazz tributes with *Singin' with the Big Bands* (1994) and *Manilow Sings Sinatra* (1998).

Copacabana was adapted into a stage musical in 1994, and *Harmony*, a musical based on the lives of the Comedian Harmonists, premiered at the La Jolla Playhouse in California in 1997. Manilow composed music for several animated features and released the concept album *Here at the Mayflower* (2001) with a musical narrative constructed around tenants in an apartment building and featuring the upbeat single "Turn Up the Radio."

Despite his distinctly unfashionable cultivation of the middle of the musical road, Manilow has persevered as a pianist, singer, arranger, composer, and producer, enjoying major triumphs in every medium of entertainment. Brushing aside the hail of critical disdain, Manilow has managed to sustain a distinctive musical legacy of unapologetic romanticism in a pop-music environment pervaded by blunt antiromanticism, angst, and ironic detachment.

SELECTIVE DISCOGRAPHY: *Barry Manilow I* (Arista, 1973); *Barry Manilow II* (Arista, 1974); *Tryin' to Get the Feeling* (Arista, 1975); *This One's for You* (Arista, 1976); *Live* (Arista, 1977); *Even Now* (Arista, 1978); *One Voice* (Arista, 1979); *Barry* (Arista, 1980); *If I Should Love Again* (Arista, 1981); *Oh, Julie!* (Arista, 1982); *Here Comes the Night* (Arista, 1982); *2:00 A.M. Paradise Café* (Arista, 1984); *Manilow* (RCA, 1985); *Swing Street* (Arista, 1987); *Barry Manilow* (Arista, 1989); *Live on Broadway* (Arista, 1990); *Because It's Christmas* (Arista, 1990); *Showstoppers* (Arista, 1991); *Hidden Treasures* (Arista, 1993); *Singin' with the Big Bands* (Arista, 1994); *Summer of '78* (Arista, 1996); *Manilow Sings Sinatra* (Arista, 1998); *Here at the Mayflower* (Concord, 2001); *A Christmas Gift* (Columbia, 2002).

BIBLIOGRAPHY: B. Manilow, *Sweet Life: Adventures on the Way to Paradise* (New York, 1987); P. Butler, *Barry Manilow* (London, 2001).

WEBSITES: www.barrymanilow.com; www.barrynet. com.

WYNN YAMAMI

AIMEE MANN

Born: Richmond, Virginia, 8 September 1960
Genre: Rock

Best-selling album since 1990: *Bachelor No. 2* (2000)

Hit songs since 1990: "That's Just What You Are," "Choice in the Matter," "Save Me"

Aimee Mann is a singer/songwriter who is equally adept at creating both unflinchingly honest songs and engaging, guitar-based pop melodies. As a solo artist and as the lead singer of the 1980s band 'Til Tuesday, she collaborated with some of the leading songwriters of her generation, including Glenn Tilbrook and Chris Difford of the British pop band Squeeze, Jules Shear, and Elvis Costello. Lyrically, Mann is known for her wry, clear-eyed observations on regret, recrimination, and the frailties of human relationships. Mann has become the poster child for the lone songwriter who has prevailed against a greedy music industry driven by hit singles.

Mann first appeared in the Boston punk band the Young Snakes, which she formed after quitting the prestigious Berklee School of Music in the early 1980s. In 1982 she left the Young Snakes and formed the synthesizer-pop band 'Til Tuesday with fellow dropout and then-boyfriend Michael Hausman. Joey Pesce and Robert Holmes joined them later, with Mann as the lead singer and primary songwriter. Their first hit song, "Voices Carry," about a woman with a not-too-nice boyfriend, propelled their debut album of the same name to gold status in seven months. The music video for the song was on constant rotation on MTV during the network's infancy, which probably helped record sales.

Epic Records signed 'Til Tuesday after they won a Boston battle-of-the-bands contest; it would be the first but not the last time Mann would find herself beholden to record companies. After 'Til Tuesday's initial success and commercially disappointing second and third albums, *Welcome Home* (1986) and *Everything's Different Now* (1989), the band broke up. Aimee Mann went solo, Hausman became her manager, and in 1993 she released her debut solo *Whatever*, on a new independent label, Imago Records.

Although *Whatever*'s batch of thoughtful rock tunes, which rely more on guitars and less on synthesizers, drew high critical acclaim, Imago went bankrupt and folded shortly thereafter. Imago still owned Mann's second album, *I'm with Stupid*, which they sold to label boss David Geffen for release in 1996 on DGC, his alternative-music imprint. Mann co-wrote much of *I'm with Stupid* with longtime producer Jon Brion. It was critically regarded as a masterpiece of instantly compelling, three-minute pop songs. Though the tone of *I'm with Stupid* was often bitter, Mann demonstrated she could convey far more with a few rhyming lines than most lyricists accomplish in a whole

Aimee Mann [CARLOS SERRAO/MICHAEL HAUSMAN ARTIST MANAGEMENT]

song. "I could talk to you till I'm blue in the face / But we still would arrive at the very same place / With you running around and me out of the race," sings Mann on "That's Just What You Are," a tune she wrote with Glenn Tilbrook and Chris Difford. The song turned into a modest hit, appearing on the soundtrack for the popular television show *Melrose Place*.

By the summer of 1998 Mann was ready to release her third album but was thrown another curve when DGC was acquired by Interscope in the Polygram-Universal merger at the end of 1998, which left some 200 artists without a record label. At first matters looked promising, but by the spring of 1999 it became clear that Interscope was looking for a hit, not "a record for her fans," as label co-chair Jimmy Iovine told the *New York Times*. At this point, Mann had already recorded most of the third album, *Bachelor No. 2*, but she needed the help of lawyers to buy back her masters from Interscope. Never one to bow to the pressures of conformity, Mann then created her own label, SuperEgo Records, and released *Bachelor No. 2* in 2000. Her label is part of the organization United Musicians, which she and musician Michael Penn (whom she married in 1998) established to help like-minded artists release albums independently.

Unsurprisingly, the songs on *Bachelor No. 2* contain double entendres that may be interpreted as excoriations of the music business, or of former lovers, or both. Filmmaker and fan Paul Thomas Anderson approached Mann with the proposal to script a film inspired by some of the songs on *Bachelor No. 2*. They had become friends when Michael Penn composed the original score for Anderson's films *Hard Eight* (1996) and *Boogie Nights* (1997). Mann agreed, and the film *Magnolia* (1999) was born from the opening line of "Deathly," a typical, emotionally self-destructive Aimee Mann lyric: "Now that I've met you / Would you object to / Never seeing each other again?" The film earned her an Academy Award nomination for Best Original Song for "Save Me." The nomination and the success of the soundtrack, which sold half a million copies, brought her music to a wider audience.

Mann and Penn spent much of 2001 and 2002 touring the United States with their act Acoustic Vaudeville, which grew out of weekly appearances at the Los Angeles club Café Largo. With comedians filling in the witty patter between songs, the tour was a sell-out success. In 2002 Mann released *Lost in Space*, a collection of midtempo pop songs tinged with whirring chamberlins and a continued preoccupation with relationships, fame, and life's disappointments. It debuted at number thirty-five on the *Billboard* 200 chart the week of its release.

SELECTIVE DISCOGRAPHY: *Whatever* (Imago, 1993); *I'm with Stupid* (Geffen, 1996); *Bachelor No. 2, or the Return of the Dodo* (SuperEgo, 2000); *Lost in Space* (SuperEgo, 2002). **With 'Til Tuesday:** *Voices Carry* (Epic, 1985); *Welcome Home* (Epic, 1986); *Everything's Different Now* (Epic, 1988). **With the Young Snakes:** *Bark Along with the Young Snakes* (Ambiguous, 1982). **Soundtrack:** *Music from the Motion Picture Magnolia* (Reprise, 1999).

WEBSITES: www.aimeemann.com; www.unitedartists. com.

CARRIE HAVRANEK

MARILYN MANSON

Formed: 1989, Fort Lauderdale, Florida

Members: Marilyn Manson, vocals (Brian Warner, born Canton, Ohio, 5 January 1969); Ginger Fish, drums (Frank Kenny Wilson, born Framingham, Massachusetts, 28 September 1966); Madonna Wayne Gacy, keyboards (Stephen Gregory Bier, Jr., born 6 March 1964); John 5, guitar (John Lowery, born Grosse Pointe, Michigan, 30 July 1971). Former members: Daisy Berkowitz, guitar (Scott Mitchell

Putesky, born East Orange, New Jersey, 28 April 1968); Olivia Newton-Bundy, bass (Brian Tutunick, born 31 March 1968); Gidget Gein, bass (Brad Stewart, born 11 September 1969); Sara Lee Lucas, drums (Fred Streithorst); Twiggy Ramirez, bass (Jeordie Francis White, born 20 June 1971); Zim Zum, guitar (Timothy Michael Linton, born 25 June 1969); Zsa Zsa Speck, keyboards (Perry Pandrea).

Genre: Rock

Best-selling album since 1990: *Antichrist Superstar* (1996)

Hit songs since 1990: "The Beautiful People," "The Dope Show"

With a penchant for stirring up controversy, Marilyn Manson was one of the most intriguing and vilified rock bands of the 1990s. Manson, led by the band's lightning-rod namesake, featured a constantly changing cast of grim-faced players who did a grinding, industrial dance of the macabre with their leader, who mixed the makeup rock of KISS with the shock tactics of the 1970s rocker Alice Cooper. With futuristic-sounding, keyboard-laden heavy metal songs such as "Irresponsible Hate Anthem" and "Antichrist Superstar," Manson provoked the ire of the religious right with his outrageous lyrics and stage antics. Arrests, concert bans, and lawsuits dogged Manson throughout the late 1990s as record sales faded and his over-the-top persona lost its shock value.

Marilyn Manson & the Spooky Kids was born in 1989 in Fort Lauderdale, Florida, the brainchild of the Ohio native Brian Warner. This middle-class son of a furniture salesman father and nurse mother was educated in a private Christian school, the strictures of which he later attributed to his desire to mock and question organized religion. Each of the group's members took a stage name that combined that of a famous celebrity with a serial killer, hence Marilyn Manson (Marilyn Monroe and Charlie Manson), was joined by guitarist Daisy Berkowitz; bassist Olivia Newton-Bundy—soon replaced by Gidget Gein; drummer Sara Lee Lucas; and keyboardist Zsa Zsa Speck.

The band released several home-recorded tapes and played locally in Florida in the early 1990s, earning a reputation for their disturbing imagery, gothic makeup, and homemade special effects. The group opened for the popular industrial rock act Nine Inch Nails in 1993, and were signed by the band's leader, Trent Reznor, to his Nothing Records label that year. Their debut album, *Portrait of an American Family*, was released in the summer of 1994.

The band's debut is rife with disturbing imagery, profane language, and a dark, cynical worldview that is

Attempts to Ban Marilyn
Manson

Accused of everything from distributing drugs to torturing animals on stage, cheering on gang rapes to endorsing Satanic views, Marilyn Manson was a favorite target for censors and conservative religious groups in the middle and late 1990s. The American Family Association regularly picketed the group's shows, and some cities attempted to pass legislation banning Manson from performing in their towns. Some, like in South Carolina, took the path of least resistance, paying the band $40,000 *not* to play in the state. When Manson joined Ozzy Osbourne's Ozzfest show in 1997, the management of Giants Stadium in New Jersey attempted to block Manson from performing; it took a federal judge's decision to secure Manson's right to perform. At one point in 1997, a Milwaukee school banned the Manson "look," citing it as a disturbance to classroom activities; in 1998 a Kentucky woman was arrested for wearing a Manson T-shirt. With the help of the American Civil Liberties Union, Manson fought back against some of the venues, suing them on First Amendment grounds. More often than not, Manson won the right to present his show, but the legal battles eventually took their toll, frequently overshadowing the music and the antiestablishment message.

thanks to a grim cover of the Eurythmics' 1980s new wave hit, "Sweet Dreams (Are Made of This)."

The stage was now set for the album that turned Manson into both an icon for disaffected, marginalized teens and a target for censors and religious leaders. The Christianity-attacking concept album *Antichrist Superstar* (1996), whose title is a play on Andrew Lloyd Webber's religious-themed rock musical *Jesus Christ Superstar*, is twisted by Manson into a story of an evil being's rise to power and the destruction of decorous, mainstream society. The album debuted at number three on the *Billboard* album charts. The allegorical tale, complete with abrasive guitars, jackhammer beats, and Manson's tortured, spooky yelling/singing, features the hit "The Beautiful People."

Thanks to grim videos in which Manson is strapped into medical torture devices amid images of decay and destruction, the group rose to superstar cult status, their black concert T-shirts a staple of high schools and rock shows. Meanwhile, Manson's stage act was drawing the ire of conservative and religious groups, who frequently attempted to ban the band from playing live, accusing Manson of everything from devil worship to immoral behavior.

Mechanical Animals (1998) represented a stylistic change for the group, with its focus on a slicker, glam-rock sound that traded the gloomier imagery of the past for a more sterile, glittery, androgynous look akin to David Bowie's Ziggy Stardust character of the early 1970s. Songs such as "Great Big White World," "The Dope Show," and "Coma White" portray a bleak, postnuclear science-fiction world of drugs and numbness.

After a period of relative quiet imposed by both the deadly shooting spree at Columbine High School in April 1999 (the two, goth-obsessed shooters were reported to have been Manson fans) and fans' rejection of the *Mechanical Animals* album and concept, Manson released a meditation on the ills of fame, guns, and violence entitled *Holy Wood (In the Shadow of the Valley of Death)* (2000). The album is a virtual cheat sheet of Manson themes, questioning the existence of God ("Godeatgod"), ridiculing the gun culture and blind patriotism ("The Love Song," "Burning Flag"), and attacking the church ("Target Audience").

The album mixes the anthemic, abrasive gothic rock of *Antichrist* with the more sedate, glam-inspired meditations of *Mechanical Animals*. Manson failed in his attempt to get a movie version of the album produced. His longtime side kick Twiggy Ramirez left the group in May 2002, just as Manson was gearing up to record a new album, *The Golden Age of Grotesque* (2003), inspired by life in 1930s Berlin.

By appealing to (mostly male) teenagers ridden with feelings of rebellion and angst, Marilyn Manson became the cultural bogeymen of the late 1990s with images meant

matched by the grim, menacing clatter of the music, which mixes the hard cadences of "industrial" dance music with the overamplified guitars of heavy metal. Manson willfully blends sacred childhood imagery such as lollipops and dolls with references to suicide, disease, apathy, drugs, and sex. The group's first ban, in Utah in 1995, was fueled by Manson's destruction of a Mormon bible on stage.

While each band member sported a disturbing, pale makeup look, it was Manson who was the visual centerpiece of the group's dark worldview. The gangly, heavily tattooed singer with the long black hair often sported heavy white makeup, colored contacts, and combinations of medical bandages and braces, lace gloves, and leather fetish lingerie. A follow-up album, *Smells Like Children* (1995), a collection of covers, remixes, and odd spoken word collages, helped put the band on the national map

to spook parents and intrigue their children. A gifted huckster, Manson took taboo subjects (drugs, sex, religion) and exploited them for their shock value, reveling in the resulting media attention and robust album sales. In the process, Marilyn Manson became an anti-hero for a generation. But, just like the tragic figures in many of his songs, even the anti-hero was subject to a fall when his antics ceased to be horrifying.

SELECTIVE DISCOGRAPHY: *Portrait of an American Family* (Nothing/Interscope, 1994); *Smells Like Children* (Nothing/Interscope, 1995); *Antichrist Superstar* (Nothing/Interscope, 1996); *Remix & Repent* (Nothing/Interscope, 1997); *Mechanical Animals* (Nothing/Interscope, 1998); *The Last Tour on Earth* (Nothing/Interscope, 1999); *Holy Wood (In the Shadow of the Valley of Death)* (Nothing/Interscope, 2000); *The Golden Age of Grotesque* (Nothing/Interscope, 2003).

GIL KAUFMAN

ZIGGY MARLEY

Born: David Marley; Kingston, Jamaica, 17 October 1968

Genre: World

Best-selling album since 1990: *The Best of Ziggy Marley and the Melody Makers (1988–1993)* (1990)

Hit songs since 1990: "All Love and Live," "Power to Move Ya," "People Get Ready"

David "Ziggy" Marley is the oldest son of reggae superstar and activist Bob Marley, the man who first brought Jamaica's reggae music to international attention and popularity. Because of Bob's early death and his son's close physical and vocal resemblance, Ziggy came to be seen as successor to his father's larger-than-life legacy.

Unlike his father, who grew up in the stench and danger of a Kingston ghetto, Marley grew up in privilege as the son of a man who was already a Jamaican institution. Yet Marley was in the house the night in 1975 that his parents were wounded by gunfire in an assassination attempt, and he saw several of his father's associates end up as victims of Jamaica's political violence.

More pleasant childhood memories include learning how to play guitar and drums from his legendary father, performing with him onstage, and accompanying him on road trips, including a journey to Zimbabwe to help fight racism there. Nicknamed "Ziggy" after the David Bowie album *The Rise and Fall of Ziggy Stardust and the Spiders* (1972), Marley, along with his siblings Stephen, Cedella, and Sharon, even recorded "Children in the Streets" (1979) with Bob Marley and the Wailers when he was ten

years old. The song was a reworking of "Children in the Ghetto" (1975); the profits went to the United Nations Children's Emergency Fund. When young Marley saw a cover story on his father in *Melody Maker* magazine, he assumed that the moniker was a description of his father rather than the publication, and the children's own group came to be known as the Melody Makers.

Although Bob Marley did not want his children to have to deal with the pressures of the music business, they did perform at family functions, including their father's own state funeral after his death from cancer at the age of thirty-six in 1981. Their debut album, *Play the Game Right* (1985), and its follow-up, *Hey, World!* (1986), received little promotion or airplay, and when the label, EMI, wanted Marley to go solo, the Melody Makers switched labels rather than break up the family act. *Conscious Party* (1988) was produced by husband-and-wife team Chris Frantz and Tina Weymouth of Talking Heads and included guest performers Keith Richards of the Rolling Stones, Jerry Harrison of Talking Heads, the Ethiopian band Dalbol, and the cast of the Broadway musical *Sarafina!* The clever kaleidoscope of styles and Marley's socially conscious yet tuneful songwriting ability spun off the hit singles "Tumbling Down" and "Tomorrow People." The album *One Bright Day* (1989) proved to be a successful follow-up.

Although Melody Maker records were never as popular in the 1990s as they had been in the late 1980s, the albums remained interesting, innovative, and energetic and saw the group mature and continue to cross-fertilize a wide variety of styles that turned many Bob Marley fans and hard-core reggae lovers against them. Drenched in the same Rastafarian faith that nourished the spirituality of his father, Marley's song lyrics are often politically motivated, dealing with themes of freedom and injustice.

In 1996 more than 300,000 people crowded into New York's Central Park to hear Ziggy Marley and the Melody Makers and other Marley family members pay tribute to Bob Marley. After two decades as the leader of the three-time Grammy Award–winning Melody Makers, Marley released his adventuresome debut solo album, *Dragonfly,* (2003), to considerable critical acclaim but also to the virtual astonishment of his fan base. Not a reggae album as such, the raw power of *Dragonfly* allowed Marley the artistic freedom he obviously had been craving.

Marley has both benefited by and been damned for his ancestry. Those who see and hear his late father in his music may be drawn to him at first, while those who listen more closely attack him for not staying true to his father's musical ideals. The criticism is a familiar one—Bob Marley was initially attacked by purists when he began adding elements of British and American rock and pop to the reggae that he performed.

SELECTIVE DISCOGRAPHY: *Dragonfly* (Private Music/RCA, 2003). **With Ziggy Marley and the Melody Makers:** *Conscious Party* (Virgin, 1988); *One Bright Day* (Virgin, 1989); *Time Has Come: The Best of Ziggy Marley and the Melody Makers* (Capital re-release, 1990); *Jahmekya* (Virgin, 1991); *Joy and Blues* (Virgin, 1993); *Free Like We Want 2 B* (Elektra/Asylum, 1995); *The Marley Family Album* (Heartbeat, 1995); *Fallen Is Babylon* (Elektra/Asylum, 1997); *Marley Magic: Live in Central Park at Summerstage* (Heartbeat/Tuff Gong, 1997); *Arthur and Friends* (Rounder, 1998); *Spirit of Music* (Elektra/Asylum, 1999); *Ziggy Marley and the Melody Makers Live, Vol. 1* (Elektra/Asylum, 2000).

BIBLIOGRAPHY: G. Hausman (ed.), *The Kebra Negast: The Lost Bible of Rastafarian Wisdom and Faith from Ethiopia and Jamaica,* introduction by Z. Marley (New York, 1997).

WEBSITES: www.ziggymarley.com; www.melodymakers.com.

DENNIS POLKOW

BRANFORD MARSALIS

Born: Beaux Bridge, Louisiana, 26 August 1960
Genre: Jazz
Best-selling album since 1990: *Mo' Better Blues* (1990)

The early 1990s witnessed the emergence of a new generation of jazz talent steeped in jazz history. Among the most inventive and talented members of this sophisticated generation, Branford Marsalis won recognition in the 1990s for his soprano and tenor saxophone playing. Among his peers, he is the most recognizable jazz saxophonist in the world, having led a house band on *The Tonight Show with Jay Leno* in the early- to mid-1990s.

The sons of Ellis Marsalis, a jazz pianist, Branford and his brothers, Delfeayo and Wynton, who also became distinguished jazzmen, began playing music as children. Unlike Wynton, whose taste in music is rather formal, Branford has always been interested in rock, R&B, and blues. Branford first played alto saxophone, studying it and other instruments at Berklee College of Music. In 1981 he joined Art Blakey's Jazz Messengers but soon moved to a small band led by brother Wynton. Branford then switched to tenor and soprano saxophone. He appeared on recordings by Miles Davis and Dizzy Gillespie and toured with Wynton's group in the United States, Japan, and Europe. He also appeared on two of Sting's albums, *The Dream of the Blue Turtles* (1985) and . . . *Nothing Like the Sun* (1987). He toured with Sting and later with Herbie Hancock. Like other members of his generation, such as Wynton and the saxophonist Joshua Redman, Marsalis's early playing drew on classic jazz sax players such as John Coltrane, Sonny Rollins, and Charlie Parker. Some critics commented that Marsalis's style was too steeped in these influences and that his early recordings—such as the classic format of *Romances for Saxophone* (1986) and the hard bebop of *Trio Jeepy* (1988)—broke no new ground.

Branford Marsalis's recordings of the 1990s answered these critics with fresh creative energy. In 1992 he began a three-year stint as musical director on *The Tonight Show with Jay Leno,* a nightly gig that made him the most recognized member of his jazz generation. During his time on *The Tonight Show,* Marsalis recorded some of his most memorable music, though he left the show after reportedly tiring of playing second fiddle to Leno. He won a Grammy Award for Best Instrumental Performance, Individual or Group, in 1993 for *I Heard You Twice the First Time,* an album that pays homage to blues-jazz fusion. It won wide audiences and critical accolades. The following year he won another Grammy for his performance on Bruce Hornsby's single "Barcelona Mona."

His most inventive album of the 1990s, however, was a rap-jazz fusion project, *Buckshot LeFonque* (1994), recorded with Gang Starr's DJ Premier. *Buckshot LeFonque* was, in many ways, the culmination of Marsalis's experiments and appearances with hip-hop and popular music artists such as Public Enemy, the Neville Brothers, and even the Grateful Dead. Fame and recognition led Marsalis to do soundtrack work throughout the decade, first on Spike Lee's *Mo' Better Blues* (1990) and Ken Burns's PBS documentary *Baseball* (1994). For that massive series, Marsalis collaborated again with Bruce Hornsby on a version of "The Star-Spangled Banner" (1995) that was nominated for a Grammy.

Throughout the 1990s, Marsalis produced compelling jazz. His highly acclaimed album *Requiem* (1998) is notable on several levels. The album was the last recording by pianist Kenny Kirkland, a brilliant musician who died before the record was completed. *Requiem* also contains seven Marsalis compositions that are both experimental and melodic. Because of Kirkland's death before completion of the album—Marsalis felt his friend and ally could not be replaced—the album sounds rough and unfinished. That less polished sound, ironically, brings Marsalis's vibrant sax playing to life on the album, making the record one of his best.

The late 1990s found Marsalis moving somewhat out of the spotlight and into academic circles. He was awarded an honorary doctorate at Beloit College and teaches in the Jazz Studies department at Michigan State University. Teaching has given Marsalis the opportunity to pursue his wide range of intellectual and artistic interests, including Shakespeare and acting. His recordings continue his exploration of various modes of music. *Creation* (2000), for instance, finds Marsalis playing with the Orpheus Chamber Orchestra on classical works by Debussy and Ravel; the album was released the same year Marsalis made recording appearances on albums with Harry Connick Jr., Sting, and Terence Blanchard.

Footsteps of Our Fathers (2002) finds Marsalis again mining the jazz tradition, though he takes risks with startling reinterpretations, some of jazz's most demanding songs. It is a bold album in which Marsalis works through signature tracks forever associated with jazz legends—including Sonny Rollins's "Freedom Suite," John Coltrane's "A Love Supreme," and Ornette Coleman's "Giggin." On the album and on the less interesting *A Jazz Celebration* (2002), recorded with his brothers and father, Marsalis breathes new life into difficult compositions, making them accessible for contemporary audiences.

Once overshadowed by his brother Wynton, Branford Marsalis became the most recognizable jazz instrumentalist of the 1990s. His eclectic range of interests, his attempts to fuse hip-hop and jazz, and his exuberant style have made him one of the most important contemporary jazz talents.

SELECTIVE DISCOGRAPHY: *Scenes in the City* (Columbia, 1984); *Royal Garden Blues* (Columbia, 1986); *Romances for Saxophone* (Columbia, 1986); *Renaissance* (Columbia 1987); *Random Abstract* (Columbia, 1987); *Trio Jeepy* (Columbia, 1989); *Crazy People Music* (Columbia, 1990); *The Beautyful Ones Are Not Yet Born* (Columbia, 1991); *I Heard You Twice the First Time* (Columbia, 1992); *Bloomington* (Columbia, 1993); *Buckshot LeFonque* (1994); *Dark Keys* (Sony, 1996); *Music Evolution: Requiem* (Sony, 1999); *Footsteps of Our Fathers* (Rounder, 2002); *A Jazz Celebration* (Rounder, 2002). **Soundtrack:** *Mo' Better Blues* (Columbia, 1990).

SHAWN GILLEN

WYNTON MARSALIS

Born: Kenner, Louisiana, 18 October 1961

Genre: Jazz

Best-selling album since 1990: *Marsalis Plays Monk: Standard Time Vol. 4* (1999)

Wynton Marsalis has been one of the world's most prominent practitioners and champions of jazz since becoming the first person to win Grammys in both jazz and classical categories with Columbia Records in 1983, and repeating the feat in 1984. Well dressed, articulate, puckish, ambitious, and hard-working, he is a virtuosic trumpeter, an accomplished composer, a persuasive classicist, a savvy media star, a hands-on bandleader, and co-founder/artistic director of Jazz at Lincoln Center, which became a full-fledged constituent of America's largest cultural performance institution in 1995. Marsalis personally conducts the Lincoln Center Jazz Orchestra annually through two full seasons and international tours while participating in a host of auxiliary events. From 1988 through 1994, he maintained a separate sextet, which has continued to perform since then, although less frequently and with changes in personnel. By 2003 Marsalis was averaging 120 performances a year. His discography since 1990 has encompassed the Pulitzer Prize–winning oratorio *Blood on the Fields* (1997); *Live at the Village Vanguard* (1999), a boxed set of seven nights with his band in a jazz club; and *In Gabriel's Garden* (1996), recordings of Baroque concertos by Bach and Purcell.

Marsalis has won nine Grammys, as well as the Grand Prix du Disque of France, the Edison Award of the Netherlands, and honorary membership in England's Royal Academy of Music. He was among America's "25 most influential people" in 1996, according to *Time* magazine. He was designated a "Messenger of Peace" by the United Nations (2001) and received a U.S. Congressional "Horizon Award" in 2002.

Wynton Marsalis is the son of the New Orleans jazz pianist and educator Ellis Marsalis, the younger brother of saxophonist Branford, and the older sibling of trombonist Delfeayo and drummer Jason. Wynton started on his career course in childhood, studied trumpet formally from age twelve, and spent time with Danny Barker, a banjo player and guitarist for Jelly Roll Morton. In high school Marsalis played with marching bands, jazz bands, funk bands, and, at the age of fourteen, performed Haydn's Trumpet Concerto with the New Orleans Philharmonic Orchestra. His mature music encompasses all these strains, intricately woven into highly self-referential narratives on jazz and the African-American cultural experience.

Marsalis entered the Juilliard School in New York City in 1979, and, with his brother Branford, a Berklee College of Music student, burst on the jazz scene that same year as a member of Art Blakey's Jazz Messengers. His debut recording, *Wynton Marsalis* (1982), cast him leading former Miles Davis band members Herbie Hancock, Ron Carter, and Tony Williams. Marsalis also encouraged "young lions": musicians born since 1960, well-versed in classic jazz (especially the bebop of the 1950s and 1960s), with virtuosic skills. Among Marsalis's protégés are

Spot Light | Marsalis Wins Pulitzer for *Blood on the Field*

In 1997 Wynton Marsalis became the first jazz-identified musician to receive the most celebrated musical award presented in the United States—the Pulitzer Prize for Music Composition—for his libretto and score for *Blood on the Field* (1997). The oratorio encompasses numerous serious and dramatic subjects relevant in both political and personal spheres, including the pressures on Africans in America seeking freedom from slavery (and by implication, the ongoing effects of slavery on African-American culture), the inevitablility of male-female power struggles, and the impact of tricksters' provocations, all evoked in a kaleidoscope of musical idioms in twenty episodes stretching over three hours. Miles Griffith and Cassandra Wilson sing the parts of the lovers, and Jon Hendricks is Juba, a wise fool. All three vocalists have husky voices, and their parts are pitched in low vocal registers. Marsalis's score is rigorously composed.

Though structured as a conventional song cycle, his orchestration seems based on the music of Duke Ellington, employing trumpet, trombone, and saxophone sections in melodic counterpoint and as a backdrop for the vocals, as classical composers use strings, brass, and woodwinds. Propulsion is generated by a jazz rhythm section—notably, trap drum kit struck at a steady but usually restrained swing. Soloists break out of the sections in brief bursts, to echo or comment on the singers' lines; the bandmembers also recite non-melodic passages of the libretto in unison, as a chorus. There are many virtuosic demands placed on individual instrumentalists as well as the entire Lincoln Center Jazz Orchestra; Marsalis's trumpet is evident throughout, almost as a character in itself. Certain episodes are programmatic, depicting the chaotic emotions at a slave marketplace, or the high-stepping of a New Orleans parade, while some songs—"You Don't Hear No Drums," "God Don't Like Ugly," "Look and See"—could stand alone. But Marsalis's work is so designed for the specific forces at his command that most other ensembles are likely to be intimidated from attempting to stage it.

drummer Jeff Watts; pianists Kenny Kirkland, Marcus Roberts, and Eric Reed; bassist Christian McBride; and trumpeters Roy Hargrove and Nicholas Payton.

Jazz, to Marsalis, is essentially an African-American-born form of expression, and an agent of progressive meritocracy bearing lessons for the authentic individual and the world. Its heroic lineage began with Louis Armstrong, another New Orleans–born trumpet player, and extends as far as Blakey and vocalist Betty Carter. In 2002 Jazz at Lincoln Center began to feature music from outside the United States, principally Cuba, Spain, and Brazil. Marsalis embraces the mid-1960s music of John Coltrane, such as *A Love Supreme* (1964), but not free jazz, electrically processed instruments, and rock-pop-hip-hop fusions.

Marsalis has promulgated his viewpoint as artistic director, fundraiser, lecturer and curator of Jazz at Lincoln Center; as consultant and interviewee throughout Ken Burns's *Jazz*, a ten-part, nineteen-hour video documentary that debuted on PBS in 2001; on the VHS/DVD release of his PBS series *Marsalis on Music* (1995); and in his twenty-six-part National Public Radio series "Making the Music," a 1996 Peabody Award winner. He tirelessly promotes jazz as a serious, important, relevant, and functional (if not commercially robust) concert music.

Stylistically, Marsalis moved through an early phase of Miles Davis emulation to develop a refined personal vocabulary based on faultless articulation and thoroughly considered ideas. Since the 1990s, he has pursued his esthetic by recording a repertoire of deceased jazz giants in addition to his own works; these recordings range from multi-episode "little big band" charts to completely notated, neoromantic and postmodern collages, as heard on his millennium composition *All Rise* (2002), recorded with Esa-Pekka Salonen conducting the Los Angeles Philharmonic Orchestra.

Marsalis is the first (and only) jazz artist to win the Pulitzer Prize for music composition (in 1997, for his oratorio *Blood on the Fields*). He has also composed for string quartet, chamber orchestra, modern dance, and ballet. Marsalis's disciplined showmanship, in conjunction with the talents of collaborative administrators, transformed Jazz at Lincoln Center from a summer concert program into a full-fledged constituent of the Lincoln Center empire, equal to its two opera companies, the New York City Ballet, the Juilliard School, the film program, and the theater company. Jazz at Lincoln Center's diverse activities under Marsalis's guidance include an annual, nationwide high school big-band competition in which contestants compete by playing Duke Ellington scores. In 2001 ground was broken for what Marsalis calls "the house that swing built," the first multiuse building designed specifically for jazz use at the world headquarters of AOL/Time-Warner in New York City.

Marsalis has authored three books and a jazz curriculum, undertaken musical diplomatic missions (leading the Lincoln Center Jazz Orchestra to China), and recorded more than forty albums in twenty years. Neither critical acclaim nor the confidence of his corporate sponsors has insured him satisfying record sales or a general audience fervent and eager for his personal productions. In 2002 Marsalis and Columbia Records let contract renewal negotiations lapse, despite the release of the prestigious project *All Rise* (2001).

Marsalis is featured on the *Marsalis Family* (2003) album with his father and brothers, a production of Branford's Marsalis Music label. In mature mid-career, Wynton Marsalis carries a unique portfolio of achievements, plus increasing responsibilities and possibilities, expectations and challenges.

SELECTIVE DISCOGRAPHY: *Think of One* (Columbia, 1983); *Hot House Flowers* (Columbia, 1984); *Tune in Tomorrow: The Original Soundtrack* (Columbia, 1990); *Standard Time, Vol. 3: The Resolution of Romance* (Columbia, 1990); *Uptown Ruler: Soul Gestures in Southern Blue, Vol. 2* (Columbia, 1991); *Blue Interlude* (Columbia, 1992); *Citi Movement* (Columbia, 1993); *In This House, on This Morning* (Columbia, 1994); *Joe Cool's Blues* (Columbia, 1995); *In Gabriel's Garden* (Sony Classical, 1996); *Blood on The Fields* (Columbia, 1997); *Marsalis Plays Monk: Standard Time Vol. 4* (Columbia/Sony Classical, 1999); *At the Octoroon Balls/A Fiddler's Tale Suite* (Columbia/Sony Classical, 1999); *Big Train* (Columbia/Sony Classical, 1999); *Mr. Jelly Lord: Standard Time Vol. 6* (Columbia/Sony Classical, 1999); *The Marciac Suite* (Columbia/Sony Classical, 1999); *Live at the Village Vanguard* (Columbia, 1999); *All Rise* (Sony Classical, 2001); *Trumpet Concertos* (Sony Classical, 2002); *The Marsalis Family* (Marsalis Music, 2003). **With Art Blakey:** *Wynton* (Who's Who in Jazz, 1988).

BIBLIOGRAPHY: W. Marsalis, *Sweet Swing Blues on the Road* (New York, 1994); W. Marsalis, *Marsalis on Music* (New York, 1995); L. Gourse, *Skain's Domain: A Biography* (New York, 2000); W. Marsalis, *Jazz in the Bittersweet Blues of Life* (New York, 2001); W. Marsalis, *Jazz at Lincoln Center: Jazz for Young People Curriculum* (New York, 2002).

WEBSITES: www.wyntonmarsalis.net; www. jazzatlincolncenter.org.

HOWARD MANDEL

RICKY MARTIN

Born: Enrique Martin Morales; San Juan, Puerto Rico, 24 December 1971

Genre: Latin, R&B, Pop

Best-selling album since 1990: *Ricky Martin* (1999)

Hit songs since 1990: "Livin' la Vida Loca," "La Copa de la Vida"

Recording a song that becomes a worldwide smash is a huge accomplishment. But when that song—coupled with a million-watt smile and some well-placed hip shakes—single-handedly launches a music revolution, as one-time child star Ricky Martin's "Livin' la Vida Loca" did in 1999, it is a rare occurrence indeed. The former Menudo member thrust his way into the world's consciousness with his mega-selling hit at the dawn of the new millennium, opening the door for a raft of Latin artists in a movement dubbed the "Latin Explosion."

Born in San Juan, Puerto Rico, in 1971, Ricky Martin was the only child of psychologist Enrique Martin and accountant Nereida Morales, who divorced when he was two years old. Martin began acting in commercials as a child, and by the time he was sixteen had already had a lifetime's worth of pop stardom. A member of the perennially youthful manufactured boy band, Menudo—which forced members to retire at age sixteen—Martin began acting and singing while in grade school, finally gaining entrance to Menudo and touring the world with the group after his third audition in 1984 at age twelve.

Martin won a Mexican Academy Award for his role in the film version of the Mexican soap opera *Alcanzar Una Estrella II*, in 1988 and in 1992 signed a deal with Sony Records, which released his self-titled debut that year. A second album, the ballad-heavy *Me Amaras* (1993), preceded Martin's move to Los Angeles to concentrate on breaking his career in the United States. The singer landed a role on the ABC soap opera *General Hospital* as singing bartender Miguel Morez and released his third album, *A Medio Vivir* (1995), produced by fellow ex-Menudo member Robi Rosa. The album opened up Martin's style by introducing some rock elements into the traditional mix of Spanish ballads and upbeat dance numbers, producing the hit "Maria." In 1997 Martin began a year on Broadway in the role of Marius in *Les Miserables*.

The Hipshake Heard 'Round the World

Already a huge star in Latin America, the personable singer released *Vuelve* (1998), which debuted at number one on *Billboard*'s Top Latin chart and contained the official song for that year's soccer World Cup championship,

Ricky Martin [PAUL NATKIN/PHOTO RESERVE]

"La Copa de la Vida" ("The Cup of Life"). The single hit the number one chart position across the globe while the album sold more than 6 million copies worldwide. With a 1999 Grammy Award for Best Latin Pop Performance, Martin was poised to cross over to an American audience, which he did in an unforgettable fashion at the February Grammy Awards ceremony.

His electrifying performance of the song, complete with leaping flames, a hip-shaking, leather-clad derriere, and a million-watt smile, launched Martin into the stratosphere. Suddenly, the singer was everywhere: magazine covers, entertainment news programs, benefit concerts, and television specials.

The hype would reach astronomical levels with the release of the Latin pop single "Livin' la Vida Loca" in the spring of 1999. The rousing, dance floor-ready celebration of a wild life was the number one single in the United States for five weeks during the summer and the album from which it was taken, *Ricky Martin* (not to be confused with his self-titled 1992 Spanish debut), entered the charts at number one. The song, which was so ubiquitous it quickly took on the quality of another Spanish smash, "The Macarena" (1996), helped the album sell more than 660,000 copies in its first week, the best ever for a Latin performer on the mainstream pop charts.

With production from Emilio Estefan Jr. and Desmond Child, *Ricky Martin* blends dance pop, rock, jazz, ska, and salsa into a world beat mix that appeals both to Martin's loyal Latin audience and to an American one primed for new sounds thanks to Martin's charisma and approachable,

Spot Light | The Latin Explosion

With a shake of the hips, a flash of his pearly whites, and a soccer chant that became a worldwide smash, Ricky Martin helped open the floodgates for the late-1990s "Latin Explosion." Following his career-making performance of "La Copa de la Vida" at the 1999 Grammy Awards, Martin released the Latin pop smash "Livin' la Vida Loca," an infectious Latin-English celebration of life that became Columbia Records' biggest-selling number one hit of all time. In the wake of Martin's success, the pop charts were suddenly flooded with Latin artists such as Jennifer Lopez, Enrique Iglesias, Marc Anthony, Chris Perez, Shakira, Luis Miguel, and Maná, some of whom were already major stars in Latin America but who had struggled to break the all-important American market. Not coincidentally, the movement came just a few years before the United States Hispanic population was expected to exceed African Americans as the country's largest minority population (2005).

photogenic image. Even Madonna was wooed to join in Martin's "Latin Explosion" by singing a duet with him on the song "Be Careful (Cuidado con Mi Corazon)." The album also produced the hit ballad "She's All I Ever Had."

Along with massive exposure came prying questions, including a repeated whisper campaign concerning Martin's sexuality. Though interviewers asked Martin to clear up the media-created confusion, the singer politely demurred, suggesting that what he does in his bedroom—he was linked romantically with Hispanic television personality Rebecca de Alba for years—was not for public consumption. Taking few chances, Martin launched his second English-language album, *Sound Loaded* (2000), with another pop romp combining Latin percussion and Western dance music, "She Bangs."

Despite stronger songs and a more eclectic, lusher sound, the album did not fare as well as its predecessor. A hastily arranged duet with red hot Anglo-Latin singer Christina Aguilera on the album's second single, "Nobody Wants to Be Lonely," and the title track, which was uncomfortably close in sound to "Livin' la Vida Loca," did not reach the fevered pitch of the previous album's singles, according to music critics. Martin retreated from the spotlight in 2001 and 2002, making sporadic appearances at charity events.

With a lifetime of experience at his fingertips, Ricky Martin was poised to break into the lucrative American market, but even the former Menudo member could never have predicted how large an entrée he would make. The success of Martin's feel-good Latin dance singles helped pave the way for a number of other Latin artists who were finally able to translate their fame to a more receptive American audience.

SELECTIVE DISCOGRAPHY: *Ricky Martin* (Sony Discos, 1991); *Me Amaras* (CBS/Sony Discos, 1993); *A Medio Vivir* (Sony Discos, 1995); *Vuelve* (Sony Discos, 1998); *Ricky Martin* (Columbia, 1999); *Sound Loaded* (Sony/Columbia, 2000); *Almas del Silencio* (Sony Discos, 2003).

GIL KAUFMAN

MARY MARY

Members: Erica Atkins (born Inglewood, California); Trecina (Tina) Atkins (born Inglewood, California).

Genre: Gospel, R&B

Best-selling album since 1990: *Incredible* (2002)

Hit songs since 1990: "Shackles (Praise You)," "In the Morning"

Building upon the success of 1990s artists such as Kirk Franklin and Yolanda Adams, the sister duo Mary Mary brought gospel music into the pop mainstream, using the sound of contemporary hip-hop and R&B to spread a message of religious salvation. A key factor in the sisters' appeal, beyond the catchy melodies and infectious beats of their records, is their emphasis on personal uplift. Avoiding harder-edged messages of repentance and judgment, Mary Mary embraces the lighter side of gospel, an approach that ensures acceptance among a wide-ranging audience.

Raised in a strict religious family in Inglewood, California, Erica and Tina Atkins spent their early years singing in church, influenced by the histrionic style of gospel legends such as the Clark Sisters and Shirley Caesar. By the mid-1990s, they were appearing on the popular television program "Bobby Jones Gospel," and touring in the gospel musical play, *Mama I'm Sorry*. Soon after, the sisters began writing songs for top gospel acts such as 702 and Yolanda Adams. Working with R&B producer Warryn Campbell, Mary Mary released its debut album, *Thankful*, in 2000. Spurred by the exuberant, driving hit,

"Shackles (Praise You)," the album crossed over to the R&B charts, earning Mary Mary a Grammy Award for Best Contemporary Soul Gospel Album. While most of *Thankful* is devoted to brash modern styles, a rousing version of the traditional gospel song "Wade in the Water" proves the sisters have not abandoned their roots.

In 2002 Mary Mary released its second album, *Incredible*, a more assured, well-rounded collection than its predecessor. While aggressive hip-hop rhythms still permeate the album, they are balanced with several songs that sport an appealing softer approach. Opening with an acoustic guitar intro that suggests the influence of folk music, "Trouble Ain't" coasts on a gentle bed of guitar, drums, and piano. Freed from the rigid hip-hop backing of their earlier work, the sisters reveal genuine vocal power and an astute understanding of harmony and collaboration. While their voices are perhaps too similar in quality to stand out from one another, both women use growls, high falsetto shouts, and other devices to give their performance variety. Like many of Mary Mary's finest songs, "Trouble Ain't" is a testament to perseverance and strength: "After you've done all that you know how / Just to keep from breaking down / Just believe it's gonna get much better after awhile." Although the song is interspersed with religious references, its inspirational message ensures a universal appeal. *Incredible* is further highlighted by the jumpy, dance-oriented title track and a warm, convincing update of 1970s gospel artist Walter Hawkins's "Thank You."

Since its 2000 debut, Mary Mary has merged gospel music with the modern styles of hip-hop and R&B, creating music that engages the body while appealing to the spirit. The duo's commercial success is a measure of the enduring power and flexibility of the gospel tradition.

SELECTIVE DISCOGRAPHY: *Thankful* (Columbia, 2000); *Incredible* (Columbia, 2002).

WEBSITE: www.mary-mary.com.

DAVID FREELAND

MA$E

Born: Mason Durrell Betha; Jacksonville, Florida, 27 August 1978

Genre: Rap

Best-selling album since 1990: *Harlem World* (1997)

Hit songs since 1990: "What You Want," "Lookin' At Me"

Like punch-drunk boxers, rap stars are forever threatening to quit the music business, only to stage triumphant returns before their public has had a chance to miss them. Mid-1990s sensation Ma$e released a pair of hit pop rap albums before

| Ma$e Joins the Ministry

Rappers retire almost as often as some legendary basketball players, but when Ma$e said he was quitting the rap game for the ministry, few doubted him. In a statement given in April 1999, two months before the release of his second album, *Double Up,* the rapper said his retirement was "effective immediately" and that he would only do spoken word engagements to promote the album. "It takes a great person to walk away from money," Ma$e told MTV News shortly after the announcement. "It takes a courageous person. It takes a person that you've never encountered. And everybody always questions what's real. 'What's real about Ma$e?' This is the realest thing you ever seen." Betha went on to found Saving a Nation of Endangered Ministries (SANE), in Atlanta in late 1999 and work toward a degree in mathematics at Clark Atlanta University. He was the featured speaker on SANE's summer 2000 nationwide crusade, Hell Is Not Full. That same year, Betha told a *Detroit News* reporter that one of the reasons he quit the music business was because of a vision he had of leading millions of people into hell with his music.

star, Killa Kam, also known as Cam'ron—Betha decided to go it alone following member Bloodshed's death in a car accident in 1996. Hoping to catch the ear of then rising producer Jermaine Dupri, Betha, calling himself "Murda Mase," traveled to Atlanta in 1996 to attend an urban music conference. Though Dupri was not charmed, another rising rap production star, Sean "Puff Daddy" (later "P. Diddy") Combs of Bad Boy Records, was. Combs approached Betha after hearing one of the rapper's demo tapes and offered him a contract.

Before releasing his debut, *Harlem World* (1997), Ma$e was already a household name thanks to his star-making cameos on hit singles by Puff Daddy ("Can't Nobody Hold Me Down"), Brian McKnight ("You Should Hold Me"), Mariah Carey ("Honey"), 112 ("Only You"), and Bad Boy's biggest star, Notorious B.I.G. ("Mo Money, Mo Problems"). His combination of laid-back, monotone rapping style and humble, dimple-cheeked good looks were at odds with the Bad Boy ethos of shiny suits, conspicuous wads of cash, flashy cars, and copious amounts of expensive champagne. Ma$e, however, eagerly embraced the luxurious lifestyle.

Ma$e joined Puff Daddy on MTV's August 1997 Video Music Awards alongside former Police singer Sting in a tribute to their recently murdered comrade, B.I.G. (born Christopher Wallace). *Harlem World*, featuring guest rapping from Jermaine Dupri, Busta Rhymes, Lil' Kim, Black Rob, and Puff Daddy, was released two months later, rocketing to the number one slot on the *Billboard* charts, selling more than 4 million copies.

With a slightly lisping delivery described by some critics as "narcoleptic," Ma$e's debut revels in a hedonistic lifestyle of women, money, and parties, polished to a high sheen by the trademark Bad Boy style, a combination of familiar song samples, uplifting rhythms, and slick, over-the-top music videos. The album includes the hits "Feel So Good" (which samples Kool and the Gang's "Hollywood Swinging") and "Lookin' at Me." Puff Daddy and Ma$e launched a highly successful world tour in support of the album in 1997.

Quitting at the Top of His Game

After his debut's success, Ma$e founded his own label, All Out Records, which debuted with the group Harlem World, featuring his sister, Stasson (also known as Baby Stase). Harlem World's debut, *The Movement*, trafficked in the same themes as Ma$e's solo work (sex, guns, and money), with tracks that aimed for mainstream, pop-oriented tastes.

Shortly before the release of his second album, *Double Up* (1999), Ma$e said in several interviews that he planned to revive his more hardcore Murda Ma$e alter ego as an antidote to the mainstream "jiggy" style of rap he had pursued with Bad Boy, which placed emphasis on

deciding that the hip-hop lifestyle was not for him. The rapper turned his back on the riches and rewards of the music business in favor of the ministry, never to return.

Mason Durrell Betha was born in Jacksonville, Florida, in 1978 into a family of six children, including his twin sister, Stasson. When Betha was six years old, his family moved to Harlem. Fearing he would be lured into the dangerous world of the New York streets, Betha's parents sent him to live with his grandparents in Florida at age fifteen, though he returned a few years later to attend the State University of New York on a basketball scholarship. In addition to his expertise on the court, Betha was encouraged by friends to work on his already impressive rapping skills, which he practiced on the bus on the way to basketball games.

After a brief stint as part of a rap collective known as Children of the Corn—along with another future rap

feel-good lyricism and endless materialistic boasting over gritty street reportage.

By the time *Double Up* was released in June 1999, Ma$e's career was already over thanks to his retirement. Either because it did not blaze any new musical trails or because the rapper was unwilling to promote it with performances, or a combination of the two, *Double Up* failed to reach its predecessor's sales success.

Ma$e burned brightly but quickly on the rap scene in the late 1990s. His flashy style of rapping quickly lost favor, but he will be forever remembered not only for his rapid ascent to fame, but for an even rarer feat: giving up on music before it gave up on him.

SELECTIVE DISCOGRAPHY: *Harlem World* (Bad Boy, 1997); *Double Up* (Bad Boy, 1999). **With Harlem World:** *The Movement* (Sony, 1999).

GIL KAUFMAN

MASTER P

Born: Percy Miller; New Orleans, Louisiana, 29 April 1970
Genre: Hip-Hop
Best-selling album since 1990: *MP da Last Don* (1998)
Hit songs since 1990: "Ice Cream Man," "I Miss My Homies," "Make 'Em Say Uhh!"

Percy Miller was one of the most significant architects of mainstream hip-hop's expansion into the South in the 1990s. The enterprising Master P confronted the industry's staunch geographical bias against the South by ignoring mainstream rap conventions altogether. Choosing to do things independently, he spent the mid-1990s perfecting the funky, bounce-driven style of gangsta rap that later made him a hugely successful regional star. He and his No Limit label carved out a unique identity in southern rap circles with their straight-to-video movies, signature album covers, and catchphrase-heavy lyrics. By 1997 Master P had proved himself to be a bankable national star as well when *Ghetto Dope* (also known as *Ghetto D*) brought the sound and style of New Orleans to the rest of the hip-hop community.

Despite his connection to New Orleans' rich hip-hop community, Master P actually split most of his youth between New Orleans and Richmond, California. In 1990 he started the No Limit label to offer something different to the patrons of his record shop, also called No Limit. He released two albums steeped in the slow-rolling funk of nearby Oakland: *Get Away Clean* (1991) and the mod-

est hit *The Ghetto's Tryin' to Kill Me* (1994). Though it seemed that the slick West Coast gangsta rap popularized by Ice Cube, Dr. Dre, and Tupac was on the decline, the success of Master P's independent releases showed otherwise. He soon moved to New Orleans, where he teamed with local producers Beats by the Pound to create an unapologetically gritty take on gangsta that emphasized southern social contexts and the region's unique vernacular. His breakout albums, *99 Ways to Die* (1995) and *Ice Cream Man* (1996), charted remarkably well considering that neither boasted a significant national radio or video hit.

The following year the No Limit empire began its national expansion with the chart-topping *Ghetto Dope* (1997) and the slapstick, straight-to-video biopic *I'm Bout It*, named after the breakthrough single of Tru, the sidegroup Master P formed with his brothers Silkk the Shocker and C-Murder. The album features the brutish sing-along hit "Make 'Em Say Uhh!" as well as the introspective ballad "I Miss My Homies." Despite Master P's novel rise from enterprising, independent regional star to national sensation, he was often criticized for his simple raps, gaudy materialism, and bouncy, bass-heavy production. The following year, Master P's threat of retirement sent *MP da Last Don* to the top of the charts, but his empire began to show signs of wear as his constant threats of retirement grew tiresome. No Limit struggled to balance its hardcore ethos with Master P's hopes for a larger presence in popular culture, as seen in his focus on the career of his son, novelty rapper Lil Romeo, and his frequent attempts to try out with professional basketball teams. By the time No Limit's more violent and aggressive crosstown rivals, Cash Money Millionaires, ascended the following year, Master P was not even the top draw in his own town.

Despite his musical missteps, Master P's outstanding vision and earnest business plan opened hip-hop to exciting new regions and sounds.

SELECTIVE DISCOGRAPHY: *Get Away Clean* (In-A-Minute, 1991); *Mama's Bad Boy* (In-A-Minute, 1992); *The Ghetto's Tryin' to Kill Me!* (No Limit, 1994); *99 Ways to Die* (No Limit, 1995); *Ice Cream Man* (No Limit, 1996); *Ghetto D* (No Limit, 1997); *MP Da Last Don* (No Limit, 1998); *Only God Can Judge Me* (No Limit, 1999); *Ghetto Postage* (No Limit, 2000); *Game Face* (No Limit, 2001).

HUA HSU

MATCHBOX TWENTY

Formed: 1996, Orlando, Florida
Members: Kyle Cook, guitar (born Frankfort, Indiana, 29 August 1975); Paul Doucette, drums (born Pittsburgh,

Pennsylvania, 22 August 1972); Adam Gaynor, guitar (born New York, 26 November 1964); Rob Thomas, vocals (born Germany, 14 February 1971); Brian Yale, bass (born Connecticut, 24 November 1968).

Genre: Rock

Best-selling album since 1990: *Yourself or Someone Like You* (1996)

Hit songs since 1990: "Push," "3 A.M.," "If You're Gone"

When matchbox twenty first burst on the music scene in 1996 with its fusion of alternative pop and 1970s-styled power rock, few critics predicted the band would be anything more than a one-hit wonder. Instead, matchbox twenty became one of the most popular American rock bands of the late 1990s, spawning a legion of imitators.

Lead singer Rob Thomas grew up an army brat, constantly relocating as his father faced reassignment and later moving back and forth between his mother's home in Florida and his grandmother's in South Carolina. Dropping out of high school at the age of seventeen, Thomas proceeded to drift throughout the American South, writing songs and singing in local bands. In Orlando, Thomas met up with bass player Brian Yale and drummer Paul Doucette; the trio performed in a variety of outfits before hooking up with guitarists Kyle Cook and Adam Gaynor to form "Matchbox 20" in 1996. The fledgling band derived its curious name after seeing a restaurant patron wearing a jersey sporting the number "20" as well as a patch that read "matchbox"; the band would later change its name to "matchbox twenty" prior to the release of its second album in 2000.

After recording a series of demos with Collective Soul producer Matt Serletic, matchbox twenty signed a recording contract with Lava Records, a subsidiary of Atlantic Records. In 1996 the band released its debut album, *Yourself or Someone Like You*. The album flopped upon release, as radio stations failed to pick up the lead single, "Long Day." In the spring of 1997, the follow-up "Push" began to make inroads with radio and the listening public. Somewhat atypical of the matchbox twenty sound because of its beefy, aggressive guitar and vocal combination, "Push" embroiled the band in a minor controversy, as some women's groups interpreted the lyrics as promoting violence toward women: "I wanna push you around, I will, I will / I wanna push you down, I will, I will / I wanna take you for granted." "Push" became a staple on MTV, even though Thomas, with his Roman-styled haircut, offered the only memorable look within the band.

As the public began to embrace matchbox twenty, critics did not take so kindly to the band. Detractors charged that the "faceless" backing band only served to show that Thomas was the only real talent of interest within the band. Many critics pegged matchbox twenty as a prototypical one-hit wonder.

matchbox twenty's third single from *Yourself or Someone Like You* silenced critics and established the band as a commercial radio force. "3 A.M.," a gentle midtempo number with a soft, galloping beat, channels the roots-rock sound of 1980s college radio bands such as R.E.M., but infuses it with the anthem-like spirit of 1970s arena rock, particularly on its memorable chorus: "And she says, 'Baby / It's 3 a.m., I must be lonely.'" Lyrically, "3 A.M." reveals Thomas's sensitive side, as he ponders the impending death of a loved one: "She says it's cold outside and she hands me my raincoat / She's always worried about things like that / She says it's all gonna end and it might as well be my fault." *Yourself or Someone Like You* would chart two more hit singles and ultimately sell 10 million copies worldwide. The band's success also spawned a host of imitators, including such bands as Train and Lifehouse.

Thomas further enhanced his profile by co-writing the number one hit "Smooth" for the rock band Santana in 1999. Broadcast Music, Inc. named Thomas its "Pop Songwriter of the Year" for that year and, at the Grammy Awards, he earned awards for Song of the Year, Record of the Year, and Best Pop Collaboration with Vocals. Interest in matchbox twenty rocketed accordingly, and pressure mounted on the band to deliver a worthy follow-up to *Yourself or Someone Like You*.

matchbox twenty released *mad season by matchbox twenty* in 2000; the album further refined the band's successful formula, while broadening its sound with keyboards and horns. The single "If You're Gone" epitomizes the musical growth. Modeled after "3 A.M.," "If You're Gone" begins with a musical whisper, allowing Thomas ample room to ruminate about the seeming futility of a relationship. Slowly building tension through the verses, "If You're Gone" reaches a crescendo for the chorus, as Thomas pleadingly sings: "If you're gone / Maybe it's time to go home / There's an awful lot of breathing room / But I can hardly move." As "If You're Gone" reaches its conclusion, a full horn section complements Thomas's powerful emoting. *mad season by matchbox twenty* avoided any sophomore slump for the band, selling 4 million copies worldwide.

The band released its third album, *More Than You Think You Are*, in 2002. Though Thomas remained the primary songwriter, band members such as Cook and Doucette emerged from the shadows to collaborate and shape the creative direction of the band's songs. Thomas's celebrity also attracted high-profile guests for the album, most notably Mick Jagger, who co-wrote the lead single "Disease."

An unlikely success story, matchbox twenty, with its accessible, friendly sound that drew from many familiar styles, confounded critics and an image-conscious public to become one of the leading purveyors of American mainstream rock in the late 1990s.

SELECTIVE DISCOGRAPHY: *Yourself or Someone Like You* (Atlantic, 1996); *mad season by matchbox twenty* (Atlantic, 2000); *More Than You Think You Are* (Atlantic, 2002).

SCOTT TRIBBLE

THE MAVERICKS

Formed: 1990, Miami, Florida

Members: Paul Deakin, drums (born Miami, Florida, 2 September 1959); Nicholas Kane, guitar (born Jerusalem, Georgia, 21 August 1954); Raul Malo, vocals, guitar (born Miami, Florida, 7 August 1965); Robert Reynolds, bass (born Kansas City, Missouri, 30 April 1962). Former member: David Lee Holt, guitar.

Genre: Country

Best-selling album since 1990: *What a Crying Shame* (1994)

Hit songs since 1990: "O What a Thrill," "There Goes My Heart"

A popular band led by expressive vocalist Raul Malo, the Mavericks were an anomaly in 1990s country. Never as smooth sounding as the more commercially successful group Lonestar, the Mavericks pioneered a highly individualistic style that drew upon traditional country instrumentation of guitar, drums, and fiddles. Malo, a distinctive and engaging singer, brought an additional perspective to the group through his Cuban-American heritage. On ballads, he combined the lush vocalizing of 1950s Cuban balladeers such as Beny Moré with the dramatic style of 1960s pop and rock crooner Roy Orbison. Backing Malo with tight, rhythmically precise playing, the group's members created an explosive yet warm sound.

The Mavericks formed in Miami, Florida, after Malo, a longtime country fan, met bassist Robert Reynolds, who shared his fondness for classic country vocalists such as Patsy Cline and Orbison. After Reynolds recruited the talents of his best friend, drummer Paul Deakin, the group began playing rock clubs in the Miami area. In 1990 the band released its independently financed debut album, which received substantial local airplay in Florida before attracting the notice of several record companies in the country capital of Nashville, Tennessee. Signing with MCA Records in 1991, the group issued its first major-label release, *From Hell to Paradise*, the next year. A rich

collection distinguished by Malo's keening tenor, the album mines country tradition with exciting results. On "This Broken Heart," a lustrous ballad complete with lonesome-sounding steel pedal guitar, Malo draws out his vocal lines in the languid style of Orbison, while the high, emotional catch in his voice recalls Moré and other Cuban balladeers. The title track, featuring several lyrics sung in Spanish, is a biting, angry critique of the Cuban revolution and the repressive government of postrevolutionary leader Fidel Castro. Overall, *From Hell to Paradise* established the Mavericks as a unique, uncompromising force in contemporary country.

In 1994 the group achieved its biggest commercial success with *What a Crying Shame*, which featured minor country hits such as "There Goes My Heart" and the title track. Lacking *From Hell to Paradise*'s energetic spark, the album nonetheless veers comfortably between swinging, up-tempo numbers and rock-influenced ballads such as "All That Heaven Will Allow," originally recorded by Bruce Springsteen.

The album's follow-up, *Music for All Occasions* (1995), combines the group's country orientation with a nostalgic penchant for 1950s pop music. "Foolish Heart," for example, features a catchy, galloping rhythmic hook as well as sugary backup vocals reminiscent of 1950s and 1960s country-pop stalwarts, the Anita Kerr Singers. While enjoyable, most critics agree the album's kitschy affability lacks the depth of its predecessors. After singing lead on a further album, *Trampoline* (1998), Malo began pursuing a solo career while remaining part of the group. Although the Mavericks did not officially disband, the group had become largely inactive by the early 2000s.

The Mavericks emboldened 1990s country with a mixture of 1950s-styled pop, rock, and Cuban balladry. Benefiting from the sparkling lead vocals of Malo, the group enjoyed a brief chart run during the mid-1990s, defying the slick trend in commercial country radio with a captivating, persuasive sound.

SELECTIVE DISCOGRAPHY: *Mavericks* (Y&T, 1990); *From Hell to Paradise* (MCA, 1992); *What a Crying Shame* (MCA, 1994); *Music for All Occasions* (MCA, 1995); *Trampoline* (MCA, 1998); *It's Now! It's Live* (MCA, 1998).

DAVID FREELAND

MAXWELL

Born: Brooklyn, New York, 23 May 1973

Genre: R&B

Best-selling album since 1990: *Now* (2001)

Hit songs since 1990: "Ascension (Don't Ever Wonder)," "Lifetime"

Along with fellow performers Angie Stone, D'Angelo, and Erykah Badu, Maxwell helped define the late 1990s "neo-soul" movement, which, veering from the tough hip-hop sound, infused modern R&B with the kinds of lush, rhythmic funk and soul grooves popular in the 1970s. Like 1980s superstar Prince, Maxwell produces, writes, and plays most of his own material, basing it on his romantic and spiritual experience. In this way, his music is more direct and personal than the slicker, heavily produced sounds of artists such as Boyz II Men and Usher. At the same time he avoids the raunchy explicitness of singers such as D'Angelo and R. Kelly, focusing instead on the romantic side of love.

Professionally Maxwell uses his middle name, keeping his full name confidential to ensure the privacy of his family. Born in Brooklyn, New York, to Puerto Rican and West Indian parents, Maxwell suffered the death of his father at an early age and found comfort through singing in church. In his teens he bought a small keyboard and began composing songs, eventually recording them as demo tapes in a professional studio. After performing on the New York club circuit in the early 1990s, Maxwell signed a contract with Columbia Records in 1994. Initially his future with Columbia seemed anything but promising. He recorded his first album, *Maxwell's Urban Hang Suite*, shortly after signing but saw it delayed for a year due to internal management problems within the company. When finally released in 1996, sales were slow until word of mouth spread. Gaining power through a hit single, "Ascension (Don't Ever Wonder)," the album eventually went platinum and was nominated for a Grammy Award.

In a 1998 interview with the BBC, Maxwell described *Urban Hang Suite* as "a rough sketch of a moment in time," based on a past romantic relationship. Unified by themes of love, matrimony, and commitment, the album has a cohesive feel further enhanced by Maxwell's influence on every track: He wrote the songs and played many of the instruments. In addition, he recruited the expertise of veteran guitarist Wah Wah Watson, whose funky style enlivened many R&B recordings of the 1970s. The most important ingredient in the album's success, however, is Maxwell's voice: Gliding and seductive, it recalls classic singers of the 1960s and 1970s such as Smokey Robinson and Curtis Mayfield. On the tender ballad "Whenever, Wherever, Whatever," Maxwell exudes the gentle purity of a choirboy, singing highly and sweetly. The lyrics reinforce one of his favorite themes, self-renunciation in love: "Take my heart and my love / Take of me all that you must." "Ascension (Don't Ever Wonder)" became the album's biggest hit on the strength of Maxwell's smooth, creamy falsetto gliding over a sensuous groove. On other

Maxwell [AP/WIDE WORLD PHOTOS]

songs, such as the sinuous "Sumthin' Sumthin,'" his voice displays a compelling tough edge more in keeping with the gritty side of R&B. Taken as a whole, the album bears a cumulative power that increases with each listen.

Performing on MTV's *Unplugged* in 1997, Maxwell proved that his initial success was no fluke. Released as a live album later that year, *Maxwell Unplugged* finds the singer expanding his horizons through an intimate, ethereal version of "This Woman's Work," a ballad originally recorded by artsy rock performer Kate Bush. Singing with subtlety and passion, Maxwell is movingly vulnerable on lines such as, "I should be crying but I just can't let it show." Referring to his sudden commercial success, Maxwell tells the live audience, "I never thought this would happen," a statement in keeping with his shy, self-effacing public personality. Although most critics felt that Maxwell's next in-studio album, *Embrya*, obscured his romantic message in obtuse songwriting and overlong tracks , his 2001 release, *Now*, was a return to form. Maxwell is at his best on "For Lovers Only," a ballad enhanced by a pedal steel guitar, an instrument usually associated with country music. Another ballad, "Lifetime," became a hit on the basis of its strong melody and Maxwell's sincere, emotive vocal delivery.

A multitalented musician who oversees each aspect of his recordings, Maxwell fashioned a reputation in the 1990s as an old-fashioned love balladeer, applying his sweet-tempered voice to supple, fluid rhythms. As he gained stardom Maxwell became a gentle sex symbol, known for music that stirred emotions while creating a backdrop for romance.

SELECTIVE DISCOGRAPHY: *Maxwell's Urban Hang Suite* (Columbia, 1996); *Maxwell Unplugged* EP

(Columbia, 1997); *Embrya* (Columbia, 1998); *Now* (Columbia, 2001).

WEBSITE: www.musze.com.

DAVID FREELAND

JOHN MAYER

Born: Bridgeport, Connecticut, 16 October 1977

Genre: Rock

Best-selling album since 1990: *Room for Squares* (2001)

Hit songs since 1990: "No Such Thing," "Your Body Is a Wonderland"

As teenage and college girls of Generation Y (the children of baby boomers) outgrew *NSYNC and the Backstreet Boys, John Mayer turned them on to more mature, thoughtful music that nevertheless retained the sentiment and soft seduction of their half-forgotten bubblegum idols.

Mayer grew up with a middle-class family in Fairfield, Connecticut, but was entranced by the idea of breaking out of the tranquil lifestyle and pursuing an individualistic life of music. He caught the music bug at age thirteen, after hearing a neighbor's cassette of the late Texas blues great Stevie Ray Vaughan. At fifteen, he started playing professionally and dropped out of high school for two years.

In 1997 he was accepted by the prestigious Berklee College of Music in Boston. While the pop rock world is notoriously unimpressed by official credentials, Berklee is one of the few institutions that has had success in formally training pop musicians. However, Mayer felt stifled by what he saw as the school's emphasis on technical virtuosity over creativity. So after three months, he moved to Atlanta, Georgia, with a friend who was originally from the city.

He found the booming metropolis an excellent live music market—plenty of people went out at night, yet audiences were not overly jaded or demanding. However, the experience separated him a bit from his blues roots. For one thing, he tended to write introspective, self-deprecating lyrics, while blues is more geared toward extroversion and accusation. Another more pragmatic hurdle was the fact that it was tough for a no-name newcomer to assemble a band. Therefore, he performed as a solo, acoustic act, which gave his repertoire some touches of the coffeehouse troubadour.

Audiences warmed up to his skillful, jazz-influenced guitar playing and his soothing, grainy voice that sounded like it was coming from someone far more mature than his years. While Mayer has always been a guitar natural, he said singing well requires a concentrated effort.

Mayer went the acoustic route for his first EP *Inside Wants Out* (1999). Drums are absent from most cuts, and the only obvious studio touch is some vocal overdubbing. Its first four tracks, "Back to You," "No Such Thing," "My Stupid Mouth," and "Neon," would show up on his debut album *Room for Squares* (2001). "Neon" is memorable for its incongruity—Mayer sings about a lover who is into "mixed drinks and techno beats" over a folksy, percolating guitar solo. His guitar playing also signals that while he may not have been interested in being the most technically proficient student, he possesses chops to spare.

He was discovered by Columbia Records subsidiary Aware at a South by Southwest Music Festival showcase in Austin, Texas, in 2000. Later that year, he began recording *Room for Squares* with producer John Alagia (Ben Folds Five, Dave Matthews Band). This time, Mayer used a full rock combo to fill out his raw inspiration. His slightly raspy voice draws comparisons to Dave Matthews, while his confessional lyrics and acoustic leanings make him seem an ideal counterpart to the other Generation Y breakout of the early 2000s, Norah Jones. His first single "No Such Thing" rocked along with an aggressive tempo and unusual but catchy chord progressions. With musings about high school memories and trying to avoid a boring fate, Mayer created an anthem for aimless yet ambitious twenty-somethings going through what he calls the "quarterlife crisis."

The second single, "Your Body Is a Wonderland," a new song not included on *Inside Wants Out*, is an acoustic-framed ballad whose success signaled pent-up demand in the pop world for direct, sexy, understandable lyrics. The song won a Grammy Award in 2003 for Best Male Pop Vocal Performance.

Mayer, now more than able to hire a backing band, showcased his well-honed performance skills on double-live *Any Given Thursday* (2003). He returns to his blues roots on the despairing "City Love" and lets bassist David LaBruyere get funky on "No Such Thing."

Millions of young people who had put away their pre-fab pop records were still in the market for enjoyable, inoffensive music. Mayer helped them through their college and young professional years with lyrics that treated them as adults and accessible melodies they could sing along with.

SELECTIVE DISCOGRAPHY: *Inside Wants Out* (Aware, 1999); *Room for Squares* (Aware/Columbia, 2001); *Any Given Thursday* (Aware/Columbia, 2003).

RAMIRO BURR

MARTINA McBRIDE

Born: Martina Mariea Schiff; Sharon, Kansas, 29 July 1966

Genre: Country

Best-selling album since 1990: *Emotion* (1999)

Hit songs since 1990: "Independence Day," "A Broken Wing," "Blessed"

Over the course of five albums released in the 1990s, Martina McBride evolved from tough country belter to sophisticated vocalist, all the while preserving her finely honed sense of musical tradition. McBride's appeal is largely due to her excellent voice, a powerful, flexible instrument capable of tenderness and resilience in equal measure. Just as important, however, is McBride's ability to support vocal talent with genuine honesty and soulfulness. Unlike contemporary pop singers such as Celine Dion and Mariah Carey, McBride never fails to sound emotionally connected with her material, even when her arrangements seem overly polished. Like fellow country star Reba McEntire, McBride gives voice to a range of female experience, finding the common threads that unite women's lives. Her emotional depth and truthfulness have earned praise from other performers as well as African-American poet and writer Maya Angelou, who professed admiration during an appearance on *The Oprah Winfrey Show.*

As a child country performer in Kansas, McBride sang regularly with her father's band. After graduating from high school she spent years working her way into the music industry, receiving a break through the influence of country superstar Garth Brooks. First selling T-shirts for Brooks during his concerts, McBride eventually became his opening act. Although McBride's 1992 debut album, *The Time Has Come,* brought critical acclaim, it was the follow-up, *The Way That I Am* (1993), that made her a country star. A first-rate collection of ballads and tough up-tempo tunes, the album features McBride's breakthrough hit, "Independence Day," a daring, angry tale of an abused wife who retaliates by setting the house on fire. Using traditional images of American patriotism to deliver a potent message, "Independence Day" finds power through McBride's gutsy interpretation as well as trenchant, unsettling lyrics: "She tried to pretend he wasn't drinkin' / But Daddy left the proof on her cheek." Skillfully tying "proof" to both its standard meaning and a descriptive term for whiskey, "Independence Day" brought a new degree of lyrical intelligence to 1990s country music. Although McBride does not write her own material, she displays a sharp gift for song selection on the album's remaining nine tracks. At times her smooth vocal tones, assured pitch, and throaty intimacy recall 1970s pop singer Linda Ronstadt, but McBride's singing also bears a toughness that links it with tough-spirited vocalists of the past such as Kay Starr and Wanda Jackson.

McBride's successive albums, beginning with *Wild Angels* (1995), are more pop-oriented, lacking the rough edge that makes *The Way That I Am* so exciting. This new smoothness is in keeping with the hit style of 1990s country, which achieved mainstream success through plush arrangements and songs emphasizing feel-good sensitivity instead of heartache. *Wild Angels* and its follow-ups, *Evolution* (1997) and *Emotion* (1999), became McBride's most successful albums, crossing over to the pop charts. While slicker than her earlier releases, these albums find McBride retaining her musical integrity on a number of fine tracks. *Wild Angels* features a rollicking version of country and rock performer Delbert McClinton's "Two More Bottles of Wine," as well as the tender "All The Things We've Never Done," a sensitive ballad of marital regret. *Evolution* achieves its best moment in another study of an abusive marriage, "A Broken Wing." While lyrically less incisive than "Independence Day," "A Broken Wing" ranks as one of McBride's most soulful performances. Singing against a gospel-styled choir that never threatens to overpower the record, McBride fashions the song as a stirring anthem of liberation. On her final "fly," McBride uses vocal power and impressive breath control to communicate spiritual release.

Although McBride was nearly forced to declare bankruptcy in 1997 because of financial problems, she maintained her reputation for hard work and consistency, hosting the television program *Celebrity Homes and Hideaways* and professing her domestic happiness with long-time husband John McBride. Speaking to the *Calgary Sun* in 1999, she attested, "I've been able to combine my career with family and I really have it all." In 2001 McBride released *Greatest Hits,* a fine summation of her contributions to modern country. Moving from gentle pop ballads to rocking dance numbers, McBride proves she has the strength to invest any type of material with her personal, heartfelt style.

With trademark versatility, Martina McBride bridged the gap between pop and traditional country in the 1990s, performing songs that appealed to fans of both styles. Singing with passion and soul, McBride reaches a broad range of listeners without compromising her musical roots.

SELECTIVE DISCOGRAPHY: *The Time Has Come* (RCA, 1992); *The Way That I Am* (RCA, 1993); *Wild Angels* (RCA, 1995); *Evolution* (RCA, 1997); *Emotion* (RCA, 1999); *White Christmas* (RCA, 1999); *Greatest Hits* (RCA, 2001).

WEBSITE: www.martina-mcbride.com.

DAVID FREELAND

PAUL McCARTNEY

Born: James Paul McCartney; Liverpool, England, 18 June 1942

Genre: Rock, Pop

Best-selling album since 1990: *Flaming Pie* (1997)
Hit songs since 1990: "Freedom"

Paul McCartney was the bassist and one of the two principal singers and songwriters of the British pop innovators the Beatles. When the group disbanded in 1970, he kicked off a solo career and became the most commercially successful solo Beatle. As a solo artist, McCartney released more than twenty albums, numerous best-of collections, several movie soundtrack songs, and occasional oddities. He enjoyed many hit singles and embarked on several stadium world tours. His album sales dwindled in the 1990s, but he remained a top box office ticket on tour. With George Harrison living in seclusion and Ringo Starr not a major player, McCartney became the public face of the Beatles. He spent the 1990s anthologizing the band's legacy for future generations. He also dodged his reputation as a soft rock hit-maker by returning to the classic rock and R&B that influenced him as a teenager. At the same time he turned heads by making two ambient techno albums under a pseudonym. McCartney was highly visible after the terrorist attacks of September 11, 2001. He wrote "Freedom," an anthem to lift American spirits, and then he embarked on a world tour that was highly praised by critics and broke box office records.

Beginnings

McCartney was born in Liverpool, England, to a father who played in a local jazz band. His mother, who died of breast cancer in 1956, would figure into many of his future songs. Growing up in the 1950s, McCartney was greatly influenced by the New Orleans piano R&B of Fats Domino, the guitar rock of Eddie Cochran, and the gospel singing style of early rock hit-maker Little Richard. McCartney met John Lennon in 1956 and they soon formed the Beatles together. He married his future musical collaborator Linda Eastman in 1969.

McCartney released his first solo album in 1970, the year the Beatles broke up. The following year he formed the group Wings, his effort to continue the splendid harmony and collaborative spirit of the Beatles. Until the band's break-up in 1981, Wings enjoyed several Top 10 hits, performed stadium tours, and recorded *Band on the Run* (1973), which remains McCartney's solo masterpiece. The songs within songs are reminiscent of his Beatles work as are the accessible hooks—from the "ho, hey-ho" chorus of "Mrs. Vanderbilt" and the shout-outs in "Jet" and "Helen Wheels" to the soulful gospel sway of "Let Me Roll It." Most critics agree *Band on the Run* is the only solo McCartney album at the level of his best Beatles work.

Experimentation

In the 1980s McCartney experimented with funk and reggae. He collaborated with an array of artists including Motown legend Stevie Wonder, pop superstar Michael Jackson, and New Wave songwriter Elvis Costello. His album sales failed to meet the expectations of a McCartney album even though he found success with his 1989 world tour.

McCartney started writing classical music at the dawn of the 1990s but it received middling reviews throughout the decade. The pop album *Off the Ground* (1993) did not yield any hit singles. In the years to come McCartney concentrated on organizing the *Beatles Anthology* project—a video documentary series, compact disc series, and hardcover book—as well as *1*, a collection of Beatles hits which became an instant best-seller.

Despite his colossal responsibility as the public face of the Beatles, McCartney managed an almost subversive flair for unpredictability. In 1994 he released an ambient techno album under the pseudonym Fireman and later collaborated with the Welsh psychedelic pop band Super Furry Animals for a collection of oddball Beatles remixes. He also made a cameo on their album chomping vegetables.

Getting Back to Where He Once Belonged

McCartney's renewed spontaneity surfaced on *Run Devil Run* (1999), in which he returns to the rock classics of his youth. He sounds the most invigorated in years singing the collection of carefree covers (plus one original) of vintage rock nuggets by Fats Domino, Buddy Holly, Little Richard, and Chuck Berry.

Critics speculated that McCartney's back-to-basics drive was inspired by the death of Linda, his wife and longtime musical collaborator, to breast cancer in 1998. He weeded the production down on his follow-up album, *Driving Rain* (2001). Although his sunny sentimentality surfaces at times, it is a deceptively dark collection of mostly sparse and quiet songs that grapple with sadness and loss. It projects the idol as just another man who lost his wife. In 2000 he released *A Garland for Linda*, a collection of modern classical originals written in Linda's honor.

After the terrorist attacks of September 11, 2001, McCartney rose to the occasion with the song "Freedom," and it became the centerpiece of a tour which grossed $70 million in the United States. The tour broke box office records and made him the highest-earning celebrity in the world. During the concert—which featured many Beatles songs—he paid separate tributes to Lennon and Harrison, who died in 2001.

Following the tour, McCartney sought to change the publishing credit he and John Lennon shared during their Beatles days. Although "Lennon/McCartney" reflected their early partnership, McCartney asserted the songwriters later wrote independently. McCartney lobbied Lennon's widow Yoko Ono to change the historical record. So no one would mistake Lennon as the writer of the McCartney ballad "Yesterday," he argued, the needed to be credited as "McCartney/Lennon." Ono refused. "I tried to ignore it, but it built into an insecurity. It became a major issue," McCartney told *Rolling Stone* magazine. On his two-disc live album, *Back in the U.S.* (2002), he switched the Beatles song credit to "Paul McCartney & John Lennon," which prompted Ono to consider legal action.

McCartney is a pioneer whose profuse songbook influenced generations of songwriters. He composes in many genres, from reggae to R&B to classical, and his music maintains an accessibility and upbeat sentimentality that are hallmarks of pop music.

SELECTIVE DISCOGRAPHY: *McCartney* (Apple, 1970); *Pipes of Peace* (Columbia, 1983); *Press to Play* (Capitol, 1986); *Off the Ground* (Capitol, 1993); *Flaming Pie* (Capitol, 1997); *Run Devil Run* (Capitol, 1999); *Driving Rain* (Capitol, 2001). **With Wings:** *Band on the Run* (Apple, 1973); *Venus and Mars* (Apple, 1975). **Soundtracks:** *Give My Regards to Broad Street* (EMI, 1984); *Spies Like Us* (Capitol, 1985); *Live and Let Die* (Capitol, 1990); *Jerry Maguire* (Sony, 1996); *Vanilla Sky* (Sony, 2001); *The Family Way* (XXI, 2003).

WEBSITES: www.paulmccartney.com; www.thebeatles.com.

MARK GUARINO

DELBERT McCLINTON

Born: Lubbock, Texas, 4 November 1940

Genre: R&B, Country, Blues, Rock

Best-selling album since 1990: *Room to Breathe* (2002)

Hit songs since 1990: "Every Time I Roll the Dice," "Good Man, Good Woman"

Highly regarded among a loyal core of fans for his musical eclecticism and soulful performance style, Delbert McClinton is an uncompromising singer, songwriter, and harmonica player who has resisted categorization during a career that spans five decades. On recordings, McClinton seamlessly fuses R&B, rock, country, and blues with his wild, rollicking sensibility. Often displaying flashes of rascally humor, McClinton adds depth to his work by allowing a softer, more vulnerable side to surface, particularly on aching ballads. Although he experienced a limited degree

of commercial success during the early 1980s, McClinton did not begin to gain wider recognition until the 1990s, when he moved to Nashville and won accolades for his high-powered blend of rock and country. Despite critical acclaim and belated popular acceptance, McClinton remains a "cult" singer—a performer who releases consistently fine albums, attracting a devoted following while falling short of pop crossover stardom.

Early Critical Success

A product of the fertile Texas music scene, McClinton grew up in Fort Worth, where he began performing in nightclubs during his teens. By the late 1950s he was playing harmonica behind blues performers such as Jimmy Reed and Bobby "Blue" Bland. In 1960 he recorded a blues single, "Wake Up Baby," and later played the distinctive harmonica part on Bruce Channel's number one pop hit, "Hey! Baby" (1962). A popular story among fans is that McClinton taught harmonica to a young John Lennon—just beginning his career with future rock legends the Beatles—during an English tour with Channel in support of the single. During the 1960s and early 1970s, McClinton performed with the group the Rondells and then as part of the duo Delbert & Glen, achieving little commercial success. Attracting increased attention as a songwriter, McClinton landed a recording contract in 1975 with the ABC label, where he released acclaimed albums such as *Victim of Life's Circumstances* (1975) and *Genuine Cowhide* (1976), two works that explore his love of classic R&B and rock from the 1950s. In 1980 he scored his only major pop hit, the horn-driven, R&B-influenced, "Givin' It Up for Your Love." After suffering a second divorce and losing his home to the Internal Revenue Service, McClinton retreated from recording for most of the 1980s.

New Popularity in the 1990s

In 1989 McClinton issued a fiery comeback album, *Live from Austin*, the success of which led to a move to Nashville and a recording contract with the country label Curb. At Curb he recorded fine albums such as *I'm with You* (1990), a simmering collection highlighted by the pulsating ballad, "I Want to Love You" and the rocking "The Real Thing." "I Want to Love You" captures the tenderness that lies beneath McClinton's grizzled surface: "I want to love you . . . let you see the frightened child inside of me, how frail a man can be." McClinton's follow-up, *Never Been Rocked Enough* (1992), features the gritty "Every Time I Roll the Dice," his first hit in more than a decade. His hoarse, shouting vocals offset by a muscular guitar part, McClinton sounds on the single like a rougher version of

1970s and 1980s rock singer Bob Seger. The album also contains "Good Man, Good Woman," a funky duet with rock star Bonnie Raitt that won a Grammy Award when included as part of Raitt's album, *Luck of the Draw* (1991). By the mid-1990s, McClinton's relations with Curb had become strained, although he continued to release fine performances such as "Tell Me About It" (1996), a spunky duet with deep-voiced country performer Tanya Tucker.

Now married to music executive Wendy Goldstein and having extricated himself from his Curb contract, McClinton signed with the small Rising Tide label to release *One of the Fortunate Few* (1997), an album critics cite as one of his finest. Containing performances that cut across a wide swath of R&B styles, the album sports a roster of high-profile guest artists such as blues legend B.B. King and R&B/gospel singer Mavis Staples. Although he did not write it, the album's opener, "Old Weakness (Coming On Strong)," captures McClinton's intensity through pounding piano and hard percussion. With a shuffling beat that recalls the style of blues legend Jimmy Reed, "Better Off with the Blues" benefits from McClinton's harmonica playing and skilled vocal phrasing. "Monkey Around" provides an ideal vehicle for his roguish sense of humor: "You made a man into a monkey / Now the monkey's gonna monkey around." Featuring liner notes by noted writer Nick Tosches, the album emerges as one of McClinton's most intelligent, well-rounded efforts.

In 2001 McClinton released *Nothing Personal*, his first album for the small Austin, Texas-based New West label. Capturing an honest, intimate feel similar to the 1990s work of country star Willie Nelson, the album is largely notable for McClinton's weathered but still powerful voice—with its oak-mellowed quality, it sounds steeped in life and experience. "When Rita Leaves" is a poignant ballad set against a simple arrangement with guitar, percussion, and restrained strings, while "Birmingham Tonight" imparts a rustic sound through use of a delicate, lonesome-sounding piano. "Livin' It Down," meanwhile, is a hard rocker in McClinton's classic style, bolstered by his trademark woebegone, humorous lyrics: "I reached out for a lifeline and she threw me a noose." Alternately passionate and languid, *Nothing Personal* won a Grammy Award for Best Contemporary Blues Album in 2001. *Room to Breathe*, another acclaimed set, followed in 2002.

A durable performer with a leathery, individualistic spirit, Delbert McClinton incorporates a diverse range of music styles into his raucous but sensitive sound. Coming close to stardom at several points during a career that began in the late 1950s, McClinton gained wider acceptance during the 1990s while maintaining his steady cult following.

SELECTIVE DISCOGRAPHY: *Victim of Life's Circumstances* (ABC, 1975); *Genuine Cowhide* (ABC,

1976); *Second Wind* (Capricorn, 1978); *The Jealous Kind* (Capitol, 1980); *Live from Austin* (Alligator, 1989); *I'm with You* (Curb, 1990); *Never Been Rocked Enough* (Curb, 1992); *One of the Fortunate Few* (Rising Tide, 1997); *Nothing Personal* (New West, 2001); *Room to Breathe* (New West, 2002).

WEBSITE: www.delbert.com.

DAVID FREELAND

AUDRA McDONALD

Born: Berlin, Germany, 3 July 1970
Genre: Vocal
Best-selling album since 1990: *How Glory Goes* (2000)

Audra McDonald's shining, expressive soprano and interpretive intelligence made her one of the brightest talents to emerge on the Broadway musical theater scene during the 1990s. Combining an opera singer's sophistication with the bold delivery of a Broadway and pop performer, McDonald achieved a vocal precision and sensitivity rare in contemporary music. By the end of the decade, her talent and versatility had allowed her to make successful transitions into television, film, and, most notably, recordings.

Born in Germany but raised in Fresno, California, McDonald began performing in local dinner theater productions at the age of nine. After attending the Roosevelt School of the Performing Arts in Fresno, she enrolled at the renowned Juilliard School of Music in New York but eventually became frustrated by the school's heavy emphasis on the classical, as opposed to popular, music repertory. Although she would later return to complete her degree, McDonald left Juilliard to accept a small role in the Broadway musical *The Secret Garden* (1991). Her big break came in 1993, when, despite fainting from nervousness during her audition, she was cast as Carrie Pipperidge in a Broadway revival of the classic 1945 musical *Carousel*. One of the few African-American actresses to play Carrie, McDonald imbued the role with a youthful luminosity, winning Broadway's prestigious Tony Award in 1994. In 1996 she earned a second Tony for her portrayal of a headstrong opera student in Terrence McNally's play *Master Class*.

The 1990s were exciting years for musical theater, with young composers such as Michael John LaChiusa, Adam Guettel, Ricky Ian Gordon, and Jason Robert Brown infusing new life into the idiom through dark narrative themes and musical elements borrowed from rock, pop, and R&B. As a performer McDonald was at the forefront of this movement, acknowledging its influence on her first album, *Way Back to Paradise* (1998), a collection of songs written by all four composers. From a commercial perspective this is a risky venture, since neither the composers nor their works are well known to the general public. Furthermore the songs, often featuring dissonant melodies and minimalist production, are largely inaccessible compared with the easy tunefulness of most pop music. In spite of these challenges, the album is a moving emotional statement tempered by McDonald's technical refinement. The singer is especially impressive on the three songs by Gordon, composed to poems by great African-American writer Langston Hughes. On "Dream Variations" her supple, high soprano soars joyously above the arrangement, bringing to life the majesty of the lyrics: "to make my arms wide in the face of the sun, dance, whirl. . . ." "Song for a Dark Girl" is a haunting account of a southern lynching that McDonald builds with a mounting sense of tragedy, while "Daybreak in Alabama" uses the metaphor of multicolored flowers to evoke a dream of racial unity. Like Hughes, McDonald within these short pieces conveys a sweeping sense of drama, a summation of the multiple joys and tragedies of African-American life. With her mature control of vocal dynamics and shading, she expresses happiness and outrage with equal power.

On her follow-up album, *How Glory Goes* (2000), McDonald combines older, well-known show tunes with contemporary material, performing the standard "Bill" with heartbreaking sincerity. By this time McDonald had also proven her skills as an accomplished dramatic actress, appearing in the 2001 television version of the award-winning play *Wit*.

Expertly balancing the precision of classical singing, the flashy glamour of Broadway, and the directness of pop, McDonald has carved out her own musical niche, championing the work of a talented generation of young composers. In the process she has established her own reputation as a gifted singer with the confidence to handle a wide range of styles and material.

SELECTIVE DISCOGRAPHY: *Way Back to Paradise* (Nonesuch, 1998); *How Glory Goes* (Nonesuch, 2000); *Happy Songs* (Nonesuch, 2002).

WEBSITE: www.audra-mcdonald.com.

DAVID FREELAND

REBA McENTIRE

Born: Chockie, Oklahoma, 28 March 1955

Genre: Country

Best-selling album since 1990: *Read My Mind* (1994)

Hit songs since 1990: "Is There Life Out There," "She Thinks His Name Was John," "How Was I to Know"

Applying her distinctive, tremulous vocals to a long run of Top 10 hits, Reba McEntire became the most successful female country performer of the 1980s and 1990s. While other singers of the 1980s faded into obscurity during the following decade, McEntire remained on top through consistently fine song selection and a warm, down-to-earth public persona. In keeping with this image McEntire imbued her songs with a refreshingly female perspective, choosing material that explored the many aspects of contemporary women's lives. Her voice, a wide-ranging instrument recalling the sound of country legend Patsy Cline, was the perfect vehicle for her songs of loss, faith, and determination. By the beginning of the millennium she had proven her resiliency, overcoming personal tragedy and finding success on the Broadway stage and television.

Early Life and Rise to Stardom

Raised on an Oklahoma cattle ranch, McEntire spent her childhood performing in rodeos with her father, professional steer rider Clark McEntire, while gaining music instruction from her mother Jackie. With her sisters she formed the group the Singing McEntires, recording a song, "The Ballad of John McEntire," that received local radio play in Oklahoma. After performing the national anthem at the National Rodeo Finals in Oklahoma City in 1974, McEntire was approached by country singer and songwriter Red Steagall, who suggested she record as a solo artist. With the blessings of her family she broke away from the Singing McEntires and, through Steagall's connections, signed a recording contract with Mercury Records in 1975. During this time she married steer wrestler Charlie Battles and completed her teaching diploma at Southeastern Oklahoma State University.

Although McEntire achieved a degree of commercial success on Mercury, her sound did not fully coalesce until moving to MCA Records in 1984. On MCA she achieved stardom through infusing her recordings with more of her tough but tender personality. Proving herself a skilled dramatic interpreter, McEntire shone on songs that cast her in a wide range of roles, from bored society wife in "Little Rock" to the neglected spouse of "Whoever's in New England" (both 1986). On the latter she establishes a new female country image for the late 1980s; neither aggressive nor overly submissive, McEntire sounds confident that her husband will come back: "When whoever's in New England's through with you / And Boston finds better things to do . . . you'll always have a place to come back to." Unfamiliar with life "up north," McEntire's character is distinctly southern, unworldly but far from naïve. Like the characters on the popular late 1980s television program *Designing Women*, McEntire epitomizes the traditional but contemporary woman of the "New South," secure in her values while approaching modern pressures with open-mindedness. In keeping with this duality, McEntire retained the country twang in her voice even as her records sounded increasingly slick and polished as the 1980s drew to a close.

The 1990s: Tragedy and Triumph

In 1990 seven members of McEntire's nine-piece band were killed in a plane crash. Devastated, McEntire released *For My Broken Heart* (1991) as a means of coming to terms with the loss. Although the songs avoid addressing the tragedy specifically, all feature characters looking back on their lives with autumnal regret. On "All Dressed up (with Nowhere to Go)," an old woman in a nursing home, forgotten by her family, waits in her Sunday finery for the ride to church that will never come. While the scene's grim irony approaches the southern gothic style of writer Flannery O'Connor, McEntire's straightforwardness grounds it in everyday experience. As such, the song is as much a statement about respect for the elderly as an exploration of loss and mortality. Even at her most adventurous McEntire remains populist, maintaining a directness that assures her ongoing appeal to country audiences. Still, her art is sometimes less simple than it appears. On "I Wouldn't Go That Far," another of *For My Broken Heart*'s highlights, she describes a late-night car ride taken in her youth: "He drove me down that old dusty road . . . he wanted me and I wanted him." At first, McEntire's character seems to be saying no to sex; only later is it apparent that she "wouldn't go that far" in love: "I didn't follow my heart." By the end, she sings with the sadness and resignation of one who has lost the great love of her life. A fine storyteller, McEntire makes listeners feel they are in private conversation with her, the soulful tug in her voice contributing to her authenticity.

In 1994 McEntire released one of her most courageous songs, "She Thinks His Name Was John," the only country hit to address the topic of AIDS. Serious without being heavy-handed, the song is all the more impressive for its lack of moralizing. "I'm not a person who judges," she told the AIDS magazine *A&U* in 2001. Like all of McEntire's best work, "She Thinks His Name Was John," gives voice to the multiple challenges women face in a changing world. During the remainder of the 1990s McEntire continued to release albums that displayed confidence and vocal growth. While her work during this period sometimes erred on the side of blandness, it never sounded less than pleasant. On *So Good Together* (1999), her voice is supple and strong, richer and less wobbly than on earlier releases. Her lower register in particular sounds full and rounded, while her tough vocal growl remains intact. On songs such as "'Til I Said It to You," she employs a skilled

sense of timing, fitting long strings of words into the rhythm without sounding rushed or strained. The same rhythmic assurance informs the bass-driven title track, which reflects McEntire's interest in other musical styles, namely rhythm and blues.

New Directions

While McEntire cut back on her recording activities after the late 1990s, she found success in the New York theater, replacing Broadway star Bernadette Peters in a revival of the classic musical *Annie Get Your Gun* in 2001. McEntire won raves from the tough New York critics for her spirited, high-strung performance. Crediting her with rescuing an otherwise labored production, the *New York Times* asserted, "She makes a highly polished performance look so easy you wonder why we aren't all Broadway stars." In the fall of 2001 she premiered her own sitcom, *Reba*, which, in keeping with McEntire's trademark realism, dealt with a mature subject: single motherhood and teen pregnancy. During this period McEntire also published two autobiographical books and continued her activities as a successful businesswoman, running Starstruck Enterprises, a combination booking, publishing, promotions, and private jet company, with second husband Narvel Blackstock. Despite her success McEntire remained chipper, funny, and engaging during interviews, seeming more like a friendly next-door neighbor than a multimillionaire performer. As if in recognition of this accessibility, McEntire attested on "I'm a Survivor" (2001) that, "I may be the queen of broken hearts / But I don't hide behind the crown"—lyrics that hold true for her entire career.

McEntire's down-home honesty and pop sophistication paved the way for successful 1990s country singers such as Shania Twain and Faith Hill. Unlike these performers, McEntire maintains close ties with her country roots, her voice never losing its twangy cadences. Ignoring trends in country music that call for hard-rock pyrotechnics, McEntire relies on subtle communication and storytelling for the effectiveness of her work, creating music that speaks to a female audience while remaining universally likable. Through her presence in other areas of the media, including television and theater, McEntire has succeeded in bringing country further into the cultural mainstream.

SELECTIVE DISCOGRAPHY: *Reba McEntire* (Mercury, 1977); *Just a Little Love* (MCA, 1984); *Whoever's in New England* (MCA, 1986); *For My Broken Heart* (MCA, 1991); *Read My Mind* (MCA, 1994); *So Good Together* (MCA, 1999).

BIBLIOGRAPHY: R. McEntire, *Reba: My Story* (New York, 1994); R. McEntire, *Comfort from a Country Quilt* (New York, 1999).

DAVID FREELAND

BOBBY McFERRIN

Born: New York, New York, 11 March 1950
Genre: Jazz, Classical
Best-selling album since 1990: *Circlesongs* (1997)

Bobby McFerrin uses his entire body and more voice than most singers when he improvises with vocalists and instrumentalists of diverse genres. The son of opera singers Sara and Robert McFerrin, Sr. (the first African-American male soloist at the Metropolitan Opera), McFerrin had piano lessons, played clarinet, and took music preparatory classes at the Juilliard School as a child. He cites Gershwin, Bach, Puccini, Verdi, Joe Williams, and Count Basie as his "first loves." He studied piano, composition, and orchestration at Sacramento State University and Cerritos College, where the pianist and soundtrack composer Dave Grusin was one of his teachers. As a teenager he formed a high school quartet that had a nationwide tour with the Ice Follies, and he played piano in a lounge band. McFerrin was especially drawn to Miles Davis's jazz-fusion breakthrough album *Bitches Brew* (1969), and he was fascinated by pianist Keith Jarrett's performances of lengthy concerts without prepared music. Yet McFerrin resisted committing to a musical career until he was twenty-seven years old, when, "during a period of intense inner searching about my creative self," he recalls hearing "not a thunderbolt, just a still, small voice saying 'You are a singer.'"

In 1978 McFerrin joined the New Orleans fusion band Astral Project and toured with the singer/lyricist Jon Hendricks. He won acclaim and notice for performances at the Playboy Jazz Festival at the Hollywood Bowl in 1980 and the Kool Jazz Festival in New York in 1981. In 1982 he performed at the Kool festival on a program introducing a generation of "young lions," including Wynton Marsalis and more than a dozen other emerging talents, recorded by Elektra/Musician. In 1983 McFerrin toured Europe as an unaccompanied vocalist using no prepared material, as documented on *The Voice* (1984).

McFerrin continues to refine his solo practice. He thumps his chest or stamps his feet for percussion and begins a wordless melody or a mid-register phrase from a Beatles' tune, a Bach invention, a bebop theme, *The Wizard of Oz*, or a kindergarten ditty such as "Itsy Bitsy Spider." He alters the timbral qualities of selected syllables by manipulating his throat, tongue, cheeks, teeth, and nasal passages. Simultaneously he summons pure high head tones as grace notes and dips into tenor, baritone, and/or bass registers until he is a split personality singing like a street corner choir or a persuasive imitation of a conventional jazz ensemble.

McFerrin also pursues creative collaborations. In 1986 he won two Grammys: for his complex vocal chart and performance of "Another Night in Tunisia" with the vocal quartet Manhattan Transfer on his album *Spontaneous Inventions* (1986), and for his duet with the pianist Herbie Hancock on the film soundtrack *'Round Midnight* (1986). He won a Best Recording for Children Grammy for *The Elephant's Child* (1987).

McFerrin's greatest fame and fortune arose from his reggae-inflected, multitracked single "Don't Worry, Be Happy," from *Simple Pleasures* (1988), which also includes layered one-man-band renditions of songs by 1960s rock bands. The track won 1988 Grammys for Song of the Year, New Song of the Year, and Best Pop Male Vocal, and it was adopted by George H.W. Bush's campaign in the 1992 presidential contest against Bill Clinton, although it was later withdrawn at McFerrin's request.

Overwhelmed by continuous touring and publicity demands, McFerrin suspended performing to study conducting with Leonard Bernstein and Seiji Ozawa. On his fortieth birthday in 1990 he led the San Francisco Symphony. He won a 1992 Grammy for a second rendition of the jazz classic "'Round Midnight" with pianist Chick Corea and mixed his original compositions with classical works in a duet program with the cellist Yo-Yo Ma on *Hush* (1992). In 1994 McFerrin was appointed music director of the St. Paul Chamber Orchestra, with which he runs a music education program; the album *Paper Music* (1995) is his conducting debut with that ensemble. *The Mozart Sessions* (1996) features Corea and the St. Paul Chamber Orchestra.

McFerrin directs Voicestra, a fourteen-piece improvising choir heard on *Medicine Music* (1990) and *Circlesongs* (1997); Hard Chorale, a quartet; and a jazz group, Bang! Zoom. He is largely unconcerned with genre distinctions and believes that anyone can make music with the voice. In concert McFerrin typically directs sections of the audience in ostinato patterns against and over which he and amateur volunteers perform solo. Although he may want to deny the uniqueness of his musical gifts, McFerrin is one of a kind.

SELECTIVE DISCOGRAPHY: *The Voice* (Elektra, 1982); *Spontaneous Inventions* (Blue Note, 1986); *The Elephant's Child* (Windham Hill, 1987); *Simple Pleasures* (EMI, 1988); *The Best of Bobby McFerrin* (Blue Note, 1990); *Medicine Music* (EMI, 1990); *Hush* (Columbia, 1992); *Play* (1992); *Bang! Zoom* (Blue Note, 1995); *The Mozart Sessions* (Sony, 1996); *Circlesongs* (1997); *Beyond Words* (Blue Note, 2002).

WEBSITE: www.bobbymcferrin.com.

HOWARD MANDEL

MAUREEN McGOVERN

Born: Youngstown, Ohio, 27 July 1949
Genre: Vocal

Best-selling album since 1990: *Baby I'm Yours* (1992)

Often billed as the "Stradivarius Voice" in honor of the famous Italian violin, Maureen McGovern is renowned for her perfect pitch, warm phrasing, and vocal range spanning several octaves. Achieving fame in the early 1970s for her hit recordings from popular Hollywood movies, McGovern reinvented herself during the mid-1980s, building her reputation as a first-class interpreter of popular songs. Having earned critical praise for her memorable roles in Broadway musicals, McGovern in the 1990s recorded sensitive tributes to famed composers such as George Gershwin and Harold Arlen. Resisting the trend in contemporary music for synthesized arrangements, McGovern favors piano and orchestral backings that showcase the lush purity of her voice.

As a child McGovern was heavily influenced by the great pop vocalists of the twentieth century, particularly Broadway and recording star Barbra Streisand. Upon graduation from high school in 1967, McGovern worked as a secretary by day while performing folk music in the evenings. In the early 1970s her activity as a rock performer in hotels and clubs brought her to the attention of 20th Century Fox Records, who signed her to a recording contract in 1972. At 20th Century Fox McGovern recorded her most famous song, "The Morning After" (1972), a number one pop hit featured in the 1972 film *The Poseidon Adventure*, a tale of passengers trapped on a capsizing ocean liner. Dubbed by press as the "disaster queen" after recording songs for similar films such as *The Towering Inferno* (1974) and *Gold* (1975), McGovern strove to overcome such limitations and began pursuing roles on the Broadway stage. In 1981 she made her Broadway debut in a revival of the classic operetta, *The Pirates of Penzance*, before winning starring roles in the musicals *Nine* (1982) and *The Threepenny Opera* (1989).

By the late 1980s and early 1990s McGovern had fashioned a career as a stylish, sophisticated interpreter of songs by legendary twentieth-century composers such as Arlen and Gershwin. Her astute rhythmic sense and flexible voice, which moves effortlessly from a high coloratura down to a rich, smoky lower register, enliven *Naughty Baby* (1989), a fine collection of Gershwin material. Switching artistic gears, McGovern released *Baby I'm Yours* (1992), an album of pop and R&B songs from the 1950s and 1960s. Rather than recreating the originals, McGovern reinterprets classic numbers such as "Sincerely" and "Anyone Who Had a Heart" using her own confident style. "It's All in the Game," a song associated with 1950s R&B and pop group the Platters, becomes in McGovern's hands an adult testimonial to life's joys and hardships.

By the end of the 1990s McGovern had recorded two further albums of pop standards, *Out of This World* (1996), a tribute to songwriter Arlen, and *The Music Never Ends* (1997), a celebration of the lyrics of writers Alan and Marilyn Bergman. Reissued in 2003 with additional songs, the latter album is a strong example of McGovern's technical agility. On "The Windmills of Your Mind," she navigates the winding, classically influenced melody with assured control of timing and mood. During this period McGovern became active in charitable causes, lending her support to the Muscular Dystrophy Association and founding Works of Heart, an organization that promotes music as therapy for those suffering from illness.

Supporting her vast talent with resilience and tenacity, McGovern reshaped her career in the 1980s, achieving an artistic rebirth through her elegant treatments of pop standards. Releasing albums notable for their rich sound and intelligent song selection, McGovern maintained her reputation in the 1990s and 2000s as a versatile, uncompromising stylist.

SELECTIVE DISCOGRAPHY: *The Morning After* (20th Century Fox, 1973); *Naughty Baby* (CBS, 1989); *Baby I'm Yours* (RCA, 1992); *Out of This World* (Sterling, 1996); *Music Never Ends* (Sterling, 1997; Fynsworth Alley, 2003); *Pleasure of His Company* (Sterling, 1998).

WEBSITE: www.maureenmcgovern.com.

DAVID FREELAND

TIM McGRAW

Born: Delhi, Louisiana, 1 May 1967
Genre: Country

Best-selling album since 1990: *Not a Moment Too Soon* (1994)

Hit songs since 1990: "Indian Outlaw," "It's Your Love," "Don't Take the Girl"

Tim McGraw began his career with all the earmarks of a one-hit wonder. But, by the end of the 1990s, the Louisiana-bred singer had succeeded Garth Brooks as country music's most successful male solo artist. The son of the major league baseball pitcher Tug McGraw, Tim grew up in Start, Louisiana, his attention divided between music and athletics. He attended Northeast Louisiana University on an athletic scholarship, and it was there that he taught himself to play the guitar. His stints at local bars and clubs fired his musical ambitions, and McGraw moved to Nashville in 1989 to pursue a career in music; within three years he signed with Curb Records and released his self-titled debut album, which spawned three minor country radio hits.

McGraw achieved major commercial success in 1994 with the release of *Not a Moment Too Soon* and its controversial single, "Indian Outlaw." A hard-charging dance number backed by a martial drumbeat, "Indian Outlaw" enraged Native American groups for what they considered to be stereotypical lyrics: "You can find me in my wigwam / I'll be beatin' on my tom-tom." Fueled by the controversy, fans purchased the single in droves. Though critics dismissed McGraw as a novelty act, "Indian Outlaw" reached number eight on the country charts as well as number fifteen on the pop charts.

With the follow-up single, "Don't Take the Girl," McGraw moved away from the hokey, redneck style of "Indian Outlaw" and positioned himself as a more serious, dramatic performer. A stirring tale of the love shared by a man and a woman from childhood, "Don't Take the Girl" showcases McGraw's robust voice and sincere, unsentimental delivery in narrating a tragedy that befalls the young: "I'll gladly take her place if you'll let me / Make this my last request." On the strength of its two hit singles, *Not a Moment Too Soon* became the year's best-selling country album.

While touring in support of his follow-up album *All I Want* (1995), which spawned three number one country singles, McGraw became romantically involved with his tour mate and fellow country singer Faith Hill. The pair married on October 6, 1996, in Rayville, Louisiana. McGraw wasted no time in making use of his wife's vocal talents: The pair recorded the duet "It's Your Love" for McGraw's 1997 album *Everywhere*. Set to plaintive violins and weepy steel guitars, the stirring "It's Your Love" celebrates the newlyweds' bliss. "It's Your Love" became *Billboard*'s most-played country single, and, on the strength of it and four other hit singles, *Everywhere* climbed to number two on *Billboard*'s pop charts.

By the time he had released *A Place in the Sun* (1999), which features the Top 10 pop hit "Please Remember Me," McGraw had effectively supplanted Garth Brooks as country's leading male artist. In part McGraw's celebrity transcended his music. His rugged good looks and "bad boy" image earned him the designation of Sexiest Country Star by *People* magazine in 2000. Moreover, McGraw's marriage to Hill further raised his profile; the pair became one of popular culture's power couples in the late 1990s, performing and appearing together at numerous award shows and benefits.

Tim McGraw [MARIA CHAVEZ]

While McGraw had evolved into a cosmopolitan celebrity, artistically he remained true to his country roots; though his music appealed to pop audiences, McGraw did not attempt to curry favor with them in the way that his wife or Shania Twain did. McGraw's music, like that of Garth Brooks, forsook raw, acoustic country instrumentation in favor of a crisp, radio-ready production that would not seem out of place on rock or pop radio. Like Brooks, however, McGraw refused to hide his vocal twang or avoid traditional country-styled lyrics, as evidenced by his songs "Don't Mention Memphis," "Give It to Me Strait," and "It Doesn't Get Any Countrier Than This." McGraw was a crossover success in the late 1990s, but there was no doubt of his true nature; while critics endlessly debated whether Twain and Hill were country or pop artists, McGraw was clearly a country artist.

McGraw released his eighth album, *Tim McGraw & the Dancehall Doctors*, in 2002. For the recording, he forsook the standard Nashville reliance on session musicians, instead calling on his touring band to capture the energy of his live performances. In a nod to his ever-broadening fan base, the album featured a cover of Elton John's pop classic "Tiny Dancer." *Tim McGraw & the Dancehall Doctors* debuted at number two on both the country and pop album charts and sold more than 2 million copies in its first three months of release.

With 25 million records sold and nineteen number one hits to his credit, McGraw has established himself not only as one of the most successful artists in the history of country music but also as a household name.

SELECTIVE DISCOGRAPHY: *Tim McGraw* (Curb, 1993); *Not a Moment Too Soon* (Curb, 1994); *All I Want* (Curb, 1995); *Everywhere* (Curb, 1997); *A Place in the Sun* (Curb, 1999); *Set This Circus Down* (Curb, 2001); *Tim McGraw & the Dancehall Doctors* (Curb, 2002).

SCOTT TRIBBLE

LOREENA McKENNITT

Born: Morden, Manitoba, 17 February 1957

Genre: New Age

Best-selling album since 1990: *The Book of Secrets* (1997)

Hit songs since 1990: "The Mummer's Dance"

Loreena McKennitt conjured rustic images of knights, forests, and pagan ceremonies with her Celtic-influenced roots-revival music. An inquisitive, nomadic artist, she explored Europe, North Africa, and the Middle East looking for sounds that would blend with her trusty harp and ringing soprano.

Born of quintessential Canadian-prairie Scotch-Irish stock, McKennitt took piano and voice lessons growing up, but thought she really wanted to be a veterinarian. She attended the University of Manitoba in Winnipeg to pursue that field; however, she was smitten with performing and composing. In 1981 she moved to Stratford, Ontario, and joined a folk music club. Several of its members were Irish, and they piqued her curiosity in Celtic music. Intrigued, she traveled to the Emerald Isle in 1982 to immerse herself in the music.

Returning to Stratford, she performed in public places for tips. She picked up *How to Make and Sell Your Own Recording,* by Diane Sward Rapaport, a book she still credits for helping her get off the ground, and began building her own music business from scratch. She founded the Quinlan Road label and released her first cassette, *Elemental* (1985). She followed that with the Christmas-themed *To Drive the Cold Winter Away* (1987) and *Parallel Dreams* (1989). She also kept a database of listeners and kept them informed of her latest projects.

By the end of the 1980s McKennitt was making more than 100,000 Canadian dollars per year on her own and was in a good position to negotiate when major labels came calling. She finally chose Warner Bros., which allowed her to keep her own label and sell her albums at shows, as she had always done.

Her Warner debut *The Visit* (1992) features pensive, serious songs that greet listeners with folksy cello, violin, and bagpipe playing. McKennitt's voice betrays a slight

Irish lilt acquired from her annual stays in Doolin, Ireland. "All Souls' Night" commemorates the Celtic New Year with slow, violin-led formality. Her voice takes on a wailing drama on "Bonny Portmore," featuring violins and bagpipes. Cementing her love for anachronistic beauty, she sets the nineteenth-century Alfred Lord Tennyson poem "Lady of Shalott" to music. With a major-key, midtempo melody, the song is a bright moment on an album full of shadows and mystery.

McKennitt turned to Spain and Morocco for inspiration on *The Mask and Mirror* (1994). The urgent "Marrakesh Night Market" pulsates with the Middle Eastern percussion instruments balalaika and dumbek. "Mystics Dream" continues the Mediterranean theme, while the traditional "Bonny Swans" and musical version of Irish poet and dramatist William Butler Yeats's poem "The Two Trees" hearken back to her Celtic roots.

A popular artist in Canada since the late 1980s, she would finally break through in the United States with *The Book of Secrets* (1997). The crossover was thanks to noted engineer/producer Nick Batt's remix of "The Mummer's Dance," one of her most rhythmic songs to date. "Mumming" refers to a tree-worship ceremony practiced by pagans. On this album she achieves a more natural, pan-New Age fusion of her disparate influences. She writes most of the material while again setting a poem to music; this time, it is a twangy, minor-key take on Alfred Noyes's "The Highwayman."

When performing live, McKennitt dazzles audiences with her strong, piercing soprano and her Troubadour Lever harp, a utilitarian pedal-free model made for the wear and tear of traveling. A few Irish music purists griped that she was a foreigner appropriating their music, but she responded that Celtic music itself is heavily informed by migration and cross-cultural influences.

In 1998 tragedy struck when her fiancé, Ronald Rees, was killed in a boating accident. Devastated, she nonetheless was determined to make something positive out of the calamity by creating and raising money for the Cook-Rees Memorial Fund for Water Search and Safety.

She also poured herself into helping new artists on Quinlan Road and in 2003 performed at a tribute event set up by her hometown of Morden. With her busy schedule, no follow-up to capitalize on *The Book of Secrets* was immediately forthcoming, though in 2003 she vowed to begin another album as soon as she had time.

McKennitt, along with artists like Enya and Michael Flatley, helped spark a revival of interest in traditional Irish music during the 1990s. She may not have convinced everyone that bagpipes are hip, but she did manage to remind listeners of the timeless beauty of acoustic string and percussion instruments.

SELECTIVE DISCOGRAPHY: *Elemental* (Quinlan Road, 1985); *The Visit* (Warner Bros., 1992); *The Mask and Mirror* (Warner Bros., 1994); *The Book of Secrets* (Warner Bros., 1997).

RAMIRO BURR

SARAH McLACHLAN

Born: Halifax, Nova Scotia, 28 January 1968

Genre: Rock

Best-selling album since 1990: *Surfacing* (1997)

Hit songs since 1990: "Possession," "Building a Mystery," "Angel"

Sarah McLachlan is a Canadian singer and songwriter with an ethereal soprano that can go from a whisper to a soar in a split second. McLachlan gained a foothold in the pop music landscape in the early 1990s with her breakthrough third album, *Fumbling Towards Ecstasy*, thanks to the success of the radio hit "Possession." McLachlan used her success to help pave the way for other female singer/songwriters when she formed an all-female touring group in 1997, which she dubbed Lilith Fair. McLachlan, who plays piano and guitar, writes songs that are honest, emotional, confessional, and other-worldly—qualities that struck a chord with thousands of young female singers and songwriters.

McLachlan's childhood in Halifax was sheltered and solitary. The daughter of Doris and Jack, an American marine biologist, she spent much of her youth writing songs. From the outset of her career at the age of nineteen, with the debut album *Touch* (1988), critics compared McLachlan's superb vocal range to other singer/songwriters, namely Tori Amos for her frankness, Joni Mitchell for her honesty, and Kate Bush for her tone.

Most critics regard her third album, *Fumbling Toward Ecstasy* (1993), as her watershed achievement. It is a mature, feminine, ethereal collection. The lyrics explore male-female relationships from the perspective of an empathetic woman who has grown to accept herself and what she may expect from others. Ironically, "Possession," a song she wrote about her experience with someone who stalked her through correspondence, became a hit single. "Possession" is a beautiful yet obsessive ode to love. It is a classic Sarah McLachlan song that remains in mid-tempo while building a tension that simmers through the surface. On the chorus McLachlan shows her range, nearly quaking on the high notes toward the end of the lyric: "I will be the one / To hold you down / Kiss you so hard / I'll take your breath away."

Spot Light | Lilith Fair: A Celebration of Women in Music

The Canadian singer/songwriter Sarah McLachlan is responsible for launching the sold-out and acclaimed Lilith Fair, a summer touring group of all-female performers from around the world. A tour with a conscience and an agenda, Lilith grossed more than $28 million, with more than $2 million going to local and national charities and nonprofit organizations such as Planned Parenthood, RAINN, and the Breast Cancer Fund. At each performance a dollar from each ticket sale was donated to a local women's shelter. McLachlan brought along heavyweight talents such as Sheryl Crow, Indigo Girls, the Dixie Chicks, the Pretenders, Natalie Merchant, Shawn Colvin, Queen Latifah, and Missy Elliott; critical favorites such as Juliana Hatfield, Me'shell Ndegéocello, and Aimee Mann; and rising stars such as Beth Orton and Nelly Furtado. Many of the women involved in Lilith Fair saw a considerable boost in their careers and record sales thanks to their involvement. Lilith Fair lasted for three years, from 1997 through 1999. Rather than push it beyond its natural course, McLachlan called it quits after 139 dates and the participation of more than 100 artists. The tour not only inspired good will and good deeds but also led to several compilation albums and a documentary, *Lilith Fair: A Celebration of Women in Music* (2002).

Following the success of *Fumbling*, which remained on the charts for more than a year and became a multiplatinum hit, McLachlan toured. In February 1997 she eloped with Ashwin Sood, who plays drums and percussion in her band. That year she released *Surfacing*, which debuted on the *Billboard* chart in the number two slot and brought her two hit songs and two Grammys: Best Female Pop Vocal Performance for "Building a Mystery" and Best Pop Instrumental Performance for "Last Dance." The ballads, "Adia" and "Angel," are lovely and ethereal offerings that enjoyed steady airplay.

Perhaps the most significant event in 1997 for McLachlan was the launching of the heralded Lilith Fair, an all-female summer tour. In its three years Lilith Fair grossed more than $20 million, some of which was donated to national and local charities in the United States and Canada. After Lilith Fair ended in 1999, McLachlan released *Mirrorball*, a live album that chronicles her 1998 tour. It bought her some time as she went on hiatus and took a break to start a family. McLachlan gave birth to a daughter, India Ann Sushil Sood, in April 2002.

SELECTIVE DISCOGRAPHY: *Fumbling Toward Ecstasy* (Arista, 1993); *The Freedom Sessions* (Arista, 1995); *Surfacing* (Arista, 1997); *Mirrorball* (Arista, 1999).

BIBLIOGRAPHY: B. Childerhorse, *From Lilith to Lilith Fair: The Authorized Story* (New York, 1998); J. Fitzgerald, *Building a Mystery: The Story of Sarah McLachlan and Lilith Fair* (Kingston, Ontario, 2000).

CARRIE HAVRANEK

JOHN McLAUGHLIN

Born: Yorkshire, England, 4 January 1942
Genre: Jazz, Classical, World
Best-selling album since 1990: *Inner Mounting Flame* (1998)

As the leader of the Mahavishnu Orchestra during the late 1960s and early 1970s, the virtuoso guitarist John McLaughlin introduced spiritual themes to the blazing speed, powerhouse rhythms, and newly emergent instruments of electric jazz-rock fusion. Since the 1990s, he has demonstrated how youthful brilliance can flower into maturity across musical genres by revisiting jazz standards and conventional formats that have inspired him, while maintaining his groundbreaking high-tech and high-energy ensembles and Shakti, the acoustic ensemble that brought Hindi classical music to rock audiences. He has also performed original chamber and symphonic works with world-class instrumentalists and orchestras.

Starting conventional piano and violin lessons at age nine, McLaughlin became enamored of the electric guitar at age eleven and largely taught himself the instrument under the influence of recordings by the Chicago blues guitarist Elmore James, the Belgian gypsy Django Reinhardt, the American modernist Tal Farlow, and other blues and swing pioneers. In London during the 1960s, McLaughlin worked with the popular, progressive bands of rockers Georgie Fame and Graham Bond, folk-rocker Brian Auger, and drummer Ginger Baker, a founding member of Cream. McLaughlin roomed with bassist Dave Holland and

was a member of the circle of jazz musicians jamming at Ronnie Scott's club. In 1969 McLaughlin released his debut album, *Extrapolation*, moved to New York City to join drummer Tony Williams's trio Lifetime, and participated in Miles Davis's breakthrough electric jazz albums *In a Silent Way* and *Bitches Brew*. Although he continued working with Davis intermittently through the 1980s, both in concert and in studio projects, McLaughlin was never formerly a Davis band member. In 1970 McLaughlin became a disciple of Sri Chimnoy, who gave him the Hindu name "Mahavishnu" after the Hindu god of sustenance, and he established the Mahavishnu Orchestra (MO) with keyboardist Jan Hammer, violinist Jerry Goodman, bassist Rick Laird, and drummer Billy Cobham. Their unique repertoire of bold, often odd-metered instrumental music excited young audiences attuned to much more basic rock fare. The MO's aura of ecstatic religiosity contrasted with prevailing presentation styles, though its dynamics were akin to those of bands exploring heightened experience through psychedelic drugs.

The original lineup of the Mahavishnu Orchestra released three albums, and, as reorganized in 1974 to include French violinist Jean-Luc Ponty, recorded two more with a string section and the London Symphony Orchestra conducted by Michael Tilson Thomas. In 1975 McLaughlin initiated Shakti, a lively acoustic ensemble drawing on traditional Southern Indian (Carnatic) music, in which he played guitar with the Indian violinist L. Shankar and the tabla (hand drums) player Zakir Hussein. During that decade McLaughlin also recorded with Carlos Santana and instituted an acoustic guitar trio with European collaborators. By the mid-1980s, when he appeared on *The Tonight Show* and in the film *'Round Midnight* (1986), both times to perform more conventional modern jazz, he had established much of the range he has subsequently pursued.

McLaughlin does not reiterate his interests; he advances them. He has pioneered the use of guitar-synthesizers and MIDI interfaces in electric jazz settings. He has promoted Hindustani musicians, including percussionist Trilok Gurtu and flutist Hariprasad Churasia, and many worthy young instrumentalists (including guitarist Dominique di Piazza; bassists Kai Eckhardt, Matthew Garrison, and Jonas Hellborg; and saxophonist Gary Thomas) in his diverse ensembles. He has adapted repertoire associated with the pianist Bill Evans and the saxophonist John Coltrane to the guitar, and has initiated classically inclined efforts, recording with the concert pianist Katia LaBeque and debuting his neo-Romantic "Mediterranean Concerto" (1988) with Tilson-Thomas conducting the London Symphony Orchestra.

Especially since the 1990s, McLaughlin has strived to bring elements of his diverse projects together. His refined lyricism is evident in the funk-oriented music of his band Free Spirits, with organist Joey DeFrancesco and soul-drummer Dennis Chambers. His Mahavishnu energy infects acoustic trio recitals with fellow guitarists Paco De Lucia and Al DiMeola, and his jazz-derived phrasing is in evidence in his Indian and classical settings. He records prolifically, alternating among his ensembles while nurturing his compositional ambitions in the chamber and orchestral genres. In 2003 McLaughlin prepared a three-movement score commissioned by choreographer Jean-Christophe Maillot for the Ballets de Monte Carlo titled "Thieves and Poets," featuring symphony orchestra and violin, cello, clarinet, classical guitar, and himself as soloist, to be recorded by I Pomeriggi Musicali Orchestra of Milan. Simultaneously, he prepared recordings of his favorite American songbook standards, including "Stella by Starlight" and "My Foolish Heart."

McLaughlin never blunts his passion or technique, and his ever-wider repertoire emphasizes the "one world" message of his earliest Mahavishnu days. From the 1970s to the turn of the twenty-first century, McLaughlin has continued to wed sacred and secular goals and pleasures. In performance, whatever his ensemble, he exudes both an immediate presence and a transporting intensity.

SELECTIVE DISCOGRAPHY: *Extrapolation* (Polydor, 1969); *Devotion* (Douglas, 1970); *My Goal's Beyond* (Rykodisc, 1970); *Inner Mounting Flame* (Columbia, 1971); *Birds of Fire* (Columbia 1973); *Apocalypse* (Columbia, 1974); *Visions of the Emerald Beyond* (Columbia, 1975); *Shakti* (Columbia, 1976); *Johnny McLaughlin, Electric Guitarist* (Columbia, 1978); *One Truth Band* (Columbia, 1978); *Belo Horizonte* (Warner Bros., 1981); *Music Spoken Here* (Warner Bros., 1983); *Mediterranean Concerto for Guitar and Orchestra* (Columbia, 1988); *The Lost Trident Sessions* (1999). **With Miles Davis:** *In a Silent Way Sessions* (Columbia, 1969); *Bitches Brew* (Columbia, 1970); *A Tribute to Jack Johnson* (Columbia, 1970); *Big Fun* (Columbia, 1972); *On the Corner* (Columbia, 1972); *You're Under Arrest* (Columbia, 1985); *Aura* (Columbia, 1985); *Concerto for Guitar & Orchestra, "The Mediterranean"* (CBS, 1990); *John McLaughlin Trio, Live at the Royal Festival Hall* (JMT, 1990); *Qué Alegría* (Verve, 1992); *Time Remembered: John McLaughlin Plays Bill Evans* (Verve, 1993); *The Free Spirits, Tokyo Live* (Verve, 1994); *After the Rain* (Verve 1995); *The Promise* (Verve, 1995); *Paco De Lucia/Al Di Meola/John McLaughlin* (Verve, 1996); *The Heart of Things* (Verve, 1997); *Remember Shakti* (Verve, 1998); *Mahavishnu Orchestra: The Lost Trident Sessions* (Columbia Legacy, 1999); *The Heart of Things: Live in Paris* (Verve, 2000); *Remember Shakti: The Believer* (Verve, 2000); *Remember Shakti: Saturday Night in Bombay* (Verve, 2001). **With the Tony Williams Lifetime:** *Spectrum: The Anthology* (Polygram, 1997).

HOWARD MANDEL

MEAT LOAF

Born: Marvin Lee Aday; Dallas, Texas, 27 September 1947
Genre: Rock
Best-selling album since 1990: *Bat out of Hell II: Back into Hell* (1993)
Hit songs since 1990: "I'd Lie for You (And That's the Truth)," "Original Sin," "I'd Do Anything for Love (But I Won't Do That)"

Meat Loaf became a 1970s superstar when he combined rock opera bombast and arena theatrics, particularly on his signature hit "Two out of Three Ain't Bad." He was a memorable performer thanks to this melodramatic style and overpowering 250-pound presence.

Born into a gospel-singing family, Meat Loaf first worked as a singer and occasional actor. His mother died from cancer when he was quite young and his father became an alcoholic. In 1967 he quit college where he was studying to be an accountant, and moved to Los Angeles to form a rock group known alternately as Meat Loaf Soul and Popcorn Blizzard. The band gained a following while opening for rockers the Who, the Stooges, and Ted Nugent.

Meat Loaf won a part in the West Coast production of the musical *Hair*. At an early 1971 tour stop in Detroit, Michigan, Meat Loaf teamed up with a singer/actress cast-mate named Stoney to record his first album *Stoney and Meat Loaf* on Motown's Rare Earth imprint. (This was later re-released as *Meat Loaf (Featuring Stoney)* in 1979.) The album met with negligible success but the pair scored on the hit single "What You See Is What You Get," which peaked at number seventy-one on the *Billboard* pop charts later that year.

After Meat Loaf moved to New York, he appeared in the off-Broadway musical *Rainbow in New York*, which ran from 1972 to 1974. He then switched roles in another off-Broadway musical, *More Than You Deserve*, written by producer, composer, and classically trained New York pianist Jim Steinman, who was impressed by Meat Loaf's powerful vocals and stage presence.

Meat Loaf landed the part of Eddie in the theatrical production in 1975 and later the movie version of Richard O'Brien's cult piece *The Rocky Horror Picture Show*. The next year he followed that up by singing on one side of Ted Nugent's album *Free for All*. Meat Loaf joined up again

Spot Light | The Bat Is Back

It was highly improbable, but Meatloaf soared back on the national scene with his hit single "I'd Do Anything for Love (But I Won't Do That)" from the direct sequel to his pompous masterpiece *Bat Out of Hell* (1971). Few rock artists have been able to resurrect the zenith of their careers to such an incredible degree. Putting their differences behind them Meatloaf and Jim Steinman reunited for *Bat Out of Hell II: Back into Hell* (1993), which peaked at number one in October 1993. All the basic elements were there—confused teen hero, histrionic singing, and arena sound. Familiar themes of youthful angst and struggle were plentiful in titles like "Life Is a Lemon and I Want My Money Back," "Out of the Frying Pan (and into the Fire)," "Objects in the Rear View Mirror May Appear Closer," and "Good Girls Go to Heaven (Bad Girls Go Everywhere)."

with Steinman on the *National Lampoon Road Show* tour and later as Steinman worked on a musical update of the Peter Pan story titled *Never Land*. But it was on the pair's masterpiece album, *Bat out of Hell* (1977) that Meat Loaf reached his critical zenith. A teen opera penned by Steinman, the music was elevated into rock lore thanks to producer Todd Rundgren's pop focus and Meat Loaf's over-the-top vocals and theatrical stage presence. The album went platinum by the end of the year, with several hit singles, including "Paradise by the Dashboard Light," "Two out of Three Ain't Bad," and "You Took the Words Right out of My Mouth."

A sequel was planned but never released as Meat Loaf was unable to record due to physical exhaustion and other problems relating to nonstop work, including film appearances in *Americathon* (1979) and *Roadie* (1980). Frustrated, Steinman released his own solo album *Bad for Good* (1981) to minimal success in England. Meanwhile Meat Loaf followed with *Dead Ringer* (1981), which included Steinman tunes and featured Cher in a duet on the title track. But gone was producer Rundgren and his pop skills. Making matters worse, almost four years had transpired since the original smash, and so the album barely dented the charts. One tune "I'm Going to Love Her for the Two of Us" peaked at number eighty-four on the *Billboard* pop charts.

In 1983 Steinman filed suit against Meat Loaf and none of his songs appeared on Meat Loaf's subsequent album, *Midnight at the Lost and Found* (1983). That and Meat Loaf's subsequent albums, *Bad Attitude* (1984) and *Blind before I Stop* (1986), fell flat. Shortly afterward, Meat Loaf filed for bankruptcy as he went into physical and psychological rehabilitation.

In 1993 Meat Loaf hooked up again with Steinman to produce *Bat out of Hell II: Back into Hell*, the long awaited sequel. The album features the original story and the usual bombastics. It produced the hit single "I'd Do Anything for Love (But I Won't Do That)" while the album peaked at number one in October 1993.

Meat Loaf then went solo again and released *Welcome to the Neighborhood* (1995) and *Rock 'n' Roll Hero* (1999) but by then the appeal of his melodramatic flair was old hat. As a team Meat Loaf, Steinman, and Rundgren struck lightning when they combined absorbing lyrics, pop sense, and over-the-top singing. But the magic of the original *Bat out of Hell* came in its camp silliness and gothic and operatic flair, an approach that did not have a long shelf life.

SELECTIVE DISCOGRAPHY: *Bat out of Hell* (Epic, 1977); *Dead Ringer* (Epic, 1981); *Bat out of Hell II: Back into Hell* (MCA, 1993); *Welcome to the Neighborhood* (Virgin, 1995).

SELECTIVE FILMOGRAPHY: *The Rocky Horror Picture Show* (1975); *Americathon* (1979); *Roadie* (1980); *Crazy in Alabama* (1999); *Fight Club* (1999).

BIBLIOGRAPHY: Meat Loaf, *To Hell and Back* (New York, 2002).

RAMIRO BURR

MEDESKI, MARTIN & WOOD

Formed: 1991, New York City

Members: Billy Martin, drums, percussion (born New York, New York, 30 October 1963); John Medeski, keyboards (born Louisville, Kentucky, 28 June 1965); Chris Wood, bass, electric bass (born Pasadena, California, 25 November 1969).

Genre: Jazz, Jazz Fusion, Alternative Rock

Best-selling album since 1990: *Shack-Man* (1996)

Hit songs since 1990: "Last Chance to Dance Trance (Perhaps)," "Jelly Belly," "Bemsha Swing/Lively Up Yourself," "Chubb Sub"

Multi-keyboardist John Medeski, drummer Billy Martin, and bassist Chris Wood formed their trio in 1991, and by indefatigably touring colleges and alternative rock-oriented venues in the United States via recreational vehicle, established its high energy, loosely structured,

Medeski, Martin & Wood. L-R: Billy Martin, John Medeski, Chris Wood [DANNY CLINCH/BIG HASSLE MEDIA]

improvisatory instrumental music as a popular genre unto itself. Medeski, Martin & Wood thereby stands as the premiere "jam band," with an enthusiastic following among young listeners and a large number of imitative ensembles formed in its wake.

Medeski, Martin & Wood's original repertoire has frequently evolved out of live "jams," launching from a basic melodic figure and simple chord progression (a "vamp") over a consistent rhythmic groove. Due to each member's personal skills as well as the spontaneous, creative interplay of the three together, a jam might last for twenty minutes or more, in the style of free-form rock bands such as the Grateful Dead or Blues Traveler (with whom Medeski has appeared as a guest artist). Essentially updating the 1950s–1960s organ trio format popularized by Jimmy Smith with rock, pop, soul, New Orleans, and reggae rhythms and a smattering of avant-garde elements, Medeski, Martin & Wood has also successfully applied its ensemble sound to jazz standards such as Duke Ellington's "Caravan" and Thelonious Monk's "Bemsha Swing," and rock anthems such as Jimi Hendrix's "Hey Joe" and Sly Stone's "Everyday People." So doing, Medeski, Martin & Wood defies categorization and eludes definitive criticism. The trio has

been described as both "too cerebral" and irresistibly funky; it enjoys a generally positive reputation in both jazz and rock segments of the music press, and wins over audiences by being at once provocative and accessible.

Medeski, Martin & Wood met during the late 1980s, while studying at New England Conservatory and/or working with like-minded musicians of the Northeast United States—among them drummer Bob Moses, saxophonist/composer John Zorn, the Lounge Lizards, the Either/Orchestra, guitarist David Fiuczynski, and guitarist Marc Ribot's bands Shrek and Rootless Cosmopolitans. Medeski is a classically trained pianist who has extended his virtuosity to electric piano, Hammond B-3 organ, an array of synthesizers, and sampling keyboards; he typically stacks them one atop another, to finger any of them simultaneously or at whim during a single solo. Wood performs on both acoustic "stand-up" bass and electric basses. Martin (also known as illy B) provides a loud, firm yet flowing beat, an interest in working with hip-hop turntablists such as DJ Logic and DJ Olive, and the addition of Latin and African percussion instruments.

Medeski, Martin & Wood first recorded as an all-acoustic ensemble (*Notes from the Underground*, 1992), but solidified itself as an electro-acoustic hybrid, as heard on its breakthrough album *Friday Afternoon in the Universe* (1994). Two years later, band members retreated to a Hawaiian shack for a month to record their best-selling album *Shack-Man* (1996), and upon its release toured on the alternative rock circuit H.O.R.D.E. (Horizons of Rock Developing Everywhere), which afforded Medeski opportunities to play with Rickie Lee Jones and the group Leftover Salmon. The next year, they performed in the prestigious Brooklyn Academy of Music Next Wave Festival, and were awarded a high-visibility, midafternoon spot at George Wein's Newport Jazz Festival. The trio also enjoyed significant success supporting guitarist John Scofield on his album *A Go Go* (1997). Scofield and Chris Wood performed as guests of Government Mule on "Sco-Mule" (from *Deep End, Volume 1*, 2002), which was nominated for a Grammy in the Best Rock Instrumental Performance category. Medeski also guested on that album.

All three Medeski, Martin & Wood principles maintain projects of their own: Among other activities, Medeski curates and produces albums for Ropeadope Records, Martin has his own Amulet Records, and Wood has collaborated with rhythm and blues saxophonist Karl Denson. Medeski, Martin & Wood's ambitious production *Uninvisible* (2002) includes spoken-word contributions by Col. Bruce Hampton and backgrounds by the five-man Antibalas Horns. Medeski, Martin & Wood songs have been used on movie soundtracks, including that of Jerry Seinfeld's feature-length film, *Comedian* (2002). In 2003, the trio traveled widely, from the University of Vermont to the Hollywood Bowl, from Calgary, Alberta, to San Sebastian, Spain. The band shows no signs of slowing the pace of its busy schedule, and there is every indication that it has more ideas to inject into its patented "jam band" format.

SELECTIVE DISCOGRAPHY: *Notes from the Underground* (hap-Jones, 1992); *It's a Jungle in Here* (Gramavision, 1993); *Friday Afternoon in the Universe* (Gramavision, 1994); *Shack-Man* (Gramavision, 1996); *Bubblehouse* EP (Gramavision, 1996); *Farmers Reserve* (Indirecto, 1997); *Combustication* (Blue Note, 1998); *Tonic* (Blue Note, 1999); *Medeski Martin & Wood Best Of (1991–1996)* (Ryko/Gramavision, 1999); *The Dropper* (Blue Note, 1999–2000); *Uninvisible* (Blue Note, 2002). **Soundtrack:** *Get Shorty* (Verve, 1995).

WEBSITE: www.mmw.net/band.jsp.

HOWARD MANDEL

The Mekons. L-R: row 1 Sally Timms, Susie Honeyman, Sara Corina; row 2 Rico Bell, Steve Goulding, Lu Edmonds; row 3 Jon Langford, Tom Greenhalgh [FRANK SWIDER/ TOUCH AND GO/QUARTERSTICK RECORDS]

THE MEKONS

Formed: 1977, Leeds, England

Members: Jon Langford, vocals, guitar, drums (born Newport, South Wales, 11 October 1957); Tom Greenhalgh, vocals, guitar (born Stockholm, Sweden, 4 November 1956); Sally Timms, vocals (born Leeds, England, 29 November 1959); Robert "Lu" Edmonds, bass, guitar, vocals (born Hertfordshire, England, 24 September 1957); Steve Goulding, drums (born South London, England); Susie Honeyman, violin; Rico Bell, accordion (born Wallasey, England); Sara Corina, bass.

Genre: Rock, Country

Best-selling album since 1990: *I Love Mekons* (1993)

The Mekons are an ever-changing collective of musicians hailing from the punk era of late-1970s England. Although they never had a hit, their relentless experimentation brought them a fiercely loyal following. The band's extensive discography includes forays into punk, folk, country, reggae, techno, synth pop, straight-ahead rock and roll, and the occasional artful pastiche combining all of the above. From the start rock critics championed the group's incendiary live shows and strident working-class politics. The Mekons associated themselves with marginalized pockets of society, performing benefits for unions and death-penalty opponents. The group has a history of bad luck with recording labels but was rejuvenated when most of its members relocated to Chicago in the early 1990s. There the Mekons were reborn, rushing out albums on the Chicago label Quarterstick, participating in numerous side projects, and enjoying a new audience that appreciated their history and eclecticism.

The founding and most consistent members of the Mekons are Jon Langford and Tom Greenhalgh. The two met while art students at Leeds University in Yorkshire. A local show by the founding British punk band the Sex Pistols inspired them both to put down their paintbrushes and pick up musical instruments—Langford learned drums and Greenhalgh the guitar. Soon they released the single "Never Been in a Riot," an irreverent response to the race conscious anthem "White Riot" by the Clash, Britain's ruling political punk band.

The Mekons were signed to Virgin but were subsequently dropped, a pattern that repeated throughout the band's career. As the band's continual reinvention was cheered by fans and the press, record companies could not figure out how to market them, or they went out of business trying. Subsequent albums hopped from label to label, some going out of print or held in limbo for years. Not until the late 1990s did most of their catalog become reissued.

The Mekons' most endurable incarnation was as a postmodern country band. *Fear and Whiskey* (1985) emerged as the blueprint for later albums and side projects. Its ghostly sound evoked archetypal American images like freight trains, outlaws, barrooms, and bleak landscapes. The Mekons continued to embrace Americana while twisting it into the perspective of a solitary outsider. The music evoked the loneliness of Hank Williams, one of country music's founders (they covered the Williams chestnut "Lost

Highway"), but with drunken dance beats and erratic punk energy. *Fear and Whiskey* became an underground classic. It helped set a path for the alternative country movement of the 1990s, led by the Illinois band Uncle Tupelo and its later offshoots, Wilco and Son Volt. The music that bloomed in that period introduced old-time country music to a new generation that recognized it shared the working-class roots of punk.

Langford, who had since switched to guitar, admitted he became obsessed by America's musical roots through trips to Nashville, Memphis, and Chicago and by compilation tapes friends made for him. "I felt like someone scuba diving for the first time, it was amazing," he told the *Chicago Daily Herald* in 1999. "What I learned about America was that you have this rich culture here but you kind of pave over it. You're moving on so fast." Still a painter, Langford honored country music icons in his artwork and had gallery showings across the United States and Great Britain.

A majority of the band relocated to Chicago by the early 1990s and began forming side projects and recording solo albums for local labels that welcomed them to their roster. By that point the Mekons had all but retired, its lineup becoming a rotating door of musicians. The stability of a new home jump-started the band creatively, and the Mekons embarked on their most fertile and experimental period. *Me* (1998) lampooned materialism and pornography within a harsh techno backdrop; *Journey to the End of the Night* (2000) was a quieter collection of melancholic songs about capitalism in decline. Although *OOOH! (Out of Our Heads)* (2002) was recorded before the terrorism of September 11, 2001, its weaving of exotic rhythms, traditional Welsh and Celtic music, and harsh biblical imagery led critics to associate it with the attack's mournful fallout.

By the end of the decade, the Mekons' creativity looked limitless. In 2002 the group celebrated its history with a three-city tour. Each night showcased a specific period in the band's career: noisy punk; honky-tonk country; and avant-garde experimentalism. The tour was a testament to the group's legacy as survivors and as relentless provocateurs.

SELECTIVE DISCOGRAPHY: *The Quality of Mercy Is Not Strnen* (Virgin, 1979); *The Mekons* (Red Rhino, 1980); *It Falleth Like Gentle Rain from Heaven: The Mekons Story* (CNT, 1982); *Fear and Whiskey* (Sin, 1985); *Edge of the World* (Sin, 1986); *Honky Tonkin* (Twin/Tone, 1987); *So Good It Hurts* (Twin/Tone, 1988); *Original Sin: The Mekons Rock 'n' Roll* (A&M, 1989); *The Curse of the Mekons* (Blast First, 1991); *I Love Mekons* (Quarterstick, 1993); *Retreat from Memphis* (Quarterstick, 1994); *United* (Quarterstick, 1995); *Pussy, King of Pirates* (Quarterstick, 1996); *Me* (Quarterstick, 1998); *Journey to the End of the Night* (Quarterstick, 2000); *OOOH! (Out of Our Heads)* (Quarterstick, 2002).

MARK GUARINO

JOHN MELLENCAMP

Born: Seymour, Indiana, 7 October 1951

Genre: Rock, Folk

Best-selling album since 1990: *The Best That I Could Do (1978–1988)* (1997)

Hit songs since 1990: "Wild Night," "Key West Intermezzo (I Saw You First)," "Peaceful World"

John Mellencamp is a musical ambassador of small-town America. His songbook is filled with hits that chronicle the voices of rural midwesterners. Until the 1990s he was mainly rooted in the classic guitar rock of 1960s bands like the Rolling Stones and Them as well as the American folk tradition of the Depression-era songwriter Woody Guthrie. Later Mellencamp branched out to experiment with electronic beats, hip-hop grooves, and work with younger performers from the rap and R&B world. Mellencamp has never strayed far from his midwestern roots. Southern Indiana remains his home base. He became an activist for the plight of family farms through the Farm Aid organization he formed with the singer/songwriters Willie Nelson and Neil Young. He also complemented his musical career through painting and directing films. By the close of the 1990s, Mellencamp had accumulated so many memorable songs that his live shows became a jukebox of career hits. He later acknowledged that his advancing age prevented him from getting the radio exposure he enjoyed in his early days, so he gave up worrying about writing hit singles. Instead, he explored folk music, connecting the politics of the day with the lives of average Americans.

Beginnings

Mellencamp was born in Seymour, Indiana, just south of the state university town of Bloomington. His childhood was marred by spina bifida, a neurological condition that cripples the spinal cord. Mellencamp survived, and by the end of his senior year of high school he had eloped with a girlfriend. He soon had a child and began a life of working odd jobs, playing in bands, and attending classes at Vincennes University. In 1975 he moved to New York in search of a record deal.

He soon met Tony DeFries, who then managed the British glam-rock icon David Bowie. DeFries helped Mellencamp get his first album released, but there was a catch. DeFries changed Mellencamp's last name to Cougar without him even knowing it. The stage name dogged Mellencamp until the early 1990s, when he was confident enough to shed it. Mellencamp's first four albums were mostly forgettable and did not sell well, though he did earn his first hit song in 1979 with "I Need a Lover."

Mellencamp was modeled as a hard-rocking rebel. His breakthrough was *American Fool* (1982). It featured three hit singles, including "Jack and Diane," which became his signature song. It told the story of two young kids from the Heartland with big dreams that were stalled by reality. The disillusionment became political with another signature hit, "Pink Houses," from *Uh-Huh* (1983). The song faced the same fate of Bruce Springsteen's "Born in the U.S.A.," released a year later. Both featured sweeping choruses that amounted to flag-waving or ironic detachment, based on the perspective of the listener. "Ain't that America / for you and me," Mellencamp sang, relating the poverty and resentment of his characters in the song's verses.

By the mid-1980s, Mellencamp had developed into a serious singer/songwriter. His album *Scarecrow* (1985) sympathized with family farmers and railed against the government-subsidized factory farms that were running them out of business. Under the Farm Aid organization he performed annual benefit concerts and telethons to raise money and awareness.

New Directions

In his song "R.O.C.K. in the U.S.A.," Mellencamp gives a shout out to his soul, funk, and rock influences from the late 1960s through the early 1970s. In 1987, with the career-changing album *The Lonesome Jubilee*, he took a new direction. Expanding his band with a fiddle player, backup singers, and accordion, Mellencamp creates pictures of contemporary small-town America and its poverty, joblessness, and vacated dreams. The bleak outlook is lifted by the musical ensemble. The songs are narratives more than testimonials, and the music swoons under the band's romantic folk-rock flourishes. A masterpiece of heartland rock, the album redefined Mellencamp's public persona.

After the quieter and more introspective album *Big Daddy* (1989), Mellencamp announced his retirement. He invested his time in painting and began production on "Falling from Grace," a feature film he directed and starred in. In it he plays a character similar to himself in Jackson County, Indiana, where he grew up. He also purchased a home in his hometown of Seymour and helped turn it into the Southern Indiana Center for the Arts.

He returned to music with *Whenever We Wanted* (1991), a straightforward rock album in the vein of his heroes the Rolling Stones. Void of social commentary, it was his first album without the name Cougar in the title. The cover art features his elaborate painting studio and Elaine Irwin, a former model who became his third wife.

In the 1990s Mellencamp became a veteran artist best appreciated for his earlier hits. His recording output was just as prolific as it had been in the preceding decade, but the sales curve showed a marked downturn. The new chapter gave him the chance to experiment and stray further from heartland rock.

Illness and Renewal

In 1994 Mellencamp suffered from a heart attack and took a year off recuperating. By 1996 he was back with *Mr. Happy Go Lucky*. The album features programmed beats supplied by the acclaimed New York DJ Junior Vasquez, best known for his work with the dance music divas Madonna, Donna Summer, and Cher. Mellencamp also added keyboardist and rapper Moe-Z, M.D., to his band. The result is a funky and more groove-oriented record. "Key West Intermezzo (I Saw You First)" became a hit, and Mellencamp's live shows became more like dance parties. He had already had a hit duet ("Wild Night") with the bassist and R&B vocalist Meshell Ndegeocello two years earlier, a recording that introduced him to a younger generation and helped to make Ndegeocello a household name. Mellencamp also performed a duet with the R&B singer India.Arie and collaborated with Chuck D of the hardcore hip-hop group Public Enemy. As a veteran rock artist playing to a core fan base, he drew praise for taking chances and exposing urban artists and new sounds to his audience.

Jumping Labels

Mellencamp jumped labels, from PolyGram/Mercury to Columbia Records, in 1999. His first-ever boxed set would come out later that year. He also made the unusual step of announcing he was co-writing a Broadway musical with the horror fiction writer Stephen King, based on an original ghost story. He was silent until early 2003, when he debuted a song on his Internet site, hinting at a new direction for his music. Featuring mandolin, acoustic guitar, fiddle, accordion, tambourine, and vocals, "To Washington" takes its melody and arrangement from Woody Guthrie, who borrowed it himself from the country music pioneers the Carter Family. Mellencamp rewrote the lyrics to reflect his dissatisfaction with President George W. Bush and his administration's campaign to wage war against Iraq in 2003. The singer told reporters the turbulent political climate prompted him to return to more stripped-down, socially conscious music.

Early in his career John Mellencamp was denounced by critics as yet another clone of American rock statesmen like Bruce Springsteen, Bob Seger, and Tom Petty. He proved, however, that he was a wholly original artist. Mellencamp's knack for combining catchy guitar hooks with snapshots of small-town America resulted in many hit songs. He turned several corners, exploring folk and country traditions and, later, the electronic beats of urban hip-hop, while never losing his connection with his midwestern roots.

SELECTIVE DISCOGRAPHY: *Chestnut Street Incident* (Mainman/MCA, 1976); *American Fool* (Poly-Gram/Mercury, 1982); *Uh-Huh* (PolyGram/Mercury, 1983); *Scarecrow* (PolyGram/Mercury, 1985); *The Lonesome Jubilee* (PolyGram/Mercury, 1987); *Big Daddy* (PolyGram/Mercury, 1989); *Whenever We Wanted* (PolyGram/Mercury, 1991); *Mr. Happy Go Lucky* (PolyGram/Mercury, 1996); *The Best That I Could Do* (1978–1988) (PolyGram/Mercury, 1997); *John Mellencamp* (Columbia, 1998); *Cuttin' Heads* (Columbia, 2001).

WEBSITE: www.mellencamp.com.

MARK GUARINO

ALAN MENKEN

Born: New York, New York, 22 July 1949

Genre: Soundtrack

Best-selling album since 1990: *Aladdin* (1992)

Composer Alan Menken has been a workhorse in the animated film industry. His toe-tapping, literate music breathed life into the once dead genre, resurrecting it to spectacular popularity. From time to time, Menken returns to his musical theater roots and achieves similar success.

Growing up in suburban New Rochelle, New York, about twenty-five minutes out of Manhattan, it was his parents' foregone conclusion that Menken would become a dentist. His father and many members of his immediate and extended family were all successful dentists. Menken did not have dental ambitions, but was influenced by the Menken family's love of music—particularly Broadway musicals. Menken studied piano and violin as a youngster and later attended New York University. He appeased his parents by studying pre-med before gravitating toward the prestigious university's music department. After graduating with a music degree, Menken supported himself by playing clubs and writing "jingles"—music for advertising campaigns. In 1978 he composed the music for an adaptation of Kurt Vonnegut's *God Bless You, Mr. Rosewater*, which played off-Broadway at New York's WPA Theatre. The show teamed Menken with playwright/lyricist Howard Ashman and initiated an exceptionally produc-

tive twelve-year creative partnership until it was interrupted by Ashman's death in 1991.

After several lukewarm stage forays, Menken met success in 1982 by combining his music with Ashman's lyrics to create, *Little Shop of Horrors*, a witty, off-the-wall show about a geeky flower shop owner and his array of man-eating plants. It became the third-longest running off-Broadway play in history and in 1986, Warner Bros. turned it into a successful film. Menken's song, "Mean Green Mother from Outer Space," written specifically for the film version of *Little Shop of Horrors*, received an Academy Award nomination for Best Song. More importantly, it brought his talent to the attention of Disney Studios who offered Menken and Ashman the opportunity to develop several animated film projects of their choosing.

Their first effort, *The Little Mermaid* (1989), was enormously well received, won two Academy Awards, and began a long string of successful Disney-produced animated films, marking a comeback for the studio and for the entire genre as well. It also began a string of Academy Awards for Menken. His next project was an eighteenth-century French tale called *Beauty and the Beast* (1991). The movie was so popular that Disney immediately made plans for its transformation into a Broadway musical. Nevertheless, *Beauty and the Beast* was shaded with sadness as Ashman died from complications of AIDS before the movie was released. In addition, the successful team had almost completed work on their third animated film, *Aladdin* (1992). Disney enlisted lyricist Tim Rice to finish the project. Rice, who was the librettist for *Evita* and *Jesus Christ Superstar*, also worked with Menken on the Broadway version of *Beauty and the Beast*, which opened in 1994 and featured eight new songs by Menken. *Beauty and the Beast* has had over 4,000 performances in its triumphant Broadway run.

Aladdin was even more successful than the previous two blockbuster films, and Menken continued reaping praise for his clever melodies that furthered the films' plot lines in the same way that theatrical musicals traditionally do. In 1992 he went back to the theater and collaborated with lyricist David Spencer on another off-Broadway success, *Weird Romance*. He also began work, with Lynn Ahrens as lyricist, on a new musical adaptation of Charles Dickens's *A Christmas Story*, which receives, since its opening in 1994, a two-month Christmas holiday performance every year in New York's Madison Square Garden Theater.

Over the next five years, Menken composed the music for an onslaught of Disney animated musicals, including *Pocahontas* (1995), *The Hunchback of Notre Dame* (1996), and *Hercules* (1997), all of which further contributed to his collection of eight Academy Awards. In 1998, Disney Studios offered Menken a ten-year multimillion-dollar contract to write music for their upcoming projects.

His *Little Shop of Horrors*, already one of the most widely produced plays in the world, circled back to New York and opened on Broadway in the summer of 2003. Additionally, Menken is at work with lyricist Glenn Slater to transform *The Little Mermaid* into a Broadway production. Along the way he has written songs for a number of other projects, most notably the theme for the film *Rocky V* (1990), and "The Measure of a Man" and "My Christmas Tree" from the hit movie *Home Alone 2* (1992). A new Disney animated musical, *Home on the Range*, is scheduled for release in 2004. Billed as a comic western, it features Menken again teaming with Slater.

Menken's music will forever be considered a principal reason for the resurgence of animated films. He was at his zenith during the years that he teamed with Ashman.

SELECTIVE DISCOGRAPHY: *Little Shop of Horrors* (stage) (Geffen, 1982); *Little Shop of Horrors* (film) (Geffen, 1986); *The Little Mermaid* (Walt Disney, 1989); *Beauty and the Beast* (film) (Walt Disney, 1991); *Lincoln* (Angel, 1992); *Aladdin* (Walt Disney, 1992); *Weird Romance* (Columbia, 1993); *Beauty and the Beast* (stage) (Wonderland, 1994); *A Christmas Carol* (MSG, 1994); *Pocahontas* (Wonderland, 1995); *The Hunchback of Notre Dame* (Wonderland, 1996); *King David* (Trunksong, 1997).

DONALD LOWE

NATALIE MERCHANT

Born: Jamestown, New York, 26 October 1963

Genre: Rock

Best-selling album since 1990: *Tigerlily* (1995)

Hit songs since 1990: "Carnival," "Wonder," "Jealousy"

Natalie Merchant began her career as the thoughtful lead singer for the folk-rock band 10,000 Maniacs. The band achieved success with a few albums and eventually broke up. Merchant, who was the primary songwriter for the Maniacs, launched a solo career in the mid-1990s and became even more successful. Her unique voice, uncompromising political opinions, and folk-rock style make for music with a social conscience.

Merchant is the third of four children of Ann and Anthony Merchant. Her mother and father divorced when she was seven, and the young Natalie lived with her mother. Eventually her mother remarried and moved the family to a commune in upstate New York, a lifestyle change that profoundly influenced Merchant psychologically. The women who lived in the commune were strong, capable, and solitary.

In 1981, at the age of seventeen, Merchant joined a local group that became 10,000 Maniacs, and she had much success on the independent, college-rock scene. The group scored several hits, such as the quirky "Like the Weather" and "Hey Jack Kerouac" from their breakthrough album *In My Tribe* (1988). They released six critically well-received albums and established an active fan base. The fans faithfully followed Merchant when she left the band in the summer of 1993. Merchant confessed that all she wanted to do growing up was leave her hometown and to expand her horizons; because the Maniacs were all from Jamestown, New York, she knew she would have to go solo.

Finding Her Voice

With her passionate, rich alto, Merchant is a songwriter who constantly absorbs the world around her; she interprets issues, people, events, and causes through song. Her self-produced debut album, *Tigerlily*, appeared in 1995. The album's title refers in part to her love of flowers, and she told *Billboard* magazine, "I love names that combine two incongruous things. It's a combination of songs which are almost fierce in power lyrically and musically, and others which are really gentle and graceful." Although *Tigerlily* is contemplative, austere, and somber, there is a light touch in the music; the arrangements and even the vocals are reined in. The first single, "Carnival," is a moody, midtempo contemplation on life: "Have I been blind? / Have I been lost inside myself and my own mind?" "Carnival" peaked at number six on the *Billboard* Top 40. *Tigerlily* is so wholly formed, it does not sound like a debut solo album; it is as if Merchant had been collecting the material in her head for years. Merchant dedicated the song "River" to her acquaintance, the promising young film actor River Phoenix, who died of a drug overdose in 1993. The album sold more than 5 million copies and peaked at number thirteen on the *Billboard* 200 chart.

No Sophomore Slump

After extensive touring both on her own and with Sarah McLachlan's Lilith Fair in 1998 and 1999, Merchant released *Ophelia* (1997), which peaked at number eight on the *Billboard* 200. Her appearances in the Lilith Fair in the summer of 1998 helped spur sales. *Ophelia*'s first single, "Kind and Generous," is Merchant's love letter to her fans. She wrote following the tremendous success of *Tigerlily*. She sings, "For everything you do / You know I'm bound / I'd like to thank you for it." The single landed in the Adult Top 40. *Ophelia*, named for the character in Shakespeare's *Hamlet* who goes mad and drowns herself, continues in the vein of *Tigerlily*, but at times with a heavier hand and heart.

In November 2001 Merchant released her third solo effort, *Motherland*, her most ambitious record to date. She co-produced the album with the well-regarded T-Bone Burnett, who has worked with Elvis Costello and the Wallflowers, and it is perhaps her most expansive work to date. Arabic influences appear in the opening track "This House Is on Fire," and there is a tango-flamenco hybrid flavor in "The Worst Thing." Though Merchant released the album in the fall of 2001, the lyrics in the title track assumed a new meaning after the terrorist attacks of September 11. She now says it feels like the death of nostalgia and dreams; she sings a plea to be "faceless, nameless, innocent, blameless and free." *Motherland*, though, is not all worldly melancholy. The positive pop gem, "Just Can't Last," suggests that life's troubles are ultimately fleeting, and that Merchant can still write a song with a light, lilting touch.

Merchant, eccentric and principled, manages to educate, inspire, and imbue her songs with a social and moral awareness. On stage at times she seems like a schoolteacher. One of her goals is to inspire people to think a little more.

SELECTIVE DISCOGRAPHY: *Tigerlily* (Elektra, 1995); *Ophelia* (Elektra, 1997); *Natalie Merchant Live in Concert* (Elektra, 1999); *Motherland* (Elektra, 2001). **With 10,000 Maniacs:** *In My Tribe* (Elektra, 1987); *Our Time in Eden* (Elektra, 1992).

CARRIE HAVRANEK

JO DEE MESSINA

Born: Framingham, Massachusetts, 25 August 1970
Genre: Country, Pop
Best-selling album since 1990: *Burn* (2000)
Hit songs since 1990: "Heads Carolina, Tails California," "I'm Alright," "Burn"

A country star with a husky, powerful voice and a mane of red hair, Jo Dee Messina was part of a wave of 1990s female vocalists, also including Trisha Yearwood and Shania Twain, who updated country music with a prominent rock and pop influence. Born and raised in New England, Messina did not fit the southern country prototype, but her brash vocals were well suited to the breezy, assured sound promoted by 1990s country radio. Overcoming significant personal obstacles to keep her career on track between albums, Messina proved that the toughness and resilience projected in her singing were genuine.

Raised in the small town of Holliston, Massachusetts, Messina longed to be a country singer from an early age, emulating the throaty, soulful style of 1970s vocalists such as Tammy Wynette and Dottie West. By her teens Messina was performing in a band with her family, becoming a well-

known act on New England's country scene. Recognizing the limited options for a country singer in the northeast, Messina decided at age nineteen to move to the country music locus of Nashville, Tennessee, where she found work singing on a radio program, "Live at Libby's." Although producer Byron Gallimore heard her on the radio and soon became a supporter, Messina's true breakthrough came in 1994 at Nashville's popular Fan Fair, an annual event where country stars mingle with their fans. Backstage with her friend, up-and-coming singer Tim McGraw, Messina spotted a Curb Records executive and joked with him, "What you guys really need over there is a redhead." Aided by further recommendations from famed producer James Stroud, Messina signed with Curb and released her self-titled debut album in 1996.

Sparked by energetic hits such as "Heads Carolina, Tails California," *Jo Dee Messina* represents the spirited, rock-driven country sound popular in the mid-1990s. While less than perfect from a technical perspective—her big voice sometimes strays off-pitch—Messina makes up for it with her directness and honesty. Her singing projects determination and self-assurance, qualities upon which she relied after her first album's run of hits had dried up. Due to the high expense of maintaining a touring band, Messina ran into severe financial problems while recording her second album. At one point she placed her house on the market, planning to declare bankruptcy and move back to Massachusetts. Fortunately the album, tellingly titled *I'm Alright*, proved an even bigger success than its predecessor, crossing over from the country to the pop charts. Messina's voice, rich and compelling in its lower register, is well served on upbeat hits such as "Bye Bye," "Lesson in Leavin'," and the likable title track, which good-humoredly alludes to Messina's on-again, off-again career success: "I'm above the below / and below the upper." By the time of her third release, *Burn* (2000), Messina had cultivated a strong rock sound, evident on tracks such as "Dare to Dream," which blares with high-voltage electric guitar.

Following a circuitous path to stardom, Messina brought a winning directness to country music of the late 1990s and early 2000s. While falling short of the crossover fame of fellow country artist Shania Twain, Messina appealed to both country and rock fans with her hard-driving vocal style and engaging series of hits.

SELECTIVE DISCOGRAPHY: *Jo Dee Messina* (Curb, 1996); *I'm Alright* (Curb, 1998); *Burn* (Curb, 2000).
WEBSITE: www.jodeemessina.com.

DAVID FREELAND

METALLICA

Formed: 1981, Los Angeles, California
Members: Kirk Hammett, lead guitar (born San Francisco, California, 18 November 1962); James Hetfield, vocals,

rhythm guitar (born Downey, California, 3 August 1963); Lars Ulrich, drums (born Gentofte, Denmark, 26 December 1963). Former members: Cliff Burton, bass (born Castro Valley, California, 10 February 1962; died Ljungby, Sweden, 27 September 1986); Ron McGovney, bass; Dave Mustaine, guitar (born La Mesa, California, 13 September 1961); Jason Newsted, bass (born Battle Creek, Michigan, 4 March 1963).

Genre: Heavy Metal, Rock

Best-selling album since 1990: *Metallica* (1991)

Hit songs since 1990: "Enter Sandman," "Until It Sleeps," "The Memory Remains"

Equal parts punk and heavy metal, Metallica pioneered the darker and faster genres known as speed and thrash metal in the early 1980s. As the decade progressed, they emerged as the premiere underground metal band and sold millions of records despite minimal airplay on radio and MTV. After adopting a slower, simpler sound in the 1990s, the group reached a mass audience. By the decade's end, Metallica was one of music's most successful acts but had alienated much of their original core audience.

Origins

When drummer Lars Ulrich and guitarist James Hetfield met in Los Angeles in 1981, they decided to form a band that reacted against the style-over-substance glam metal, which was quickly gaining popularity on the Sunset Strip in Los Angeles. They recruited guitarist Dave Mustaine and bassist Ron McGovney and began making music influenced by British heavy metal bands like Iron Maiden, Motorhead, and the lesser-known Diamond Head. The latter band's driving irregular rhythms and dark tone were the most direct influence on Metallica's sound. They took Diamond Head's heavily distorted but technically precise rhythmic guitar style and sped it up to a blistering pace. By using two bass drums simultaneously, Ulrich augmented the tempo to unthinkable speeds. These elements of extreme velocity combined to develop Metallica's distinct version of speed metal.

Los Angeles was not quite ready for them, but similar-sounding metal was gaining popularity in the San Francisco Bay Area. The band relocated there to get Cliff Burton, the bassist of local band Trauma, to join them. A solid fan base grew rapidly. Their widely circulated demotape, *No Life 'Til Leather,* prompted a record deal with underground label, Megaforce, on one condition: They must move to New York City.

Shortly after arriving on the East Coast, the band dismissed Mustaine because of behavioral problems. He went on to form Megadeth, one of the top speed-metal rivals of Metallica throughout the 1980s. The competition between the two bands was often heated and personal because of Mustaine's unceremonious departure. His replacement was Kirk Hammett.

With the lineup of Ulrich, Hetfield, Burton, and Hammett in place, Metallica released its debut album, *Kill 'Em All* (1983). The album creates an ominous and mesmerizing world with lightning-quick rhythms, Hetfield's coarse growl, and the use of the notably eerie Phrygian musical scale.

Underground Stardom

The band's next two albums, *Ride the Lightning* (1984) and *Master of Puppets* (1986), were more accomplished. Having Hammett from the beginning of the creative process allowed him to develop a more melodic and classically virtuosic guitar sound to complement Hetfield's pounding strums. Hetfield's vocals remained abrasive, but he introduced more melody and showed an aptitude for more conventional singing during the balladlike verses of "Fade to Black" and "Welcome Home (Sanitarium)." The songs dealt with suicide and mental illness, respectively, and represented a major step forward in lyrical maturity. *Master of Puppets* was hailed a masterpiece by even the unlikeliest critics. It cracked the Top 30 of the *Billboard* album chart and became the first platinum speed-metal album.

As the band's career soared to new heights, tragedy struck during a tour of Sweden in November 1986: The group's bus was in a horrible accident, and the band's bassist, Cliff Burton, was killed. After an anguished hiatus, Metallica chose to continue. Jason Newsted, a fervent Metallica fan and leader of the Phoenix-based band Flotsam and Jetsam, took Burton's place. Following a five-song EP of covers, *Garage Days Re-Revisited* (1987), the group released their most ambitious album to date, . . . *And Justice for All* (1988). With its bleak outlook at a decaying society, thin production, epic songs averaging more than seven minutes, and sophisticated compositions, it is a challenging listen. It cracked the Top 10 and swiftly went platinum.

After years of resistance, Metallica finally decided to shoot their first music video for "One," near the end of 1988. The song is based on the Dalton Trumbo novel *Johnny Got His Gun,* about a hospitalized war veteran who loses his sight, voice, hearing, and limbs but maintains total consciousness. Using scenes from the film version of the book and stark black-and-white performance footage, "One" was a disturbing tour de force. Medium rotation on MTV pushed the song to become one of the most unlikely Top 40 hits in *Billboard* history. Despite the crossover success, Metallica's uncompromising methods kept them in solid standing with their longtime fans.

Metallica. L-R: James Hetfield, Lars Ulrich, Jason Newsted, Kirk Hammett [PAUL NATKIN/PHOTO RESERVE]

Blockbuster Success

Having difficulty reproducing the complicated songs from . . . *And Justice for All* onstage, and uncertain how to refine its complex sound any further, Metallica decided to scale back on its self-titled 1991 release. With shortened, simplified, and significantly slower songs, it was a more straightforward album that was destined to reach a larger audience. Though the first single and video, "Enter Sandman," was ominous, its throbbing, repeated riff and verse-memorable chorus structure made it a hit. Selling a half million copies and peaking at number sixteen on the *Billboard* Hot 100, it became the group's most popular anthem.

The album's next two singles, "The Unforgiven" and "Nothing Else Matters," demonstrated a commercial side of Metallica not seen before. The former features a hefty guitar crunch in the verses that leads to a gentle pop chorus. The latter is the band's first love song, complete with a string section. Only "Holier Than Thou" and "Through the Never" approach the velocity of past efforts, while "Sad but True," "Don't Tread Me," and "The God That Failed" forge new territory with bass-heavy grooves and plodding guitars. Those characteristics were indicative of much of the nu-metal to follow in the 1990s and thereafter.

Metallica's new direction naturally disappointed some die-hard fans, but it introduced the band to a sub-stantially larger audience. *Metallica* debuted at number one, sold 3 million copies in its first two months, 6 million by the end of 1992, and 12 million by the end of decade. Its tremendous success generated new interest in previous albums and pushed all of them to multiplatinum status.

After incessant touring and some much-needed time off, the band felt heavy pressure to follow up their self-titled album. Instead of fearlessly trailblazing as they had always done, Metallica chose to assimilate to the 1990s alternative rock look and sound with *Load* (1996). The album's first video, "Until It Sleeps," presents all four members with short hair, with Hammett and Ulrich donning glam makeup. Similar images fill the album's liner notes, and the cover sports an updated, less menacing logo. They toned down the threatening, doomsday attitude and replaced it with a safer, more transparent, and occasionally bluesy sound. This distancing from the Metallica of the past surprised and disappointed many, but it did not prevent the album from debuting at number one, quickly selling 3 million copies, and yielding another gold single, "Until It Sleeps." The next year the group followed with *Re-Load*, a collection of songs that did not make it onto *Load* and some newly written material. Though somewhat of a rehash of the previous album, it offers a few new twists and found similar success.

After a five-year gap between albums in the middle 1990s, Metallica kept up an album-a-year pace in the late 1990s. *Garage Inc.* (1998) was a double-album of covers, some previously recorded and some new, paying tribute to artists ranging from Bob Seger and Lynyrd Skynyrd to early, more direct influences such as Diamond Head and the Misfits. *S&M* (1999) was another double disc that captured the band performing Metallica classics and two new songs with the San Francisco Symphony. The album once again attracted a new audience while acknowledging their classical influences. Both sold millions, garnered solid airplay, and reaffirmed the band's immense popularity, establishing them as one of the top-selling acts of the 1990s.

At the beginning of the new millennium, Metallica's headlines shifted from its music to its legal battles. The group garnered a litigious reputation by suing companies like Victoria's Secret and Pierre Cardin for trademark infringement over the use of the band's name. They also sued Amazon.com over sales of a bootleg album and released *Garage Inc.* partially as an attempt to prevent unauthorized dissemination of their rare material. It was no surprise then, when they filed suit against the online music distribution company Napster in April 2000 for facilitating the illegal trading of their copyrighted music. Lars Ulrich hand-delivered thirteen boxes of legal paperwork containing the names of over 300,000 users who had traded Metallica's music illegally. Though legally justified, Ulrich's antics seemed unfashionable and greedy for a rock star who had sold nearly 50 million albums. His actions caused a major backlash among some fans and fellow musicians. Metallica settled with Napster and praised them for attempting to run a legitimate business that thwarted the sharing of unauthorized, copyrighted material.

With all the distractions stalling Metallica's musical growth, and a longstanding ban on side projects, Newsted became frustrated and left the band. He promptly formed Echobrain, released an album with them, and then joined Canadian progressive metal legends Voivod. In April 2001 Metallica entered the recording studio to start work on a new album without a bassist. Three months later all progress ceased as James Hetfield entered rehab for alcoholism and other addictions. Five months later he returned to the group, and they readied an eighth studio album for 2003 release. Galvanizing speed metal into a viable underground institution, Metallica transcended its genre to become one of rock's most enduring forces. After years of boldly defining new directions in heavy metal, the band eventually made mainstream concessions to maintain longevity. Thriving long after most of their contemporaries had floundered, Metallica has left a legacy as one of the greatest rock bands of the 1980s, 1990s, and beyond.

SELECTIVE DISCOGRAPHY: *Kill 'Em All* (Megaforce/ Elektra, 1983); *Ride the Lightning* (Elektra, 1984); *Master of Puppets* (Elektra, 1986); *. . . And Justice for All* (Elektra, 1988); *Metallica* (Elektra, 1991); *Garage, Inc.* (Elektra, 1998).

BIBLIOGRAPHY: M. Putterford, *Metallica: In Their Own Words* (Chester, New York, 2000); K. J. Doughton, *Metallica Unbound: The Unofficial Biography* (New York, 1993).

WEBSITES: www.metallica.com; www.metclub.com; www.encycmet.com.

DAVE POWERS

PAT METHENY

Born: Lee's Summit, Missouri, 12 August 1954
Genre: Jazz
Best-selling album since 1990: *Speaking of Now* (2002)

Pat Metheny is among the most distinctive and popular guitarists to have emerged from the electric jazz fusion of the 1970s. Metheny finds common cause with mainstream jazz veterans such as drummer Roy Haynes, fellow-guitarists John Scofield and Bill Frisell, iconoclasts such as saxophonist/theorist Ornette Coleman and discontinuous improviser Derek Bailey, and percussionists from foreign countries such as Brazil, Martinique, Cameroon, and Mexico. He also adapts material by pop-jazz artists such as singer Norah Jones as well as the Choir of the Cambodian Royal Palace.

Metheny began as a trumpeter, like his older brother Mike, but switched to guitar at age fourteen when his teeth were fitted with braces. Inspired by guitarist Wes Montgomery, he attended University of Miami and was appointed a guitar instructor by his second semester. He taught guitar at Berklee College of Music (Boston) starting in 1973, instructing the likes of Al Di Meola, Mike Stern, and Bern Nix. Metheny also joined the band of Berklee instructor and vibraphonist Gary Burton, along with bassist Jaco Pastorius and drummer Bob Moses, who were his trio mates on his debut album, *Bright Size Life* (1975). In 1977 he established the Pat Metheny Group with former Miami classmates Mark Egan (bass) and Danny Gottlieb (drums), and Lyle Mays (keyboards), who remains Metheny's writing partner. The German label ECM supported Metheny's approach, issuing ten albums in nine years. The guitarist/composer's broad melodies, open harmonies, and expansive, soothing performances gained a large, young following.

Though Metheny recorded in some combinations that did not employ all of his group members, his own sound— including warm, fleet guitar playing—was a constant. His efforts to establish more mainstream jazz credentials included an eighteen-month tour and double LP recording, '80–'81 (1981), with saxophonists Michael Brecker and Dewey Redman, bassist Charlie Haden, and drummer Jack DeJohnette. On *Rejoicing* (1984) he features Haden and drummer Billy Higgins, and on *Question and Answer* (1990) he improvises freely with bassist Dave Holland and masterly drummer Roy Haynes. But Metheny's *Song X* (1996), an inspired collaboration with innovative composer/saxophonist Ornette Coleman, is the cornerstone of his credibility with fans who discount his earlier, so-called "pastel" efforts.

In the late 1980s Metheny became infatuated with Brazil, and two of his recordings, *Still Life/(Talking)* (1987) and *Letter from Home* (1989), reflect that country's landscape and ecology. The increasing sophistication of his compositions and his use of guests to supplement his group's members were well served by the glossy productions a new label, Geffen Records, afforded him. However, his growing dissatisfaction with Geffen may have prompted such extreme projects as *Zero Tolerance for Silence* (1993), in which he wrenches dissonances out of his instrument.

Since 1990 Metheny has repeatedly ventured into new territory, including sideman responsibilities in ensembles led by drummer Roy Haynes and pianist Herbie Hancock, among others. He has been amply bestowed with Grammy Awards, taking Best Jazz Fusion Performance honors in 1982, 1983, 1984, 1987, and 1989; Best Instrumental Composition (other than Jazz) in 1990; Best Contemporary Jazz Performance, Instrumental in 1992, 1993, 1995, and 1998; and Best Jazz Instrumental Performance, Soloist, in 2000 for the track "(Go) Get It." Given the constancy of the honors, one senses that Metheny is recognized for being Metheny, the crossover guitarist. However, his musicality has impressive range, and he conveys distinctly different content when addressing serious American folk melodies in duet with Charlie Haden on *Beyond the Missouri Sky* (1997), booting up a rock track such as "The Roots of Coincidence," or involving himself with high-powered peers on the collective album *Like Minds* (1999).

Metheny's core audience proves its loyalty by following their star through his unpredictable turns; he rewards them by alternating darker, more difficult projects with lighter, more accessible ones. Since contracting with Warner Bros. in 1997, he has produced multilayered, detailed soundscapes such as the double Grammy Award–winning *Imaginary Day* (1997), the film score to Wim Wenders's *A Map of the World* (1997), and the Pat Metheny Group's *Speaking of Now* (2002). *One Quiet Night* (2003) is his first solo acoustic guitar album, sure to appeal to his devotees and also to attract new listeners.

Metheny's entire career has been a journey of exploration, launched from his Midwestern roots toward even more ambitious and comprehensive territory. Whether performing acoustic solos or conjuring grand, exotic soundscapes with the members of his group, his personal imprint as guitarist and composer represents increasingly global expeditions.

SELECTIVE DISCOGRAPHY: *Pat Metheny Group* (ECM, 1978); *80/81* (ECM, 1981); *The Falcon and the Snowman* (EMI, 1984); *Song X* (Geffen, 1986); *Secret Story* (Geffen, 1992); *Zero Tolerance for Silence* (Geffen, 1992); *I Can See Your House from Here* (Blue Note, 1994); *We Live Here* (Geffen, 1996); *Quartet* (Geffen, 1996); *Imaginary Day* (Warner Bros., 1997); *A Map of the World* (Warner Bros., 1999); *Like Minds* (1999); *Trio 99–00* (Warner Bros., 2000); *Speaking of Now* (Warner Bros., 2002); *One Quiet Night* (Warner Bros., 2003). **With Gary Burton:** *Like Minds* (Concord, 1998). **With Jack DeJohnette:** *Parallel Realities* (MCA, 1990). **With Charlie Haden:** *Beyond the Missouri Sky* (Verve, 1996).

HOWARD MANDEL

GEORGE MICHAEL

Born: Yorgos Kyriatou Panayiotou; Bushey, England, 25 June 1963

Genre: Rock, Pop

Best-selling album since 1990: *Older* (1996)

Hit songs since 1990: "Freedom 90," "Fast Love," "Jesus to a Child"

From an early age George Michael wanted to be a star and worked hard to achieve his goals. Born to a Greek Cypriot father and English mother, and called Georgios Panayiotou, he was a geeky teenager with seemingly little going for him. In 1975 he met the more handsome and stylish Andrew Ridgeley at Bushey Meads Comprehensive and subsequently they formed the teen duo Wham! This was after Michael had gone on a diet, changed his name, and worked on improving his looks. By 1986 Michael and Ridgeley were achieving hit after hit with songs that embraced a wide range of musical styles. Their pop videos captured the spirit of the time by purveying stylish images of boys having a good time.

As the songwriter and lead singer of Wham!, Michael had a talent for writing songs with a wide appeal, and it was on the basis of this strength that he was able to launch a solo career in 1987. His first album, *Faith*, was an international success that sold more than 10 million copies and spawned several hit singles. The album was clearly targeted toward an American public in the stylistic thrusts of powerful tracks such as "Faith," "Father Figure," and "Hard Day." The songwriting displays a maturity that had immediate appeal among listeners. *Faith* proved more popular than his next album, *Listen Without Prejudice*, which was released in 1990. Although the album sold quite well, it was a commercial disappointment for Michael, and the follow-up album, *Volume 2*, was shelved. In 1992 Michael contributed to the all-star compilation charity album, *Red Hot + Dance*, with one of his songs, "Too Funky," making it to the Top 20.

Michael's career in the 1990s was characterized by struggles of many kinds. His legal battle with Sony ended in his defeat; Michael said that he would refuse to release any more records if he lost the case. Following this incident Michael signed with the music division of DreamWorks, having bought himself out of the Columbia contract. His much-awaited third album, *Older,* was released in 1996 but struggled to reach the same heights of commercial success that his first album had achieved. Nevertheless, this album is highly polished and slick in its production and consists of eleven well-crafted songs. In contrast to the style of songwriting found on his previous albums, *Older* emphasizes more laid-back and peaceful ballads. In all the tracks there is a sense of confidence in the performance, which is both stylish and reflective. In tracks such as the elegiac "Jesus to a Child," Michael allows his emotions on love and death to flow forth with great clarity. In the title track, there is a sense of retrospection in the lyrics as Michael yearns for his lost youth. Throughout the song, the reverbed vocal line is cushioned by lush strings, gentle piano comping, trumpet interjections, and a slow rock beat that transports the feelings with the greatest ease. In the most upbeat track of the album, "Fastlove," there is an ironic slant on the sentiments of commodified love. The camp humor of the musical style is enhanced by the more than blatant use of the disco hit, "Forget Me Not," with its jerky high-pitched chorus line and irresistible rhythmic pull. The promo video to this song, which was aired countless times on MTV, offers an interpretation of the song that is playful, insolent, and autoerotic.

At the end of 1998, the album *Ladies & Gentlemen*, a two-disc compilation of thirty-one songs, came out. In no uncertain terms this album documents Michael's career since his break up with Wham! in 1986. On the first disc there is a collection of slower ballads; on the second there are more flashy, dance-pop numbers.

In 1999, the album *Songs from the Last Century* was released by Virgin. It is a cover album co-produced with Phil Ramone that features a range of popular standards,

such as "My Baby Just Cares for Me," "Brother Can You Spare a Dime," and "The First Time Ever I Saw Your Face." All the arrangements are gentle and intimate, set to a combo of guitar, bass, drums, and piano. The diverse instrumentation includes big band, orchestra, and a rock band.

In 1998 Michael was arrested in a public toilet near his home in Beverly Hills for so-called lewd conduct. In a clever move, the singer appeared on CNN and publicly declared his homosexuality with a great deal of self-parody. Paradoxically, this incident only served to increase his popularity. In 2002 he released two hit singles, "Freek!" and "Shoot the Dog," both accompanied by satirical videos. In "Freek!," the use of techno-based pop with the occasional depersonalized American country drawl, set in a glossy yet sleazy production, stands in dramatic contrast to the songs from the album *Songs from the Last Century*. "Shoot the Dog" was released following his much publicized political retort and attack on the Blair-Bush alliance prior to the Iraq War. The political satire of this song is drawn out through the funky music. The song is in a line of strong political statements that Michael has expressed through his music.

SELECTIVE DISCOGRAPHY: *Faith* (Epic, 1987); *Listen Without Prejudice, Vol.1* (Epic, 1990); *Older* (DreamWorks/Virgin, 1996); *Ladies & Gentleman: The Best of George Michael* (Epic, 1998); *Songs from the Last Century* (Aegean/Virgin, 1999).

STAN HAWKINS

MIDNIGHT OIL

Formed: 1976, Sydney, Australia; Disbanded 2002

Members: Peter Garret, vocals (born Sydney, Australia, 16 April 1953); Rob Hirst, drums, vocals (born Sydney, Australia, 3 September 1955); Jim Moginie, guitar, keyboards (born Sydney, Australia, 18 May 1956); Martin Rotsey, guitar (born Sydney, Australia, 19 February 1956); Dwayne "Bones" Hillman (born New Zealand, 7 May 1958). Former member: Andrew James, bass.

Genre: Rock, Pop

Best-selling album since 1990: *Blue Sky Mining* (1990)

Hit songs since 1990: "Blue Sky Mine"

Midnight Oil, the Australian rock band, was introduced to U.S. audiences through their hit "Beds Are Burning" (1987), considered one of the most potent political rock songs of all time. The band had already been around for over ten years fighting for the environment and social justice, especially the rights of the Australian Aborignes. Midnight Oil took their self-appointed role as advocates seriously, and they used their breakthrough fame to promote their convictions in unconventional ways. Their live shows were distinctive for their firebrand blend of activism, hard guitar rock, and the hyper energy of their front man, Peter Garrett. Thrusting his wiry, seven-foot frame into every pocket of the stage, Garrett created a incomparable performance picture.

Garrett was an unlikely band front man in more ways than one. He had earned a law degree when the band first came together in the late 1970s, during the height of punk rock. The band distinguished themselves by their fiercely independent streak. They created their own record label, Powderworks, and booked their own tours across Australia, many of them benefits. Midnight Oil quickly developed a loyal following. They signed to Columbia Records in 1983, and their major label debut, *10,9,8,7,6,5,4,3,2,1* (1983), sat on the charts for two years. Garrett made news in 1984 when he ran unsuccessfully for a seat on the Australian senate.

The band's international breakthrough was *Diesel and Dust* (1987). The music was politically charged, anthemic rock with polished hooks perfect for radio airplay. The music, most significantly the hit single "Beds Are Burning," spoke for the plight of the Aborigines who had been disenfranchised by colonization and suffered from land rights issues, particularly the mining of uranium on their land. Most Americans however, were not even aware of the music's message, which Garrett admitted was subversive. The album and subsequent videos introduced a wider U.S. audience to Garrett—his lanky demeanor, shaven head, and intense body maneuverings.

The band became known for staging impromptu concerts, most famously in front of the Exxon building in New York in 1990, a year after the disaster of the breakup of the oil tanker *Exxon Valdez*, in waters off Alaska, which resulted in the worst oil spill in U.S. history. In the 1990s Midnight Oil regularly played benefits for Greenpeace, the international environmental organization, and Garrett became president of the Australian Conservation Foundation. The band was invited to perform for the closing ceremonies of the Summer Olympics in Sydney in 2000. While performing "Beds Are Burning," each band member opened his jacket to reveal the word "sorry" written on his shirt, a gesture that made waves for politicizing the moment. It was meant to draw attention to the struggles of the Aborigines.

By then Midnight Oil had evolved into a pop-oriented band, as evidenced by the release of their most nonpolitical album, *Breathe* (1996). Their albums received mostly warm reviews, but the band was playing to a small, dedicated following. Columbia shifted priorities, and by the late 1990s devoted minimal effort to marketing the group. The band signed with Liquid Records, an independent label in Minneapolis. Liquid released *Capricornia* (2001), an accessible and upbeat pop album meant to reconnect with the core audience. From 2001 into the next year, Midnight Oil embarked on an ambitious club tour of the United States, playing sold-out shows in most cities. In late 2002 Garrett announced his retirement to become a full-time environmental activist. The rest of the band continued under a different name.

While most bands pay lip service to activism, Midnight Oil integrated social concerns fully into everything they did. Paving the way for politically conscious groups like Rage Against the Machine, System of a Down, and Fugazi, Midnight Oil remained committed to making music that could change people's lives. The band staked their reputation on live shows that were always exhilarating.

SELECTIVE DISCOGRAPHY: *Midnight Oil* (Powderworks, 1978); *Head Injuries* (Powderworks, 1980); *Bird Noises* EP (Powderworks, 1980); *Place Without a Postcard* (Powderworks, 1981); *10,9,8,7,6,5,4,3,2,1* (Columbia, 1983); *Red Sails in the Sunset* (Columbia, 1984); *Species Deceases* EP (Columbia, 1985); *Diesel and Dust* (Columbia, 1987); *Blue Sky Mining* (Columbia, 1990); *Scream in Blue Live* (Columbia, 1992); *Earth and Sun and Moon* (Columbia, 1993); *Breathe* (Sony/Work, 1996); *20,000 Watt R.S.L.—The Columbia Collection* (Columbia, 1997); *Redneck Wonderland* (Columbia, 1998); *The Real Thing* (Sony, 2000); *Capricornia* (Liquid, 2001).

WEBSITE: www.midnightoil.com.

MARK GUARINO

MIDORI

Born: Osaka, Japan, 25 October 1971
Genre: Classical

Midori's career started dramatically on the last day of 1982 at the age of eleven when conductor Zubin Mehta invited her to perform the Paganini Concerto as surprise guest soloist with the New York Philharmonic at the orchestra's traditional New Year's Eve concert. The slight girl performed flawlessly with a maturity and refinement well beyond her years, and the audience responded by jumping to its feet. The concert quickly became a modern musical legend, and overnight Midori became a star.

She first picked up the violin at the age of three in Osaka, Japan, studying and practicing with her mother, Setsu Goto, herself an accomplished violinist. At the age of six she made her concert debut in Osaka, and three years later came to the Juilliard School in New York to study with Dorothy Delay. When she was ten, the Hayashibara Foundation made her the lifelong loan of a rare 1734 Guarnerius del Gesu violin.

The music world has a longstanding fascination with child prodigies, and Midori was *the* child prodigy of the 1980s, performing with major orchestras and some of the biggest names in classical music. She became a media darling, finding herself the object of intense media attention. In addition to her concerts she was booked on mainstream entertainment shows such as *The Tonight Show* and on *Sesame Street*, and was the subject of interviews on Cable News Network, CBS Sunday Morning, and on French, Japanese, German, and British television.

In 1986 the Midori legend grew again when, during her debut performance at Tanglewood (in Bernstein's *Serenade*) with the Boston Symphony and Leonard Bernstein, she broke two strings and ended up playing three different violins before the piece ended, never missing a note. The next day a story about the concert landed on the front page of the *New York Times* under the headline "Girl, 14, Conquers Tanglewood with 3 Violins."

In 1990 she made her Carnegie Hall debut, which was recorded and issued as a live recording to wide acclaim. In 1991 she was back at Carnegie for the concert hall's historic 100th Anniversary concert, which was recorded and broadcast around the world. In 1992 she performed for another worldwide television audience in a performance from the Olympic Winter Games in Albertville, France.

That year she also set up a nonprofit foundation called Midori & Friends, to promote arts education in New York City; she devotes a significant part of her schedule to working on the foundation. In the mid-1990s, she surprised many of her fans by enrolling at New York University, graduating with a degree in psychology and gender studies.

In 2001 Midori was awarded the prestigious Avery Fisher Prize, and in 2002 she was named Instrumentalist of the Year by Musical America. With pianist Robert McDonald she has recorded much of the solo violin literature, and has performed and recorded with many of the world's top orchestras.

Music prodigies often have a difficult time making the transition to mature artist, but after a period of introspection in her twenties, Midori seems to have accomplished it with ease. Many critics note a deepening of her musicianship as her interests have broadened.

SELECTIVE DISCOGRAPHY: *Tchaikovsky, Shostakovich: Violin Concertos, with Claudio Abbado and the Berlin Philharmonic* (Sony, 1998); *Midori—Live At Carnegie Hall,* with pianist Robert McDonald (Sony, 1990).

WEBSITE: www.gotomidori.com/english/index.html.

DOUGLAS MCLENNAN

THE MIGHTY MIGHTY BOSSTONES

Formed: 1985, Boston, Massachusetts

Members: Dicky Barrett, vocals (born Providence, Rhode Island, 22 June 1964); Tim Burton, saxophone; Ben Carr, dancer (born Boston, Massachusetts, 16 May 1968); Roman Fleysher, saxophone; Joe Gittleman, bass (born Boston, Massachusetts, 6 April 1970); Lawrence Katz, guitar; Chris Rhodes, trombone; Joe Sirois, drums (born North Andover, Massachusetts, 25 January 1972). Former members: Nate Albert, guitar (born Cambridge, Massachusetts, 26 November 1971); Tim Bridewell, trumpet; Dennis Brockenborough, trombone (born Delaware, 19 December 1970); Josh Dalsimer, drums; Kevin Lenear.

Genre: Rock

Best-selling album since 1990: *Let's Face It* (1997)

Hit songs since 1990: "Where'd You Go?," "The Impression That I Get"

The Mighty Mighty Bosstones were one of the pioneers of the American ska movement, which exploded in the mid-1990s and gave the Boston band its first taste of commercial success.

The Bosstones formed in 1985, with an original lineup consisting of Tim Bridewell (trumpet), Dicky Barrett (vocals), Nate Albert (guitar), Joe Gittleman (bass), Josh Dalsimer (drums), and Tim "Johnny Vegas" Burton (saxophone), plus dancer Ben Carr. The band released its debut album *Devils Night Out* in 1990 on Taang! Records. The Bosstones' sound derived from Jamaican ska, a horn-driven style of reggae that first came to prominence in the 1960s and that British bands such as Madness and English Beat brought to the masses in the early 1980s. The Mighty Mighty Bosstones' version of ska was decidedly unique in its incorporation of heavy-metal and punk influences.

The Bosstones cultivated a grassroots following through their high-energy live performances, which often saw the band fully decked out in plaid suits. They played more than 300 shows a year for much of the 1990s. The Bosstones' accessibility and loyalty to their fan base stood in stark contrast to the standoffishness of grunge bands in vogue at the time and helped forged rabid devotion to the group.

After a lineup change in which drummer Joe Sirois, saxophonist Kevin Lenear, and trombonist Dennis Brockenborough joined the band, with Bridewell and Dalsimer departing, the Bosstones signed to Mercury Records in 1993. They scored their first commercial coup in 1995, appearing in the movie *Clueless*. Featured as a house-party band in the movie, the Bosstones perform two songs: "Someday I Suppose" and "Where'd You Go?"

As ska-influenced bands such as No Doubt and Sublime came to dominate the charts in 1997, interest in the Bosstones surged. *Let's Face It* (1997) became the band's best-selling album, and the single "The Impression That I Get" nearly topped the modern rock charts. "The Impression That I Get," an infectious up-tempo number with reggae guitars and blurting horns, charmed listeners with its decidedly self-effacing lyrical approach, in which the narrator muses about his ability to confront adversity: "I'm not a coward, I've just never been tested / I'd like to think that if I was, I would pass." As the music reaches a powerful crescendo in the chorus, Barrett lets out a guttural heavy-metal growl that leads into the chorus.

After the success of *Let's Face It*, the Bosstones experienced more lineup shifts, as Lenear and Albert departed, the latter to finish his education at Brown University; the band added Roman Fleysher (saxophone) and Lawrence Katz (guitar) as their replacements. At the height of the ska craze, the Bosstones played to festival-sized audiences as part of the Lollapalooza Tour, but, as interest in the musical movement began to wane, the band returned to more familiar club environs. In 1998 the Bosstones celebrated their roots by releasing *Live at the Middle East*, recorded during the band's annual five-night "Hometown Throwdown" in Boston.

Though perhaps underappreciated for their important musical influence, the Bosstones continued to hold the respect, devotion, and adoration of their fans.

SELECTIVE DISCOGRAPHY: *Devils Night Out* (Taang!, 1990); *More Noise and Other Disturbances* (Taang!, 1991); *Don't Know How to Party* (Mercury, 1993); *Question the Answers* (Mercury, 1994); *Let's Face It* (Mercury, 1997); *Pay Attention* (Island/Def Jam, 2000); *A Jackknife to a Swan* (SideOneDummy, 2002).

SCOTT TRIBBLE

LUIS MIGUEL

Born: Luis Miguel Gallego Bastery; San Juan, Puerto Rico, 19 April 1970

Genre: Latin

Best-selling album since 1990: *Romance* (1991)

Hit songs since 1990: "Ayer," "No Sé, Tú," "Amarte Es Un Placer"

Luis Miguel oozes class, swagger, and charm whether he's belting out mariachi standards, seducing with an orchestral ballad, or indulging the old folks with a 1950s bolero. Born to the Spanish singer Luisito Rey and the Italian model Marcella Bastery, Luis Miguel grew up in Mexico City. After adolescence he had only a distant relationship with his parents, who divorced in 1986; his father died in 1992. Miguel recorded his first album, *Un Sol*, in 1982, becoming a popular child star with the bubble-gum hits "Tú y Yo" and "1 + 1 = 2 Enamorados."

In 1990, Luismi, as fans call him, made a fortuitous leap to bolero music, recording the nostalgia-filled *Romance*. The album was a gamble—he risked alienating young fans and seeming insincere to older listeners. But Latin music was ready for a revival of the bolero, a slow but rhythmic ballad form, framed by acoustic guitar, that enjoyed its heyday in the 1950s. Often the boleros were performed by trios that played guitars and sang in harmony. With producer Armando Manzanero, a legendary Mexican songwriter, Luismi made the boleros modern and upscale by bringing in an orchestral backdrop. His forceful, dramatic tenor breathed new life into the sentimental, poetic lyrics. *Romance* contains classic tracks such as "Contigo en la Distancia," originally recorded by the late Mexican singing and acting legend Pedro Infante, and new boleros such as "No Sé, Tú," written by Manzanero. The album sold more than 1 million copies in the United States alone.

During the 1990s, Miguel's releases alternated between bolero fare and Latin adult contemporary. In 1993 he returned with *Aries*, a pop album that featured the symphonic power ballad "Ayer." In a symbolic baton-passing and a rare performance in English, Luis Miguel sang with his hero Frank Sinatra on "Come Fly with Me" for Sinatra's 1994 *Duets II*. Some people saw more than a little Sinatra in Luis Miguel's cocky charisma, his ability to transcend teen-idol status, and his conservative tastes in music.

Like his previous efforts, *Mis Romances* (2001) displays Luis Miguel's perfectionism as a singer and producer. He is backed by the Royal Philharmonic Orchestra throughout and virtuoso Cuban émigré trumpeter Arturo Sandoval on the energetic "La Ultima Noche." "Amor, Amor, Amor" is a brassy, uptempo Vegas-styled update of Julio Iglesias's 1970s hit.

With sales figures showing that fans were beginning to go into been-there-done-that mode with his series of similarly titled bolero tributes, Luis Miguel stood at a crossroads at the start of the new century. Most likely he still has the youth, popularity, and talent to make stylistic adjustments.

SELECTIVE DISCOGRAPHY: *Romance* (WEA Latina, 1991); *Aries* (WEA Latina, 1993); *Segundo Romance* (WEA Latina, 1994); *Romances* (WEA

Latina, 1997); *Amarte Es un Placer* (WEA Latina, 1999); *Mis Romances* (WEA Latina, 2001).

RAMIRO BURR

LIZA MINNELLI

Born: Los Angeles, California, 12 March 1946
Genre: Vocal
Best-selling album since 1990: *Gently* (1996)

Liza Minnelli [GREG GORMAN/J-RECORDS-BIFF WARREN]

Along with fellow chanteuse Barbra Streisand, Liza Minnelli is one of the last pop singers to embody an old-fashioned sense of showmanship, or "chutzpah." Show business is in her blood: She is the daughter of legendary singer Judy Garland and film director Vincente Minnelli. Mirroring a pattern of her late mother's career, Minnelli's ongoing tabloid publicity has often threatened to overwhelm her sizable artistic achievements. Yet, as her finest work shows, Minnelli is a full-fledged performer with intrinsic star quality. If her albums have sometimes disappointed, it is because the relatively constrained medium of recording cannot always contain her; she relies on the expansiveness of the stage to put her larger-than-life performances across.

Raised in an environment of glittering celebrity—legendary pop singer Frank Sinatra was the first person to visit her as an infant—Minnelli had adulthood thrust upon her at an early age. "My life has been lived in front of the press," she told the U.K. *Guardian* in 1996. "I was born and someone took a picture and it's been that way ever since." Her parents divorced when she was five, and by age twelve Minnelli had become caregiver to her fragile, unstable mother, managing the household and even purchasing a stomach pump as a precaution against Garland's many suicide attempts with pills.

Broadway, Film, and Television Stardom

Moving to New York with her parents' encouragement in the early 1960s, Minnelli soon won Broadway's Tony Award for her performance in the musical *Flora, the Red Menace* (1965), in which her luminous performance of "A Quiet Thing" was a highlight. Overcoming the death of her mother in 1969 and the breakup of her marriage to singer/songwriter Peter Allen the next year, Minnelli achieved stardom with the 1972 film version of the Broadway musical *Cabaret*. Her brassy portrayal of second-rate nightclub singer Sally Bowles, trying to survive amidst the desperation of the Weimar Republic in 1930s Berlin, was unforgettable, earning her an Academy Award for Best Actress. The same year she released *Liza with a "Z,"* a live

album from her television special of the same name. The album, her most commercially successful release, displays Minnelli at her best: sharp, exuberant, and funny, with an engaging, somewhat dizzy stage presence. During the early 1980s she was often out of the spotlight due to drug and alcohol problems, but she overcame them by the end of the decade, touring extensively and recording an album with English pop group the Pet Shop Boys. In addition, throughout the 1980s Minnelli appeared in some memorable film roles, most notably *Arthur* (1981).

Taking Risks in the 1990s

While no longer the superstar of two decades earlier, Minnelli by the mid-1990s was a seasoned, venerable artist with the power to select and oversee her own projects. Always more renowned for her stage performances than her recordings, Minnelli took a career risk in 1996 with the release of *Gently*, an album of classic pop songs featuring a sparse, restrained arrangement—quite different from the large-scale orchestration accompanying her in live shows. Since age, drugs, and cigarettes have worn Minnelli's voice markedly, the choice to feature her in such an unadorned setting is a bold one.

Critics have observed that Minnelli is a blunt vocalist: She is frequently off pitch and has trouble sustaining phrases, often cutting them off with a dusky croak. Nonetheless, she performs *Gently*'s songs with ample dramatic skill. "In the Wee Small Hours," a song associated with her old friend Frank Sinatra, appeals to Minnelli's fans as especially moving. Coming in after a sensitive, two-minute piano solo, Minnelli strips the lyrics down to their barest essentials, imparting to lines such as "that's the time you miss him most of all" a soul-baring fragility. On "Embraceable You," a song taught to her as a child by famed pop and jazz vocalist Ella Fitzgerald, she is smoky and dark, delivering, critics remarked, an almost frighteningly deep interpretation. The album is not entirely serious, however: On "Close Your Eyes," she plays with the lyrics and melody in a light-hearted manner, suggesting a jazz singer's sense of improvisation. While critics noted a few misfires—she sounds too rough around the edges on her duet with smooth-voiced 1950s singer Johnny Mathis, for example—*Gently* displays a new artistic maturity.

In late 1999 Minnelli returned to the scene of her mother's greatest performances—the Palace Theater in New York—in *Minnelli on Minnelli*, a show featuring classic songs from musicals directed by her father, who died in 1986. On the live album of the same name, released in 2000, Minnelli often sounds winded but manages to summon her familiar bravado on songs such as "What Did I Have That I Don't Have." Minnelli's career has continued to be nurtured by a loyal, largely gay male fan base fond of her dramatic persona and style. Reviewing a 2002 performance at the Royal Albert Hall in London, the U.K. *Independent* caustically remarked, "When she drank a glass of water, [her fans] roared. And when she emerged in a tiny black costume stretched to danger point . . . and asked, 'Does this look all right?' they said yes." Other reviews of the engagement were more positive, with critics noting her slimmed-down appearance, renewed vocal energy, and magnetic power. The *London Evening Standard* perceptively noted the symbiotic quality existing between Minnelli and her fans: "There is still the sense that she needs all the help she can get from the audience. Their adoration is not merely requested; it is essential." Minnelli's engagement at Royal Albert Hall came on the heels of her much-publicized wedding to music and television producer David Gest, whom she credited with helping her survive a 2001 bout with encephalitis during which she nearly died.

Beyond the tormented family history, bouts with drugs, and ongoing tabloid speculation over her private life, Minnelli should be noted for her drive and tenacity, a performer who embodies the old maxim, "The show must go on." As an artist, she possesses a communicative power lacking in many singers, even in those with technically finer voices. Soulful and generous, Minnelli approaches music as she does life: head-on, with a do-or-die enthusiasm that pulls fans into her idiosyncratic world. She has earned her reputation as a show-biz survivor.

SELECTIVE DISCOGRAPHY: *Liza! Liza!* (Capitol, 1964); *Liza with a "Z"* (Columbia, 1972); *Results* (Epic, 1989); *Liza Minnelli Live from Radio City Music Hall* (Sony, 1992); *Gently* (Angel, 1996); *Minnelli on Minnelli* (Angel, 2000); *Liza's Back* (J-Records, 2002).

SELECTIVE FILMOGRAPHY: *The Sterile Cuckoo* (1969); *Cabaret* (1972); *New York, New York* (1977); *Arthur* (1981); *That's Dancing!* (1985); *Stepping Out* (1991).

DAVID FREELAND

KYLIE MINOGUE

Born: Melbourne, Australia, 28 May 1968
Genre: Rock, Pop
Best-selling album since 1990: *Light Years* (2001)
Hit songs since 1990: "Better the Devil You Know," "Spinning Around," "Can't Get You Out of My Head"

Kylie Minogue has managed to retain her status as an international pop icon since the late 1980s. After appearing on several Australian television programs, she gained national fame with the popular Australian soap opera series *Neighbours*, a hit in the United Kingdom as well. During a charity performance Minogue decided to sing the song "Loco-Motion," made famous by Little Eva. A tape of this performance was submitted to a record company called Mushroom, which grabbed the opportunity to release a single by a young TV star. Few would have guessed that this song would become a number one hit in Australia in 1987.

Mushroom Records' relationship with the London songwriting factory Stock Aitken and Waterman (SAW) soon led to Minogue's first English number one hit, "I Should Be So Lucky," and second number one in Australia. Following this success, SAW took over production of all her songs and videos and re-recorded "Loco-Motion," which reached the Top 10 in the United States. Minogue's success as a pop star resulted in her leaving *Neighbours*. In 1990 against SAW's advice, she decided to opt for a more sexy and sensual image in the promo video for "Better the Devil You Know." Following the success of this video, and her insistence for more of a say in her lyrics, she left SAW and released two albums with Brothers in Rhythm, *Kylie Minogue* (1994) and *Impossible Princess* (1997). During this period Minogue's contact with a range of other artists, such as Michael Hutchence, Nick Cave, and the Pet Shop Boys, had a profound effect on her musical development that was most discernible in the album *Impossible Princess*, in which she draws on the rock-oriented style of Britpop and dance-based numbers. In the track "Some Kind of Bliss," the melodic content of her vocal lines is warm and sensitively delivered, with Minogue's expressive tone convincing and sincere. Throughout the album her vocal tone is mature and polished, a far cry from the shrill squeakiness of her early material.

By 2000 Minogue had been encouraged by the Pet Shop Boys to change to their Parlophone label. This move paid off as she succeeded in reestablishing her status in Europe with the release of *Light Years*, an exciting compilation of catchy disco, Europop, and dance-driven tracks. The hits "Spinning Around" and "Your Disco Needs You," co-written by Robbie Williams and Guy Chambers, firmly established her credibility within dance-based pop. Moreover, *Light Years* contributed significantly to the revival of disco at the turn of the twenty-first century, with Minogue in a strong position as a leading international pop artist.

Minogue sustained her status by releasing *Fever* (2001), another hit album that remained in the dance-based disco vein of her previous album. The single "Can't Get You Out of My Head" became a smash hit in the United States, her first major success there in fifteen years. In the United Kingdom this song helped win her two BRIT Awards in 2002, one for Best International Female Artist and the other for the *Fever* album, which was recognized as Best International Album. Other hits on this album include "Burning Up," "Love Affair," and "Come into My World," all catchy numbers that abound with an energy that draws on Euro-dance-pop grooves.

While Minogue has not achieved the same status as Madonna, nevertheless she has demonstrated tenacity in maintaining her position at the top. By reinventing her playful image countless times and working with a creative team of musicians and producers to create catchy pop songs and fun videos, she has emerged as one of the most successful artists in Europe and Australia at the beginning of the twenty-first century.

SELECTIVE DISCOGRAPHY: *Kylie* (Geffen, 1988); *Enjoy Yourself* (1989); *Rhythm of Love* (Mushroom 1990); *Let's Get to It* (Mushroom, 1991); *Kylie Minogue* (De-Construction, 1994); *Impossible Princess* (De-Construction, 1997); *Intimate & Live* (Mushroom, 1999) *Light Years* (Parlophone, 2000); *Fever* (Parlophone, 2002).

STAN HAWKINS

JONI MITCHELL

Born: Roberta Joan Anderson, 7 November 1943
Genre: Folk, Rock, Jazz
Best-selling album since 1990: *Turbulent Indigo* (1994)

Hit songs since 1990: "Night Train Home," "The Magdalene Laundries," "Stormy Weather"

Joni Mitchell's artistic achievement places her in the vanguard of recent popular music, no mean attainment for a woman in a male-dominated industry. Her folk roots and focus on the power of the lyric bear comparison with a performer like Bob Dylan, yet Mitchell is more than just a female version of that giant of the rock scene. While she has operated in that similar singer/songwriter mode, her constant striving for new ways to shape and present her work marks her as a singular talent.

Canadian Beginnings

Growing up in rural Canada, Mitchell studied painting in Calgary and then moved to Toronto in 1964. She learned to play guitar and began to play the role of roaming troubadour in the folk tradition made fashionable by artists such as Woody Guthrie and then Bob Dylan. In 1965 she married a fellow singer, Chuck Mitchell, with whom she also performed. Her striking good looks helped attract attention to her collection of potently original work, featuring unusual guitar tunings and delivered in a voice that swooped memorably into the upper registers. She began to build a reputation in bars and coffee houses. She met the established folksinger Tom Rush, who recorded a Mitchell original, "The Circle Game," which also became the title track of his next album. Other leading folk performers were aware of Mitchell's talents, with Judy Collins recording a version of her song "Both Sides Now" in 1967.

Greenwich Village Coffee Houses

When her marriage ended that same year, she moved to New York, forging a name in the coffee houses of Greenwich Village but also travelling to England at the encouragement of the noted producer Joe Boyd. However, it was only after Mitchell's encounter with David Crosby, a former member of the renowned rock band the Byrds, that her star began to ascend. Crosby, a well-known practitioner of offbeat guitar-tunings himself, became her lover and then produced her debut LP, *Song to a Seagull*.

It was a promising yet not fully formed introduction to Mitchell's art; it was on her second collection, *Clouds* (which featured "Chelsea Morning" and "Both Sides Now," the latter an international hit in the hands of Collins), that she really began to carve out a career of major proportions. By the time *Ladies of the Canyon* was released in 1972, Mitchell was the major female singer in a musical revolution that blended folk and rock forms and witnessed the emergence of dozens of singer/songwriters.

The album showcases such classic Mitchell compositions as "The Circle Game," the environmental anthem "Big Yellow Taxi," and a song that captured the spirit of the times, "Woodstock," a celebration of the 1969 rock festival.

With *Blue* (1971) Mitchell created perhaps the archetypal album of the era: a collection of fragile, introspective songs that celebrated love and commemorated loss in equal measure. Her relationship with Graham Nash—now a colleague of Crosby's in Crosby, Stills, and Nash—was one of the affairs she reflected on in this landmark LP, which seemed to distill the essence of the new California and its growing community of folk-inclined hippies.

Goddess of Confession

But Mitchell was quick to cast off the status of the goddess of confession, muse to other rock stars, and a mere chronicler of heartbreak. *For the Roses* (1972) hinted at a fuller, lusher, and more ambitious sound with strings, horns, and woodwind augmenting her voice, guitar, and piano. On *Court and Spark* (1974), the vision was pursued with even greater vigor. With the jazz saxophonist Tom Scott and his band LA Express in tow, Mitchell concocted an epic contemplation of stardom and its downside; "Free Man in Paris" and "Down to You" move away from the autobiographical, drawing on observations of a new gallery of characters centered in Los Angeles.

The following year *The Hissing of Summer Lawns* proved a stunning climax to this period—jazz and tribal rhythms sat comfortably with the remarkable folk melodies that Mitchell had always invented with such facility. "The Boho Dance," "The Jungle Line," and "Don't Interrupt the Sorrow" had critics gasping, yet her mature sophistication began to distance her from the paying public. *Hejira* (1976), showcasing the rising star of the jazz bass Jaco Pastorius, was almost as good, but it fared less well commercially. By the time of *Don Juan's Reckless Daughter* (1977), an ambitious, sprawling double release, and the brave but challenging *Mingus* (1979), a reinterpretation of work by the great jazz bass player Charlie Mingus, Mitchell had set course on a route that left her girlish romanticism far, far behind.

Since then, Mitchell has retrenched. Her albums in the past two decades have harked back to her styles of the early and mid-1970s, and even earlier still. The dramatic progression she so clearly sought in that decade—from folkie balladeer to sophisticated social commentator to cosmopolitan purveyor of sounds that embraced rock, jazz, and world influences—had stalled. *Wild Things Run Fast* (1982), *Dog Eat Dog* (1985), and *Chalk Mark in a Rain Storm* (1988) share the lyrical richness of their predecessors but seemed to mark time.

In this period Mitchell did expand her range of collaborators, engaging the synthesizer master Thomas Dolby to produce *Dog Eat Dog* and enlisting contributions from Peter Gabriel, Billy Idol, Willie Nelson, and Tom Petty on *Chalk Mark in a Rain Storm*; it seemed that if her interest in jazz had been sidelined, she was still eager to bring flavors as diverse as country and punk to her work. The decade also saw a significant personal and musical development. Mitchell married for the second time, shortly after the release of *Wild Things Run Fast*, and her new husband, the bassist Larry Klein, became a key figure in the production of her recorded work.

Acoustic Stylings Revisited

Night Ride Home (1991) saw the decade begin with Mitchell revisiting some of the acoustic stylings that had marked her success at the end of the 1960s. Hailed as a return to roots and a return to form, the recording focuses on her vocal strengths and her acoustic guitar playing. One of the reasons for this stripped-down version was that she had built a studio in her Bel Air home; although there were contributions from Wayne Shorter, the focus of the work rested on Mitchell's shoulders. The title track expresses a certain optimism, countered by the more melancholic moods of "Two Grey Rooms."

A three-year silence, bridged only by a cameo appearance on the second album by emerging British singer Seal, was broken in 1994 with the arrival of *Turbulent Indigo*, an album that would see Seal return the favor on the track "How Do You Stop"; the song earned Mitchell a Grammy for Best Pop Album. Her separation from Klein, shortly before the release of *Turbulent Indigo*, did not result in his exclusion from the collection, which he co-produced. The album was, however, made in the same home studio, a circumstance that resulted in emotional tensions that were, perhaps, reflected in the vivid title. Some of the material ventures into socially fraught issues: "The Magdalene Laundries" covers the incarceration of Irish women by the Catholic Church, and "Not to Blame" is a powerful anti-rape piece.

Since then, aside from the 1998 album *Taming the Tiger*, Mitchell has been treading water professionally, with a number of recordings drawing on her past material. In 1996, in a unique move, she simultaneously issued a pair of albums that summarized her career output: *Hits*, which gathers her more familiar work, and *Misses*, a collection of her best lesser-known songs. *Taming the Tiger* saw her operating again with Klein and Shorter, expressing longing on "Man from Mars" and bemoaning abandon on "Crazy Cries of Love."

Lavish Rearrangements

In 2000 Mitchell issued *Both Sides Now*, an album of standards, including "You're My Thrill," "Stormy Weather," and "Answer Me, My Love," alongside new takes on her own title tune and her composition "A Case of You." She followed it with *Travelogue* (2002), a double set, which employs a full orchestra to recreate some of her finest moments in a series of lavish rearrangements. With the London Symphony Orchestra, conducted by Vince Mendoza, she creates new versions of "Woodstock," "The Last Time I Saw Richard," "God Must Be a Boogie Man," and nineteen other pieces of her work. It also became her valedictory set; she revealed, in magazine interviews, her intentions to retire from recording and quit the business— "a corrupt cesspool," in her words—late that year.

In considering Joni Mitchell's legacy, one must not overlook her painting—several of her album covers, including *Clouds, Mingus, Wild Things Run Fast,* and *Travelogue,* feature her visual art; her images were also used in the 2001 movie *Vanilla Sky.* But that is a mere footnote to her magnificent musical achievement, which was a huge influence on her own generation of popular music makers and those who followed. Amy Grant and Janet Jackson have sourced her songs for hits of their own, and performer/composers such as Prince, Alanis Morissette, Tori Amos, and Shawn Colvin have paid tribute to Mitchell as an inspiration, a songwriter, and a personal role model. Few artists can claim to have captured the tenor of an era in song—or in any other art form, for that matter—as memorably or as movingly as Joni Mitchell did during her apogee in the late 1960s and early 1970s.

SELECTIVE DISCOGRAPHY: *Song to a Seagull* (Reprise, 1968); *Clouds* (Reprise, 1969); *Ladies of the Canyon* (Reprise, 1970); *Blue* (Reprise, 1971); *For the Roses* (Asylum, 1972); *Court and Spark* (Asylum, 1974); *The Hissing of Summer Lawns* (Asylum, 1975); *Hejira* (Asylum, 1976); *Mingus* (Asylum, 1979); *Wild Things Run Fast* (Geffen, 1982); *Night Ride Home* (Geffen, 1991); *Turbulent Indigo* (Reprise, 1994); *Hits* (Reprise, 1996); *Misses* (Reprise, 1996); *Travelogue* (Warner Bros., 2002).

BIBLIOGRAPHY: B. Hinton, *Joni Mitchell: Both Sides Now* (London, 1996); S. Luftig, *The Joni Mitchell Companion: Four Decades of Commentary* (New York, 2000); K. O'Brien, *Shadows and Light* (London, 2001).

WEBSITE: www.jonimitchell.com.

SIMON WARNER

MOBY

Born: Richard Melville Hall; New York, New York, 11 September 1965
Genre: Rock, Electronica
Best-selling album since 1990: *Play* (1999)

Hit songs since 1990: "Bodyrock," "Southside," "We Are All Made of Stars"

The mainstream success of the iconoclastic vegan, substance-free, and born-again Christian artist Moby is one of the big surprises of the techno-electronica music subculture of the late 1990s. Moby was born Richard Melville Hall. (His middle name refers to his lineage: Moby is a great-great-great-nephew of Herman Melville, author of the great American novel *Moby Dick.*) Moby spent a good portion of the 1990s recording techno-electronica albums using synthetic instruments such as keyboards, synthesizers, sampling equipment, and software that helped him loop, double-track, and create unusual textures. After releasing a few albums that fared well in the United Kingdom and on the U.S. dance music charts, he surprised himself and his record label with the album *Play* (1999), which sold more than 2 million copies in the United States and tens of millions of copies worldwide.

Moby was born and lived in Harlem until the age of two, when his father was killed in a car accident. In 1967 he moved with his mother to an apartment in Darien, Connecticut. He also lived briefly in San Francisco, and returned to Darien to live with his grandparents when he was four years old. Moby's mother is his primary musical influence; she worked as a doctor's aide by day and as a keyboard player in a band by night. By the age of ten Moby was playing guitar, smoking marijuana, and performing in a band. By 1983 he acquired his first four-track recording device. "This is when I realized I could finish songs by myself," he writes on his website, "and that I didn't need to be so reliant on other musicians." Shortly after this realization, Moby fell in love with dance and techno music. He moved to New York City in 1989 and started to DJ at clubs. He shopped around his demo tape to record labels to no avail until Instinct Records signed him in 1990. His dance music fared well and garnered him a small following. Moby became known during the rave craze of the early 1990s, when all-night music and experimentation with drugs at urban clubs became the fashion.

The Making of Moby

By the time Moby released his first album, the wild days were behind him and he became an avowed vegan (abstaining from all animal products, including meat and cheese). He experienced a spiritual awakening. In 1995 he signed with Elektra and released his major-label debut album *Everything Is Wrong,* which *Spin* magazine named Album of the Year. This eclectic record, with the twenty-three-minute-long religious-techno tune "Hymn," won

Spot Light | *Play*

From television commercials for Nissan cars and Nordstrom department stores to an Oliver Stone movie, *Any Given Sunday* (1999), the songs from Moby's album *Play* helped swell sales of the album to double platinum within two years of its release. The album, with its samples of blues and folk recordings, gained momentum through word of mouth, but it could not break through the rigid, niche-oriented playlists of American radio stations. It was the commercial licensing of every single song from *Play,* however, and Moby's nonstop two years of touring that really boosted his visibility. Surprisingly, the idea to license his songs came from Moby himself; he and managers Marci Weber and Barry Tyler devised a plan to garner attention for Moby's music, but little did they know the full impact such a maneuver would have. By 2001 it seemed as if Moby was everywhere. To date, *Play* has gone platinum in about twenty-five countries, shocking and remarkable for an album so eclectic and off the beaten path. The album has sold more than 10 million copies worldwide and earned him three Grammy Award nominations.

pioneer of world music. The lead-off track, "Honey," samples from a song by Bessie Smith, the great blues singer of the 1920s. The track "Run On" features slide guitar and haunting piano with samples from a 1943 classic Gospel tune, "Run On for a Long Time." A current of sadness and suffering runs throughout the album. The universality of such emotions made an impact on millions of listeners.

Moby organized a major tour for summer 2001 and invited a bunch of seemingly disparate artists such as the eclectic singer Nelly Furtado, DJ Paul Oakenfold, the Roots, and Incubus. He continued the tour in the summer of 2002, leading up to the release of *18* later that year. Thanks to the high sales of *Play, 18* hit number one on the *Billboard* electronic charts. It reached number one on the *Billboard* Canadian chart, and it peaked at number four on the *Billboard* 200 chart. It went platinum in the United States. Like *Play, 18* strikes a sad, bluesy, soulful chord. Yet it is far more contemplative, and mournful. Particularly notable are "Extreme Ways," which Moby sings, and the mellow, synthesizer-rich title track.

Moby's albums are best appreciated when listened to as a whole, which is ironic, because the snippets of songs from *Play* made their way all over U.S. television ads and movie trailers. Nevertheless, Moby is an original in the field of electronica. His roots are deep, his spirit is adventurous, and his music is emotionally resonant.

SELECTIVE DISCOGRAPHY: *Everything Is Wrong* (Elektra, 1995); *I Like to Score* (Elektra, 1997); *Play* (V2, 1999); *18* (V2, 2002).

WEBSITE: www.moby.com.

CARRIE HAVRANEK

critical praise. In 1996 Moby began to suffer from acute panic attacks during the recording of his album *Animal Rights.* This less danceable album tanked (in terms of sales) and left fans confused. At the same time Moby's mother was diagnosed with fatal lung cancer. In 1997 Moby released an album of musical score compositions cleverly titled *I Like to Score.*

Pushing *Play*

Elektra dropped Moby from their roster shortly after the release of *I Like to Score.* He recorded a follow-up and shopped it around. *Play* (1999) was released by V2 Records, and the album's success gradually snowballed, thanks to radio play, extensive commercial licensing, and good word of mouth. When Moby began his tour to support the album, he played to a handful of people at a record store; by the end of the tour, he was playing to thousands in arenas. The album utilizes early African-American field recordings made by Alan Lomax, legendary folklorist and

MONICA

Born: Monica Arnold; Atlanta, Georgia, 24 October 1980
Genre: R&B, Pop
Best-selling album since 1990: *The Boy Is Mine* (1998)
Hit songs since 1990: "The Boy Is Mine," "Don't Take It Personal"

Monica's appealing vocals and youthful presence helped make her one of the most exciting rhythm and blues stars of the late 1990s. Like her teenaged contemporary Brandy, Monica is equally convincing on up-tempo dance tracks and winsome ballads, working with a series of hot producers to capture a mature, up-to-date sound. Although the two singers performed as a duet on one of the biggest pop hits of the 1990s, "The Boy Is Mine," Monica has not enjoyed Brandy's commercial consistency, due in large part to the long

Monica [JOSHUA JORDAN/J-RECORDS-BIFF WARREN]

time span between her album releases. This situation belies the extent of Monica's talent—she possesses a fuller, more powerful voice than Brandy, and her best performances are marked by genuine vocal technique recalling her years as a child gospel singer.

Raised in a suburb of Atlanta, Monica was singing professionally by the age of ten, performing with the gospel group Charles Thompson and the Majestics. During a talent show performance at age twelve, Monica impressed producer and record executive Dallas Austin with her version of pop star Whitney Houston's hit 1980s ballad, "The Greatest Love of All." Signing Monica to Arista Records, Austin took several years to craft her debut album, *Miss Thang* (1995). Only fourteen years old at the time of its release, Monica sounded mature and assured, tackling the tough hip-hop grooves of the hit "Don't Take It Personal" with conviction. On an updated version of soul singer Latimore's 1970s hit, "Let's Straighten It Out," Monica and fellow teen pop star Usher trade vocal lines in soulful collaboration. Singing well-timed cries of "Whoa . . . yeah," Monica invests the song with an edge of gospel-styled immediacy.

Although Monica's second album, *The Boy Is Mine*, did not appear until 1998, it became her biggest success

on the basis of the smash title song and the seductive hit, "The First Night." Like the late-1990s work of female R&B group Destiny's Child, "The First Night" is underscored by an abiding sense of self-respect, as Monica tells a prospective boyfriend, "I should make a move but I won't . . . I don't get down on the first night." On the pop-influenced ballad, "Inside," Monica suggests the extent of her vocal abilities, handling key changes with ease and emphasizing lyrics with precision and tenderness. Unlike many contemporary R&B performers who sing off-key, Monica approaches her songs with an assured sense of pitch and timing. After the release of *The Boy Is Mine*, Monica took time off "to relax and enjoy my life," as she explained on her website. In 2003 she revealed that her hiatus was also a result of the death of her boyfriend, who shot and killed himself while in her presence in 1999.

Monica's third album, *All Eyez on Me*, was scheduled for release in 2002 but was cancelled due to Internet piracy. The album, re-titled *After the Storm*, was finally released in 2003 and earned immediate radio exposure through the catchy single, "So Long."

In the late 1990s, Monica's impressive vocal ability and engaging recordings fully justified her star status. Unlike other young singers of her generation, who survive more on looks than talent, Monica possesses true depth and range. Her 1990s recordings will endure as fine examples of tough, modern R&B.

SELECTIVE DISCOGRAPHY: *Miss Thang* (Arista, 1995); *The Boy Is Mine* (Arista, 1998); *After the Storm* (J-Records, 2003).

WEBSITE: www.monica.com.

DAVID FREELAND

JOHN MICHAEL MONTGOMERY

Born: Danville, Kentucky, 20 January 1965
Genre: Country
Best-selling album since 1990: *Kickin' It Up* (1994)
Hit songs since 1990: "I Swear," "I Can Love You Like That"

John Michael Montgomery represents the pop end of the 1990s country axis, his unassuming voice and slick albums more suggestive of 1970s rock group the Eagles than hard-driving country singers of the past such as Merle Haggard. Although his early work attempted to capture some of the toughness associated with the "new traditionalist" movement in 1980s and early 1990s country—propagated by artists such as George Strait and Alan Jackson—that influence wore off after his first few albums. By the mid-1990s, country music as a whole had turned in a smoother direction, and Montgomery was at the vanguard of this change with tuneful hits such as "I Swear" and "I Can Love You Like That." Unlike his contemporary Martina McBride, who sought to balance her traditional roots with the new popularity of country-pop, Montgomery changed his image little from album to album. In this way, he typifies the country "hunk in a hat" popular in the 1990s, his appeal largely derived from startlingly blue eyes, dimples, and a toothy smile.

Growing up in Danville, Kentucky, Montgomery initially learned guitar playing from his father. Joined by his drum-playing mother, Montgomery performed in the family band from an early age and took over as lead singer at seventeen when his parents divorced. Discovered while singing at the Austin City Saloon in Lexington, Kentucky, Montgomery signed with Atlantic Records and released his debut album, *Life's a Dance*, in 1992. A well-rounded collection of catchy ballads and swinging uptempo tunes, it brought Montgomery a degree of commercial success, although critics agree his occasional attempts at an aggressive neo-traditional style sound forced. His voice, weak in its upper register and sometimes off-pitch, is more suited to less demanding pop songs, such as the gentle "I Swear," a centerpiece of his second album, *Kickin' It Up* (1994).

By the time of his self-titled third release in 1995, Montgomery had hit upon a successful formula for each album: several lighthearted, humorous songs such as "Sold (The Grundy County Auction Incident)," with most of the remaining tracks given over to plush ballads with greeting-card sentiments, such as the smash hit, "I Can Love You Like That" (1995): "You like romantic movies / you never will forget / the way you felt when Romeo kissed Juliet." Later albums show little sign of artistic growth; despite its title, *Brand New Me* (2000) is more of the same thing, comprised largely of mawkish ballads such as "The Little Girl." Appeasing the religious, right wing element of country's fan base, the lugubrious song begins with parents who "never took the young girl to church," then details the horrors that ensue: drugs, physical abuse, and, eventually, spouse killing and suicide. By the song's end, the girl has experienced religious salvation due to foster parents who introduce her to Sunday school.

John Michael Montgomery helped steer country music in an increasingly pop direction in the 1990s. While performers such as Dolly Parton sought a return to their country roots, or worked to integrate their traditional impulses within contemporary formats, Montgomery has largely maintained his unchallenging country-pop style throughout his career.

SELECTIVE DISCOGRAPHY: *Life's a Dance* (Atlantic, 1992); *Kickin' It Up* (Atlantic, 1994); *John Michael Montgomery* (Atlantic, 1995); *What I Do the Best* (Atlantic, 1996); *Leave a Mark* (Atlantic, 1998); *Home to You* (Atlantic, 1999); *Brand New Me* (Atlantic, 2000); *Pictures* (Warner Bros., 2002).

WEBSITE: www.johnmichael.com.

DAVID FREELAND

ALANIS MORISSETTE

Born: Ottawa, Ontario, 1 June 1974
Genre: Rock
Best-selling album since 1990: *Jagged Little Pill* (1995)
Hit songs since 1990: "You Oughta Know," "Hand in My Pocket," "Ironic"

Alanis Morissette parlayed some serious anger toward an ex-boyfriend into superstardom, emerging as one of the leading female singer/songwriters of the late 1990s.

Child Star

Born in Ottawa, Morissette took to music from an early age, learning to play the piano at the age of six and writing her first song at the age of nine. In 1985, she joined the cast of Nickelodeon's *You Can't Do That on Television*, a sketch comedy show. After two years, Morissette left the show to pursue a musical career.

Morissette signed a recording deal with MCA Records at the age of sixteen and released her debut album *Alanis* in 1991. *Alanis*, along with the follow-up album *Now Is the Time* (1992), cast Morissette in the vein of female pop singers such as Debbie Gibson, Belinda Carlisle, and Tiffany, offering up bubbly, disposable pop numbers for mainstream audiences. Both albums were hits in Canada, and Morissette earned the Most Promising Female Artist at Canada's Juno Awards; the young singer, however, failed to garner much attention outside her homeland.

Looking to jumpstart her career, Morissette moved to Los Angeles in 1994. While there, she met producer Glen Ballard, whose previous collaborators included Michael Jackson, Paula Abdul, and the band Wilson Phillips. Morissette and Ballard soon after began writing songs together. Though both hailed from the pop world, their new songs were darker and edgier than what dominated the airwaves, particularly from female singer/songwriters of the day. In 1995 Morissette released *Jagged Little Pill*, the culmination of her writing and recording sessions with Ballard.

| "You Oughta Know"

The song "You Oughta Know" catapulted Alanis Morissette to stardom, but, despite public clamoring for details on the song's inspiration, Morissette has never revealed the identity of its subject. In an interview with the *Toronto Sun* shortly after the release of the single, Morissette fueled speculation that the song was indeed about a particular person and not a lyrical abstraction: "I haven't heard from him, and I don't think he knows. Which sort of says a lot about him. The ironic thing is, if anybody questions whether it's them I'm writing about, that means something in and of itself. People who were kind and honest and full of integrity throughout the process of making this album wouldn't question whether they were in that song because they would know." Most public speculation centered on Morissette's ex-beau Dave Coulier, star of the hit television series *Full House*. Morissette and Coulier met at the 1992 National Hockey League (NHL) All-Star game in Montreal, where Morissette performed the national anthem, and the pair dated for more than a year. Other sleuths cited *Friends* star Matt LeBlanc, former Morissette songwriting partner Leslie Howe, NHL player Mike Peluso, and Coulier's *Full House* co-star Bob Saget—all of whom Morissette dated at one time or another. Morissette may indeed never reveal the subject of "You Oughta Know." As the singer/songwriter herself said: "I'm not going to deny or say yes to that, because I think it is wrong. I sort of laugh at it. . . . The truth is, I am never going to tell who it was about."

A Musical Sensation

The lead single from *Jagged Little Pill*, "You Oughta Know," quickly established Morissette as a household name in the United States. An angry, propulsive rhythm (courtesy of Red Hot Chili Peppers bass player Flea and guitarist Dave Navarro) sets the stage for Morissette's seething rant against a former boyfriend who betrayed her: "And every time you speak her name / Does she know how you told me you'd hold me / Until you died, till you died?" The raw emotion of "You Oughta Know" fueled speculation as to the identity of the song's antagonist, and Internet sites devoted to solving the mystery quickly sprang forth. MTV further sparked interest in Morissette by elevating the fresh-faced singer, with her spidery long hair and steely gaze, to visual icon status.

Morissette struck gold as well with the follow-up singles "Hand in My Pocket" and "Ironic." On the former, hypnotic drum machines, ambient guitars, and a warbling harmonica frame Morissette's lyrical exploration of her own contradictions: "I feel drunk, but I'm sober / I'm young, and I'm underpaid." Morissette lost some of her artistic credibility with the latter single, an acoustic number that reached a feverish intensity on the memorably wailed chorus; critics (and English teachers) mocked the singer for her skewed understanding of irony, citing lyrics such as: "A traffic jam when you're already late / A no-smoking sign on your cigarette break."

Despite her detractors, Morissette became a revelation to mainstream radio, which had not yet heard a female singer/songwriter with such a raw, alternative sound. *Jagged Little Pill* was a huge success, selling 30 million records worldwide. Morissette also eventually won over many of her critics, scoring Grammy Awards for Album of the Year (*Jagged Little Pill*) and Song of the Year ("You Oughta Know").

The highly anticipated follow-up album *Supposed Former Infatuation Junkie* (1998) confirmed that Morissette was not a musical flash-in-the-pan. The work was less angry and more spiritually reflective than its predecessor, in large part due to Morissette's pilgrimage to India prior to the recording of the album. The lead single "Thank U," a haunting midtempo ballad, shows Morissette at peace with herself and her relations. *Supposed Former Infatuation Junkie* debuted at number one on the album charts and ultimately sold more than 7 million copies.

Morissette took a short break from her musical career to pursue her interest in cinema. She appeared in two films by director Kevin Smith: *Dogma* (1999) and *Jay and Silent Bob Strike Back* (2001). In *Dogma*, Morissette had a memorable cameo as a female God; she reprised the role for the latter film.

In 2002 Morissette released her third album, *Under Rug Swept*. The singer once again found herself in the middle of a public debate as a result of her highly personal lyrics. In the deceptively bright-sounding lead single "Hands Clean," Morissette revisits a teenage relationship with an older man: "Ooh this could be messy / But you don't seem to mind." Though shocked by Morissette's forthright discussion of statutory rape, the public nevertheless bought *Under Rug Swept* in droves; the album, like its predecessors, became a multimillion seller.

With her captivatingly honest lyrics, Morissette held the attention of music audiences worldwide throughout the late 1990s and established herself as a commercially successful female artist.

SELECTIVE DISCOGRAPHY: *Jagged Little Pill* (Maverick/Reprise, 1995); *Supposed Former Infatuation Junkie* (Maverick/Reprise, 1998); *Alanis Unplugged* (Maverick, 1999); *Under Rug Swept* (Maverick, 2002).

SELECTIVE FILMOGRAPHY: *Dogma* (1999); *Jay and Silent Bob Strike Back* (2001).

SCOTT TRIBBLE

MORPHINE

Formed: 1990, Cambridge, Massachusetts; Disbanded 1999

Members: Mark Sandman, lead vocals, 2-string bass guitar, keyboards (born 24 September 1952; died 3 July 1999); Dana Colley, baritone and tenor saxophones (born 17 October 1961); Billy Conway, drums (born 18 December 1956). Former member: Jerome Dupree, drums (born 9 November 1956).

Genre: Rock

Best-selling album since 1990: *Cure for Pain* (1993)

In an era ruled by guitar-driven grunge rock, Morphine was a band without a guitarist. The trio's minimalist sound and guttural grooves evoked midnight passion, foreboding scenarios, and abstract dreams. Its sensual, bluesy music was often compared to the nightmarish qualities of the experimental films of David Lynch, or the crime fiction of Jim Thompson. College airplay and positive press made the group one of the 1990s' best-respected cult bands.

Morphine emerged out of Treat Her Right, a conventional blues group headed by bassist and vocalist Mark Sandman. Saxophonist Dana Colley lived near Sandman and the two began to experiment together, creating what would become their signature sound. Sandman's deadpan voice sat in the same low octaves as Colley's baritone saxophone, and together they worked to supplant a lead guitar line. Surprised to discover such a minimal approach led to wider possibilities, they enlisted area drummer Jerome Dupree to complete the trio. In 1991 Morphine released its debut album *Good* on the independent label Accurate/Distortion. Rykodisc Records re-released *Good* the next year and Morphine received its first batch of solid reviews and college airplay across the country. *Good* was named Independent Album of the Year at the 1992 Boston Music Awards. Soon after, Dupree was replaced by Treat Her Right drummer Billy Conway.

Morphine's second album, *Cure for Pain* (1993), pushed the band into the mainstream and a word-of-mouth campaign that led to international tours, national press, and shows booked on large outdoor festival stages and lengthy residencies in small clubs.

Much of the fascination with Morphine revolved around its distinctive sound without a guitar, the signature instrument in rock. Morphine looked more like a jazz combo. "[Guitars] don't really matter," Conway told the *Chicago Daily Herald* in 1997. "Jerry Lee Lewis played piano and he rocked and Little Richard rocked. There's no law I know of that rock and roll has to have a guitar. I think the [rock] attitude is hopefully reflected in [the playing style] and hopefully we deliver the song in the proper package."

In 1996 Morphine jumped to DreamWorks, a major label, and the following year the group released its fourth album *Like Swimming*. By that point Sandman's lyrics had grown darker, with images appearing to have been transcribed from dreams. "I swam out as far as I could swim 'til I was too tired to swim anymore and then tried to get my strength back," Sandman sings on the song "Empty Box." Despite a push from DreamWorks, the album failed to bring Morphine big commercial success. On July 3, 1999, while on tour in Rome to promote the album, Sandman died onstage of a heart attack.

Morphine left a deep vault. In 2000 the posthumous album *The Night* was released, followed by the live album *Bootleg: Detroit*. In early 2003 Rykodisc released a best-of collection that included unreleased material. Conway and Colley toured as Orchestra Morphine in 2000 to say goodbye to fans. In 2002 they debuted as Twinemen, a new trio featuring singer Laurie Sargent.

Morphine's unusual sound and Sandman's wry, sobering vocals distinguished the band from its peers. Its albums tried to redefine the essential elements of rock.

SELECTIVE DISCOGRAPHY: *Good* (Rykodisc, 1992); *Cure for Pain* (Rykodisc, 1993); *Yes* (Rykodisc, 1995); *B-Sides and Otherwise* (Rykodisc, 1997); *Like Swimming* (DreamWorks, 1997); *The Night* (DreamWorks, 2000); *Bootleg: Detroit* (Rykodisc, 2000); *The Best of Morphine 1992–1995* (Rykodisc, 2003).

WEBSITE: www.morphine3.com.

MARK GUARINO

VAN MORRISON

Born: George Ivan Morrison; Belfast, Northern Ireland, 31 August 1945

Genre: Rock

Best-selling album since 1990: *The Best of Van Morrison* (1990)

Singer/songwriter Van Morrison has compiled a tremendous volume of work since first recording in the 1960s and he remains one of contemporary music's most intangible stars. Morrison's soulful, sometimes spiritual music is influenced by a wide array of styles, including those of his Irish roots, and goes beyond clear-cut description. Additionally, his reticent personality and disdain for stardom have cast him publicly as an enigma. Linked by the masses to his pop hit, "Brown-Eyed Girl" and a few other radio staples, Morrison's entire song canon contains some of the preeminent poetry of post-1960s music.

Early Genius

Growing up, Morrison was exposed to a variety of musical styles by his mother who was an opera and, later, jazz singer, and his father, who was a fervent collector of seminal blues and folk recordings. By age fifteen, Morrison was adept on the guitar, saxophone, and harmonica and began playing in Belfast professionally with a variety of rhythm and blues groups. He eventually caught on as a saxophonist with a traveling show band, the Monarchs, who played throughout the United Kingdom. He left the Monarchs in 1964 to play his own music with a group of musicians in Belfast who shared similar artistic passions. They named the band Them. They released two albums, *Them* (1965) and *Them Again* (1966), which introduced the United States to Morrison specifically by the oft-covered hit, "Gloria."

After Them broke up, Morrison returned to Belfast where his songs caught the attention of producer Bert Berns. Berns convinced Morrison to come to New York and record some of them as singles. On the strength of "Brown-Eyed Girl," which had become a hit, Berns, without Morrison's approval, compiled the songs on an album titled *Blowin' Your Mind* (1967). Morrison's fury over this situation fueled his distrust of the record industry, a sentiment he has never released. Morrison recovered by recording *Astral Weeks* (1968). Using a jazz quartet for backing, *Astral Weeks* took just two days to record, but the result was a stunning album hailed by critics then and now as one of the most important recordings of contemporary music. *Astral Weeks* featured Morrison's literate Belfast-placed poetry combined with an emotional mélange of folk, blues, and jazz tinged with Celtic import. The album established Morrison as a creative genius, an expressive singer, and a star—albeit a reluctant one—on the rise.

Morrison recorded ambitiously, releasing sixteen albums throughout the 1970s and 1980s. Most of the hits came in the early 1970s, a time when his music continued to be a mix of jazzy rhythm and blues with Irish overtones. They include "Moondance," "Domino," "Wild Night," and the love ballad "Tupelo Honey." In the 1980s, Morrison's music took a spiritual turn and his songs often professed a devotion to a higher power. His most noteworthy albums of that period were *Irish Heartbeat* (1988), which includes backing by Ireland's exceptional folk band, the Chieftains, and *Avalon Sunset* (1989), which contains "Have I Told You Lately"—made popular once again when pop singer Rod Stewart recorded it for a smash hit.

The Reticent Star

These two albums marked a comeback of sorts for Morrison and he built even more momentum for the 1990s with the successful *The Best of Van Morrison* (1990). He also continued his propensity for releasing nearly an album per year with *Enlightenment* (1990), *Hymns to the Silence* (1991), and *Too Long in Exile* (1993).

Another puzzle throughout Morrison's career is his concert work, where forming a rapport with the audience has never been a top priority. While most performers direct their energy out to the audience, Morrison seems to bring his inward, showing concern only for the music itself. The effect of this prudence can make him appear clumsy, shy, or even hostile at different times and critics have been harsh on Morrison for this character trait. However, his muscular tenor colors and blends into songs like a musical instrument and few singers inject their music with the inner passion that Morrison brings to the stage. He extends that passion into his lyrics that are often inspired by the works of poets such as William Blake, William Butler Yeats, T. S. Eliot, and many others. He has released three live albums and *A Night in San Francisco* (1994) is the one that critics often cite as his best live effort.

Morrison paired with Linda Gail Lewis, the sister of early rock legend Jerry Lee Lewis, to record a collection of country and blues standards with *You Win Again* (2000). Jerry Lee Lewis was a major influence for Morrison and working with his sister allowed that stimulus to bear fruit. Lewis plays piano and sings on this recording, which features John Lee Hooker's signature song, "Boogie Chillen," and three by Hank Williams—"Jambalaya," "Why Don't You Love Me," and the title track. All of Morrison's albums normally carry a theme and this one communicates Morrison's root influences.

Morrison returned to his own compositions in *Down the Road* (2002). The album is a full-circle return to the rhythm and blues swing of his earliest music and features thirteen Morrison originals in addition to his version of the much-rendered classic, "Georgia on My Mind." He belts some powerful blues on "Talk Is Cheap."

Van Morrison was inducted into the Rock and Roll Hall of Fame in 1993. He has written and recorded more than 500 songs in his career. A dedicated gypsy poet, Morrison takes his music to the people, which has always been more comfortable for him than leading with any aspect of his persona.

SELECTIVE DISCOGRAPHY: *Astral Weeks* (Warner Bros., 1968); *Moondance* (Warner Bros., 1970); *Tupelo Honey* (Warner Bros., 1971); *Saint Dominic's Preview* (Warner Bros., 1972); *Hard Nose the Highway* (Warner Bros., 1973); *Veedon Fleece* (Warner Bros., 1974); *A Period of Transition* (Warner Bros., 1977); *Wavelength* (Warner Bros., 1978); *Common One* (Warner Bros., 1980); *Beautiful Vision* (Warner Bros., 1982); *Celtic Swing* (Phonogram, 1985); *No Guru, No Method, No Teacher* (Mercury, 1986); *Avalon Sunset* (Polydor, 1989); *Hymns to the Silence* (Polydor, 1991); *Too Long in Exile* (Polydor, 1993); *A Night in San Francisco* (Polydor, 1994); *Days Like This* (Polydor, 1995); *How Long Has This Been Going On?* (Verve, 1996); *The Healing Game* (Polydor, 1997); *The Philosopher's Stone* (Polydor, 1998); *Back on Top* (Virgin, 1999); *Down the Road* (Polydor, 2002). **With the Chieftains:** *Irish Heartbeat* (Mercury, 1988). **With Linda Gail Lewis:** *You Win Again* (Virgin, 2000). **With Them:** *Them* (Parrot, 1965); *Them Again* (Parrot, 1966).

BIBLIOGRAPHY: K. Altman, *No More Mr. Nice Guy!* (London, 1999); B. Hinton, *Celtic Crossroads: The Art of Van Morrison* (London, 2000).

DONALD LOWE

MORRISSEY

Born: Steven Patrick Morrissey; Manchester, England, 22 May 1959
Genre: Rock
Best-selling album since 1990: *Bona Drag* (1990)
Hit songs since 1990: "Interesting Drug," "We Hate It When Our Friends Become Successful," "More You Ignore Me, the Closer I Get"

Few singers in the pantheon of alternative rock music rival the enigmatic British recording artist Morrissey. Since his debut in 1983 as the lead singer of the band the Smiths, he has remained a mystery both to fans and to critics. Is he the moody, maudlin, melismatic singer he often comes across as in his jangly, guitar-driven songs? Or is he the politically minded activist who passionately pursues causes and who reminded people that "Meat Is Murder"? Is Morrissey homosexual, as rumored? Or is he unwaveringly celibate, as he has publicly declared? These questions only seem to add to his mystique.

Morrissey's concerts are transcendent experiences. Both male and female fans go to great lengths to com-

Morrissey [PAUL NATKIN/PHOTO RESERVE]

municate with him by tossing flowers, bras, T-shirts, boxer shorts, or themselves toward the stage. On stage he appears in an Elvis Presley–like pompadour, with brooding good looks and emotional ruminations. His songs contain snappy titles like "Last of the Famous International Playboys," "We Hate It When Our Friends Become Successful," and "Hairdresser On Fire." Famously private, Morrissey boasts an amazingly loyal fan base and appeals equally to people of different races, genders, and sexual preferences. Though many critics believe that Morrissey's solo work does not compare to his music with the Smiths, his fans would probably disagree.

A Solitary Childhood

Son of a night security guard and a librarian, Morrissey has recalled his childhood as turbulent and marked by extensive periods of staying indoors. His parents split when he was seventeen years old, and his black-humor lyrics were influenced by his solitary upbringing. He spent time with poetry and music and became a fan of the American actor James Dean and the Irish dramatist Oscar Wilde. When Morrissey and guitarist Johnny Marr met in 1982 and formed the Smiths, they created one of the most revered indie bands in Britain. Morrissey was often provocative and blunt in interviews, and he associated himself with somewhat unusual and controversial issues, such as vegetarianism and animal rights. By the time the

Smiths broke up and Morrissey embarked on a solo career, he had a massive following in the United States.

With the release of his solo album *Viva Hate* (1989), the title a reference to the bitter split with Marr and the Smiths, Morrissey scored a couple of hit singles, including the beautifully morose "Everyday Is Like Sunday" and the catchy, obsessive love song "Suedehead." In "Suedehead" Morrissey implores, "Why do you come here? / And why do you hang around?" The song introduced him to a wide American audience; and its forlorn romantic story struck a chord with scores of misfit, lovelorn youth.

Bona Drag (1990), his second album, is a compilation; it surveys various troubling issues but is not really a wholly conceived album. *Kill Uncle* (1991), his next release, was dismissed by critics who thought it unremarkable and perhaps even deliberately turgid. Yet the album features the lovely and haunting "Driving Your Girlfriend Home," the jaunty rockabilly-like "Sing Your Life," and the humorous, vivid, and snide "King Leer."

At His Sly Best

Fans and critics alike were vindicated by *Your Arsenal* (1992). The album features electric guitars and aggressive tempos. *Your Arsenal* just barely missed the *Billboard* Top 20 (at number twenty-one); its successor, *Vauxhall and I* (1994), reached number eighteen on its release. Many critics feel that *Vauxhall and I* shows Morrissey at his post-Smiths best. He sounds vulnerable, appreciative, and somewhat satisfied: from the lead-off track "Now My Heart Is Full" to the wise "Hold On to Your Friends," in which he sings, in second person, "Don't feel so ashamed to have friends." For someone whose career seemed to revolve around adopting a glib posture, these lyrics seemed like a personal revelation.

The last significant single Morrissey released was the midtempo charmer "The More You Ignore Me, the Closer I Get," which landed on the *Billboard* Top 40 Mainstream, reached number one on the Modern Rock Tracks, and made number forty-six on the *Billboard* Top 100. The insidious guitar line and witty lyrics are classic Morrissey: "I'm now a central part of your mind's landscape / Whether you care or do not." The ambiguous, double-entendre is effective: Is he taking potshots at record executives, or a lover?

Shortly after the release of *Vauxhall and I*, Morrissey seemed to disappear from the pop scene, spending time in court and battling record labels. He jumped to BMG Records for the lackluster *Southpaw Grammar* (1995) and then to Mercury for the equally flaccid *My Early Burglary Years* (1998). Although he has sold out Los Angeles' Hollywood Bowl faster than the Beatles, Morrissey never achieved monumental record sales. Nevertheless, his complex and uncompromising persona won him deeply loyal fans.

SELECTIVE DISCOGRAPHY: *Viva Hate* (Reprise, 1988); *Bona Drag* (Sire, 1990); *Kill Uncle* (Reprise, 1991); *Your Arsenal* (Reprise, 1992); *Vauxhall and I* (Reprise, 1994): *Southpaw Grammar* (Reprise, 1995); *Maladjusted* (Mercury, 1997); *My Early Burglary Years* (Reprise, 1998). **With the Smiths:** *Meat Is Murder* (Sire, 1985); *The Queen Is Dead* (Sire, 1986); *Strangeways, Here We Come* (Sire, 1987); *Louder Than Bombs* (Sire, 1987).

CARRIE HAVRANEK

SHAWN MULLINS

Born: Atlanta, Georgia, 8 March 1968

Genre: Rock

Best-selling album since 1990: *Soul's Core* (1998)

Hit songs since 1990: "Lullaby," "What Is Life"

Singer/songwriter Shawn Mullins enjoyed a brief moment in the commercial spotlight as his quirky folk-pop song "Lullaby" became a radio sensation.

Mullins was born in Atlanta in 1968; his mother was a schoolteacher and his father worked in the railroad industry. Mullins took to music at an early age, learning to drum when he was four years old. He subsequently became adept at playing piano, cello, bass, and guitar and formed his first band at the age of twelve. When he was a freshman in high school, Mullins became acquainted with Amy Ray, then a local performer and later a member of the popular folk duo the Indigo Girls. Ray appeared at a career day sponsored by Mullins's high school and encouraged the young Mullins to pursue a career in music.

Before committing to music full time, Mullins served for two years in the U.S. Army Airborne Infantry. While in the military, Mullins released his first album on his own SMG label. After leaving the military, Mullins recorded a host of albums for SMG and became a regular on the Atlanta club circuit. He gradually gained a following with his intimate performances, highlighted by his folksy guitar playing and his half-sung/half-spoken vocal style. In 1997 Mullins received the award for Best Acoustic Artist at the Atlanta Music Awards.

Columbia Records signed Mullins to a contract and, in 1998, released *Soul's Core*, Mullins's most recent independent effort. At the time, singer/songwriters were enjoying unprecedented success on mainstream radio, due in large part to the popularity of the Lilith Fair tour, which highlighted female singer/songwriters. Mullins's quirky single "Lullaby" offered radio programmers a male counterpart to artists such as Jewel and Sheryl Crow and quickly became a surprise Top 10 hit. "Lullaby" bounces along to a jaunty acoustic guitar, while Mullins—in a departure from traditional pop radio fare—alternates between speaking and singing the lyrics. The song posits Mullins as a struggling heartland artist in Los Angeles: "I told her I ain't so sure about this place / It's hard to play a gig in this town and keep a straight face / Seems like everyone here's got a plan / It's kind of like Nashville with a tan." For the choruses, Mullins breaks into a lilting falsetto and offers a hopeful counterpoint to the otherwise dark lyrics: "Everything's gonna be alright / Rock-a-bye." On the strength of its hit single, *Soul's Core* ultimately sold 1 million copies.

Mullins followed up *Soul's Core* with a high-profile appearance on the soundtrack to the Adam Sandler film *Big Daddy* (1999), offering up a faithful cover of George Harrison's "What Is Life." As interest in Mullins peaked, Columbia released an anthology of his earlier works titled *The First Ten Years* (1999). Mullins released his first true major label album in 2000, but *Behind the Velvet Sun* failed to garner major interest, largely because the work lacked a hit single along the lines of "Lullaby." Critics also bemoaned the album's slick, pop arrangements, charging that Mullins had forsaken his roots and unique crossover style.

SELECTIVE DISCOGRAPHY: *Better Days* (SMG, 1992); *Big Blue Sky* (Rainy Day, 1994); *Eggshells* (SMG, 1996); *Soul's Core* (Sony, 1998); *Beneath the Velvet Sun* (Columbia, 2000). **Soundtrack:** *Big Daddy* (Sony, 1999).

SCOTT TRIBBLE

MYSTIKAL

Born: Michael Tyler; New Orleans, Louisiana, 16 January 1975

Genre: Hip-Hop

Best-selling album since 1990: *Ghetto Fabulous* (1998)

Hit songs since 1990: "Y'all Ain't Ready Yet," "Ain't No Limit," "Neck Uv Da Woods"

Throughout the 1990s, southern-based hip-hop gained commercial dominance by forging a fresh new sound from prominent synthesizers, complex rhythms, and drawling raps laced with regional slang. Mystikal was among a number of New Orleans–based rappers to win nationwide exposure during this time. Arguably one of the most talented artists to emerge from New Orleans gangsta rap impresario Master P's No Limit label, Mystikal spent the latter half of the decade developing a tongue-twisting, confrontational style of rapping that would propel him to great success early in the twenty-first century.

Although he was immersed in the New Orleans hip-hop scene from his early teens, Mystikal's rap career began in earnest when he returned to his hometown after a tour in the Gulf War. In 1995 he released a self-titled debut through local independent label Big Boy. The album was successful enough to attract the attention of New York-based Jive Records, which added a few new tracks to *Mystikal* and re-released it as *Mind of Mystikal* in 1996.

The backing tracks on *Mind of Mystikal* do little to deviate from the dominant sound of the time, the laid-back, melodic production style known as G-funk and pioneered by the L.A.-based rapper/producer Dr. Dre. Mystikal does, however, manage to distinguish himself from leading G-funk emcees such as Snoop Dogg and Warren G. In contrast to their lazy, sing-songy flow, he delivers his rhymes in rapid-fire bursts punctuated by James Brown–like shouts. The sound is aggressively new enough to lend weight to the obligatory boasts of superior microphone skills, such as this typically densely packed passage from "Here I Go": "I wreck beaucoup crews / with the words I use / I'm 'bout to be feelin' like ZZ hill cuz I'm screamin' and screamin' and singin' the blues." *Mind of Mystikal* became an underground rap hit, eventually going gold.

This success was enough to attract the attention of Mystikal's New Orleans neighbor, Percy Miller. Better known as Master P, Miller had spent the early 1990s steadily releasing cheaply produced gangsta rap through his No Limit label. Although No Limit records received no play on MTV or radio, grassroots sales turned the label into a mini-empire. Fortuitously, Mystikal signed with No Limit just as it was breaking through to huge mainstream success, thanks to Master P's sixth solo album, *Ghetto D*, and the soundtrack to the No Limit-produced home video *I'm Bout It*. Mystikal contributed the track "What Cha Think" to the latter, and in November 1997 No Limit released *Unpredictable*.

Unpredictable's more polished production significantly improves upon its predecessor, showcasing Mystikal's menacing bark over stripped-down beats and jazz-tinged bass. Mystikal, for his part, distinguishes himself as a more talented writer and rapper than many of the often-generic emcees in the No Limit stable. On "Ain't No Limit," eerie strings and distorted chants serve as the backdrop to Mystikal's inventive, referential boasts: ". . . you talking weirder than Elvis Presley / I'm trying to blow out bigger than the jaws of Dizzy Gillespie." *Unpredictable* proved to be a commercial breakthrough for Mystikal, selling 1 million copies and creating major anticipation for his follow-up. Deviating little from the formula of the album before it, *Ghetto Fabulous* (1998) debuted nearly at the top of the album charts and also went platinum.

Like all No Limit albums, both *Unpredictable* and *Ghetto Fabulous* are at least as much about reinforcing the

No Limit brand as they are about developing the career of the individual artist. In 2000, feeling the constraints of having to be a "team player," Mystikal left No Limit to return to Jive, which released his fifth album, *Let's Get Ready*. The move proved commercially and artistically fruitful. The lead single, "Shake Ya Ass," memorably harnesses the potential of Mystikal's voice as an instrument in its own right, playing his staccato outbursts off sparse, funky beats and a smooth, falsetto refrain. It was the biggest single of his career to date and ultimately drove sales of the album to the 2 million mark. In late 2001, Mystikal released his sixth album, *Tarantula*, which garnered two Grammy Award nominations.

As one of the main artists to benefit from and subsequently drive the ascendance of southern hip-hop in the 1990s, Mystikal developed a sound that would propel him to mainstream success at the turn of the decade.

SELECTIVE DISCOGRAPHY: *Mystikal* (Big Boy, 1995); *Mind of Mystikal* (Jive, 1996); *Unpredictable* (No Limit, 1997); *Ghetto Fabulous* (No Limit, 1998); *Let's Get Ready* (Jive, 2000); *Tarantula* (Jive, 2001).

BIBLIOGRAPHY: Editors of *Rap Life* Magazine, *Master P: Forever Bout It: The Life and Times of Percy Miller, The Ghetto Bill Gates* (New York, 2001).

WEBSITE: www.bigtruckrecords.com.

MATT HIMES

NAS

Born: Nasir Ben Olu Dara Jones; Brooklyn, New York, 14 September 1973

Genre: Hip-Hop

Best-selling album since 1990: *It Was Written* (1996)

Hit songs since 1990: "Street Dreams," "Got Ur Self a Gun"

Nas is widely viewed as a once-and-future street prophet, who repeatedly wavers between exercising his substantial artistic gifts and downplaying them in order to seek widespread appeal.

The son of acclaimed Jazz musician Olu Dara, Nas first came to the attention of hip-hop fans as "Nasty Nas" performing a guest verse on Main Source's 1991 single "Live at the Barbeque." The song brought him instant notoriety for his relaxed-yet-intense vocal delivery, as well as for his willingness to violate one of hip-hop's strongest, yet least noted, rules against insulting Christianity. "When I was twelve," he rhymes, "I went to hell for snuffing Jesus."

In April 1994, he released his first album, *Illmatic*, which critics consider to be one of the all time great hip-hop albums. The album's lyrics have an internal rhythmic momentum that Nas uses to intensify the strength of his already powerful observations. With an eye for the telling poetic detail, Nas addresses various aspects of the street life with informality and empathy.

After such a nuanced and artistic debut, fans were shocked by Nas's second album, *It Was Written* (1996), which openly embraced a pop sensibility. On the strength of the first single "Street Dreams" (based on the Eurythmics' 1983 pop hit "Sweet Dreams (Are Made of This)"), *It Was Written* ultimately reached number one on the *Billboard* 200.

The following year, Nas adopted the name Nas Escobar in tribute to Colombian drug lord Pablo Escobar, and created a group called the Firm with rappers Foxy Brown, Nature, and AZ. The group released a self-titled album, dealing primarily with drug themes, which failed to inspire his core fans.

Nas released two albums in 1999, *I Am . . .*, which reached number one on the *Billboard* 200, and *Nastradamus*. *I Am . . .* contains one of Nas's most controversial songs, "Hate Me Now," in which he berates the fans who have criticized his materialism: "My bad, should I step out my shoes? / Give 'em to you?" To add insult to injury, the song features a guest appearance from Sean "Puff Daddy" Combs, widely seen as the most shamelessly commercial rap artist of the era.

In 2001, Nas released *QB Finest*, a compilation album that features his crew, Bravehearts, and produced only one hit, the sexually indulgent "Oochie Wally."

Just when Nas seemed to have committed himself to a career as a sexually explicit pop star, he became embroiled in a conflict with Brooklyn-based rapper Jay-Z. As each emcee began to release songs responding to each other's insults, the hip-hop community took increasing note of the fact that, in his anger, Nas was crafting rhymes that recalled the quality and intensity of his earliest efforts.

Energized by his public feud with Jay-Z—and the public reaction to it—Nas released *Stillmatic* in late 2001, its

Spot Light | *Illmatic*

Illmatic (1994) is considered to be one of the quintessential New York hip-hop albums, a rare blend of insightful lyricism and straightforward sample-heavy music. Released in an era dominated by the relaxed, synthesizer-based West Coast "G-Funk" of Dr. Dre and Snoop Dogg, *Illmatic*—along with *Enter the Wu-Tang: (36 Chambers)* by Wu-Tang Clan—returned hip-hop's focus to the East Coast. Nas's style on this album is defined by his poetic observations of everyday life and the social and political realities that they implied. The song "One Love," is written in the form of a letter to an imprisoned friend. By concentrating on details, the song manages to simultaneously portray both the isolation of prison and the difficulties of life on the outside: ". . . Yo, guess who got shot in the dome-piece? / Jerome's niece, on her way home from Jones Beach / it's bugged. . . ." This album also breaks with hip-hop tradition by forgoing the use of a single producer/disc jockey to construct the instrumental settings for Nas's lyrics, instead using many different producers to create a unique sound for each song. In the wake of *Illmatic*'s success, this approach soon became standard practice among hip-hop artists.

title a reference to his intention to resume the style of his first album. This release was soon followed by *The Lost Tapes,* a compilation of outtakes from 1998 to 2001, and *God's Son,* both released in 2002. These three albums are widely seen as a return to form for Nas, much to the delight of the hip-hop community.

For many hip-hop fans, Nas embodies the contradictions of the form. His refusal to be defined as either an artist or a pop star has brought him a great deal of criticism, along with an equivalent portion of respect.

SELECTIVE DISCOGRAPHY: *Illmatic* (Sony/Columbia, 1994); *It Was Written* (Sony/Columbia, 1996); *The Firm* (Sony/Columbia, 1997); *I Am . . .* (Sony/Columbia, 1999); *Nastradamus* (Sony/Columbia, 1999); *QB Finest* (Sony/Columbia, 2001); *Stillmatic* (Sony/Columbia, 2001); *The Lost Tapes*

(Sony/Columbia, 2002); *God's Son* (Sony/Columbia, 2002).

JOE SCHLOSS

YOUSSOU N'DOUR

Born: Dakar, Senegal, 1 October 1959
Genre: World
Best-selling album since 1990: *The Guide (Wommat)* (1994)

Singer, drummer, bandleader, and composer Youssou N'Dour is the most important, successful, and influential African performer on the world music scene. A superstar and national hero in his native Senegal, N'Dour originated and coined the term "mbalax," that unique style of Senegalese dance music that took the music world by storm in the mid-1980s and has remained popular in the three decades since N'Dour began performing it.

Born in the rough Medina section of Dakar, the capital of Senegal, N'Dour's father was a mechanic and his mother was a female gawlo or griot, a West African troubadour who would sing of the region's royal history, family sagas, and oral traditions. Encouraged by his mother, N'Dour began singing as a child and became sought after for circumcision parties and gatherings. By the age of twelve, he was performing in theater, in music groups, and on radio broadcasts; by age fourteen, N'Dour had already earned the nickname "The Little Prince of Dakar."

In 1975, after joining the Star Band, the best-known Senegalese pop band of the time, the sixteen-year-old N'Dour became the star attraction of the act before forming his own breakaway group, Étoile de Dakar, two years later, and then Super Étoile de Dakar in 1981. The unique feature of these bands was that they drew upon the traditional sabar drum ensemble, which uses pitched drums dialoguing in suddenly fluctuating cross-rhythms and transposing these rhythms to electric lead guitar, rhythm guitar, and synthesizers. The rhythm guitar usually takes the role of the rhythm of the mbung mbung drum, and N'Dour began referring to this style of music as mbalax, the Wolof word for rhythm; N'Dour is credited with the invention of mbalax, which remains the dominant style of Senegalese music.

When Super Étoile began performing in the West, the mbalax craze moved with it and ignited enormous interest in this unique import from Senegal and the singer so associated with it. Peter Gabriel heard N'Dour at a London club in 1984 and was so taken with him that he used him on his *So* (1986) album, singing a duet with him on the hit single "In Your Eyes," which was also later used in

(1994), N'Dour's trademark mbalax sound was starting to take a backseat to even bigger production values and ever-increasing Western-style pop and rock elements; the multiplatinum single "7 Seconds" was recorded with hip-hop singer Neneh Cherry, jazz saxophonist Branford Marsalis makes an appearance, and a cover of Bob Dylan's "Chimes of Freedom" is included.

Joko (2000) actually appeared in two configurations: an American version subtitled *The Link*, which includes pop duets with Sting and Wyclef Jean, and an international release subtitled *From Village to Town*, which omits Sting and Jean and substitutes genuine mbalax. This marketing strategy continues on N'Dour's releases of Afro-pop albums for Western audiences and smaller, Senegalese-oriented releases on his own Jololi label.

Just as many critics had dismissed N'Dour as having sold out and abandoned his African roots, *Nothing's in Vain* (2002) appeared as a largely acoustic and the most African-oriented Western album N'Dour had released in over a decade. Yet even when N'Dour chooses to embed himself within the hackneyed trappings of Western pop music, he is able to generate interest because of the sheer resonance and tonal beauty of his tenor voice.

SELECTIVE DISCOGRAPHY: *Nelson Mandela* (Polygram, 1990); *Set* (Virgin, 1992); *Eyes Open* (Sony, 1992); *Lion* (Virgin re-release, 1992); *The Guide (Wommat)* (Chaos/Columbia, 1994); *Immigrés* (Worldbeat/Virgin re-release, 1995); *Ba Tay* (Jololi, 1995); *Inedits 84–85* (Celluloid/Melodie, 1997); *Best of the 80s* (Melodie, 1998); *Special Fin D'annee Plus* (Jololi, 1999); *Joko* (Nonesuch/Elektra, 2000); *Le Grand Bel, Vol. 1 and 2* (Jololi, 2000); *Lii* (Jololi, 2000); *Rewmi* (Jololi, 2000); *St. Louis* (Jololi, 2000); *Nothing's in Vain* (Nonesuch/Elektra, 2002); *The Rough Guide to Youssou N'Dour & Étolie de Dakar* (World Music Network, 2002). **With Peter Gabriel:** *So* (Universal re-release, 2002). **With Paul Simon:** *Graceland* (Warner Bros. re-release, 1997). **Soundtracks:** *Passion: Music for the Last Temptation of Christ* (Geffen, 1989); *The Wild Thornberrys Movie* (Jive, 2002).

BIBLIOGRAPHY: J. Cathcart, *Hey You! A Portrait of Youssou N'Dour* (Whitney, England, 1989); Y. N'Dour and É. De Dakar, *The Rough Guide to Youssou N'Dour & Étolie De Dakar*, abridged edition (New York, 2003).

WEBSITE: www.youssou.com.

DENNIS POLKOW

Youssou N'Dour [PAUL NATKIN/PHOTO RESERVE]

the film *Say Anything* (1989). Gabriel generously had N'Dour accompany him on his subsequent world tour both to sing with Gabriel and to open the shows with the Super Étoile; Gabriel also used N'Dour in his score for Martin Scorsese's film *The Last Temptation of Christ* (1988).

With the release of the album *Immigrés* (1985) in Europe and in the United States (1988), N'Dour became firmly established as the most popular African performer on the world music scene, a reputation also bolstered by his drumming contributions on Paul Simon's *Graceland* (1986). In 1988 N'Dour performed as part of Amnesty International's "Human Rights Now!" campaign, a forty-four-day, five-continent world tour kicked off by a special London concert in which N'Dour performed with Gabriel, Bruce Springsteen, Sting, and Tracy Chapman at Wembley Stadium.

With the album *Lion* (1989), which includes a duet with Gabriel, N'Dour began deliberately courting Western audiences quite effectively with glossy production values and some token English lyrics while continuing to sing in French and his native Wolof. That approach continued with *Eyes Open* (1992), recorded for director Spike Lee's record label. By the time of *The Guide (Wommat)*

NELLY

Born: Cornell Haynes, Jr.; Austin, Texas, 2 November 1978
Genre: Rap

Best-selling album since 1990: *Country Grammar* (2000)

Hit songs since 1990: "Country Grammar," "Hot in Herre"

New York, Los Angeles, and Atlanta have long been the key cities of the hip-hop world, but with the surprise success of his 2000 major-label debut, *Country Grammar*, the St. Louis rapper Nelly put the Midwest on the map. With a colorful crew of fellow rappers called the St. Lunatics, the photogenic Air Force brat added St. Louis to the rap map by unleashing a string of sing-songy, instantly accessible party anthems such as "Hot in Herre" and "Country Grammar." Like the Wu-Tang Clan a decade earlier, the solo success of Nelly was intended as a stepping-stone for the solo careers of his mates in the St. Lunatics.

Cornell Haynes, Jr., the youngest son of an Air Force sergeant, was born in Texas in 1978 and raised in Spain before landing in St. Louis, Missouri, where his parents divorced when he was eight. The young Cornell bounced between eight different schools and almost as many homes as a child; fearing her son was being led astray by older friends, Nelly's mother moved the family to the suburban University City, Missouri.

At fifteen Nelly formed the group the St. Lunatics with his brother, City Spudd, and his high school friends Kyjuan, Ali, Murphy Lee, and Jason. In 1996, the group had a regional hit with the self-produced song, "Gimmie What Ya Want," which sold more than 7,000 copies, but the release failed to elicit any offers from record labels. Meanwhile, Nelly continued to pursue his parallel passion, baseball, playing shortstop in the St. Louis Amateur Baseball Association and attending training camps for the Atlanta Braves and Pittsburgh Pirates.

Hoping to repeat the success of New York's nine-member Wu-Tang Clan—a hard-core rap collective that debuted with a group album and later launched more than half a dozen successful solo careers—the group pushed the handsome, charismatic Nelly to the fore, hoping to secure a solo deal that would allow him to bring his cohorts along. The ploy was a success: Nelly was signed by Universal Records in 2000 and released his debut album, *Country Grammar*, that year.

The album, which debuted in the *Billboard* top five, produced one of the biggest hits of the year in the title track, which featured a sly funk bass line and nursery rhyme chorus ("I'm going down, down baby, yo' street in a Range Rover / Street sweeper baby, cocked ready to let it go / Shimmy shimmy cocoa what? Listen to it pound"). A combination of St. Louis boosterism, party lyrics, and bluster, the song not only put St. Louis on the rap map, but it also made Nelly a star. Although initially thought of as a novelty act, Nelly's debut sold more than 8 million copies.

A Tribute to a Jailed Friend Becomes a Fashion Statement

Not only did Nelly bring a distinctive Midwestern twang to the rap game, he also brought an album's worth of insider slang, some of which became common parlance thanks to hits such as "E.I."—which introduced the title phrase, translated as "Bring it on!"—and "mo," St. Louis slang for a friend. With City Spudd (a.k.a. Lavell Webb) serving a ten-year sentence for robbery, Nelly paid tribute to his incarcerated St. Lunatic by always wearing a Band-Aid under his left eye, a bizarre fashion accouterment that became part of the rapper's signature look, as did backward baseball jerseys.

Nelly swept up the Best New Artist and Album of the Year trophies at the 2000 *Source* magazine awards. He performed beside Britney Spears, the Rolling Stones, and *NSYNC at the January 2001 Super Bowl, and he joined Destiny's Child and Eve on an MTV-sponsored summer tour. In 2001 Nelly launched his Vokal clothing line and participated in the debut album from the St. Lunatics, *Free City*. The rapper had a hit with the boast-heavy track, "#1," from the *Training Day* soundtrack, released in September 2001, and had a co-starring role in the film *Snipes*.

Though the St. Lunatics' album did not reach the level of success of Nelly's debut, Nelly proved he was not a one-hit wonder by beginning 2002 with another hit, a remix of *NSYNC's "Girlfriend." The first single from his second solo album, *Nellyville*, proved that the St. Louis rapper was no fluke. Again employing his penchant for slurring consonants and spelling words his own way, "Hot in Herre" became another ubiquitous summer anthem, blaring nonstop from pop, hip-hop, and R&B radio. The Neptunes-produced party song, which encouraged the shedding of clothing, was another pop-rap confection with an intensely catchy chorus and smooth, confident rapping from Nelly. The number one album sold some 5 million copies.

With a sitcom in development and more movie roles on the horizon, Nelly closed out 2002 by spinning out yet another big hit, "Dilemma," a love ballad featuring the Destiny's Child member Kelly Rowland singing the R&B chorus. When radio programmers began playing it, the track turned into a smash hit, forcing Rowland to move up the release of her first solo album to capitalize on the song's success.

Nelly became a superstar with his smooth flow and sing-along choruses, leading some to criticize the rapper for his pop-leaning tastes. Nevertheless, the allure of his songs was undeniable, as was his impressive feat of shining the world's attention on a city that turned into a hip-hop gateway.

SELECTIVE DISCOGRAPHY: *Country Grammar* (Universal, 2000); *Nellyville* (Universal, 2002); **With the St. Lunatics:** *Free City* (Universal, 2001).

WEBSITE: www.nelly.net.

GIL KAUFMAN

WILLIE NELSON

Born: Abbott, Texas, 29 April 1933

Genre: Country

Best-selling album since 1990: *The Great Divide* (2002)

Hit songs since 1990: "There You Are," "Maria (Shut Up and Kiss Me)," "Mendocino County Line"

One of the first country artists to successfully write and perform his own songs, Willie Nelson spent a decade penning hits for others before recording a series of groundbreaking solo albums beginning in the 1970s. As influenced by jazz and pop as by country, Nelson has displayed wide-ranging imagination, his singing and guitar playing reflecting subtlety, precision, and heart. As a songwriter, Nelson creates aching portraits of people trapped by circumstances; his weathered, nasal voice and idiosyncratic sense of timing provide the ideal foil for his material. Overcoming personal problems such as the loss of his house and battles with the Internal Revenue Service (IRS), Nelson has retained his talent and prolificacy, recording challenging, boundary-pushing albums through the late 1990s and beyond. His gentle and unassuming artistic persona only partially hides a flinty, renegade spirit; this contrast sparks his recordings and gives them life.

Raised by their grandparents in rural Texas, Nelson and older sister Bobbie were encouraged to play instruments from an early age, Bobbie taking up the piano, Willie the guitar. After graduating from high school Nelson entered the U.S. Air Force, but was forced to leave due to chronic back problems. In 1954 he moved to Fort Worth, Texas, working as a disc jockey and performing in local nightclubs and bars. Two years later, he recorded his first single, "Lumberjack," which eventually sold a respectable 3,000 copies due to extensive local radio play. After writing the hit "Family Bible" for country singer Claude Gray in 1960, Nelson moved to the music industry locus of Nashville, Tennessee, writing hits for country stars such as Patsy Cline and Ray Price. Word of Nelson's talent for detailed, incisive writing quickly spread,

and by the mid-1960s his songs had been recorded by rock and R&B artists such as Roy Orbison, Joe Hinton, and Timi Yuro. During this period Nelson also released his own albums, although his restrained performance style clashed with the string-heavy "Nashville Sound" then predominating country music. In the early 1970s, after a fire destroyed his Nashville home, Nelson returned to Texas, leaving the music business and unsuccessfully venturing into pig farming.

Country Stardom

Nelson's lawyer, Neil Rushen, encouraged him to record for Atlantic Records, a major rhythm and blues label making a foray into country music. Two albums resulted from the association, including the classic *Phases and Stages* (1974). Recorded with an R&B band in Muscle Shoals, Alabama, the album is conceived as a song cycle detailing the breakup of a relationship from both points of view. On songs such as "Washing the Dishes," Nelson displays his talent for concision and psychological complexity: "Learning to hate all the things / That she once loved to do / Like washing his shirts / And never complaining / Except of red stains on the collars." Moving to Columbia Records in 1975, Nelson released the album *Red Headed Stranger,* dealing with the unusual subject of a preacher on the run after murdering his wife and her lover. So minimalist in sound that Columbia executives initially thought they were listening to a demo version, the album is challenging and intellectually satisfying. Spurred by the wistful hit, "Blue Eyes Crying in the Rain," it solidified Nelson's reputation as a performer, bringing him crossover success among a rock and pop audience.

Nelson's newfound popularity tied in with the burgeoning "outlaw" movement, a loose collective of performers who eschewed the orchestrated Nashville Sound for a more swinging, traditional style based on fiddles, drums, and guitar. After being characterized as an "outlaw," Nelson surprised the public by recording *Stardust,* an album of popular standards from the 1930s and 1940s. By the early 1980s Nelson was a bona fide pop star, recording smooth, radio-friendly hits such as "On the Road Again" (1980) and "Always on My Mind" (1982). His success, however, was checkered by battles with the IRS. In the late 1980s, $16 million in debt after investing in faulty tax shelters, Nelson was allowed to pay off the agency with income from two albums that were recorded quickly and sold via television commercials.

New Directions in the 1990s

With many of his troubles behind him, Nelson recorded with undiminished spirit and energy in the 1990s, creating what critics describe as some of his most powerful work. *Across the Borderline* (1993) is a high-profile collaboration with several renowned rock artists, including Bob Dylan and Sinéad O'Connor. On songs such as "She's Not for You" Nelson creates a rich mood with dexterous guitar playing and deeply felt vocals. After several albums for small labels, Nelson signed with Island Records in 1996 and released *Spirit,* an album critics cite as one of his most exciting, rewarding works. Beautifully executed, the album derives its power from the balance of sound and quiet space. With sister Bobbie's churchy piano imparting a feel of rustic sincerity, "I'm Not Trying to Forget You (Anymore)" is classic Nelson, melodic with an ironic sense of humor: "I've been trying to forget someone / That my heart still adores / So I'm not trying to forget you anymore." Like many of his best songs, "I'm Not Trying to Forget You (Anymore)" is lined by a mordancy that contrasts with Nelson's gentle surface. Fans and critics find other tracks equally impressive: "She Is Gone" demonstrates a fine understanding of collaboration, with Bobbie's piano and Nelson's emotive guitar taking turns in richly textured solos, while the instrumental "Mariachi" features subtle shifts of tempo and volume, building slowly to a climax that is arresting in its muted intensity.

Turning to producer Daniel Lanois for his follow-up album, *Teatro* (1998), Nelson again created a series of elegant, atmospheric songs. This time, however, his effectiveness is undercut slightly by Lanois's penchant for unusual aural effects such as echoed percussion. Unlike other country artists who rely on producers to provide a strong, defining musical stamp, Nelson works best in a laid-back, casual style that displays his virtuosity unadorned. Still, the album features several memorable tracks, such as the haunting "Home Motel," a quiet song with vivid, poetic imagery: "I'm gonna hang a neon sign with letters big and blue / Home motel on lost love avenue." Like many of Nelson's best songs, "Home Motel" conjures a sadness built upon loss and resignation. Over the course of his career this resignation emerges as one of Nelson's most powerful attributes, a sign of obduracy rather than weakness. The 1980s and 1990s were marked by other career highlights: In 1988 he published his autobiography and in 1998 he was a recipient of the prestigious Kennedy Center Honors. This period also saw his arrest for marijuana possession in 1994. Nelson used the occasion to speak out for marijuana's legalization, criticizing the government's War on Drugs program. The story that Nelson once lit a marijuana joint during an invited visit to the White House in the 1970s only added to his iconoclastic legend.

Exerting his individualistic spirit, Nelson carved out new territory at the turn of the millennium, recording a collection of blues-based songs, *Milk Cow Blues* (2000) and a children's album, *Rainbow Connection* (2001). Despite the inclusion of juvenile material such as "Playmate" and "I'm Looking Over a Four-Leaf Clover," *Rainbow Connection* bears a universality that appeals to adults. Critics hailed the title track, often associated with children's television character Kermit the Frog, as a revelation. Strumming gently on guitar, Nelson uncovers melodic complexities and emotional currents missing from the better-known version. The sophisticated contours of Nelson's playing point to his early jazz influences, particularly Belgian guitarist Django Reinhardt. Detailed in spite of its simple surface, "Rainbow Connection" captures a sense of innocence and yearning for hope that, while childlike, transcend boundaries of age.

In 2002 Nelson released *The Great Divide,* a collaboration with hot young performers such as hip-hop artist Kid Rock and R&B star Brian McKnight. With its high-profile roster, *The Great Divide* became Nelson's most commercially successful album in years, although critics have said Nelson himself often gets buried in the flashy production. Still, the album's hits, "Maria (Shut Up and Kiss Me)" and "Mendocino County Line," a duet with country singer Lee Ann Womack, attest to Nelson's continued relevance within contemporary country music. With older, more traditional country artists such as Loretta Lynn and George Jones being pushed off the charts in favor of younger, pop-oriented performers, Nelson's tenacity and endurance are admired by fans and critics alike.

Surviving the many transformations country music has undergone since the 1960s, Nelson has retained a distinctive sound without sacrificing his popularity. His finely etched renderings of love and loss find expression in his dry, grainy voice, quiet phrasing, and assured guitar playing. Regarded as an American original, Nelson has held his ground, recording consistently inventive works that defy categorization. His style, tender yet rooted in a core of toughness, remains uniquely his own.

SELECTIVE DISCOGRAPHY: . . . *And Then I Wrote* (Liberty, 1962); *Phases and Stages* (Atlantic, 1974); *Red Headed Stranger* (Columbia, 1975); *Stardust* (Columbia, 1978); *Always on My Mind* (Columbia, 1982); *Across the Borderline* (Columbia, 1993); *Spirit* (Island, 1996); *Teatro* (Island, 1998); *Milk Cow Blues* (Island, 2000); *Rainbow Connection* (Island, 2001); *The Great Divide* (Universal, 2002).

BIBLIOGRAPHY: W. Nelson and B. Shrake, *Willie: An Autobiography* (New York, 1988); W. Nelson, *The Facts of Life and Other Dirty Jokes* (New York, 2002).

WEBSITE: www.willienelson.com.

DAVID FREELAND

AARON NEVILLE

Born: New Orleans, Louisiana, 24 January 1941
Genre: R&B, Pop

Best-selling album since 1990: *The Grand Tour* (1993)

Hit songs since 1990: "The Grand Tour," "Use Me"

With his trademark high falsetto voice, Aaron Neville is a unique talent in popular music. Influenced by the flowing style of 1950s and 1960s vocalist Sam Cooke, Neville uses his sweet, flexible voice to embellish his songs with *melisma,* the singing of multiple notes within a syllable. While Neville during the 1960s and 1970s remained a "cult" singer, little known outside of his native New Orleans, he succeeded in crossing over to the popular mainstream in the 1980s and 1990s. Since that time, he has recorded everything from country to gospel, keeping his unique sound intact.

Raised in a rough section of New Orleans, Neville's early life was difficult, marked by drug addiction and time in jail. Although a tough youth, Neville was a devoted Roman Catholic who frequently sang gospel music in church. He began recording around 1960, but it was his 1966 hit, the catchy "Tell It Like It Is," that gave him his first dose of rhythm and blues success. In the 1970s he teamed with brothers Arthur, Charles, and Cyril to form the group the Neville Brothers; together they released a series of critically acclaimed albums, in particular *Yellow Moon* (1989), an inventive fusion of R&B, rock, and gospel that critic Robert Christgau called "their masterpiece." During the 1980s Neville pursued solo projects in addition to working with his brothers, recording a hit duet, "Don't Know Much" (1989), with pop and rock star Linda Ronstadt. A smooth pop ballad that received extensive airplay on mainstream radio, the song earned Neville a solo contract with A&M Records.

Neville's first album for A&M, *Warm Your Heart* (1991), is a well-rounded collection displaying his facility with different types of material. "Angola Bound," a tough song culled from Neville's prison experiences, features a classic "second line" sound, a shuffling type of rhythm unique to New Orleans music. On the atmospheric "It Feels Like Rain" Neville creates a mood of warm intimacy through vocal understatement, achieving a kind of quiet power. The spiritual "I Bid You Goodnight" features Neville backed with a strong choir, his voice floating ethereally over the arrangement. Despite the diversity of material on *Warm Your Heart,* the production is smooth and uncluttered, giving the album a cohesive feel. Subsequent albums of the 1990s steered Neville into more of a mainstream pop direction, although his vocal performances were always compelling. In 1993 he had a hit on the country charts with a first-rate version of "The Grand Tour," a song associated with country legend George Jones. The high-pitched tug in Neville's voice was well suited to the country idiom, pushing the single into *Billboard*'s Top Country chart. Neville fulfilled a lifelong dream in 2000, releasing his first gospel album, *Devotion.* On traditional spiritual numbers like "Mary Don't You Weep" and "Banks of the River Jordan," Neville's classic falsetto remains in fine form.

With a gentle voice that belies his large physical frame, Aaron Neville has proven his talent time and again in a variety of musical settings. Perhaps the most commercially successful singer to come out of New Orleans, he is seen by critics as a gifted representative of that city's rich musical heritage.

SELECTIVE DISCOGRAPHY: *Warm Your Heart* (A&M, 1991); *The Grand Tour* (A&M, 1993); *The Tattooed Heart* (A&M, 1995); *Devotion* (EMI Gospel, 2000). **With the Neville Brothers:** *Fiyo on the Bayou* (A&M, 1981); *Yellow Moon* (A&M, 1989); *Valence Street* (Columbia, 1999).

WEBSITE: www.aaronneville.com.

DAVID FREELAND

NEW EDITION

Formed: 1982, Boston, Massachusetts; Disbanded 1990; Re-formed 1996

Members: Ricky Bell (born Boston, Massachusetts, 18 September 1967); Michael Bivins (born Boston, Massachusetts, 10 August 1968); Bobby Brown (born Boston, Massachusetts, 5 February 1969); Ronnie DeVoe (born Boston, Massachusetts, 17 November 1967); Johnny Gill (born Washington, D.C., 22 May 1966); Ralph Tresvant (born Boston, Massachusetts, 16 May 1968).

Genre: R&B, Pop

Best-selling album since 1990: *Home Again* (1996)

Hit songs since 1990: "Hit Me Off," "I'm Still in Love with You"

Beginning its career as an innocent sounding spin-off of early 1970s group the Jackson 5, New Edition enjoyed a highly successful string of teen-oriented pop hits before toughening its sound in the late 1980s, laying the groundwork for 1990s hip-hop. After the group disbanded in 1990, members Bobby Brown and Johnny Gill pursued successful solo careers; in addition, the group Bell Biv DeVoe, comprised of three New Edition members, emerged at the forefront of the rhythmic, uptempo, "New Jack Swing" sound of the early 1990s. In 1996, after Bell Biv DeVoe's popularity had declined, all six members of New Edition reunited for the hit album *Home Again.*

Formed in the Roxbury section of Boston, Massachusetts, New Edition's initial members were Ricky Bell, Michael Bivins, and Bobby Brown, elementary school classmates who began performing together in order to earn spending money. After enlisting friend Ralph Tresvant as a fourth member, the group began winning local talent shows. Adding one additional member, Ronnie DeVoe, in 1980, the young singers performed a successful engagement at Boston's Strand Theatre, where their version of the Jackson 5's 1970 hit "The Love You Save" impressed music producer Maurice Starr. Signing the quintet to his small Streetwise label, Starr crafted an immediate hit with "Candy Girl" (1983), a charming teen-pop confection in which Tresvant's voice sounded remarkably similar to that of a young Michael Jackson. Parting with Starr in 1984, New Edition signed with MCA Records and released hits such as "Cool It Now" (1984) and "Mr. Telephone Man" (1985). Brown left the group in 1986 to pursue a successful solo career. His replacement, Johnny Gill, sang with New Edition on rhythmic, sharper-edged hits such as "If It Isn't Love" (1988).

In 1990 after New Edition had temporarily disbanded, Ricky Bell, Michael Bivins, and Ronnie DeVoe formed the highly successful group, Bell Biv DeVoe. Scoring a hit with the aggressive, sexually charged song "Poison" (1990), the group sounded vastly different from the sweet-tempered, boy-next-door image New Edition had proffered in the 1980s. The thumping funk rhythms and sinuous bass of "Poison" represented the best of "New Jack Swing," a sound that would inform the hip-hop and R&B of the 1990s. Riding the crest of Bel Biv DeVoe's success, Bivins helped develop the career of 1990s R&B stars Boyz II Men, a group strongly influenced by New Edition's assured harmonies and slick stage presence. During the early 1990s, former New Edition members Brown, Tresvant, and Gill released solo hits that combined hip-hop rhythms with smooth R&B balladry.

By the mid-1990s, Brown, Gill, Tresvant, and Bell Biv DeVoe were all experiencing difficulty keeping up with the newest trends in R&B, which was moving toward aggressive sounding hip-hop and, alternately, more traditionally styled "neo-soul." In a much-publicized move, all six members reunited for *Home Again* (1996), an album that re-cemented New Edition's position as a viable force in contemporary R&B. "Hit Me Off," a number one R&B smash that crossed over to the pop charts, sports a hard, driving beat and a sophisticated sense of group interplay, with the members switching off on vocal leads. The album's other big hit, "I'm Still in Love With You," features smooth backing harmonies and a devotional message in keeping with Boyz II Men's romantic style. Although New Edition's commercial success had again diminished by the end of the 1990s, the group announced in October 2002 that it had signed a recording contract

with the Bad Boy label, owned by hip-hop pioneer Sean "P. Diddy" Combs.

Surviving many incarnations, New Edition remained one of the most influential R&B groups of the 1980s and early 1990s. The group has often proved its resilience, resurfacing after long periods of inactivity. By 1996 New Edition was again at the forefront of modern R&B, releasing hits that combined gentle harmonizing with the tough sound of hip-hop.

SELECTIVE DISCOGRAPHY: *Candy Girl* (Streetwise, 1983); *New Edition* (MCA, 1984); *All for Love* (MCA, 1985); *Heart Break* (MCA, 1989); *Home Again* (MCA, 1996). As Bel Biv DeVoe: *Poison* (MCA, 1990); *BBD* (Universal, 2001).

DAVID FREELAND

NEW ORDER

Formed: 1980, Manchester, England

Members: Gillian Gilbert, vocals, keyboards (born Manchester, England, 1961); Peter Hook, bass (born Manchester, England, 13 February 1956); Stephen Morris, drums (born Macclesfield, Cheshire, England, 28 October 1957); Bernard Sumner, vocals (Bernard Dicken; born Salford, Manchester, England, 4 January 1959).

Genre: Electronic, Rock

Best-selling album since 1990: *Republic* (1993)

Hit songs since 1990: "World in Motion," "Regret," "World (The Price of Love)"

New Order, the innovative synthesizer pop band, formed in the mid-1980s in the wake of the New Wave movement, which emphasized dance music that relied on keyboards and programmed synthesizer loops. New Order grew out of the influential New Wave group Joy Division, which collapsed after the suicide of its lead singer, Ian Curtis, in 1980. Surviving members, vocalist Bernard Sumner (also known as Bernard Albrecht), Peter Hook, and Stephen Morris, picked up the pieces and created New Order in 1981. In so doing, they became one of the most influential 1980s bands. Tinkering with New Wave, they forged a new sound from synthesizers, effects-processed guitars, and real drums, rather than drum machines; they created an alternative kind of dance music that brought together elements of disparate genres.

New Order received much media attention because of Curtis's death. Their first single, "Ceremony," was written when they were Joy Division though it was released under the name New Order. Their desire to explore electronic music and its incumbent technologies surfaced in songs like "Temptation," a Top 40 hit in England. Committed to the club culture, the band became part owners in the Manchester nightclub Hacienda, which went on to become one of the most well-known dance clubs in England.

Mixing Elements

Combining dance music with slightly morose lyrics, New Order exploited the music's therapeutic possibilities. The epic "Blue Monday," released in 1983 in a 12-inch format, with Sumner's cool and plain vocals, is a signature song. It became the biggest-selling single in U.K. music history. Continuing the twisted bittersweet love song theme, New Order put together one of their most popular dance hits, "Bizarre Love Triangle," for their 1986 album *Brotherhood*. It enjoyed new life on the *Billboard* charts ten years later, thanks to its inclusion in their album *Best of New Order* (1995).

Much of New Order's music has been repeatedly remixed, even during their heyday, which was a relatively new practice in the mid- to late 1980s. New Order broke ground by collaborating with New York hip-hop producer Arthur Baker on "Confusion" (1983) and "Thieves Like Us" (1984). In true dance style, these singles went on for nearly six minutes, but New Order was not aiming for heavy duty radio play: The clubs were their audience.

The mixing and remixing continued with updated versions of their singles, one by renowned R&B producer Quincy Jones, who set his handiwork to the previously released "Blue Monday." Pet Shop Boys producer Stephen Hague co-wrote and mixed the single "True Faith," which helped to boost the song up to number three on the Hot Dance Music/Club Play chart. In 1987 the band collected and released their best singles as *Substance: The Singles 1980–1987*. They even caught the attention of filmmakers. New Order appeared in pivotal scenes in 1980s films such as *Pretty in Pink* (1986) and *Bright Lights, Big City* (1988).

Two years later they issued *Technique* (1989), an album with nine bass- and drum-driven tracks, tinged with gravelly, ragged guitar work. With tracks like "Fine Time" it is clear from the start that this is a different, more fully engaged band. The ferocity, energy, and intricacy indicate an ensemble hitting its stride. *Technique* mixes lean dance-pop songs, guided by deft guitar work with club-ready electronic tracks, such as "Fine Time" and "Round and Round." The album peaked at number thirty-two on the *Billboard* Top 200 chart in the year of its release.

Shortly after the release of *Technique*, New Order had a surprise hit single, "World in Motion," which went to number one in England. The song serendipitously became a national anthem because the band is accompanied by England's World Cup soccer team on the track.

A New Decade, a New Sound

In 1993 New Order released the bright and vibrant *Republic*, and though it did not spawn a host of singles, it peaked at number eleven on the *Billboard* 200 and sold more than 500,000 copies. Buoyed by the straight-ahead, unequivocal, pop-dance track "Regret," the band's first bona fide radio hit in the United States, *Republic* is the band's most mainstream effort to date.

New Order never officially broke up, but band members took time off after *Republic* to engage in side projects. Sumner left the group and formed the band Electronic with the Pet Shop Boys and ex-Smiths member, guitarist Johnny Marr; Hook formed Revenge, while partners Gilbert and Morris went on to create a duo they called the Other Two. New Order issued a new album after a lengthy absence, cheekily titled *Get Ready* (2001). It peaked at number two on *Billboard*'s Top Electronic Albums chart, although the album seemed no more electronically oriented than its predecessors. It was hailed by critics and well liked by fans as the welcome return of a band that had disappeared for too long. The guitar-and-reverb-drenched "Crazy" fared well on the dance music charts. An intriguing, layered sound pervades *Get Ready*.

Although New Order was most prolific in the 1980s, the band created their most memorable work at the cusp of the 1990s. They are best known for innovating the way guitars and electronic music work together to create unerringly danceable songs.

SELECTIVE DISCOGRAPHY: *Power, Corruption and Lies* (Qwest/Warner Bros., 1983); *Substance* (Qwest/Warner Bros., 1987); *Technique* (Qwest/Warner Bros., 1989); *Republic* (Qwest, 1993); *Best of New Order* (Warner Bros., 1995); *Get Ready* (Warner Bros., 2001); *International: Greatest Hits* (Warner Bros., 2003).

SELECTIVE FILMOGRAPHY: *Pretty in Pink* (1986); *Bright Lights, Big City* (1988).

CARRIE HAVRANEK

RANDY NEWMAN

Born: New Orleans, Louisiana, 28 November 1944
Genre: Rock, Pop, Soundtrack
Best-selling album since 1990: *Bad Love* (1999)

Randy Newman never enjoyed big commercial success but his songbook is considered one of pop music's treasures. Composed in multiple styles—in particular theatrical show tunes and New Orleans R&B—Newman songs offer the perspective of loners and lowlifes. They illuminate the humanity of characters with humor and compassion, and in doing they have helped shape the direction of contemporary songwriting.

Newman spent his early childhood in New Orleans, and his best work often views elevated moments in southern history through the eyes of ordinary people. His self-effacing humor and knack for irony help his work endure through countless cover versions by other artists. In the 1990s Newman emerged as a sought-after film composer, and he won an Academy Award in 2002. In between films, he experimented with a musical based on the classic dramatic German poem *Faust* by Johann Wolfgang Von Goethe. In 1999 his first album after eleven years received critical accolades and prompted Newman to make live appearances accompanied only by a piano.

When he turned seventeen, Newman was already a published songwriter. Although he was raised in New Orleans, his family moved to Los Angeles in his early years. His uncles, Alfred, Emil, and Lionel Newman, were already there, working as Academy Award–winning film composers. Newman dropped out of college to work on staff for a local music publisher, writing hits for artists like Three Dog Night, Dusty Springfield, Peggy Lee, and Harry Nilsson, who recorded an entire album of Newman's songs.

In 1968 Newman released his debut album. As he honed his skills in the years to come, Newman would write songs that were both pain-ridden and humorous. His songs would be populated by racist southerners, young urban professionals, music industry opportunists, misfits, pimps, soldiers, legendary Louisiana governor Huey Long, and God. His songs might take place at the beginning of time, during the great Mississippi flood of 1927, or in hell. As much as his songs knew no bounds, he wrote under an umbrella of styles, using lush orchestrations or spare piano. "Short People," a hit in 1976, drew controversy for bigotry when in fact it was sniping at bigotry itself.

Newman entered the 1990s on the heels of *Land of Dreams* (1988), one of his most commercially successful albums. This work looked with nostalgia at his southern roots as it attacked Wall Street greed, blind patriotism, and the shallowness of hip-hop. Aside from instrumental scoring, Newman wrote songs for family movies like *Toy Story* (1995) and *James and the Giant Peach* (1996) that were considerably cheerier than his more personal work. He received fifteen Academy Award nominations and in 2002 he finally won Best Song for "If I Didn't Have You," from the film *Monsters Inc.* (2001).

In 1995 Newman released *Randy Newman's Faust*, a concept album that told the story of Goethe's hero, but in a contemporary setting. In Newman's version, Faust is a slovenly college student with rock star dreams who ends up selling his soul to the devil. After a tryout run at the La Jolla Playhouse in La Jolla, California, the musical opened at the Goodman Theatre in Chicago in 1996. Like most of Newman's work, it explores deep themes such as the omnipotence of God and the purpose of suffering in the world.

Newman closed the decade with a comeback album, *Bad Love* (1999). Considered one of his best, it features songs about patriotism, capitalism versus communism, divorce, and the challenges of learning history's lessons. The songs convey both pessimism and optimism, self-effacement and tenderness. Newman explores intricate themes in simplest ways, often with humor and grace.

Newman's instrumental scores are often compared with American masters like Aaron Copeland and George Gershwin.

SELECTIVE DISCOGRAPHY: *Randy Newman* (Reprise, 1968); *12 Songs* (Reprise, 1970); *Sail Away* (Reprise, 1972); *Good Old Boys* (Reprise, 1974); *Little Criminals* (Warner Bros., 1977); *Born Again* (Warner Bros., 1979); *Trouble in Paradise* (Warner Bros., 1983); *Land of Dreams* (Reprise, 1988); *Randy Newman's Faust* (Reprise, 1995); *Bad Love* (DreamWorks, 1999). **Soundtracks:** *The Natural* (Warner Bros., 1984); *Parenthood* (Warner Bros., 1989); *Walt Disney's Toy Story* (Disney, 1995); *James and the Giant Peach* (Disney, 1996); *A Bug's Life* (Disney, 1998); *Toy Story 2* (Disney, 1999).

WEBSITE: www.randynewman.com.

MARK GUARINO

NEXT

Formed: 1992, Minneapolis, Minnesota

Members: T-Low (Terrance Brown; born 7 June 1974); Tweety (Raphael Brown; born 28 January 1976); R.L. (Robert Lavelle Huggar; born 2 April 1977).

Genre: R&B

Best-selling album since 1990: *Welcome II Nextasy* (2000)

Hit songs since 1990: "Butta Love," "Too Close"

Next brought a new degree of sexual explicitness to 1990s R&B, taking the seductive harmony style popularized by Boyz II Men and applying it to songs that usually required heavy editing for radio airplay. Despite the group's blatant raunchiness, Next gave evidence of a strong gospel background, especially in the tough, sophisticated harmonies that drove hits such as

Next. L-R: Left to right: Tweety, R.L., T-Low [MARC BAP-TISTE/J-RECORDS-BIFF WARREN]

"Too Close" and "Butta Love." Although Next occasionally mixed declarations of love with its aggressively sexual messages, for the most part it held on to the same erotic formula, which critics maintain began to wear thin after three albums.

Next formed after brothers Terrance and Raphael Brown (known respectively as T-Low and Tweety) were introduced to Robert Lavelle Huggar (R.L.) through their uncle, the director of a local gospel choir. The singers were soon taken under the wing of gospel and R&B performer Ann Nesby, who acted as their manager. In 1994 the group recorded a demo at the Minneapolis studio of Jimmy Jam and Terry Lewis, one of the top producing teams in 1980s and 1990s R&B. The demo came to the attention of Naughty By Nature rap group member Kay Gee, who signed Next to his new Divine Mill label, a subsidiary of Arista Records.

The group's first album, *Rated Next*, appeared at the end of 1997 and became an immediate hit on the basis of daring lyrics and Kay Gee's tough-sounding production. Sporting some of the most danceable grooves of any 1990s R&B album, *Rated Next* creates a compellingly erotic atmosphere. All three singers are strong vocalists, and their muscular interplay gives the album a powerful air of gospel urgency. The hit "Too Close," in which tight harmonies are layered over a 1970s- and 1980s-styled funk beat, is one of the album's highlights, although "Butta Love" and "Cozy" are equally appealing. While the dense funk beat never wavers, the album's limited theme—expressed in titles such as "Penetration" and "Sexitude"—threatens to become tedious long before the final track.

Although Next ran the risk of overkill in the same way that 1970s soul singer Barry White approached self-parody with his erotic, spoken-word love ballads, the group continued on the same path with its follow-up album, *Welcome II Nextasy* (2000). On the driving hit single, "Wifey," the group extols the virtues of an adventurous spouse who knows "when to flip it street freak"—"freak" being a motif that recurs in various forms throughout the album. Just how little the group changed from first album to second is evident in the song titles. For example, *Rated Next*'s "Phone Sex" was replaced by "Cybersex" on the follow-up, complete with silly lyrics suggesting the group may not be entirely serious: "I want your PC / Sit on my laptop." In 2002 the group released its third album, *The Next Episode*, on J-Records, a label newly created by former Arista chief Clive Davis. In keeping with its predecessors, the album sports dense beats and lyrics that leave little to the imagination.

Next epitomizes the aggressive side of contemporary R&B, drawing upon the harmonic traditions of gospel to push boundaries of lyric and theme. Even when severely edited for radio, Next's records became hits on the basis of their irresistible funk grooves and sly, assertive vocals.

SELECTIVE DISCOGRAPHY: *Rated Next* (Arista, 1997); *Welcome II Nextasy* (Arista, 2000); *The Next Episode* (J-Records, 2002).

DAVID FREELAND

NICKELBACK

Formed: 1996, Hanna, Alberta

Members: Chad Kroeger, vocals, guitar (born Hanna, Alberta, 15 November 1974); Mike Kroeger, bass (born Brooks, Alberta, 25 June 1972); Ryan Peake, guitar (born Calgary, Alberta, 1 March 1973); Ryan Vikedal, drums (born Brooks, Alberta, 9 May 1975). Former member: Brandon Kroeger, drums (born Hanna, Alberta).

Genre: Rock

Best-selling album since 1990: *Silver Side Up* (2001)

Hit songs since 1990: "How You Remind Me," "Too Bad," "Never Again"

Though one of many successful commercial hard rock bands of the late 1990s, Nickelback outdid its competitors by scoring a number one single with the bitter "How You Remind Me."

Nickelback began its career as a cover band in native Hanna, Alberta, located northeast of Calgary. Tiring of playing other acts' songs, singer/guitar player Chad Kroeger wrote a batch of his own songs, borrowed four thousand dollars, and moved to Vancouver to record them in a studio. Kroeger's band mates—brother Mike (bass), Ryan Peake (guitar), and cousin Brandon Kroeger (drums)—joined him in Vancouver in 1996. The band independently released the full-length album Curb and embarked on a tour across Canada.

In 2000, after replacing the departing Brandon Kroeger with new drummer Ryan Vikedal, Nickelback released The State. The band benefited from new Canadian radio content requirements that emphasized homegrown talent, and the single "Leader of Men" became a hit. "Leader of Men" hints at Nickelback's ultimately successful commercial formula, with chorus-laden guitars and the Kroeger brothers' dark, vocal harmonies. Nickelback subsequently scored high-profile opening slots for acts such as 3 Doors Down, Fuel, and Creed. Roadrunner Records, a subsidiary of Island Records, snapped up the band and re-released The State; the album ultimately sold 500,000 copies.

The band's much-anticipated third album and first true major label album, Silver Side Up, appeared in 2001. It was an immediate hit, selling nearly 200,000 copies in its first week alone. The lead single "How You Remind Me" was a sensation. Set to ferocious guitars, "How You Remind Me" finds Kroeger growling kiss-off lines to a former lover ("It's not like you to say sorry / I was waiting on a different story / This time I'm mistaken / For handing you a heart worth breaking") around the song's central lyrical hook: "This is how you remind me." With "How You Remind Me," Nickelback topped both the U.S. and Canadian singles charts simultaneously—the first act to do so since the Guess Who, with its classic anthem "American Woman" in 1970.

The follow-up single "Too Bad," inspired by Kroeger's own childhood, became an MTV staple and penetrated mainstream radio, despite its angry, hard-rocking tone, which features the rapid-fire chorus: "It's too bad / It's too late / There's no time to rewind / Let's walk / Let's talk." On the strength of its hit singles, Silver Side Up ultimately sold 6 million copies worldwide. Nickelback was celebrated in its native Canada, earning Best Group, Best Rock LP, and Best Single ("How You Remind Me") honors at Canada's Juno Awards in 2002. The band also received Grammy Award nominations for Best Rock Song and Best Rock Performance by a Duo or Group.

The success of Silver Side Up led to various high-profile collaborations for Nickelback. Chad Kroeger—along with Saliva front man Josey Scott, Theory of a Dead Man guitarist Tyler Connolly, and Pearl Jam drummer Matt Cameron—recorded "Hero" for the Spider-Man soundtrack in 2002; Chad Kroeger also appeared as a guest vocalist on Santana's album Shaman (2002).

SELECTIVE DISCOGRAPHY: Curb (Roadrunner, 1996); The State (Roadrunner, 2000); Silver Side Up (Roadrunner, 2001). Soundtrack: Spider-Man (Sony, 2002).

SCOTT TRIBBLE

STEVIE NICKS

Born: Stephanie Lynn Nicks; Phoenix, Arizona, 26 May 1948
Genre: Rock
Best-selling album since 1990: Timespace: The Best of Stevie Nicks (1991)
Hit songs since 1990: "Edge of Seventeen"

Singer/songwriter Stevie Nicks rapidly gained international prominence in 1975 when she became a vocalist for the supergroup Fleetwood Mac. She followed Janis Joplin as one of rock's leading female singers and enhanced that credential by forging a successful solo career despite suffering personal chaos. Famous for her unique stage presence and an inimitable voice, Nicks has managed to juggle a solo career with occasional dalliances in Fleetwood Mac.

Nicks lived in more than a half-dozen major cities during her formative years. Her father was a successful businessman whose career required that the Nicks family move wherever his promotions took him. Consequently, she spent a great deal of time with her grandfather, a colorful character, who in his earlier days made his living as a pool shark and moonlighted as a country and western guitar player and singer. He taught Nicks to sing duets with him, and when she was sixteen, her parents bought her a guitar. She wrote her first song, about a relationship with a boyfriend that went awry, soon after.

Nicks first met guitarist/singer Lindsey Buckingham while attending high school in Palo Alto, California. They played together in a band called Fritz, became lovers, and in 1970 moved to Los Angeles, where Nicks cleaned houses and worked as a waitress to support Buckingham's songwriting career. After hearing their debut album duet, Buckingham/Nicks (1973), Fleetwood Mac drummer Mick Fleetwood invited them to join the band, which at the time was in shambles. Fleetwood Mac became an immediate sensation with the addition of Nicks and Buckingham, whose soft-rock talents proved to be a perfect tonic for the band's discordant chemistry. (Fleetwood did not originally want Nicks and agreed only because Buckingham refused to join the group without her.)

Thrust into the role of singer and focal point of Fleetwood Mac, Nicks captured her essence as a freewheeling mystic sorceress of rock. Clad in flowing chiffon gowns with wispy blonde hair floating about her head, she danced and grooved emotionally to each song. Her sense of style influenced an entire generation of women's fashion tastes. Nicks's unrestrained alto possesses a distinctive rasp and folksy phrasing that perfectly suited the moody rock sounds of Fleetwood Mac in hits such as "Dreams" and "Rhiannon." In 1977, during the tour for the monumentally successful album *Rumours* (1977), she and Buckingham acrimoniously split up. Yet, both persisted on in the band. During this time Nicks developed a cocaine habit.

The 1980s were both flourishing and tumultuous for Nicks as she made successful strides in her solo career but suffered several personal setbacks. Her first solo album, *Bella Donna* (1981), immediately went platinum and contained several hits, including a duet with rocker Tom Petty, "Stop Draggin' My Heart Around," and another with then-boyfriend, singer Don Henley, "Leather and Lace." In the 1980s she recorded three more solo albums, all of which went platinum, and recorded two with Fleetwood Mac. The decade was a whirlwind of touring and recording. Nicks's messy breakup with Buckingham was further complicated by her affair with Mick Fleetwood and an eight-month marriage to Kim Anderson, the widowed husband of her best friend who had died from leukemia. Nicks's million-dollar cocaine use began to wear down the cartilage in her nose, threatening her singing voice. She finally checked herself into the Betty Ford Clinic and emerged clean, only to become addicted to prescription drugs. She entered the 1990s as a rock superstar, but overweight, broken-hearted, and drug-addicted.

After recording *Behind the Mask* (1990) with Fleetwood Mac and releasing a compilation album of solo work, *Timespace* (1991), Nicks sought help in another rehabilitation stint and finally conquered her drug addiction. She began to reclaim her health and was able to lose the weight, which had begun to make her too self-conscious to perform.

In 1993 Nicks, having announced that she had left Fleetwood Mac for good, began aggressively moving on with her solo career. Her fifth studio release, *Street Angel* (1994), put her back on the scene, although the album's sales paled in comparison to her earlier releases. She also performed a track, "Somebody Stand by Me," for the soundtrack to the 1995 film *Boys on the Side*.

In 1996 Nicks returned to Fleetwood Mac as the core members of the group—including Buckingham—prepared for a 20th Anniversary Tour of the album *Rumours*, which has sold more than 30 million copies worldwide. To kick off the tour, Fleetwood Mac held an intimate concert on a Los Angeles soundstage in 1997 and released a live

recording of that show in an album titled *The Dance* (1997). One of Nicks's noteworthy Fleetwood Mac songs, "Landslide," came from that album, giving the pretty ballad another turn as a hit single. This, she announced, was to be her last foray with Fleetwood Mac.

Nicks revisited her signature sound in the solo release *Trouble in Shangri-La* (2001). The album features work from her new pal, singer Sheryl Crow, who co-produced five songs from the album. Nicks called on several cronies to guest on this thirteen-song album, such as singer/songwriter Sarah McLachlan, singer Macy Gray, Natalie Maines of the Dixie Chicks, and Tom Petty's guitarist, Mike Campbell.

In 2002 Fleetwood Mac regrouped and Nicks found herself once again on stage with Buckingham. The band released a studio recording, *Say You Will* (2003), and supported it throughout the year with an extensive tour.

Stevie Nicks survived the excesses and trappings of rock stardom and remains an important contemporary artist into her fifties—not an easy feat, especially for a female in an industry that promotes youthful stars as intensively as it devours them.

SELECTIVE DISCOGRAPHY: *Bella Donna* (Atlantic, 1981); *Wild Heart* (Atlantic, 1983); *Rock a Little* (Atlantic, 1985); *Other Side of the Mirror* (Atlantic, 1989); *Timespace* (Atlantic, 1991); *Street Angel* (Modern Atlantic, 1994); *Trouble in Shangri-La* (Warner Bros., 2001).

BIBLIOGRAPHY: E. Wincentsen, *Stevie Nicks: Rock's Mystical Lady* (New York, 1995).

DONALD LOWE

NINE INCH NAILS

Born: Trent Reznor; Mercer, Pennsylvania, 17 May 1965
Genre: Rock, Industrial
Best-selling album since 1990: *The Downward Spiral* (1994)
Hit songs since 1990: "Wish," "Closer," "Hurt"

Despite the revolving door of talent that backs him onstage, Nine Inch Nails is and always has been the private pursuit of Trent Reznor. The ambitious singer and multi-instrumentalist was responsible for bringing the pulsing, relentless rhythms of industrial music to the mainstream. With his best-selling album, *The Downward Spiral* (1994), Reznor proved that albums filled with bleak, melancholy, and occasionally masochistic themes could still top the charts. With this perverse formula of sonic aggression and lyrical angst,

Reznor and his Nine Inch Nails band helped redefine alternative rock in the 1990s.

Reznor's initial hopes were quite modest. A young fan of new wave and industrial dance music, Reznor began recording his own music in 1988 with the timid hope of eventually releasing a 12-inch single, most likely for a label in industrial-friendly Europe. But when he sent his demo to various American labels, almost all the labels showed interest in signing him. He eventually settled on TVT. Released in November 1989, Pretty Hate Machine slowly became one of the most important alternative rock albums of the 1990s. Though influential industrial bands like Skinny Puppy, KMFDM, and Ministry had experienced modest success in the 1980s and 1990s by appealing to fans of heavy metal, Nine Inch Nails's well-timed and perfectly executed debut had a lasting impact on the landscape of popular culture.

The band's success did not come quickly. Though he recorded Pretty Hate Machine all by himself, Reznor assembled a backing band consisting of childhood friend Chris Vrenna on drums, guitarist Richard Patrick, and a host of different keyboardists. They toured constantly. Reznor hoped the album would cross over to alternative rock fans unfamiliar with the bruising rhythms of industrial music, and the first sign of this scheme's success was the modest popularity of its lead single, "Down in It." The song was a surprise hit among fans of modern rock and dance music. The guitar-heavy "Head Like a Hole," which had initially been the album's first single, gained a new life and the angst-riddled, anti-authority anthem became a staple on MTV.

Realizing they had a minor hit on their hands, TVT pressured Reznor for an ambitious follow-up and exerted control over the next album's creative direction. Resistant to TVT's meddling, Reznor instead spent his time brainstorming ideas for his next album and collaborating on obscure one-off projects with Pigface and Al Jourgensen from Ministry.

The Industrial Revolution

The band's biggest break came with its placement on the inaugural Lollapalooza tour in 1991. The traveling summer festival was wildly successful thanks to its angst-ridden and anti-authority attitude. Lollapalooza exposed thousands of American teens to Reznor's confrontational live persona and the wall of sound produced by Vrenna, Patrick, and newly permanent keyboardist James Woolley. During the tour, "Head Like a Hole" reentered the charts and Pretty Hate Machine stayed on the album charts for nearly two more years, selling more than 1 million copies. Along with Nirvana's Nevermind (1991) and the Lollapalooza tour itself, Pretty Hate Machine was a defining document of the aggressive sound and disaffected suburban ennui that would fuel alternative rock's rise throughout the decade.

After considerable legal wrangling, Reznor secured a release from TVT in 1992 and signed with Interscope, which allowed him to start his own imprint, Nothing. He released the Broken (1992) EP and a companion EP of remixes, Fixed (1992). Each suggested that Reznor had not spent the years since recording Pretty Hate Machine idly. He had channeled his frustration and animosity against the industry into darker, heavier cuts like "Happiness Is Slavery" and "Wish" (which won a Grammy Award for Best Heavy Metal Performance). Broken debuted in the Top 10 and foreshadowed the preoccupation with sado-masochistic imagery that would typify Reznor's later work. A series of extremely violent videos were issued alongside the EPs, though few of them were released commercially.

Reznor prepared for his eagerly anticipated follow-up by relocating to Los Angeles and building a studio in the house where actress Sharon Tate was murdered by Charles Manson's cult. Reznor later claimed ignorance to this coincidence, but it no doubt added to his own cult of personality. Patrick had left the band to form Filter and Reznor added guitarist Robin Finck and bassist Danny Lohner to fill out the band's sound. The success of The Downward Spiral (1994) owed as much to its subtle themes and textures as it did to the band's outlandish image. The album debuted at number two and went multiplatinum shortly thereafter. Whereas Broken had been built on bursts of jagged heavy metal guitars and full-frontal shock value, The Downward Spiral was a carefully conceived concept album that borrowed heavily from 1970s progressive rock and shrouded all of its hurt and melancholy in delicate, sophisticated tapestries of noise. The shocking "Closer"—and its sexually graphic and offensive chorus—became one of the most unlikely hits of the year, and it was followed up the charts by the morose ballad "Hurt."

The year was a busy one for Reznor. Nine Inch Nails played an unforgettable set at that summer's 25th anniversary Woodstock concert. The band distinguished itself not only for its furious, inspired playing, but also because Reznor and his mates had covered themselves in mud prior to taking the stage. Later that year, Reznor provided the soundtrack for Oliver Stone's controversial Natural Born Killers (1994) and contributed vocals to Tori Amos's second album, Under the Pink (1994). The next year, Reznor and his again revamped band (featuring new keyboardist Charlie Clouser) went on tour with legendary rocker David Bowie. Reznor also recorded a bleak cover of Joy Division's "Dead Souls" for the soundtrack of The Crow (1993) and released an alternate edition of remixes entitled Further Down the Spiral (1995).

The Inward Spiral

Confronted with his sudden stardom, Reznor retreated to his new studio in New Orleans, Louisiana, and considered his next move carefully. Perhaps exhausted by his own career, Reznor threw himself into producing *Antichrist Superstar* (1996), the second album for his Nothing signee Marilyn Manson. The album made Manson a star but it did not help Reznor with his own writer's block. In 1997 his childhood friend Vrenna left the band and, though Reznor worked on the soundtrack for David Lynch's *Lost Highway* (1997), he could not figure out a direction for Nine Inch Nails's third full-length album.

Two years later he released the double compact disc *The Fragile* (1999). Not only is this album bleaker than his previous work, Reznor also took the opportunity to lash out at all the industrial metal acts he felt had swiped the Nine Inch Nails aesthetic, especially the recently estranged Marilyn Manson. Though many consider *The Fragile* to be Reznor's most studious album, its stint on the charts was brief: It debuted at number one, but massive expectations—as well as a fickle, metal-obsessed musical climate that Reznor himself had helped institute—suggested that Reznor's dour, hyper-obsessive industrial compositions were no longer pop currency. By the time *The Fragile*'s companion remix set, *Things Falling Apart* (2000), and a live disc, *And All That Could Have Been* (2002), were released, pop music had found more accessible ways to convey Reznor's message of angst and loathing. His disdain for the spotlight and passion for heady, detail-oriented arrangements may have cost these albums sales, but it was Reznor's pioneering hand in finding a niche for the sonic and emotional aggression of industrial rock in America's pop charts that made him one of the decade's most vital figures. The message had gone mainstream, but his music was left behind.

SELECTIVE DISCOGRAPHY: *Pretty Hate Machine* (TVT, 1989); *Broken* EP (Nothing/Interscope, 1992); *Fixed* EP (Nothing/Interscope, 1992); *The Downward Spiral* (Nothing/Interscope, 1994); *The Fragile* (Nothing/Interscope, 1999); *Things Falling Apart* (Interscope, 2000); *And All That Could Have Been* (Nothing, 2002). **Soundtracks:** *Natural Born Killers* (Interscope, 1994); *The Crow* (Atlantic, 1994); *Lost Highway* (Interscope, 1997).

HUA HSU

NIRVANA

Formed: 1987, Aberdeen, Washington

Members: Kurt Cobain, vocals and guitar (born Hoquiam, Washington, 20 February 1967; died Seattle, Washington, 5 April 1994); Krist (Chris) Novoselic, bass (born Compton, California, 10 May 1965); Dave Grohl, drums (born Warren, Ohio, 14 January 1969).

Genre: Rock

Best-selling album since 1990: *Nevermind* (1991)

Hit songs since 1990: "Smells like Teen Spirit," "Come As You Are," "All Apologies"

In fewer than three years, Nirvana became the centerpiece of a major revolution in popular musical taste, the effects of which can be felt to this day. The guitarist/composer Kurt Cobain led this dynamic trio toward mainstreaming the punk rock style that became known as grunge. With Nirvana's success in the early 1990s, alternative rock moved into the hearts and minds of a whole generation. Like Buddy Holly, Jimi Hendrix, and too many musical innovators before him, Kurt Cobain did not live to see the full effects of Nirvana's musical legacy, which still lives on.

Cobain's Childhood and Teenage Trials

Kurt Cobain was born into a working-class family in an economically depressed community in the state of Washington. An apparently happy child who showed considerable artistic ability, he saw his family fall apart by the time he was eight years old. His parents' separation and divorce were traumatic events for the young Kurt. Thereafter he lived at times with both parents, then with other relatives and friends. During his teens he endured periods of homelessness, sleeping wherever he could. By the ninth grade he was into alcohol and marijuana, soon followed by harder drugs.

As he passed through adolescence into young manhood, his personal relations were strained. Eventually all that seemed to matter was composing music and playing it on the guitar, skills in which he was largely self-taught. A high school dropout who never held any job for very long, Cobain eventually found a musical soul mate in the bassist Krist Novoselic. In 1987, the drummer Aaron Burckhard (Dave Grohl became Nirvana's drummer later), Cobain, and Novoselic formed the trio that eventually altered the direction of the music world.

Forging a Style

The musical roots of Nirvana lay in the soil of punk rock, though their style came to be known as grunge. Among other things, it shared with punk rock a tendency toward alternating slow and fast, soft and loud passages. By comparison with popular groups of the 1980s—even harder-edged ones like Guns N' Roses—Nirvana's music was dissonant and frenetic, with a guttural bass underlining, liberal distortion effects, and a heavy drum line. At the same time, however, Cobain's compositions had a quieter, more lyrical side. Such work provided respite from more intense tracks in the two major studio albums

Nirvana. L-R: Dave Grohl, Kurt Cobain, Krist Novoselic [S.I.N./CORBIS]

Nirvana cut. In one of his published journals, Cobain provided the best description of the Nirvana style: "Nirvana try to fuse punk energy with hard rock riffs, all within a pop sensibility."

The Sub Pop label in Seattle had become important to all alternative musicians in the artistically fertile northwest region of the country. Signing with them marked Nirvana's first serious recognition by the business side of the music industry, giving them the opportunity to become better known. Although the label lacked the resources to promote its records widely, Nirvana had already attracted considerable attention through their concerts and other performance dates in the region. Their first effort was a single featuring "Love Buzz" on side A and "Big Cheese" on B, both of which would reappear in *Bleach*. "Love Buzz"—originally recorded by the Dutch group Shocking Blue—became a signature song for Nirvana in their early concert dates. In subject matter and style these numbers and the others cut for the album come remarkably close to the Nirvana that debuted on the national scene a few years later.

Bleach, the first Nirvana album, came out in vinyl in 1989 from Sub Pop. The album title comes from an advertisement recommending drug users to "bleach" their needles before reusing them in order to ward off the HIV virus. Like many of the verbal elements in Nirvana's albums, it was chosen almost at random by Cobain when he had to come up with a title. The songs on *Bleach* range from the lightweight, mildly outrageous "Floyd the Barber," inspired by a character on the television series *The Andy Griffith Show*, to the dark and angry "Scoff," a punkish retort to someone in authority. Though a few tracks seem too slight to merit inclusion, the album has surprises like the romantic, Beatles-like "About a Girl," inspired by Cobain's girlfriend of the time. Generally, however, the music on *Bleach* shares many of the characteristics of alternative rock associated with the Sub Pop label. I. It is a mix of punk rock and heavy metal with lyrics expressing the concerns and outlook of what became known as Generation X. Cobain gave a voice to those who felt cheated by what their parents and society had told them they had to believe in. As a result, they grew angry over their failed search for something to replace those false values.

Nirvana Tops the Charts

Bleach, for all its promise, did not fully realize the group's ensemble power or Cobain's talents as a composer/musician. That promise was realized in 1991 with the release of *Nevermind.* In their combination of punkish fury, garage-band rock, heavy-metal riffs, and melodic inventiveness, these tracks set the tone of the 1990s. It was a jolt of originality unrivaled until the flowering of hip-hop and rap later in the decade.

For this album Nirvana signed with David Geffen's label, with a large advance payment and a guarantee of widespread publicity. The original pressing of *Nevermind* was 50,000 copies; by the end of the year it was selling 400,000 copies a week, and by January 1992 it had reached the number one spot on the *Billboard* chart. "Smells Like Teen Spirit," the lead track, became one of the most frequently played songs on college and alternative radio. The music video, featured on MTV, drew a record number of requests. A member of the popular 1980s heavy-metal band Mötley Crüe, in Los Angeles for a recording session, heard it one day as he headed home on the freeway. He was quoted later as saying he knew then that rock in the style of the Crüe was over. Something new had begun. It was another of those events in the history of popular music, like the emergence of Elvis and the Beatles, that seemed inevitable.

"Smells Like Teen Spirit" begins quietly enough, with a restless motif in the bass behind the melody line. The lyric pattern is verse-chorus-verse, with the instrumental volume increasing at the point of each chorus. During the chorus, Cobain's vocalism, subdued in the verse sections, becomes an angry shout. By the end of the track, the chorus has reached maximum intensity, with certain lines repeated over and over. Internally, the lyric lacks the kind of logic that shows in its structure. Some of it clearly seems aimed at the pressures felt in performance, as in the refrain line: "Here we are now, entertain us." Some lines seem to be there solely for the sake of the rime, as later in the chorus, where a series of randomly chosen words ends with "My libido / Yay, a denial." Whatever individual parts suggest, overall it is the music that carries the song, not the lyric. To put it another way, the lyric seems absolutely right in spite of its inconsistencies when it is heard in its musical context. In general, this characterizes most of the tracks in *Nevermind* and the other albums Nirvana released after they became internationally famous in the early 1990s.

Grunge Attitude

With every new development in rock comes a new look. Eighties groups had glammed in much-permed long hair, spandex shorts, and high tops. After the transcendent success of "Teen Spirit" and *Nevermind,* Kurt Cobain appeared unwashed and ungroomed on *Saturday Night Live* in a T-shirt advertising an unknown band, jeans with holes at the knees, Converse shoes, and crudely dyed hair. His appearance epitomized not only the grunge look, replicated by countless numbers of teens throughout the country, but also the grunge attitude. This was an "in your face," response that spoke volumes about a whole generation.

Nevermind gives this attitude musical expression, and defines it with various permutations. "In Bloom," the second track on the album, hits the fan who does not have a clue what Nirvana is up to, the one who merely wants to be entertained by "all the pretty songs." By contrast, "Come as You Are" is a low-key invitation to participate in the musical experience "as a friend, as an old enemy." "Breed" kicks the tempo up a notch, with a characteristic repetition of music and lyric that becomes truly obsessive by the next track, "Lithium," with its chilling chorus ending in the phrase, "I'm not gonna crack." "Polly"—a song Cobain reworked from an earlier version—deals with a celebrated kidnap and rape case and is written from the viewpoint of the perpetrator. "Territorial Pissings" spins off (in the voice of Krist Novoselic) a 1960s song, "Get Together," popularized by the Youngbloods, with Cobain voicing the perspective of an alien. "Drain You" describes parasitic relationships; "Lounge Act" and "Stay Away" parody musical trends Cobain found inimical to his artistic values. "On a Plain" returns to more personal themes and the difficulty of giving them expression in words; finally, in a quiet, codalike ending, "Something in the Way" takes the listener to the world of the homeless living beneath a bridge. An additional hidden track, purely instrumental, with feedback from the guitars, comes a full nine minutes after the last labeled track on the CD. It provides a fitting end to Nirvana's most important album.

The album *Incesticide* followed toward the end of 1992. After more than a year of ceaseless public attention and booming sales, Nirvana issued a collection documenting its recorded presence in early demos, compilations, and covers—in short, a history of the band from its earliest recorded beginnings to the point at which it became a major musical force. Part of the impetus for the album was Cobain's increasing doubts about the very success Nirvana was experiencing. The essential attitude of the alternative rocker was to remain outside the mainstream of music and society. Groups like Guns N' Roses or Mötley Crüe were supposed to be at the center of the stage, while indie musicians played in cellars and garages. Now all that had changed, and Cobain never felt completely comfortable with it. As happens so frequently in American popular culture, the outsider had moved inside by becoming a commodity. Cobain had to think that, in the words of his journal, "We can pose as the enemy to infiltrate the mechanics of the system." Otherwise, they would be selling out. That was what he came to believe he had done.

With *Nevermind* (1991), their first release from a major label, Nirvana put the punk rock sound at the center of the musical stage. In the 1970s the British group the Sex Pistols had begun the first wave of punk sensibility, a deliberately outrageous mixture of offensive lyrics backed by repetitive sounds. American groups like the Talking Heads and the Ramones, centered at the New York club CBGB's, furthered the punk esthetic; as good as they were, however, it was the garage bands in the Seattle area who finally realized the movement's full potential. Nirvana's raw energy and walloping riffs carried it to the core of a generation. When Nirvana came along, teens caught the spirit in the same way that earlier generations had followed the sound of the Beatles or Bob Dylan in the 1960s.

With the musical success he continued to doubt, Cobain's personal life changed. During the recording sessions for *Nevermind*, he met Courtney Love of the group Hole. They married early in 1992 and had a child in August of that year. Although Cobain had found in Courtney someone he truly loved, and in their child, Frances Bean, a sense of personal redemption, he continued to have serious problems with drug addiction. He was by then a habitual heroin user. He also suffered from suicidal tendencies that had shown up a number of times in his family. During the next two years, the many sides of his conflicted personality caused distress and pain to those who cared for him, and uneasiness in those who managed his career. He frequently overdosed on drugs, often just short of death. More than once during this time he had to be resuscitated. Cobain's problems notwithstanding, Nirvana remained the band of the moment. Its concerts sold out worldwide. This fanatic following of the group repelled Cobain. He tired of the constant performing and lack of privacy. In a pattern set early in his life, he wanted to withdraw from everything, but, because of his career, he could not. Drugs seemed to give him one way out of his dilemma.

As a way of reasserting its essential punkishness, the band created its controversial third album, *In Utero*, released in September 1993. It moved instantly to the top of the charts. As in previous efforts, a number of the songs address Cobain's feelings about being a rock star, while others deal with longstanding differences with his family. The violent imagery of "Aneurysm" and the controversial "Rape Me" are matched by the snarling dissonances of this music, which peak in the wildly frenetic "Pennyroyal Tea." The gentler, more lyrical side of Cobain surfaces in the Courtney-inspired "Heart Shaped Box." The last line of the last track, "All Apologies," encapsulates Cobain's emotional state at that time: "All alone is all we are." *In Utero* was the last Nirvana album to be released in Cobain's lifetime.

The Sudden End

While on tour in 1994, Cobain overdosed in Rome on a combination of the drug Rohypnol and champagne. Back in California later in the month, he entered a rehab center in Los Angeles. On April 1 he climbed a wall to escape, and four days later, at his home near Seattle, he isolated himself in the green house. After a strong hit of heroin, he committed suicide with a blast from a shotgun. He was twenty-seven years old. Among the last words on his suicide note was the phrase, "Better to burn out than fade away."

Two albums were issued posthumously. *Unplugged in New York*, recorded during Nirvana's live performance on the MTV show in the fall of 1993, is a frequently touching compilation of covers and selected Cobain songs delivered with an acoustic sound only occasionally captured elsewhere in their recorded work. *From the Muddy Banks of the Wishkah* (a Seattle-area river), issued two years later, is yet another compilation, this time of previously unreleased live performances. Along with some stray tracks, pirates, and a recently released single left out of the *In Utero* sessions (over which a legal battle developed), these albums completed the recorded legacy of the most important group of the early 1990s.

SELECTIVE DISCOGRAPHY: *Bleach* (Sub Pop, 1989); *Nevermind* (DGC, 1991); *Incesticide* (DGC, 1992); *In Utero* (DGC, 1993); *Unplugged in New York* (DGC, 1994); *From the Muddy Banks of the Wishkah* (DGC, 1996).

BIBLIOGRAPHY: C. Crisafulli, *Teen Spirit: The Stories Behind Every Nirvana Song* (New York, 1996); M. Azerrad, *Come as You Are: The Story of Nirvana* (New York, 2001); C. R. Cross, *Heavier Than Heaven: A Biography of Kurt Cobain* (New York, 2001); K. Cobain, *Journals* (New York, 2002).

ARCHIE LOSS

NO DOUBT

Formed: 1987, Orange County, California

Members: Tom Dumont, guitar (born Los Angeles, California, 11 January 1968); Tony Kanal, bass (born Kingsbury,

London, England, 27 August 1970); Gwen Stefani, vocals (born Fullerton, California, 3 October 1969); Adrian Young, drums (born Long Beach, California, 26 August 1969). Former members: John Spence, vocals (born 1969; died Anaheim, California, 21 December 1987); Eric Stefani, keyboards (born Fullerton, California, 17 June 1967).

Genre: Rock

Best-selling album since 1990: *Tragic Kingdom* (1995)

Hit songs since 1990: "Just a Girl," "Spiderwebs," "Don't Speak"

No Doubt first came to prominence as part of the mid-1990s ska revival, but transcended the movement to become one of rock music's most successful mainstream radio acts.

Orange County Origins

The band had its origins in Orange County, California. Siblings Eric and Gwen Stefani and friend John Spence shared a common affection for British ska bands of the early 1980s such as Madness and English Beat; the trio, which came to be known as "No Doubt" after one of Spence's favorite expressions, incorporated ska's frenetic, horn-driven reggae styling into its developing sound. Eric Stefani manned the keyboards, while Spence and Gwen Stefani shared vocal duties.

No Doubt brought its raucous music to the Anaheim party circuit, relentlessly gigging and, in the process, securing a sizable cult following. To flesh out its sound, the band added bass player Tony Kanal and, later, guitarist Tom Dumont and drummer Adrian Young. In December 1987 Spence committed suicide, leaving Gwen Stefani alone at the microphone.

Interscope Records signed No Doubt to a recording contract in 1991 and released the band's self-titled debut the following year. The album barely made a splash on alternative radio, which was then dominated by the dark and moody sounds of grunge acts such as Nirvana and Soundgarden. A national tour also flopped, and Interscope temporarily withdrew its financial support of the band. No Doubt took a further hit when founding member Eric Stefani left the band to pursue a career in animation.

One More Chance

Interscope gave the band one final opportunity to prove itself in the studio; the band responded with what would become *Tragic Kingdom*, released in 1995. The album served to document another setback that the band had experienced during its recording, namely the breakup of Gwen Stefani and Kanal, who had dated for seven years. The album was a slow mover at first, but ultimately the single "Just a Girl" landed in MTV's coveted Buzz Bin. MTV audiences embraced "Just a Girl," seizing upon its

driving, propulsive guitar riff as well as Stefani's lyrical beef with men who sought to constrain her existence: "'Cause I'm just a girl, little ol' me / Don't let me out of your sight / I'm just a girl, all pretty and petite / So don't let me have any rights / Oh . . . I've had it up to here!" With her unique fashion style that juxtaposed athletic wear with traditional Indian jewelry, Stefani quickly became the band's visual reference point.

The band also scored hits with "Spiderwebs" and "Don't Speak," the latter topping the singles charts. "Spiderwebs" fuses the band's ska influence with punk-rock sensibilities, with Dumont's guitars alternating between frenetic reggae upstrokes and heavy distortion-laden riffs. The ballad "Don't Speak" generated significant interest as a result of its curious video, which depicts Kanal, Dumont, and Young ostracizing Stefani for what they consider disproportionate media coverage of her; the video's subtext was rooted in fact, as the band apparently nearly broke up at the height of its success because of the inter-band divisions.

No Doubt benefited from an increased public awareness and interest in ska music in the mid-1990s, largely the result of the Offspring and the Mighty Mighty Bosstones having made minor inroads in commercial radio in the preceding years. No Doubt's success bolstered the movement, and a host of other ska-influenced acts such as Sublime, Less Than Jake, and Save Ferris experienced their first mainstream airplay.

It was five years before No Doubt released *Return of Saturn* (2000), the much-anticipated follow-up to *Tragic Kingdom*. *Return of Saturn* represented a great leap forward for the band, in terms of musical and lyrical development. The band retained its ska sensibility, but broadened its sound, incorporating the sound of 1980s new wave music as well as modern electronic flourishes. Stefani's lyrics touched on more adult themes, including her desire to marry and have a family. The song "Marry Me" garnered much attention, as gossip columnists seized on Stefani's seemingly telegraphed plea to current boyfriend (and future husband) Gavin Rossdale of the band Bush: "I can't help that I liked to be kissed / And I wouldn't mind if my name changed to Mrs." The hit single "Simple Kind of Life," the first song for which Stefani composed the music in addition to writing the lyrics, also resonated with listeners in its emotional honesty: "And all I wanted was a simple thing, a simple kind of life."

Stefani made a pair of high-profile collaborations with Eve and Moby, fueling speculation that she would soon depart No Doubt for a solo career, but the band's lineup remained intact for *Rock Steady*, released in 2001. The album, recorded in Jamaica, featured a decided reggae vibe, a not-so-subtle nod to the band's ska origins. The lead single "Hey Baby," with its call-and-response engagement

| *Tragic Kingdom* (1995)

Much like Fleetwood Mac's landmark album *Rumours* (1977), No Doubt's *Tragic Kingdom* fascinated audiences with its frank expression of inter-band turmoil. In the case of *Tragic Kingdom,* it was the breakup of singer Gwen Stefani and bass player Tony Kanal that served as the flashpoint during the recording of the album. Stefani and Kanal had dated for seven years before breaking up prior to the recording of *Tragic Kingdom.* Their breakup occasioned a flood of intense, highly personal lyrics from Stefani. On songs such as the hit single "Don't Speak," Stefani wallows in confusion and self-doubt: "I really feel I'm losing my best friend / I can't believe this could be the end." On other tracks such as "Happy Now?," Stefani angrily lobs lyrical salvos at Kanal: "No more leaning on your shoulder / I won't be there, no more bother." Kanal and Stefani remained professionals throughout the ordeal, completing the recording of the album. The pair's friendship survived the painful breakup, and they would ultimately come to joke about their highly public split. In the promotional video for "Ex-Girlfriend" from *Return of Saturn* (2000), for instance, the pair struggle to kill each other before falling out a window together.

with listeners ("All the boys say, 'Hey baby, hey baby, hey' / Girls say, 'Hey baby, Hey Baby, hey'") was a major hit, as were the follow-ups "Hella Good" and "Underneath It All." *Rock Steady* sold 2 million copies and earned the band its first Grammy Award.

No Doubt surprised many critics by shaking off the limitations of ska and evolving a powerful and unique mainstream sound. And, by charting three consecutive smash albums for the band, mainstream audiences illustrated their willingness to follow No Doubt in its continued development.

SELECTIVE DISCOGRAPHY: *No Doubt* (Interscope Records, 1992); *Tragic Kingdom* (Trauma/Interscope Records, 1995); *Return of Saturn* (Interscope Records, 2000); *Rock Steady* (Interscope Records, 2001).

SCOTT TRIBBLE

THE NOTORIOUS B.I.G.

Born: Christopher Wallace; Brooklyn, New York, 21 May 1972; died Los Angeles, California, 9 March 1997
Genre: Hip-Hop
Best-selling album since 1990: *Life after Death* (1997)
Hit songs since 1990: "Juicy," "Big Poppa," "Hypnotize"

In the early 1990s the New York–based rapper the Notorious B.I.G. exploded onto a hip-hop scene then dominated by "G-Funk," the synthesizer-laden, funk-based style pioneered by the West Coast rapper and producer Dr. Dre. The Notorious B.I.G.'s gritty, unromanticized tales of urban crime injected a note of reality into G-Funk's over-the-top and often facile celebration of the pleasures of "gangsta" life. B.I.G.'s charisma and skill as a storyteller created an instant critical and commercial sensation, re-establishing East Coast rap as a vital force in hip-hop and paving the way for New York–based rappers such as Nas and Jay-Z. The Notorious B.I.G.'s murder in 1997 cut short a career just reaching its prime.

Up from the Streets

Born in the Bedford-Stuyvesant section of Brooklyn, New York, Christopher Wallace began rapping with local groups while still a teenager, taking the name Biggie Smalls in reference to his imposing height and girth. An able but indifferent student, he dropped out of high school at age seventeen, and his subsequent career as a crack dealer resulted in a nine-month stint in a North Carolina jail. A demo tape he made shortly after his release got him a brief write-up in the respected hip-hop magazine *The Source*. The article attracted the attention of Uptown Records producer Sean "Puffy" Combs, who immediately signed Biggie. When Combs left Uptown a short time later to form his own label, Bad Boy, he took Biggie with him. In 1993 the Notorious B.I.G., as he was now known, made his debut as a guest rapper on remixes of the Mary J. Blige singles "Real Love" and "What's the 411?" He soon followed these with his first solo track, "Party and Bull****," which was heard on the soundtrack of the movie *Who's the Man* and generated much anticipation for his debut album.

Released in September 1994, *Ready to Die* stands as one of the landmark albums of 1990s hip-hop. Although New York was universally acknowledged as the cradle of hip-hop culture and music, by the early 1990s the hard-edged beats and socially conscious rhymes of East Coast rap had largely been supplanted in popularity by the lazy melodic grooves and gleefully amoral "gangsta" posturing of West Coast G-Funk. On *Ready to Die* the Notorious

B.I.G. takes G-Funk-style crime narratives and infuses them with wit and emotional depth, delivering tightly constructed yet seemingly effortless rhymes over Combs's slick, pop-oriented production. On the album's first single, "Juicy," the Notorious B.I.G. spins an autobiographical rags-to-riches tale over a sample of Mtume's huge R&B hit from 1983, "Juicy Fruit," conveying the contrast between his old and new lives with skillful economy: "We used to fuss when the landlord dissed us / No heat, wonder why Christmas missed us / Birthdays was the worst days / Now we sip champagne when we thirst-ay." A sample of another R&B hit from 1983, the Isley Brothers' "Between the Sheets," anchors the album's second single, "Big Poppa," an upbeat boast of sexual prowess that became the Notorious B.I.G.'s signature song. *Ready to Die* counterbalances its carefree celebrations of sex, crime, and material wealth with more sober-minded tracks. "Warning" depicts the paranoia that accompanies sudden wealth and fame, while "Things Done Changed" casts a melancholy, nostalgic eye on a deteriorating city neighborhood: "Back in the days, our parents used to take care of us / Look at em now, they even f****** scared of us." The overall result is an album of considerable richness and complexity, unified by the Notorious B.I.G.'s consistently authoritative storytelling. Appropriately, *Ready to Die* had an immediate impact on hip-hop and popular music, selling 4 million copies and turning the Notorious B.I.G. into a star.

In late 1994 the Notorious B.I.G. married a Bad Boy label mate, the R&B singer Faith Evans. He spent the following year bolstering the success of *Ready to Die* with guest spots on tracks by artists such as Total, R. Kelly, and Michael Jackson. He also used his newfound clout to launch Junior M.A.F.I.A., a rap group consisting of some of his childhood friends. In 1996 the Junior M.A.F.I.A. member Lil' Kim launched a successful solo career under the tutelage of the Notorious B.I.G., with whom she began an affair.

Rivalry and Murder

With the Notorious B.I.G.'s success Bad Boy challenged Los Angeles–based Death Row Records as hip-hop's dominant label, sowing the seeds for an intense East Coast/West Coast rivalry. In November 1994 the Death Row artist—and former friend of the Notorious B.I.G.—Tupac Shakur was shot several times in the lobby of a Manhattan recording studio. Shakur accused the Notorious B.I.G. and Combs of masterminding the attack. Although the two denied this, Shakur held a grudge and in 1996 recorded "Hit 'Em Up," a scathing, personal attack on the Notorious B.I.G., Bad Boy, and the entire East Coast scene. In September 1996 Shakur was murdered in an unsolved drive-by shooting in Las Vegas. Speculation linked the Notorious B.I.G. to Shakur's death. Six months later, on

March 9, 1997, the Notorious B.I.G. was gunned down in Los Angeles. The two deaths rocked the hip-hop community, leading to an extensive, long-term soul-searching regarding the violence permeating rap music and the rap industry.

In death, the Notorious B.I.G., like Shakur, came to be regarded as a kind of hip-hop martyr. This image enhanced the immense respect he already enjoyed as an artist and increased the already-high anticipation of his second album, *Life after Death*, which was released three weeks after the Notorious B.I.G.'s murder. A sprawling double album of twenty-four tracks, *Life after Death* enlisted a wide array of producers and guest artists in a successful attempt to expand upon the pop-friendly yet gritty hip-hop style of *Ready to Die*. It was also a stunning commercial success. It debuted at number one on the charts, selling 700,000 copies in its first weeks and ultimately going eleven-times platinum. Its first two singles, "Hypnotize" and "Mo Money Mo Problems," made the Notorious B.I.G. the first artist to have two posthumous number one hits. Moreover, Combs's and Evans's tribute to the Notorious B.I.G., "I'll Be Missing You," became one of the most successful singles of 1997. *Born Again* (1999), a collection of previously unreleased tracks, was also a commercial success, debuting at number one and selling 2 million copies.

The Notorious B.I.G. brought a fresh and distinct voice to hip-hop in the 1990s, expanding the genre both as an art form and as a commercial powerhouse. While his success restored the relevance the East Coast hip-hop scene had lost during the rise of West Coast rap, it also helped engender a bitter and murderous rivalry between the two coasts that divided hip-hop.

SELECTIVE DISCOGRAPHY: *Ready to Die* (Bad Boy, 1994); *Life after Death* (Bad Boy, 1997); *Born Again* (Bad Boy, 1999).

BIBLIOGRAPHY: C. Scott, *The Murder of Biggie Smalls* (New York, 2000); R. Sullivan, *Labyrinth* (New York, 2002).

WEBSITES: www.notoriousonline.com; www.badboy online.com.

MATT HIMES

*NSYNC

Formed: 1995, Orlando, Florida

Members: James Lance Bass, vocals (born Clinton, Mississippi, 4 May 1979); Joshua Scott Chasez, vocals (born Washington, D.C., 8 August 1976); Joseph Anthony Fatone, vocals (born Brooklyn, New York, 28 January 1977); Christopher Alan Kirkpatrick, vocals (born Clarion, Pennsylvania, 17 October 1971); Justin Randall Timberlake (born Memphis, Tennessee, 31 January 1981).

*NSYNC. L-R: Joey Fatone, Lance Bass, Justin Timberlake, Chris Kirkpatrick, Joshua Scott "JC" Chasez [PAUL NATKIN/PHOTO RESERVE]

Genre: Rock, Pop

Best-selling album since 1990: *No Strings Attached* (2000)

Hit songs since 1990: "I Want You Back," "Bye, Bye, Bye," "Pop"

One of the most successful pop groups of the late 1990s and early 2000s, *NSYNC built a large, devoted audience by performing R&B-based vocal music. With the help of MTV, especially the show *Total Request Live*, *NSYNC launched their music and faces into the world's living rooms. *NSYNC albums contain a mixture of upbeat dance numbers and ballads; singles representing both styles have held positions at the top of the charts. Their songs combine the group's distinctive mixture of plaintive solo singing, close harmonies, and, especially on later albums, intricate pop production. *NSYNC's good looks and flashy presentation appeal to their core audience, whose public face consists largely of preteen and teenage girls.

Prior to the formation of *NSYNC in 1995, Justin Timberlake and JC Chasez worked together as cast members of the Disney Channel's *Mickey Mouse Club*, which was filmed in Orlando, Florida. After a brief relocation to Nashville, the two returned to Orlando, where they met Chris Kirkpatrick, who was singing in a doo-wop group at Universal Studios along with Joey Fatone. The idea to form a group was Kirkpatrick's; with the addition of Fatone, they began to perform in clubs throughout Orlando. Still missing a bass singer, they located Mississippian Lance Bass with the help of Timberlake's vocal coach, and the group was complete. According to *NSYNC lore, their name originated with Timberlake's mother, who (with the use of Bass's nickname Lansten) formed "*NSYNC" with the last letter of each member's first name. True or not, the name describes their musical aesthetic well.

The Early Days: Big in Germany

In 1996 the group caught the eye of the impresario Louis J. Pearlman, known as the man behind the creation of the 1980s boy band New Kids on the Block. At the time Pearlman was also handling the Backstreet Boys, the first hugely popular American boy band of the late 1990s. Pearlman orchestrated *NSYNC's early successes. He signed *NSYNC to RCA records and released the band's first single in Germany; the Backstreet Boys had already found popularity in Europe. In 1997 *NSYNC had their first European hit with the dance number "I Want You Back." The song, which begins, "You're all I ever wanted / You're all I ever needed / So tell me what to do now / 'Cause I want you back," established one of *NSYNC's most popular lyrical themes: boy had girl, boy lost girl, boy begs girl to come back. *NSYNC followed the success of "I Want You Back" with a smash European tour. In 1998, after the Backstreet Boys hit it big in the United States, *NSYNC released their first album, *NSYNC, in America.

"Alternative" rock—made popular in the early 1990s by bands like Nirvana and Pearl Jam—faded in the late 1990s. At the same time the popularity of the Backstreet Boys and British girl group the Spice Girls shifted listeners' attention to pop music. *NSYNC's success demonstrated that the market could sustain more than one boy band. While the arrangements on *NSYNC lack the quirkiness of later releases, this early album established their appeal to a large, youthful fan base with plenty of disposable income. In addition, their ballads, including "(God Must Have Spent) a Little More Time on You," found a receptive audience on Adult Contemporary radio stations. *NSYNC's group harmonization owes much to the virtuosic style established by the popular African-American boy group Boyz II Men. This style favors ornamented, polished singing over the raw edges of rock. On *NSYNC the group adds elements imported from European dance music, such as the techno beat on "I Need Love." Later albums use dance beats derived more from hip-hop.

The popularity of *NSYNC has always been based in a loyal audience of teenage girls. To that end *NSYNC carefully projects a slightly androgynous, nonthreatening sexual appeal, and their songs are more romantic than sexual, more suggestive than explicit. Through prudent marketing, the individual personalities of *NSYNC members balance their playful group image. This allows fans to position themselves both as part of something larger than themselves (*NSYNC fans) and as individuals with unique interests (by becoming a "Justin fan" or "Lance fan"). However, the success of *NSYNC depends as much on their musical choices as their icon status.

In 1999 following the quick release of a Christmas album, *NSYNC initiated a lawsuit against Pearlman's Trans Continental Management in order to extricate themselves from their contract. While *NSYNC framed this lawsuit in terms of artistic freedom, many in the industry labeled the band greedy. They weathered these accusations, settled out of court, and signed to Jive Records, the home of Britney Spears and, again, the Backstreet Boys. In the process the group kept their manager from Trans

Spot Light | Celebrity

In the creation of Celebrity (2001), especially the single "Pop" and the title track, *NSYNC followed the adage to write what you know. Not the first meditation on the problem of being fabulously famous, Celebrity nevertheless manages to sound fresh without departing from the formula the band established on previous albums. It successfully continues *NSYNC's willingness to experiment with pop production while exploring a juxtaposition of aural imperfections, such as feedback and high-end pop production, that depart from their previous releases. In a mark of their increased artistic control, JC Chasez or Justin Timberlake share writing credits on all but three tracks. Timberlake also takes production credits on several songs, including the first single, "Pop." When "Pop" hit the airwaves in 2001, it sounded like nothing else on pop radio. "Pop" pays homage to Michael Jackson's Thriller (1982) and uses stylized hip-hop production techniques. Written by Timberlake and Wade J. Robson, the song is simultaneously a tribute to pop music ("Feel it when your body starts to rock / Baby you can't stop / And the music's all you got / This must be pop") and a declaration of the band's musical freedom. "Pop" upends expectations of what a boy band could and should sound like, especially at the point halfway through where it breaks into a mostly instrumental jam. This instrumental section, heavy on sampled guitars and beat box (also performed by Timberlake), introduces the new sounds found throughout Celebrity.

Continental, Johnny Wright. *NSYNC's next release was titled No Strings Attached (2000), a jab at their legal difficulties: The cover depicts the five members as life-sized puppets, strings and all. At the time of its release, No Strings Attached set the record for most albums sold in the first week of release—2.4 million, a figure that topped the Backstreet Boys' sophomore effort, Millennium (1999).

Musically, No Strings Attached represents a significant step forward for the group, although many of the producers and songwriters from their first albums remained on board. Group harmonization appears with a greater frequency on the upbeat numbers, as in the opening of the first track (and single), "Bye Bye Bye." The solos—sung by the tenors Timberlake and Chasez—depend less on reverb. By removing this echolike effect, the voices stand out rather than blend into the background. *No Strings Attached* perfects their pop formula with its careful mixture of wistful love ballads, novelty tracks, and party songs.

International Success at the Turn of the Century

Throughout 2000 and 2001 it seemed that at least one member of *NSYNC appeared weekly on MTV's popular show *Total Request Live*, each time accompanied by thousands of screaming fans on the streets below the studio in which the show is filmed. Their takeover of MTV was facilitated by a series of creative videos for the singles from *No Strings Attached*. The video for "Bye Bye Bye" continues the puppet theme from the cover of the album and features the band members dancing and singing while suspended on strings. By bringing the voices of *NSYNC into their viewer's homes on an hourly basis, MTV played a substantial role in cementing the group's position at the center of American popular culture.

Although *NSYNC's music has evolved over the course of their four full-length albums, many variables have stayed the same. For example, romantic ballads remain prominent on each album, and many of them have placed on both Top 40 and Adult Contemporary charts. These songs feature full, soothing harmonies that engulf the listener, juxtaposed with solo singing that personalizes the song. The lyrics allow the younger listener to imagine herself within the life of a man, while the soothing harmonies assuage their fear of adult relationships. In "This I Promise You," written by the 1980s pop star Richard Marx, Timberlake's solo manages to convey both vulnerability and compassion through a combination of almost-straining high notes and his voice's rich texture. The upbeat dance numbers often share the ballads' lyrical themes, especially romantic vulnerability and yearning for true love.

*NSYNC strives to outdo other pop groups in every way, especially in album and ticket sales. Their live shows offer an assortment of spectacles not unlike Disney-produced Broadway shows such as *The Lion King*. In the course of differentiating themselves from other boy bands, *NSYNC has repeatedly emphasized their creative input on albums. Indeed, both Chasez and Timberlake contributed songs to *No Strings Attached* and *Celebrity* (2001). Fans often defend their preference for *NSYNC in terms of the band's seeming authenticity and superior artistic merit when compared to other boy bands. Several tracks on their 2001 release, *Celebrity*, confront the terms of *NSYNC's fame directly. *Celebrity* sold well but did not break sales records, as *No Strings Attached* did. Many found its lyrics about the problems of fame self-indulgent, but the album also includes several fun, adventurous tracks. Following the release of *Celebrity* and the supporting tour, *NSYNC went on hiatus while the band members explored solo projects and acting careers.

*NSYNC positioned itself at the center of pop music trends at the tail end of the twentieth century. By incorporating sounds from a variety of musical genres, they forged a sound already familiar yet always new. This combination, along with the flair of their presentation style, makes them popular with preteens, teenagers, and adults alike.

SELECTIVE DISCOGRAPHY: *NSYNC* (RCA, 1998); *No Strings Attached* (Jive, 2000); *Celebrity* (Jive, 2001).

WEBSITES: www.nsync.com; www.nsync-world.com.

CAROLINE POLK O'MEARA

PAUL OAKENFOLD

Born: London, England, 30 August 1963
Genre: Dance, DJ, Electronica
Best-selling album since 1990: *Bunkka* (2002)
Hit songs since 1990: "Planet Rock," "Southern Sun," "Starry-Eyed Surprise"

Working in a genre notorious for its velvet-rope snobbery, Oakenfold attempted to fuse upscale dance music with accessible pop and deliver it to the masses.

Oakenfold's appreciation for popular music stems from listening to his father's Beatles and Rolling Stones records as a child. He also admired glam-rockers T-Rex and R&B by Marvin Gaye and the Isley Brothers. He spent his early twenties as a promoter for a record label's rap division. However, his epiphany came in 1987, on a birthday trip to the legendary Spanish resort of Ibiza, known for its gorgeous sunsets. He found a scene that featured a melting pot of hip European dance music, but a more laid-back, people-friendly atmosphere than the urban clubs he'd frequented in London.

By then a disc jockey (DJ), Oakenfold incorporated the Mediterranean sounds of Ibiza into his club sets back in England. He also produced English dance group Happy Mondays. But his big break came in 1992, when he rescued the U2 song, "Even Better Than the Real Thing," whose original version was sliding down the charts. His innovative remix was, in fact, "better than the real thing" to British ears and made number eight on the country's pop chart. This led to Oakenfeld opening for part of U2's *Zooropa* tour (1993).

He went on to form his own label, Perfecto, and make remixes for British pop-rockers Boy George and Massive Attack. Beginning in 1996 he spent eighteen months as the resident DJ for Liverpool megaclub Cream. Although his rising stardom meant he could have made more money doing short stints at many clubs worldwide, he preferred introducing new music every week to a loyal audience. When he did tour, he maintained his accessible vision, revising his setlist on the fly as he took the crowd's pulse.

His album *Tranceport* (1998) actually comprises songs by other artists; it is an attempt to recreate what an Oakenfold DJ set would sound like. As the title suggests, the music is from dance music's trance subgenre, considered the genre's most simple and pop-oriented subset. At its worst, it can be banal and predictable, but Oakenfold avoids clichéd tracks, picking songs by genre innovators like Paul van Dyk ("Rendezvous") and Gus Gus ("Purple"). Full of square-wave synthesizer blasts, vocal sampling, and fluctuating keyboard sounds, the album features seamless between-song transitions and an unstoppable groove.

The sweeping, twenty-one-track *Ibiza* (2001) reflects his eclecticism and Ibiza's all-encompassing vibe, with remixes of Radiohead's "Idioteque" and U2's "Beautiful Day" among the usual trance fare. In 2001 Oakenfold toured the United States, including the Midwest, not a region known for its disco fever. However, he was well received in the region's midsize clubs.

With his egalitarian bent, a bid for pop crossover was inevitable, and it happened with *Bunkka* (2002). Oakenfold considers it his first real solo album, since it contains original songs instead of remixes of others' work. Guest artists include Nelly Furtado and Perry Farrell, former Jane's

Addiction front man. While a competent dance/pop album in the vein of Moby, *Bunkka* does not possess the muscular energy of Oakenfold's DJ efforts. However, the optimistic single "Starry-Eyed Surprise," with its cheerful guitar hook and soothing rap, became Oakenfold's first mainstream hit, reaching number forty-one on the *Billboard* Hot 100.

Never one to worry with insular notions of genre purity, Oakenfold has been an excellent ambassador for dance music. He has helped keep the genre viable in the United States and expand it in Europe with his crowd-pleasing sets and his willingness to work with artists outside his niche.

SELECTIVE DISCOGRAPHY: *Tranceport* (Kinetic, 1998); *Swordfish: The Album* (Sire, 2001); *Ibiza* (Perfecto, 2001); *Bunkka* (Maverick, 2002).

RAMIRO BURR

OASIS

Formed: 1991, Manchester, England

Members: Noel Gallagher, guitar, vocals (born Manchester, England, 29 May 1967); Liam Gallagher , vocals (born Manchester, England, 21 September 1972); Alan White, drums (born London, England, 26 May 1972); Andy Bell, bass (born Cardiff, Wales, 11 August 1970); Gem Archer, guitar (Colin Murray Archer, born Hunwich, County Durham, England, 29 May 1967). Former members: Paul "Bonehead" Arthurs, guitar (born Manchester, England, 23 June 1965); Paul "Guigsy" McGuigan, bass (born Manchester, England, 9 May 1971); Tony McCarroll, drums (born Manchester, England, 4 June 1971).

Genre: Rock

Best-selling album since 1990: *Definitely Maybe* (1994)

Hit songs since 1990: "Cigarettes and Alcohol," "Wonderwall," "Don't Look Back in Anger"

For a time in the mid-1990s, the British rock group Oasis appeared to be an unstoppable force. Riding on the crest of the Britpop wave, the Manchester band outgunned most of their rivals at home and built a sizable following in the United States.

Uncertain Start

Oasis was formed in 1991 in a city that had a powerful reputation as a rock center on the strength of recent acts such as Joy Division, the Smiths, New Order, the Stone Roses, and the Happy Mondays. Oasis had an uncertain start; they were originally called Rain, a reference to a Beatles song, and were then renamed for a little known British live venue called Swindon Oasis. The group featured Paul McGuigan, Paul Arthurs, Tony McCarroll, and the younger Gallagher brother, Liam.

Musical Coup D'etat

The older Gallagher brother, Noel, was working as a roadie for a band from the same part of the world, the Inspiral Carpets. He saw his brother's band play and was far from impressed. Invited to manage the act, Noel proposed a different strategy: He would come in as guitarist and songwriter. This musical coup d'etat saw him become the principal creative force in the group, the de facto leader.

Combining rock attitude with a pop sensibility, Oasis quickly made their mark. In 1993 they attracted the attention of the independent record company boss Alan McGhee, whose Creation label had already enjoyed success with the Jesus and Mary Chain. McGhee saw the Gallaghers' group play a powerful set at the notable Glasgow venue King Tut's Wah Wah Club. The gig was significant because the band had received no invitation to perform, but the promoter reportedly gave in to threats that the club would be wrecked if the group was not allowed on stage. Such behavior hinted that Oasis might be the new Sex Pistols, the notorious act that had ignited the flame of British punk in the mid-1970s. The prospect resulted in early music press interest and stimulated broader newspaper interest in the band's activities.

That gig clinched a deal with Creation, and Sony handled the act outside the United Kingdom; hence the band pulled off a useful trick: They drew a cult following because they appeared to be an indie group with a small label, whereas they were actually benefiting from the commercial muscle of Sony, one of the most powerful global record concerns.

In 1994 the group issued their debut single, "Supersonic," which enjoyed a modest Top 40 placing. The next four singles were bona fide hits: "Shakermaker" stalled just outside the British Top 10, but "Live Forever," "Cigarettes and Alcohol," and "Whatever" all seized positions in the upper reaches of the chart.

Album's Spectacular Impact

When the group unveiled their first album, the results had even more spectacular impact. *Definitely Maybe* (1994) became one of the fastest-selling debut releases of all time, entering the British charts at number one and emerging as one of the great success stories of the decade.

Heading to Japan and then the United States to build momentum outside the U.K., Oasis quickly began to show the strains of touring. When they played a disappointing gig in Los Angeles, Noel Gallagher departed, suggesting he was determined to quit the group. Although the wound was stitched, early 1995 saw the first of a number of departures from the original quintet. While "Some Might Say" reached number one in the United Kingdom in the spring of that year, it proved a swan song for the drummer,

Spot Light | "Wonderwall"

The song "Wonderwall" has become Oasis's defining piece. For the band it is an anthem both treasured and burdensome. In 2002 Noel Gallagher threatened to leave the stage of a gig unless the audience stopped joining in on the song. But as a major hit on both the U.S. and U.K. charts, it is likely to be one of the group's most enduring legacies. Thought to be a tribute to Noel's girlfriend at that time, Meg Matthews (later his wife and then his ex-wife), the song reflects on the uncertainties of a love affair. "Backbeat the word was on the street / That the fire in your heart is out," the lyric reveals but contains a strong plea: "I don't believe that anybody / Feels the way I do about you now"; the lovers thus reaffirm their affections. With a title inspired by a George Harrison solo album, "Wonderwall" has attracted the attention of other artists, too. Within weeks of its emergence as a hit, an act called Mike Flowers Pops rearranged the song as an easy-listening vocal tour de force. A little later Thom Yorke of Radiohead contributed, with the Posies, to a surprising tribute: an impromptu live performance of the piece on Canadian radio.

McCarroll, who had clashed with the two Gallaghers. His replacement was Alan White, who debuted with the band at the Glastonbury Festival that summer.

By August 1995, as the Britpop phenomenon peaked, the two leading bands in the movement, Oasis and Blur, clashed head-on. The period had seen a string of new groups emerge on the British scene, many of whom featured a classic four- or five-piece, guitar-led lineup that presented upbeat pop with a potent rock rhythm, creating styles and sounds that had made the U.K. a pop superpower in the 1960s. Supergrass and Pulp, but most notably Oasis and Blur, made guitar acts fashionable once more.

Oasis versus Blur

When Oasis and Blur announced that rival singles would be issued on the same day in 1995, the media transformed the chart struggle into a contemporary version of the Beatles versus Rolling Stones contests. Amid press headlines and acrimony between the artists involved, Blur's "Country House" entered at number one to hold off the challenge of Oasis's "Roll with It."

The battle intensified in the coming months as the Gallaghers and Damon Albarn became involved in a war of words, a strategy that kept both groups in the public eye. Noel later turned down a prestigious Ivor Novello songwriting prize because it had been jointly awarded to his rivals.

Toward the end of 1995, the band's second album, *(What's the Story) Morning Glory?*, immediately topped the U.K. charts; by early 1996 the record had peaked at number four in the United States. Meanwhile, "Wonderwall," the song that became Oasis's signature, raced to the number two position in the U.K. in December 1995.

By now the group was accelerating toward triumph around the world. The single "Don't Look Back in Anger" made an appearance at the top of the U.K. charts; Maine Road, the soccer ground that is home to the Gallaghers' beloved Manchester City, hosted a legendary Oasis gig featuring two consecutive nights at Knebworth in front of more than 200,000 fans.

Noel's Vocal Stint

When they took part in MTV's popular *Unplugged* series—minus a temporarily absent Liam, whose laryngitis meant that Noel took over vocal duties—their place in the aristocracy of rock and their foothold in the American market seemed quite secure. Attempts to solidify their U.S. stature stalled, however, because of infighting, problems in personal relationships, and an aborted tour. When the group did return to the United States, it was to support U2, a clear sign that the seat of power was in the possession not of Oasis but their Irish counterparts.

Slowing Momentum

When the group's third album, *Be Here Now* (1997), was released to some lukewarm reviews, the wind in Oasis's sails seemed to have calmed. While the record initially sold well in the U.K. and the United States, it proved not to have the staying power of the first two albums and seemed to portend a decline in the band's fortunes. Nonetheless, the group had hardly stalled. "Do You Know What I Mean," "Stand By Me," and "All Around the World" were high-placed U.K. singles, and "Champagne Supernova" and "Don't Go Away" gave the band a pair of U.S. hits.

New Members

Personnel changes transformed the band. In 1999 Arthurs left the group and was replaced by the former Heavy Stereo guitarist Gem Archer. Then ex-Ride member Andy Bell took over bass duties from the departing McGuigan. It seemed that all was not running smoothly in the Oasis camp.

Yet the albums kept coming. *Standing on the Shoulder of Giants* (2000) featured "Go Let Out," providing the band with another U.K. number one, and *Heathen Chemistry* (2002) spawned a string of Top 10 successes, including the Indian-influenced "Hindu Times." It appeared that the demons that had haunted the Gallaghers at the height of their fame were finally being held at bay.

After more than a decade of gigging and recording, Oasis have become a familiar fixture on the British charts and retain a substantial international following. While their glory days may be behind them, their core fan base has stuck with the group through its ups and downs. Yet the group seems to have squandered an opportunity to attain the heights reached by the Beatles in the United States a generation earlier. Unwilling to play the obligatory industry games, they have left a legacy not as significant rock innovators but as rabble-rousers with the talent to skillfully ape the composing styles of their heroes, John Lennon and Paul McCartney.

SELECTIVE DISCOGRAPHY: *Definitely Maybe* (Epic, 1994); *(What's the Story) Morning Glory?* (Epic, 1995); *Be Here Now* (Epic, 1997); *Standing on the Shoulder of Giants* (Epic, 2000); *Heathen Chemistry* (Epic, 2002).

BIBLIOGRAPHY: M. Krugman, *Oasis: Supersonic Supernova* (London, 1997); D. Cavanagh, *The Creation Records Story: My Magpie Eyes Are Hungry for the Prize* (London, 2001).

WEBSITE: www.oasisinet.com.

SIMON WARNER

THE OFFSPRING

Formed: 1984, Garden Grove, California

Members: Bryan "Dexter" Holland, vocals (born Long Beach, California, 29 December 1966); Greg Kriesel, bass (born Glendale, California, 12 January 1965); Kevin "Noodles" Wasserman, guitar (born Los Angeles, California, 4 February 1963); Ron Welty, drums (born Long Beach, California, 1 February 1971).

Genre: Rock, Punk

Best-selling album since 1990: *Smash* (1994)

Hit songs since 1990: "Come Out and Play," "Self-Esteem," "Pretty Fly for a White Guy"

The Offspring turned punk's nihilism on its head with lyrics just as likely to satirize itself or its fans as the "establishment."

The group's willingness to subvert punk, whose calling card is supposedly its subversion, can be found in its roots. Bryan Holland and some friends were unable to crash a 1986 concert by seminal Los Angeles punk band Social Distortion, and afterward vowed to form their own band. It seemed like a sour-grapes boast, but Holland actually learned the guitar and the following year formed Manic Subsidal, which would by 1989 become Offspring.

Playing a fusion of surf rock and skate-punk, the band was discovered in 1989 by Bad Religion founder and Epitaph Records owner Brett Gurewitz. He released the group's debut *Offspring* (1989), which sold a modest 3,000 copies. In the meantime, the members kept the band going on the side as they attended college. Drummer Ron Welty earned an electronics degree, bassist Greg Kriesel a finance degree, and Holland a master's degree in molecular biology. In an interview, Holland knowingly tweaked punksters as "smart kids trying to pretend they're not."

Ignition (1992) followed, selling a respectable 100,000 copies but not impressing the members enough to quit their jobs or studies. But the group's third album, *Smash* (1994), hit at just the right time—MTV was helping create a punk revival by hyping bands like Rancid and Green Day, and Offspring had accessible, offbeat material that unintentionally fit the new trend while not seeming like a clone of the others.

The first single "Come Out and Play" opened the doors, while the follow-up "Self-Esteem" kept the momentum going. Critics agree "Self-Esteem" does not win any points for musical originality—it is a "lafadoso" song, that is, a song that uses the typical 1990s alternative rock repeating bass line of la, fa, do, and so. However, the biting lyrics about an insecure guy who keeps coming back to an unfaithful girlfriend struck a vein among many teenagers, while the cheeky double entendre, "I took her back and made her dessert," maintains punk irreverence. The third single "Gotta Get Away" features a black and white video that portrays the mosh pit with stark drama. More musically complex than "Self-Esteem," the song tickles album rock fans' ears with its crunchy guitar and Holland's relatively melodic singing.

Selling about 5 million copies in the United States, *Smash* became the best-selling independent album in history. But Offspring jumped to major label Columbia, while Gurewitz accused the band of going corporate. With the band's Columbia debut *Ixnay on the Hombre* (1997), it seemed that Gurewitz would get the last laugh. The group's sense of humor is muted, and "Change the World" expresses disillusionment with Gurewitz.

However, *Americana* (1998) represents a return of the mischievous spark. The first single "Pretty Fly (for a White Guy)" pokes fun at suburban kids who pretend to be gangsta rappers, while "Why Don't You Get a Job" takes

SELECTIVE DISCOGRAPHY: *Smash* (Epitaph, 1994); *Ixnay on the Hombre* (Columbia, 1997); *Americana* (Columbia, 1998); *Conspiracy of One* (Columbia, 2000).

RAMIRO BURR

OL' DIRTY BASTARD

Born: Russell Tyrone Jones, a.k.a. Osirus; Brooklyn, New York, 9 May 1970

Genre: Rap

Best-selling album since 1990: *Return to the 36 Chambers: The Dirty Version* (1995)

Hit songs since 1990: "Shimmy Shimmy Ya," "Got Your Money"

In a genre where poker-faced solemnity is paramount, Russell Jones is a tragic hip-hop clown of Shakespearean proportions. The erratic, unpredictable rapper, known variously as Ol' Dirty Bastard, Dirt Dog, Big Baby Jesus, and Osirus, rose to fame in the early 1990s as a member of the pioneering New York rap troupe the Wu-Tang Clan. With the release of his profane, soul-inspired solo debut, *Return to the 36 Chambers: The Dirty Version* (1995), Jones seemed destined for solo stardom as well. Felled by weapons possession charges, multiple drug arrests, and incarcerations, the rapper ended up in prison, his career in a shambles.

Born in Brooklyn, New York, in 1969, Russell Jones, a welfare child, helped form the Staten Island–based hip-hop group the Wu-Tang Clan in 1992 with his cousins Robert Diggs (a.k.a. RZA) and Gary Grice (a.k.a. Genius). The group's debut album, *Enter the Wu-Tang (36 Chambers)* (1993), was one of the most influential rap albums of the 1990s. With its unique meld of multiple strong rap styles, martial arts imagery, and gritty production style, the album was meant as a launching pad for the solo careers of its nine members. Prior to the album's release, Jones was convicted of second-degree assault in New York; in 1994 he was shot in the stomach by another rapper in Brooklyn following a street argument.

Jones, billed as Ol' Dirty Bastard, released his solo debut album, *Return to the 36 Chambers: The Dirty Version*, in 1995. Built on RZA's patented dark, piano-sampling production style, the album is a maniacal compilation of Jones's singing styles: aggressive sung-spoken rapping, warbling soul crooning, and vulgar stream-of-consciousness rants. "Brooklyn Zoo" and "Shimmy Shimmy Ya" helped the album sell 500,000 copies; its success led to guest work on a remix of Mariah Carey's 1995

"Come Out and Play"

While Rancid bragged about relieving the rich of their valuables on "Salvation" and Green Day dissed the workaday world on "Longview," the other mid-1990s punk breakout, Offspring, got its first hit with a more conservative point of view, criticizing gang culture and a lenient justice system. "Come Out and Play" contains all the sloppy musical credentials of punk: Vocalist Bryan Holland ominously speaks, but does not quite rap, the verses about kids going to school with guns. The chorus kicks in with a three-note hard rock guitar riff, while Holland does his best not to overenunciate. However, Holland is the rare punk rocker who expresses a dim view of the young male trend toward heightened machismo and sensitivity to slights: "Hey, man, you talking back to me? / Take him out." He also mocks the idea of trying teenagers as juveniles: "You're under 18 / you won't be doing any time." The song, which first made airplay charts in July 1994, does not follow traditional punk ideology. Unfortunately, it foreshadows the increase in school gun violence during the late 1990s. The Offspring would go on to make more blunt and often humorous statements about American life, but this serious indictment of youth culture and the juvenile justice system put it on the map.

---

aim at slackers over a whimsical groove that recalls the Beatles' "Ob La Di."

Conspiracy of One (2000) continues in the same vein, with the band rocking out over fast-paced, mosh-pit ready tunes, but much of the material seems to merely borrow from past inspiration. In a typically irreverent move, the band announced in 2003 that its forthcoming album would be titled *Chinese Democracy*, which Guns N' Roses had announced several years earlier would be the title of its long-delayed album. "You snooze, you lose," Holland quipped.

Offspring dealt with the contradictions of being a mainstream punk band with humor and aplomb, and argued that there were more things for rebellious rockers to skewer than just the police, school, and parents.

song "Fantasy." Among other songs, Ol' Dirty Bastard contributed the intensely scatological "Dog S***" track to the Wu-Tang's hit second album, *Wu-Tang Forever* (1997).

In November 1997 the twenty-eight-year-old rapper—the father of thirteen children—was arrested for failing to pay almost a year's worth of child support for his three children with wife Icelene Jones. It was the beginning of a career-ending spiral of legal problems.

By 1998 Ol' Dirty Bastard was known more for his unpredictable behavior than for his rapping. Within a few months in early 1998, Ol' Dirty Bastard launched his "Dirty Wear" clothing line, helped save a four-year-old girl from being crushed by a car, and, one night later, interrupted the Grammys during an acceptance speech by rocker Shawn Colvin with a shout of "Wu-Tang is for the children!"

In September, he was arrested for terrorist threats after harassing a security guard at the House of Blues in Los Angeles. Two weeks later, he was removed from the Four Seasons Hotel in Berlin for lounging on a balcony in the nude. In November 1998 Ol' Dirty Bastard pled guilty to threatening to kill his ex-girlfriend. In January 1999 he was pulled over by New York police and allegedly fired shots at the officers, leading to an arrest for attempted murder and criminal weapon possession; police, however, were never able to produce any physical evidence in the case, which was dismissed a month later.

Ol' Dirty Bastard's troubles were hardly over, though. When he was found wearing bulletproof body armor in California in March—an illegality for convicted felons—the rapper became the first person arrested under the new law. Within the next six months, ODB was twice arrested in New York for driving without a license—once with a small amount of crack cocaine in his vehicle; jailed in California for failing to pay bail in the House of Blues case; and arrested once again in New York for driving with a suspended license and possession of marijuana and twenty vials of crack. An arrest warrant was issued in California for failure to appear in the bullet-proof vest case just before the rapper entered a drug rehabilitation program in August.

Amid his string of arrests, Ol' Dirty Bastard released his second solo album, *Nigga Please* (1999). The album features the minor old school soul hit "Got Your Money," and a comically overwrought piano jazz cover of "Good Morning Heartache," a song popularized by the legendary jazz vocalist Billie Holiday.

In early 2000 Ol' Dirty Bastard was sentenced to a Los Angeles drug treatment facility from which he escaped in October, two months shy of his release. He was on the lam for a month, secretly recording new material with RZA and performing at a record release party for the Wu-Tang

Clan in New York in November, somehow escaping without incident. He was apprehended a few days later at a McDonald's in Philadelphia while signing autographs; Ol' Dirty Bastard was later extradited to New York on drug possession charges. In April 2001 he was sentenced to two to four years in prison by a New York Supreme Court judge.

A greatest hits compilation, *The Dirty Story: The Best of Ol' Dirty Bastard*, was released in August 2001. March 2002 saw the release of *The Trials and Tribulations of Russell Jones*, a slipshod album of previously unreleased songs and material recorded while he was on the lam. With his legal troubles overshadowing his musical output, both albums were duds, effectively closing the door on Jones's career.

A tragic figure, Russell Jones blazed a bizarre path across the 1990s hip-hop scene until his inner demons and drug addiction resulted in a career-ending prison sentence.

SELECTIVE DISCOGRAPHY: *Return to the 36 Chambers: The Dirty Version* (Elektra, 1995); *Nigga Please* (Elektra, 1999); *The Dirty Story: The Best of Ol' Dirty Bastard* (Elektra, 2001); *Trials & Tribulations of Russell Jones* (D3, 2002). **With Wu-Tang Clan:** *Enter the Wu-Tang Clan (36 Chambers)* (Loud Records, 1993); *Wu-Tang Forever* (Loud/RCA, 1997); *The W* (Columbia, 2000).

GIL KAUFMAN

112

Formed: 1995, Atlanta, Georgia

Members: Michael Keith (born Atlanta, Georgia, 18 December 1978); Daron Jones (born Atlanta, Georgia, 27 December 1977); Quinnes "Q" Parker (born Atlanta, Georgia, 24 March 1977); Marvin "Slim" Scandrick (born Atlanta, Georgia, 25 September 1979).

Genre: R&B

Best-selling album since 1990: *Part III* (2001)

Hit songs since 1990: "Only You," "Love Me," "It's Over Now"

The group 112 was one of the most successful acts to emerge on the Bad Boy label run by R&B impresario Sean "Puffy" Combs during the 1990s. 112 began as a smooth harmony outfit inspired largely by 1990s R&B group Boyz II Men. On early releases all four members display strong vocal skills, using rich, full harmonies to imbue love ballads with a sense of urgency. By the time of their third album in 2001, however, the group had largely jettisoned their gentle ballad approach for a tougher sound in keeping with the harder-edged current in modern R&B. Although publicized conflicts with Combs and Bad Boy hindered 112's career during the early 2000s, the group managed to retain its popularity, patching up differences with the label by the beginning of 2003.

112 was formed by four high school classmates in their hometown of Atlanta, Georgia, and they began by performing at church functions. During the early 1990s they earned the notice of the management team Courtney Sills and Kevin Wales, which introduced the group to Combs. Christening the teenaged singers 112 (after a popular nightclub in Atlanta), Combs spearheaded production on the group's self-titled debut album in 1996. Although the bulk of *112* consists of sweet-sounding ballads such as "Cupid" and "I Will Be There," the album's biggest hit, "Only You," is a seductive dance track, driven by a thumping bass and the members' creamy harmonies. While the album's material lacks the distinction of Boyz II Men's finest work, it is enhanced by 112's vocal professionalism, polished through years of singing in church choirs. In 1998 the group returned with *Room 112*, an album that structurally mirrored its predecessor: lush, pleading ballads interspersed with the occasional dance track. Although it boasted substantial hits in "Love Me" and "Anywhere," critics expressed disappointment in the group's unchallenging adherence to formula.

112 changed directions for *Part III* (2001), an album cited by many critics as the group's finest. Sporting a flashier, more funk-oriented sound than previous efforts, *Part III* features production by the group member Daron Jones. On groove-based songs such as "Dance with Me" and "Peaches and Cream," the group incorporates the type of techno-electronic sound favored in the early 2000s by the hit R&B producer Rodney Jerkins. "It's Over Now" ranks as one of the group's strongest singles, its aching and dramatic mood propelled by assertive harmonies and a haunting arrangement of strings, guitar, and jittery rhythm.

Unfortunately, the group's success was soon hampered by legal battles. In February 2002 the four members signed a new recording deal with Def Jam Records, claiming that their contract with Bad Boy had expired. Combs immediately filed an injunction, insisting that the group was still signed to Bad Boy. During the publicity that ensued, 112's members accused Combs of holding them to the terms of an onerous 1996 contract. Finally, in early 2003, the case was settled, with Bad Boy and Def Jam agreeing to handle 112 jointly, splitting profits on the group's future releases. At the same time, 112 announced plans to record its fourth album.

Finding success in the 1990s singing Boyz II Men–influenced love ballads, 112 had evolved by the early 2000s into a forward-thinking R&B group determined to establish trends rather than follow them.

SELECTIVE DISCOGRAPHY: *112* (Bad Boy, 1996); *Room 112* (Bad Boy, 1998); *Part III* (Bad Boy, 2001).

WEBSITE: www.one12.com.

DAVID FREELAND

ORGANIZED NOIZE

Formed: Atlanta, Georgia
Members: Rico Wade (born Atlanta, Georgia, 26 February 1972); Pat "Sleepy" Brown; Raymon Murray
Genre: Hip-Hop
Hit songs since 1990: "Waterfalls"

Organized Noize is a hip-hop production outfit with a Southern niche. Their music blends elements of Parliament-Funkadelic with a soulful and sometimes futuristic sound. Their eccentric and intricate soundscapes helped catapult groups like OutKast and TLC, and Southern hip-hop in general, to the national forefront.

Organized Noize established Atlanta, Georgia, as a rap music hub distinct from the Northeast and West Coast. Whereas most rap producers utilize sampled bits of previously recorded songs in their tracks, Organized Noize crafts entirely original songs. Their producers, including Rico Wade, discovered the rap duo OutKast, whose debut album, *Southernplayalisticadillacmuzik* (1994), displayed a laid-back, funky, and grounded sound. The album went platinum and announced OutKast as a formidable hip-hop act.

Always difficult to pigeonhole, Organized Noize provided a different sound to a growing roster of clients. With "Waterfalls," they gave TLC a huge hit; and their work on OutKast's follow-up album, *Atliens* (1996), is as otherworldly and digital as *Southernplayalisticadillacmuzik* is regional and visceral. Organized Noize tracks remain steeped in soul. They furthered their work in rhythm and blues by producing a hit for En Vogue: "Don't Let Go (Love)" for the *Set It Off* soundtrack (1996).

The production team expanded into an umbrella of Atlanta-based artists they call the Dungeon family, which includes OutKast, Goodie Mob, and rappers Cool Breeze and Backbone, producing in their studio, the Dungeon. In 1996, they secured a record label production deal with Interscope. After failing to release a hit album under that label, Interscope and Organized Noize parted ways in 1999.

Having learned well from Organized Noize, OutKast began producing most of their own songs. The production trio had nominal credit on OutKast albums *Aquemini* (1998) and *Stankonia* (2000), and the influence of Organized Noize on these efforts is evident. *Stankonia* was

TLC's "Waterfalls" brought Organized Noize to national attention, and it remains their most popular production. It was released as the third single from the female trio's runaway triumph, *Crazysexycool* (La Face, 1994). "Waterfalls" is a metaphor for foolish pursuits, and in it, the ladies of TLC caution young people against irresponsible actions that might result in tragedies like gun violence and AIDS. Its lyrical content was starkly different for the fun-loving TLC, and Organized Noize responded with an entirely unique sound. Although TLC was best known for youthful rhythms steeped in R&B and rap, Organized Noize fashioned a sophisticated track that crisscrosses generations and genres. "Waterfalls" is built on a funky guitar that borrows as much from country music traditions as it does from blaxploitation films of the 1970s. The melody is calm and soothing. The entire effect imparts an older, sophisticated sound, which underscores TLC's role as social educators. Organized Noize's deft production also sets off a rap verse by Lisa "Left Eye" Lopes, which has become one of her best-loved performances. "Waterfalls" is both TLC and Organized Noize's most critically acclaimed work. It garnered 1996 Grammy Award nominations for Best Pop Performance by a Duo or Group with Vocal and one of the Recording Academy's biggest honors, Record of the Year. "Waterfalls" helped TLC win the Best R&B Album statue that same year.

nominated for a 2002 Best Album Grammy and won the Best Rap Album Award. In 2002 Organized Noize added "Saturday (Oooh!)," a hit song for another Atlanta native, Ludacris, to its list of accomplishments.

Although Organized Noize is not as prolific as hip-hop producers the Neptunes or Timbaland, they are as influential. Organized Noize's groundbreaking work with OutKast helped to broaden the sound spectrum of hip-hop to include styles typically ignored in the Northeast and West Coast scenes.

DARA COOK

BETH ORTON

Born: Norfolk, England, 14 December 1970
Genre: Rock, Pop
Best-selling album since 1990: *Daybreaker* (2002)
Hit songs since 1990: "She Cries Your Name," "Stolen Car," "Concrete Sky"

Beth Orton began in the British trip-hop dance scene, which melded hip-hop beats with trippy, atmospheric touches, usually achieved with synthesizers and drum programming. As a solo artist with a haunting, reedlike voice, she combined a love of folk music with ethereal, otherworldly synthesizer touches. Prior to her solo career she appeared as a guest vocalist on albums by the U.K. electronica duo the Chemical Brothers. On her own she produced three solo albums and various collaborations.

Though Orton has an unmistakable singing voice, she started out wanting to be an actress. It was not until she met fellow Briton, William Orbit, a producer and mixer known for his work with rock stars Sting and Madonna, that she turned to singing. Impressed by her speaking voice, Orbit invited her into the studio to record a song. He introduced her to people in the music business, and in 1996 she released a debut album, *Trailer Park*, to critical acclaim. Though Orton did not tour to support the album—she opened for other artists—she developed a strong following. By the time she released her second album, *Central Reservation* (1999), her debut had sold 90,000 copies in the United States. Steady airplay on Triple A (Adult Album Alternative) radio stations helped ignite sales. The single "She Cries Your Name," a haunting song with cellos, minimal rhythmic touches, and acoustic guitar, proved to be a breakthrough.

In 1997 *Rolling Stone* magazine named *Trailer Park* one of the top ten albums of the year. Orton's lyrics can be elliptical and abstract, but also touched with wisdom. In the bluesy, slow tempo piano tune "Sweetest Decline," she sings, "What's the use in regrets? / They're just things we haven't done yet / What are regrets? They're just lessons we haven't learned yet."

Orton's third album, *Daybreaker* (2002), possesses a spirited crispness and buoyancy that earlier efforts lacked. Although some critics considered it overproduced, others found *Daybreaker* a lovely record that brings Orton's crackling alto to the fore. On *Daybreaker* Orton collaborates with revered country singer Emmylou Harris and the prolific alternative country singer/songwriter Ryan Adams.

Though Orton emerged from the dance scene, her own music is ethereal and spare, combining the best of acoustic instruments with the processed sounds of syn-

Beth Orton [VALERIE PHILIPS/ASTRALWERKS]

thesizers and backbeats. Orton demonstrated that the honest delivery of folk music could bring a humanizing touch to the chilly, otherworldly aspects of electronic music.

SELECTIVE DISCOGRAPHY: *Trailer Park* (Dedicated/Heavenly, 1996); *Best Bit* EP (Heavenly, 1997); *Central Reservation* (Heavenly/Arista, 1999); *Daybreaker* (Astralwerks/Heavenly, 2002).

CARRIE HAVRANEK

JOAN OSBORNE

Born: Anchorage, Kentucky, 8 July 1962
Genre: Rock
Best-selling album since 1990: *Relish* (1995)
Hit songs since 1990: "One of Us," "Right Hand Man"

One of the most exciting female singers to emerge in the 1990s, Joan Osborne sings in a powerful style that owes a heavy debt to soul and R&B. While best known for her gentle, folk-influenced 1995 hit, "One of Us," Osborne is a versatile artist, proving her facility with styles ranging from pop to tough blues. During the mid-1990s Osborne was linked with popular female rock singers such as Sheryl Crow and Alanis Morissette, even though her idiosyncratic approach did not easily fit into any genre. Long gaps between albums, as well as marketing challenges stemming from her unique sound, hindered Osborne's career after "One of Us." Still, she remained a challenging performer unafraid to take musical chances.

Born in Kentucky in 1962, Osborne did not entertain thoughts of singing professionally until the early 1990s, after moving to New York to study film. Visiting a blues bar with an open mic for amateur performers, she was prompted after a few drinks to sing a rendition of jazz vocalist Billie Holiday's classic "God Bless the Child." Overcoming nerves, she began appearing at open mic events around town, writing songs and developing her unique hybrid of blues, soul, and rock. After recording two albums for her own label, Womanly Hips, she signed with Mercury Records and released her 1995 breakthrough work, *Relish*. Singing a varied collection of material, much of it written with guitarist Eric Bazilian, Osborne revealed a hard-edged vocal personality that was bracing and memorable. On the driving "Right Hand Man," she recalls the scabrous, desperate style of 1960s rock singer Janis Joplin, while the classic blues song "Help Me" is marked by her sinewy, dark-hued phrasing. Osborne's fame was secured, however, with "One of Us," a catchy song that speculates on the various human guises God might take: "What if God was one of us / Just a slob like one of us." Although the tone of the song is serious, even reverential, right-wing Christian groups protested its characterization of God as a "slob." The mild controversy only abetted the song's success: By 1996 it had been nominated for a Grammy Award, spurring sales of *Relish* past the 2 million mark.

Osborne took a long time to deliver a follow-up to *Relish,* focusing instead on live tours and acting as spokesperson for organizations such as Planned Parenthood. Osborne's support of the pro-choice Planned Parenthood brought her additional controversy when an anti-abortion group staged a boycott of her recordings in late 1998. Leaving Mercury, Osborne signed with Interscope Records to release the long-awaited *Righteous Love* in 2000. While the album features a smoother, more polished sound than its predecessor, none of its songs stand out with the hit-making charisma of "One of Us." Unfortunately *Righteous Love* quickly dropped from sight, a commercial disappointment. Moving to a smaller label, Compendia, Osborne switched gears by releasing *How Sweet It Is* (2002), a pleasing collection of covers of R&B songs from the 1960s and 1970s.

Osborne left a lasting impression on 1990s rock music, combining gritty, intense vocals with incisive songwriting. Never a prolific artist, Osborne has used her

Joan Osborne [JIMMY LENNER JR./COMPENDIA MUSIC]

recordings to explore a broad scope of musical interests, creating highly personal work that demands appreciation on its own terms.

SELECTIVE DISCOGRAPHY: *Soul Show* (Womanly Hips, 1991); *Blue Million Miles* EP (Womanly Hips, 1993); *Relish* (Blue Gorilla/Mercury, 1995); *Early Recordings* (Mercury, 1996); *Righteous Love* (Interscope, 2000); *How Sweet It Is* (Compendia, 2002).

WEBSITE: www.joanosborne.com.

DAVID FREELAND

OZZY OSBOURNE

Born: John Michael Osbourne; Birmingham, England, 3 December 1948

Genre: Heavy Metal, Rock

Best-selling album since 1990: *Live & Loud* (1993)

Hit songs since 1990: "Mama, I'm Coming Home"

Renowned as one of the most outrageous performers in rock music, vocalist Ozzy Osbourne's marathon with substance abuse never kept him from finding fresh methods to market his career. He emerged as a rock star in the 1970s as a member of Black Sabbath, translated that success into a solo career, and parlayed it all into a blockbuster reality television show. In equal turns fascinating and revolting, Osbourne has spun all publicity into good publicity. Many credit him with being the founder of heavy metal rock.

A Musical Escape

Osbourne's thirst for attention took shape while growing up in a family of six children in the coarseness of industrial Birmingham, England. His parents were laborers in the manufacturing trades and their family lineage was rife with alcoholism and mental illness. Osbourne's youth was spent in habitual trouble and he was once arrested for burglary, landing briefly in Birmingham's Winson Prison. At fourteen, he joined a local band called the Black Panthers, and sang with several other club bands before meeting up with school chum, guitarist Tony Iommi. They formed Black Sabbath, the name of a Boris Karloff movie. Their intent was to follow the blues/rock path of Led Zeppelin and other English bands on the rise. However, a record company imposed Satanist symbols on their first album cover, branding them as disciples of the occult. This association with devil worship still clings to Osbourne and, despite his occasional claims to the contrary, is an image that he recurrently fosters.

Black Sabbath was hugely successful, launching the singer as one of the world's most famous rock stars. Eventually Osbourne's drug and alcohol abuse made him unmanageable even by Black Sabbath's standards and they fired him in 1978. Expected by many to drift into obscurity, a savvy business manager, Sharon Arden, whom he would marry in 1982, convinced Osbourne to embark on a solo career. His first album, *Blizzard of Oz* (1981), went platinum. His subsequent albums also sold well and Osbourne was once again on top of the rock and roll heap. Nevertheless, life was far from trouble-free. Osbourne simultaneously caught flak and drew fans for his macabre stage shows and much publicized social behavior. He hired a dwarf to toss around on stage, hurled raw meat at his audience, killed a litter of cats, defecated in an elevator, urinated on the Alamo, and bit the head off a live dove in a record company executive's office. Animal activists, concerned parents, and religious factions, outraged over what they perceived as devil worship, badgered his tours. Adoring fans would lob dead animals at him—frogs, snakes, cats, dogs—midconcert, predicating one of the most infamous incidents in rock history. During a concert in Des Moines,

| MTV's *The Osbournes*

The Osbournes distinguishes itself from a throng of other reality television programs because the family is so famous and outrageous. It offers an inside look at the personal lives of Ozzy Osbourne, his wife Sharon, and two of their children, a daughter, Kelly, and a son, Jack. An adopted son, Robert, also appears, but their oldest daughter, Aimee, has refused to take part. *The Osbournes* displays an abnormal family dealing with normal family issues. They demonstrate few behavior boundaries and manage their lives with the help of personal assistants, trainers, and other handlers. Yet, similar to many households, a hierarchy survives. Sharon rules the roost, albeit with biting wit and sarcasm. Osbourne dodders around with a "deer-in-the-headlights" expression, trying to reign in his hyperactive teenagers. As a burned-out rocker whose past is littered with debauchery of every nature, he gets little reverence for his disciplinary efforts. The kids are caught up in the malaise of adolescent fantasy. Viewers watch the Osbournes argue, swear, laugh, scream, cry, eat, and sleep as they go about their lives. *The Osbournes* took a turn for the serious but was not deterred when Sharon developed colon cancer and Osbourne battled alcoholism.

Iowa, a fan tossed a live bat on stage. Certain that it was rubber, Osbourne bit the bat's head off. Osbourne's ensuing rabies treatment delayed the tour. Later, Osbourne fought lawsuits over his culpability in teenage suicides regarding his song "Suicide Solution." The song is about the dangers of drinking alcohol but is often interpreted as advocating suicide. Osbourne was exonerated.

In 1991, after multiple rehab stays, Osbourne took sobriety seriously. His album *No More Tears* (1991) features a softer sound than previous work. It contains a pretty ballad, "Mama, I'm Coming Home," which recognizes his desire to return to his wife after time on the road. During the tour that followed *No More Tears*, Osbourne decided to retire and spend more time with his family, which included two daughters and a son from his marriage to Sharon, and three children from an earlier marriage who

lived elsewhere. He punctuated his retirement with a live album, *Live & Loud* (1993), that contains music from the highly publicized *No More Tears* tour. It was promoted as the last chance for Osbourne's legions of fans to see him perform and was a major financial success. Months later, Osbourne, restless from life at home, broke his retirement, and went into the studio to begin preproduction for *Ozzmosis* (1995).

Settling Down (Sort Of)

Along the way, Osbourne received his first Grammy Award in 1993 for Best Metal Rock Vocal Performance with the funky, hard-driving, "I Don't Want to Change the World," off *Live & Loud*. Critics often overlook the fact that Osbourne is an engaging rock singer. However, some are quick to recognize that his voice is high and true, carrying a musical whine that mixes an agreeable measure of wit with his intense, edgy style. In a genre of music where vocals often take a backseat to the distorted sound, Osbourne's voice always sits up front.

With retirement a distant memory, Sharon, credited as the driving force behind her husband's career, created Ozzfest in 1996. This assembly of various heavy metal groups with Osbourne as headliner gambled that there was still interest in heavy metal rock. Osbourne spiced up Ozzfest by offering a consumer-friendly package replete with tattoo parlors, body piercing, dominatrixes, psychic readings, and opportunities for fans to meet the bands. It was phenomenally successful and continued to be produced year after year.

In 2001 Osbourne released *Down to Earth*, his first new album in six years. It received glowing reviews. A ballad off the album, "Dreamer," performed in the vein of John Lennon's "Imagine," presents the paradox of Osbourne advocating peace and harmony throughout the world. Other songs on the album characteristically flirt with spooky afterlife themes. That autumn he promoted the album with a tour originally titled "Black Xmas." The name was changed to "Merry Mayhem" in the aftermath of the September 11 terrorist attacks. To honor a solo career that has produced the sale of over 70 million albums, Osbourne received a star on the Hollywood Walk of Fame.

In another odd twist, Sharon secured a deal with the MTV network to film the Osbourne family in their daily routines. Ridiculed from the onset and marked for failure, the weekly-aired show, titled *The Osbournes*, won an Emmy Award for Outstanding Reality Programming in 2002. The family signed a $20 million deal for the 2003 season. A plethora of profitable merchandising materials from the show has resulted, such as books, and the release of a collection of favorite household songs called *The Osbourne Family Album*. Osbourne and Sharon renewed wedding vows on New Year's Eve 2002, celebrating twenty years of marriage.

Osbourne is a true survivor in a musical battlefield frequently recognized for short-lived success, shattered lives, and death. Labeled rock's Prince of Darkness, Osbourne and his wife's knack to successfully promote themselves has shed a bright light on financial balance sheets.

SELECTIVE DISCOGRAPHY: *The Blizzard of Oz* (CBS, 1980); *Diary of a Madman* (CBS, 1981); *Speak of the Devil* (CBS, 1982); *Talk of the Devil* (CBS, 1982); *Bark at the Moon* (CBS, 1983); *The Ultimate Sin* (CBS, 1986); *Tribute* (CBS, 1987); *No Rest for the Wicked* (CBS, 1988); *Just Say Ozzy* (CBS, 1990); *No More Tears* (Sony, 1991); *Live & Loud* (Sony, 1993); *Ozzmosis* (Sony, 1995); *The Ozzman Cometh* (Sony, 1997); *Down to Earth* (Epic, 2001); *Live at Budokan* (Epic, 2002).

BIBLIOGRAPHY: G. Johnson, *Ozzy Osbourne* (New York, 1985); C. Clerk, *Ozzy Osbourne: Diary of a Madman* (New York, 1990); H. Shaw, *Ozzy Talking: Ozzy Osbourne in His Own Words* (New York, 2002).

DONALD LOWE

OUR LADY PEACE

Formed: 1992, Toronto

Members: Duncan Coutts, bass (born Ontario, 4 February 1970); Raine Maida, vocals (born Ontario, 18 February 1970); Steve Mazur, guitar; Jeremy Taggart, drums (born Ontario, 7 April 1975). Former members: Chris Eacrett, bass (born Canada, 1971); Mike Turner, guitar (born Bradford, Ontario, 5 June 1967).

Genre: Rock

Best-selling album since 1990: *Clumsy* (1997)

Hit songs since 1990: "Superman's Dead," "Somewhere Out There"

Our Lady Peace made brief waves in alternative hard rock circles in the late 1990s with the hit "Superman's Dead."

While at the University of Toronto, criminology student and part-time singer Raine Maida hooked up with fellow student Mike Turner, an English major who played guitar. The pair recruited Chris Eacrett, a marketing student and bass player from nearby Ryerson University, as well as Jeremy Taggart, a seventeen-year-old jazz drummer, to round out its lineup. The quartet became known as Our Lady Peace, taking its name from a 1943 poem by American poet Mark Van Doren.

The band's demos attracted the attention of Sony Music Canada, which quickly snapped up the group. In

1995 Our Lady Peace released its debut album *Naveed*. The band enjoyed a minor alternative-radio hit with the hard-charging rocker "Starseed." On *Naveed* the band openly celebrates classic-rock influences such as Led Zeppelin, considered anathema to the raw, hard rock sounds favored by the grunge acts of the day. Our Lady Peace enhanced its profile by appearing as openers on fellow Canadian Alanis Morissette's *Jagged Little Pill* tour.

Our Lady Peace enjoyed its biggest success with the release of *Clumsy* in 1997. With grunge fading in popularity, Our Lady Peace's style of hard rock found a wider audience. The surging "Superman's Dead" became the band's biggest hit, winning over fans with Maida's memorable, high-register wailing on chorus: "Alone I'm thinking / Why is superman dead / Is it in my head." On the strength of "Superman's Dead," *Clumsy* sold more than 2 million copies.

The band's subsequent two releases *Happiness Is Not a Fish That You Can Catch* (1999) and *Spiritual Machines* (2001) were hits in the band's native Canada, but failed to generate much interest in the United States. In part, hard rock had once again outmoded Our Lady Peace's sound, with acts such as Creed and Staind ushering in a period of bleak and moody, ballad-oriented hard rock.

Our Lady Peace resurfaced on American radio in 2002 with the minor hit "Somewhere Out There" from the album *Gravity*. A lush midtempo ballad, "Somewhere Out There" aimed at reaching pop audiences. Critics assailed the album for its bland hard rock, which belied the initial promise of the band.

Though, for the most part, hailed by reviewers for its smart and infectious style of hard rock, sustained commercial success eluded Our Lady Peace in the 1990s.

SELECTIVE DISCOGRAPHY: *Naveed* (Sony, 1995); *Clumsy* (Sony, 1997); *Happiness Is Not a Fish That You Can Catch* (Sony, 1999); *Spiritual Machines* (Sony, 2001); *Gravity* (Columbia, 2002).

SCOTT TRIBBLE

OUTKAST

Formed: 1992, Atlanta, Georgia

Members: Andre "Dre"/"Andre 3000" Benjamin (Andre Lauren Benjamin, born Atlanta, Georgia, 27 May 1975); Antwan "Big Boi" Patton (Antwan Andre Patton, born Savannah, Georgia, 1 February 1975).

Genre: Rap

Best-selling album since 1990: *Stankonia* (2000)

Hit songs since 1990: "Ms. Jackson," "Rosa Parks," "The Whole World"

OutKast, the Atlanta-based rap group, is one of the most eclectic and original forces in hip-hop music. Although their music differs from prevailing hip-hop styles, it is as commercially successful as more formulaic efforts.

Andre "Dre" Benjamin and Antwan "Big Boi" Patton met as competing rappers in high school. They decided to team up and were soon discovered by the production team Organized Noize, an affiliation that facilitated their signing with LaFace Records. OutKast's debut album *Southernplayalisticadillacmuzik* (1994) revels in a casual, laid-back style, notable in the calm, funky pace of the lead single "Player's Ball." The album went platinum. The follow-up was the futuristic-sounding *ATLiens* (1996), whose biggest hit was "Elevators (Me & You)." It chronicles the group's ascendance with a sobering summation from Dre: "I live by the beat like you live check to check / If you don't move yo' feet then I don't eat, so we like neck to neck."

Dre and Big Boi began to individualize themselves as unique personalities. Dre dressed like a younger George Clinton. He often performed wearing wigs and an odd array of clothes, including skirts, and his subject matter was philosophical. Big Boi boasted a traditional hip-hop image of athletic gear and mainstream rhyme topics, including the travails of life in the ghetto. OutKast acknowledged these distinctions in the group's third album, *Aquemini* (1998). The title signifies an amalgam of Big Boi and Dre's astrological signs, Aquarius and Gemini respectively. OutKast began producing most of their own songs on this album, with Organized Noize assuming a supporting role. The effort received a rave review in *The Source* magazine, which hailed it as a hip-hop classic. The album includes the jazzy "SpottieOttieDopaliscious," the Clinton-featured

funk cut "Synthesizer," and a hard-core single with Raekwon, "Skew It on the Bar B." The raucous, folksy, and harmonica-assisted "Rosa Parks" brought controversy. Rosa Parks herself, a central figure in the U.S. civil rights movement, threatened to sue OutKast over the song's content. The case was dismissed in 1999.

After the turn of the millennium, Dre changed his name to "Andre 3000." OutKast released another major album, *Stankonia* (2000). The work is replete with a variety of sounds, from drum and bass on the political "B.O.B." (which stands for "Bombs over Baghdad"), to salsa on "Humble Mumble," to funk on "Ms. Jackson," a soulful, organ-enhanced apology to an ex-girlfriend's mother. "Ms. Jackson" became a number one pop single. By 2001, OutKast had amassed enough hits to release a greatest hits collection: *Big Boi and Dre Present . . . OutKast.* A new song on the album, "The Whole World," featuring rapper Killer Mike, is a sweeping statement on the testy state of the universe. In 2002, OutKast won two Grammy Awards for Best Rap Performance by a Duo or Group for "Ms. Jackson" and Best Rap Album for *Stankonia.* In a significant event for the group, OutKast was nominated in the broad categories Album of the Year and Record of the Year. In 2003, they won another Grammy Award for Best Rap Performance by a Duo or Group for the song "The Whole World." They also began work on a double album, *Speakerbox/The Love Below.*

SELECTIVE DISCOGRAPHY: *Southernplayalisticadillac-muzik* (LaFace, 1994); *ATLiens* (LaFace, 1996); *Aquemini* (LaFace, 1998); *Stankonia* (LaFace, 2000); *Big Boi and Dre Present . . . OutKast* (LaFace, 2001).

DARA COOK

P | p
P

JIMMY PAGE

Born: James Patrick Page; Heston, Middlesex, England, 9 January 1944

Genre: Rock

Best-selling album since 1990: *No Quarter: Jimmy Page and Robert Plant Unledded* (1994)

One of the most illustrious guitar players in all of rock music, Jimmy Page became famous when the band that he created, Led Zeppelin, went on to become the consummate hard rock group of the 1970s. Before their breakup in 1980, Page's leadership, remarkable guitar skills, and imaginative song writing enabled Led Zeppelin to sell more than 100 million records. The respect he receives because of his association with Led Zeppelin has afforded Page leeway in exploring various musical dalliances through the years, although none of them has taken firm root.

The Led Zeppelin Years

Page received a Spanish guitar when he was thirteen, became inspired by rock icon Elvis Presley, and by the time he turned fifteen had already gained a reputation around London as a talented guitarist. He was asked to join a touring rock group, Neil Christian & the Crusaders; however, the travel began making him ill so he left after two years and decided to study painting at an art college. Soon after, inspired by London's burgeoning 1960s blues/rock scene, Page dropped out of art school. He learned to read music and became a notable studio musician who was comfortable playing pop, jazz, country, rockabilly, and especially the blues. Some of the artists whose records he played on included the Rolling Stones, the Who, Tom Jones, Donovan, and the Kinks.

In 1966 the Yardbirds, who had already replaced guitarist Eric Clapton with Jeff Beck, asked Page to join, and he accepted the offer. The Yardbirds were just beginning to tap into the potential of having both Beck and Page when Beck quit. Page took over the guitar duties, but the Yardbirds broke up in 1968 with concert obligations unfulfilled. Page quickly comprised a band called the New Yardbirds that included bassist John Paul Jones, drummer John Bonham, and an unheard-of singer named Robert Plant, and finished the concert tour. Afterward, they renamed the group Led Zeppelin. The name derives from a nasty remark by drummer Keith Moon of the British band, the Who, wherein he said that the band "would sink like a lead balloon." Led Zeppelin proceeded to record nine monumentally successful albums.

Originally a strictly blues-influenced band, Led Zeppelin added a heavy, louder style known later as hard rock or heavy metal. Other bands used their blueprint to create various brands of heavy metal rock, but no one found as much variety in the genre as Led Zeppelin. Page experimented with different guitar tunings and added elements of jazz in addition to ethnic folk sounds such as Indian, Arabic, and Celtic. Some of their hits included "Stairway to Heaven," "Over the Hills and Far Away," and "Whole Lotta Love." In 2000 the cable music channel VH1 compiled a list of the 100 Greatest Hard Rock Artists and Led Zeppelin was named number one. They also earned a rowdy reputation, and eventually drugs and other excesses took their toll. Page became hooked on heroin in the band's last ragged years and in 1980 Bonham died of

| Task Brasil

While on tour in Brazil promoting the album *No Quarter* (1994), Page witnessed a small civil war taking place within view of his hotel room window. He was awestruck by the suffering, particularly that of the street children. In an effort to help, he donated over 130,000 pounds to Task Brasil, a U.S. nonprofit organization designed to provide unfortunate Brazilian children, often homeless, with the attention and love that they need. Task Brasil used the donation to build a house affectionately called "Casa Jimmy," in which children could live in a safe environment. Page continues to work with Task Brasil, organizing fundraising activities such as auctions of rock memorabilia and performing concerts on behalf of the organization.

alcoholism. Led Zeppelin disbanded two months later. Despondent, Page quit playing guitar for more than a year.

Guest Guitar God

Page emerged in 1982 to compose the soundtrack to the movie *Death Wish II*. He was also a guest at various concerts and fundraisers, sharing the stage a few times with Britain's two other guitar legends, Clapton and Beck. In a 1985 concert for the human rights cause, Live Aid, the three remaining Led Zeppelin members thrilled the music world by reuniting briefly, with pop superstar Phil Collins on drums, at a stadium performance in Philadelphia, Pennsylvania.

In 1984 Page formed the Firm with singer Paul Rodgers of the group Bad Company. The Firm released two moderately strong selling albums before disbanding in 1986. Further fueling hopes of a Led Zeppelin reunion, Page performed with Plant, Jones, and John Bonham's son, Jason, on drums at New York's Madison Square Garden in 1988 to celebrate Atlantic Records' twenty-fifth anniversary. Page also appeared on Plant's solo album, *Now & Zen* (1988), and Plant returned the favor by singing "The Only One" on Page's first solo effort, *Outrider* (1988).

In 1990 the news that Page was planning a full-scale project with Plant buoyed hopes that Led Zeppelin was reforming. However, the project fell through so Page joined with singer David Coverdale, formerly of Deep Purple, to release *Coverdale/Page* (1993). The album, which sounds similar to Led Zeppelin's early work, clearly displays Page's trademark strength of creating funky rock riffs and winding guitar solos. The album sold moderately well but a large-scale promotional tour was cancelled and the two never recorded another album.

The next year, Page and Plant finally came together, without bassist Jones, to release an acoustic collection of songs, *No Quarter: Jimmy Page and Robert Plant Unledded* (1994), which MTV brought into their popular rock acoustic venue, *Unplugged*. The album contains three new releases and several Led Zeppelin songs, although it bypasses many of their most popular releases. *No Quarter* combines their rock/blues influence with a Middle Eastern flavor to create what was described as a "world" music sound. Backing Page instrumentally is a Moroccan/Egyptian ensemble and, on a few songs, the London Symphony Orchestra. While it was not the kind of reunion that Led Zeppelin fans had wished for, the album sold over 1 million copies and spawned a sold-out world tour. One of the album's highlights is a new version of the majestic "Kashmir." In 1998 Page reworked the song yet again in collaboration with rap artist Sean "Puff Daddy" Combs, successfully combining rap and rock music into the movie soundtrack hit "Come with Me" from the film *Godzilla* (1998).

In 1995 Led Zeppelin was inducted into the Rock and Roll Hall of Fame. Neil Young and Joe Perry and Steven Tyler of Aerosmith joined Page and Plant on stage for a raucous jam at the induction festivities. This was the second induction for Page, as the Yardbirds were honored in 1992.

Page combined with Plant again on a much-hyped collection of new songs, *Walking into Clarksdale* (1998). Unfortunately, the album neither grabbed new listeners' attention nor inspired Led Zeppelin fans, who had all but given up on a true reunion of the legendary band. *Walking into Clarksdale* sold poorly and Page went off to guest with the hard rock group the Black Crowes. These young rockers seemed to bring out the best in Page. He played ferocious guitar on their songs as the Black Crowes roared back with renderings of Led Zeppelin material. A live album, *Live at the Greek* (2000), resulted. Page continued to tour with the Black Crowes in 2001, but a back injury forced him to bow out midway through. Page owns his own recording studio and continues to record and tour. Due to his ample body of work as a studio musician, numerous compilation albums featuring his playing keep cropping up. In addition, he is an active fundraiser for the organization Task Brasil.

With a sleepy, self-satisfied expression, confidently grooving on the music's beat, his guitar slung low below the hip, few performers look more comfortable on a rock stage than Jimmy Page. His agile guitar skills have long been the benchmark for what being a rock guitarist entails. The scant efforts spent by Page toward a pure solo career in favor of collaborating probably echo back to his early musical roots as a noteworthy studio musician.

SELECTIVE DISCOGRAPHY: *Outrider* (Geffen, 1988); *Before the Balloon Went Up* (Dressed to Kill, 1998); *Rock and Roll Highway* (Thunderbolt, 2000); *Bury the Axe* (Dressed to Kill, 2002). **With the Black Crowes:** *Live at the Greek* (TVT, 2000). **With David Coverdale:** *Coverdale/Page* (A&M, 1993). **With the Firm:** *The Firm* (Atlantic, 1985); *Mean Business* (Atlantic, 1986). **With Robert Plant:** *No Quarter: Jimmy Page and Robert Plant Unledded* (Atlantic, 1994); *Walking into Clarksdale* (Atlantic, 1998). **Soundtracks:** *Death Wish I* (1974); *Death Wish II* (Swan Song, 1982); *Death Wish III* (1985); *Godzilla* (Sony, 1998).

BIBLIOGRAPHY: T. Horkins, *Led Zeppelin* (New York, 1998); S. Davis, *Hammer of the Gods* (New York, 2001); R. Cole with R. Trubo, *Stairway to Heaven: Led Zeppelin Uncensored* (New York, 2002).

DONALD LOWE

BRAD PAISLEY

Born: Glen Dale, West Virginia, 28 October 1972

Genre: Country

Best-selling album since 1990: *Part II* (2001)

Hit songs since 1990: "He Didn't Have to Be," "Me Neither"

With his easygoing manner and all-American good looks, Brad Paisley represents the new breed of gentle country singer popular in the 1990s and 2000s. Like his contemporaries Tim McGraw and Kenny Chesney, Paisley comes across as loyal and steadfast—a sharp contrast to the hard-drinking, hell-raising country singers of the 1960s and 1970s. What saves Paisley from becoming another "hat act"—a sardonic term for country artists whose appeal derives from tight jeans and a cowboy hat—is his sensitive songwriting. On self-penned hits such as "He Didn't Have to Be" Paisley captures an honesty and directness that set him apart from other young performers. His songs of fatherhood and matrimonial loyalty are well conveyed by his attractive, if modest, voice and adept guitar playing.

Raised in the small West Virginia town of Glen Dale, Paisley received his first guitar, a present from his grandfather, at age eight. By his early teens he was performing regularly on "Jamboree USA," a weekly country radio program on WWVA in Wheeling, West Virginia. The experience led to steady work as an opening act for legendary country performers such as George Jones and Little Jimmy Dickens. While studying music administration at Nashville's Belmont University, Paisley secured a songwriting deal with EMI, a major music publishing company, and began issuing demo recordings of his own work. In 1999 he signed with Arista Records and released his debut, *Who Needs Pictures*, an assured album that provides a good indication of the range of his talents.

Comprised mostly of his own songs, *Who Needs Pictures* sports a well-rounded selection of material and styles. On the opening track, "Long Sermon," Paisley demonstrates his engaging, homespun sense of humor: "There ain't nothin' that'll test your faith / Like a long sermon on a pretty Sunday." Other songs, such as "It Never Woulda Worked Out Anyway," recall the up-tempo "western swing" sound popularized in the 1990s by country star George Strait. The lighthearted "Sleepin' on the Foldout" tells the story of a man forced by his wife to spend a night on the porch. For tough country singers of the past such as Jones, this punishment might have been the result of drinking, gambling, or philandering. In Paisley's case, the worst thing he has done is to clean fish instead of visiting his wife's family. More henpecked than devilish, Paisley imbues modern country music with a refreshing dose of sweetness. Perhaps the album's finest moment is the hit "He Didn't Have to Be," in which Paisley's character moves from reminiscing fondly about his stepfather to thinking about his own fatherhood: "I hope I'm at least half the dad / That he didn't have to be." The song, sentimental but never cloying, points to Paisley's talent for expressing small details that speak to the broader passages of everyday life.

Now a bona fide country star, Paisley released his follow-up album, *Part II*, in 2001. On the whole *Part II* is as strong as its predecessor, although on certain tracks Paisley's emphasis on lyrical cuteness begins to sound hokey. On "Two People Fell in Love," for instance, he gets bogged down in trite details: "Right now at a picnic shelter down by Cain Creek / You'll find potato salad, hot dogs, and baked beans." On the other hand, the title track is one of his strongest efforts, a well-arranged ballad with a memorable theme built around sequels to popular Hollywood movies: "Why can't love be more like that / Where the best ones get a second chance." Paisley's voice has developed nicely, his lower range sounding deeper and more assured than on his debut. Like "The Nervous Breakdown" on his first album, *Part II* features an instrumental track, "Munster Rag," that showcases his nimble guitar playing. On this track, as well as "Too Country," a group performance with country legends Jones, Bill Anderson, and Buck Owens, Paisley proves that his youthful approach is balanced by a respect for the traditions of the past.

In contrast with country stars of previous generations, Brad Paisley avoids themes of heartbreak and loss, detailing instead with the joys and small disappointments of day-to-day life. At his best, Paisley evinces an honesty and sweetness that wrap his recordings with an appealing layer of humanity. If his music sometimes seems overly cheerful it is most likely because, as one of the most successful young performers in country music, Paisley has very little to complain about.

SELECTIVE DISCOGRAPHY: *Who Needs Pictures* (Arista, 1999); *Part II* (Arista, 2001).

WEBSITE: www.bradpaisley.com.

DAVID FREELAND

EDDIE PALMIERI

Born: Bronx, New York, 15 December 1936
Genre: Latin, Jazz, World
Best-selling album since 1990: *Obra Maestra* (2000)
Hit songs since 1990: "Muneca"

Eddie Palmieri was dubbed "the sun of Latin music" in the early 1970s for his searingly brilliant style, which fused advanced jazz ideas with New York–inflected Afro-Cuban rhythms. His musical star has shone brightly since childhood; he made a Carnegie Recital Hall debut on a classical piano piece at the age of eleven. Since the death of his colleague Tito Puente in 2000, Palmieri has reigned as the leading exponent of Latin jazz for serious listening and social dancing.

Cuban dance bands embraced modern jazz elements as early as the 1940s, when the Havana-born Mario Bauza mentored Dizzy Gillespie. Latin-influenced jazz was a staple of post–World War II ballrooms, succeeding the popular swing bands in several major cities of the United States. Palmieri's uncle Chino had a dance band in which Eddie had his first job as a teenage timbales player; his brother Charlie, older by nine years, was already a recognized Latin keyboardist and arranger by the mid-1950s, when Eddie entered the scene around New York's Palladium Theater in Spanish Harlem. His apprenticeship culminated in membership in the Tito Rodriguez Orchestra from 1958 to 1960.

In 1961 Eddie Palmieri introduced Conjunto La Perfecta, pitting two burly trombones against the precision of the traditional flute-led charanga band. He retained the dynamic lineup of piano, bass, timbales, clavé sticks, and congas with which Cuban music spins its compelling polyrhythms. The ensemble, built around the horn charts of the trombonist Barry Rogers, was scoffed at as elephantine (Charlie called it "the trombonga"), but La Perfecta re-charged urban Latin music for the 1960s.

Though Palmieri is deeply grounded by Afro-Cuban dance band traditions and Yoruba-derived rhythms, he admires Duke Ellington, Charlie Parker, Thelonious Monk, Miles Davis, McCoy Tyner, and jazz modernism in general; he chooses for his band musicians whose improvisational skills can stretch his challenging arrangements. Of the five La Perfecta albums, two are collaborations with innovative vibraphonist Cal Tjader; they are landmarks of Latin jazz that introduce production techniques their producer, Creed Taylor, marketed in the mid-1970s as "smooth jazz." Palmieri influenced jazz musicians such as Herbie Mann and colleagues such as Mongo Santamaria's arranger, Marty Sheller, and the Fania All-Stars composer/arranger/producer/bandleader Johnny Pacheco.

After La Perfecta dissolved in 1968, Palmieri concocted new combinations, most often playing piano in the center of jazz orchestra-sized ensembles. He has long been a talent scout, discovering vocalists and instrumentalists who have sustained strong careers, such as the singers Ishmael Quintana and Cheo Feliciano, the percussionists Nicky Marrerro and Giovanni Hidalgo, the bassists Andy Gonzalez and John Benitez, and the baritone saxophonist Ronnie Cuber. He can boast such crossover innovations as the edgy convergence of heated Latin music and black rhythm and blues of the band Harlem River Drive as documented on the album *Live at Sing-Sing* (1972).

He writes cutting melodies for horns and dark, edgy harmonies that suggest tension and stress; he was an early adapter of electric basses, electric pianos, and synthesizers, although after the mid-1980s he returned to less processed and/or amplified instrumentation. A small, wiry, talkative, intense figure, Palmieri excels at improvising dramatic, out-of-time introductions, breaks or codas in contrast to his players' fast, hot solos and the vivid, swirling ensemble passages he pens.

Palmieri won his first Grammy Award in the newly created Latin Record of the Year category in 1976, for the album *Sun of Latin Music* (1974). He protested the release of his next album, *Unfinished Masterpiece* (1976), but it, too, won a Grammy. Each of his next five albums, issued between 1978 and 1987, was a Grammy nominee, and in each he refined his recipe, adding or reshaping elements of rhythm and blues, avant garde jazz, a dialect from this or that outpost of the African diaspora, and Afro-Cuban music.

In the early 1980s Palmieri relocated to Puerto Rico, but found his Eddie Palmieri Orchestra excluded from the best bookings, despite Grammy wins in the category Best

| Palmieri Establishes Latin Jazz Grammy

In 1976, the year the Grammys first conferred an award for Best Latin Album, the honor went to Eddie Palmieri for *The Sun of Latin Music*. He won again the next year, for *Unfinished Masterpiece*. He also won Grammys in the strangely titled category "Best Tropical Performance" for *Palo Pa' Rumba* (1984), *Solito* (1985), and *La Verdad* (1988), and he has been nominated innumerable times, in both Latin, salsa, and jazz categories. But as a board member since 1993 of the National Academy of Recording Arts and Sciences, New York chapter, Palmieri argued that Latin jazz, the genuine hybrid, was no longer his alone, but rather a genre with much creativity and innovation deserving its own recognition. He was obviously persuasive; the first Grammy for "Best Latin Jazz Performance" for albums by solo artists, duos, or groups, vocal or instrumental (compilations not eligible) was presented in 1995 to Cuban-born, Miami-based trumpeter Arturo Sandoval's *Danzon*. Palmieri was a contender that year for his *Palmas* and again in 1996 for *Arete,* which was beaten out by *Antonio Brazileiro* (1995), the last album by Brazilian bossa nova star Antonio Carlos Jobim.

for Latin jazz band, in clavé (a fundamental beat of two and three strokes, in rapid succession). For a JVC Jazz Festival performance at Carnegie Hall in the late 1990s, he rewrote a concert by Wolfgang Amadeus Mozart for the combined forces of his band and Puente's. Their collaborative album, *Obra Maestra* (2000), an extravaganza featuring a twenty-six-piece all-star ensemble, was a Grammy winner for "Best Salsa Performance." It was also Tito Puente's last recording.

As younger Latin artists and audiences gravitate toward pop and disco dance styles and incorporate West Coast-Mexican influences, Palmieri asserts his jazz links with ensembles of excellent horn players such as the alto saxophonist Donald Harrison, the trumpeter Brian Lynch, and the trombonist Conrad Herwig, a lineup represented on several of his recordings of the 1990s. On *La Perfecta II* (2002), Palmieri revisited some of his 1960s breakthrough material, giving it subtle new gloss. His albums convey much of his energy, but his music is best experienced live.

Despite his originality, continued Grammy Awards recognition, the devotion of hard-core fans, the interest of more mainstream markets, his rigorous performance schedule, and his unrivaled claim of Latin jazz kingpin, Eddie Palmieri has not achieved household-name recognition or overwhelming records sales. But his restless creativity is well recognized for advancing the art and pleasures of Latin music

SELECTIVE DISCOGRAPHY: *Live at Sing-Sing* (Tico, 1972); *Unfinished Masterpiece* (Musical Production, 1979); *Sueno* (Intuition, 1982);); *La Verdad: The Truth* (Fania, 1987); *Salsa-Jazz-Descargas-Exploration* (Musical Productions, 1991); *EP* (Fania, 1993); *Palmas* (Elektra, 1993); *Palmieri and Tjader* (Tico, 1993); *The Sun of Latin Music* (Musical Production, 1995); *Arete* (RMM, 1995); *Live* (RMM, 1999); *La Perfecta II* (Nonesuch, 2002); *El Rumbero del Piano* (RMM, 1998); **With Tito Puente:** *Obra Maestra* (2000). **With Cal Tjader:** *El Sonido Nuevo: The New Soul Sound* (Verve, 1967).

HOWARD MANDEL

Tropical Latin Performance for *Palo Pa' Rumba* (1983) in 1984, *Solito* (1984) in 1985, and *La Verdad* (1987) in 1988. Returning to New York, he contracted with Nonesuch Records in 1990, hoping to reach beyond his urban Latin fan base to a sophisticated, adventurous record market. Though he retains his core listenership and enjoys nearly unanimous raves from the music press, Palmieri's Latin jazz has not achieved mainstream American acceptance comparable to reggae or Brazilian pop. His genre is ghettoized, as in the way it has been used to represent New York Latinos on film soundtracks for Brian DePalma's *Carlito's Way* (1993) and Spike Lee's *Crooklyn* (1994).

In the 1990s Palmieri promulgated his theory that Latin rhythms can be applied "scientifically" to many strains of composition from Western Classical tradition to good effect; to prove it he embarked on adaptations of Johann Sebastian Bach and Ludwig van Beethoven pieces

PANTERA

Formed: 1981, Dallas, Texas

Members: "Dimebag" (formerly "Diamond") Darrell Abbott, guitar (born Dallas, Texas, 20 August 1966); Vinnie Paul Abbott, drums (born Dallas, Texas, 11 March 1964); Philip Anselmo, vocals (born New Orleans, Louisiana, 30 June 1968); Rex "Rocker" Brown, bass (born Graham, Texas, 27 July 1964).

Genre: Heavy Metal, Rock

Best-selling album since 1990: *Vulgar Display of Power* (1992)

Hit songs since 1990: "Planet Caravan," "Cat Scratch Fever," "Revolution Is My Name"

One of the most intense metal bands to ever hit number one on *Billboard*'s album chart, Pantera became synonymous with the outer limits of rock aggression.

The group was formed by high school friends in Dallas. All the original members have remained except for vocalist Terry Glaze, who was replaced by David Peacock and finally Philip Anselmo, who joined in 1986. Pantera churned out a trio of clichéd metal albums from 1983 to 1985 whose only hints of future success came with Abbott's expert guitar solos.

Cowboys from Hell (1990) smartly avoids the gaudy quasi-Satanic imagery that typified the band's obscure 1980s output. With superb timing, they got the glam and big hair out of their system before they found fame. The album still contains some vestiges of 1980s excess, with Anselmo's voice at times rising to a shriek on the searing ballad "Cemetery Gates" and the apocalyptic "Shattered." But Anselmo's roaring vocals and the industrial-strength guitar and drum attack on "Psycho Holiday" and "The Art of Shredding" make it clear that this is no-hair band.

Vulgar Display of Power (1992) cemented Pantera's reputation as metal's rising stars, perhaps Metallica's heir apparent. The CD received virtually no airplay but caught on thanks to MTV, touring, and word-of-mouth. Speed metal "F***ing Hostile" is a half-sung, half-screamed polemic against religion and police who bust more tokers than muggers. Using two bass drums, Vinnie Paul Abbott creates a militaristic rhythmic blast that earned him the nickname "the Brick Wall."

By 1993 Pantera was a household name among headbangers, and with Metallica taking its time between albums, Pantera's emergence as a talented and uncompromising counterpart was welcome news to fans dismayed to see grunge grabbing the spotlight. *Far Beyond Driven* (1994) was a number one debut—the group had never even had an album in the Top 40 before. The group's high commercial watermark of the 1990s, it continues the group's trend toward bleaker, more antisocial themes. On "Good Friends and a Bottle of Pills," Anselmo languidly drawls a sordid tale of drug use and sex over jagged guitar riffs, while "Strength Beyond Strength" dramatizes a drug pusher's grandiose boasts. However, the album did mark the group's first foray onto mainstream radio, with their cover of the Black Sabbath ballad "Planet Caravan" reaching number twenty-one on *Billboard*'s Mainstream Rock Tracks chart.

Pantera eased off a bit for *The Great Southern Trendkill* (1996), which contains three ballads ("10's," "Floods," and "Suicide Note, Pt. 1"), but the predictability of the heavier songs makes this far less essential than previous 1990s efforts. In July 1996, Anselmo, who sang, "I've done it all but tap the vein" on *Far Beyond Driven*, collapsed after a heroin overdose and nearly died. However, he quit the drug cold turkey, surviving the harrowing withdrawal that accompanies the experience. After devoting time to side projects, Pantera scored an unexpected airplay hit in 1999 with its cover of Ted Nugent's "Cat Scratch Fever" for the *Detroit Rock City* soundtrack.

Pantera returned to its full-blast attack for *Reinventing the Steel* (2000), which made number four on the *Billboard 200*. The album shows a band content to churn out its trademark sound for longtime fans, without worrying about staying up-to-the-minute on alternative metal trends. After *Reinventing the Steel*, Pantera went on hiatus for a few years as members again returned to side projects. But they all insisted Pantera was still a going concern.

Pantera's ability to bridge 1980s guitar-hero riffing and 1990s mosh-pit headbanging helped keep metal alive and relevant during its mid-1990s slump and influenced alternative metal youngbloods like Tool and Korn.

SELECTIVE DISCOGRAPHY: *Cowboys from Hell* (Atlantic, 1990); *Vulgar Display of Power* (East West, 1992); *Far Beyond Driven* (East West, 1994); *Reinventing the Steel* (East West, 2000). **Soundtrack:** *Detroit Rock City* (Polygram, 1999).

RAMIRO BURR

PAPA ROACH

Formed: 1993, Vacaville, California

Members: Dave Buckner, drums (born Vacaville, California, 29 May 1976); Tobin Esperance, bass (born Vacaville, California, 14 November 1979); Jerry Horton, guitar (born Vacaville, California, 10 March 1975); Jacoby Shaddix, vocals (born Vacaville, California, 28 July 1976).

Genre: Nu-Metal, Rock

Best-selling album since 1990: *Infest* (2000)

Hit songs since 1990: "Last Resort," "She Loves Me Not," "Broken Home"

Packaging rap and hardcore-tinged rage into melodic pop structures made Papa Roach's brand of heavy metal stand out from contemporaries at the turn of the millennium. More immediate than plodding nu-metallers and more meaningful than posturing rap-rockers, the band's soaring anthems cathartically rallied millions of kids affected by the dissolution of the nuclear family. A decision to tackle more personal and adult topics by their third album, though, compromised Papa Roach's following.

During high school in the Northern California town of Vacaville, vocalist Jacoby Shaddix, guitarist Jerry Horton, drummer Dave Buckner, and bassist Will James formed Papa Roach in 1993. With San Francisco–based Faith No More's blend of progressive metal, funk, and rap as a primary influence, they developed a dedicated local following through explosive live performances and Shaddix's unpredictable, onstage behavior.

After self-producing and self-releasing two EPs, the band dismissed James due to his inability to commit to full time work with them. His replacement, Tobin Esperance, was a longtime roadie for the band. With this lineup they recorded their debut album, *Old Friends from Young Years* (1997), and released it on their own Onion Hardcore label. Tracks from the album ended up in heavy rotation on independent and college radio stations in the area, and the band was soon touring with up and coming aggressive rock acts such as Incubus, Powerman 5000, and Sevendust. The exposure eventually led to a deal with DreamWorks Records.

Sales of their major label debut *Infest* (2000) were modest in the first month, as was rock radio response for the lead single "Last Resort." Then in June, the "Last Resort" video became a staple on MTV's *Total Request Live*, a teen-targeted daily video countdown. The song's lyrics explicitly deal with a youth expressing suicidal tendencies that began after losing his mother. With rap-like verses "Would it be wrong / Would it be right / If I took my life tonight / Chances are that I might," and a fiery sing-along chorus, "'Cause I'm losing my sight / Losing my mind / Wish somebody would tell me I'm fine," it was a runaway hit. The band's candid darkness and empathy for dysfunctional adolescent situations garnered it a similar audience to Korn, whose gloomy terror had been balancing out the sugary pop on MTV's airwaves for the last couple of years. Though the album's next two singles "Broken Home" and "Between Angels and Insects" failed to match the success of "Last Resort," *Infest* sold 3 million copies.

During the group's multiplatinum run, front man Shaddix used the abbreviated name Coby Dick. He reverted back to his birth name Jacoby Shaddix prior to *Lovehatetragedy*'s 2002 release. The change was indicative of Papa Roach's new sound and lyrical approach. They chose to further downplay their already subtle rap tendencies and opted for more straightforward hard rock. Plus, Shaddix shifted the focus from teen angst to his own marital strife. The catchy "She Loves Me Not" was a successful first single, but the more mature direction was inherently less interesting to the legions of youth who identified with more adolescent topics. As a result, the album blended in with much of the current rock and failed to match the success of *Infest*.

Though not as wildly popular, for a brief time Papa Roach's unabashed dealings with childhood scars infiltrated American teens in the same way Korn, Linkin Park, and Eminem's music did.

SELECTIVE DISCOGRAPHY: *Old Friends from Young Years* (Onion Hardcore, 1997); *Infest* (DreamWorks, 2000); *Lovehatetragedy* (2002).

WEBSITES: www.paparoach.com; www.papa-roach.com.

DAVE POWERS

DOLLY PARTON

Born: Locust Ridge, Tennessee, 19 January 1946

Genre: Country

Best-selling album since 1990: *Eagle When She Flies* (1991)

Hit songs since 1990: "Eagle When She Flies," "Rockin' Years"

In many respects Dolly Parton is the quintessential country singer; her poor upbringing in the Smoky Mountains of Tennessee and subsequent rise to fame are the components of country legend. Over the years Parton has managed to retain the girlish innocence and sweet soprano voice that propelled her to stardom, even when her records veered toward glitzy overproduction. More than contemporaries such as Reba McEntire and Barbara Mandrell, Parton makes country stardom a personal statement, decorating herself with glittering rhinestones, towering blonde wigs, and pounds of makeup. At her core, however, Parton is still that simple mountain girl from Tennessee, and her best recordings reflect this contrast between wide-eyed child and knowing adult. While she moved away from a pure country sound in the late 1970s, devoting her energies to slick pop music, Parton returned to traditional country in the 1990s and produced some of the finest work of her career.

Country Beginnings and Pop Stardom

Born in the Tennessee mountain town of Locust Ridge, Parton is the fourth of twelve children. Her farmer parents, possessing little cash, paid the doctor who delivered her with cornmeal. As a child in the 1950s Parton sang on radio and television programs in nearby Knoxville. In 1966, at the age of twenty, she signed with Nashville-based Monument Records and recorded her first hit,

Dolly Parton [HARRINGTON/SUGAR HILL RECORDS]

"Dumb Blonde," the next year. Although the real-life Parton was crafty and intelligent, the sexy "Dumb Blonde" image stuck, informing the public's perception throughout her career. In the late 1960s she appeared on a television program with country star Porter Wagoner, with whom she enjoyed several duet hits.

Recording solo by the early 1970s, Parton created a remarkable series of country hits, many of which she wrote herself. Drawing upon her childhood experiences, Parton painted tender, loving portraits of her family in "Coat of Many Colors" (1971) and "My Tennessee Mountain Home" (1973). The former, one of her most beloved recordings, describes a coat her mother, too poor to afford clothes, stitched for her out of old rags. When she gets to school the other children laugh at her, even though in Parton's assessment, "I felt I was rich / And I told them of the love / my mama sewed in every stitch." The song, performed in Parton's bell-clear soprano, is a masterpiece of country sentiment, memorable for its ingenuous depth of feeling. Other songs of this period, such as the haunting

"Jolene" (1974), deal with adult themes of marital insecurity and jealousy. In 1977 Parton hit with "Here You Come Again," a glossy pop record that brought her new popularity with a mainstream audience.

Parton spent much of the 1980s cultivating her pop base and largely ignoring her longtime country fans, although her soulful work on *Trio* (1987), an album recorded with fellow singers Linda Ronstadt and Emmylou Harris, was a refreshing exception. During these years Parton also established a career as a movie actress, performing in the films *9 to 5* (1980), *The Best Little Whorehouse in Texas* (1982), and *Rhinestone* (1984). Always down-to-earth and cheerful, she exhibited a witty, self-deprecating sense of humor, telling interviewers, "I'm not offended by dumb blonde jokes because I know that I'm not dumb. I also know I'm not blonde."

Return to Country Roots

The 1990s witnessed Parton's gradual return to pure country music, a movement that began with the release of *White Limozeen* in 1989. Produced by country artist Ricky Skaggs, the album benefits from traditional country instrumentation of guitar, steel pedal, banjo, and fiddle, as well as Parton's renewed vocal commitment. *Eagle When She Flies* (1991) features the hit title song, an ode to female perseverance and strength: "She's a woman / She knows how to dish it out / Or take it all." *Slow Dancing with the Moon* (1993) is another highlight among Parton's early 1990s recordings. Critics hailed Parton for her childlike grace and simplicity on the expressive title track, her feathery voice supported by a restrained but powerful arrangement. Other songs, such as the lilting "I'll Make Your Bed," reveal a playful sensuality only hinted at in Parton's earlier work: "I'll love you to sleep at night, wake you with a kiss / things that I can't do, I swear you won't miss." Still, Parton's finest music of the 1990s was yet to come. In 1998 she recorded *Hungry Again* after spending time meditating and fasting in a remote mountain cabin. Composed entirely of her own material, the album finds Parton exploring a range of country music styles, from tough, 1950s-styled honky-tonk to religious gospel, with assurance and maturity.

The subtle, restrained sound and traditional country arrangements of *Hungry Again* paved the way for Parton's next release, *The Grass Is Blue* (1999). The album represents a bold artistic step for Parton in that it is her first recording of bluegrass, a traditional country music style characterized by fast banjo playing and tight vocal harmony. While bluegrass has a dedicated following, it is singularly out of place within the contemporary, pop-driven country music industry—an indication of just how much risk Parton was taking in recording the album.

To a greater extent than any of Parton's previous work, *The Grass Is Blue* speaks to her Appalachian childhood and formative musical influences, even when the material is not strictly bluegrass in nature. Beginning with a mournful fiddle solo, pop songwriter Billy Joel's "Travelin' Prayer" is refashioned as a deep bluegrass piece, with Parton sounding, critics noted, more relaxed and loose than she has in years. Approaching the song with power and soul, Parton ends by singing a high-pitched yodel. "Cash on the Barrelhead" is a deep country blues, while "Silver Dagger" conjures an air of mystery through potent use of lyrical imagery. Renouncing her true love for a life of celibacy, Parton's character describes the opposition of her mother: "In her right hand is a silver dagger / She says that I can't be your bride." The harrowing story digs into the dark history and superstition of Parton's mountain upbringing, revealing the mysterious, secretive woman who has always been there, hidden beneath the false eyelashes and layers of makeup. On the up-tempo "I'm Gonna Sleep with One Eye Open" she communicates with the trenchant precision of a blues singer, shouting with emotional urgency. Finally, Parton displays her mastery of gospel music on "I Am Ready," the album's closing track. In what critics describe as an expertly timed performance, Parton offers a powerful display of gospel *melisma*, a vocal technique in which multiple notes are sung within the same syllable. Brimming with freedom and release, *The Grass Is Blue* is further enlivened by the nimble banjo picking of Jim Mills.

Building upon the album's surprise popularity—it reached the Top 30 on the country album charts and also dented the pop charts—Parton quickly recorded two more bluegrass collections, *Little Sparrow* (2001) and *Halos & Horns* (2002). The latter contains a fine gospel version of rock group Led Zeppelin's 1970s hit, "Stairway to Heaven."

The homespun, traditional mountain woman and flamboyant Las Vegas–styled diva form equally important elements of Parton's musical personality. She is both the small-town girl dreaming of life in the big city and the glittering woman who is no longer sure of what she wants once she gets there. After years of pop stardom, Parton's renewed artistic fulfillment came through a return to her roots, allowing her to record the soulful bluegrass music closest to her heart.

SELECTIVE DISCOGRAPHY: *Hello, I'm Dolly* (Monument, 1967); *Coat of Many Colors* (RCA, 1971); *Jolene* (RCA, 1974); *Here You Come Again* (RCA, 1977); *Trio* (Warner Bros., 1987); *White Limozeen* (Columbia, 1989); *Eagle When She Flies* (Columbia, 1991); *Slow Dancing with the Moon* (Columbia, 1993); *Hungry Again* (Decca, 1998); *The Grass Is Blue* (Sugar Hill, 1999); *Little Sparrow* (Sugar Hill, 2001); *Halos & Horns* (Sugar Hill, 2002).

SELECTIVE FILMOGRAPHY: *9 to 5* (1980); *The Best Little Whorehouse in Texas* (1982); *Rhinestone* (1984); *Steel Magnolias* (1989); *Unlikely Angel* (1997).

BIBLIOGRAPHY: A. Nash, *Dolly: The Biography* (New York, 2003).

DAVID FREELAND

MANDY PATINKIN

Born: Mandel Patinkin; Chicago, Illinois, 30 November 1952

Genre: Vocal

Best-selling album since 1990: *Dress Casual* (1990)

Singer/actor Mandy Patinkin thrives on artistic challenges. The result is a cross-media career that has seen Patinkin create over thirty diverse film roles; perform in a broad range of stage musicals, classics, and contemporary comedies; and portray a doctor on a popular primetime television series. Wedged within this wide array of work are several solo recordings displaying what many critics feel Patinkin does best: sing.

Patinkin grew up in Chicago, and started singing at eight years old in the choir of the synagogue that his parents attended. He acted in local theater productions before leaving Chicago to attend the University of Kansas. Against his parents' wishes that he return home to work in the family scrap metal business, Patinkin transferred to New York City's prestigious performing arts college, the Juilliard School, in 1972. He left after two-and-a-half years to pursue a professional acting career. Although he had not focused on musical endeavors for several years, Patinkin was cast in the Broadway production of the musical *Evita* in 1979. He portrayed Che Guevara, the play's narrator, and won a Tony Award for Outstanding Featured Actor in a Musical.

This success led to a string of starring musical roles, and gained Patinkin a reputation as a showy, expressive performer whom some critics have lambasted for letting his song interpretations overshadow the music. His performances are memorable for their embellished physicality and stylized note phrasing. Patinkin has only had a few film roles that have utilized his singing, but his unique eccentricity informs all of his work whether he sings or not. His film portrayal of a Spanish swordsman on a revengeful quest in *The Princess Bride* (1987) proved unforgettable as millions of the film's viewers memorized Patinkin's phrasing of his characters' oft-repeated comic line, "Hello. My name is Inigo Montoyo. You killed my father, prepare to die." Moreover, vocally, he can be equally unforgettable. Patinkin contrasts a powerful yet tender tenor with a low baritone rumble, enabling him to cover a remarkable range of song styles. At times, he adds musical cries or yelps into his phrasing for interpretation.

His first solo recording, *Mandy Patinkin* (1989), displays an eclectic mix of music mostly from a concert repertoire titled *Dress Casual*, that later received a showing on Broadway. He followed with an ambitious thirty-one-song release, *Dress Casual* (1990), again displaying his voraciously daring musical approach. Yet, for all of Patinkin's panache, which recalls the style of singer Al Jolson, his concerts are marked by their simplicity. They include minimal staging, lighting or scenery and Patinkin is often casually clad in a sweater and sneakers.

Patinkin offers a more subtle side to his pure tenor in his next two recordings, *Experiment* (1994) and *Oscar & Steve* (1995). *Experiment* contains eighteen songs, including his rendition of Harry Chapin's, "Taxi," and the sky-high "Bring Him Home" from *Les Miserables*, which Patinkin handles masterfully. Patinkin is considered the foremost male interpreter of Stephen Sondheim's music and he exhibits that talent on *Oscar & Steve*. His exuberant stylings of Oscar Hammerstein's songs comprise the rest of the album.

The Yiddish-language *Mamaloshen* (1998) marked a return to Patinkin's flamboyant side. Patinkin did not speak a word of Yiddish until 1990. He learned the language on a promise to legendary theater producer, Joe Papp, who had long encouraged Patinkin to record the album, whose title means "mother tongue." *Mamaloshen* contains classic Yiddish songs in addition to some other interesting musical finagling: Yiddish versions of "The Hokey Pokey," "Take Me Out to the Ballgame," and "Supercalifragilisticexpialidocious"—from the film *Mary Poppins* (1964).

Patinkin won an Emmy Award in 1996 for his portrayal of Dr. Jeffrey Geiger on the popular television series *Chicago Hope*, but left the show having worked on it for only two years. He chose, instead, to spend more time with his wife and two sons who were located in New York. *Chicago Hope* was shot in Los Angeles. Later, he rejoined the show on a guest basis to continue portraying the humanistic Dr. Geiger on and off until the show's end in 1999.

He released a sixth solo album, *Kidults* (2001), a compilation of music appropriate for both children and adults. One of Broadway's newest stars, Kristin Chenoweth, joins him for three songs on the compilation of Broadway and pop songs. Patinkin paid a tribute to Sondheim with a live thirty-four-song concert recording of Sondheim songs, with *Sings Sondheim* (2002).

Patinkin keeps a busy concert schedule and maintains his presence as one of New York's busiest stage and film actors, choosing to perform in roles that allow him to explore his creativity. While it is always difficult to predict what his next musical move might encompass, Patinkin never seems to stray too far from a Sondheim melody or lyric.

SELECTIVE DISCOGRAPHY: *Mandy Patinkin* (Sony, 1989); *Dress Casual* (Sony, 1990); *Experiment* (Nonesuch, 1994); *Oscar & Steve* (Nonesuch, 1995); *Mamaloshen* (Nonesuch, 1998); *Kidults* (Nonesuch, 2001); *Sings Sondheim* (Nonesuch, 2002). **Broadway Cast Recordings:** *Evita* (MCA, 1979); *Sunday in the Park with George* (RCA, 1984).

SELECTIVE FILMOGRAPHY: *The Big Fix* (1978); *Yentl* (1983); *Daniel* (1983); *The Princess Bride* (1987); *Dick Tracy* (1990); *True Colors* (1991); *Music of Chance* (1993); *Men with Guns* (1998); *The Adventures of Elmo in Grouchland* (1999).

DONALD LOWE

LUCIANO PAVAROTTI

Born: Modena, Italy, 12 October 1935

Genre: Classical

Best-selling album since 1990: *Romantica: The Very Best of Luciano Pavarotti* (2002)

Hit songs since 1990: "Nessun dorma!" from Puccini's "Turandot"

Luciano Pavarotti is the most celebrated operatic tenor since Enrico Caruso. His name is a household word and is as adored and respected outside of the opera world as within it. Pavarotti's remarkable four-decade career has included spectacular triumphs at virtually every major opera house in the world. Through his many best-selling recordings and videos, his television and film appearances, and his eagerness to bring opera to a wider public by performing operatic arias in sold-out sports arenas and outdoor stadiums, Pavarotti has been heard by more people and has done more to promote interest in opera than any singer in the genre's history.

Tenor by Birth and Climb to the Top

Pavarotti was born on the outskirts of Modena, Italy. The doctor who delivered him is said to have declared upon hearing his first cry that he would grow up to be a tenor. No prediction could have been more pleasing to his father Fernando, a baker by trade but himself a tenor in the town's chorus. Young Pavarotti grew up listening to and mimicking his father's voice as well as his vast opera recording collection. By the age of four, it is said that Pavarotti would regularly climb up on the kitchen table and sing "La donna è mobile" from Verdi's *Rigoletto*.

The young Pavarotti joined his father in singing in the town chorus and was soon studying with Arrigo Pola, and later with Ettore Campogralliani, who were the only voice teachers Pavarotti ever had. Though all agreed that Pavarotti's voice showed remarkable promise, he chose to attend teaching college rather than pursue a career in the arduous and uncertain world of professional singing.

A superb soccer player in his youth, Pavarotti worked as an elementary school gym and math teacher and an insurance salesman for a living while continuing to pursue his love of singing on the side. In 1961 Pavarotti won the Achille Peri Prize, which opened the door for him to make his professional debut as Rodolfo in Puccini's *La bohème* first in Reggio Emilia, and then one by one across the regional opera houses of Italy. Two years later, Pavarotti was in London as an understudy to his childhood idol Giuseppe di Stefano for the same role at Covent Garden, stepping in when di Stefano became ill both for the per-

formance and for a "Live from the Palladeum" television broadcast that was seen by 15 million British viewers.

Conductor Richard Bonynge soon engaged Pavarotti to sing alongside his wife, soprano Joan Sutherland, which began an extraordinary nearly thirty-year partnership that lasted until Sutherland's retirement in 1990. Bonynge had been systematically revitalizing demanding *bel canto* coloratura roles for Sutherland and Pavarotti's high range, sterling clarity, and rich timbre were the perfect complement to Sutherland's highly ornamented stratospheric singing. The couple's appearances in Donezetti's *La Fille du Régiment* at Covent Garden in 1966, at La Scala in Milan in 1968, and at the Metropolitan Opera in New York in 1972 were nothing less than sensations for Pavarotti. For the first time in the modern era, a tenor sang out in full voice and with complete confidence and beauty all nine of the high C's in the treacherous aria "Pour mon âme, quel destin!" Even the most finicky opera lovers were stunned and gave the tenor explosive, rock concert-like ovations while dubbing Pavarotti the "King of the High C's."

Reaching a Wider Public and Using Amplification

The Pavarotti phenomenon reached its artistic peak in the mid-1970s, when the Teflon tenor seemed to be virtually invincible in his consistent ability to produce glorious sounds while enthusiastically walking the tenor tightrope in sold-out opera houses in more than sixty countries. In an effort to accommodate the myriad fans that wanted a live Pavarotti encounter, Pavarotti began performing recitals and concerts in front of huge audiences in concert halls, arenas, city squares, stadiums, and parks. In 1980 more than 200,000 people attended Pavarotti's concert performance of *Rigoletto* in New York's Central Park and in 1991 more than 250,000 British Pavarotti enthusiasts—including Prince Charles and Princess Diana—stood out in the rain in London's Hyde Park to hear him. In 1986 Pavarotti traveled to China to sing *La bohème* and performed a televised concert in the Great Hall of the People in Beijing that was seen by more than 100 million Chinese viewers. More than half a million people jammed into Central Park to hear Pavarotti sing a 1993 concert that was televised live via satellite across the world.

The downside of these constant outdoor concerts and arena appearances became Pavarotti's increasing dependence on amplification as his voice began to wane in intensity and range. These shortcomings could be compensated for through clever sound mixing and Pavarotti began curtailing his appearances in staged operas and legitimate concert halls. When he did agree to appear in unamplified venues, cancellations became frequent and vocal problems began to emerge. Many of the same audiences who had so adored him as the "King of the High C's" were quick to turn on Pavarotti when he would crack a high note or when his diminished natural projection was such that he was barely audible above an orchestra.

At the 1990 World Cup of soccer in Rome, Pavarotti and his colleague and nearest tenor rival Plácido Domingo gave their colleague José Carreras a triumphant welcome back in a live televised outdoor concert following Carreras's dramatic recovery from leukemia. The resulting recording and video, called *The Three Tenors,* became an international cultural phenomenon that has been widely repeated, emulated, and even parodied.

In 1992 Pavarotti and several rock and pop artists redefined crossover by giving a massive outdoor concert for charity in his hometown of Modena. Called "Pavarotti & Friends," Sting, Zucchero, Lucia Dalla, the Neville Brothers, Aaron Neville, Suzanne Vega, Mike Oldfield, Brian May, and Bob Geldof performed both pop and classical music individually and with each other. The concert included Pavarotti and Sting singing a duet of Franck's "Panis angelicus" and the entire group joining Pavarotti in a sing-along finale of "La donna . . . mobile." Purists balked, but the resulting video and compact disc were enormously successful and Pavarotti & Friends became a regular event, attracting some of the biggest names in the music business. Princess Diana attended the 1995 concert for the children of Bosnia, which featured U2's Bono and the Edge along with U2 producer and the Velvet Underground's Brian Eno, Meat Loaf, Michael Bolton, and Dolores O'Riordon of the Cranberries. The event culminated with a Bolton-dominated "Nessun dorma!" sing-along finale. The 1996 "War Child" concert attracted Eric Clapton, Elton John, Liza Minnelli, Joan Osborne, and Sheryl Crow, and featured a sing-along finale of John's "Live Like Horses."

By the 1998 concert for the children of Liberia, pop music producer Phil Ramone began producing the music and film director Spike Lee began directing the films of the Pavarotti & Friends concerts. The Liberian benefit included Celine Dion, the Spice Girls, Jon Bon Jovi, Natalie Cole, the Corrs, Vanessa Williams, Trisha Yearwood, and Stevie Wonder. Wonder wrote a song for the occasion, "Peace Wanted Just to Be Free," which he sang in duet with Pavarotti as a finale to the proceedings. The 1999 concert to benefit Guatemala and Kosovo featured Mariah Carey, Joe Cocker, Gloria Estefan, B.B. King, Boyzone, Ricky Martin, and Lionel Richie. In some truly unusual moments, Pavarotti even provided improvisational humming alongside of King in "The Thrill Is Gone" and provided the hook for a Ritchie-led "We Are the World" finale. His Holiness the Dalai Lama of Tibet attended the 2000 benefit for Cambodia and Tibet, which included the Eurythmics, Tracy Chapman, Savage Garden, George

Michael, Enrique Iglesias, and an "All You Need Is Love" sing-along finale.

Perhaps to complement such eclectic extravaganzas, Pavarotti did occasionally acquiesce to take on new artistic challenges late in his career. In 1991, for instance, Pavarotti sang his first ever performances of Verdi's *Otello,* the crown jewel of dramatic Italian tenor roles that would have been an enormous challenge for Pavarotti, a lyric tenor, to take on even in his prime. The occasion was the retirement of longtime Chicago Symphony Orchestra music director Sir Georg Solti, and concert performances took place in Orchestra Hall in Chicago and Carnegie Hall in New York, which were recorded live for compact disc release. The recorded results are mediocre, at best, and in live performance there were moments of near disaster. Though Pavarotti had hoped to one day perform *Otello* in the opera house, his vocal problems with the role kept that from occurring.

Pavarotti's highly anticipated formal retirement from operatic performance was to have been another dramatic tenor role—Puccini's *Tosca*—at the Met in 2002, but it never came to be. The tenor sang the dress rehearsal but cancelled the performance mere hours before he was to go on. His manager begged Pavarotti, who said he was suffering from the flu, to at least show up to take a bow for those who had paid as much as $1,800 a seat to hear his final operatic performance, but Pavarotti refused. Pavarotti will turn seventy in 2005, and in 2002 jokingly announced that as of that milestone birthday he would no longer be singing, even in the shower. Yet Pavarotti's father sang well into his eighties, and cynics point out that a few more high C's may well be squeezed out of him beyond that date with enough public demand, financial incentive, and, of course, amplification.

SELECTIVE DISCOGRAPHY: Giordano, *Andrea Chénier* (Decca re-release, 1984); Donizetti, *Lucia di Lammermoor* (Decca re-release, 1985); Donizetti, *L'elisir d'amore* (Deutsche Grammaphon, 1990); *O Holy Night* (Decca re-release, 1990); *O Sole Mio* (Decca re-release, 1990); *Passione* (Decca re-release, 1990); *Pavarotti at Carnegie Hall* (Decca re-release, 1990); *Volare* (Decca re-release, 1990); Boito, *Mefistofele* (Decca re-release, 1990); Donizetti, *L'elisir d'amore* (Decca re-release, 1990); Donizetti, *La Fille du Régiment* (Decca re-release, 1990); Mascagni, *Cavelleria Rusticana/Leoncavallo/ Pagliacci* (Decca re-release, 1990); Puccini, *La bohème* (Decca re-release, 1990); Puccini, *Madama Butterfly* (Decca re-release, 1990); Puccini, *Tosca* (Decca re-release, 1990); Puccini, *Turandot* (Decca re-release, 1990); Rossini, *Guglielmo Tell* (Decca re-release, 1990); Verdi, *Requiem* (Decca re-release, 1990); Verdi, *Il trovatore* (Decca re-release, 1990);

Verdi, *Rigoletto* (Decca re-release, 1990); *Verismo* (Decca re-release, 1990); Verdi, *La traviata* (Decca re-release, 1991); Verdi, *Otello* (Decca, 1991); *Pavarotti in Hyde Park* (Decca, 1992); Puccini, *Manon Lescaut* (Decca, 1993); Puccini, *Tosca* (RCA, 1993); Verdi, *Don Carlo* (EMI Classics, 1994); *Pavarotti in Central Park* (Decca, 1995); Puccini, *La bohème* (Opera D'Oro, 1997); Verdi, *I Lombardi* (Decca, 1997); Verdi, *Rigoletto* (Deutsche Grammaphon, 1998); *Live Recital* (Decca, 2001); Puccini, *Luisa Miller* (Decca re-release, 2001); Verdi, *Un ballo in maschera* (Decca re-release, 2001); *The Pavarotti Edition* (Decca, 2001). **With other artists:** *Pavarotti & Friends* (Decca, 1993); *Pavarotti & Friends 2* (Decca, 1995); *Pavarotti & Friends Together for the Children of Bosnia* (Decca, 1996); *Pavarotti & Friends for the Children of Liberia* (Decca, 1998); *Pavarotti & Friends for Guatemala and Kosovo* (Decca, 1999); *Pavarotti & Friends for Cambodia and Tibet* (Decca, 2000).

BIBLIOGRAPHY: L. Pavarotti with W. Wright, *Pavarotti: My Own Story* (New York, 1981); J. Kesting, *Luciano Pavarotti: The Myth of the Tenor* (London, 1992); L. Pavarotti with W. Wright, *Pavarotti: My World* (New York, 1995).

WEBSITE: lucianopavarotti.com.

DENNIS POLKOW

PAVEMENT

Formed: 1989, Stockton, California; Disbanded 1999

Members: Mark Ibold, bass (born 1967); Scott Kannberg, guitar (born 1967); Stephen Malkmus, songwriter, vocals, guitar (born Santa Monica, California, 30 May 1966); Bob Nastanovich, drums (born 1968); Steve West, drums (born 1967). Former member: Gary Young, percussion (born Marmaroneck, New York, c. 1954).

Genre: Rock

Best-selling album since 1990: *Crooked Rain, Crooked Rain* (1994)

Hit songs since 1990: "Cut Your Hair," "Gold Soundz," "Shady Lane"

The off-kilter harmonies and nearly discordant guitar playing of the band Pavement made a huge impact on the mid-1990s independent rock scene popular with college students and disaffected twentysomethings. Under the direction of singer and guitarist Steve Malkmus, the lyrics lean toward the episodic, elliptical, and purposefully obscure. Pavement songs start off in a nearly atonal manner and end in a paroxysm of guitar

squalls, with Malkmus occasionally screaming the vocals. The band enjoyed decent record sales on the Matador label, and broke up in 1999 to pursue other interests.

College dropouts Malkmus and Scott Kannberg formed Pavement as a studio project in 1989 and quickly added three members, Gary Young, Bob Nastanovich, and Mark Ibold, to round out the band; Young left in 1993 after their debut release *Slanted and Enchanted* (1992). Sam West replaced him. Critics and college indie rock fans praised the band for its free-for-all guitar playing and vague lyrics. *Crooked Rain, Crooked Rain* (1994) followed the debut, and it had a near-hit with the song "Cut Your Hair," in which Malkmus cautions a girl against cutting her hair to impress her no-good, punk boyfriend. The song, with its chorus of "oooh-ooh-oohs" in the background, is goofy and anthemic, yet it reached number ten on *Billboard*'s Modern Rock chart in 1994. The sprawling nature of the album, from the country rock of "Range Life" and the improvisational, jazzy, space-age tune "5 – 4 = Unity" exemplifies the band's modus operandi: Anything is fair game.

Malkmus told Greg Kot of the *Chicago Tribune*, "I never felt like we needed to reach 'the next level,' whatever that is. We're doing well at the level we're at." This principled defiance pervades Pavement's songwriting. Examples include the quirky, experimental, eighteen tracks of *Wowee Zowee* (1995), the melodic and engaging "Shady Lane" from *Brighten the Corners* (1997), and *Terror Twilight* (1999), the band's swan song, which surprisingly landed in the United Kingdom Top 20.

Pavement never aimed to "make it big" and they remained firmly within in the lo-fi independent rock world of the mid- to late 1990s. They tossed off songs with a casual but insouciant style, and not without making a mark on American underground music before their breakup.

SELECTIVE DISCOGRAPHY: *Slanted and Enchanted* (Matador, 1992); *Crooked Rain, Crooked Rain* (Matador, 1994); *Wowee Zowee* (Matador, 1995); *Brighten the Corners* (Matador, 1997); *Terror Twilight* (Matador, 1999).

CARRIE HAVRANEK

PEARL JAM

Formed: 1990, Seattle, Washington

Members: Jeff Ament, bass (born Big Sandy, Montana, 10 May 1963); Matt Cameron, drums (born San Diego, California, 28 November 1962); Stone Gossard, guitar (born Seattle, Washington, 20 July 1966); Mike McCready, guitar (born Seattle, Washington, 5 April 1965); Eddie Vedder, vocals (born Chicago, Illinois, 23 December 1964). Former members: Dave Abbruzzese, drums (born 17 May 1968); Jack Irons, drums; Dave Krusen, drums.

Genre: Rock

Best-selling album since 1990: *Ten* (1991)

Hit songs since 1990: "Alive," "Jeremy," "Better Man"

Pearl Jam is one of the most respected mainstream rock bands to have come out of the 1990s. Because the band was rooted in Seattle at the time grunge rock began to gel, Pearl Jam became known, after Nirvana, as the genre's most popular proponent. As the 1990s wore on the band evolved into a serious arena-rock act. Although their album sales dwindled over the years, nevertheless they retained a dedicated following and the esteem of their older rock peers.

Roots and Early Growth

Pearl Jam's roots date to the mid-1980s, when the bassist Jeff Ament and the guitarist Stone Gossard played in the Seattle band Green River. When Green River split in 1987, Ament and Gossard enlisted the singer Andrew Wood and formed Mother Love Bone. The group released their debut, *Apple*, on a major label in 1990. Wood died of a heroin overdose soon thereafter, and Ament and Gossard formed another band. This time they brought in the guitarist Mike McCready and the drummer Dave Krusen, and together they recorded a demo. Through a friend it wound up in the hands of the singer Eddie Vedder, who recorded his own lyrics and vocals over the tape and sent it from his home in San Diego back to Seattle. Vedder was quickly hired. In early 1991 the band (then named Mookie Blaylock, after a professional basketball player) began to tour and started recording a debut album *Ten*, which appeared later that year. During this time the group changed its name to Pearl Jam, reportedly in honor of a favorite recipe by Vedder's great-grandmother Pearl. (Vedder later said the band simply liked the word *pearl*.)

Big Seller

Ten became Pearl Jam's biggest-selling album, and it defined what came to be labeled "grunge." The music's monstrous guitar riffs mirrored 1970s arena rock, and the alienation expressed in Vedder's lyrics was rooted in the postpunk of the 1980s. The antirock attitude and Everyman fashion (flannel and jeans, usually) helped usher in "alternative rock," a newly coined niche in commercial radio that distanced itself from the formulaic and glossy pop metal of the previous decade. Unlike the raw, dense sound of their Seattle peers Alice in Chains and Soundgarden, Pearl Jam's debut featured songs with big, memorable choruses, perfect for radio, like "Alive" and "Jeremy." Their accessibility and earnestness made them one of the most popular band of the grunge era.

Spot Light | Pearl Jam Takes on Ticketmaster

A turning point in Pearl Jam's career came when it launched a legal battle against the ticketing giant Ticketmaster, which *Time* magazine ended up calling "rock 'n' roll's holy war." The band filed a memorandum with the Antitrust Division of the U.S. Department of Justice in May 1994. After buying Ticketron in 1991, Ticketmaster had become the largest distributor of tickets to major venues in cities nationwide. Pearl Jam charged that Ticketmaster was a monopoly and that the exorbitant service fees it tacked on to each ticket unnecessarily elevated concert prices. In defiance they canceled their 1994 summer tour to promote their album, *Vs.* Instead, Jeff Ament and Stone Gossard testified at hearings before the U.S. Congress in June. When touring commenced the following year, the band relied on smaller ticketing agencies, which forced them to play alternative venues not contracted with Ticketmaster. The tour was limited to only twelve cities, and skipped some major markets. The venues it did play were too small to accommodate fan demand. By then the Justice Department had decided that Ticketmaster did not pose a threat to the concert industry and cited several small competitors that were on the rise to give consumers a choice. Time has borne out Pearl Jam's claims, however. As of 2003 Ticketmaster remained the dominant ticketing agency for all major concerts. The three- to six-dollar service fees that Pearl Jam had initially complained about had risen to eight- to eleven-dollars per ticket.

Pearl Jam ended up relying on Ticketmaster for subsequent tours, but the public battle marked the beginning of the band's self-regulated retreat from the promotional spotlight. The band never appeared to promote a new album or tour on MTV and, except for occasional appearances on *The Late Show with David Letterman,* avoided talk shows and award ceremonies.

Even though *Ten* was a huge hit and immediately put the band in the public eye, it was still the sound of a band just learning how to make music together. The songwriting credits were strictly divided between Vedder's lyrics and Gossard's music. The two follow-up albums—*Vs.* (1993) and *Vitalogy* (1994)—were stronger and more eclectic, the results of a band whose members had grown comfortable with one another. *Vs.* is a grunge hallmark for its monster riffs and heartfelt soul. It is stocked with psychologically ripe anthems like "Go" and "Glorified G." The ballad "Elderly Woman Behind the Counter in a Small Town" became a staple of their live shows.

Vitalogy was the band's first album to follow the suicide death of Nirvana front man Kurt Cobain. Battling manic depression and ill prepared to become spokesperson for a generation, Cobain retreated into heroin addiction. While his songs drowned in self-pity, Pearl Jam's were driven by romantic fury, which Cobain routinely mocked. A much darker album than the previous two, *Vitalogy* mocks the commodification of celebrity by the media, as in "Not for You." "If you hate something / Don't you do it too," Vedder bellows. "Nothingman" is a plaintive ballad about a lost soul, whereas "Immortal" hints at the pedestal Cobain refused to sit on. The album also features experiments with sound collage ("Hey Foxymophandlemama, That's Me") and a paranoid rant accompanied by accordion ("Bugs"). The album's lasting power is thunderous rockers like "Corduroy," a bracing band mission statement, and "Whipping," which rails against the violence created by the prolife movement. By this time Vedder had become more than just another grunge howler. He was a steely singer who could convey complex emotions and subtlety. *Vitalogy* is Pearl Jam's epic statement, full of brooding beauty and blazing conviction.

Expanding Audience

As Pearl Jam continued to release albums, they started connecting with the baby-boom generation. Vedder was invited to sing at a concert honoring Bob Dylan, and he filled in for the late Jim Morrison when the Doors were inducted into the Rock and Roll Hall of Fame in 1993. He toured with Pete Townshend of the Who and Neil Finn of Crowded House and appeared on their respective live albums. A few months after Vedder inducted Neil Young into the Rock and Roll Hall of Fame in 1995, Pearl Jam and Young headed into a Seattle studio and recorded *Mirror Ball*, a collection of new Young songs backed by the band. Even as late as 2002, Pearl Jam opened special club dates for the Who.

By the late 1990s Pearl Jam had created a prolific body of work. Grunge had vanished from the spotlight. The best-selling groups of that era either had broken up or had members fall victim to drug-related deaths. Pearl Jam itself was

experiencing its share of diminishing sales—the band's 2000 album *Binaural* sold 715,000 copies whereas *Ten* had peaked with 8.9 million; despite this decline, the group showed no signs of falling apart. In fact, critics contended that the band had become more tightly knit. Unlike most bands they had undergone hardly any personnel changes except for a continually revolving drummer position, which rotated from Krusen to Matt Chamberlain to Dave Abbruzzese to Jack Irons to Matt Cameron.

No longer faced with the pressure of selling huge amounts of records, the band steadily released albums that were not experimental but were consistently strong collaborative efforts. Starting with *Vitalogy* in 1994 and continuing with *Riot Act* in 2002, Pearl Jam cemented its sound, which combined Vedder's abstract lyrics and dark vocal texture with Gossard's and McCready's compelling guitar arrangements, hooks, and monster grooves.

The band endured because they often took breathers for solo projects. In 1991 the entire band plus Soundgarden singer Chris Cornell recorded under the name Temple of the Dog for a tribute album memorializing Wood. Ament formed the band Three Fish and released two albums. McCready formed the Rockfords and released a single album; he also recorded with Layne Staley, the lead singer of Alice in Chains, under the name Mad Season. Vedder played drums on tour for Hovercraft, his wife's band, and also performed solo during political rallies for Ralph Nader, the Green Party presidential candidate in 2000. Gossard released his debut solo album, *Bayleaf*, in 2001.

Pearl Jam remained a top concert draw, routinely selling out tours in the United States and overseas. Bolstered by a loyal fan base, the band released seventy-two complete shows from its 2000 world tour. Each double- and triple-disc set documented a specific show and was sold at discount price. Fourteen of the shows ended up on the *Billboard* 200 charts. According to *Billboard*, the entire project sold 1.29 million copies. The band continued the practice for its 2003 world tour.

One major setback to their 2000 tour was the death of nine fans fatally crushed during a festival set in Roskilde, Denmark, on June 30, 2000. Pearl Jam was cleared of blame and later recorded the song "Love Boat Captain" to reach out to the families of the victims. The band vowed never to play festivals or to allow open floor seating at any of their shows.

Pearl Jam helped to define the grunge rock movement in the early 1990s and evolved into a tightly knit, successful arena rock group. Remaining together while other bands of their ilk fell apart, Pearl Jam took pains to sustain an audience and to demonstrate how a band with multiplatinum success can still put passion into its music.

SELECTIVE DISCOGRAPHY: *Ten* (Epic, 1991); *Vs.* (Epic, 1993); *Vitalogy* (Epic, 1994); *No Code* (Epic,

1996); *Yield* (Epic, 1998); *On Two Legs* (Epic, 1998); *Binaural* (Epic, 2000); *Riot Act* (Epic, 2002).

WEBSITE: www.pearljam.com.

MARK GUARINO

MURRAY PERAHIA

Born: New York, New York, 19 April 1947
Genre: Classical

Murray Perahia is one of the most accomplished pianists of his generation. During the 1990s, as piano recital series across the United States found it increasingly difficult to survive, Perahia was one of the few pianists who consistently managed to fill concert halls. His evolution as an artist has been steady, deliberate, and on his own terms.

Born in New York, Perahia began studying the piano at the age of three. At five he was studying with Jeanette Haien, who coached him through graduation from the High School of Performing Arts. He attended Mannes College of Music, graduating with degrees in conducting and composition, and studied piano privately with Mieczyslaw Horszowski and Artur Balsam.

Perahia was invited by the pianist Rudolf Serkin to the Marlboro Festival in Vermont, where he had the opportunity to work and perform with some of the biggest names in the classical music world—among them cellist Pablo Casals, Serkin, Alexander Schneider, and the Budapest String Quartet. For a year he was Serkin's teaching assistant at the Curtis Institute in Philadelphia.

In 1968 Perahia made his Carnegie Hall debut and in 1972 he won the prestigious Leeds International Piano Competition, which launched his international career. The prize came with numerous concert dates in prestigious venues, but Perahia turned down about half of them, saying that he really was not ready.

In 1973 he played his first concert at the Aldeburgh Festival, meeting and working with Benjamin Britten and Peter Pears, and accompanying Pears in lieder recitals. In 1975 he won the $50,000 Avery Fisher Prize. In the 1970s he also struck up a friendship with pianist Vladimir Horowitz, who had a profound impact on him.

In 1976 Perahia moved to London, and from 1981 to 1989, he served as co-artistic director of the Aldeburgh Festival, working with Oliver Knussen and Stuart Bedford. In 1990 his career suffered a setback when he got a paper cut on his right thumb. It became infected so he took antibiotics, which made him sick. When he stopped the drugs, his thumb swelled up, and doctors made him quit

playing the piano for four years. He used the time to study and analyze music, and, when he returned to performing, his musicianship had deepened.

At the beginning of his career Perahia was known for his mastery of piano color and his ability to create a multidimensional palette of sound. Unlike many pianists, he felt little need to perform everything, preferring to stick to the repertoire he felt he understood best. Mozart, Chopin, and Schubert were favorites. After his hiatus, however, he began to delve into heavier repertoire, and critics noted the extra heft. He also began exploring Bach seriously, recording all the keyboard concertos, the *Goldberg Variations* and the *English Suites*. His recording of the *Suites* earned him a Grammy Award for Best Instrumental Performance in 1998. His recording of the Chopin Ballades won him a Gramophone Award in 1995.

Perahia has recorded the complete Mozart, Beethoven, and Chopin concertos. His chamber-music recordings include a 1989 Grammy-winning disc of Bartok's Sonata for Percussion and Two Pianos with Sir Georg Solti. In 2000 he was named principal guest conductor of the Academy of St. Martin's in the Fields and performs with the group as conductor and soloist.

Perahia is not a virtuoso in the traditional sense, though he has plenty of technical fire. He is not an intellectual pianist in the mode of a Serkin or Alfred Brendel. And he is not a grand romantic in the tradition of Arthur Rubenstein. What he brings to the keyboard is a sense of poetry and a distinctive sound harnessed to a deep understanding of the music he chooses to perform. Impeccably tasteful and uncompromising, Perahia is nevertheless one of the world's most popular classical pianists.

SELECTIVE DISCOGRAPHY: *Bach: Goldberg Variations* (Sony, 2000); *Bach: English Suites, Nos. 1, 3, 5* (Sony, 1998); *Chopin: 4 Ballades* (Sony, 1995); *The Aldeburgh Recital* (Sony, 1991).

DOUGLAS MCLENNAN

ITZHAK PERLMAN

Born: Tel Aviv, Israel, 31 August 1945
Genre: Classical

Itzhak Perlman is the leading violinist of the late twentieth and early twenty-first centuries and one of the most recognized classical artists in the world. His international career has included performances with every major orchestra, and at every major classical festival and concert venue in the world, and his recordings and videos have been honored with the highest awards in the music business.

Itzhak Perlman [PETER ADAMIK/ANGEL RECORDS]

Born in Israel in 1945, Perlman received his early musical training in Tel Aviv. At the age of four he was struck with polio, which left him unable to walk unassisted. In 1958 he came to New York to study with Ivan Galamian and Dorothy Delay at the Juilliard School.

His first major attention came with a performance of "Flight of the Bumblebee" on *The Ed Sullivan Show* at the age of thirteen. A win at the prestigious Leventritt Competition in 1964 launched his international career. He received additional attention in the press when the rare Guarnerius del Gesu violin he had been loaned by Juilliard for the competition was stolen after the awards while he was backstage (the instrument was later recovered in a pawn shop).

In 1987 he accompanied the Israel Philharmonic on a historic tour to Warsaw and Budapest; it was the first performances by the orchestra in Eastern Bloc countries. This was followed by a visit with the orchestra to the Soviet Union in 1990. A documentary of this trip, *Perlman in Russia*, won a 1992 Emmy Award for Outstanding Classical Program in the Performing Arts, the first of four Emmys Perlman has won.

Perlman has performed and recorded with most of the leading musicians and orchestras of the day, including Isaac Stern, Yo-Yo Ma, Daniel Barenboim, Lynn Harrell, Leonard Bernstein, Jessye Norman, Zubin Mehta, and Seiji Ozawa. He has recorded all of the standard violin literature in more than 130 releases, and has won fifteen Grammy Awards, the first in 1977 for a recording of Vivaldi's *The Four Seasons*, and the fifteenth in 1995 for an album of American music featuring works by Leonard Bernstein, Samuel Barber, and Lukas Foss.

In 1995 in honor of his fiftieth birthday, a twenty-one-CD boxed set, *The Itzhak Perlman Collection*, was released featuring a "definitive" collection of violin music. The recordings feature a selection of major violin works of the baroque, classical, romantic and twentieth century, including chamber music and concertos.

Perlman has been a frequent performer on television—including several broadcasts of *Live from Lincoln Center* and the Public Broadcasting Service (PBS) specials *A Musical Toast* and *Mozart by the Masters*, both of which he hosted. He has been an occasional guest on *The Tonight Show*, *The David Letterman Show*, and *Sesame Street*. In 1994 he hosted a Three Tenors live broadcast from Dodger Stadium in Los Angeles.

In film, he collaborated with composer John Williams on Williams's Academy Award–winning score for Steven Spielberg's film *Schindler's List* (1993), performing all of the violin solos. The soundtrack from the movie was a best-seller.

Having conquered most of the challenges of the classical violin world, in the 1990s Perlman expanded his activities, performing with Klezmer bands in Mexico and at major North American music festivals. He recorded an album of Klezmer music, and a PBS special, *In the Fiddler's House*, about his adventures with Klezmer music, was filmed in Poland in 1995 and won an Emmy the following year.

With his wife Toby, in the mid-1990s he founded the Perlman Music Program in New York, which identifies young musicians ages eleven to eighteen and supports them with musical instruction. A film about Perlman's work at the school, *Fiddling for the Future*, won another Emmy in 1999.

Perlman also began to conduct, appearing in the late 1990s as conductor/soloist with the Chicago Symphony, the Philadelphia Orchestra, the Los Angeles Philharmonic Orchestra, and others. In 2001 he began an appointment as Principal Guest Conductor of the Detroit Symphony.

Among his many honors are Musical America's Musician of the Year (1980), the National Medal of Liberty (1986) presented by President Ronald Reagan, and the National Medal of Arts (2000) presented by President Bill Clinton.

Perlman's eloquence as a performer, his warm tactile musicianship, unerring sense of musicality, and expansive personality have attracted millions of fans. He is a big man physically, and he engulfs his instrument, making his violin playing seem easy. He is also an eloquent communicator and gifted teacher, both with a violin in his hands and without. He brings a curiosity to his work that shows in his playing and in his choice of projects, and he is a passionate advocate and spokesman for people with disabilities.

SELECTIVE DISCOGRAPHY: *The Itzhak Perlman Collection* (EMI, 1995); *The American Album* (EMI, 1995). **Soundtrack:** *Schindler's List* (MCA, 1993).

DOUGLAS MCLENNAN

THE PET SHOP BOYS

Formed: 1981, London, England

Members: Neil Tennant, vocals (born Gosforth, England, 10 July 1954); Chris Lowe, keyboards (born Blackpool, England, 4 October 1959).

Genre: Rock, Pop

Best-selling album since 1990: *Very* (1993)

Hit songs since 1990: "Can You Forgive Her," "Go West," "Absolutely Fabulous"

The Pet Shop Boys have spent almost two decades essentially exploring the possibilities of electro pop, a style that first emerged in the early 1980s but one that has served the duo well for most of their time together. Relying principally on a combination of synth riffs, drum-machine rhythms, and well-crafted vocals, they have consistently revealed that rare ability to produce original material with a strong pop ethos. Beneath the sugar-coated melodies and enticing dance-floor beats, the pair have offered an engaging and entertaining commentary on everyday life—from the vagaries of romance to the mysteries of sexual ambiguity, from the numbing banality of suburbia to the excitements of the metropolis.

Getting Started

Although the popular music journalist Neil Tennant and the architecture student Chris Lowe first met by chance in a hi-fi shop in 1981, it was two years before they truly embarked on their recording careers. Tennant took advantage of a New York trip to interview Sting to make contact with the disco producer Bobby "O" Orlando. After hearing a demo tape that Tennant and Lowe had put together, an impressed Orlando encouraged them to begin recording seriously.

At the time, pop music in the United Kingdom was undergoing some seismic shifts. The New Romantics and the emergence of MTV had returned glamour to center stage after the dark nihilism of punk; the synthesiser had temporarily sidelined the guitar, permitting bands like the Human League, Soft Cell, and Depeche Mode to apply the new technology in pursuit of chart success. The climate seemed right for the Pet Shop Boys to make their mark.

Yet their initial push proved fairly fruitless as "West End Girls" (1984) and "Opportunities (Let's Make Lots of Money)" (1985) failed to make an impression. But early disappointments were swept aside when, late in 1985, "West End Girls" was revamped and re-released to become the number one single in the United Kingdom, repeating the feat in the United States early the next year.

The remaining years of the 1980s saw the Pet Shop Boys visit the Top 10 in Britain routinely—"Suburbia," "It's a Sin," "What Have I Done to Deserve This," "Heart," and "So Hard" all enjoyed high sales and high placings. In the United States, if their success rate was lower, they nevertheless kept up their American profile with songs like "Opportunities" and "Always on My Mind."

Gathering a strong following both in the mainstream market and among gay fans—the group's determined unwillingness to reveal their sexual inclinations merely added to the appeal and the mystery—they also transcended their singles ascendancy by releasing albums: *Please* (1986), *Actually* (1987), and *Introspective* (1988), which won the accolades of critics.

Their rocketing profile led them to work closely with the divas Dusty Springfield and Liza Minnelli; Tennant also collaborated with Bernard Sumner of New Order, a band that had been a large influence on the Pet Shop Boys. Spanning the worlds between pop, indie, and the rising club culture, the Pet Shop Boys seemingly could do no wrong.

Ambitious Projects

By now Tennant and Lowe possessed the financial security and artistic confidence to pursue a range of ambitious projects. The album *Behavior* (1990) saw them jettison the superficial frivolities of their earlier work; "So Hard," "Being Boring," and "Jealousy" replaced exuberance with a more mature and melancholic approach.

But they never plowed the same furrow for very long, and, even when they attempted surprising arrangements, which recalled the excesses of Euro disco, the Pet Shop Boys merely attracted critical comment on their ability to deliver the ironic without blowing their credibility.

They continued these unlikely pursuits when the album *Very* (1993) spawned a number two U.K. hit—a cover of the Village People's "Go West"—and their image, in stage shows and videos, became increasingly outrageous. As concerned with artistic style as they were with musical merit, the group worked alongside the acclaimed British filmmaker Derek Jarman on their occasional but invariably lavish live productions.

Yet their extended run of British success was not mirrored in the United States. Short of single entries, the critically acclaimed *Very* barely cracked the Top 20 in

America. Meanwhile, in 1994, the group took part in the Stonewall Equality shows at the Albert Hall in London, joining Elton John, Sting, and others and, in part, answering criticisms that they had not shown sufficient support for gay issues. That same year, "Absolutely Fabulous," a tribute to the U.K. television comedy series, also enjoyed British Top 10 status.

No new material emerged until 1996, when *Bilingual* grasped the vogue for Latin rhythms and granted the duo a further U.K. smash in "Se A Vide E (That's the Way Life Is)." Tennant was also pursuing a solo project, overseeing an album of songs by the late British songwriter/playwright Noel Coward. The resulting collection, *20th Century Blues* (1998), gathered stars like the Divine Comedy and Marianne Faithfull and stressed the Pet Shop Boys' interest in the theatrical tradition.

The album *Nightlife* (1999) included a major club hit in "New York City Boy." On the strength of renewed American interest, the Pet Shop Boys toured the United States for the first time in eight years. Yet their main concern, as the decade drew to close, focused on a project for the stage. Working alongside the playwright Jonathan Harvey, they penned the songs for a show called *Closer to Heaven*, which enjoyed a West End run during most of 2001.

The busy pair still had time to record and release a further album of their own in spring 2002—*Release*, featuring guitar contributions from ex-Smiths Johnny Marr and a Lennon/McCartney-like track in "I Get Along." The project that proved that their vibrant brand of pop retained an enduring attraction.

Much analyzed but often evasive in their interviews, the Pet Shop Boys have developed a unique aura, built on a Midas-like touch as recording artists but further stimulated by their other creative statements: the clothes they wear, the stage postures they assume, and the images they present on video.

Camp, kitsch, very English, witty, and *postmodern* are among the adjectives that have been applied to the phenomenon of Neil Tennant and Chris Lowe. Nonetheless, despite the visual and psychological games they have played, they remain, primarily, tunesmiths and craftsmen in the great Tin Pan Alley tradition.

SELECTIVE DISCOGRAPHY: *Please* (EMI America, 1986); *Actually* (EMI America, 1987); *Introspective* (EMI America, 1988); *Behavior* (EMI America, 1990); *Discography: The Complete Singles Collection* (EMI America, 1991); *Very* (Capitol, 1993); *Bilingual* (Sire, 1996); *Nightlife* (Sire 1999); *Closer to Heaven* (featuring the Original Cast) (Sony, 2002); *Release* (Parlophone, 2002).

BIBLIOGRAPHY: C. Heath, *Literally* (London, 1992); P. Docherty and T. White (eds.), *Design for Performance: Diaghilev to the Pet Shop Boys* (London, 1996).

WEBSITE: www.petshopboys.net.

SIMON WARNER

BERNADETTE PETERS

Born: Bernadette Lazzara; Queens, New York, 28 February 1948
Genre: Vocal
Best-selling album since 1990: *I'll Be Your Baby Tonight* (1996)

Bernadette Peters combines remarkable singing skills and hair-triggered comic timing with a sultry sexuality to make her one of music's most unforgettable stars. A throwback to the days when performers could do it all—sing, dance, and act—Peters is as equally comfortable on a Broadway stage as she is on a movie set. She has placed more prominence on her recording career since the 1990s.

Urged into the arts by her working-class parents, Peters began performing at the age of three and was a veteran of several plays and television programs, including *The Horn & Hardart Children's Hour* and *Name That Tune*, before she was teenager. Her mother, concerned that their family's surname, Lazzara, would limit the performer to ethnic roles, changed it to Peters when she was ten. The name was derived from her father's first name. Shortly after, Peters began landing major roles in regional and touring stage productions, generally in musicals. After time off to attend a private high school, Peters returned to show business and hit the ground running. She was cast in numerous Broadway and off-Broadway shows, garnered several awards and enough visibility for a viable attempt at the big screen. She moved to Hollywood and immediately received accolades for performances in several supporting roles, including a memorable turn as a naïve secretary in *The Longest Yard* (1974). She teamed with comedian Steve Martin in leading roles for two films: *The Jerk* (1979) and an avant-garde musical, *Pennies from Heaven* (1981). While critics had misgivings about both films, her performances were highly acclaimed. She returned to Broadway the following year and began adeptly juggling Tony Award–winning success in shows such as Andrew Lloyd Webber's *Song and Dance* and Stephen Sondheim's *Sunday in the Park with George* amid an ongoing television and film career.

While performing in the Broadway show *The Goodbye Girl*, a stage remake of Neil Simon's hit film of the

Bernadette Peters [FLROOZ ZAHEDI/ANGEL RECORDS]

eral humorous dispatches characteristic of the pouty-styled performer.

Peters won her second Tony Award for Best Actress in a Musical (the first was from *Song and Dance* in 1985) when she returned to Broadway in a revival of Irving Berlin's *Annie Get Your Gun* in 1999. She followed that with more movie roles and Emmy-nominated guest appearances on the television sitcom *Ally McBeal* before recording *Bernadette Peters Loves Rodgers and Hammerstein* (2002). Although she is more closely associated with the work of Sondheim, this thirteen-song album serves as her tribute to what many critics consider the greatest songwriting team in Broadway musical history.

In March 2003 Peters began performances on Broadway in the revival of the musical *Gypsy*. In *Gypsy*, she embarked on one of American theater's supreme female musical roles, Rose, the meddling stage mother of two daughters in a traveling vaudeville troupe. The performance earned her a Tony award nomination for Best Actress in a Musical.

Peters's achievements in film, in television, and as one of Broadway's most prolific performers have probably distracted her from maintaining the kind of recording career that someone of her talent warrants.

SELECTIVE DISCOGRAPHY: *Bernadette* (MCA 1992); *I'll Be Your Baby Tonight* (Angel Classics, 1996); *Sondheim, Etc.* (Angel Classics, 1997); *Bernadette Peters Loves Rodgers and Hammerstein* (Angel Classics, 2002). **Broadway Cast Recordings:** *Sunday in the Park with George* (RCA, 1984); *Into the Woods* (RCA, 1988); *Annie Get Your Gun* (Angel Classics, 1999).

SELECTIVE FILMOGRAPHY: *The Longest Yard* (1974); *The Jerk* (1979); *Pennies from Heaven* (1981); *Heart Beeps* (1981); *Slaves of New York* (1989); *Pink Cadillac* (1989); *Cinderella* (1997); *Prince Charming* (2001); *Let It Snow* (2001); *Bobbies Girl* (2002); *It Runs in the Family* (2003).

DONALD LOWE

same name, Peters released *Bernadette* (1992). The album contains a collection of thirteen previously released songs from her debut album, *Bernadette Peters* (1980), and *Now Playing* (1981). It features little of the Broadway fare that fans recognize her for in favor of an eclectic mix of country ballads and period rock styles. It does feature her signature, "Broadway Baby" sung in Peters's distinctive lisp.

Peters's voice is lilting, often with a seductive rasp on the back end of notes. She can power songs forward in a soprano belt or make them tenderly balance to-and-fro on the thin edge of sound and silence. Her Grammy-nominated release, *I'll Be Your Baby Tonight*, (1996) contains an assortment of songs from many popular artists, including Bob Dylan who wrote the album's title song. Peters chooses to give the Dylan classic a strong blues touch. The album also contains songs from such noted musicians as Sam Cooke, the Beatles, Billy Joel, Lyle Lovett, and Eric Clapton, among others. Also included are sprinklings of Broadway music including Sondheim's poignant "No One Is Alone." Peters injects *I'll Be Your Baby Tonight* with her strong acting and interpretive skills making all the songs seem uniquely hers.

In 1997 Peters recorded a fifteen-song live album of her first concert at Carnegie Hall, *Sondheim, Etc.* (1997), which was a benefit for the Gay Men's Health Crisis. The album contains mostly Sondheim songs and features sev-

TOM PETTY AND THE HEARTBREAKERS

Formed: 1974, Gainesville, Florida

Members: Ron Blair, bass (born Macon, Georgia, 16 September 1952); Mike Campbell, lead guitar (born Gainesville, Florida, 1 February 1954); Steve Ferrone, drums (born Brighton, England, 25 April 1950); Tom Petty, lead vocals, guitar (born Gainesville, Florida, 20 October 1953); Benmont Tench, keyboards (born Gainesville, Florida, 7 September 1954). Former members: Howard (Howie) Epstein, bass (born Milwaukee, Wisconsin, 21 July

1955; died Santa Fe, New Mexico, 23 February 2003); Stan Lynch, drums (born Gainesville, Florida, 21 May 1955).

Genre: Rock

Best-selling album since 1990: *Tom Petty and the Heartbreaker's Greatest Hits* (1993)

Hit songs since 1990: "Learning to Fly," "Mary Jane's Last Dance," "Free Girl Now"

Tom Petty and the Heartbreakers have managed to achieve longevity in the notoriously fickle rock music business without ever reinventing themselves. Instead, they have relied on strong songwriting, a myriad of musical influences, and an unaffected approach to produce top-selling albums and an extensive list of hit singles. Although the band's leader, Tom Petty, has embarked on solo ventures and other members of the group have worked on projects outside of the Heartbreakers, they have remained a cohesive group with minimal personnel changes since emerging in 1976. Tom Petty and the Heartbreakers earned a reputation for stubbornly standing up for themselves whenever they have felt threatened professionally or artistically.

Learning to Fly from Gainesville

The son of an insurance salesman in Gainesville, Florida, Tom Petty began playing in an assortment of bands as a teenager. He was a big fan of the Beatles and was inspired early on, when at the age of eleven he met Elvis Presley. He left school at seventeen to join a band called Mudcrutch with guitarist Mike Campbell and keyboardist Benmont Tench. After exhausting all local venues, Mudcrutch left for Los Angeles in search of a record deal. The band broke up, but Shelter Records, a label cofounded by the singer/songwriter Leon Russell, showed interest in Petty as a solo artist. Petty received the opportunity to write songs alongside Russell, gaining important experience while also jamming with other bands. Meanwhile, Campbell and Tench formed a group with other Gainesville-bred musicians, drummer Stan Lynch and bass player Ron Blair.

Now a seasoned singer/songwriter with a record deal, Petty rejoined his former mates, and they decided to let him front the band. Their first album, *Tom Petty and the Heartbreakers* (1976), featured ten short, hard-hitting songs that quickly arrived at their raw musical essence. Because of the album's vibrant energy, many people mistook the band as part of the surging "new wave" rock scene from England. While America was slow to catch on to Tom Petty and the Heartbreakers, England fell in love with them. The single "Breakdown" from their debut helped them gain popularity, and by the time their triumphant

third album, *Damn the Torpedoes* (1979), was released, the band had begun playing stadium-size concert venues and enjoying superstardom. *Damn the Torpedoes* followed a stormy chapter of legal entanglements for the band as they adamantly fought the forced transfer of their song copyrights and royalties after the conglomerate MCA purchased Shelter Records. They doggedly stood their ground, even declaring bankruptcy, before a judge ruled in their favor. *Damn the Torpedoes* contains nine songs, six of which gained major radio airplay. The album features some of their signature songs, such as "Refugee," "Don't Do Me Like That," "Even the Losers," and "Here Comes My Girl."

Tom Petty and the Heartbreakers, led by the straightforward charm of Petty, built on their image as no-frills musical craftsmen by racking up hit after hit in their ensuing albums throughout the 1980s. Critics referred to them as America's most famous garage band. The band's intelligent blending of various musical styles, particularly 1960s folk, enabled them to create a unique brand of catchy heartland rock. The Byrds, the Rolling Stones, and Bob Dylan were influences as were blues, southern, and even psychedelic rock. Petty's expressive vocal work manifests a pleasing nasal sincerity, a more musical version of Dylan's voice. Petty's appearance—long blond hair parted down the middle in a 1970s-style—has never changed. Tom Petty and the Heartbreakers' material is often playful and sometimes political, but it is always lyrically straightforward and guitar-led. Campbell's rhythm and solo guitar work adroitly balances between pop jingle-jangle and dirty hard rock. Other hits from the 1980s include "Woman in Love," "You Got Lucky," "Waiting," and "Don't Come Around Here No More."

In 1988 Petty took time off from the Heartbreakers to be the youngest member of the Traveling Wilburys, a supergroup consisting of like-minded old pros Roy Orbison, Bob Dylan, George Harrison, and Jeff Lynne. They were a novelty group with fake names all ending in Wilbury—Petty was Charlie T. Jr. Wilbury—but their music was for real. The Traveling Wilburys won a 1990 Grammy for Best Rock Performance by a Group. Petty's two-album dalliance as a Wilbury gave him impetus to record a solo album. He released *Full Moon Fever* (1989), which went triple platinum and produced three hit singles: "Free Fallin'," "Runnin' Down a Dream," and his signature anthem, "I Won't Back Down." Campbell played guitar and helped produce the album.

Together Forever

Although the Heartbreakers were initially upset with Petty's recording on his own, they continued as a group and released *Into the Great Wide Open* (1991). The album features two more hits, "Learning to Fly" and "Into the Great Wide Open," and kept the band on its sure-footed

Spot Light | Petty's Many Battles

Tom Petty and the Heartbreakers have always been a band of unbending convictions—artistic, political, and personal. After their victory over MCA Records for copyrights and royalties in 1978, the band girded for another battle with MCA in 1981, when the record company tried to raise album prices of their third release, *Hard Promises,* from $8.98 to $9.98. Tom Petty publicly decried the change, encouraging fans to complain and threatening to retitle the album *$8.98.* The record company lowered the price. In 1987, he fought and won his case against a tire company that used a song that sounded like one of Petty's. He forced the 2000 presidential campaign of George W. Bush to stop using his song "I Won't Back Down" in their rallies. Petty constantly battles concert promoters over the price of tickets in an effort to keep them affordable. The high cost of food, souvenirs, and parking at his concerts alarms him, too. He refuses corporate sponsorship and shuns limousines. Petty was reportedly delighted when the title track of his album, *The Last DJ* (2002), which protests the death of free-form radio, was banned on many radio stations.

creative force within the band. Additionally, he developed into a well-respected music industry producer who helped to revive the careers of singer/songwriters John Prine and Carlene Carter. The Heartbreakers fired Epstein before the summer 2002 tour, citing Epstein's unmanageable personal habits as the reason. Blair returned as his replacement. On February 23, 2003, Epstein died of a heroin overdose.

After *Wildflowers* Petty announced that he would never record again without the rest of the band. They released their twelfth album, *Echo* (1999), a success that contained another hit single: this time a frolicking rocker, "Free Girl Now." In that same year, Tom Petty and the Heartbreakers received a star on the Hollywood Walk of Fame. In 2001, millions of TV viewers watched as they performed a somber, memorable version of Petty's solo hit, "I Won't Back Down," on the entertainment industry-sponsored fundraiser, *A Tribute to Heroes,* which benefited the victims of the September 11, 2001, terrorist attacks. In 2002 Tom Petty and the Heartbreakers were inducted into the Rock and Roll Hall of Fame.

Throughout their career, Tom Petty and the Heartbreakers have done their best to stand up for the common person, often railing against rising ticket and album prices. The 2002 studio release, *The Last DJ* (2002), a concept album, exemplified Petty's disgust with corporate greed and the deterioration of pop music culture. The title song, which sardonically laments the replacement of radio disc jockeys with preselected musical formats, was banished by radio stations across the country. The lyrics mourn, "And there goes the last DJ, who says what he wants to say. . . ." Ever true to themselves, Tom Petty and the Heartbreakers have thrived on a rare combination of mass appeal and a stubborn stylistic commitment to say what they want to say.

SELECTIVE DISCOGRAPHY: *Tom Petty and the Heartbreakers* (Shelter, 1976); *You're Gonna Get It* (Shelter, 1978); *Damn the Torpedoes* (Backstreet, 1979); *Hard Promises* (Backstreet, 1981); *Long after Dark* (Backstreet, 1982); *Southern Accents* (MCA, 1985); *Let Me Up (I've Had Enough)* (MCA, 1987); *Into the Great Wide Open* (MCA, 1991); *Echo* (Warner Bros., 1999); *The Last DJ* (Warner Bros., 2002).

DONALD LOWE

path of success. Their first compilation album, *Tom Petty and the Heartbreakers, Greatest Hits* (1993), went quadruple-platinum. One of the two previously unreleased songs on the album, "Mary Jane's Last Dance," went on to win MTV's 1994 Best Male Video Award.

Petty released what is considered a second solo album, *Wild Flowers* (1994), although he was musically backed by nearly every member of the Heartbreakers. Like his first solo effort, *Wildflowers* went triple-platinum. It contains three radio staples, including "You Don't Know How It Feels," which brought Petty a 1995 Grammy Award for Best Male Rock Performance.

In 1994 drummer Stan Lynch left the band and veteran drummer Steve Ferrone replaced him. This marked only the second personnel change for the Heartbreakers. In 1982 Howie Epstein had replaced bassist Ron Blair. Epstein, who had worked with Dylan, Warren Zevon, and Stevie Nicks, immediately became a strong

LIZ PHAIR

Born: Elizabeth Clark Phair; New Haven, Connecticut, 17 April 1967

Genre: Rock

Best-selling album since 1990: *Whip-Smart* (1994)

Hit songs since 1990: "Never Said," "Supernova"

With a mix of the profane and the profound, Chicago singer/songwriter Liz Phair exploded onto the music scene in 1993 with one of the most critically acclaimed debut albums of all time, *Exile in Guyville*. A brash, lo-fidelity statement of sexual and emotional liberation, the album was hailed as a triumph for its feminist rock storytelling and was a bellwether for an emerging group of confessional, late 1990s female singer/songwriters.

Elizabeth Clark Phair was born in 1967 and adopted by medical researcher Dr. John Phair and teacher Nancy Phair, who moved the family to Winnetka, Illinois, in 1976. Growing up in the posh Chicago suburb, Phair studied piano and sought to further her arts education by majoring in art history at one of the Midwest's most liberal, arts-oriented colleges, Ohio's Oberlin College.

Phair got involved in the music scene at Oberlin, continuing her musical education during a stint in San Francisco with her college friend, Chris Brokaw, who later became the guitarist for the independent rock band Come. Brokaw prodded Phair to record some of the songs she had played for him, which the singer did in 1991 using a guitar and a simple four-track recording machine at her parent's home. Her two, fourteen-track "Girlysound Tapes" made their way to Brokaw, but also began circulating on the underground rock scene. After Come were signed to leading independent label Matador, Brokaw gave Phair's tapes to the label's co-founder, Gerard Cosloy, who signed Phair to a contract in 1992.

Phair left Winnetka for the grittier Wicker Park neighborhood in Chicago, home to a thriving visual and musical arts community. The singer was living off the money she earned selling her charcoal sketches when she teamed up with rising producer/drummer Brad Wood, bassist Leroy Bach, and guitarist Casey Rice to record her eighteen-track debut, *Exile in Guyville*, in late 1992.

Loosely intended as a track-for-track answer to the Rolling Stones' 1972 magnum blues opus, *Exile on Main Street*, Phair's album is a blast of fresh air aimed at knocking the stuffing out of the testosterone-heavy Wicker Park music scene, dubbed "guyville" in a song by Phair's pals in the Chicago band Urge Overkill.

Suffused with a lifetime of relationship issues, questions of self-worth, and playfully twisted perspectives on gender roles, critics labeled the album a lyrically blunt, sometimes profane, and at times confusing declaration of freedom and female empowerment. In interviews, Phair gamely played up the often contradictory roles of sex symbol, feminist godhead, and apathetic independent rocker. The music has a spontaneous quality, with songs such as "Shatter" slowly developing over a murky bed of low-burbling bass and acoustic guitar while other songs are built on eerie piano playing and abstract time signatures.

With a dull-edged, lower register voice that teeters on the brink of boredom, odd guitar turnings, and spare arrangements, the album is a triumph in understatement, leaving Phair to make the grand declarations with her lyrics, as in the folk rock "Divorce Song." Her voice quavering and sullen, Phair sings, "And when I asked for a separate room / It was late at night / And we'd been driving since noon."

The album became a sensation, with a hit college radio single in "Never Said" and an Album of the Year Award from New York's weekly the *Village Voice* and *Spin* magazine. The sole bump in Phair's road to stardom was her crippling stage fright, which led the already unkind Chicago press to lambaste her during her rare, and admittedly shaky, live appearances.

Phair released her second album, *Whip-Smart* (1994), which was given a major-label push thanks to Matador's recently signed distribution deal with Atlantic Records. The high-energy single "Supernova," with its slick production and classic rock guitar solo, signals that this album is not a mere sequel to Phair's debut. With cleaner, more precise production on the album as a whole, songs such as the acerbic opener "Chopsticks" and the ballad "Nashville" retain Phair's blunt lyrical honesty and quirky guitar-playing style.

Phair attempted to tour in support of the album, but canceled a string of dates due to nerves. The mini-album, *Juvenilia* (1995), features several re-recordings of songs from the "Girlysound Tape," as well as a cover of the Vapors' "Turning Japanese." The song "Rocket Boy" appears on the soundtrack to *Stealing Beauty* (1996) but for several years Phair retreated from the spotlight, marrying film editor Jim Staskausas in late 1995 and giving birth to a son, James Nicholas Staskausas, in December 1996.

The Girlysound Singer Grows Up

Phair began work on her third album with R.E.M. producer Scott Litt in 1996, eventually scrapping the sessions due to her dissatisfaction with their direction. When she finally emerged with *Whitechocolatespaceegg* (1998), a full five years after her lauded debut, Phair was a changed woman. In place of the lo-fidelity songs about casual sex and emotional turmoil were brighter, more pop rock-oriented songs, Rolling Stones–like blues rock and several songs about the joys of motherhood.

Despite the changes, there is still evidence of the old Phair including a jubilant song about being abused and liking it ("Johnny Feelgood"), a song about insane relatives ("Uncle Alvarez"), and a rollicking blues song ("Baby Got Going") that sexualizes a train ride. Rather than diminish the power of Phair's songwriting, the refreshingly straightforward pop, blues, and calypso-flavored arrangements bring focus to her quirky character studies ("Big Tall Man").

Phair overcame her stage fright and joined the all-female Lilith Fair tour in the summer of 1998 and launched a headlining tour that fall. She filmed a cameo in the movie "Cherish" (2002) and sang backup on Sheryl Crow's hit, "Soak up the Sun." By the end of 2002 Phair had nearly completed her first new album in five years, which was tentatively slated for a 2003 release.

With her confessional songwriting and home-schooled performance style, Phair brought intense focus to the already burgeoning mid-1990s Chicago music scene. Her blunt lyrics and hands-on approach to writing and producing her music also created an entrée for such strong female singer/songwriters as Alanis Morissette and Fiona Apple to reach a mass audience.

SELECTIVE DISCOGRAPHY: *Liz Phair* (Capitol, 2003); *Exile in Guyville* (Matador, 1993); *Whip-Smart* (Matador, 1994); *Juvenilia* EP (Matador, 1995); *Whitechocolatespaceegg* (Matador/Capitol, 1998).

GIL KAUFMAN

SAM PHILLIPS

Born: Leslie Phillips; East Hollywood, California, 28 June 1962

Genre: Rock

Best-selling album since 1990: *Martinis and Bikinis* (1994)

Hit songs since 1990: "I Need Love," "Baby, I Can't Please You," "Zero, Zero Zero"

Not to be confused with the legendary Sun Records producer Sam Phillips, singer/songwriter Sam Phillips got her start in contemporary Christian music. She quickly switched genres early in her career, with her first pop album *The Indescribable Wow* (1988). Critics acknowledge Phillips has never quite received the accolades and record sales that her talent as a songwriter merits. With a penchant for witty, cerebral love songs that recall 1960s pop influences such as the Beatles and the Beach Boys, Phillips is a psychologically incisive songwriter who knows that a touch of levity adds the right portion of irony.

Phillips grew up in Glendale, California, the second of three children. Her given name is Leslie, but her nickname was Sam. Phillips was exposed to myriad cultural

arts: painting, dancing, singing, and piano. By the time Phillips was a teenager she was writing her own songs. It proved an effective coping mechanism as she watched her parents' marriage dissolve. By the time Phillips was twenty-two, performing as Leslie Phillips, she was selling a quarter million copies with her gospel-flecked records.

Phillips fled the Christian scene, which she found too confining, and recorded two albums before her Grammy Award–nominated *Martinis and Bikinis* (1994). Hailed by critics as smart, consistently melodic, and at times surprising, the album is her most acclaimed release. It garnered a near hit with "I Need Love." With its insidious hook, and textbook verse-chorus-verse structure, it is one of her most structured pop songs. It is also one of her best, illustrating her world-weary wisdom and deft sense of wordplay. "I need love / Not some sentimental prison / I need God / Not the political church," she sings out in the chorus. Its weighty sentiments belied their light delivery and poet's attention to rhyme and rhythm.

Phillips's third album, the beautifully produced *Omnipop (It's Only a Flesh Wound Lambchop)* (1996), features collaborations with members of the band R.E.M. and witty stabs at the entertainment business and politics. After *Omnipop*, Phillips took a break and switched labels from Virgin Records to Nonesuch, a prestigious label known for its roster of high-caliber, left-of-center talent. Phillips released *Fandance* (2002), her most unadorned album.

Phillips is married to guitarist and producer T Bone Burnett, who produced her final Christian album, and has worked with her on her rock albums. She is the kind of artist whose music is too smart for commercial radio, but has found a home with fans of Triple A (Adult Album Alternative) radio.

SELECTIVE DISCOGRAPHY: *The Indescribable Wow* (Virgin, 1988); *Cruel Intentions* (Virgin, 1991); *Martinis and Bikinis* (Virgin 1994); *Omnipop (It's Only a Flesh Wound Lambchop)* (Virgin, 1996); *Fandance* (Nonesuch, 2001).

CARRIE HAVRANEK

PHISH

Formed: 1983, Burlington, Vermont

Members: Trey Anastasio, guitar, vocals (born Forth Worth, Texas, 30 September 1964); Jon Fishman, drums, vocals (born Philadelphia, Pennsylvania, 19 February 1965); Mike Gordon, bass, vocals (born Boston, Massachusetts, 3 June 1965); Page McConnell, keyboards (born Philadelphia, Pennsylvania, 17 May 1963). Former member: Jeff Holdsworth, guitar (born 14 November 1963).

Genre: Rock

Best-selling album since 1990: *A Live One* (1995)

Phish. L-R: Page McConnell, Trey Anastasio, Jon Fishman, Mike Gordon [AP/WIDE WORLD PHOTOS]

Phish is a phenomenon more than a band. It became a major stadium touring act by the late 1990s without having to make its way through conventional commercial channels like radio airplay, music videos, or corporate sponsorship. Instead, Phish blossomed in popularity due to grassroots organizing, a thriving Internet culture, and intensive touring. The band specializes in improvisational music and its lure is through its live shows more than its albums. Phish is the most successful band continuing the legacy of the Grateful Dead, the longtime San Francisco collective that groomed its own subculture from the late 1960s through the early 1990s. Phish helped

contribute to its own mythology through a number of hallmarks such as marathon live shows, unusual cover choices, Halloween shows featuring setlists covering entire albums by other artists, and a dress-wearing drummer known to "solo" by running a vacuum cleaner onstage. Phish announced a hiatus in 2000, but after a series of solo projects from its respective members, the band was back on the touring circuit in late 2002.

Guitarist Trey Anastasio, drummer Jon "Fish" Fishman, and bassist Mike Gordon met as freshmen at the University of Vermont. With sophomore and guitarist Jeff Holdsworth (who left soon after), the group played its first show at a basement party in 1983. Keyboardist Page

McConnell, a student at nearby Goddard College and already a fan of the band, joined two years later. After a few years honing their sound at college parties, the group recorded its debut *Junta* (1988) to sell as a cassette at live shows. They then started touring outside Vermont, playing up and down the East Coast and later in Colorado and Utah. After an album on an independent label, the group was signed to Elektra, a major label, in 1992.

Grassroots Success

The Internet factors heavily in Phish's success. The rate of Internet development parallels the band's growth. When phish.net was introduced the band's popularity boomed. The website allowed the band to connect directly with fans. The Internet fostered tape trading and allowed for band minutiae to be archived and discussed. A subculture surrounding the band was nurtured without the conventional aid of radio airplay or cable television. Phish's popularity grew under the radar of the mainstream media. By 1996 Phish was already playing arenas. That year the band grossed $17 million and played forty-nine U.S. shows, including its biggest show yet, to 75,000 people in Plattsburgh, New York, on the heels of their most popular album, *Billy Breathes* (1996).

Phish is intrinsically linked to the Grateful Dead, the pioneering psychedelic group known for improvisational music, a subculture of devoted fans, and a touring life that stretched for thirty years. When leader Jerry Garcia died in 1995, the Dead had been headlining arenas, their popularity mainly due to live shows since they never sold many records and had only one Top 10 hit. Although dozens of bands thrived in the wake of the Dead, none did so with as much success as Phish.

Like the Dead, Phish expertly juggles rock, jazz, country, funk, bluegrass, pop, and spacey instrumental ambience. The group brings these styles together with simple lyrics and uses their songs as frameworks for improvisation.

Aside from their originals, they actively school themselves in rock history, peppering setlists with covers. (In 1994 they began an annual Halloween tradition of covering entire albums.) Phish live shows are dance parties with long stretches of improvisation that often feature giant inflatable objects. The group fostered their popularity by sanctioning arena sections to be reserved for tape recording. During this time the band played large outdoor festivals and multiple nights at stadiums. For New Year's Eve 1999, they played a record six hours, from midnight to dawn at the Big Cypress Seminole Indian reservation in Florida.

Much of Phish's jamming spirit is fused into their studio albums, although *The Story of the Ghost* (1998) and *Farmhouse* (2000) are considered their most song-oriented

work yet. Phish made only one video ("Down with Disease") in the 1990s and never had a major hit song.

Ruling the Touring Industry

By the end of the decade, Phish had become one of the biggest names in rock. It grossed more than $61 million in ticket sales in 1999 and 2000. In 2000 the group announced a temporary hiatus due to exhaustion. Apparently there was one lesson from the Grateful Dead they did not want to learn: "A part of what killed Jerry Garcia was the bigness of what the Dead became. He couldn't stop touring. It's the antithesis of what I want to happen," McConnell told a reporter in 2003.

After releasing side projects over the course of a year, the group reunited in late 2002 and picked up where it left off, but at a decidedly slower pace and with ample room set aside for rest and solo interests.

Phish proved a rock band could reach monumental success by reaching out to fans directly, rather than through the established media. Its populist attitude spawned a subculture of devoted fans and made it phenomenally successful on tour. The band's prolific output of live albums, studio work, official bootlegs, and side projects helped whet fans' appetites, and the live shows redefined the psychedelic dance experience originally established by the Grateful Dead.

SELECTIVE DISCOGRAPHY: *Junta* (Phish, 1988); *A Picture of Nectar* (Elektra, 1992); *A Live One* (Elektra, 1995); *Billy Breathes* (Elektra, 1996); *The Story of the Ghost* (Elektra, 1998); *Farmhouse* (Elektra, 2000); *Round Room* (Elektra, 2002).

WEBSITES: www.phish.com; www.phish.net.

MARK GUARINO

PINK

Born: Alecia Moore; Doylestown, Pennsylvania, 8 September 1979

Genre: R&B, Pop, Rock

Best-selling album since 1990: *Missundaztood* (2001)

Hit songs since 1990: "Get the Party Started," "Just Like a Pill"

After her moderately successful debut album, R&B singer Pink somehow convinced her record company that her image was due for an overhaul. Though a new artist of Pink's caliber and age generally doesn't have much sway, the teenage singer prevailed, switching from the girlish R&B pop singer of *Can't Take Me Home* (2000), to the edgy, confessional pop rocker of

Missundaztood (2002), a transition that gained her a massive audience and indelible pop hits with songs such as "Get the Party Started" and "Just Like a Pill."

Pink was born Alecia Moore in Doylestown, Pennsylvania, a small town just outside of Philadelphia. At thirteen, the singer—who had adopted the childhood name Pink as a professional moniker either as a result of her dyed pink hair or a childhood incident in which she had her pants pulled down and her cheeks blushed pink—began rapping with her friend Skratch's local rap group, Schools of Thought.

After seeing the fourteen-year-old singer perform her weekly five-minute set at Philadelphia's Club Fever, an MCA Records representative tapped Pink to complete the line-up of the short-lived R&B girl group Basic Instinct. After the dissolution of the group, Pink was asked to complete the three-singer line up of yet another girl group, Choice, signed to LaFace Records.

Choice, too, would flounder, but the relationship with LaFace would not, eventually bringing Pink to the attention of the label's co-founder, "L.A." Reid, thanks to her songwriting skills. As a girl, Pink had been turned on to folksingers such as Bob Dylan and Don McLean by her guitar-playing father, James, and the songwriting bug had never left her. Reid paired Pink with producer Daryl Simmons, who asked the singer to write a chorus for the song "Just to Be Loving You," which rekindled Pink's interest in songwriting.

Reid signed Pink to LaFace as a solo artist and placed her in the studio with his partner, Babyface, and Simmons, who helped shape the singer's solo debut, *Can't Take Me Home*. The album, on which Pink co-wrote half the tracks, sold more than half a million copies thanks to the hit "There You Go," a brassy kiss-off to a former boyfriend. Songs such as "Split Personality" and "Hell Wit Ya" are classic late-1990s R&B, imbued with thumping machine-like beats, thick bass lines, and a sprinkling of hip-hop slang.

The album established Pink alongside such teenage pop singers as Britney Spears and Christina Aguilera, as well as edgier R&B artists such as TLC and Kelis, but, thanks to her cropped pink hair, tattoos, and street-inspired sartorial style, Pink's image was less refined than that of her peers. A mix of skateboarder, techno raver, and rocker, the somewhat tepid music on the album failed to live up to Pink's wild child image.

Teaming with Mya, Lil' Kim, and Christina Aguilera, Pink was part of one of the biggest worldwide pop hits of 2001, a remake of Patti LaBelle's "Lady Marmalade," from the soundtrack to the film *Moulin Rouge*. In the video, the quartet are dressed in risqué lingerie, with Pink emerging as the flashiest, most alluring member of the impromptu supergroup; the song won a 2002 Grammy Award for Best Pop Collaboration with Vocals. It was the beginning of a career makeover that would put Pink securely in her element.

Taking Control and Bursting into Superstardom

True to her rock roots, Pink teamed with her musical hero, ex-4 Non Blondes singer Linda Perry—who had a semi-hit with the 1993 rock song "What's Up?"—to write half of the songs for *Missundaztood*. The Perry-penned disco pop anthem, "Get the Party Started," exploded onto the charts upon its release. Even though critics called it pure ear candy, Pink's vocals are noticeably more raw and the production is more progressive than the songs on the singer's debut.

The songs on *Missundaztood* are noticeably more personal, none more so than the hit dance rock song "Don't Let Me Get Me." The litany of personality flaws and life lessons ("Everyday I fight a war against the mirror / Can't take the person staring back at me / I'm a hazard to myself") includes a line in which Pink complains about being compared to Britney Spears and a section in which she playfully chides boss Reid about his career advice ("L.A. told me / You'll be a pop star / All you have to change / Is everything you are.") With more rock guitars, guest appearances from Aerosmith singer Steven Tyler and Bon Jovi guitarist Richie Sambora, as well as songs about her struggles as a hell-raising child, *Missundaztood* clicked with fans, selling more than 4 million copies.

Pink celebrated her liberation by touring as an opening act for retro rocker Lenny Kravitz during the summer of 2000 and, in the fall, recording a song for the soundtrack to *Charlie's Angels: Full Throttle* (2003), as well as filming a cameo for the film.

At the tender age of nineteen, music industry newcomer Pink took hold of her career and stopped being the person her handlers told her to be. The results were a hit R&B/rock album and rebel girl image that connected with millions of fans and secured a second chapter to Alecia Moore's story.

SELECTIVE DISCOGRAPHY: *Can't Take Me Home* (Arista, 2000); *Missundaztood* (Arista, 2002).

WEBSITE: www.pinkspage.com.

GIL KAUFMAN

PINK FLOYD

Formed: 1965, London, England

Members: David Gilmour, guitar, vocals (born Cambridge, England, 6 March 1944); Nick Mason, drums (born Birmingham, England, 27 January 1945); Richard Wright, keyboards, vocals (born Surrey, England, 28 July 1945). Former members: Syd Barrett, guitar, vocals (born Cambridge, England, 6 January 1946); Roger Waters, bass, vocals (born Surrey, England, 6 September 1944).

Genre: Rock

Best-selling album since 1990: *Is There Anybody Out There? The Wall: Live 1980–1981* (2000)

One of the most popular progressive rock bands in the world, Pink Floyd has broken almost every convention in popular music. The band laces long, slow-paced rock compositions with distracting sound effects and pessimistic lyrics, an unusual recipe for success in the music business. Pink Floyd's most important albums, with a few exceptions, rarely produced hits, yet it has become one of the most enduring icons in rock and roll. Its signature recording, *Dark Side of the Moon* (1973), stayed on the *Billboard* 200 chart for more than fourteen years. The album continues to attract listeners: In 1991 *Dark Side of the Moon* returned to the charts in *Billboard*'s pop catalog category and remained in its Top 10 throughout the 1990s. Part of Pink Floyd's success is due to the fact that few bands sound better on expensive stereo equipment or better suit FM radio's album-oriented format (AOR). Although the band peaked in the 1970s, the 1990s were somewhat notable years for current and former members. Remaining members of the group released four albums and mounted a highly successful American tour. Songs like "Money," "Wish You Were Here," and "Comfortably Numb" remain staples on American classic rock radio stations.

Early Days: The Barrett Years

Pink Floyd formed in 1965 when Roger Waters, Nick Mason, and Richard Wright, architecture students in London, met guitarist Syd Barrett. The group began as an R&B cover band, but soon carved out distinctive psychedelic songs and lyrics that explored heightened states of perception and madness. Once the band hit the pub circuit in London, its shows featured slide shows and other lighting effects. Its earliest albums, *The Piper at the Gates of Dawn* (1967) and *A Saucerful of Secrets* (1968), reveal the creative influence of Barrett who wrote the band's early singles such as "Arnold Layne" and "See Emily Play."

The Peak Years

Barrett left Pink Floyd in 1968 when LSD use damaged his already fragile mental state. His absence would haunt the band for a decade. He was replaced with gui-

tarist David Gilmour. Barrett's loss changed the direction of the band away from tight psychedelic pop hits to its trademark dirges and conceptual albums. The group's first albums with Gilmour—*Ummagumma* (1969), *Atom Heart Mother* (1970), and *Meddle* (1971)—were uneven, though each album contains a handful of gems. *Dark Side of the Moon* (1973) brought the band recognition, particularly in the United States, and turned the group into progressive rock's first best-selling behemoth. A loosely organized concept album, the record comments pessimistically on modern stresses associated with time, money, war, and madness. The album also marks bassist Waters's emergence as the band's major creative force, though every group member gets composition credits for various tracks. *Dark Side of the Moon* also embodies Pink Floyd's mature sound: long, dour songs punctuated by sound effects, mumbling voices, and Gilmour's thundering guitar solos. "Money," the album's principal hit in 1973, has been on steady rotation on FM stations since the day it hit the charts. More than 30 million copies of the album have been sold, placing it among the top three best-selling albums in music history.

Following *Dark Side of the Moon*, Pink Floyd released a classic series of follow-up albums. *Wish You Were Here* (1975), a tribute to Barrett, *Animals* (1977), and *The Wall* (1979) all met with popular acclaim and were followed by sophisticated concerts that featured crashing airplanes, gigantic floating animals, and complex light shows. The band's fame reached its peak in the United States with the release of *The Wall* (1982), a film starring the Boomtown Rats' Bob Geldof. It is remarkable for its animated sequences and recreation of World War II–era London. Wright left the band shortly after the film's release, citing differences with Waters. Tensions between Waters and the rest of the group led to his quitting the band after the release of *The Final Cut* (1983). The remaining members of Pink Floyd released *A Momentary Lapse of Reason* (1987). Wright rejoined the band first as a contract player in 1987, and then as a full-time member in 1994.

The Quiet 1990s

In the 1990s the band released only one studio album, *The Division Bell* (1994), a largely unremarkable album that nonetheless reached the top spot in the charts in the first weeks of its release. Pink Floyd's music without Waters tends to be more ambient, up-tempo, and musical, whereas Waters's late work with Floyd and in his solo career has grown wordy and caustic.

The most notable Pink Floyd event of the 1990s was not an official Pink Floyd event. In 1990 Waters led an ensemble cast, including Sinéad O'Connor, Joni Mitchell, and Van Morrison, through a version of *The Wall* at the crumbling remains of the Berlin Wall. The event received worldwide attention. The original album traces the roots of a mental breakdown of a self-absorbed rock star who becomes metaphorically walled off from himself and his fans. Played in a completely different, arguably inappropriate, context, *The Wall—Live in Berlin* (1990), may be the strangest attack on political repression ever recorded.

Always the subject of urban myths, *Dark Side of the Moon* gained a strange notoriety in the 1990s when fans started playing it alongside *The Wizard of Oz*. Floyd fans have spent hours comparing the album to the 1939 classic film *The Wizard of Oz* and publishing their analysis on websites. It is claimed, for example, that Floyd's "Great Gig in the Sky" begins when the tornado first appears in the film. At the moment "Great Gig" ends, Dorothy and her house land in Oz. "Money," one of Floyd's most famous songs, begins at the moment when the film turns from black and white to color. The band denies any intentional connections between its album and the film.

Other Pink Floyd releases of the 1990s were live albums and compilations that cashed in on the band's enduring success. The most notable were the box set *Shine On* (1992), which contains all eight of the band's original lineup albums, and *P.U.L.S.E.* (1995), a live recording of a 1994 tour featuring a live performance of *Dark Side of the Moon*. In 1996 Pink Floyd was inducted into the Rock and Roll Hall of Fame. The year 2003 saw yet another release of a repackaged version of *Dark Side of the Moon*, this time remastered for 5.1 sound on the thirtieth anniversary of its release.

Although Pink Floyd's creative heyday is long past, the regrouped band continues to fill stadiums and sell collections of its material. Its classic albums continue to attract new generations of fans who delight in the group's spacey pessimism and brilliantly produced sound.

SELECTIVE DISCOGRAPHY: *The Piper at the Gates of Dawn* (Capitol, 1967); *A Saucerful of Secrets* (Capitol, 1968); *Ummagumma* (Capitol, 1969); *Atom Heart Mother* (Capitol, 1970); *Relics* (Capitol, 1971); *Meddle* (Capitol, 1971); *Dark Side of the Moon* (Capitol, 1973); *Wish You Were Here* (Capitol, 1975); *Animals* (Capitol, 1977); *The Wall* (Capitol, 1979); *A Collection of Great Dance Songs* (Capitol, 1981); *Works* (Capitol, 1983); *The Final Cut* (Capitol, 1983); *A Momentary Lapse of Reason* (Columbia, 1987); *Delicate Sound of Thunder* (Columbia, 1988); *Shine On* (Columbia, 1992); *The Division Bell* (Columbia, 1994); *P.U.L.S.E.* (Columbia, 1995); *Is There Anybody Out There? The Wall: Live 1980–1981* (Sony, 2000). **Soundtrack:** *Music from La Vallee: Obscured by Clouds* (Capitol, 1972).

SHAWN GILLEN

PIXIES

Formed: 1986, Boston, Massachusetts; Disbanded 1993

Members: Kim Deal, bass, vocals (born Dayton, Ohio, 10 June 1961); Black Francis, lead vocals, guitar (Charles Michael Kitteridge Thompson, IV, born Long Beach, California, 1965); David Lovering, drums (born Boston, Massachusetts, 6 December 1961); Joey Santiago, guitar (born Manila, Philippines, 10 June 1965).

Genre: Rock

Best-selling album since 1990: *Death to the Pixies* (1997)

Hit songs since 1990: "Dig for Fire," "Head On"

The Pixies never notched a number one record or placed a video in heavy rotation, but their unmistakable influence can be heard in many of the alternative rock acts from the 1990s that did. Nirvana inherited the dramatic soft-to-loud song structures from the Pixies, and nearly every novelty hit about spaceships owes a debt to the short-lived band. With an intriguing sound that combined surf rock, psychedelia, post-punk noise, and pop hooks, the Pixies found favor with critics and college students but were never embraced by the mainstream public. They broke up on the cusp of the alternative-rock explosion, leaving four albums and a legacy that was solidified by a wave of reissues and archive albums.

Charles Thompson and Joey Santiago, roommates at the University of Massachusetts, began playing music together in the mid-1980s. The pair added the bassist Kim Deal and the drummer David Lovering, Thompson adopted the stage name Black Francis, and the Pixies began playing shows in Boston. Black Francis proved to be a strict bandleader, whipping the players into shape quickly enough to start recording studio tracks before the close of their first year. The resulting songs, known as "The Purple Tape," caused a stir in the underground scene, and the English label 4AD released eight of the tracks as *Come On Pilgrim* in 1987. The following year, the band recorded the full-length *Surfer Rosa* (1988) and quickly amassed a small but ardent group of admirers.

Surfer Rosa displays the Pixies' talents in full bloom: Santiago's screeching blasts of guitar noise, Lovering's meaty drumming, and the combination of Deal's delicate vocals with Black Francis's manic, possessed shouting, all wrapped in giddy pop song structures. Most of the tracks are built on their signature dynamic: softly strummed chords that build to a thunderous eruption, lending an apocalyptic air to Black Francis's lyrics (sometimes sung in Spanish) of surreal sexual and religious imagery. The result is strange, riveting, fun, and utterly original.

Pixies. L-R: David Lovering, Black Francis, Joey Santiago, Kim Deal [S.I.N./CORBIS]

The band immediately joined the ranks of top post-punk innovators like Sonic Youth and Husker Du, and embarked on their first headlining tour. The album *Doolittle* followed in 1989. Marked by stronger hooks and less abrasive production, it led to brief MTV exposure for the single "Hear Comes Your Man." While the Pixies' audience in America remained cult-sized, their popularity exploded in Great Britain, where the album peaked at number eight on the pop album charts.

The Pixies began the 1990s with a short break, during which Deal formed the Breeders with Tanya Donelly from Throwing Muses and released the album *Pod* (1990). Late 1990 saw the release of the third Pixies album, *Bossanova*. The record is a departure from the full-out rock of their previous work. It features an expansive, stretched-out sound and an emphasis on nuanced playing. Many of the songs reflect Black Francis's interest in UFOs and aliens, as well as the bold, twangy guitar sound of surf rock. "Down to the Well" and "The Happening" are sci-fi epics that evoke the cold nocturnal desert chill of the legendary UFO crash site in Roswell, New Mexico. "Dig for Fire" and "Allison" provide twisted-pop charm, and the album closes with the dreamy ballad "Havolina."

Although the band remained on the fringe in their native country, *Bossanova* brought them even greater success in England. Though not as revered as *Surfer Rosa* or *Doolittle*, *Bossanova* was replete with the atmospheric soundscapes that inspired the experimental sounds of English bands like Blur and Radiohead.

During the *Bossanova* tour, Black Francis grew increasingly frustrated with Deal's lack of professionalism, and Deal responded with pointed quips throughout the shows. Tension between the two mounted, and an American tour was canceled. Black Francis went to work writing a new album and called the group to Paris in early 1991 to record. During the sessions, Black Francis exercised his authority as lead songwriter and sole creative force, shutting out any Deal contributions save for bass duties. The resulting album, *Trompe le Monde* (1991), is an abrasive affair: The music is breathless, but somewhat clipped. Nevertheless, *Trompe* is an enthralling album and boasts a handful of the band's most rousing songs, including the straight-ahead rock of "Letter to Memphis" and an incendiary cover of Jesus and Mary Chain's "Head On." The album was heavily promoted, but yet again the Pixies failed to catch fire with a broad American audience. Ironically, the record was released on the heels of Nirvana's *Nevermind*, which supplanted the Pixies on the alternative-rock throne.

The Pixies supported U2 on the Zoo TV tour in 1992 and then went on another hiatus. Black Francis changed his name to Frank Black and released an eponymous solo album in the summer of 1993. During an interview with the BBC, he announced the breakup of the Pixies; he informed the rest of the band later that day. Kim Deal went on to record with the Breeders and scored a major hit with the album *Last Splash* (1993). Deal dabbled with different bands and took nearly ten years to record a follow-up to *Last Splash*; Black released a string of well-received albums with his band the Catholics.

In 1997 Elektra released *Death to the Pixies 1987–1991*, a greatest hits compilation packaged with a blistering live concert recording. The release kicked off a Pixies renaissance marked by constant name-dropping by younger bands and an English documentary film. A collection of live outtakes, *Pixies at the BBC* (1998) and *Complete B Sides* (2001), followed. The independent label spinART repackaged the original "Purple Tape" in 2002 as *Pixies*. This constant stream of releases is a testament to the Pixies' influence and the enduring strength of their work. Few bands have been as energetic, experimental, and tuneful at the same time. Indeed, their albums still sound like transmissions from the future, emanations from an alternate-rock universe where twisted intelligence and fun go hand in hand.

SELECTIVE DISCOGRAPHY: *Come On Pilgrim* (4AD/Elektra, 1987); *Surfer Rosa* (4AD/Elektra,

1988); *Doolittle* (4AD/Elektra, 1989); *Bossanova*
(4AD/Elektra, 1990); *Trompe le Monde* (4AD/Elek-
tra, 1991); *Death to the Pixies 1987–1991*
(4AD/Elektra, 1997); *Pixies at the BBC* (4AD/Elek-
tra, 1998); *Complete B-Sides* (4AD, 2001); *Pixies*
(spinART, 2002).

WEBSITE: www.pixies4ad.com.

SEAN CAMERON

ROBERT PLANT

Born: Robert Anthony Plant; West Bromwich, Staffordshire, England, 20 August 1948

Genre: Rock

Best-selling album since 1990: *No Quarter: Jimmy Page & Robert Plant Unledded* (1994)

Hit songs since 1990: "Hurting Kind (I've Got My Eyes on You)," "Calling to You"

Singer Robert Plant rose to superstardom as the lead singer for Led Zeppelin, whom many consider the greatest hard rock band in history. Plant endured personal tragedy and the letdown of Led Zeppelin's breakup to prove detractors wrong with a successful solo career that has outdistanced the other two living members of the band.

Stairway to the Top

Plant entered hastily into musical prominence when Yardbird guitarist Jimmy Page discovered him toiling with a regional band in Birmingham at a local college. Page was searching for a singer to join himself and bassist John Paul Jones to form the New Yardbirds. Plant recommended his pal John Bonham as drummer and the foursome began making rock and roll history in 1968 under the name Led Zeppelin. Until their breakup in 1980, Led Zeppelin sold more than 50 million albums (that total has grown to more than 100 million in 2003) and set the standard for the hard rock genre. They built on their blues/rock beginnings by infusing groundbreaking musical innovation into their sound. Plant gained a reputation for his screeching vocals, high moans, and sexy stage presence. He also wrote most of the band's lyrics, leaning heavily on Celtic mysticism to create songs with rich imagery, including one of rock's ultimate anthems, "Stairway to Heaven." Although never a favorite of critics, Led Zeppelin ruled the rock and roll universe for nearly ten years until their excessive lifestyle—sex, drugs, and rock and roll personified—began taking its toll.

In 1977 Plant suffered tragedy when his young son, Karac, died of a severe stomach infection. Led Zeppelin cancelled their world tour and Plant went into seclusion.

Robert Plant [SANDRINE DULEMO AND MICHAEL LABAICA/UNIVERSAL RECORDS]

He emerged sixteen months later and the band began to pick up momentum only to fold after Bonham died suddenly following a night of heavy drinking in 1980. That officially ended Led Zeppelin, although rumors and hopes for their reunion exist into the new millennium. In 2000, VH1 selected the band for the number one slot on its program *100 Greatest Hard Rock Bands*.

Plant spent the 1980s in a catch-22—trying to capitalize on his Led Zeppelin fame, while also distancing himself from the band to forge an identity as a solo artist. His first effort, *Pictures at 11* (1982), showed a revitalized Plant. The album features Phil Collins on drums and it spawned Plant's first solo hit, a slashing rock tune titled, "Burning Down One Side." He released a second album, *The Principle of Moments* (1983), which produced another hit, "Big Log." Plant followed with a world tour that was incessantly plagued by his audiences' lust for Led Zeppelin music. Plant appeased them at times, but for the most part stubbornly stuck to his own set list.

Except for a dalliance with a supergroup called the Honeydrippers (which featured Jimmy Page, guitarist Jeff Beck, and keyboardist Paul Shaffer), Plant found definition and confidence as a solo artist with four solo albums through the 1980s, scoring his best success with *Now and Zen* (1988). Incidentally, the Honeydrippers released one record, a compilation of just five 1950s-era songs. One of them, an old hit by Phil Phillips & The Twilights, "Sea of Love" (1959), surprised the band when it became a huge success. Plant, Page, and Jones teased Led Zeppelin fans by reuniting for a few songs in 1985 at a Live Aid Concert and for a poorly played set in 1988 at Madison Square Garden for Atlantic Records' fortieth anniversary bash.

The Song Remained the Same

By 1990 Plant's solo career was firmly established. His next two releases, *Manic Nirvana* (1990) and *Fate of Nations* (1993), were moneymaking and listeners began to stop comparing Plant's music to Led Zeppelin. Even when Plant performed Led Zeppelin songs in his concerts, he did it more for the joy of reliving them than out of necessity to keep his audience happy. His albums feature a mix of diverse rock that contains altering rhythms and dashes of non-rock instruments like mandolins and harps. Plant's voice is one of rock music's most notable. Its high tones and guttural wails drip with breathy impertinence and Plant utilizes his wide range like an instrument, making it ebb and flow with the tide of the music.

To the delight of Led Zeppelin fans, Plant and Page made good on a much-hyped reunion and their first effort was an album on the MTV live acoustic venue, *Unplugged*. Their release, *No Quarter: Jimmy Page and Robert Plant Unledded* (1994), contains mostly lesser known Led Zeppelin songs and features some new material classified as "new world" music. Plant's howl at the top of "Since I've Been Loving You" evokes an entire decade of Led Zeppelin music, although, bravely, little else on this album does. Most of the music reflects Plant's affinity for exploring the remote parts of the world and his fascination with Middle Eastern cultures and Celtic lore. He is accompanied not only by Page, but also by an eleven-piece Egyptian orchestra, an authentic Moroccan ensemble, and the London Symphony Orchestra. (Jones is not included.) The album's highlight is a whirling rendition of "Kashmir." Plant and Page also rework versions of other Led Zeppelin fare such as "No Quarter," "Thank You," "Gallows Pole," and "Four Sticks." Plant and Page promoted the successful selling album with a world tour that lasted on and off for nearly two years. They interrupted their tour in 1995 to perform with Steven Tyler and Joe Perry of Aerosmith and Neil Young at Led Zeppelin's induction ceremony into the Rock and Roll Hall of Fame.

Plant paired again with Page for his next recording effort, *Walking into Clarksdale* (1998). This time the duo wrote new material, but the long anticipated album disappointed many listeners and sales were low. While Plant had somewhat stepped out of the shadow of Led Zeppelin in his solo career, the combination of Plant and Page together could not. Fans excused the creative innovation of the first album, but expected more of their seminal sound from *Walking into Clarksdale*. For many listeners it was trou-

bling that the album contains barely a trace of blues. The album's title is a reference to Clarksdale, Mississippi, often credited as the birthplace of the blues—the music of Plant and Page's youth. Instead, the album sticks to aesthetically charged rock with leanings once again toward Middle Eastern sounds.

After five years of touring off and on with Page, Plant began playing very small venues in the United Kingdom with a group composed of old friends, Priory of Brion. They played a repertoire of mostly 1960s folk, pop, and acid rock songs. Shortly after, he traveled the same back roads with a different band of his assemblage called Strange Sensation. His exploration of 1960s music continued and his next solo release, *Dreamland* (2002), contains his renditions of ten songs from that genre including the often done classic, "Hey Joe," and Bob Dylan's "One More Cup of Coffee."

Since his rush to fame in 1968, little of Plant's look and singing style have changed. He still has golden locks hanging near the waist of his tall frame. Plant has been successful, as music trends change, to resist any major attempts to reinvent his style, choosing instead to let the trends adapt to him.

SELECTIVE DISCOGRAPHY: *Pictures at 11* (Atlantic, 1982); *The Principle of Moments* (Atlantic, 1983); *Shaken 'n' Stirred* (Atlantic, 1985); *Now and Zen* (Atlantic, 1988); *Manic Nirvana* (Atlantic, 1990); *Fate of Nations* (Atlantic, 1993); *No Quarter: Jimmy Page & Robert Plant Unledded* (1994); *Walking into Clarksdale* (Atlantic, 1998); *Dreamland* (Atlantic, 2002).

BIBLIOGRAPHY: T. Horkins, *Led Zeppelin* (New York, 1998); S. Davis, *Hammer of the Gods* (New York, 2001); R. Cole and R. Trubo, *Stairway to Heaven: Led Zeppelin Uncensored* (New York, 2002).

DONALD LOWE

IGGY POP

Born: James Newell Osterberg; Muskegon, Michigan, 21 April 1947

Genre: Rock

Best-selling album since 1990: *Brick by Brick* (1990)

Singer Iggy Pop's "no holds barred" performing style in the late 1960s with his band Iggy and the Stooges was a precursor to punk rock; most critics credit him with originating the genre, which arrived over a half decade later. It is remarkable that Iggy survived the rowdy ferocity of his early days. Sometimes forgotten in the zaniness surrounding his persona is that Iggy is a witty, intelligent songwriter and a skillful manipulator of live audiences. He has also acted in a variety of film and television roles.

Iggy Pop grew up in Ann Arbor, Michigan, and was named after his father, James Osterberg. Both of his parents were schoolteachers. He aspired to be a blues drummer and moved to Chicago as a teenager to be closer to the blues scene. In 1967 he returned to Ann Arbor and tracked down his high school classmates, bassist Dave Alexander, guitarist Ron Asheton, and his brother, drummer Scott Asheton. Osterberg changed his name to Iggy Pop and became the lead singer. They named the band the Psychedelic Stooges, later shortened to the Stooges. While other 1960s groups were singing about love, peace, and harmony, the Stooges quickly made a name for themselves by disharmoniously blasting songs about violence, death, destruction, drugs, and life's malaise. Their stage anarchy included ear-splittingly loud guitars and Iggy's thrashing around on stage while smearing raw meat or peanut butter (some rock observers claim feces) over his body. The thin and emaciated singer showed no hesitancy in diving headfirst into the audience, hurling himself on to shattered glass, or fist fighting with audience members.

After recording two albums, rampant drug use forced the Stooges to disband in 1970. In an effort to beat his own addiction to heroin, Iggy moved to London where he met rocker David Bowie. Bowie produced the Stooges' third and last release, Raw Power (1973). All three albums are considered rock classics by critics, and another release, Metallic K.O. (1976), a recording of their last concert appearance, was released after the band was already in the annals of rock history. The Stooges disbanded in 1974 and Iggy moved to Los Angeles, California, where his mother discovered him wandering the streets in search of a drug fix. She helped place him in a mental institution. Bowie, who was having his own drug struggles, found Iggy and the two musical malcontents decided to move to Germany in an effort to help each other get clean of drugs.

Bowie produced and wrote material for Iggy's next album. He replaced Iggy's earlier grunge with a more refined synthesized rock sound for Iggy's next two releases, The Idiot (1977) and Lust for Life (1977). Despite recurring drug and alcohol problems, this kick-started Iggy's career and he went on to achieve recording success throughout the 1980s. In light of the vile punk rock and heavy metal that came after the Stooges, Iggy, for the first time in his career, began to sound closer to the mainstream.

He built on that trend into the 1990s with the successful album Brick by Brick (1990), which showcases Iggy as a straightforward song interpreter. The album turns introspective and reflects on issues within Iggy's control instead of his characteristic helpless rage. He sings about a determination to do better in "I Won't Crap Out" and

is undoubtedly influenced by his own history of homeless wandering when he sings "Home." In moments when he is not screaming, Iggy's voice possesses a clear and appealing sound.

After the raw, edgy releases, American Caesar (1993) and Naughty Little Doggy (1996), Iggy collaborated with the jazz trio Medeski, Martin & Wood on Avenue B (1999). The album is the farthest departure in Iggy's career. Four of the thirteen songs are meditatively spoken monologues over classical orchestration and the rest are ballads such as the wistful title track or the straight-faced humor in "Nazi Girlfriend."

Fans who attend Iggy's concerts to see him wriggle, writhe, and scream might be surprised to know that his songs have been used in both beer and athletic shoe advertisements. Iggy has also forged a career as an actor and has appeared in numerous films, including The Color of Money (1986), The Crow (1993), Dead Man (1995), City of Angels (1998), and roles on television shows such as The Adventures of Pete and Pete and Star Trek: Deep Space Nine. He also wrote the score to the cult movie favorite Repo Man (1983). His album Beat 'Em Up (2001) made longtime fans happy by returning to the seminal sound of his pre-punk days. Iggy reunited with the Stooges for a concert in California in the spring of 2003.

It is doubtful that many rock superstars anticipate growing old while in the throes of fame, and it is interesting to witness the variety of ways that superstars from the 1960s and 1970s have dealt with middle age and beyond. Iggy Pop, whose physical shape and size have changed little through the years, continues growing to new musical heights.

SELECTIVE DISCOGRAPHY: The Idiot (RCA, 1977); Lust for Life (RCA, 1977); TV Eye (RCA, 1978); New Values (Arista, 1979); Soldier (Arista, 1980); Zombie Birdhouse (Animal, 1982); Blah Blah Blah (A&M, 1986); Instinct (A&M, 1988); Brick by Brick (Virgin, 1990); American Caesar (Virgin, 1993); Naughty Little Doggie (Virgin, 1996); Avenue B (Virgin, 1999); Beat 'Em Up (Virgin, 2001). With the Stooges: The Stooges (Elektra, 1969); Fun House (Elektra, 1970); Raw Power (Columbia, 1973); Metallic K.O. (Skydog, 1976).

BIBLIOGRAPHY: J. Ambrose, Iggy Pop: The Biography (New York, 2002).

DONALD LOWE

THE PRETENDERS

Formed: 1978, London, England

Members: Martin Chambers, drums (born Hereford, England, 4 September 1951); Andy Hobson, bass (born

Swinton, England, 20 November 1962); Chrissie Hynde, vocals, guitar (born Akron, Ohio, 7 September 1951); Adam Seymour, guitar, vocals (born Leicester, England, 17 January 1961). Former members: Pete Farndon, bass (born Hereford, England, 2 June 1952; died London, England, 14 April 1983); James Honeyman-Scott, guitar (born Hereford, England, 4 November 1956; died London, England, 16 June 1982); Robbie McIntosh, guitar (born Hereford, England, 1 January 1950); Malcolm Foster, bass (born Gosport, England, 13 January 1956).

Genre: Rock

Best-selling album since 1990: *Last of the Independents* (1994)

Hit songs since 1990: "I'll Stand by You," "Night in My Veins"

The Pretenders emerged from the London music scene in the late 1970s with a personalized style encompassing punk angst, reggae grooves, and pop craftsmanship. The principal songwriter and lead vocalist, Chrissie Hynde, led the group with a forceful and self-assured stage presence. After three successful albums, the group incurred the tragic loss of both guitarist James Honeyman-Scott and bassist Pete Farndon. Hynde continued to record with various studio musicians and by the mid-1990s had recruited a stable group. In this incarnation, the Pretenders reestablished their hard rock aesthetic with critically acclaimed albums and strong performances at the Lilith Fair festival and on tour with the Rolling Stones.

Hynde grew up in Akron, Ohio, and attended Kent State University for three years. In 1973 she moved to London and worked as a music critic for *New Musical Express*. Dissatisfied with the job and the music scene, she moved back to Akron and joined the group Jack Rabbit. Hynde returned to London three years later and, through the assistance of Malcolm McLaren (manager for the punk band the Sex Pistols), she was hired to play guitar in Masters of the Backside. Although dismissed, she continued to perform with various bands and honed her songwriting skills, eventually recording a demo tape and signing with Real Records.

With the help of producer Nick Lowe, Hynde recruited Farndon, Honeyman-Scott, and session drummer Gerry Mackleduff to form the Pretenders. Their cover version of Ray Davies's (of the band the Kinks) "Stop Your Sobbing" breached the U.K. charts and was followed by the pleasantly melodic "Kid." After the addition of drummer Martin Chambers, the group recorded their eponymous debut album, *The Pretenders* (1980). The first single, "Brass in Pocket," was an immediate success and hit number one in the United Kingdom and number fourteen in the United States. The song begins with a hypnotic guitar riff in a lan-

guid tempo that gradually builds to the chorus. The lyrics present a self-assured woman in pursuit of a man: "I'm gonna have some of your attention. Give it to me." The accompanying music video, which depicts Hynde as a waitress in a diner, was placed in constant rotation by MTV and gained the group a wide American audience.

Due to heavy demand, the group quickly released the aptly titled *Extended Play* EP (1981) with its single, "Talk of the Town." After a busy touring schedule, the Pretenders moved to Paris and recorded their second album, *The Pretenders II* (1981). On June 14, 1982, Farndon was asked to leave the group due to his constant use of heroin and cocaine. In a strange twist of fate, Honeyman-Scott died of a drug overdose two days later. The remaining members, Hynde and Chambers, rallied together and produced the wistful "Back on the Chain Gang," dedicated to Honeyman-Scott. Before this album could be completed, the group suffered the news of Farndon's drug-related death in April 1983.

Crawling through the 1980s

Learning to Crawl, which alludes to Hynde's infant daughter with Ray Davies and the band's tentative activity after the tragedies, was finally released in 1984. The album went platinum and featured the raucous "Middle of the Road," with its incendiary guitar and harmonica solos. During this time, Hynde married Jim Kerr of the pop group Simple Minds and gave birth to her second daughter. The relationship soon dissolved and Hynde eventually married Colombian sculptor Lucho Brieva in 1997.

After the album release the group was effectively dismantled and Hynde enjoyed success on her own, recording a cover of Sonny and Cher's "I Got You Babe" with UB40. The next two albums were released under the Pretenders moniker but were largely solo efforts by Hynde with uneven results. In 1994 the group was reinvented with the addition of guitarist Adam Seymour and bassist Andy Hobson, and the subsequent album, *Last of the Independents*, was hailed as the return of the Pretenders. While songs such as "Hollywood Perfume" and "Rebel Rock Me" recalled the energy of their earlier efforts, the album was significantly marred by innocuous ballads. "Night in My Veins" exhibits a pleasant harmonic progression with a steady drum groove. Although the melody is shapeless, Hynde's performance is memorable with the rapid line, "Even if it's," followed by "just the night in my veins." The surprise hit from the album was the ballad, "I'll Stand by You," with its piano introduction, predictable melodic phrasing, and backing gospel choir.

Renewing Their Rock Aesthetic

The Pretenders released the acoustic live album, *The Isle of View* (1995), with imaginative arrangements of previous material. With *¡Viva El Amor!* (1999), the Pretenders reasserted their rock aesthetic with the biting commentary of "Popstar" and the rugged energy of "Legalize Me" with guitarist Jeff Beck. Hynde reveals outstanding vocal prowess in "One More Time" and a supple intimacy in Silvio Rodríguez's "Rabo de Nube." The ballad, "From the Heart Down," exhibits some of Hynde's most poignant lyrics: "You sink into my flesh like a knife," and "Longing hurts the teeth like something sweet." Although this album went largely unnoticed, it represents one of the band's strongest releases.

In 1999 the group performed at the Lilith Fair, a festival centered around female musicians. As an outspoken crusader for PETA (People for the Ethical Treatment of Animals), Hynde was arrested in March 2000 in a protest against the Gap clothing store. Although she spent a night in jail, the protest was a success, with the Gap changing its policy toward illegal leather products.

The Pretenders' next album, *Loose Screw* (2002), highlights the group's signature rock sound merged with reggae beats and textures. The album features imaginative bass lines, varied sonic textures, and an overall clean production. "You Know Who Your Friends Are" begins with a rollicking bass line and guitar delay, sliding subtly into the chorus. The vocal line is relaxed and conversational with gentle melismas. The reggae-saturated single, "Complex Person," exhibits a hypnotic melody centered around certain key notes and concludes with an unexpected harmonic change. The confessional "Nothing Breaks Like a Heart" wistfully describes the complications of human relationships: "I want you more than before, so I conceal it." During this time, the Pretenders reached another milestone by performing with the Rolling Stones in their U.S. concerts.

Hynde's innovative songs fueled the Pretenders through various incarnations. The original quartet presented edgy rock songs coupled with a remarkably melodic approach. With the tragic loss of Honeyman-Scott and Farndon, the group sputtered in the late 1980s and early 1990s, only to reemerge with a powerful new lineup in the mid-1990s. While Hynde generally eschewed the designation of female rock star, she undoubtedly challenged the orthodoxy of rock gender roles through her stalwart persona and performances.

SELECTIVE DISCOGRAPHY: *The Pretenders* (Sire, 1980); *Extended Play* EP (Sire, 1981); *The Pretenders II* (Sire, 1981); *Learning to Crawl* (Sire, 1984); *Get Close* (Sire, 1986); *The Singles* (Sire, 1987); *Packed!* (Sire, 1990); *Last of the Independents* (Warner Bros., 1994); *The Isle of View* (Warner Bros., 1995); *¡Viva El Amor!* (Warner Bros., 1999); *Loose Screw* (Artemis, 2002).

WEBSITE: www.pretendersband.com.

WYNN YAMAMI

PRINCE

Born: Prince Rogers Nelson; Minneapolis, Minnesota, 7 June 1958

Genre: R&B, Pop, Rock

Best-selling album since 1990: *The Love Symbol Album* (1992)

Hit songs since 1990: "Cream," "Sexy M.F.," "The Most Beautiful Girl in the World"

Prince is one of the most versatile and talented musicians in the history of pop music. Not only is he an accomplished instrumentalist on keyboards, bass, lead guitar, and drums, but he is also an original singer with a range that stretches from low, gruff bass notes to screechy high falsetto tones. Notably, in all of his first five albums, Prince played all the instruments on his own. His fame is also due to an identity that is inimitable. His flamboyant appearance blurs so many boundaries that he might be best described as postmodern androgyne. Throughout his career he has transgressed sexual, gender, and musical norms.

Prince grew up in Minneapolis, where only a small portion of the population was black. Named after his father, a black-Italian jazz musician, Prince was a self-taught musician playing drums, guitar, piano, and bass. He formed his first band, Grand Central, while in high school in 1972. Grand Central became Champagne, and they recorded with Chris Moon. This led to Prince's leaving the band and writing songs and working for Moon for the next two years. He recorded demos and tracks for Linster Willie's (aka Pepe Willie) band, 94 East, prior to his first major break, a self-production deal with Warner Bros. Signing him up for a six-figure advance in early 1978, Warner Bros. permitted Prince to write, produce, and perform all of his albums. This was an unprecedented agreement not only because of his age (he was only twenty), but also because of his race. The only black artist prior to him to be allowed artistic freedom was Stevie Wonder, and that was only after he had been signed to Motown Records for ten years.

On his debut album, *For You* (1978), his brash rock style fuses with soul and funk to cater to a predominantly black audience. While this album did not chart, his next one, *Prince* (1979), managed to chalk up the hit "I Wanna Be Your Lover." With the release of his third album, *Dirty Mind* (1980), his songs became so sexually explicit that they lost radio coverage, bewildering a white audience. It was with album number four, *1999* (1983), and the hit "Little Red Corvette" that Prince achieved major international attention. Thanks to heavy MTV coverage, this song made it into the American Top 10 and, together with Michael Jackson's "Billie Jean," became the first breakthrough for

Spot Light | *Diamonds and Pearls*

Diamonds and Pearls (1991) is one of Prince's most stylistically innovative albums and in many ways signifies where pop music was at the end of the twentieth century. The thirteen songs of this album present a range of styles and musical idioms expressed through technical devices. With each song one experiences a complete shift in style. For example, from track six, "Strollin'," to track seven, "Willing and Able," there is a dramatic change from a simple, relaxed swing drive to an animated and humorous township jive—the influence of South African township could not be more obvious. With stylistic changes come significant shifts in a range of other elements such as studio production, instrumentation, harmonic flavor, and rhythmic impetus. In songs such as "Cream," it is possible to detect at least five contrasting styles: blues, classic rock, funk, soul, and boogie. Most notable is Prince's levels of musical intensity, which are captured by his characteristic confidence in delivery. In the track "Walk Don't Walk," the musical energy is harnessed to a relaxed tempo and conventional diatonic chord progressions. The intensity of this track is encapsulated in its leisurely, easygoing, and positive feel, which is a direct result of a medium tempo within a ballad style. In the final track, "Live 4 Love (Last Words from the Cockpit)," it is difficult not to pick up on Prince's characteristic humor as he opens the song with a melodramatic, robotic vocal countdown with unmistakable allusions to Earth, Wind & Fire in the bass and rhythm parts. Stylistic diversity reaches a most intense level in this track as Prince draws on techno, hard-rock, funk, soul, rap, pop, and house.

a black pop artist on MTV. From the outset, Prince's fans were as varied as he, with different social, racial, and cultural backgrounds. When planning his first tour in 1979, he insisted that his band be multiracial and include both men and women. The ideology behind this decision increased his popularity and helped him gain a wide following all over the world.

In 1984 his success continued with the album *Purple Rain,* which accompanied a movie of the same name in which he starred. Three singles from the album became hits: "When Doves Cry," "Let's Go Crazy," and "Purple Rain." Through the 1980s Prince released an album each year. From this period the album that stands out most is the solo double album *Sign o' the Times,* which resulted in a film featuring Prince performing live. Demonstrating a high degree of individuality, the songs off this album deal with themes of sex, love, salvation, and God. The 1980s ended with the release of one of Prince's strangest singles, from the first *Batman* film. This hit, entitled "Batdance," made it to number one, helping the album *Batman* to sell more than 14 million copies worldwide.

Following the low-key reception of *Graffiti Bridge* in 1990, *Diamonds and Pearls,* released the next year, was a success. With his formidable funk band, the New Power Generation, featuring gospel-soul singer Rosie Gaines, Prince was able to produce a rich selection of songs that drew on a wide breadth of styles.

The next two albums, *Love Symbol* (1992) and *Come* (1994), did not live up to their predecessors musically. It was as if the emphasis was more on raunchiness and sexual explicitness, with all the eccentricity surrounding Prince at this stage, than on the quality of the musical writing. The media hype surrounding Prince in 1993 had to do with the change of his name. He renamed himself as an unpronounceable icon and then became "Victor," and finally changed over to TAFKAP (The Artist Formerly Known as Prince). Soon it was disclosed that these name changes involved his heated dispute with Time Warner over his contract. In February 1994, following a major setback with Warner and a distribution deal, Prince's Paisley Park Records went out of business. What resulted was a release of the poignantly beautiful hit, "The Most Beautiful Girl in the World," from his next album, *The Beautiful Experience,* which was released on independent labels around the world in 1994. However, Prince still had to honor his contract with Warner and issued the *Black Album* and *Come* in addition to a set of greatest hits, *The Hits.* Full of resentment toward Warner Bros., Prince wrote SLAVE on his cheek for a photo session and went on tour with this strong statement.

In 1995 *The Gold Experience* album was released, featuring songs with which he had toured. This material continued to attempt to shock, sensationalize, and provoke reactions. The next album, *Chaos and Disorder,* was his last obligation to Warner and consists mainly of P-funk jam numbers with an abundance of guitar soloing by Prince. At this stage it was announced that Prince's band, the New Power Generation, would be touring no longer.

With his new label, NPG, distributed by EMI, the three-disc album *Emancipation* was released in 1996. Consisting of thirty-six tracks, this album is the longest in duration produced by Prince. The music stands as a testament to his versatility as a producer and musician, drawing on influences from jazz, R&B, rock, funk, pop, and dance styles. One of the features that stands out most throughout this album is the complexity of the artist's jamming style, which gives the album a sense of extravagance and celebration. Not quite the commercial success he had hoped it would be, Prince banked on his next album, *Crystal Ball*, to do better. Released in 1998, the album proved to Prince and his fans how difficult it is to distribute records independently through websites. As a result sales were disappointing, as they were for his next album, *New Power Soul*.

In 1999 Prince released the remix collection *1999 (The New Master), The Vault: Old Friends 4 Sale* and *Rave Un2 the Joy Fantastic*. In December 1999 his publishing contract with Warner-Chappell expired, and Prince reverted to his original name. From 2000 to 2003 he went on successive small-town tours in the United States and Europe promoting his albums *Rave Un2 the Joy Fantastic, The Beautiful Experience* (2001), and *The Rainbow Children* (2001). All these tours were relatively low-level events compared to the spectacle of his former tours.

Despite a slump in popularity and drop in record sales at the turn of the millennium, Prince nevertheless continues to occupy a central position in the pop industry as one of the most musically innovative artists of all time. During the 1980s and 1990s he emerged as a highly eccentric and influential artist with promo videos and live concerts that were pioneering for their time. Prince's brand of pop—a hybrid of funk, rock, jazz, R&B, and dance-pop—is unique and distinguishable through both its mode of performance and its pathbreaking production, which has had a major impact on the development of popular music worldwide.

SELECTIVE DISCOGRAPHY: *For You* (Warner Bros., 1978); *Prince* (Warner Bros., 1979); *Dirty Mind* (Warner Bros., 1980); *Controversy* (Warner Bros., 1981); *1999* (Warner Bros., 1983); *Purple Rain* (Warner Bros., 1984); *Parade* (Paisley Park, 1986); *Sign o' the Times* (Paisley Park, 1987); *The Black Album* (Paisley Park, 1987); *Lovesexy* (Paisley Park, 1988); *Batman* (Warner Bros., 1989); *Graffiti Bridge* (Pasiley Park, 1990); *Diamonds and Pearls* (Paisley Park, 1991); *The Love Symbol Album* (Warner Bros., 1992); *Gold Experience* (Warner Bros., 1995); *Chaos & Disorder* (Warner Bros., 1996); *Emancipation* (NPG, 1996); *New Power Soul* (NPG, 1998); *Rave Un2 the Joy Fantastic* (Arista, 1999); *Crystal Ball* (NPG, 1999); *The Rainbow Children* (Redline, 2001).

STAN HAWKINS

JOHN PRINE

Born: Maywood, Illinois, 10 October 1946
Genre: Country
Best-selling album since 1990: *The Missing Years* (1991)

Since 1971 singer/songwriter John Prine has enchanted his loyal fan base and earned the respect of industry peers with clever, literate, narrative-driven story songs. A gifted lyricist with a wry, understated wit, Prine writes sad songs that seem funny, and humorous songs rife with heartbreak. Prine has never attained huge commercial success, but he did improve album sales when he formed his own record company.

Although they lived in the Chicago suburbs, Prine's parents had a strong connection to Kentucky coal country. His father moved them north to escape that way of life, but they visited relatives in the summers and frequented a small western Kentucky town named Paradise that Prine made famous in a song by the same name. At the age of fourteen, Prine learned some guitar chords and began writing songs. His influences were Hank Williams and Roger Miller. After serving two years in the Army in West Germany, he returned to his job with the postal service and frequented Chicago's folk clubs. In 1969 friends coerced Prine into performing at one of the clubs, and he played three songs: "Sam Stone," "Hello in There," and "Paradise." (All three appear on his debut album.) His performance convinced the club's owner to hire Prine regularly, and he emerged as part of Chicago's music scene, secured a record deal, and released his first album, *John Prine* (1971). The album drew raves; Prine's songs, many written as a teenager, seemed wise beyond his years. "Hello in There" examines loneliness and senility from the point of view of the song's elderly male character. He sings, "Me and Loretta, we don't talk much more / She sits and stares out the back door screen." Prine's tasteful avoidance of rhyming the two lines displayed songwriting confidence and maturity. Prine was among the first songwriters to chronicle the plight of Vietnam War veterans; his "Sam Stone" is the melancholy tale of a heroin-addicted vet who returns home with a "Purple Heart and a monkey on his back." In addition, few songwriters can turn a phrase in the way that Prine can. One example of this talent is heard in "Spanish Pipedream," an amusing romp about a draft-dodging soldier and a topless dancer who go on to live happily ever after. It begins, "She was a level-headed dancer, on the road to alcohol, and I was just a soldier, on the way to Montreal."

Prine's Twain-like sensibility caught critics' attention, and he was dubbed, along with a handful of other budding folk artists, as a contender to become the "New Bob

Dylan." This short-lived phenomenon originated from a *New York Times* article; one of the other candidates, Loudon Wainwright III, lampooned the concept and invoked Prine's name in his 1992 song, "Talking New Bob Dylan."

Unfortunately, *John Prine* sold poorly, as did subsequent albums. However, his music built a loyal following that allowed Prine a steady small-venue concert career. Along the way, he altered his style to appease record companies, drawing on country rock and rockabilly on *Common Sense* (1975) and *Pink Cadillac* (1979). These gambits failed to widen his audience, however. A disillusioned Prine found himself without a record label and contemplating retirement before he made the bold move of creating his own record company, Oh Boy Records, in 1980. Four years later, he released his first album, *Aimless Love* (1984). He continued his comeback with the Grammy-nominated *German Afternoons* (1985).

Prine waited six years to release his next studio recording, *The Missing Years* (1991), which included guest work by Tom Petty and Bruce Springsteen. To the delight of many in the music industry who long recognized Prine's contributions, *The Missing Years* won a 1991 Grammy Award for Best Contemporary Folk Album. Howie Epstein, the bass player for Tom Petty and the Heartbreakers, produced the album and seemed to find just the right mix for Prine, who has never been hailed as a great vocalist. The appealing twang in Prine's singing style suggests much more of his Kentucky heritage than his Chicago upbringing.

After *John Prine Christmas* (1994), a droll, offbeat album of eight loosely gathered songs (some of them relating to the holiday season), Prine released the critically acclaimed *Lost Dogs and Mixed Blessings* (1995). Again, Epstein managed to combine Prine's exquisite wordplay with a punchy beat. The album is a typical blend of Prine's funny and sad songs, including "Ain't Hurtin' Nobody," wherein Prine sings, "Six million seven hundred thousand and thirty-three lights on, you think someone could take the time to sit down and listen to the words of my song." In "Lake Marie," Prine talks most of the lyrics, at one point confessing, "Many years later we found ourselves in Canada trying to save our marriage and perhaps catch a few fish, whatever came first."

In 1997 Prine's career was interrupted by throat cancer. He spent the next year in treatment, and, after winning a clean bill of health, released the Grammy-nominated *In Spite of Ourselves* (1999). Prine wrote only the album's title track and pulled the rest of the sixteen songs from classic country music. Additionally, he performed the songs as duets with some of his favorite female singers, including Iris Dement, Trisha Yearwood, Emmylou Harris, and Lucinda Williams. The title track is part

of the soundtrack to the film *Daddy and Them* (2003), in which Prine also has an acting role. He spent 2003 extensively touring.

Prine is an esteemed songwriting talent whose songs have been recorded by industry heavyweights such as Bette Midler, Bonnie Raitt, Nanci Griffith, Johnny Cash, Kris Kristofferson, and John Denver. "Paradise" has been recorded by twenty-four different artists and "Angel from Montgomery" by seventeen. While major commercial success has eluded him, Prine is treasured by his small army of fans and fellow musicians.

SELECTIVE DISCOGRAPHY: *John Prine* (Atlantic, 1971); *Diamonds in the Rough* (Atlantic, 1972); *Common Sense* (Atlantic, 1975); *Bruised Orange* (Asylum, 1978); *Pink Cadillac* (Asylum, 1979); *Storm Windows* (Asylum, 1980); *Aimless Love* (Oh Boy, 1984); *German Afternoons* (Oh Boy, 1985); *The Missing Years* (Oh Boy, 1991); *Lost Dogs and Mixed Blessings* (Oh Boy, 1995); *In Spite of Ourselves* (Oh Boy, 1999).

DONALD LOWE

THE PRODIGY

Formed: 1990, Braintree, Essex, England

Members: Liam Howlett, producer (born Braintree, Essex, England, 21 August 1971); Maxim Reality, vocals (born Keith Palmer, Cambridgeshire, England, 21 March 1967); Keith Flint, dancer, vocals (born England, 27 March 1969). Former member: Leeroy Thornhill, dancer (born Essex, England, 8 October 1968).

Genre: Rock

Best-selling album since 1990: *The Fat of the Land* (1997)

Hit songs since 1990: "Firestarter," "Breathe," "Smack My Bitch Up"

In 1997, on the strength of the album *The Fat of the Land*, the Prodigy brought to popular radio a new musical style called electronica, which fused techno, rock, and dance music and relied heavily on samples from the music of other artists.

By the age of nineteen, Liam Howlett was already a veteran of the British underground music scene, having produced and released his own music, which was heavily influenced by rave culture. Raves, all-night parties that combined loud techno music and drugs, were spawning a growing subculture in England, and Howlett, in his music, attempted to capture the excitement of that young and subversive scene. Howlett met up with dancers Keith Flint and Leeroy Thornhill, and with them formed the Prodigy in 1990. The trio performed in clubs and at raves, with

Flint and Thornhill serving to rile up crowds while Howlett played his music. The British label XL picked up the Prodigy and issued the band's self-produced first release *What Evil Lurks* in 1991, along with a host of singles. The Prodigy expanded its sound by adding rapper Maxim Reality to the lineup in 1993.

Music for the Jilted Generation, released in 1995, gave the band its biggest success in England, but also saw the band move away from its rave-style sound and toward a more complex fusion of rock and techno sounds. With his spiky hair and ample piercings, Flint physically embodied this fusion and gradually emerged as the band's visual icon.

Flint was also the catalyst for the band's biggest single, "Firestarter," released in 1996. In his first-ever vocal on record, Flint spews the lyrics with memorable ferocity: "I'm the bitch you hated, filth infatuated / Yeah, I'm the pain you tasted, fell intoxicated." "Firestarter," with its booming drum-and-bass style, its siren-like guitar samples, as well as its wailing vocal catcalls courtesy of Flint, was an immediate British hit and gradually made its way across the Atlantic. With its fresh sound, "Firestarter" was a revelation to mainstream U.S. radio, and the single became a surprising hit. The Prodigy's subcultural look resounded with MTV audiences as well, and the station moved the band into heavy rotation.

"Firestarter" had embroiled the Prodigy in minor controversy for its seeming endorsement of arson; the follow-up "Smack My Bitch Up" brought even more attention to the band. The pulsing "Smack My Bitch Up" is largely an instrumental track, featuring only the single, oft-repeated lyric: "Change my pitch up, smack my bitch up." The lyrics enraged women's groups, which charged that the song inspired violence toward women. MTV ultimately removed the promotional video for "Smack My Bitch Up" from its rotation, sparking a debate on censorship and further cementing the Prodigy in popular consciousness.

The Prodigy's penchant for controversy, coupled with the band's radical new sound, helped *The Fat of the Land* reach number one on the *Billboard* album charts—a first-ever achievement for an "electronica" act, as the genre would be dubbed by the media. *The Fat of the Land* ultimately sold 10 million copies worldwide.

In the years following *The Fat of the Land,* electronica lost much of its radical appeal, as acts such as Moby brought a less harsh, more mainstream flavor to the genre; as a result, the Prodigy largely faded from view. The band did not put forth any new music until 2002, when it released the U.K. single "Baby's Got a Temper," which generated little excitement.

Though its popular success stemmed largely from a single album, the Prodigy possess a formidable legacy, having almost single-handedly introduced a bold, new style into American popular music.

SELECTIVE DISCOGRAPHY: *Experience* (Elektra, 1992); *Music for the Jilted Generation* (Mute, 1995); *The Fat of the Land* (XL, 1997).

SCOTT TRIBBLE

PUBLIC ENEMY

Formed: 1982, Long Island, New York

Members: Chuck D, lead rapper (Charles Ridenhour, born Roosevelt, New York, New York, 1 August 1960); Flavor Flav, rapper (William Drayton, born Roosevelt, New York, New York, 16 March 1959); Terminator X, DJ (Norman Lee Rogers, born New York, New York, 25 August 1966). Former member: Professor Griff, minister of information (Richard Griff).

Genre: Hip-Hop

Best-selling album since 1990: *Fear of a Black Planet* (1990)

Hit songs since 1990: "911 Is a Joke," "Brothers Gonna Work It Out," "Can't Truss It"

Chuck D, the leader of Public Enemy, said that his group set out to "destroy popular music," but the group accomplished something far more profound: They pushed hip-hop to the outer limits and thereby rewrote the rules for all forms of pop music. Their classic period lasted only a few years, but throughout the 1990s they remained a potent voice of dissent in both the worlds of politics and music.

The Founding Vision

Public Enemy emerged in 1982 as a concept dreamed up by Charles Ridenhour, a student and DJ at Adelphi University in Garden City, New York. Along with his friends Hank Shocklee and Bill Stephney, he recorded a track titled "Public Enemy No. 1," which caught the attention of the producer Rick Rubin, a co-founder of the hip-hop label Def Jam. Ridenhour adopted the name Chuck D and began constructing his vision of a group that would operate as a hip-hop advance guard, blending the language and image of a revolutionary army with radical and inventive beats. He enlisted Shocklee as his producer (who dubbed his production crew "The Bomb Squad"), his friends Norman Lee Rogers (DJ Terminator X) on turntables and William Drayton (Flavor Flav) as a second rapper and comic foil, and his fellow Nation of Islam member Richard Griff (Professor Griff) to command the group's backup dancers, the Security of the First World.

Public Enemy. L-R: Chuck D, Flavor Flav [PAUL NATKIN/PHOTO RESERVE]

Believing the Hype

With their revolutionary image and manifesto in place, the group released *Yo! Bum Rush the Show* in 1987 to critical praise but very low sales. The group made an enormous artistic and commercial leap with their follow-up, *It Takes a Nation of Millions to Hold Us Back* (1988), widely considered one of the finest hip-hop albums ever made.

Shocklee perfected Public Enemy's sonic palate, an invigorating collage of hard funk, sirens, and industrial noise that succeeded both as dance music and avant-garde art. Chuck D emerged as a powerful rapper, delivering afrocentric political rants in a deep sonic boom; Flavor Flav perfected his court-jester persona, delivering gallows humor commentary on Chuck D's dead serious statements. They courted controversy from the white establishment for their antigovernment lyrics ("Both King and X they got ridda both" from "Rebel without a Pause"), and they drew praise from critics of all races for the unflinching honesty of their music. At the height of their power, the group made its

first in a string of embarrassing public relations missteps when the *Washington Times* quoted and published Professor Griff's anti-Semitic invective. Chuck D promptly fired his friend and set to work on a new album.

Fear of a Black Planet was released in the spring of 1990 and garnered excellent reviews and sales. The album boasts a fuller, funkier sound, building on the frenetic production of *Millions* with an even more innovative sampling strategy. The single "911 Is a Joke," a seriocomic tale of urban injustice delivered with expert timing by Flavor Flav, shot to the top of the pop singles charts, and incendiary tracks such as "Burn Hollywood Burn" (featuring raps by Ice Cube and Big Daddy Kane) and "Brothers Gonna Work It Out" cemented Public Enemy's reputation as the most danceable political band in the world. No active group pushed hip-hop (or music in general) so far, and their influence would soon cross over into commercial rock.

Apocalypse 91 . . . The Enemy Strikes Black (1991) provided another triumph for the band, and their mix of rebellion and charged beats produced forceful tracks like "Can't Truss It" and "Shut Em Down." Their collaboration with the heavy metal band Anthrax on a remake of the *Millions* track "Bring the Noize" expanded their audience to heavy metal fans and predated the rap-rock trend of the late 1990s. Sadly, *Apocalypse* was the last album of their classic period—it was released just as hip-hop audiences began to swoon over the more laid-back West Coast sound of gangsta rap. By the time they released *Muse Sick-N-Hour Mess Age* in 1994, the band seemed hopelessly outdated as rap trends began to fall in and out of favor in a matter of months. It did not help that *Muse Sick* was a scattered affair hampered by Flavor Flav's increasingly erratic behavior and troubles with the police. The album produced the bouncy single "Give It Up" and promptly faded from the charts.

Faced with a crisis in popularity and group cohesion, Chuck D recorded a solo album, *The Autobiography of Mistachuck*, in 1996 and released his autobiography in 1997. With renewed energy Chuck D reassembled the group and the Bomb Squad, and recorded the soundtrack to Spike Lee's movie *He Got Game* (1998). The album reestablished Public Enemy for an audience that had long forgotten them, proving that they could warm up to the stripped-down productions and quicker rhyme schemes of the newer hip-hop era and dust younger acts with their cutting intelligence. The single "He Got Game" bests the repetitive style of Puff Daddy and his cohorts with a simple loop from Buffalo Springfield's "For What It's Worth" that propels Chuck D and Flavor Flav's biting lyrics on the exploitation of black culture by big business. The album sounds fresh and placed them back in the good graces of the critics.

Apostle of the Internet

As the MP3 format for music downloading rose in popularity in the late 1990s, Chuck D recognized the potential for taking music directly to the audience without the involvement of a major corporate label. He severed ties with Def Jam and released a new Public Enemy album, *There's a Poison Goin' On . . .* (1999), on the Internet before it was available in stores. Driven by a renewed political vitriol, the album harks back to the busy production style of Public Enemy's classic period. Chuck D quickly emerged as the most vocal advocate of Internet distribution, switching his political agenda from battling racism to taking on the music industry. While many major artists spoke out against piracy and lost profits, Chuck D spoke for smaller artists and the populist power of the medium and encouraged fans to download music rather than feed the corporate powers.

In 2002 Public Enemy released *Revolverlution*, an album that combines Chuck D's Internet obsession with a reflective view of Public Enemy's achievements. The album plays like a fan-assembled mix with its blend of new tracks, live recordings, and interview snippets. While not as cohesive or innovative as the classic albums, *Revolverlution* updates Public Enemy's mission by combining populism with revolutionary attitudes and styles. Although they may never recapture their former artistic glory, the group has become a vigilant watchdog of the abuses of corporate America.

SELECTIVE DISCOGRAPHY: *Yo! Bum Rush the Show* (Def Jam, 1987); *It Takes a Nation of Millions to Hold Us Back* (Def Jam, 1988); *Fear of a Black Planet* (Def Jam, 1990); *Apocalypse 91 . . . The Enemy Strikes Black* (Def Jam, 1991); *Greatest Misses* (Def Jam, 1992); *Muse Sick-N-Hour Mess Age* (Def Jam, 1994); *He Got Game* (Def Jam, 1998); *There's a Poison Goin' On . . .* (Play it Again, 1999); *Revolverlution* (Koch, 2002).

WEBSITE: www.publicenemy.com.

SEAN CAMERON

PUDDLE OF MUDD

Formed: 1993, Kansas City, Missouri

Members: Douglas John Ardito, bass (born Concord, Massachusetts, 10 March 1972); Paul James Phillips, guitar (born Brunswick, Georgia, 26 June 1976); Wesley Reid Scantlin, vocals, guitar (born St. Joseph, Missouri, 9 June 1973); Greg David Upchurch, drums (born Houma, Louisiana, 1 December 1973).

Genre: Rock

Best-selling album since 1990: *Come Clean* (2001)

Hit songs since 1990: "Blurry," "Control"

In just a few short years, Puddle of Mudd singer Wes Scantlin went from sneaking backstage at rock shows to headlining his own concerts and selling 1 million copies of his band's hard rock major label debut *Come Clean* (2001). The story of how the Missouri native rose to the top invariably runs through his dogged pursuit of Limp Bizkit singer Fred Durst and a batch of emotionally charged, grunge rock-inspired songs that drew immediate comparisons to a previous decade's tragic rock idol, the late Kurt Cobain of the band Nirvana.

Scantlin had been trying to make a career with his band, Puddle of Mudd, for more than five years. Named after the band's rehearsal space, which had flooded one day when the Mississippi River overflowed its banks, leaving a puddle of mud, the group had slogged it out with a rotating group of members since the early 1990s. After half a decade of frustration and one locally released mini-album (*Stuck*, 1994) and one full length (*Abrasive*, 1997) with original members Jimmy Allen, Sean Sammon, and Kenny Burkett, the singer broke up the group in 1999 and was preparing to move to New Orleans and marry his ex-girlfriend.

When a friend suggested Scantlin attend the 1999 Limp Bizkit–headlined Family Values tour when it came to town, Scantlin made up a fake backstage pass and attempted to track down Bizkit singer and budding label honcho Fred Durst. Though Scantlin failed to find Durst, he did manage to get his last copy of Puddle of Mudd's demo tape into the hands of Durst's bodyguard. Three weeks later, Durst flew Scantlin to Los Angeles and signed him to his Flawless label. When Durst found a backing band to replace the players Scantlin had fired just a few months before, he jokingly referred to the new group as the first "rock and roll boy band."

Scantlin's new cohorts were not new to the music business, either. Drummer Greg Upchurch had played with acclaimed Los Angeles band Eleven and performed as part of former Soundgarden singer Chris Cornell's live band, while bassist Ardito had been in the group Cellophane and was interning at Interscope Records when Durst tapped him for Puddle of Mudd. Guitarist Paul Phillips, formerly of the punk band Happy Hour, was an old friend of Durst's from Jacksonville, Florida.

Though studio veteran Josh Freese played drums on Puddle of Mudd's debut, *Come Clean*, Upchurch later became a full-time member.

Blue-Collar Rock That Struck a Chord

Unlike Durst's nu-metal band, which synthesized hard rock and hip-hop beats, Puddle of Mudd are rock traditionalists, relying on the basic guitar, bass, drums setup, and a charismatic lead singer on *Come Clean,* which debuted in the *Billboard* Top 10 in its first week of release. With Scantlin's gravelly voice frequently compared to Cobain's, and with the quiet verse/loud chorus formula employed to perfection by Cobain's band, Puddle of Mudd unleashed one rock anthem after another with songs such as the raunchy breakthrough hit "Control."

The song is among the first Scantlin wrote upon moving to Los Angeles to relaunch the group, inspired by his ex-girlfriend and a relationship that had run its course. "I need to feel you / You need to feel me / I can't control you / You're not the one for me, no / I can't control you— You can't control me / I need to feel you, so why's there even you and me?," he growls in the song. Durst had a cameo in and directed the video for the song, a bombastic number with grinding guitars and Scantlin's pained, shout/singing.

In a strange bit of irony, Scantlin was arrested in March 2002 for a roadside altercation with his fiancée, Michelle Rubin, which eerily mirrored the plotline for the "Control" video, in which Scantlin has a heated argument with his video girlfriend. Police did not pursue charges against the singer. In another hit song, the power-pop-meets-grunge ditty "She Hates Me," Scantlin laments another messy relationship gone sour.

Side by side with the hard rocking songs on the album are dreamy, string-laden acoustic ballads such as "Drift & Die" and "Blurry," yet another chronicle of failed relationships and emotional abuse. In the video for the latter, Scantlin, in his uniform of classic rock T-shirt, jeans, and backward baseball cap, is shown playing with a young boy who appears to be the same age as his four-year-old son Jordan.

After touring the world for much of 2001, including stints on the 2001 Family Values tour with Stone Temple Pilots, Linkin Park, and another platinum-selling Durst discovery, Staind, as well as a performance with Durst and Led Zeppelin's Jimmy Page at the MTV Europe Awards, Puddle of Mudd were slated to enter a studio to work on the follow-up to *Come Clean,* expected for release in 2003.

Scantlin went from being a construction worker, cook, dishwasher, and frustrated musician to a rock star and million-selling artist over the course of the 1990s. When Durst put together a band for Scantlin, their major label debut landed in the *Billboard* Top 10 and Scantlin was able to take the pain of failed relationships and turn it into hard rock gold.

SELECTIVE DISCOGRAPHY: *Stuck* (V&R, 1994); *Abrasive* (Hardknocks, 1997); *Come Clean* (Flawless/Interscope, 2001).

WEBSITE: www.puddleofmudd.com.

GIL KAUFMAN

$$Q \left|\begin{matrix} q \\ \mathbf{Q} \end{matrix}\right.$$

QUEENS OF THE STONE AGE

Formed: 1997, in Palm Springs, California

Members: Joshua Homme, vocals, guitar; Nick Oliveri, vocals, bass; Mark Lanegan, vocals, guitar (born in Ellensburg, Washington, 25 November 1964); Dave Grohl, drums (born Washington, D.C., 14 January 1969).

Genre: Rock

Best-selling album since 1990: *Songs for the Deaf* (2002)

Hit songs since 1990: "The Lost Art of Keeping a Secret," "Feel Good Hit of the Summer," "No One Knows"

Combining Lollapalooza cynicism with Woodstock hedonism, Queens of the Stone Age used macho guitar riffs and booty-shaking rhythms to appeal to a wider-than-average swath of rock fans.

The band's leaders, Joshua Homme and Nick Oliveri, had plenty of experience with taking the pulse of a crowd before forming the band. They had performed together in Kyuss, a hard-rock band that lasted from 1987 to 1995; they were famous for playing "generator parties" in the Southern California desert—the ultimate in punk shows. Admission was free; anyone, including unsavory characters, could and did attend, and the party lasted as long as the generator did. Homme and Oliveri credit the gigs for forcing them to develop an expansive sound to compensate for the desert's lack of acoustical reverb.

The band's name comes from a 1991 Kyuss recording session in which the producer Chris Goss jokingly christened Kyuss members "queens of the stone age," a wordplay on their being "stoned or whatever," Oliveri

recalled. They were also hoping the name would hint at a stylistic shift and alienate some of the more aggressive mosh-pit mavens who frequented Kyuss concerts.

Their debut album, *Queens of the Stone Age* (1998), rocks with a neo-retro vibe, with lascivious guitar licks conjuring Jimi Hendrix or the Guess Who and Homme's clear, declarative vocals recalling Bad Company. Oliveri, in contrast, is the bad cop, screaming his lyrics for the metalheads. "If Only" features a catchy hook and driving cymbals, signaling that the group has learned a thing or two about groove. The hip-shaking concept hits and misses; the drums on "Walkin' on the Sidewalks" bash instead of propel, while the guitar is slightly clunky.

The promising debut got the group signed to a major label, Interscope, and the Queens set to work on their follow-up. *Rated R* (2000) gave the group its first radio hit, "The Lost Art of Keeping a Secret," an uptempo slice of driving Southern rock. The album maintains its predecessor's nostalgic feel while sprinkling in new elements. The live favorite "Feel Good Hit of the Summer" is a pro-drug anthem that simply lists seven mind-altering substances, punctuating the last one, cocaine, with an aggressive guitar attack. "Better Living Through Chemistry," a similarly themed tune, incorporates Eastern stringed instruments. The calmer, midtempo "Auto Pilot" uses a metronomic, British Invasion-derived beat and sunny harmonies.

The band's rebellious lyrics weren't just a front; they earned a wild reputation on tour. Homme fractured his hand in 2001 during a postgig fight at a Melbourne, Australia, bar. Oliveri, for his part, played wearing nothing but shoes. In 2002 the stunt got Oliveri arrested in Rio de Janeiro,

Brazil. Fans loved the group's anything-goes bent, because it applied to them as well—the band took a laissez-faire attitude towards amateur taping of concerts. That policy, however, prevented the Queens from testing new material in person for fear that a bootleg version of a not-yet-recorded song would make its official release anticlimactic.

Their third release, *Songs for the Deaf* (2002), adds star power with the addition of the drummer Dave Grohl (Nirvana, Foo Fighters) and the vocalist/second guitarist Mark Lanegan of the Screaming Trees. The playing is more technically proficient, and the music rocks harder than before. "No One Knows," which combines classic rock production with a bouncy, repetitive modern-rock guitar hook, became the group's second radio hit. Homme is more audacious about his technical prowess this time out, picking out sixteenth-note riffs on "First It Giveth" and machine-gun thirty-second-note licks on the power-pop "A Song for the Dead." The addition of the legendary Grohl to a semifamous band seemed too good to be true, and sure enough, he left the group during its 2003 tour to rejoin the Foo Fighters. However, the group expected the departure and carried on, signing up to play the main stage at the 2003 Lollapalooza.

Homme proclaimed he was making music "sweet enough for the chicks and heavy enough for the dudes." Stereotypes aside, the group did have an uncanny ability to revel in rock's most notorious excesses while appealing to everyone from Black Sabbath diehards to matchbox twenty fans.

SELECTIVE DISCOGRAPHY: *Queens of the Stone Age* (Loosegroove, 1998); *Rated R* (Interscope, 2000); *Songs for the Deaf* (Interscope, 2002).

RAMIRO BURR

QUEENSRŸCHE

Formed: 1981, Bellevue, Washington

Members: Chris DeGarmo, guitars (born Wenatchee, Washington, 14 June 1963)—in band from 1981–1998; Kelly Gray, guitar; Eddie Jackson, bass (born Robstown, Texas, 29 January 1961); Scott Rockenfield, drums, percussion (born Seattle, Washington, 15 June 1963); Geoff Tate, vocals (born Stuttgart, West Germany, 14 January 1959); Michael Wilton, guitars (born San Francisco, California, 23 February 1962).

Genre: Heavy Metal, Rock

Best-selling album since 1990: *Empire* (1990)

Hit songs since 1990: "Silent Lucidity," "Jet City Woman," "Bridge"

Throughout the 1980s and 1990s, Queensrÿche became one of the most successful and enduring forces in progressive heavy metal. With Geoff Tate's operatic vocals, complex, minor-key guitar progressions, and gothic harmonies, choirs, and orchestrations, the group conjured dark images of despair, unrest, and rebellion. Coupled with social and political commentary, they amassed a large cult following by the late 1980s. Their greatest commercial successes, though, came in the early 1990s with softer love songs. Despite broadening their fan base temporarily, Queensrÿche remained relevant throughout the decade by returning to their heavier sound.

In 1981, at a time when many guitar-heavy acts were making lighthearted music about sex and partying, some progressive bands were continuing in the more cerebral direction of Judas Priest. That year, in the Seattle, Washington, suburb of Bellevue, guitarists Chris DeGarmo and Michael Wilton decided to form a band that leaned towards the latter. By recruiting their high school friend Geoff Tate, who possessed tremendous vocal strength comparable to Judas Priest's Rob Halford and Iron Maiden's Bruce Dickinson, they solidified their chances to compete with those heavyweights. Eddie Jackson, another friend, and drummer Scott Rockenfield, a neighbor, rounded out their lineup.

The band eventually signed to EMI records and released the albums *Queensrÿche* (1983), *The Warning* (1984), and *Rage for Order* (1986). Each release was increasingly accomplished, and their popularity grew. Then, in 1988, they unleashed the concept album masterpiece *Operation: Mindcrime*. The lyrics describe a main character whose disillusionment with Reagan-era America leads him to an anarchist group. The group convinces him to assassinate religious and political leaders as a romantic subplot develops. A major underground success, the album spent a year on the *Billboard* 200 and sold more than 1 million copies.

With its commentary on drug-related gang wars, the ominous first single and title track from *Empire* (1990) suggests that Queensrÿche were picking up where they left off with *Mindcrime*. Much of the album, though, is slicker and more accessible than their previous work. The harder-edged heavier singles, "Empire" and "Best I Can," were minor hits, but the lighter, latter releases—"Jet City Woman," "Another Rainy Night (Without You)," and the majestic, orchestral ballad "Silent Lucidity"—were bigger. "Silent Lucidity" received heavy airplay on MTV and mainstream rock radio, and eventually crossed over to become a Top 10 pop hit. Propelled by six charting singles, the album sold more than 3 million copies and became the band's greatest commercial success.

On their 1991 Building Empires Tour, Queensrÿche bravely chose to downplay the album that made them famous. Though songs from *Empire* and earlier work were played, the focus of each set was the performance of *Operation: Mindcrime* in its entirety, accompanied by related visuals on giant screens. In October *Operation: Livecrime* was released on video and CD. The decision to cater to core fans was the key element to the group's survival throughout the decade.

By the end of the year, their hometown of Seattle produced the no-frills grunge revolution, which overturned the regime of heavy metal excess. In the ensuing years, many pop-metal contemporaries unsuccessfully attempted to acclimate to the changing rock landscape; others quit or were dropped from their major label deals. By taking time off and reverting to their more progressive, *Mindcrime*-era sound with the eventual release of *Promised Land* (1994), Queensrÿche remained vital. The album debuted at number three on the *Billboard* 200 and sold 1 million copies. Though the band's popularity slowly decreased throughout the latter half of the decade, their songs continued to receive modest radio play. Their next albums, *Hear in the Now Frontier* (1997) and *Q2K* (1999) garnered decent sales.

With intellectual and challenging music, Queensrÿche emerged as one of the most distinctive metal bands of the 1980s and 1990s. The group sustained a lengthy career by maintaining a consistent sound before and after a brief venture into the mainstream.

SELECTIVE DISCOGRAPHY: *Rage for Order* (EMI America, 1986); *Operation: Mindcrime* (EMI America, 1988); *Empire* (Capitol, 1990); *Promised Land* (Capitol, 1994).

WEBSITES: www.queensryche.com; www.geofftate.com.

DAVE POWERS

R r
R

R.E.M.

Formed: 1980, Athens, Georgia

Members: Peter Buck, guitar (born Berkeley, California, 6 December 1956); Mike Mills, bass, backing vocals (born Orange, California, 17 December 1958); Michael Stipe, lead vocals (born Decatur, Georgia, 4 January 1960). Former member: Bill Berry, drums (born Duluth, Minnesota, 31 July 1958).

Genre: Rock

Best-selling album since 1990: *Automatic for the People* (1992)

Hit songs since 1990: "Losing My Religion," "Everybody Hurts," "What's the Frequency, Kenneth?"

As the first American alternative rock band to achieve mass appeal, R.E.M. cultivated an audience by remaining true to their postpunk roots, constantly challenging themselves as well as their fans. By fusing jangly guitars with cryptic lyrics that evoked the dark spirit of the deep South, they created a signature sound that appealed to critics and college students throughout the 1980s. After the success of their major-label debut, *Green* (1988), they spent the next several years retooling their approach, leading to unlikely but spectacular commercial and artistic success. The albums *Out of Time* (1991) and *Automatic for the People* (1993) sold millions of copies, despite their dark and challenging material. The band then branched out even farther with the gritty guitar rock of *Monster* (1995) and the electronica-inspired *Up* (1998). They endured health problems and the departure of an original member, Bill Berry, to remain one of rock's most relevant and creative bands.

Southern Roots

R.E.M. started in the college town of Athens, Georgia. Mike Mills and Bill Berry had been playing music together since attending high school in Macon, Georgia, and Michael Stipe and Peter Buck bonded over their shared musical taste at a local record store. The two pairs of friends eventually got together and started to play cover songs in an abandoned church. Soon they began composing original material, adopting the name R.E.M. and joining the new wave of inventive Southern postpunk bands that included the B-52s and Pylon. Though all the band members developed quickly as musicians, the thrust of the R.E.M. sound became Buck's jangly, 1960s-style guitar playing and Stipe's mumbled singing and non sequitur lyrics. They toured relentlessly, and their popularity increased exponentially. In the summer of 1981, they recorded the single "Radio Free Europe," which, despite its very small pressing of 1,000 copies, was named Independent Single of the Year by the *Village Voice*.

From *Murmur* to *Monster*

After the success of "Radio Free Europe" and the EP *Chronic Town* (1982), the band recorded its first full-length album, *Murmur*, for the independent label I.R.S. in 1983. It was released to similarly enthusiastic reviews, culminating with a best album nod from *Rolling Stone* magazine. That an independent band from Georgia could accomplish this feat, beating out such heavy hitters as Michael Jackson and the Police, seemed revolutionary. The music is complex and haunting, with strong rhythms derived from English postpunk, and the unique combination of Buck's bright guitar lines and Stipe's passionate vocals. It seems to be distilled from the same sources as the novels of William Faulkner, resulting in a juxtaposition of lush beauty and Southern madness. While other American underground guitar acts of the era explored the possibilities of abrasive noise, R.E.M. concentrated on developing a signature voice, by turns melancholy and gorgeous.

R.E.M. recorded four more albums for I.R.S. and scored a Top 10 single in 1987 with the song "The One I Love" from the album *Document* (1987). The following year they signed to Warner Bros. and released *Green* (1988). The album is an extension of the sound they developed throughout their independent years, amplified by an aggressive production that favors the guitars and drums. They notched hits with the playful "Stand" and the foreboding "Orange Crush." They embarked on an extensive world tour that left them exhausted.

While on break from touring, the band began to develop songs that sounded nothing like their previous work. Many took this to be a sign of concert burnout, as the band stated that they would not tour in support of the new material. Though seemingly a gesture aimed at alienating their fans, *Out of Time* (1991) emerged as their biggest-selling and most personal album to date. The songs evoke the pastoral Georgia setting of its recording, with Buck abandoning the electric guitar almost completely for acoustic instruments. The lush single "Losing My Religion," a somber meditation on faith driven by Buck's mandolin, rocketed to the top bracket of the pop charts, despite (or perhaps because of) the fact that it sounded like nothing else on the radio. Stylistically, *Out of Time* is all over the map, from the funk assault of "Radio Song" (complete with a rap by KRS-One) to the magisterial pop of "Near Wild Heaven." The album represents a revamped R.E.M., dipping into new sounds and genres, and finding their feet as a band all over again.

The band continued this eclectic streak with the moody *Automatic for the People* (1992). Not as awkward as moments of *Out of Time*, the album finds R.E.M. at the peak of their considerable powers. Many of its most memorable songs merge a sullen tone with invigorating instrumentation, such as the highly textured melancholy of "Sweetness Follows" and the gorgeous piano ballad "Nightswimming." These down moments are balanced out by the dizzy pop of "The Sidewinder Sleeps Tonight," and the crunchy country rock of "Man on the Moon." "Everybody Hurts" emerges as the band's most direct ballad, a simple and affecting wail for hope against hope propelled by Stipe's most soulful vocal performance. Closing with the hopeful pocket symphony

Spot Light | The *Monster* Tour

Michael Stipe liked to joke that R.E.M. would eventually break up on stage at the stroke of midnight, New Year's Eve 2000. The series of health problems that plagued their worldwide *Monster* tour of 1995, however, seemed calculated to turn that prediction into reality a few years ahead of schedule. The *Monster* tour marked R.E.M.'s return to the road after a hiatus of nearly six years. With a full slate of dates in North America and Europe, it was the band's most ambitious tour, and their first since rising to international fame. The troubles began at a March date in Lausanne, Switzerland, when drummer Bill Berry collapsed ninety minutes into the show, suffering from a brain aneurysm. Berry was saved from death by emergency surgery, and the band resumed the tour in May. Two months later Mike Mills underwent surgery to remove an intestinal tumor; in August the tour was interrupted yet again as Stipe went under the knife for an emergency hernia-removal procedure. Despite these obstacles, the tour was a massive commercial success and featured the band in top form. Along the way they recorded the brilliant *New Adventures in Hi-Fi* (1996), their final album with Berry on drums. Although he maintains that the *Monster* experience did not influence his decision, Berry left the band and retired to his Georgia farm before the recording of *Up* (1998). Ever stalwart, the band pressed on and recorded the album not with a new drummer but with electronic beats and drum loops in their most experimental work to date.

"Find the River," *Automatic* stands as R.E.M.'s most stunning accomplishment.

By 1994 R.E.M. was ready to return to the road and celebrated this new spirit with the amped-up guitar rock of *Monster* (1994). The album is not as accomplished as its predecessor, but it boasts yet another new direction for the band as they try their hand at the sludgy guitar dynamics that ruled American rock at the time. Their creativity shines through the feedback, as evidenced by the supremely catchy "What's the Frequency, Kenneth?" and the sleazy glam-rock ode "Crush with Eyeliner." The band embarked on a massive and successful world tour that was marred by health emergencies, including a brain aneurysm suffered by Berry and surgeries for Mills and Stipe.

During the *Monster* tour, the band recorded songs in several cities that were compiled and released as *New Adventures in Hi-Fi* (1996). The album plays like an alternative greatest hits collection, with the band revisiting the various styles of their entire catalog and producing some of their best stand-alone songs. "Leave" is an angry lament played over a sample of a siren. "Undertow" finds the band employing Buck's raging guitars more effectively than anything on *Monster*, backing Stipe's visceral lyrics about emotional and/or physical drowning with expert force. "E-Bow the Letter," a duet with Patti Smith, recalls the lush balladry of *Out of Time*, and the bittersweet "Electrolite" evokes the warm Southern tone of their early albums with a simple, elegant piano arrangement.

New Adventures

Shortly after the release of *New Adventures in Hi-Fi*, the longtime drummer Berry announced that he was leaving the band. Facing an uncertain future as a trio, R.E.M. commenced a fractious period that culminated in the release of *Up* (1998). Despite the reported friction during its recording, the record is remarkably breezy, their most experimental effort to date. The band dabbles in the sonic textures of electronica, adding warmth to the cold, mechanical structures of "Lotus" and "Airportman." The effect is surprisingly effective, with Stipe especially opening up and having fun with the album's array of new sounds, especially on the jittery "Hope." For added effect they replicate the sound of the Beach Boys on "At My Most Beautiful" and even take a detour back to jangle pop for the anthemic "Daysleeper." The band returned to the road once again, playing selections from their entire catalog and performing the new material with surprising élan.

In 2001, R.E.M. released their twelfth album, *Reveal*, which was marked by further but more comfortable sonic experimentation. The single "Imitation of Life" displays a conscious joining of the old and new R.E.M. aesthetic: a soaring, jangly chorus undercut with electronic details. The songs lack the live immediacy of their past work, but the focus on studio craft suits the nature of the new material. As its title suggests, *Reveal* invites close listening with deep rewards for the R.E.M. faithful and rock/pop fans alike.

R.E.M. have earned the rare combination of critical and commercial plaudits throughout their career. It is nearly impossible to imagine a rock landscape devoid of their ever-innovative presence.

SELECTIVE DISCOGRAPHY: *Chronic Town* (EP) (IRS, 1982); *Murmur* (IRS, 1983); *Reckoning* (IRS, 1984); *Fables of the Reconstruction* (IRS, 1985); *Life's Rich Pageant* (IRS, 1986); *Dead Letter Office* (IRS, 1987); *Document* (IRS, 1987); *Eponymous* (IRS, 1988); *Green* (Warner Bros., 1988); *Out of Time* (Warner Bros., 1991); *Automatic for the People* (Warner Bros., 1992); *Monster* (Warner Bros., 1994); *New Adventures in Hi-Fi* (Warner Bros., 1996); *Up* (Warner Bros., 1998); *Reveal* (Warner Bros., 2001).

WEBSITE: www.remhq.com.

SEAN CAMERON

RADIOHEAD

Formed: 1987, Oxford, England

Members: Colin Greenwood, bass (born Oxford, England, 26 June 1969); Jonny Greenwood, guitar (born Oxford, England, 5 November 1971); Ed O'Brien, guitar, vocals (born Oxford, England, 15 April 1968); Phil Selway, drums (born Hemingford Grey, Cambridgeshire, England, 23 May 1967); Thom Yorke, vocals, guitar (born Wellingborough, Northamptonshire, England, 7 October 1968).

Genre: Rock

Best-selling album since 1990: *Kid A* (2000)

Hit songs since 1990: "Creep," "Paranoid Android," "Karma Police"

Following the Britpop boom of the mid-1990s, when bands like Oasis and Blur threatened to leave a sizable mark on the United States, a group that actually fulfilled the promise emerged in their wake. Radiohead escaped the ghetto of cultdom to become one of the most important new rock acts to emerge from the British Isles since Ireland's U2 in the 1980s. In a series of ever-developing albums, Radiohead revived memories of the progressive rock experimentalists of the late 1960s, winning comparisons to early innovators such as Pink Floyd. But they have managed to avoid the confining straitjacket that such associations could have created for them. Instead, in a decade of fervent and sometimes challenging invention, they established their own unique place in the contemporary rock firmament.

Beginnings

Formed initially as On a Friday in the late 1980s, Radiohead are a rare British band because their members have benefited from university education. Only Jonny Greenwood, younger brother of Colin, lacks a degree—he dropped out of Oxford University after three months to pursue the group's possibilities at the beginning of the 1990s.

Originally a gathering of school friends, the band adopted its current identity in 1991 as the various individuals returned to their home city of Oxford after

Thom Yorke of Radiohead [PAUL NATKIN/PHOTO RESERVE]

graduation: Thom Yorke had studied English and fine art in Exeter, Phil Selway had studied English and history at Liverpool, Ed O'Brien had been to Manchester, and Colin Greenwood had done literature at Cambridge.

Attention Grabbing

Still performing as On a Friday, they began to attract the attention of the talent scouts, and in the fall of 1991, the quintet was snapped up by the EMI subsidiary Parlophone, the Beatles' original U.K. label. In early 1992 they adopted their new name, Radiohead, a reference to a song by Talking Heads. Radiohead's intense, unsettling music-making set them apart from the mainstream scene. While their music employed elements of guitar-fueled alternative rock, their use of other, more experimental production techniques and melancholic lyrical content allowed the group to stand out from the crowd. At first, the band struggled to live up to Parlophone's faith as the EP *Drill* (1992) stalled commercially and the singles "Creep" (1992) and "Anyone Can Play Guitar" (1993) made scant impression.

Yet there were some promising signs—critical reaction to the early work had been quite positive, and, when the first album, *Pablo Honey* (1993), came out, it scrambled into the lower reaches of the Top 30. More significantly, it included the song "Creep," an unnerving slice

of self-pity that found its way on to U.S. college radio, where its mood—a searing blend of outsider anguish and jagged guitar noise—resonated with listeners and gave the group a Top 40 hit. Before 1993 had drawn to a close, the debut album had been certified platinum in the United States.

In 1994 Radiohead built on this platform, playing important summer festivals at Glastonbury and Reading, undertaking an intensive U.K. tour, and beginning work in the fall on their second album. The resulting collection, entitled *The Bends* (1995), produced by John Leckie, clinched a Top 10 album placing in the U.K. and drew interest in the United States.

The new album spawned a number of notable hits with "Fake Plastic Trees" (also included on the movie soundtrack to *Clueless*), "Street Spirit (Fade Out)," and "Just" all scoring in the U.K. Top 20. The latter track also left its mark on MTV with a bleak but diverting video, directed by Jamie Thraves, of a man lying on the sidewalk. Such dark and disturbing images became increasingly associated with the band's single-minded approach to their craft.

Benefit Album

Summer 1995 saw Radiohead support R.E.M. on a U.S. tour, opening further avenues in America. Shortly afterwards, Yorke found common cause with former Roxy Music star and producer Brian Eno on a compilation benefit album, *Help!*, aimed at raising funds for charitable efforts in strife-torn Bosnia. In the following months the band joined tours with Soul Asylum and, in the summer of 1996, Alanis Morissette, who was including her own version of "Fake Plastic Trees" in her set.

The third album was recorded at a medieval mansion in Bath, England. With a working title of "Ones and Zeroes," a reference to the binary language of computers, the result was the impressive *OK Computer* (1997). It is an ambitious affair that blends a rock format with studio trickery, eliciting comparisons to Pink Floyd and prompting press speculation that it signalled a progressive rock resurrection. Trailed by an epic single, the six-and-a-half minute "Paranoid Android"—a passing reference to a character in Douglas Adams's sci-fi novel *The Hitch-Hiker's Guide to the Galaxy*—the album prompted the most critically favorable reception so far.

Other tracks from the album placed in the U.K. Top 40. "Karma Police" and "No Surprises" were typical pieces in the *OK Computer* jigsaw: maudlin, mysterious, and introspective but also strangely sinister. Much of the writing and lyrical content seemed to owe something to Yorke's long-term interest in Outsider Art—paintings and other artworks created by untrained, sometimes mentally unstable, practitioners.

Spot Light | "Creep"

If any song transformed Radiohead from unknowns with potential into stars in the making, it was "Creep." A song with more than a note of self-pity, even self-loathing, the piece quickly became associated with its singer, Thom Yorke. It tells the tale of unrequited romance and focuses on the sense of inadequacy the rejected lover suffers: "But I'm a creep, I'm a weirdo / what the hell am I doing here?" It was when this most unlikely of rock classics began to attract the attention of radio stations in San Francisco and then in Los Angeles in 1993 that Radiohead knew it would become one of their signature songs. One problem that faced Yorke was the general assumption that the song was autobiographical. When Yorke was asked, "Are you the 'Creep' guy?," the group would retort, "Yeah, we're the 'Creep' guys."

Band of the Year

Questioned in some quarters for an apparent obsession with the downbeat, the miserable, and the doom-laden, the record nonetheless seemed to distill the spirit of the moment. In the United States, the magazines *Spin* and *Rolling Stone* both named Radiohead band of the year in 1997. In the time before the recording of their eagerly anticipated follow-up, the band fully exploited the opportunities offered by the Internet, offering previews of most of the new set's tracks via MP3 files. So effective was the tactic in building consumer fascination that the new recording *Kid A* (2000) entered the U.S. charts at number one.

Produced by the band with Nigel Godrich, *Kid A* took the band farther away from the rock structures featured on earlier releases. The three-guitar attack, which had been employed to potent effect on the first trio of albums, was now largely sidelined as electronic washes wrapped Yorke's disembodied vocals in an ethereal soundscape.

The opener, "Everything in Its Right Place," sets the tone with waves of keyboards at its core, while "The National Anthem," a storming, stomping, bass-heavy track with the artillery of the brass leading from the front, is an assault on the senses. In contrast, the fragile tones of "Idioteque" entices rather than ensnares the listener.

Companion Edition

It would not be long before another album appeared from the same recording sessions. The following summer, *Amnesiac* (2001) provided a companion collection to *Kid A* and, if anything, suggested an even darker setting. Although the band insisted that the new record was more than mere outtakes from the original project, the rationale for issuing a further set of songs was never fully explained.

Nonetheless, there was no discernible decline in quality. *Amnesiac* was more moving and haunting than its predecessor, with the extraordinary "Packt Like Sardines in a Crushd Tin Box," a plaintive and desperate plea, leading into a maze of melancholy cameos; the terse domestic drama of "Morning Bell," an amended reprise of a *Kid A* track; and the mournful, contemporary blues of "Life in a Glasshouse," replete with the New Orleans stylings of Humphrey Lyttelton's traditional jazz band.

Late in 2001, the rush of releases continued as *I Might Be a Wrong: Live Recordings* completed a trio of related recordings. It features live performances recorded around Europe and offers some of the finest bits of *Kid A* and *Amnesiac*, including "The National Anthem" and "Like Spinning Plates."

Legacy

During the 1990s Radiohead managed to avoid the mainstream. They attained success on their own, idiosyncratic terms, side-stepping the star-making machinery—the standard promotional interview, for example—and pursuing an agenda of their own that included uncompromising videos and band images that rejected the merely photogenic. Distanced from the Britpop surge, with its strong tendency to nostalgia, the band followed an increasingly experimental line. At one stage it seemed that they might be at the heart of a progressive rock revival, but then they moved to another stage by sculpting a pair of minimal, electronically based albums. They earned high ratings from the critics, who seemed to yearn for a band that takes chances and has the courage to risk failure at a time when the popular music scene was driven by the visual cliché, the machismo of rap, and the guitar posturing of nu-metal.

Radiohead managed to break a 1990s pattern of U.K. groups routinely stumbling at the challenge of the huge U.S. market; Radiohead surmounted this hurdle through a shrewd use of the Internet as a promotional tool. A band of originality and intelligence, Radiohead has left an indelible mark on the evolution of rock music.

SELECTIVE DISCOGRAPHY: *Pablo Honey* (Capitol, 1993); *The Bends* (Capitol, 1995); *OK Computer* (Capitol, 1997); *Kid A* (Capitol, 2000); *Amnesiac* (Capitol, 2001); *I Might Be Wrong: Live Recordings* (Capitol, 2001); *Hail to the Thief* (Capitol, 2003).

BIBLIOGRAPHY: S. Malins, *Radiohead: Coming Up for Air* (London, 1997); M. Randall, *Exit Music: The Radiohead Story* (London, 2000); J. Doheny, *Radiohead-Karma Police: The Story Behind Every Song* (London, 2002); M. Clarke, *Radiohead* (London, 2003).

WEBSITE: www.radiohead.com.

SIMON WARNER

RAGE AGAINST THE MACHINE

Formed: 1991, Los Angeles, California; Disbanded 2000

Members: Tim Commerford, bass (born Irvine, California); Tom Morello, guitar (born New York, New York, 30 May 1964); Zack de la Rocha, vocals (born Long Beach, California, 12 January, 1970); Brad Wilk, drums (born Portland, Oregon, 15 September 1968)

Genre: Rock

Best-selling album since 1990: *Rage Against the Machine* (1992)

Hit songs since 1990: "Killing in the Name," "Bulls on Parade," "People of the Sun"

Few bands in the history of popular music have blended righteousness and rock as potently as the volatile group Rage Against the Machine. With bombastic messages and left-wing political stances that matched the fiery sound of their music—a combination of heavy metal guitars and hip-hop lyrics and beats—Rage Against the Machine stood as one of the most principled, socially and politically active bands of the 1990s. The formula, however, proved too volatile, and the band collapsed in 2000 under the pressure of the internal tensions between its members.

The nucleus of Rage Against the Machine was formed in Los Angeles in 1991 by a pair of young men from politically active, socially progressive families. The singer Zack de la Rocha is the son of the Mexican muralist Beto. The band gelled when de la Rocha met the guitarist Tom Morello, whose father had served as a member of the Mau Mau guerrilla organization that had freed Kenya from colonial rule in the 1960s. Morello's mother, Mary, was a schoolteacher who later formed the anticensorship organization Parents for Rock & Rap.

Morello and de la Rocha, along with the singer's friend, the bassist Tim Commerford, joined with the drummer Brad Wilk to release a self-produced twelve-song cassette in early 1992 featuring the incendiary gun-violence song "Bullet in the Head," which later appeared on the band's major label debut. Featuring the combination of de la Rocha's mesmerizing, high-energy stage presence and Morello's ostentatious guitar playing, the cassette sold more than 5,000 copies through the group's fan club and at concerts.

After getting assurances that they would be free to express their opinions in song, the band signed with Epic Records, which released their self-titled debut in November 1992. The album is a musical hand grenade, with de la Rocha shouting and rapping his lyrics to songs such as "Bombtrack" and "Freedom," while Morello manipulates his guitar to sound like everything from an air raid siren to a turntable. Though rock with a hip-hop edge became de riguer by the late 1990s, in 1992 Rage's combination of abrasive rock energy and a hard-rapping style was bracing and unconventional.

The album's highlight is the explosive hit single "Killing in the Name," which features the lyrics, "Some of those that work forces / Are the saints that burn crosses." The song contains all of the elements that helped the album sell more than 4 million copies: Morello's alternately funky, heavy metal, and electronic-sounding guitar playing; de la Rocha's shouted, impassioned vocals; and Wilk and Commerford's ominous rhythm tracks. After a year the album climbed to number seventy on the *Billboard* charts with little or no airplay, but it rebounded in December with the band's first MTV-aired video, for the song "Freedom."

With liner notes that read like a political manifesto, the group made it clear that their music had a message; they supported groups such as the prochoice Rock for Choice, FAIR (Fairness and Accuracy in Reporting), and the activists campaigning for the release of the African-American journalist and activist Mumia Abu-Jamal.

Whispers of the group's demise dogged them when a follow-up album was slow to come. The rumors were fueled by their admitted reluctance to spend time together when not performing or recording. But the group silenced doubters with *Evil Empire* (1996), a blistering album that entered the *Billboard* charts at number one, launching the strident hit single "Bulls on Parade." Their April 1996 appearance on *Saturday Night Live* was cut from two songs to one when the band ended a song by attempting to hang an inverted American flag—a sign of distress—on their amplifiers. Like their first effort, the second album's liner notes mention that every note was created by just bass, guitar, drums, and voice; Morello's guitar once again sounding like everything from a keyboard to a turntable to a video game.

De la Rocha's lyrics burn with a renewed intensity on tracks such as "Vietnow," "Revolver," and "Down Rodeo," on which his intricate wordplay touches on topics ranging from media manipulation to immigrant labor without resorting to blunt, obvious imagery.

A fall 1997 tour with popular rap group the Wu-Tang Clan fell apart after one week, with the rappers dropping out. Toning down the ferocity a notch, the band included a meditative cover of Bruce Springsteen's Steinbeck homage, "The Ghost of Tom Joad," on its self-titled home video released in November of 1997.

The group's third album, *The Battle of Los Angeles* (1999), also debuted at number one on the *Billboard* chart, preceded by the single "Guerilla Radio." Recorded in just one month, it is the group's most fully realized effort to date, with Morello's gigantic, eclectic guitar riffs complementing de la Rocha's even more rap-like lyrical delivery on songs such as "Calm Like a Bomb" and "Mic Check."

De la Rocha announced plans to record a solo album in early 2000, and the group played a riot-marred, explosive set outside the Democratic National Convention in August. Just a month after a drunken Commerford was arrested for climbing a set piece and interrupting an acceptance speech by Limp Bizkit at the MTV Video Music Awards in September, de la Rocha announced his departure from the group, citing breakdowns in communication. *Renegades*, an album on which the group covers songs by rappers Eric B. Rakim and EPMD and protest rockers Bob Dylan and MC5, was released in December.

Rage Against the Machine was one of the most beloved, outspoken, and hard-rocking bands of the 1990s. Never content to create mere entertainment, the group sought to educate, uplift, and provoke with their sophisticated, radical songs and activities, melding 1960s political commitment with a thoroughly contemporary 1990s sound.

SELECTIVE DISCOGRAPHY: *Rage Against the Machine* (Epic, 1992); *Evil Empire* (Epic, 1996); *The Battle of Los Angeles* (Epic, 1999); *Renegades* (Epic, 2000).

GIL KAUFMAN

BONNIE RAITT

Born: Burbank, California, 8 November 1949

Genre: Rock

Best-selling album since 1990: *Luck of the Draw* (1991)

Hit songs since 1990: "Something to Talk About," "I Can't Make You Love Me," "Love Sneakin' Up on You"

Performing a unique hybrid of blues, rock, and R&B, Bonnie Raitt earned critical praise beginning in the early 1970s, when her good taste, eclectic musical sensibility, and strong voice informed a series of highly personal recordings. One of the few women to excel at "bottleneck"

guitar playing—in which the musician plays with a metal or glass device placed over a finger of the left hand—Raitt brought to her music a genuine respect for the traditions of the past, updating them with a sharp, sensuous modern edge. In 1989, after recording for nearly two decades, she finally gained mainstream recognition with *Nick of Time*, an album that spawned several hits and Grammy Awards. During the 1990s Raitt continued to refine her style, releasing hits that emphasized her strengths as a subtle balladeer. These successes notwithstanding, Raitt rarely diluted the tough power of her sound, thereby limiting her ongoing commercial presence as the 1990s progressed. A dedicated activist as well as musician, Raitt in the 1990s worked tirelessly to gain recognition and financial assistance for overlooked pioneers of R&B music.

Early Critical Acclaim

The daughter of singer John Raitt, famous for his performances in classic Broadway musicals such as *Carousel* (1945) and *The Pajama Game* (1954), Raitt learned guitar at the age of twelve, developing an early love for blues music. Entering Radcliffe College in 1967, Raitt began performing in coffeehouses and clubs, eventually working as an opening act for blues performer John Hammond. Manager Dick Waterman signed her in the late 1960s, arranging for her to appear on bills with his other clients, classic blues singers Howlin' Wolf, Sippie Wallace, and Mississippi Fred McDowell. Signing to Warner Bros. Records in 1971, Raitt released a series of albums that garnered critical acclaim but little popular acceptance. *Give It Up* (1972) is one of the most notable of Raitt's early works, enlivened by tough, assertive blues such as "Love Me Like a Man" and the tender ballad "Love Has No Pride." Throughout the 1970s, Raitt worked with a series of producers on albums that veered from tough R&B to sophisticated pop, all without commercial success—although a 1979 version of 1960s rock singer Del Shannon's song "Runaway" was a minor hit. Dropped by Warner Bros. in 1986, Raitt signed with Capitol Records and began working with Don Was, best known as part of the R&B group Was (Not Was) and as producer for the funky rock group the B-52s. *Nick of Time* (1989) was Raitt's breakthrough, an album on which her diverse musical impulses coalesced into a polished but gritty sound. Featuring the hit singles "Thing Called Love" and "Have a Heart," *Nick of Time* won a Grammy Award for Album of the Year.

1990s Stardom

Raitt's newfound commercial prominence expanded in the early 1990s, with her follow-up to *Nick of Time*, *Luck of the Draw* (1991), becoming her best-selling release to date. On the insistent, subtly rocking hit, "Something to Talk About," Raitt finds an ideal outlet for her frisky, likable persona; the song proved so popular that Hollywood producers borrowed its title for a 1995 movie. On the album's second big hit, "I Can't Make You Love Me," Raitt reveals her talents as a gentle ballad singer, building power in her performance through expert timing and vocal control. The song is one of the rare singles to appeal to fans of both hard rock and smooth, "adult contemporary" pop—a measure of Raitt's taste and sensitivity. Elsewhere on the album, Raitt duets with R&B-influenced rock performer Delbert McClinton on "Good Man, Good Woman," a funky track underscored by percolating guitar rhythms. Raitt also proves herself a songwriter of the highest rank, penning the tough, sexually themed "Tangled and Dark" as well as the moving ballad "All at Once," on which she alternates between somber and uplifting passages with consummate skill. The song also represents one of Raitt's most affecting, honest moments on record, her lyrics pointing to a new level of maturity: "Had a fight with my daughter / She flew off in a rage / The third time this week / Don't tell me it's the age." During this period of her career, Raitt found personal contentment, giving up drugs and alcohol and marrying actor Michael O'Keefe in 1991 (the couple divorced at the end of 1999).

After working with Was on *Longing in Their Hearts* (1994), an album similar in sound and style to its two predecessors, Raitt released a smoldering live set, *Road Tested* (1995), before switching to the production team of Mitchell Froom and Tchad Blake for *Fundamental* (1998). Although commercially disappointing—none of its singles succeeded in charting—*Fundamental* stands as one of Raitt's most stimulating albums. Froom and Blake, known for their work with rock artists such as Elvis Costello and Suzanne Vega, provide Raitt with a full, dense sound and a gritty edge. The album's opener, "The Fundamental Things," is lean and streamlined, featuring relaxed, simmering horns that fall in line with the song's back-to-basics message: "Let's run naked through the city streets / we're all victims of captivity." "Round & Round" is a roots-oriented blues number, sporting rustic-sounding percussion and Raitt's fine bottleneck guitar work, while "Spit of Love," "I Need Love," and the shuffling "Meet Me Half Way" all rank as tough, uncompromising blues-inflected rock. Critics note that the album's most powerful moment, however, is the brooding "Lovers Will," a song penned by rock artist John Haitt, one of Raitt's favorite writers. Set against a simmering bed of organ, horns, and heavy drums, "Lovers Will" is a dark yet colorful tale of desire and abjection: "Who'll take the only hearts they got, and throw 'em into the fire / who'll risk their own self-respect in the name of desire . . . lovers will." Through-

out the song Raitt uses her cool, biting vocals to balance intensity with resignation.

During the 1990s Raitt was heavily involved with the Rhythm & Blues Foundation, an organization that honors overlooked pioneers of R&B. Serving as board member and emceeing benefit events each year, Raitt has given awards to many of her artistic forebears, such as New Orleans–based vocalist Irma Thomas and Ruth Brown, one of the biggest R&B stars of the early 1950s. A member of the liberal Quaker religious tradition, Raitt in the 1990s also lent her support to environmental and antiwar causes. In 2002 she released *Silver Lining,* handling most of the production duties herself. Beginning with the loose, rocking R&B groove of "Fool's Game" and continuing through the pounding, raucous "Gnawin' on It," the album provides a well-rounded portrait of Raitt's many talents and interests, although it lacks *Fundamental*'s succinct power.

Bonnie Raitt's passion, commitment, and expansive talent have earned her a special place in American popular music. One of the few female slide guitar players, and an early proponent of eclecticism in rock, Raitt pursued her artistic interests for decades before capturing a mainstream audience in the early 1990s. By the beginning of the millennium, Raitt was producing her own albums and overseeing her career with undiminished vigor.

SELECTIVE DISCOGRAPHY: *Bonnie Raitt* (Warner Bros., 1971); *Give It Up* (Warner Bros., 1972); *The Glow* (Warner Bros., 1979); *Nick of Time* (Capitol, 1989); *Luck of the Draw* (Capitol, 1991); *Longing in Their Hearts* (Capitol, 1994); *Road Tested* (Capitol, 1995); *Fundamental* (Capitol, 1998); *Silver Lining* (Capitol, 2002).

WEBSITE: www.bonnieraitt.com.

DAVID FREELAND

RAKIM

Born: William Griffin Jr.; Wyandanch, New York, 28 January 1968
Genre: Rap
Best-selling album since 1990: *The 18th Letter* (1997)
Hit songs since 1990: "What's on Your Mind" (with Eric B.), "It's Been a Long Time"

In the mid-1980s Rakim broke the conventional, uneven staccato delivery of rap with a new flow that was smooth and direct. His spiritual and complex rhymes often read like poetry, rewarding the scrutiny of the printed page.

Born in Long Island, New York, Rakim converted to Islam at age sixteen and changed his name to Rakim Allah.

A year later he met Eric B., a disc jockey and producer, and they released their independent debut *Paid in Full* (1987). The contrast between disc jockey and rapper gives the album its edge. Eric B. sounds as if he created his dance-ready beats in a crowded nightclub, while Rakim seems to have composed his lyrics comfortably seated, listening to soft jazz. Indeed, Rakim often wrote his rhymes while lounging to soothing instrumentals. The debut's title track is the model for all of rap's rags-to-riches stories, one of the genre's popular themes. "Thinking of a master plan / There ain't nothing but sweat inside my hand" is not just Rakim's coming-of-age tale, but the whole history of hip-hop. The album was a cultural watershed and went gold. Eric B. and Rakim signed to MCA Records for a reported sum of $1 million and in doing so helped usher in the commercial era of hip-hop.

In *Follow the Leader* (1988), their second album, Rakim and Eric B. diverged further, to radiant effects. Here, Eric B.'s soundscapes are more urgent and frenetic while Rakim's words are more calm and introspective. By 1990, the release year of Rakim's third album with Eric B., *Let the Rhythm Hit 'Em*, the world of hip-hop was enthralled by new exotic sounds, like those of Native Tongue groups De La Soul and the Jungle Brothers. Nevertheless, *Let the Rhythm Hit 'Em* glitters with originality, particularly the mystical realism of "The Ghetto," and the soulful dignity of "Mahogany."

Don't Sweat the Technique (1992) was Rakim's last album with Eric B., and the only one not to win a gold or platinum plaque. It features the clever word play of "Know the Ledge" and "The Punisher," but fans were beginning to doubt Eric. B's musical ability to showcase Rakim's extraordinary talents, and the duo split. Rakim emerged years later with a solo effort, *The 18th Letter* (1997), which entered the *Billboard* pop charts at number four. *The 18th Letter* did achieve a cohesive sound due to Rakim's retention of producers who catered to hardcore hip-hop fans, DJ Premier of Gang Starr, Pete Rock, and Clark Kent. This album adheres to the fundamentals of hip-hop, using old school cut and scratches, and underscoring Rakim's affinity for 1980s rap, with the rapper assuming the role of elder statesman, particularly on "It's Been a Long Time" and "Remember That."

The Master (1999) attempts to echo the flashy sound of late 1990s hip-hop. Rakim reaches beyond his typical zone of underground producers and straightforward delivery. He slows down his cadence on "Flow Forever" and attempts a pop hook on "Finest Ones." These efforts confused die-hard fans and failed to convert new ones. *The Master* did not achieve gold status.

Regardless of record sales, Rakim has made steady contributions to hip-hop. While many rappers jump from topic to topic in their rhymes, Rakim adheres to poetic cohe-sion, weaving single images throughout his songs, like the cinema theme in "The Saga Continues," from *The 18th Letter* (1997). Poet Sonia Sanchez considers Rakim a gifted artist and she recites his rhyme, "Casualties of War," during her own readings.

Recent years have found Rakim linked to Dr. Dre, the great hip-hop producer. Together, they created the 2002 hit single "Addictive" with artist Truth Hurts. Nearly every contemporary rapper, from Eminem to Nas, expressed an indebtedness to Rakim. Many artists, critics, and long-term fans consider him one of the most influential rappers of all time.

SELECTIVE DISCOGRAPHY: *Paid in Full* (4th & Broadway, 1987); *Follow the Leader* (UNI, 1988); *Let the Rhythm Hit 'Em* (MCA, 1990); *Don't Sweat the Technique* (MCA, 1992); *The 18th Letter* (Universal, 1997); *The Master* (Universal, 1999).

DARA COOK

RANCID

Formed: 1990, Albany, California

Members: Tim Armstrong, guitar, vocals (born Albany, California); Lars Frederiksen, guitar, vocals (born Campbell, California, 30 August 1971); Matt Freeman, bass (born Albany, California); Brett Reed, drums (born Albany, California).

Genre: Rock

Best-selling album since 1990: *And Out Come the Wolves* (1995)

Hit songs since 1990: "Salvation," "Ruby Soho," "Timebomb"

Of the neo-punk bands that popped onto MTV in the brief mid-1990s revival, Rancid was the group that hewed closest to punk tradition. Lefty guitarist Armstrong delivered his lyrics with a slurred, faux British accent accompanied by a mischievous sneer, while guitarist Frederiksen and bassist Freeman offered bright harmonies and spry licks. The group's members were already seasoned performers by the time fame hit and managed to take their brief burst of stardom in stride.

Armstrong and Freeman had been part of Bay Area punk group Operation Ivy in the late 1980s. For Rancid the pair brought in experienced local drummer Reed. Interestingly, Green Day front man Billie Joe Armstrong performed a gig with the group before Frederiksen became a permanent member. He also co-wrote early track "Radio, Radio, Radio." The group's material got the attention of Epitaph Records founder and Bad Religion guitarist Brett Gurewitz, who signed Rancid in 1992. Their debut CD,

Rancid (1993), is straight-ahead punk and brought in second guitarist/vocalist Frederiksen. The album features "Hyena," a simple skate-punk track that showcases the band's exuberance and self-assuredness but leaves no doubt that the group was a few hooks short of a hit.

Nationwide recognition came with their follow-up, *Let's Go* (1994); MTV placed the video for "Salvation" in heavy rotation. Reflecting the punk/rebel ethos, the song takes a tongue-in-cheek look at envy of the rich. It is also true to punk's penchant for repetition, as the group plays the hook "come on baby, won't you show me what you got there" fourteen times in fewer than three minutes.

And Out Come the Wolves (1995) delivers on the promise of "Salvation" with a pair of irresistible punk-pop hits: the ska/reggae flavored "Timebomb" and the Clash-inspired "Ruby Soho." "Timebomb" sets the vivid story of a doomed drug dealer against an incongruently sunny hook: "black coat, white shoes, black hat, Cadillac, the boy's a time bomb." "Ruby Soho" may have the same missing-my-girl theme as KISS's "Beth," but with its energetic "destination unknown" hook, it avoids the schmaltz and insularity that the topic tends to provoke. Both songs made the Top 15 on *Billboard*'s Modern Rock Tracks chart. The album title refers to the label bidding war that followed *Let's Go*. However, Rancid remained with Epitaph, preferring the creative autonomy it offered. The label might not have been multinational, but its hard-earned reputation and quality lineup meant that Rancid's CDs were not hard to find.

A major label likely would have been pressuring the group during 1996 to get something out as soon as possible. The group participated in that year's Lollapalooza but didn't exactly strike while the iron was hot, waiting until 1998 to return with *Life Won't Wait*. The title was prophetic, because neo-punk was no longer the flavor of the month. Green Day was on lite-rock stations with a ballad, while Offspring was staying on the radio with quasi-novelty tunes. Meanwhile, Rancid stuck to their guns, but the album's first single, "Bloodclot," didn't possess the hooks that characterized the group's earlier heights.

The title and the music on *Rancid* (2000) are a return to the past, featuring straight-ahead, super-fast punk rock without the Caribbean influences. Seventeen of the twenty-two tracks clock in at fewer than two minutes. During the early 2000s, Rancid concentrated on grooming new acts via their Hellfire subsidiary of Epitaph. Though not known for their trailblazing, Rancid did stay true to the punk ethic and churned out some unforgettable music.

SELECTIVE DISCOGRAPHY: *Let's Go*, (Epitaph, 1994); *And Out Come the Wolves,* (Epitaph, 1995); *Life Won't Wait*, (Epitaph, 1998); *Rancid* (Epitaph, 2000).

RAMIRO BURR

SIMON RATTLE

Born: Liverpool, England, 19 January 1955
Genre: Classical

Simon Rattle is the most highly sought-after conductor of his generation. He took the City of Birmingham Symphony Orchestra (CBSO) from a provincial band with a history of problems and built it into one of the more respected and accomplished orchestras in Britain. His high standing in the orchestral world was confirmed in 1999, when he was appointed music director of the Berlin Philharmonic.

Rattle was born in Liverpool in 1955 and spent much of his childhood studying music and organizing his family in informal music performances. He appeared as a percussionist with the Royal Liverpool Philharmonic at the age of eleven, put together his first professional orchestra at the age of fifteen, and later became conductor of the Merseyside Youth Orchestra. At sixteen he began studies at the Royal Academy of Music in London, and at nineteen he won the John Player International Conducting Competition. He became the assistant conductor of the Bournemouth Symphony and Sinfonietta and then landed the same jobs with the Royal Liverpool Philharmonic, the BBC Scottish Symphony, and the Rotterdam Philharmonic. During this time he guest-conducted the London Sinfonietta, Philharmonia and London Philharmonic.

Rattle's big break came in 1980, when he was appointed principal conductor and artistic advisor to the ailing City of Birmingham Symphony Orchestra. He and the orchestra manager, Ed Smith, embarked on an ambitious program to turn the orchestra around. The charismatic Rattle worked closely with musicians, training the ensemble in music that ranged across the orchestral literature. Programs were carefully balanced between familiar classics and challenging twentieth-century fare, and audiences responded enthusiastically.

As the orchestra's abilities improved, critics took notice, the City of Birmingham responded with increased financial support, and EMI signed the orchestra for a series of highly regarded recordings. As its reputation spread, the orchestra also began touring— through Europe, to North and South America, and Asia. In 1991 the orchestra built a brilliant new concert home.

Rattle became a highly sought-after guest conductor and began working with many of the world's major orchestras. He was appointed principal guest conductor of the Los Angeles Philharmonic (1981–1994), and principal guest conductor of the Orchestra of the Age of Enlightenment. He worked regularly with the Boston Symphony

Simon Rattle [THERISIA LINKE/ANGEL RECORDS]

Spot Light | *Towards the Millennium*

The gods of classical music prefer that a piece of music be around for several decades (even centuries) before it is declared a classic. In some circles, music from the first two decades of the twentieth century is still considered shocking. Through the 1990s Simon Rattle embarked on a decade-by-decade survey of the serious music of the twentieth century— *Towards the Millennium.* Each year's program was Rattle's vote for the most significant music composed in a decade of the century. How do you represent the music of ten years in one program? Given the swirling eddies and simultaneous currents of musical styles that came and went during the century, it is an impossible task. Yet it is just this kind of ambitious personal history that can begin to stitch together a narrative of an era. The last of these concerts, performed in the beginning of 2000, included Hans Werner Henze's *A Tempest,* Gyorgy Ligeti's Violin Concerto, Simon Holt's *Sunrise's Yellow Noise,* and Michael Tippett's *The Rose Lake.* Haven't heard of some of them? Let a few decades go by.

and Philadelphia Orchestra as well as several European ensembles, but his guest conducting was limited because of his commitment to the CBSO.

Throughout the 1990s Rattle was courted by major orchestras interested in signing him up as music director. But he stayed in Birmingham for eighteen years, a remarkable tenure given his expanding career. In Birmingham Rattle had an opportunity to build something, and his star status helped give the orchestra the resources he needed to record and mount ambitious repertoire such as his decade-by-decade survey of music of the twentieth century. He and the orchestra were also frequently on television, notably in a series called *Leaving Home,* which featured Rattle talking at length about the music of the twentieth century. By the time Rattle left Birmingham as music director in 1998, he had conducted the orchestra in 934 concerts and more than 10,000 hours of rehearsals. He also made more than sixty recordings, picking up numerous awards.

For a few years Rattle enjoyed grazing on a succession of well-regarded projects while speculation mounted about which orchestra might be able to snag him as its music director. Rumors had him heading to Philadelphia or Boston, but in 1999 Rattle accepted the job as music director of the Berlin Philharmonic beginning in 2002.

Rattle is the complete package as a music director. As a musician he has an insatiable curiosity that spans the earliest music (he is an expert conductor of music performed on period instruments) to the thorniest modern compositions. He holds modern masters such as Boulez and Messaien in the kind of high regard usually reserved for Beethoven and Brahms and Mozart.

As a conductor he brings a penetrating mind, a charismatic style, and a personal passion for music. He is comfortable with the colossal repertoire of Mahler and Bruckner but seems equally at home with a Haydn symphony. As an ambassador for his profession, he is one of the best arguments for a musical tradition that can keep on renewing itself. It is no surprise that when Rattle finally took up his new post leading the Berlin Philharmonic in the fall of 2002, he was greeted as a major celebrity in a city rich with culture. Even as he began his new post, there were signs that an orchestra with a long and distinguished tradition would be transformed by its new music director.

SELECTIVE DISCOGRAPHY: *Mahler: Symphony 10, Berliner Philharmoniker* (Angel, 2000); *Rattle Directs 20th Century Orchestral Masterworks* (Capitol, 1994); *John Adams Harmonielehre; The Chairman Dances; Tromba lontana; Short Ride in a Fast Machine, City of Birmingham Symphony Orchestra* (EMI, 1994).

BIBLIOGRAPHY: N. Kenyon, *Simon Rattle: From Birmingham to Berlin* (London, 2002).

WEBSITE: www.simon-rattle.de.

DOUGLAS MCLENNAN

COLLIN RAYE

Born: DeQueen, Arkansas, 22 August 1959

Genre: Country

Best-selling album since 1990: *I Think about You* (1995)

Hit songs since 1990: "Little Rock," "In This Life," "Love, Me"

Collin Raye's appealing tenor voice, which in its grittiness recalls Don Henley of the 1970s rock band the Eagles, graced a long string of country hits during the 1990s. Softer than Alan Jackson yet falling short of John Michael Montgomery's sticky sentimentality, Raye used his songs to tackle difficult social issues such as alcoholism and child abuse. Over the course of his career Raye has proven his versatility with performances that range from pure country to sophisticated pop balladry.

Growing up in Arkansas, Raye and his brother Scott frequently performed with their mother, a well-known local country singer who opened for stars such as Elvis Presley and Johnny Cash when they came to town. In the late 1970s the siblings formed the Wray Brothers Band, enjoying a minor country hit with the single "Reason to Believe" (1983). After the group disbanded, Raye was signed to Epic Records as a solo performer. His first album, *All That I Can Be* (1990), was a solid effort highlighted by "Love, Me," which hit number one on the country charts in 1992. The sentimental song, in which the narrator describes the death of his grandmother, became a favorite at funerals—its lyrics have often been carved in tombstones. On the hit "In This Life" (1993), in which a man ruminates upon his imminent wedding, Raye again displayed his ability to craft heartfelt, convincing songs marking life's passages. Not surprisingly, the song was soon a popular choice for wedding receptions.

In 1994 Raye moved in a more challenging direction with "Little Rock," an unsparing portrait of an alcoholic struggling to get his life on track. With lines such as "I haven't had a drink in 19 days," "Little Rock" brought a new level of realism to country music, putting a human face on a misunderstood disease. Given that alcohol has historically been represented in country lyrics as a palliative for depression, Raye deserves credit for his honesty and courage in tackling this subject. By the mid-1990s Raye had become known for addressing at least one social issue per album. *The Walls Came Down* (1998), for instance, features "The Eleventh Commandment," a harrowing account of child physical and sexual abuse: "she's so ashamed she's Daddy's secret love." At the same time, Raye became a spokesperson for Childhelp USA, an outreach organization for abused children. Although Raye's

2000 album, *Tracks*, sports a mainstream country-rock production in keeping with the hit sound of late 1990s artists such as Shania Twain, his next release, *Can't Back Down* (2001), is a more versatile set that combines a varied array of musical impulses. On "I Can Let Go Now," a heavily orchestrated pop ballad, Raye delivers one of his subtlest performances, his voice displaying softness, range, and flexibility.

Although Raye performs all types of material with conviction, he was best known in the 1990s for daring songs that set a new standard for lyrical maturity in country music. His earnest, pleading voice informs his songs of life, love, and death with an unwavering layer of sincerity.

SELECTIVE DISCOGRAPHY: *All That I Can Be* (Epic, 1990); *In This Life* (Epic, 1992); *Extremes* (Epic, 1994); *I Think about You* (Epic, 1995); *The Walls Came Down* (Epic, 1998); *Tracks* (Epic, 2000); *Can't Back Down* (Epic, 2001).

DAVID FREELAND

RED HOT CHILI PEPPERS

Formed: 1983, Los Angeles, California

Members: Michael "Flea" Balzary, bass (born Melbourne, Australia, 16 October 1962); John Frusciante, guitar (born New York, New York, 5 March 1970); Anthony Kiedis, vocals (born Grand Rapids, Michigan, 1 November 1962); Chad Smith (born St. Paul, Minnesota, 25 October 1962). Former members: Jack Irons, drums (born Los Angeles, California, 18 July 1962); Arik Marshall, guitar (born Los Angeles, California, 13 February 1967); Cliff Martinez, drums; Dave Navarro (born Santa Monica, California, 7 June 1967); Jack Sherman, guitar; Hillel Slovak (born Haifa, Israel, 13 April 1962; died Los Angeles, California, 25 June 1988).

Genre: Rock

Best-selling album since 1990: *Blood Sugar Sex Magik* (1991)

Hit songs since 1990: "Under the Bridge," "Give It Away," "Scar Tissue"

Through three drummers and a revolving lineup of guitarists, the core of the Red Hot Chili Peppers remained vocalist Anthony Kiedis and bassist Flea. Their innovative mix of funk, punk, rap, and rock shattered musical barriers and established a large cult following by the end of the 1980s. In the early 1990s, they became superstars and their music gracefully matured into the new millennium, despite countless obstacles. The group's evolution from reckless, party band to mellow, sensitive rockers was shocking but organic,

Red Hot Chili Peppers. L-R: Anthony Kiedis, Chad Smith, John Frusciante, Michael "Flea" Balzary [PAUL NATKIN/PHOTO RESERVE]

and a great testament to their talent, creativity, and appeal.

In the late 1970s, the four founding members of the Red Hot Chili Peppers were high school classmates at Fairfax High School in Los Angeles. During school, Michael Balzary, who soon changed his name to Flea, played trumpet and loved jazz music. Guitarist Hillel Slovak introduced him to rock and punk and taught him the bass. The two formed a band called Anthym with drummer Jack Irons. Aspiring actor and poet Anthony Kiedis occasionally read some of his work before their shows.

After Flea left to join the punk band Fear, and Slovak and Irons continued as the renamed What Is This?, the four reunited in 1983 as Tony Flow & the Miraculous

Majestic Masters of Mayhem. Their music was influenced by the raw and aggressive but musically adept punk of contemporary Los Angeles bands like Black Flag, the Minutemen, and X, as well as the ambitious 1960s and 1970s funk of bands like Parliament-Funkadelic and Sly and the Family Stone and artists like Stevie Wonder. With spastic energy and outrageous antics, the buzz their live show created turned to frenzy when they performed an encore one night wearing nothing but socks on their genitalia. They were signed to EMI Records, but Slovak and Irons left the band to return to What Is This?, their longer-running and more serious project.

Guitarist Jack Sherman and drummer Cliff Martinez played on their self-titled debut, *Red Hot Chili Peppers* (1984). The band felt the album failed to capture their onstage vigor, so they asked Parliament-Funkadelic leader George Clinton to produce their follow-up, *Freaky Styley* (1985). With Slovak returning and two of James Brown's band members, saxophonist Maceo Parker and trombonist Fred Wesley, contributing horn parts throughout, the 1985 effort is the Red Hot Chili Peppers album that most resembles the 1970s funk that influenced them. It became a sizable hit on college radio and indie-rock scenes, but it still failed to capture the unbridled punch of their live show.

Jack Irons's return to the band on *The Uplift Mofo Party Plan* (1987) marked the only album with all four original members performing. Producer Michael Beinhorn, most noted for his co-production on Herbie Hancock's electronic, jazz-funk fusion album *Future Shock* (1983), was finally able to capture the band's intensity on record. By abandoning the more conventional use of horns, they developed the uncharted blend of Flea's inventive slap-bass funk, Slovak's raucous but understated guitars, and Kiedis's rapid fire rapping. Just as the Red Hot Chili Peppers' music was coalescing, their personal lives were shattered by Slovak's death from a heroin overdose on June 25, 1988. The event caused Irons to leave the band for the last time and created an uncertain future for the Red Hot Chili Peppers.

The Golden Lineup Comes Together

After some time off, Kiedis and Flea decided to re-form the band. Upon hearing eighteen-year-old John Frusciante play guitar at an audition for the band Thelonius Monster, they discovered he was heavily influenced by and had perfected Hillel Slovak's style. His addition to the band was obvious. Replacing Irons was more challenging, but after auditioning several drummers, they settled on Chad Smith.

The revamped group reentered the studio with Beinhorn and recorded *Mother's Milk* (1989). The album's first single, "Knock Me Down," was an upbeat but sobering homage to Slovak, and became their first modern rock hit. A rambunctious cover of Stevie Wonder's "Higher Ground" followed with similar success, and the album became the Red Hot Chili Peppers' commercial breakthrough. By March 1990, it was certified gold and led to a contract with Warner Bros. Records.

For the first time in the band's history, the same four members remained when work for their fifth album began. They chose a new producer, though, Rick Rubin. His work with Run-D.M.C., Beastie Boys, Public Enemy, and L.L. Cool J made him largely responsible for the popularization of hip-hop. He had also worked with the intense, heavy metal band Slayer. Rubin, who would produce their next four albums, and the band turned a supposedly haunted mansion in the Hollywood Hills into a recording studio and emerged with the masterpiece *Blood Sugar Sex Magik* (1991).

The playful party romp "Give It Away" was the lead single and became a wildly popular anthem. Its repeated instructions "What I've got you've got to get it put in you / Reeling with the feeling don't stop continue" are indicative of the overt sexual energy that oozes out of tracks like "Suck My Kiss," "Apache Rose Peacock," "Sir Psycho Sexy," and the steamy "Blood Sugar Sex Magik." In a similarly playful vein, the wicked and mysterious "If You Have to Ask," "Funky Monks," and "Mellowhip Slinky in B Major" boldly blaze uncharted trails in funk. "The Power of Equality" and "The Righteous and the Wicked" show a more socially conscious, but equally energetic side. The most notable new facet revealed on the album, though, is the gentler, more melodic reflections found on "Breaking the Girl," "I Could Have Lied," and "Under the Bridge." The latter relives Kiedis's battles with drug addiction and was a monster smash, peaking at number two on the *Billboard* Hot 100 and selling over half a million copies. Its success propelled the album to number three on the album chart, peaking almost eight months after its release. Eventually, the landmark work sold more than 7 million copies in the United States. Due to its tremendous range and innovation, it is regarded by some to be one of the best albums of the 1990s.

The group's massive popularity became extremely difficult for the young Frusciante to handle, so he coped with hard drugs and erratic behavior. He abruptly quit the band in May 1992, just weeks before they were to headline the traveling alternative music festival, Lollapalooza. The band continued on with replacement guitarist Arik Marshall and completed the highly successful tour that also included alternative rock heavyweights Pearl Jam and Soundgarden, industrial metal mainstays Ministry, and premier gangster rapper Ice Cube.

Neither Marshall nor his brief successor, Jesse Tobias, were an apt fit for the band, so in September 1993, Dave Navarro joined. As a member of seminal rock group Jane's Addiction, his guitar work balanced ferocious heavy metal riffs with atmospheric psychedelia creating a unique, influential style. To assimilate with the Red Hot Chili Peppers, his playing was often more reserved on *One Hot Minute* (1995). The album had a daunting task: following up a brilliant, multiplatinum smash, after a four-year absence, with a new guitarist. Considering the odds, it was a successful effort with hits "Warped," "My Friends," and "Aeroplane." Despite quality live performances, the band's creative chemistry was questionable with Navarro. Another recovering heroin addict, his supposed relapses and desire to pursue other projects led to his departure from the band in April 1998.

The Golden Lineup Reunites

Magically, the same month, John Frusciante returned to the group after his near-death experience with heroin addiction. Clean, sober, and revitalized, he brought a renewed sense of hope to the future of the Red Hot Chili Peppers. As a result, they released the largely successful *Californication* (1999). Though the album has a fair amount of sexually charged, up-tempo grooves, it also reveals a surprising amount of maturity through softer, sweet-harmony ruminations. In fact, the singles "Scar Tissue," "Otherside," and "Californication" all crossed over to the Adult Top 40 chart, in addition to having major success in modern rock and Top 40 radio, and on MTV. Reaching an older audience was an astonishing progression for a band best known for hyperactivity, nearly naked performances, and recurring drug abuse. The band's mellowing progressed further on *By the Way* (2002). The beautiful effort demonstrated Kiedis's most accomplished vocals and elegant harmonies from John Frusciante.

Despite multiple lineup changes, drug addiction, and death, the Red Hot Chili Peppers repeatedly established themselves as one of rock's most original bands. Both their party funk and soothing ballads are truly unique and immediately recognizable. Though each incarnation of the group made solid contributions to the band's and alternative music's progression, the lineup of Anthony Kiedis, Flea, John Frusciante, and Chad Smith established itself as the most cohesive and accomplished.

SELECTIVE DISCOGRAPHY: *Freaky Styley* (EMI America, 1985); *The Uplift Mofo Party Plan* (EMI America, 1987); *Mother's Milk* (EMI America, 1989); *Blood Sugar Sex Magik* (Warner Bros., 1991); *One Hot Minute* (Warner Bros., 1995); *Californication* (Warner Bros., 1999); *By the Way* (Warner Bros., 2002).

BIBLIOGRAPHY: D. Thompson, *The Red Hot Chili Peppers* (New York, 1993).

WEBSITE: www.redhotchilipeppers.com.

DAVE POWERS

JOSHUA REDMAN

Born: Berkeley, California, 1 February 1969
Genre: Jazz

Jazz writers in the early 1990s called tenor saxophone player Joshua Redman the most important musician to emerge in the genre since trumpet legend Wynton Marsalis. Redman's string of popular albums and well-received tours have lived up to the hype. He has received some criticism for the cloying, traditional acoustic jazz sound of his early albums. Redman's twenty-first century recordings, however, such as *Passage of Time* (2001) and *Elastic* (2002), find him exploring new musical terrain and leaving his somewhat conservative be-bop image behind.

The son of the distinguished saxophonist Dewy Redman, Joshua was raised in New York City. His mother, Renee Shedroff, a Russian/Jewish dancer, encouraged his musical leanings by enrolling him in world music classes at the Center for World Music. As a child he also heard recordings by his father and master sax players such as Dexter Gordon, Sonny Rollins, and John Coltrane. At age ten, he began playing tenor sax.

Redman was a distinguished student. He graduated first in his high school class. He then went on to Harvard University, from which he graduated summa cum laude in 1991. While at Harvard he played with the university jazz band and spent his summers jamming with musicians from the prestigious Berklee College of Music, but his earliest intentions were to study medicine and then law.

Although he was accepted to Yale Law School, Redman began devoting himself to music after graduation and moved to New York City. In 1991 he won the Thelonius Monk International Jazz Saxophone Competition and landed a recording contract. A year later he was voted Best New Artist in the 1992 *Jazz Times* readers' poll. His self-titled debut, *Joshua Redman* (1992), is a collection of Redman originals and jazz standards such as "Salt Peanuts," "Body and Soul," and "Tinkle Tinkle." Seemingly aware that some critics might find his acoustic style of jazz too staid, Redman asked in liner notes that his listeners "do not attempt to place it in a camp to which it does not belong, in the midst of a battlefield which should not exist." The album was a hit with critics and listeners, garnering Redman *Rolling Stone*'s Hot Jazz Artist Award of 1993 and the 1993 *Downbeat* Critics Poll for Number One Tenor Saxophonist (Talent Deserving Wider Recognition).

Redman's recordings following his debut tended to tread familiar ground. *Wish* (1994) is notable because it includes some startling songs with guitarist Pat Metheny and two live tracks recorded with Metheny at the Village Vanguard. *Timeless Tales* (1998), a collection of American popular music culled from legends such as Rodgers and Hammerstein, Bob Dylan, and Joni Mitchell, marked a new phase in Redman's recording career. Later albums such as *Passage of Time* (2001) experiment with loosely organized conceptual songs. *YaYa3* (2002), a side project Redman completed with drummer Brian Blade and keyboardist Sam Yahel, documents Redman's less ambitious but looser style and his adept soprano sax playing. *Elastic* (2003) is his most ambitious recording, incorporating a variety of electric sounds and an eclectic list of contemporary influences such as Björk, Radiohead, Weather Report, and Prince.

Redman's new moves on *Yaya3* and *Elastic* suggest he has moved past the pressures of his early acclaim. Drawing on new influences and working in new settings,

Redman is poised to become one of jazz's great mainstream innovators.

SELECTIVE DISCOGRAPHY: *Joshua Redman* (Warner Bros., 1992); *Wish* (Warner Bros., 1994); *Moodswing* (Warner Bros., 1994); *Spirit of the Moment: Live at the Village Vanguard* (Warner Bros., 1995); *Freedom in the Groove* (Warner Bros., 1996); *Timeless Tales* (Warner Bros., 1998); *Beyond* (Warner Bros., 2000); *Passage of Time* (Warner Bros., 2001); *Yaya3* (Loma, 2002); *Elastic* (Warner Bros., 2002).

WEBSITE: www.joshuaredman.com.

SHAWN GILLEN

LOU REED

Born: Lewis Alan Reed; Brooklyn, New York, 2 March 1942

Genre: Rock, Pop

Best-selling album since 1990: *Magic and Loss* (1992)

Lou Reed is a pivotal figure in the creation of the New York rock sound. As a founding member of the Velvet Underground in the 1960s, he chronicled that decade with songs that journeyed into the worlds of drugs and sexual hedonism. His bleak urban street tales countered the sunny optimism associated with the psychedelic scene blossoming on the West Coast with bands like Jefferson Airplane and the Grateful Dead. Reed's primitive song structures, groove talking vocals, and experiments with white noise cemented his image as the original art rock hipster. Even though the Velvet Underground was never commercially successful, it proved greatly influential. Reed's solo career was marked by sharp turns in image and musical style. He entered the 1990s on the heels of *New York* (1989), a critically praised comeback.

Reed grew up in Long Island, New York, and moved to Manhattan after college to pursue a career as a songwriter and a poet. In 1964 he met John Cale, a classically trained violinist. After recruiting drummer Moe Tucker and bassist Sterling Morrison, a year later the group met Andy Warhol, a founder and major figure in the pop art movement. Warhol became their manager. He added singer/actress Nico to the band and pushed them to explore more primitive themes. The band's best work utilized minimal chords and tempos. It spoke of alienation and the discord of modern urban life. The Velvet Underground's albums sold poorly but are now considered ahead of their time, foretelling the abrasion and stripped-down ethos that would define punk rock.

Reed's solo career began in 1971. His debut, *Transformer* (1972), produced "Walk on the Wild Side," his only Top 20 single. Over the years, he would prove to be rock's most reliable chameleon, changing his public image as much as he did the music he made. Reed's subsequent albums included heavy-metal, commercial pop, glam rock, singer/songwriter folk, and grating electronic noise. By the time the 1980s rolled around he was touted as an innovator by bands including Sonic Youth and R.E.M. Reed kicked off the third chapter in his career with *New York* (1989), a gritty but accessible collection of songs that assessed the problems plaguing his hometown in recent years: the AIDS crisis, racism, and homelessness. *New York* signaled Reed's renewed viability and it was his first Top 40 album in fifteen years.

Reed entered the 1990s an established icon. He and Cale reunited to release *Songs for Drella* (1990), which they dedicated to Warhol who died in 1987. He organized a reunion of the Velvet Underground, which toured Europe and recorded a live album. Back in the United States, the band dissolved a second time after a dispute over who would produce their upcoming MTV *Unplugged* special, which was promptly cancelled. Upon their induction into the Rock and Roll Hall of Fame in 1996, they reunited a second time to play the ceremony.

By this time, Reed assumed the role of an art rock intellectual who demonstrated that dark and complex sentiments can be expressed clearly using the basic framework of two guitars, bass, and drums. He published two books of his lyrics over the years and went on spoken word tours. He also made some of his most harrowing music. *Magic and Loss* (1992) contemplated mortality and the many dimensions of loss. Tapping into both pain and humor, the album is considered one of Reed's best. Although *Set the Twilight Reeling* (1996) moved in a nostalgic pop direction, he returned to making raw rock music with *Ecstasy* (2000). Horns, electric violin, and a massive amount of guitar distortion complement the despair, rage, and overt sexuality in the lyrics.

The Raven (2003), released both as a single and double album, was originally conceived as companion music to *POE-try*, a theater project with stage director Robert Wilson. It married Reed's bleak vision with the writings of Edgar Allan Poe, an American writer who greatly influenced the French symbolist poets. The album features Reed originals and Poe's fiction and poetry read by actors and set to music. The sparse production, backdrop of distorted guitar and electronics, and mixture of overlapping voices are all ratcheted high with the dramatic tension of a surreal radio play. The album was considered a fascinating, if peculiar, musical journey.

Reed elevated hedonism to high art. As the founder and lead singer of the Velvet Underground, he used rock music to find the poetry in modern-day misery and urban decay. Throughout his unpredictable career, he relentlessly explored new styles in a multitude of genres.

SELECTIVE DISCOGRAPHY: *Transformer* (MCA, 1972); *Berlin* (RCA, 1973); *Sally Can't Dance* (RCA, 1974); *Metal Machine Music* (RCA, 1975); *Street Hassle* (Arista, 1978); *The Blue Mask* (RCA, 1982); *New York* (Sire, 1989); *Magic and Loss* (Sire, 1992); *Set the Twilight Reeling* (Reprise, 1996); *Perfect Night Live in London* (Reprise, 1998); *Ecstasy* (Reprise, 2000); *The Raven* (Reprise, 2003).

WEBSITE: www.loureed.com.

MARK GUARINO

DIANNE REEVES

Born: Detroit, Michigan, 23 October 1956

Genre: Jazz

Best-selling album since 1990: *The Grand Encounter* (1996)

Dianne Reeves is an accomplished vocalist with a rich and agile voice that she brings to mainstream and smooth jazz, pop-soul, Brazilian repertoire, and African rhythms, straddling genres rather than integrating them into a single coherent identity. Self-described as a "jazz artist who explores other kinds of music," she pays homage to the late jazz singers Sarah Vaughan and Betty Carter, claims the veteran trumpeter Clark Terry as her mentor, and has been produced by her cousin, the jazz keyboardist George Duke. She has also toured with the Brazilian pianist and pop composer Sergio Mendes, the singer Harry Belafonte and as a member of fusion bands (Caldera, Night Wings) that realized onstage the heavily crafted studio productions of instrumental jazz that gets commercial radio airplay.

Reeves's family is musical: her father was a singer and her mother a trumpet player. During the years she was growing up in Denver, her uncle, a classical bassist, influenced her musical interests. She began singing and playing piano in her mid-teens and was noticed by Clark Terry during a performance by her high school band at the National Association of Jazz Educators Convention in Chicago in 1973. Terry invited her to perform at the Colorado Jazz Party in 1973 and the Wichita Jazz Festival in 1979, and he appears as a guest soloist on the most traditionally jazz oriented of her recordings, *The Grand Encounter* (1996).

Reeves moved to Los Angeles after one year at the University of Denver, and freelanced as a studio session singer. In 1980 she co-founded Night Flight with the pianist Billy Childs, who has remained her frequent producer and/or musical director.

Reeves worked her way through the troupes of Sergio Mendes (1981–1983) and then Harry Belafonte (1983–1986). After a brief residence in New York, she returned to Los Angeles, where she resumed activities with session players of West Coast commercial and pop music. *The Palo Alto Sessions, 1981–1985* (reissued in 1996) demonstrates her wide vocal range, clear articulation, mastery of phrasing, and interpretive breadth. She sings the standard "My Funny Valentine" with a diva's self-composed drama and treats "Be My Husband" as an African-American chant, bare of artifice. She often employs effusive melisma and relies more often on layers of percolating grooves than on a driving rhythm section.

In the late 1980s Reeves performed at a memorial concert honoring Duke Ellington and performed at the Mt. Fuji Jazz Festival in Japan with the big band of the drummer Art Blakey. These occasions launched her into the international jazz festival circuit, where she has appeared with the Philip Morris Superband under the direction of the bluesy pianist Gene Harris and with Quincy Jones at the Montreux International Jazz Festival from 1980 until 1995.

Reeves was named Creative Chair for Jazz by the Los Angeles Philharmonic Association in 2002; she is responsible for creating jazz programs at the Hollywood Bowl and Walt Disney Concert Hall. She is the first woman among a handful of jazz leaders to have become the artistic director of a major jazz institution, joining such illustrious company as Joshua Redman at SFJazz, Terence Blanchard at the Thelonious Monk Institute of Jazz Performance at the University of Southern California, and Wynton Marsalis at Lincoln Center in New York.

Reeves's status as a concert, club, and festival attraction in the United States and abroad is dependent on not only her vocal delivery but her choice of material that will be acceptable to a large, general audience. She has expanded on her personal esthetic and core listenership by embracing songs written and/or made famous by Leonard Cohen, Joni Mitchell, Milton Nascimento, Cole Porter, Mongo Santamaria, and George Gershwin, among others.

SELECTIVE DISCOGRAPHY: *Never Too Far* (EMI, 1991); *I Remember* (Blue Note, 1993); *Art & Survival* (EMI America, 1993); *Quiet after the Storm* (Blue Note, 1994); *The Grand Encounter* (Blue Note, 1996); *That Day . . .* (Blue Note, 1998); *Bridges* (Blue Note, 1999); *In the Moment: Live In Concert* (Blue Note, 2000); *The Calling: Celebrating Sarah Vaughn* (Blue Note, 2001); *The Best of Dianne Reeves* (Blue Note, 2002).

WEBSITE: www.diannereeves.com.

HOWARD MANDEL

LIONEL RICHIE

Born: Tuskegee, Alabama, 20 June 1949

Genre: R&B, Pop

Best-selling album since 1990: *Louder Than Words* (1996)

Hit songs since 1990: "Do It to Me," "Don't Wanna Lose You"

A gentle romantic crooner, Lionel Richie achieved stardom in the 1980s and early 1990s by applying his wistful vocals to a hit series of tender love songs. Best known for his ballads, Richie also excelled at up-tempo dance numbers that exuded a good-time party atmosphere. With his soft-spoken, conservative manner Richie came across as the romantic guy next door, an everyman who shunned sexual explicitness in favor of love, dedication, and unity. Due to a combination of personal problems and changing trends in popular music, Richie lost his popular foothold as the 1990s progressed, but took steps to regain it near the end of the decade.

Richie was raised on the campus of Alabama's prestigious Tuskegee Institute, where his grandmother gave classes in classical piano and his mother taught elementary school. In the early 1970s, while attending college at Tuskegee, Richie joined the soul and funk group the Commodores, which went on to become one of the most commercially successful groups of the decade. By the end of the 1970s Richie was taking a larger role within the group, writing and singing lead on several of its most popular songs, including "Three Times a Lady" (1978) and "Still" (1979). In 1982 Richie left the Commodores for a solo career and made his career breakthrough with *Can't Slow Down* (1983), which sold over 10 million copies. On songs like the party anthem "All Night Long (All Night)" and the love ballads "Hello," "Penny Lover," and "Stuck on You," *Can't Slow Down* perfectly captured the feel-good, upwardly mobile atmosphere of the early 1980s, before AIDS exerted its stranglehold on the nation's consciousness. "Hello," one of the most popular singles of 1984, is a prime example of Richie's greeting-card lyrical approach: "I long to see the sunlight in your hair / And tell you time and time again how much I care."

After a follow-up album, *Dancing on the Ceiling* (1986), Richie virtually dropped from sight, embroiled in a prolonged divorce from his first wife, Brenda, the muse who inspired some of his most successful songs. Brenda's allegations, which included charges of spousal abuse, flew in the face of Richie's nice-guy image. After additional troubles—throat problems, losing a best friend to AIDS, the death of his father—Richie took a self-imposed hiatus from the music industry in 1987, a break that lasted nearly a decade. He managed to score a final number one rhythm and blues hit in 1992 with "Do It to Me," an energetic midtempo song that recalled the sweet feel of his 1980s hits, but otherwise fell out of the public spotlight.

By the time Richie came back on the scene in 1996, a lot had changed within the music industry. The romantic courtliness informing his best work had fallen out of fashion, giving way to the frank sexual wordplay of artists such as D'Angelo. Seeking to keep his style fresh, Richie released a comeback album, *Louder Than Words* (1996), that enlisted the services of hot 1990s producers and writers Kenneth "Babyface" Edmonds and Jimmy Jam & Terry Lewis. Although the years had frayed Richie's smooth baritone, *Louder Than Words* features several self-penned ballads, including "Nothing Else Matters" and "Don't Wanna Lose You," that capture his former warmth and honesty. On the other hand, critics found the up-tempo "I Wanna Take You Down" to be an awkward attempt at contemporary raunchiness. Singing lines such as, "Let's go deep undercover . . . you choose the style," Richie sounds forced and uncomfortable.

In 1998 Richie released a follow-up album, *Time*, featuring one of the best ballads of his comeback years, "I Hear Your Voice." Against a lush backdrop of strings and female voices supplying breathy "oohs" and "aahs," Richie emotes over the pain of a lost love: "I thought I'd finally learned to get on with my life / Then it all comes back . . . I hear your voice." Echoing the tactic employed decades earlier on "Still," Richie even speaks the final line, "I hear your voice," in a hushed whisper, a potentially saccharine moment made memorable by Richie's sincerity. In 2001 Richie signed with a new label, Island, and released *Renaissance*, a collection of mostly up-tempo tracks designed to push him even further in a contemporary direction. *Encore*, a live album containing new performances of his biggest hits, followed in 2003.

With his heartfelt songs and simple, direct singing, Lionel Richie is a down-to-earth, likable pop star, with the talent to tap into the current of human feeling. Speaking to the *Washington Post* in 2001, he accurately summarized his appeal: "I write about love. It's the only topic that does not go out of style. . . . I write songs that people can relate to in their everyday lives."

SELECTIVE DISCOGRAPHY: *Lionel Richie* (Motown, 1982); *Can't Slow Down* (Motown, 1983); *Dancing on the Ceiling* (Motown, 1986); *Louder Than Words* (Mercury, 1996); *Time* (Mercury, 1998); *Renaissance* (Island, 2001); *Encore* (Universal, 2003).

WEBSITE: www.lionelrichie.com.

DAVID FREELAND

SVIATOSLAV RICHTER

Born: Zhitomir, Ukraine, 20 March 1915; died Moscow, Russia, 1 August 1997

Genre: Classical

Sviatoslav Richter was one of the greatest Russian pianists of the twentieth century, and his death in 1997 at the age of eighty-two marked the end of an era of virtuoso pianists. Richter was a kind of anti-career performer, a musician intent on going his own way and who disliked tying himself down to the obligations of touring and recording. His performances were spontaneous and unpredictable, in keeping with his dislike for routine.

Richter grew up in Odessa and was largely self-taught on the piano. He could memorize music at sight, and by the age of eight was playing opera scores. As a teenager he became a rehearsal pianist.

In 1937 he enrolled at the Moscow Conservatory, where he studied with the legendary teacher Heinrich Neuhaus. After hearing Richter play, Neuhaus pronounced the young pianist a genius and declared there was nothing he could teach him. In 1940 Richter made his Moscow debut, giving the first-ever performance of Prokofiev's Sixth Sonata. The composer was so impressed, he gave Richter the Seventh, Eighth, and Ninth sonatas to premiere, and dedicated the Ninth to him.

In the 1940s and 1950s Richter won almost every major award for artists in the Soviet Union, including the Stalin Prize in 1949. He toured extensively in the 1950s, but was only permitted to travel in Iron Curtain countries. His recordings, however, became highly prized in the West.

In 1958 he was on the jury of the Tchaikovsky Competition, then considered the world's top piano competition. Richter was so enthusiastic about the young Van Cliburn's performance that he awarded him 100 points out of a possible 10, an over-the-top gesture that won him no friends.

In 1960 Richter was finally allowed to travel to the West to perform. His New York debut—which consisted of a marathon series of seven recitals in ten days at Carnegie Hall—was the sensation of the music season. A busy schedule of concerts and recordings followed, until, only a few seasons later, the pianist decided he did not like the concert lifestyle, and drastically cut back his schedule. This, of course, only increased intense public interest in his playing.

He established an annual festival in Tours, France, in 1964 and spent thirty summers there. He toured and recorded erratically. He disliked telephones and airplanes and preferred to travel by car or rail. He recorded at night, and often canceled sessions and concerts. In 1980, after suffering an embarrassing memory lapse in a concert, he began performing most of his concerts using a score.

In the 1980s and 1990s he generally performed on a whim, often scheduling appearances on short notice. His life was haphazardly managed, and whenever he needed money he'd schedule a concert. In the 1990s, his performances attracted a cult of Richter followers who tried to keep track of where he was performing and who eagerly traded recordings of his concerts. He preferred small concert venues, and the quality of his performances varied considerably. His last concert was in Lubeck, Germany, in 1995.

Richter was a unique and unpredictable artist who challenged his listeners both with his interpretations and his eclectic choice of repertoire. Though he never formally taught, his influence on a generation of younger pianists was profound, and he attracted a large and loyal following.

SELECTIVE DISCOGRAPHY: *Richter Rediscovered* (RCA, 2001); *Sviatoslav Richter in the 1950s* (Parnassus, 2002).

BIBLIOGRAPHY: B. Monsaingeon, *Richter: Notebooks and Conversations* (Princeton, NJ, 2002).

DOUGLAS MCLENNAN

LEANN RIMES

Born: Jackson, Mississippi, 28 August 1982

Genre: Country

Best-selling album since 1990: *Blue* (1996)

Hit songs since 1990: "Blue," "One Way Ticket," "How Do I Live"

Following in the footsteps of precocious country singers of the past such as Brenda Lee and Tanya Tucker, LeAnn Rimes achieved stardom at an extremely young age—thirteen. Catapulting to fame with her first single, "Blue" (1996), Rimes exhibited a strong, confident voice, marked by a maturity that belied its years. Instantly earning critical comparisons to late country legend Patsy Cline, Rimes became country music's most promising young star, her career largely shaped and guided by her father, Wilbur. Echoing a pattern that characterized the early career of Lee, however, Rimes's follow-up releases indicated a lack of artistic direction; largely abandoning her country audience, Rimes actively pursued the pop market, choosing material that many critics dismissed as inappropriate. By 2000 Rimes was making efforts to forge her own personal and artistic independence, engaging in prolonged lawsuits with her father and record label. While Rimes's publicized troubles had a delaying effect on her recording career, she resolved these disputes in 2002, releasing a new album that celebrated her adulthood with a clean-edged pop sound.

Childhood Stardom

Spending her early years in Jackson, Mississippi, Rimes won her first talent contest at the age of five, having exhibited an ability to sing on pitch before she could talk. When she was six her father, a salesman of oil-field pipe, and mother, a devout Baptist who worked at a hair salon to help pay bills, moved Rimes to Dallas, Texas, in order to spur her performing career. Setting up a recording studio in the family's small, two-bedroom apartment, Wilbur rehearsed and coached his daughter each night. By the early 1990s Rimes was singing the National Anthem at Texas Rangers baseball games and appearing on the popular television program *Star Search*. In 1994, having recorded an album in a small New Mexico studio, she met Dallas disc jockey Bill Mack, who decided to help promote her career. Mack presented Rimes with a song, "Blue," that he had originally written years before for Cline, whose death in a plane crash had prevented her from recording it. The next year, Mack arranged for Rimes to sign with Curb Records, a label known for its tough, shrewd business practices. In a move that would later come back to haunt Rimes, Curb had a court remove the "disability of minority" provision in her contract, ensuring that she would be prevented from backing out of the agreement once she turned eighteen.

Blue, Rimes's debut for Curb, was a resounding hit, selling 7 million copies and winning her a Grammy Award for Best New Artist. A solid, professional sounding country album, *Blue* is highlighted by Mack's hit title track, in which Rimes recalls Cline's spirited style through expressive, yodeling vocals. Like Lee and Tucker before her, Rimes exhibits an uncanny maturity, belting with the strength and power of an adult. Equally impressive is the full-bodied tone of Rimes's voice, which displays richness and warmth, particularly in its lower register. Proving her facility with a range of country styles, Rimes handles the up-tempo rhythm of the hit, "One Way Ticket," with ease, and duets with country legend Eddy Arnold on "Cattle Call." The song, pairing country's oldest, most venerable performer with its youngest, qualifies as one of *Blue*'s most charming, satisfying moments. Eager to capitalize on the album's success, Curb quickly unearthed Rimes's 1994 demo album and repackaged it as *Unchained Melody: The Early Years* (1997). During these years Rimes worked to the point of exhaustion, making almost 500 live appearances between 1996 and 1998.

Prepared to conquer the lucrative pop market, Rimes recorded "How Do I Live," a ballad by hit songwriter Dianne Warren, for the soundtrack to the film *Con Air* (1997). Although it was rejected by the film's producers in favor of a version by country star Trisha Yearwood, Rimes's recording became a pop crossover smash, remaining on the *Billboard* charts for a record-breaking sixty-nine weeks. Having reached the peak of her fame, Rimes included the song on her next album, *You Light Up My Life: Inspirational Songs* (1997). This time, critics were less kind to Rimes, claiming that her voice was wasted on covers of slick pop songs such as the title track, best known from the hit 1977 recording by pop singer Debby Boone. A perplexing selection of material also informed Rimes's next album, *Sittin' on Top of the World* (1998). Sporting the now-standard production credit of Wilbur C. Rimes, the album contains an awkward cover of "Purple Rain," the 1984 hit by R&B innovator Prince. Rimes returned to her earlier country sound for *LeAnn Rimes* (1999), although the album features only one original song, the spirited hit "Big Deal." By this point, critics were pointing to both Wilbur Rimes and Curb Records as forces likely inhibiting Rimes from reaching her full artistic potential.

Personal Conflict and Legal Battles

In May 2000, prompted by questions from her new boyfriend, television actor Andrew Keegan, Rimes and her mother (now divorced from her father) arranged for accountants to investigate Wilbur Rimes's business finances. Discovering that her father had assigned himself a 31 percent producer's fee, a 30 percent management fee, and a 10 percent guardian fee, Rimes and her mother sued, claiming that her father's company had usurped at least $7 million over the course of five years. At the same time, Rimes sued Curb Records in an attempt to break free of her onerous 1996 contract, which, due to the removal of the disability of minority provision, committed her to twenty-one albums instead of the industry standard of seven. During the acrimonious proceedings that ensued, the public was treated to dramatic allegations of adultery, theft, alcoholism, and promiscuity. Appearing on *The Tonight Show with Jay Leno*, Rimes denounced her latest album on Curb, *I Need You* (2001), encouraging audiences not to buy it. At one point during the trial proceedings with Curb, she turned to her father and mouthed, "I hate you." In 2002, after nearly two years of bad press, Rimes, now living in Los Angeles, settled with her father out of court. In a sign of improving relations, Wilbur attended her wedding that year to dancer Dean Sheremet.

Losing her suit against Curb Records, Rimes released *Twisted Angel* (2002), a pop album that presents her as a full-grown, independent woman. Writing much of the album's material, Rimes includes lines on "Suddenly" that celebrate her new adulthood: "It's Independence Day, I'm free / And it's a strange place to be." The barbed lyrics of "Life Goes On" seem directed at her father, ex-boyfriend Keegan, and others who lost her trust: "You sucked me in then played my mind / Just like a toy you would crank and wind." Her powerful voice undiminished, Rimes brings a new bite to these songs, performing them with a liberated sense of vigor. While making note of the album's arresting lyrics, however, reviewers criticized its pop sound as bland and overly produced. In its review, rock magazine *Rolling Stone* expressed a longing for the Rimes country sound of the past: "Let's hope Nashville will take her back, and quick."

SELECTIVE DISCOGRAPHY: *Blue* (Curb, 1996); *Unchained Melody: The Early Years* (Curb, 1997); *You Light Up My Life: Inspirational Songs* (Curb, 1997); *Sittin' on Top of the World* (Curb, 1998); *LeAnn Rimes* (Curb, 1999); *I Need You* (Curb, 2001); *Twisted Angel* (Curb, 2002).

WEBSITE: www.leannrimes.com.

DAVID FREELAND

THE RIPPINGTONS

Formed: 1987

Members: Scott Breadman, percussion; Russell Freeman, guitar, keyboards, programmer, arranger, composer, producer (born Nashville, Tennessee, 11 February 1960); Bill Heller, keyboards (born Long Island, New York); Dave Karasony, drums (born California); Eric Marienthal, saxophone (born Sacramento, California, 19 December 1957); Kim Stone, bass. Former members and featured guests: David Benoit, piano, keyboards (born Bakersfield, California, 1953); Brandon Fields, saxophones (born Marion, Indiana, 26 December 1957); Kenny G, saxophones (born Seattle, Washington, 6 July 1956); Tom Gannaway, guitar; Dave Grusin, keyboards (born Denver, Colorado, 26 June 1934); Omar Hakim, bass (born New York, New York, 12 June 1959); Howard Hewitt, vocals; Bob James, keyboards (born Marshall, Montana, 25 December 1939); Jimmy Johnson, bass; Gregg Karukas, keyboards; Jeff Kashiwa, saxophone; Dave Kochanski, keyboards; Dave Koz, saxophone, Electric Wind Instrument (born Los Angeles, California, 27 March 1963); Tony Morales, drums; Mark Portmann, keyboards; Nelson Rangell, saxophone (born Denver, Colorado); Steve Reid, percussion; Kirk Whalum, saxophone (born Memphis, Tennessee, 11 July 1958); Peter White, guitar.

Genre: Jazz

Best-selling album since 1990: *Black Diamond* (1997)

The Rippingtons are less a standing ensemble than a musical unit assembled on a per-project recording and/or touring basis to realize the arrangements of founder Russ Freeman (not to be confused with a West Coast-based cool jazz pianist of the same name, born in 1926). Freeman first convened a group of well-known pop-jazz musicians—including David Benoit, Brandon Fields, and Kenny G—under the name the Rippingtons for a recording commissioned by the Japanese Alfa label. Released in the United States as *Moonlighting* (1987) on the label Passport, the album enjoyed considerable radio airplay and such gratifying sales as to necessitate the institution of a band to follow up its success.

Freeman has played guitar since age ten, professionally since age fifteen, and studied twentieth century music at California Institute for the Arts in Valencia, California, from 1978 to 1979. He recorded *Nocturnal Playground* (1985), featuring Brandon Fields, in a style that foreshadowed the Rippingtons, though the Rippingtons' style is often regarded as "genre-defining" for its glossy mix of piquant guitar phrases, perky electronic and synthesized keyboard backdrops, and surging saxophone statements, supported by steady, rock-pop drum patterns and quasi-Afro-Caribbean percussion accents. In its employment of technically adept if impersonal studio session players and complex studio production techniques, the Rippingtons are comparable to such other highly produced and enduring pop-instrumental outfits as Spyro Gyra (founded in 1974).

What most characterizes these bands is the interchangeability of the musicians who participate in them—and indeed, the Rippingtons and Spyro Gyra have had members in common. Whereas most traditional forms of jazz value strong personal contributions from ensemble members, even avid, expert listeners are challenged to denote changes in the personnel of the Rippingtons. Perhaps this is the derivation of the genre term "smooth jazz": Quirks of individuality are smoothed out. Kim Stone has been in the Rippingtons since 1989 (after four years in Spyro Gyra), and Scott Breadman, who began his association as a substitute keyboardist in 1987, claims he is the only member of the Rippingtons besides Russ Freeman who has worked with every other member of the Rippingtons. However, one is hard-pressed to isolate either Stone's or Breadman's unique contributions to the band's sound, as every instrumental part is sanded to fit the overall design.

Freeman himself demonstrates considerable deftness in guitar fingerings, an ear for the selection of electric keyboard voicings, and a seemingly natural knack for the kaleidoscopic arrangement of diverse instruments emerging from then receding back into multilayered, often anthem-like arrangements. The Rippingtons' percussionist performances are frequently lauded; the band's rhythms tend to be sprightly, rather than heavy-handed. Still, there is little of significance in terms of thematic material, emotional content, or improvisational variation to distinguish one track by the Rippingtons from another. Several of the ensemble's dozen albums are titled after real or imagined destinations: Kilimanjaro, paradise, Monaco, "across America," the tropics. The albums' music affords these locales little more depth or distinction than a postcard.

The Oasis Awards, which recognize excellence in smooth jazz/crossover instrumental music categories, named the Rippingtons Group of the Year in 2001 and 2002, and awarded them for Achievement in Video in 1999. *Jazziz* magazine called the Rippingtons' debut *Moonlighting* "the number one most influential contemporary jazz album of all time." Besides the Rippingtons, Russ Freeman recorded *Drive* (2002) and the Christmas album *Holiday* (1995) under his own name, though with musicians from the Rippingtons. In 1994 he and Brandon Fields established their own record company, Peak, as a subsidiary of GRP, which released the first eight albums by the Rippingtons.

SELECTIVE DISCOGRAPHY: *Welcome to the St. James's Club* (GRP, 1990); *Curves Ahead* (GRP, 1991); *Weekend in Monaco* (GRP, 1992); *Live in L.A.* (GRP, 1992); *The Best of the Rippingtons 1987–1993* (GRP, 1993); *Black Diamond* (Windham Hill, 1997); *Live! Across America* (Windham Hill, 1999); *Topaz* (Windham Hill, 1999); *Life in the Tropics* (Peak, 2000).

WEBSITE: www.rippingtons.com/index2.shtml.

HOWARD MANDEL

LEE RITENOUR

Born: Hollywood, California, 11 January 1952

Genre: Jazz, Funk, Fusion

Best-selling album since 1990: *Between the Sheets* (1993)

Hit songs since 1990: "Get Up, Stand Up"

Lee Ritenour is a native Californian at the center of Los Angeles contemporary jazz, rock, pop, fusion, and studio activities. A flexible guitarist with an identifiable sound, he has contributed to some 2,000 jazz and pop recording sessions, and is a first-call instrumentalist for artists seeking support or collaboration in their high-profile Los Angeles concerts at venues such as the Hollywood Bowl or the Dorothy Chandler Pavilion.

Ritenour is a breezy, melodic improviser who enjoys rhythmic but not heavy-handed material from the 1960s to the 2000s. He has produced all-star tribute albums for Jamaican singer/songwriter Bob Marley and Brazilian bossa nova songwriter/pianist Antonio Carlos Jobim on the i.e. music imprint he established in 1997, in association with GRP Records. He has also recorded several homages to his guitar hero Wes Montgomery. These three stylistically dissimilar musicians, and most of those with whom Ritenour has worked in a variety of genres, are proponents of noticeably propulsive though not loud or domineering beats.

Ritenour started playing guitar as a child, becoming good enough to record with the Mamas and the Papas singing group when he was sixteen years old. He studied privately with guitarists Joe Pass and Howard Roberts at Hollywood's Guitar Center and attended the University of Southern California School of Music (which promoted him from student to guitar instructor when he was twenty-one and has honored him as Alumnus of the Year). Ritenour's father encouraged him to pursue music, and he was impressed at an early age by jazz guitarist Kenny Burrell as well as Montgomery, Los Angeles–based rock bands such as the Byrds, Canned Heat, and the Flying Burrito Brothers, and rock icons Jimi Hendrix and Eric Clapton.

Though classically trained, Ritenour was equally drawn to playing jazz, rock, and pop, and has said, "Fusion was, for me, the best of both worlds." He claims to have listened closely not only to soloists, but also to their orchestral backgrounds, and says his pursuit of sophisticated melodies, harmonies, and rhythms led him to Brazilian music. This type of music was among his chief musical interests in the 1980s, when Brazilian stars Caetano Veloso, Ivan Lins, Joao Bosco, and Djavan made guest appearances on his albums *Portrait* (1987), *Festival* (1988), and the Grammy Award–winning *Harlequin* (1994).

Ritenour's crossover accomplishments are unique. His classical collaboration with Grusin, *Two Worlds* (2000), in which he and the pianist perform works by Johann Sebastian Bach, Bela Bartók, and Heitor Villa-Lobos besides originals and American folk standards such as "Shenandoah," was at the top of *Billboard*'s classical music chart for fifty-one weeks. That album's popularity is matched by the sales histories of the four 1990s releases by the jazz/classical/soft fusion ensemble he co-founded, Fourplay. The quartet's eponymous debut (1991) held first place on *Billboard*'s contemporary jazz chart for thirty-three weeks, and, like its second and third efforts, *Between the Sheets* (1993) and *Elixer* (1995), went gold. Upon establishing i.e. music, his record company, Ritenour turned his Fourplay chair over to Larry Carlton. Ritenour has fleet fingers and seems to use light-gauge strings on the thin, hollow-bodied Gibson model ES-335 electric guitar he favors, for a well-articulated, sometimes feathery sound.

His setup is comparable to that of Carlton, who also prefers the Gibson ES-335, as heard on their duet album *Larry & Lee* (1994).

Ritenour also has collaborated on record and onstage with pianists Dave Grusin and Bob James, saxophonists Gato Barbieri, Tom Scott, and Ernie Watts, fellow guitarists Larry Carlton, George Benson, B.B. King, and Earl Klugh, pianist Herbie Hancock, drummers Harvey Mason and Alphonse Mouzon, vocalists Patti Austin, Al Jarreau, and Will Downing, and producer Quincy Jones, among many others. In rock, he has been a stalwart of Steely Dan, Seals and Crofts, and Leo Sayer. He has recorded multiple albums with Aretha Franklin, the Four Tops, the Pointer Sisters, Barbra Streisand, Melissa Manchester, and Barry White.

Recording under his own name, with Grusin, or in James's quartet Fourplay, Ritenour has earned multiple Grammy Award nominations, gold and platinum sales for several of his albums, frequent top placement in polls, and high marks for radio airplay, especially on New Adult Contemporary (NAC)–formatted stations. His version of Bob Marley's "Get Up, Stand Up" was a number one track added to NAC playlists in 2001, according to *Radio & Records*, a weekly newspaper covering those industries.

Given the sum of Ritenour's interests—classic technique attached to modern melodies and understated rhythms that are informed by contemporary popular idioms—Brazilian music seemed a promising vehicle for his future music. Indeed, Ritenour was prominently featured on two volumes of guitarist/harmonica player Toots Thielemans's *Brazil Project* (1992 and 1993); and on *Alive in L.A.* (1997), the one in-concert album in his catalog, Ritenour performs his original tune "Rio Funk." However, there is no sure prediction of the music he will develop, as he apparently abandons no music that he has ever studied or performed; rather, he mixes every idea and all available elements into his personal fusion.

SELECTIVE DISCOGRAPHY: *First Course* (Epic, 1976); *Captain Fingers* (Epic, 1977); *Rio* (GRP, 1979); *The Best of Lee Ritenour* (Epic, 1980); *Harlequin* (GRP, 1984); *Rit, Vol. 1* (Elektra, 1985); *Stolen Moments* (GRP, 1990); *Fourplay* (Warner Bros., 1991); *Collection* (GRP, 1991); *Wes Bound* (GRP 1993); *Between the Sheets* (Warner Bros., 1993); *Elixir* (Warner Bros., 1995); *Larry and Lee* (GRP, 1995); *The Best of Fourplay* (Warner Bros., 1997); *A Twist of Jobim* (i.e. music, 1997); *Alive in L.A.* (GRP, 1997); *This Is Love* (i.e. music, 1998); *Two Worlds* (Decca, 1999); *A Twist of Marley* (GRP, 2001); *Rit's House* (GRP, 2002); *The Very Best of Lee Ritenour* (GRP, 2003).

WEBSITE: www.leeritenour.com.

HOWARD MANDEL

THE ROLLING STONES

Formed: 1962, London, England

Members: Mick Jagger, vocals (Michael Philip Jagger; born Dartford, England, 26 July 1943); Keith Richards, guitar, vocals (born Dartford, England, 18 December 1943); Ron Wood, guitar, vocals (born Hillingdon, England, 1 June 1947); Charlie Watts, drums (born Islington, England, 2 June 1941). Former members: Brian Jones, guitar (Lewis Brian Hopkins-Jones; born Cheltenham, England, 28 February 1942; died London, England, 3 July 1969); Mick Taylor, guitar (born Hertfordshire, England, 17 January 1948); Bill Wyman, bass (born London, England, 24 October 1936).

Genre: Rock

Best-selling album since 1990: *Voodoo Lounge* (1994)

Next to the Beatles, the Rolling Stones were the most important musical group to emerge from the so-called "British Invasion" of the 1960s. Distinguished from the Beatles in style as well as substance, the Stones early on developed a bad-boy image that would stick to them forever. From the first, they epitomized rebellion and cool eroticism in a way that made their music speak directly to the alienated youth culture of the late 1960s and early 1970s. In this respect, they reached the ears and hearts of political and social radicals more emphatically than the Beatles did.

However, if the only thing their music did was to convey such messages, it would long ago have joined history with many other groups of the period—of significance then, but not now. The Stones were also a first-rate rock and roll band, the British group that did most with the traditional American musical form, the blues. It was "Rolling Stone," a number by Chicago bluesman Muddy Waters, that gave the group its name, and it was the Chicago blues style—faster paced than the blues of the Mississippi Delta from which it was derived—that shaped the group's efforts in the genre. The combination of Mick Jagger's sexy vocals and Keith Richards's Chuck Berry–influenced guitar licks gave the group an edge over all competitors as the Beatles closed shop in 1970. The self-styled "world's greatest rock and roll band" was born.

The Stones Begin to Roll

Two school chums, friends from boyhood, formed the core of the Rolling Stones. Keith Richards and Michael (Mick) Philip Jagger first met in primary school in 1950, but it was ten years before they encountered each other again and realized they shared an enthusiasm for American rock and roll and blues. By 1963 the group—by then including Brian Jones on guitar, Bill Wyman on bass, and Charlie Watts on drums—cut its first single, Chuck Berry's

The Rolling Stones. L-R: Ron Wood, Mick Jagger, Charlie Watts, Keith Richards, Bill Wyman [PAUL NATKIN/PHOTO RESERVE]

"Come On," which reached number twenty-one on the British charts. By January of the following year the Stones' cover of Buddy Holly's "Not Fade Away" made it to the number four spot. The Stones had found their audience, and they began to roll.

As the Beatles began their first, sensational American tour in February 1964, the Stones presented a musical alternative. They didn't sing songs about holding hands or other high school events, at that time the core of the Beatles' repertory. Virtually from the beginning, the Stones went for the jugular, with songs that dealt explicitly with sex and violence. They also perfected a style, in the person of Jagger, of strutting, in-your-face sexuality that became (by the 1970s) the trademark of every lead singer in every major rock group in the Western world.

Jagger's performance style takes the sensual moves and gestures once associated only with certain black performers to their logical extreme. When he sang "(I Can't Get No) Satisfaction" he made it clear what he wanted, and how much. By contrast, the Beatles, even as they moved into their hippie phase, looked more like choirboys. At the same time, Richards's guitar work took the style of the most important black guitarist of the 1950s, Chuck Berry, and

married it to the urbane and more than slightly decadent lyrics increasingly typical of the group.

Altamont and After

Early hits in the Stones' songbook like "Time Is on My Side" (1964) and "Heart of Stone" (1965) capture the blues tradition as surely as any other work of the period. "(I Can't Get No) Satisfaction" (1965) became not only their signature song but, in the opinion of many, the best rock and roll song ever. "Street Fighting Man" (1968) became an anthem of the radical activists of that year, while "Sympathy for the Devil" (also from the *Beggars Banquet* [1968] album) was the closest the Stones would get to a philosophical and political statement, with its topical references and special meanings for the young and hip.

That message seemed less definite after the Altamont disaster of December 1969. On the heels of a highly successful United States tour, the Stones promised their California fans a free concert at a venue near San Francisco. On the advice of the Grateful Dead's guitarist Jerry Garcia, members of the motorcycle gang Hells Angels were hired as security guards. The result was one death by stabbing and many others injured, as the Angels mercilessly beat random members of the audience. They also lobbed unopened 16-ounce beer cans in the air, laughing as they hit the stoned hippies, and even attacked members of the group Jefferson Airplane as they were about to perform on stage.

This disastrous event, combined with the mysterious death by drowning of band member Jones just before it, hurt the band's reputation as it was reaching a peak, but the 1970s saw a recovery with classic, sometimes controversial albums like *Sticky Fingers* (1971), the double-album *Exile on Main Street* (1972), and *Black and Blue* (1976). As the Stones moved on to the 1980s and 1990s, their music continued in a similar vein, with increasingly profitable tours and commercial connections.

The Stones as an Institution

Now an institution, the Stones went through a period in which Jagger and Richards became alienated from each other, yet still managed to produce albums that either went to the top of the charts or near it. With Ron Wood in the group, and Wyman gone by the early 1990s, the Stones remained as popular as ever, their tours raking in larger and larger revenues. The tour for *Steel Wheels* (1989), an album with nothing new to offer musically, grossed some $140 million, and the stakes continued to rise.

Rock and roll has always been a get-rich-quick business, inextricably tied to capitalist goals. Nonetheless, the Stones opened themselves up to criticism for ticket costs and commercial links, which have become endemic in the rock concert world. Musically, the 1990s saw riches that the preceding decade did not produce. In fact, three Stones albums of the 1990s would rank with the best work the Stones ever did.

Voodoo Lounge (1994) made it to the second place on the album charts and won the Stones their first ever Best Rock Album award in that year's Grammy Awards. Songs like "Love Is Strong" and "Sparks Will Fly" proved popular with audiences, and the *Lounge* tour topped any that preceded it with a gross of some $295 million. *Stripped* (1995), the live album from the tour, includes in acoustic format performances of old and new songs as well as covers like a version of Bob Dylan's "Like a Rolling Stone."

A new multimillion-dollar deal with Virgin Records, which began with the *Voodoo Lounge* album, led to the re-release of some classic Stones sets, and also the long mothballed *Rock & Roll Circus* (1996), a soundtrack and concert film originally produced for the BBC in the late 1960s featuring leading players of the period like John Lennon, Yoko Ono, and Eric Clapton. Among the reissues that the Virgin deal engendered, this was surely one of the most interesting.

Bridges to Babylon (1997) was another high point in the band's history, with a tour that *Rolling Stone* magazine

called one of the peaks of the decade, a landmark in arena-staged rock concerts and a top grosser to the tune of $337 million worldwide. The legacy of blues, R&B, and soul remains as strong as ever in *Bridges*, but there are also touches of other musical styles, for instance, the rap passage in "Anybody Seen My Baby?" and the reggae in "You Don't Have to Mean It" (sung by Richards). The album was nominated for the Best Album category in the 1998 Grammy Awards, and was followed, as usual, by the live tour album *No Security* the same year.

As the Stones move into their fifth decade—vying for longevity with established rockers Bob Dylan, Paul McCartney, and Eric Clapton—they have begun doing private party shows which, per performance, are costing billionaire birthday boys more than $10 million a date. Early in 2003, they played the birthday party of billionaire David Bonderman, a wealthy Texan, for $11.65 million, joining other luminaries, including the Eagles and Bob Dylan, who also play private parties.

The Stones released *Forty Licks* (2002), an anthology of work from their recorded beginnings to the present—a "Best of the Stones" selection that supersedes previous issues of the same kind. Rehearing past work only confirms, for their many die-hard fans, the truth of that self-styled designation from the late 1960s: "The World's Greatest Rock & Roll Band."

SELECTIVE DISCOGRAPHY: *Beggars Banquet* (London, 1968); *Sticky Fingers* (Rolling Stones/Atlantic, 1971); *Exile on Main Street* (Rolling Stones/Atlantic, 1972); *Black and Blue* (Rolling Stones/Atlantic, 1976); *Voodoo Lounge* (Virgin, 1994); *Stripped* (Virgin, 1995); *Rock & Roll Circus* (Virgin, 1996); *Bridges to Babylon* (Virgin,1997); *No Security* (Virgin, 1998); *Forty Licks* (Virgin, 2002).

BIBLIOGRAPHY: S. Davis, *Old Gods Almost Dead: The 40-Year Odyssey of the Rolling Stones* (New York, 2001); B. Wyman and others, *Rolling with the Stones* (2002).

ARCHIE LOSS

SONNY ROLLINS

Born: Theodore Walter; New York, New York, 7 September 1930

Genre: Jazz

Best-selling album since 1990: *Saxophone Colossus* (1991)

Sonny Rollins is universally acclaimed as a jazz icon, one of few vital elders of an uncompromising modern musical tradition still active early in the twenty-first century. A formidable physical presence, he is as vigorous and incisive a melodic improviser in his seventh decade as he was in the late 1940s when he apprenticed among the first generation of be-boppers, musicians reacting against the complacency of the big swing dance bands by introducing new harmonic and melodic complications in small combos. Rollins is a survivor of the era of Charlie Parker, Dizzy Gillespie, and Thelonious Monk, a man who had played as an equal with deceased heroes such as Clifford Brown, Miles Davis, and John Coltrane. But he belies his age. In live performance, especially, he outshines the most promising and/or accomplished younger jazz stars with whom he appears.

Rollins was born and raised in Harlem, the African-American neighborhood of Manhattan that was a cultural hothouse during his childhood and youth. Rollins's family was steeped in music: His father was a career navy man, often at sea or living in Annapolis, Maryland, but as an amateur clarinetist he may have encouraged his children's musical interests; his mother bought Rollins his first instrument, an alto sax. Rollins was also influenced by his uncle, who played saxophone and listened to jazz, his older sister who was a church singer and pianist, and his older brother, a violinist who became a physician rather than pursue symphonic opportunities.

Rollins studied piano at age eight, took private saxophone lessons on Manhattan's 48th Street Music Row, and harmony classes in grammar school but was essentially self-taught. He absorbed the jazz language of neighbors such as saxophonist Coleman Hawkins and pianist Bud Powell, with whom he made one of his first recordings, *The Amazing Bud Powell, Volume 1* (1949). He became a professional musician after playing tenor sax for two years. His initial coterie included drummers Arthur Taylor, Art Blakey, and Max Roach, trombonist J. J. Johnson, trumpeter Miles Davis, alto saxophonist Jackie McLean, and vibist Milt Jackson—all of whom went on to establish high standards of jazz excellence and dedication.

From the 1950s through the early 1970s, Rollins had a roller-coaster career, marked by memorable recordings with all-star ensembles, triumph over heroin addiction, assiduous practice of his instrument, investigation of extended harmonies and the far reaches of thematic development as well as mastery of the American popular songbook. Rollins ceaselessly challenged himself, several times retreating from public activity to hone his style (he was discovered during one hiatus practicing in seclusion at night on the Williamsburg Bridge) and/or undertake spiritual disciplines including Rosicrucianism, zen, yoga, and Buddhism. Originally identified with the be-bop process of inventing new songs by extending basic blues and famil-

iar chord progressions into atypical shapes, Rollins experimented with free-form jazz, pianoless combos, and Caribbean dance rhythms (he's especially fond of calypsos; his mother was born in the Virgin Islands). He took up soprano saxophone, worked with electric guitarists, recorded *Tattoo You* (1980) with the Rolling Stones, and engaged in lengthy, unaccompanied introductions and codas, climaxing in a full length a capella concert at Manhattan's Museum of Modern Art (*The Solo Album*, 1985).

Leading a small ensemble for the past thirty years whose personnel, instrumentation, format, and repertoire has remained consistent though not static, Rollins was renowned in the 1990s for the extraordinary immediacy of his concerts (he preferred brief engagements to week-long club bookings). He was antipathetic toward studio recording, though his twenty-one albums since 1972 were all issued by the Milestone label, and since 1980 he co-produced them with his wife, Lucille. Rollins's most recent albums represent him realistically, but only occasionally generate the unbound excitement of his live performances. Critics and fans agree *Plus Three* (1995) is one of the most satisfying of his 1990s recordings. On the album, veteran pianist Tommy Flanagan collaborates on quartet revisions of the Dinah Washington hit "What a Difference a Day Makes" and Nat "King" Cole's "Mona Lisa."

Rollins won his first Grammy Award, in the Jazz Instrumental Album category, in 2002 for *This Is What I Do*. It was his first time as a Grammy nominee in any performance category; he was previously nominated as a composer for his soundtrack to *Alfie* (1966) and as a liner note writer in 1994. Rollins's *The Complete Prestige Recordings* (1992), comprising sessions recorded from 1949 through 1956, were reissued as a seven-CD boxed set in 1992, and many of his older albums—including *Tenor Madness* (1956) in which he battles his saxophone colleague John Coltrane—maintain steady sales as single-disc reissues.

SELECTIVE DISCOGRAPHY: *Here's to the People* (Milestone, 1991); *Saxophone Colossus* (Original Jazz Classics, 1991); *The Complete Prestige Recordings* (Prestige, 1992); *Old Flames* (Milestone, 1993); *Plus Three* (Milestone, 1995); *Global Warming* (1998); *This Is What I Do* (2000).

BIBLIOGRAPHY: E. Nisenson, *Open Sky: Sonny Rollins and His World of Improvisation* (New York, 2001).

WEBSITE: www.geocities.com/BourbonStreet/Delta/4733.

HOWARD MANDEL

THE ROOTS

Formed: 1987, Philadelphia, Pennsylvania
Members: ?uestlove, drums (Ahmir Khalib Thompson, born 20 January 1971); Black Thought, vocals (Tariq Trotter,

born Philadelphia, Pennsylvania, 3 October 1973); Hub, bass (Leonard Hubbard); Malik B., vocals (Malik Abdul-Basit); Ben Kenney, guitar; Kamal, keyboard; Scratch, human beatbox. Former members: Josh Abrams, bass; Scott Storch, keyboards; Rahzel, the Godfather of Noyze, beatbox (Rahzel M. Brown).

Genre: Hip-Hop

Best-selling album since 1990: *things fall apart* (1999)

Hit songs since 1990: "What They Do," "You Got Me"

The Roots. L-R row 1: Tariq "Black Thought" Trotter; row 2: Kamal, Rahzel M. Brown, Scratch, Ahmir "?uestlove" Khalib Thompson [PAUL NATKIN/PHOTO RESERVE]

With a bohemian image, experimental attitude, and jazz-influenced sound, the Roots are standard bearers for the neo-soul and alternative rap genres, although they tend to reject such labels. They are also considered pioneers in the use of live instrumentation in hip-hop.

The Roots' origins can be traced to the Philadelphia High School for Creative Performing Arts, where drummer ?uestlove and vocalist Black Thought met as students in 1987. After gathering other like-minded instrumentalists, they formed a group called the Square Roots, and began to perform around the city.

By the time their first album, *Organix*, was released in 1993, they had shortened their name to the Roots and developed a reputation for intense and varied live shows, something of a rarity in hip-hop at that time. It was this reputation, and the strength of the first album, that led to their major-label debut, *do you want more?!!!??!*, in 1995. The album was embraced by many listeners who were suspicious of the turn that mainstream hip-hop had taken toward materialism and violence. The Roots, by contrast, presented a more intellectual approach to both music and lyrics, though they carefully avoided both cliché and pretentiousness. They soon began to amass an evolving coterie of side musicians, including keyboardist/producer Scott Storch and human beatbox (one who uses one's voice to create percussion sound) Rahzel, the Godfather of Noyze.

illadelph halflife was released in 1997 and cemented the band's appeal to a broad cross section of the hip-hop audience. The devotion of their fan base only increased with the establishment of the Roots' website, www.okayplayer.com, one of the first attempts by a hip-hop group to use the Internet to establish a direct relationship with those who enjoyed their music. In fact, those who used the website soon began referring to themselves as "okayplayers" and became a distinct social group within the hip-hop community.

In 1999 the Roots released their biggest-selling album, *things fall apart*. The title was intended to compare the hip-hop world to colonial Nigeria as portrayed in Chinua Achebe's 1958 novel of the same name. True to its title, the album takes a poignant, nostalgic look at an earlier era of hip-hop, yearning for lost innocence and seeking redemption through music and romantic love. Their unabashed tribute to love—the single "You Got Me"—won them a Grammy Award for Best Rap Performance by a Duo or Group.

Later that year, the Roots became one of the few hip-hop groups to release a live album. Its title, *The Roots Come Alive*, is a reference to *Frampton Comes Alive* (1976) by the rock guitarist Peter Frampton—one of the best-selling pop albums in history. The apparently ironic reference demonstrates both the breadth of the Roots' listening habits as well as their ambivalent attitude toward commercial success.

After three years of silence, the Roots released *Phrenology* in 2002. A challenging work that contains echoes of hardcore punk rock and Nigerian Afrobeat, *Phrenology* was eagerly embraced by the Roots' fans.

Intelligent, forward-looking, and thoroughly grounded in the diversity of the African-American musical tradition, the Roots have shown that an audience exists for challenging, live hip-hop.

SELECTIVE DISCOGRAPHY: *Organix* (Remedy, 1993); *do you want more?!!!??!* (Geffen, 1995); *illadelph halflife* (Geffen, 1997); *things fall apart* (MCA, 1999); *The Roots Come Alive* (MCA, 1999); *Phrenology* (MCA, 2002).

JOE SCHLOSS

MSTISLAV ROSTROPOVICH

Born: Baku, Azerbaijan, 27 March 1927
Genre: Classical

Mstislav Rostropovich is not only a great musician and a great artist, he is also one of the leading cultural voices of the twentieth century. A preeminent cellist, he has been the inspiration for and champion of dozens of major works for his instrument by some of the leading composers of his day. As a conductor, he has led many of the world's leading orchestras and served as music director of Washington, D.C.'s National Symphony. As an artist he has been an outspoken champion of cultural causes and human rights.

Rostropovich began studying the piano at the age of four with his mother, then added the cello, studying with his father Leopold, who had been a student of Pablo Casals in Paris, France. He enrolled in the Central Music School in Moscow, Union of Soviet Socialist Republics (USSR), and made his public debut at age thirteen performing the Saint-Saëns Cello Concerto. He continued at the famed Moscow Conservatory, where he added conducting to his studies. He studied composition with Russian composer Dmitry Shostakovich, and also met and befriended Russian composer Sergei Prokofiev.

As a wave of repression hit, Prokofiev and Shostakovich were banned from the conservatory and the country's musical life. But Rostropovich stayed loyal, helping Prokofiev work on his cello concerto and becoming close friends with Shostakovich. Over the next several years, Rostropovich—considered a rising star by the Soviet regime—toured extensively as a cellist, also making his debut as a conductor in Gorky in 1961, conducting Prokofiev's Symphony No. 5.

In 1955 he married star Bolshoi soprano Galina Vishnevskaya, who was a rising star, beginning not only a personal relationship but a major musical partnership as well. Rostropovich has frequently accompanied Vishnevskaya on the piano. Through the 1960s, the couple lived next door to Shostakovich in Moscow. In 1967 Rostropovich met dissident writer Alexander Solzhenitsyn and in 1969, when Rostropovich discovered his new friend in difficult circumstances, invited him to move in. Solzhenitsyn won the Nobel Prize for Literature in 1970 and the Soviet authorities pressured Rostropovich to evict the writer. Instead, Rostropovich wrote an open letter to the press, protesting, and overnight his stellar career was shut down.

New Start in the West

After Solzhenitsyn's arrest and expulsion from the USSR in 1974, Rostropovich applied to leave the coun-

Mstislav Rostropovich [SASHA GUSTOVE/ANGEL RECORDS]

try and settled in Paris, where the family heard in 1978 that their Soviet citizenships had been revoked. Being banished was not an impediment to either Rostropovich's or Vishnevskaya's career. Their reputations had preceded them and they were treated as major artists in the West, invited to perform in the world's great concert halls and becoming bigger stars than they had been at home.

Rostropovich's musicianship is marked by its warmhearted intensity, commanding tone, and formidable technique. He is a player who strongly resonates with the music he performs, and his musical appetite is large and inclusive. He has performed the entire cello repertoire and has been personally responsible for considerably expanding it through his numerous commissions from composers.

A champion of the music of colleagues, he has premiered numerous important additions to the cello repertoire. Shostakovich, Prokofiev, Benjamin Britten, Witold Lutoslawski, Aram Khachaturian, James MacMillan, and others have written cello works for him, and he has premiered numerous other pieces. His repertoire includes some fifty cello concertos.

As a conductor, Rostropovich also tirelessly promoted the work of his friends. He gave the premiere of the original version of Prokofiev's opera *War and Peace* and with his long association with the London Symphony, Rostropovich mounted major festivals dedicated to the music of Shostakovich, Prokofiev, and Britten. In 1977 he was appointed music director of Washington, D.C.'s National Symphony Orchestra, a post he held for seventeen seasons.

In 1990, seventeen years after leaving the Soviet Union, he led the National Symphony on an historic tour of Russia. The following year, during an attempted coup in August at the Russian Parliament, he flew to Moscow to be in the Parliament building in support of his friend, Russian President Boris Yeltsin. He was hailed as a national hero, and though he has been offered back his citizenship by the new Russian government, he has declined, preferring to travel on a Swiss visa.

After stepping down as music director of National Symphony in 1994, he became the orchestra's conductor emeritus, and he has continued to conduct there regularly. Released from his duties with the orchestra, he stepped up his cello career, producing a series of well-regarded recordings. His 1995 recording of Bach's solo Cello Suites is a landmark, selling more than 250,000 copies.

Rostropovich is one of the most decorated musicians alive today: He holds more than forty honorary degrees and has received 130 major awards from thirty countries, including the Lenin and Stalin Prizes, the French Legion of Honor, membership in the Academy of Arts of the French Institute, the Presidential Medal of Freedom in the United States, a Kennedy Center Honor, and the International League of Human Rights Award. His ability to express himself both through his music and as a "citizen of the world" make him one of the most important artists of his time.

SELECTIVE DISCOGRAPHY: *Bach: Cello Suites 1–6* (EMI, 1995). **With David Oistrakh:** *Brahms: Double Concerto (Concerto in A Minor for Violin and Cello)* (EMI, 1970). **With Rudolf Serkin:** *Brahms: Sonata for Cello and Piano in E Minor, Op. 38 and Sonata in F, Op. 99* (Deutsche Gramophon, 1980).

BIBLIOGRAPHY: M. Rostropovich and G. Vishnevskaya, *Russia, Music, and Liberty: Conversations with Claude Samuel* (New York, 1995).

DOUGLAS MCLENNAN

RUN-D.M.C.

Formed: 1982, Queens, New York; Disbanded 6 November 2002

Members: Run, vocals (born Joseph Simmons, 14 November 1964); D.M.C. (born Darryl McDaniels, 31 May 1964);

Jam Master Jay (born Jason Mizell, 21 January 1965; died Queens, New York, 30 October 2002).

Genre: Rap

Best-selling album since 1990: *Down with the King* (1993)

Hit songs since 1990: "What's It All About," "Down with the King," "It's Like That"

From its infancy in New York clubs, hip-hop has become as much a part of the international pop music scene as disco and rock, indelibly altering American culture. Much of the credit for those accomplishments goes to Run-D.M.C., the first group to expose rap to middle America.

Run, D.M.C., and Jam Master Jay grew up in Hollis, a middle-class neighborhood of Queens. They managed to be around at some of rap's seminal moments in the late 1970s. Clubs would play instrumental disco records, and DJs would start rhyming lines over the repetitive passages to keep people's attention. Russell Simmons, Run's older brother and one of rap's most important impresarios, managed the pioneering rapper Kurtis "Son of Kurtis" Blow. In 1977 Run became Blow's DJ, spinning records while Blow rapped. Run's trademark was to add variety by spinning hard rock records instead of the usual disco fare, a change that altered the course of pop music. D.M.C. was attracted to lyric writing. Meanwhile, Jam Master Jay cut his teeth DJing at impromptu street parties where teens would plug speakers into street lights.

Rap Pioneers

The group's debut album, *Run-D.M.C.* (1984), found instant favor among fans of the fledgling genre. Run and D.M.C. show excellent timing, trading lead lines in the middle of a line or even a word. Their rhymes seem simplistic by today's standards, but tracks like "It's Like That" and "Sucker MCs" display an indomitable, youthful creative energy. The single "Rock Box" became the first rap video played on MTV; the album was the first rap record to go gold, with sales surpassing 500,000 copies. The group went on to many other firsts, such as becoming the first rap group to appear on the cover of *Rolling Stone* and the first to appear on *Saturday Night Live*.

The band appeared with the Fat Boys in the movie *Krush Groove* (1985), although Run-D.M.C.'s members later said they were embarrassed by it. That year the group released their sophomore album, *King of Rock* (1985), which uses more rock guitar and featured the singles "King of Rock" and "You Talk Too Much."

The band's big breakout came with *Raising Hell* (1986), which contains the seminal rap-rock fusion song, "Walk This Way," featuring Aerosmith's Steven Tyler and Joe Perry. The two groups created a template that many other bands, from the Beastie Boys to 311 to Linkin Park,

Run-D.M.C. L-R: Jason "Jam Master Jay" Mizell, Darryl "D.M.C." McDaniels, Joseph "DJ Run" Simmons [AP/WIDE WORLD PHOTOS]

followed to the heights of mainstream pop success. The song made number four on the Hot 100, announcing to mainstream America that rap had arrived. The hip-shaking "You Be Illin'" and "It's Tricky" also became hits and showed that "Walk This Way" was not a fluke.

The group seems to plateau with *Tougher Than Leather* (1988). They continued their heavy-hitting, hook-filled rap-rock fusions with Rick Rubin-produced tracks like "Mary, Mary" and "Miss Elaine." But rap fans had begun to drift toward more street-oriented hip-hop by groups like the Geto Boys and Public Enemy. Accompanying the album's release was a movie of the same title. A ham-handed blaxploitation flick starring Rick Rubin and the band, it was derided for its crude stereotypes and misanthropic violence. The album sold over 1 million copies, but the movie tanked.

Meanwhile, the Beastie Boys had picked up the rap-rock mantle for suburbia and Run-D.M.C. decided to reconnect with its base. *Back from Hell* (1990) ditches Rubin and the guitars, opting for self-production, stripped-down beats, and a harder edge. In a departure from the group's previously clean image, the lead track, "Sucker DJs," drops a thirteen-letter expletive early on. The midtempo track "Ave." talks about hanging out "with a

quart in our hand" when the street suddenly erupts in violence. During the early 1990s, when gangsta rap and bubblegum rap were ascendant, Run-D.M.C. seemed hopelessly middle-of-the-road, enunciating its lyrics enough for white fans to understand but rhyming too earthily for soccer moms to approve. The album didn't even go gold.

Fading Popularity

Some thought Run-D.M.C. was a 1980s relic that would fade away. But the group returned for a last hurrah on *Down with the King* (1993). Trading the syncopated breakbeats for a more muscular, booming vibe, the group returns to the forefront with a little help from hot producers like Q-Tip and Kay Gee. The first single, the title track, "Down with the King," with its more aggressive vocal style and anthemic chorus, became the group's biggest hit on the pop charts since "Walk This Way."

In 1994 Run became an ordained Baptist minister but continued to perform with the band. An unexpected boost came in 1998 when a remix of "It's Like That" by the New York producer Jason Nevins became a huge dance hit. The group achieved another milestone later that year by performing at the White House for President Clinton's Gala for Special Olympics—quite a coup for a group whose mid-1980s concerts had stoked the ire of the Parents' Music Resource Center, whose leader Tipper Gore was by then the wife of the vice president. The song that Run-D.M.C. performed for the event, "Christmas in Hollis," made the rap charts over Christmas 1999.

During the late 1990s, the group set out to recover its roots, announcing it was preparing *Crown Royal*, an album that featured many of the new rock groups that were indebted to 1980s rap/rock hybrids. D.M.C. was less than enthusiastic about the project. He said he felt like he was outgrowing rap's youthful energy. He spoke to the press about being influenced by Bob Dylan and the Grateful Dead. A late 1999 release date came and went with no album in sight. The anticipated reunion with Aerosmith failed to materialize, though the two groups performed "Walk this Way" together at the 1999 MTV Video Music Awards. Expectations remained high for the album. After all, the rap/rock fusion was the happening subgenre.

Finally arriving in April 2001, *Crown Royal* features an all-star guest list including Nas, Fred Durst of Limp Bizkit, and Stephan Jenkins of Third Eye Blind. D.M.C. only appears on a few tracks. Despite the heavy hitters, critics and fans shunned the album. "It's Over," featuring Jermaine Dupri, coasts in self-congratulatory mode. Fans wanted to hear something more energetic and forward-thinking, especially after an eight-year recording hiatus. The title track, featuring Durst, offers more of the same, including the awkward line "I'm the reason rap sales started climbing." No singles from the album charted in *Billboard*.

Tragic Ending

As the band headed back to touring and mentoring young artists, no one could have guessed that tragedy was about to strike. On October 30, 2002, Jam Master Jay was shot and killed while playing video games at his recording studio. Several months passed without an arrest despite a reward fund of over $60,000, though friends and relatives suspected the murder was committed or at least ordered, by someone he knew. The tragic loss of Jam Master Jay brought an end to Run-D.M.C.. However, the group's legacy remained undimmed. A who's who of rock and rap paid tribute to him, and in 2003 his protégé 50 Cent became the hottest new star in rap. Run-D.M.C. didn't invent rap and didn't take it to its notorious extremes, but they helped to turn what some thought was a passing fad into an international powerhouse. In the mid-1980s they created the fusion of rock and rap that was so influential a decade later on the college rock scene.

SELECTIVE DISCOGRAPHY: *Run-D.M.C.* (Profile, 1984); *King of Rock* (Profile, 1985); *Raising Hell* (Profile, 1986); *Tougher than Leather* (Profile, 1988); *Back from Hell* (Profile, 1990); *Down with the King* (Profile, 1993); *Crown Royal* (Arista, 2001).

RAMIRO BURR

RUSH

Formed: 1968, Toronto

Members: Geddy Lee, bass, lead vocals, keyboards (Gary Lee Weinrib, born Toronto, Ontario, 29 July 1953); Alex Lifeson, guitar (Alex Zivojinovich, born Surnie, British Columbia, 27 August 1953); Neil Peart, drums (born Hamilton, Ontario, 12 September 1952). Former member: John Rutsey, drums (born Toronto, Ontario, 1953).

Genre: Rock

Best-selling album since 1990: *Roll the Bones* (1991)

Hit songs since 1990: "Dreamline"

Rush, the progressive rock trio, is the most successful rock group ever to come out of Canada. Since their debut album in 1974, Rush has changed their style several times although the band's personnel has never been altered. Known for their distinctive sound, largely due to bassist/singer Geddy Lee's piercing vocals, Rush endured drummer Neil Peart's devastating personal misfortune in the late 1990s to regroup and record again.

Formed in 1968 by guitarist Alex Lifeson and drummer John Rutsey, Rush started out primarily as a heavy blues/rock band. They added bassist/vocalist Geddy (pronounced with a hard "G") Lee in 1971 and toured throughout Canada prior to finding success when their debut album, *Rush* (1974), began getting American airplay. Lifeson's heavy guitar riffs and furious solos in addition to Lee's extremely high-pitched vocals reminded many listeners of early Led Zeppelin. Interest in the band grew and they made plans for their first American tour, although Rutsey dropped out for health reasons related to diabetes. In a hurried and fateful audition process, they selected Neil Peart (formerly of a band called Hush) as their drummer, receiving more than they had bargained for as the erudite Peart began actively writing songs and changing the band's direction. Consequently, instead of becoming lost in a sea of blues/rock boogie bands that mostly washed out by the 1980s, Rush went on a fruitful progressive bend with science fiction-styled themes and lengthy songs that flirted with rock opera.

Their fourth release, *2112* (1976), an intricate concept album based on the works of writer Ayn Rand, catapulted the band into stardom and they began filling stadiums with faithful fans. Throughout the 1970s, Rush's albums, despite little radio play and harsh treatment by critics for their over-the-top themes in addition to Lee's shrill voice, sold well, mostly due to their relentless touring. Nevertheless, the band hit their peak in the 1980s by switching gears again, creating synthesized albums containing softer, shorter songs with contemporary themes. This formula produced their best-known songs, standard radio fare like "The Spirit of Radio" and "Freewill" from *Permanent Waves* (1980) and their biggest hit, "Tom Sawyer," from *Moving Pictures* (1981), which also included the popular "Limelight."

After a decline in record sales as the 1980s wound down, Rush decreased their use of synthesizers and revisited the heavier sounds of the first albums. They garnered critical acclaim and scored successful sales on their next release, *Roll the Bones* (1991). The album featured the hit "Dreamline," and the album went on to become Rush's fastest seller ever up to that point. They followed with *Counterparts* (1993) and another success, *Test for Echo* (1996), before the band was forced to take a hiatus.

In August 1997, Peart's nineteen-year-old daughter, Selena, his only child, was killed in a car accident. The close-knit band put everything on hold in order for Peart to deal with his grief. Then in July of the following year, Peart's wife, Jackie, died after a short battle with cancer. Both Lifeson and Lee, devout family men themselves, proclaimed that Rush would not work again until and unless Peart felt ready to resume. Replacing him was never an issue. Peart grieved by going on an extended motorcycle sojourn, a spiritual trip that took him all over the North American continent. He recorded this cathartic experience in a published memoir, *Ghost Rider: Travels on the Healing Road* (2002).

In late 2001 the trio assembled in a studio for the first time in almost six years and began creating the album *Vapor Trails* (2002). They worked communally during the creative process putting the songs together piece by piece after Lifeson and Lee would gather in one part of the studio working on music and Peart would muse alone in a different studio room creating lyrics. *Vapor Trails*, the band's twenty-first album, received critical acclaim for its less grandiose, more personally styled lyrics and fresh sound. Rush promoted *Vapor Trails* with an extensive tour.

In 2003 Rush was getting ready to release a concert DVD of the *Vapor Trails* tour. Also included is footage from their *Test for Echo* tour. They postponed the earlier planned DVD from that tour due to Peart's misfortunes. Additionally, in 2003, the band was inducted into the Canadian Music Industry Hall of Fame, a tribute usually bestowed only to music industry insiders. They had earlier received induction into the Canadian Music Hall of Fame in 1994.

Throughout their thirty-year career, Rush, more than any other three-piece rock group, has imaginatively pushed musical boundaries. Their daring commitment to heavy-themed concept music made them a critics' whipping post but also cemented their following with legions of fans worldwide who often question why Rush has not been given entrance into America's Rock and Roll Hall of Fame. Further validity of Rush's importance is witnessed in the emulation of their musicianship by alternative rock bands such as Primus, Tool, and Smashing Pumpkins.

SELECTIVE DISCOGRAPHY: *Rush* (Moon, 1974); *Fly by Night* (Mercury, 1975); *Caress of Steel* (Mercury, 1975); *2112* (Mercury, 1976); *All the World's a Stage* (Mercury, 1976); *Permanent Waves* (Mercury, 1980); *Moving Pictures* (Mercury, 1981); *Signals* (Mercury, 1982); *Grace under Pressure* (Mercury, 1984); *Power Windows* (Mercury, 1985); *A Show of Hands* (Mercury, 1989); *Chronicles* (Atlantic, 1990); *Roll the Bones* (Atlantic, 1991); *Test for Echo* (Atlantic, 1996); *Vapor Trails* (Atlantic, 2002).

BIBLIOGRAPHY: R. Telleria, *Rush: Merely Players* (Kinston, Ontario, 2002).

DONALD LOWE

RUSTED ROOT

Formed: 1990, Pittsburgh, Pennsylvania

Members: Michael Glabicki, lead vocals/guitar; Jenn Wertz, vocals, guitars, percussion; Liz Berlin, vocals, guitars, percussion; Jim Donovan, drums, percussion, vocals; Patrick Norman, bass, guitar, baritone, vocals, percussion; John Buynak, electric guitar, percussion, flute.

Genre: Rock, Pop

Best-selling album since 1990: *When I Woke* (1994)

Hit songs since 1990: "Send Me on My Way"

Rusted Root may be known to most pop-music fans as the one-hit wonder behind "Send Me on My Way," but the neo-hippie sextet enjoys a secure following among jam-band connoisseurs. Michael Glabicki was inspired to form a world-beat group after a 1988 trip to South America. The group has kept a constant lineup except for Jenn Wertz, who went solo from 1994 to 2001. While the group's all-white lineup caused some to complain that it was ripping off African and Latin rhythms, Rusted Root was actually following in the footsteps of generations of fusionists who believe that music has no boundaries.

The group gained local notoriety with their 1990 debut album *Cruel Sun*, which contains "Send Me on My Way." The opening track, "Primal Scream," sets the new-agey stage with mandolin and tribal drumming. Glabicki and Wertz sing co-ed melodies, like a young Fleetwood

Mac. Clocking in at seven minutes and fifty-six seconds, "Tree" signals the group's tendency to jam on and on like the Grateful Dead. Meanwhile, Rusted Root honed its live chemistry, gaining experience around Pittsburgh at several 1990–1991 anti–Gulf War rallies.

Cruel Sun's regional success got the band a deal with a major label, Polygram, which released the group's 1994 follow-up *When I Woke*. The album also contained "Send Me on My Way," which the label believed had potential as an out-of-left-field hit single. With its sunny flute line and "I want to hold my little hand" lyrical hook, the tune quickly became a radio favorite with teenagers. The single made number seventy-two on the Hot 100 and was used in kids' movies *Matilda* and *Ice Age*. But the album starts off with the rousing "Drum Trip," featuring the polyrhythmic virtuosity of Donovan, a respected African percussion expert who gives workshops around the country. Much of the rest of the album is composed of folk rock, featuring the harmonies of Glabicki, Berlin, and Wertz. A typical example is "Ecstasy," a fiery jam whose lyrics denounce capitalism and the military.

The follow-up album, *Remember* (1996), was produced by Jerry Harrison, who worked with Live and the Crash Test Dummies. The album lacked a hit single, but it is full of melodic album tracks thanks to Glabicki's improving songwriting. The album *Rusted Root* (1998) gels only sporadically, with the band lacking their usual chemistry and Glabicki taking center stage. However, they return to their past glory on a hip-shaking cover of the Rolling Stones' "You Can't Always Get What You Want." *Welcome to My Party* (2002) is an improvement, marking the return of Wertz and When I Woke producer Bill Bottrell. The group adopts a funkier, more guitar-based sound with standouts including "Union 7" and the folksy, romantic ballad "Blue Diamonds."

By making high-quality music that's just a little too quirky for Top 40, Rusted Root may have unintentionally hit on a perfect formula. Their moderate success and loyal, long-term fan base allow them to tour regularly and do what they love without the surreal pressures of superstardom.

SELECTIVE DISCOGRAPHY: *Cruel Sun* (Ignition, 1990); *When I Woke* (Polygram, 1994); *Remember* (Polygram, 1996); *Welcome to My Party* (Universal, 2002).

RAMIRO BURR

SADE

Born: Helen Folsade Adu, Ibadan, Nigeria, 16 January 1959

Genre: Rock, R&B

Best-selling album since 1990: *Love Deluxe* (1992)

Hit songs since 1990: "No Ordinary Love," "Kiss of Life," "By Your Side"

The music of Sade (pronounced SHAH-day) is synonymous with soulful, sultry sophistication. Sade and her band made their first impact in the mid-1980s with the albums *Diamond Life* (1984), which helped to earn her the Grammy Award for Best New Artist in 1985; *Promise* (1985); and *Stronger Than Pride* (1988), which went platinum after just two weeks of release. After a four-year hiatus Sade released the album *Love Deluxe* (1992), whose track "No Ordinary Love" notched a 1993 Grammy Award for Best R&B by a Duo or Group with Vocal.

Sade was born Helen Folsade Adu (Sade is a diminutive of Folsade) in Nigeria. Her Nigerian father was a professor of economics, and her British mother was a nurse. She grew up in England and developed a strong interest in jazz, soul, and funk music by the time she was a teenager. Interested in pursuing a career in fashion design, she entered into the music business, like many successful singers, by accident. The manager of a London funk group called Pride asked her to audition as a backup singer, mostly because of her good looks. (She lacked any experience or formal training as a singer.) Sade was well received and soon developed her own following after teaming up with Pride saxophonist Stuart Mathewman. Epic picked up the newly formed band Sade by the end of 1983.

By the 1990s Sade had released several albums with Top Ten hits, but she did not enjoy the unrelenting public attention. Exhausted and burned out from worldwide tours, the late 1980s found Sade living in Spain in an unhappy marriage to the documentary filmmaker Carlos Scola. Her marriage lasted a year and, after its dissolution in 1990, she moved back to London. Two years later, she released *Love Deluxe*, a collection of mellow, soulful, and jazzy contemplations on love and relationships. The album became her best-selling release. From the sultry love song "No Ordinary Love" to the soulfully jubilant "I Couldn't Love You More," the album celebrates hard-won love and personal struggle.

In 1995 Sade took time off to have a baby with her partner Rob Morgan. In 2000 she was back in the public eye with *Lovers Rock*, another classic albeit pared-down batch of jazz-influenced love songs. The album debuted at number three on the *Billboard* chart. Its stunning success is remarkable considering the commercial climate, which at the time was shaped by teenybopper and bubble gum pop. But few, if any, rival Sade's soulful, understated style. She contrasts sharply with the overtly emotional, melismatic delivery of other R&B singers. In 2001 *Lovers Rock* earned Sade her third Grammy, for Best Pop Vocal Album.

In a career marked by alternating periods of huge success and extended respites from the music business, Sade has extracted maximum returns from a minimalist vocal technique. She weds a world-weary coolness to emotional honesty through a smoky, alluring voice.

SELECTIVE DISCOGRAPHY: *Diamond Life* (Epic, 1984); *Promise* (Epic, 1985); *Stronger Than Pride* (Epic, 1988); *Love Deluxe* (1992, Epic); *Best of Sade* (Epic, 1996); *Lovers Rock* (Epic, 2000); *Lovers Live* (Epic, 2002).

CARRIE HAVRANEK

SALT-N-PEPA

Formed: 1985, New York, New York

Members: Sandy "Pepa" Denton, vocals (born Kingston, Jamaica, West Indies, 9 November 1969); Cheryl "Salt" James, vocals (born Brooklyn, New York, 8 March 1964); Dee Dee "Spinderella" Roper, vocals, turntables (born New York, New York, 3 August 1971).

Genre: Hip-Hop

Best-selling album since 1990: *Very Necessary* (1994)

Hit songs since 1990: "Let's Talk about Sex," "Whatta Man," "Shoop"

The female rap trio Salt-N-Pepa debuted in the mid-1980s and made their mark in a male-dominated genre. The first major all-female rap crew, they combined pop sensibility, playfully feminist lyrics, and sexual swagger to become some of the first rap artists to achieve mainstream success, anticipating hip-hop's commercial ascendance in the 1990s. Unlike many of their 1980s contemporaries, Salt-N-Pepa managed to benefit from hip-hop's increasing popularity, extending their career well into the 1990s and enjoying the greatest critical and commercial reception of their career with their fourth album, *Very Necessary* (1993).

Starting Out

Cheryl "Salt" James and Sandra "Pepa" Denton met in the mid-1980s while working in a department store in their native Queens. Their co-worker and Salt's boyfriend, Hurby "Luv Bug" Azor, asked the duo to rap on a track he was working on for an audio production class. Entitled "The Show Stopper," the resultant track was a female response to the extremely popular Doug E. Fresh single "The Show" and featured James and Dento making fun of preening, overconfident men, a theme they returned to throughout their career. Released as a single in the summer of 1985 under the name Super Nature, "The Show Stopper" became an underground hit, leading to a record contract with independent label Next Plateau. The duo,

newly named Salt-N-Pepa after a line from "The Show Stopper," released their debut album, *Hot, Cool & Vicious*, in 1986. The album was produced by Azor, who was also Salt-N-Pepa's manager, and featured a DJ, Pamela Greene.

Hot, Cool & Vicious yielded three minor hits in 1987, "My Mic Sounds Nice," "Chick on the Side," and a rap remake of the Otis Redding-Carla Thomas hit "Tramp." Although their raps were simple, Salt-N-Pepa delivered them with winning verve, and their equally sassy stage show (complete with male strippers) soon brought them a loyal local audience. This audience expanded when Cameron Paul, a San Francisco DJ, started playing his own remixed version of the *Hot, Cool & Vicious* track "Push It." Released nationwide as a single, the slinky and sexy "Push It" became a huge pop hit and eventually became one of five songs nominated for the first ever Best Rap Performance Grammy in 1989. When it was announced that this new portion of the awards would not be televised, Salt-N-Pepa, along with fellow nominees LL Cool J and DJ Jazzy Jeff and the Fresh Prince, interpreted it as a slight against hip-hop and boycotted the event.

Meanwhile Salt-N-Pepa had replaced Greene with DJ Spinderella and rushed into the studio in 1988 to release a hastily produced second album, *A Salt with a Deadly Pepper*. The album featured a few more rap remakes of old R&B songs, one of which ("Shake Your Thing") became a minor hit. Although *A Salt with a Deadly Pepper* eventually went double platinum, it proved less fresh than its predecessor and seemed to confirm the hip-hop community's general view of Salt-N-Pepa as pop crossover artists with little to say.

Taking Control

Salt-N-Pepa began the 1990s by contradicting this view. As they commenced work on their third album, Salt, Pepa, and Spinderella took over some creative control from Azor, who had been credited with all the songwriting up to that point. The result was their breakthrough album, *Black's Magic*, released in March 1990. True to its cover, which features the trio surrounded by the images of black music icons, *Black's Magic* features a funky R&B-based sound. Although this stylistic turn improved Salt-N-Pepa's credibility in hip-hop, it did nothing to diminish their appeal with pop audiences, who responded to their sassy wit and frank sexuality. The album's first single, "Expression," neatly summarizes the group's playful and confident message of female empowerment: "I express myself on every jam / I'm not a man, but I'm in command / Hot damn, I got an all-girl band." "Expression" topped the rap charts for eight weeks. Another single, "Do You Want Me," was also a hit, but it was the catchy safe-sex anthem "Let's Talk about Sex" that really struck a chord with audiences.

The song was fortuitously in keeping with the then-prevalent efforts at AIDS awareness and was eventually reworked as "Let's Talk about AIDS" as part of a televised public-service campaign.

In the three years it took Salt-N-Pepa to produce a follow-up to *Black's Magic*, the trio parted ways with Azor (whose relationship with Salt had also ended), and each became a mother. Despite the three-year lag, the album they finally released managed to build upon the artistic breakthrough achieved by its predecessor. Released in October 1993, *Very Necessary* grounds itself in the same pop-friendly, R&B-infused hip-hop that made *Black's Magic* so successful while updating the sound to make it sexier and more sophisticated. *Very Necessary* provides ample opportunity for Salt-N-Pepa to showcase their feminist yet lighthearted take on female sexuality, particularly in its pair of singles, "Shoop" and "Whatta Man." While "Let's Talk about Sex" amounted to a cautionary tale about promiscuity, "Shoop" is an unabashed celebration of lust in which the females do the ogling: "Ummm, you're packed and you're stacked 'specially in the back / Brother, wanna thank your mother for a butt like that." On "Whatta Man" Salt-N-Pepa team up with female R&B group En Vogue for a celebration of monogamy that is equally concerned with carnal pleasures: "My man gives real loving, that's why I call him Killer / He's not a wham-bam-thank-you-man, he's a thriller / He takes his time and does everything right / Knocks me out with one shot for the rest of the night." Both of these singles hit the pop Top 10 and resulted in impressive sales for the album. A third single, "None of Your Business," did not chart as well but went on to win Salt-N-Pepa a Grammy for Best Rap Performance in 1995.

Very Necessary proved to be the peak of Salt-N-Pepa's career. It took them four years to follow it up with *Brand New* (1997), and by the time they did, their trademark ribaldry sounded tame compared to the hardcore antics of newer female rappers such as Lil' Kim and Foxy Brown (whom Salt-N-Pepa had no doubt inspired). Although *Brand New* was considered a solid album and eventually went gold, it lacked the impact of their earlier efforts.

Salt-N-Pepa's success as females in the once male-dominated rap industry paved the way for later female rappers such as Missy Elliott and Lil' Kim. Their success as rappers in crafting clever and catchy songs able to connect with the pop mainstream paved the way for hip-hop in general, helping it transcend color and cultural barriers to become one of the dominant forms of 1990s popular music.

SELECTIVE DISCOGRAPHY: *Hot, Cool & Vicious* (Next Plateau, 1986); *A Salt with a Deadly Pepa* (London, 1998); *Black's Magic* (London, 1990); *Very Necessary* (London, 1993); *Brand New* (London, 1997).

MATT HIMES

CARLOS SANTANA

Born: Autlan de Navarro, Jalisco, Mexico, 20 July 1947
Genre: Rock
Best-selling album since 1990: *Supernatural* (1999)
Hit songs since 1990: "Smooth," "Maria, Maria," "The Game of Love"

Guitarist Carlos Santana is one of the surviving electric-guitar "gods" who descended on rock in the late 1960s. Known for wresting a rainbow of sounds from the instrument, Santana set himself apart from contemporaries by pioneering a well-received Latin-influenced rock sound. Additionally, his strong spiritual beliefs have added mystical elements to his music. Santana's career met incredible success as the new millennium began.

To Woodstock through Tijuana

Santana's major musical influences were his father, who was a professional violinist in a mariachi band, and the bustling nightclubs of Tijuana, Mexico, where his family settled in the 1950s. As a child, Santana understood that his life's purpose would be music, and after dabbling initially with the violin, he put it down to concentrate on guitar. Santana gained valuable experience playing 1950s American blues and rock in Tijuana before moving to San Francisco, California, in 1963 to join his family, who had settled there in 1961. In San Francisco, Santana found a burgeoning musical scene, rich in many styles, including psychedelic rock, blues, folk, and Latin jazz. He formed the Santana Blues Band and they stood out among a flood of bands in the city's musical overflow by fusing Latin rhythms with elements of blues and jazz to become a local favorite of the growing hippie culture. The band, whose name was shortened to Santana, also caught the ear of illustrious promoter, Bill Graham, and he quickly elevated their status by booking them into his famous concert arena, the Fillmore West. Although interest in Santana (the band) by record companies was already abundant, they waited until their triumphant exposure at the renowned Woodstock concert in 1969 to talk business. They captivated the 500,000 concertgoers with a driving jam of, "Soul Sacrifice" and afterward signed with Columbia Records. Santana began recording a string of successful albums, which included hit songs such as "Black Magic Woman," "Evil Ways," "Everybody's Everything," and "Oye Como Va." The band went through several personnel changes after the third album, *Santana III* (1970), and began influencing their sound with more jazz, picking up jazz drummer extraordinaire, Buddy Miles, for the next three albums.

Meanwhile, Carlos, who had catapulted to stardom in a very short time, grew increasingly distressed over the casualties of rock music's excessive trappings, particularly the substance abuse. The deaths of rock notables such as Janis Joplin and Jim Morrison, in addition to guitarists Jimi Hendrix and Duane Allman, forced him to rethink his lifestyle. He sought spiritual guidance from Indian guru Sri Chinmoy, which linked him with fellow Chinmoy devotee, guitar whiz Jon McLaughlin. They collaborated on the jazz-inclined and spiritually filled *Love, Devotion and Surrender* (1973). Santana stopped following Chinmoy in 1982 but remains very open about spirituality and his journey to serve a higher power with his music.

Eventually the name Santana became synonymous with both the band and the guitarist as he continued to tour and record throughout the 1970s and 1980s, backed up by a revolving cast of supporting players. While his ensuing recording efforts continued to do well, none of them reaped the commercial success of the first three. However, Santana toured extensively throughout the 1980s and remained a huge concert draw wherever he played.

A Supernatural Success

After the release of *Spirits Dancing in the Flesh* (1990), Santana switched record labels, hoping to infuse his recording career with increased spiritual breadth and commercial success. His next album, *Milagro* (1992), is dedicated to Bill Graham and celebrated jazz trumpeter Miles Davis. *Milagro* received positive critical acclaim and further defined Santana's unique rock sound, which some classify under the recently coined genre "world music." However, Santana brought his ethnically fused sound into rock well before there was any name for it. Only a handful of rock guitarists—Jeff Beck, Eric Clapton, and the late guitarists Roy Buchannon and Jimi Hendrix—seem truly as "one" with their instrument as Santana. His fretwork combines smooth speed with impeccable taste and whether ferocious or simple, it always seems perfectly placed. His guitar hangs slightly higher than most rock players wear theirs, especially some of the strutting greats such as Jimmy Page, Keith Richards, and Joe Perry, and he cradles and coerces notes from it as if it were a fluid object. Santana's playing is blues informed, but he shifts easily into melodic major scales or the abandon of free-formed jazz as heard in his work with McLaughlin. Only Beck competes in musical range.

Santana included his brother, guitarist Jorge Santana, and a nephew on *Santana Brothers* (1994) and then waited five years before releasing his next recording. This marked a period during which Santana seemed to be gliding gracefully off into the sunset. He did tours with other legends like Bob Dylan and Beck while revisiting Woodstock in 1994 for the Woodstock II reunion concert. He was a special guest on blues great John Lee Hooker's hit album *Chill Out* (1995) and watched in wonderment, like many others, as the elderly Hooker enjoyed the greatest success of his career. Santana was honored with a star on the Hollywood Walk of Fame in 1996 and in 1998 was inducted into the Rock and Roll Hall of Fame.

Prior to the release of *Supernatural* (1999), Santana spoke of a dream in which he saw himself working with a younger set of players. (Santana may also have been dreaming about John Lee Hooker's success.) Afterward, he informed his record company that he was not content with merely rehashing his old sound. Santana wanted to push forward with a new pop sound and embark on a mission to spread his gift and spiritual message to a wider, younger audience. Using the recipe of success du jour—teaming legends with up-and-comers—Santana co-wrote and performed with Dave Matthews, Lauryn Hill, Wyclef Jean, and Rob Thomas of matchbox twenty. The results were staggeringly successful. *Supernatural* went on to sell more than 11 million copies and serve up a megahit, the salsa-styled "Smooth," which Thomas sings. Santana's guitar work is riveting, full of rich tones that enhance and blend with the album's vocals and rise majestically in the solos. Santana took very little credit for his accomplishment and instead attributed it to the positive vibe from his fellow performers and a spiritual power. The ever-modest Santana filled his arms with nine Grammy Awards for *Supernatural*, including Album of the Year in 2000. In his thirty-plus-year career, Santana had won only one other Grammy, in 1988, for Best Rock Instrumental on *Blues for Salvador* (1988).

It would be hard to imagine Santana's heavenly success with *Supernatural* as anything but a career peak. In his follow-up album, *Shaman* (2002), he continued to bridge music cultures with a Latin-funk sound. Again, Santana features several guest stars, most notably opera star Plácido Domingo. Thomas does not perform on this album, but he wrote several songs and Michelle Branch sings the album's single, "The Game of Love." Branch appeared with Santana at the pregame musical extravaganza for the 2003 Super Bowl.

In an industry rife with selfishness and brash behavior, Santana is a refreshingly humble, good-natured soul, someone more concerned about humanity than album sales. Long respected as a godlike guitar player, Santana prefers to think of his guitar's luminosity as a direct link to a higher power.

SELECTIVE DISCOGRAPHY: *Santana* (Columbia, 1969); *Abraxas* (Columbia, 1970); *Santana III*

SPOTLIGHT: Santana's Milagro Foundation

Carlos Santana is an artist who believes that it is his responsibility to use music to help the world. In 1998 Santana and his wife Deborah, in response to the many requests that they receive for donations to help those in need, formed the Milagro Foundation. (*Milagro* means "miracle.") With the help of a board of directors, the Milagro Foundation uses funds secured from concert proceeds and individual or corporate donations to assist children of all ages who are deemed to be at risk or in need of supportive intervention, providing education, arts programs, and health services throughout the world. The foundation supplies countless grassroots organizations (nonprofit groups functioning on a budget of less than $1 million) with stipends of up to $10,000.

(Columbia, 1971); *Caravanserai* (Columbia, 1972); *Carlos Santana & Buddy Miles Live!* (Columbia, 1972); *Love, Devotion, Surrender* (Columbia, 1973); *Lotus* (Columbia, 1975); *Moonflower* (Columbia, 1977); *Zebop* (Columbia, 1981); *Havana Moon* (Columbia, 1983); *Freedom* (Columbia, 1987); *Blues for Salvador* (Columbia, 1987); *Spirits Dancing in the Flesh* (Columbia, 1990); *Milagro* (Polydor, 1992); *Sacred Fire* (Polydor, 1993); *Santana Brothers* (Polygram, 1994); *Supernatural* (Arista, 1999); *Divine Light* (Arista, 2001); *Shaman* (Arista, 2002).

BIBLIOGRAPHY: M. Shapiro, *Carlos Santana: Back on Top* (New York, 2000); S. Leng, *Soul Sacrifice: The Story of Santana* (London, 2000).

DONALD LOWE

SAVAGE GARDEN

Formed: 1996, Brisbane, Australia

Members: Darren Hayes, vocals (born Brisbane, Australia, 8 May 1972); Daniel Jones, guitar, keyboard (born Essex, England, 22 July 1973).

Genre: Rock

Best-selling album since 1990: *Savage Garden* (1997)

In the late 1990s Australian duo Savage Garden had women of all ages swooning with their unabashedly romantic pop tunes, and, judging from the band's massive chart success, had a solid male following as well.

Daniel Jones and Darren Hayes met while Jones was auditioning singers for his cover band in Queensland, Australia. Suitably impressed with Hayes's performance, Jones left his band to pursue a recording contract with Hayes in tow. The new duo called themselves "Savage Garden," after novelist Anne Rice's description of a vampire lair. Savage Garden signed to the local label JDM and released its self-titled debut album in Australia in 1997. American radio stations soon after picked up the song "I Want You," and Columbia Records signed Savage Garden to a U.S. distribution deal.

With its breezy international feel and electronic-influenced dance sound, "I Want You" harks back to early 1990s chart-toppers Roxette and Ace of Base. The tune features a pulsing drum-machine backbeat as well as an appealingly romantic approach that is both seductive and well-reasoned: "Conversation has a time and a place in the interaction of a lover and a mate / But the time of talking, using symbols, using words can be likened to a deep sea diver who is swimming with a raincoat." Hayes's rapid-fire delivery of such lines, coupled with the simple and memorable chorus ("Oooh, I want you / I don't know if I need you / But, ooh, I'd die to find out"), made "I Want You" a major international hit and established Savage Garden as a force on the pop charts.

The follow-up single, "Truly Madly Deeply," outdid its predecessor, climbing all the way to number one on the *Billboard* singles chart. Sung in a high register by Hayes to a beat of a simple drum machine, "Truly Madly Deeply" honors romantic commitment: "I want to stand with you on a mountain / I want to bathe with you in the sea / I want to lay like this forever / Until the sky falls down on me." In addition to scoring on the mainstream pop charts, "Truly Madly Deeply" was a hit on adult contemporary radio. Savage Garden's mild electronic-tinged sound was sufficient to attract younger listeners, but not so dominant as to scare off adult audiences; fans of adult contemporary music came to make up much of Savage Garden's domestic audience.

On the strength of three hit singles, Savage Garden went on to sell 10 million copies of its debut album worldwide. The band continued its winning streak with the release of *Affirmation* in 1999. The lead single "I Knew I Loved You" hit number one on the pop charts. A romantic ballad built around Hayes's tender crooning and

Jones's shimmering guitars, "I Knew I Loved You" aimed straight for the romantic gut: "I knew I loved you before I met you / I think I dreamed you into life / I knew I loved you before I met you / I have been waiting all my life." The promotional video for the song features actress Kirsten Dunst as Hayes's love interest and garnered major airplay on MTV.

Affirmation yielded several more radio hits, but, within two years of its release, Savage Garden decided to part ways. Hayes soon after embarked on a solo career.

Savage Garden enjoyed more chart success in its brief four-year recording career than most bands achieve over the course of a career. The band left in its wake not only a string of memorable pop hits but also an enduring mark on the adult contemporary market, which became more open to modern, electronic-influenced music.

SELECTIVE DISCOGRAPHY: *Savage Garden* (Columbia, 1997); *Affirmation* (Columbia, 1999).

SCOTT TRIBBLE

SCARFACE

Born: Brad Jordan; Houston, Texas, 9 November 1969

Genre: Hip-Hop

Best-selling album since 1990: *The Fix* (2002)

Hit songs since 1990: "A Minute to Pray and a Second to Die," "Now I Feel Ya," "Smile"

Scarface emerged from the Houston-based gangsta rap group the Geto Boys in the early 1990s to launch a solo career, establishing the template for the southern thug rapper later followed by artists such as Juvenile and Master P. His unflinching depiction of inner-city desperation, coupled with deeply personal introspection, marked him as one of the finest lyricists in hip-hop. While the extreme violence of those lyrics and his seeming indifference to mainstream success prevented Scarface from crossing over to a wider audience, his loyal southern fan base helped him maintain a consistent level of success throughout the decade. His credibility within the hip-hop community won him the support of more mainstream artists such as Tupac Shakur and Dr. Dre and landed him a job heading up the new southern subsidiary of the legendary rap label Def Jam, Def Jam South. By the early 2000s he was excelling both in his new role as an executive (he signed the hugely successful rapper Ludacris) and as an artist, enjoying the greatest critical and com-

mercial success of his career with his seventh solo album, *The Fix* (2002).

Brad Jordan began rapping in his native Houston in the mid-1980s under the name Akshen, releasing music on the local hip-hop label, Rap-A-Lot. In the late 1980s the Rap-A-Lot founder James "Lil' J" Smith asked Akshen to join a rap group he had formed called the Geto Boys. In 1990 Akshen, Willie D, Bushwick Bill, and DJ Ready Red released their debut album as the Geto Boys: *Grip It! On That Other Level*. The album caught the attention of the well-known producer and co-founder of the legendary Def Jam hip-hop label, Rick Rubin, who signed the Geto Boys to his new Def American label and put together a reworked version of their debut entitled *Geto Boys*, a collection of grim, nihilistic dispatches from Houston's infamous Fifth Ward neighborhood that seem aggressively indifferent to mainstream approval. Every track revels in graphic depictions of sex and violence, from little person Bushwick Bill's comical sexual boasting in "Size Ain't S***" to the gleefully misogynistic "Gangsta of Love" to the brutal tale of a psychopath's killing spree in "Mind of a Lunatic." This last track prompted Geffen Records to refuse to distribute the album unless it was toned down, anticipating the censorship troubles that later dogged hip-hop artists Ice T and 2 Live Crew. Rubin refused and released *Geto Boys* through Giant Records. Thanks to the publicity-generating controversy surrounding it, *Geto Boys* was a solid success.

In 1991 the Geto Boys released their second album, *We Can't Be Stopped*, the cover of which features a gruesome photograph of Bushwick Bill fresh from shooting out his eye in a failed suicide attempt. This repulsive yet powerful image echoes the music within. Like its predecessor, *We Can't Be Stopped* tempers its amoral celebration of crime and extreme violence with notes of sadness and despair. Nowhere is this balance struck more effectively than on the album's eerie single "Mind Playing Tricks on Me," which contrasts a jaunty Isaac Hayes guitar sample with spooky vignettes exposing the desperation and paranoia underlying the "gangsta" lifestyle. "Mind Playing Tricks on Me" became an underground hit, and helped *We Can't Be Stopped* to sell 1 million copies.

Although the reception of *We Can't Be Stopped* inspired each member of the group to pursue solo careers, it was only Akshen, now going by the name Scarface (an alter ego he first employed on the Geto Boys' debut album), who enjoyed substantial and long-term success. In late 1991 he released *Mr. Scarface Is Back*. Dispensing with some of the cartoonish eagerness to shock characterizing his work with the Geto Boys, the album presents a loosely connected series of emotionally nuanced and richly detailed narratives of inner city life that highlight Scarface's impressive talent as a storyteller.

Mr. Scarface Is Back closes with the single "A Minute to Pray and a Second to Die." Anchored by a haunting Marvin Gaye sample and the remorseful refrain from which it takes its title, the track memorably shifts the focus away from Scarface's swaggering "gangsta" persona to cast him as an impartial yet melancholy observer, helpless to change the meaningless cycle of violence surrounding him: "He used to hustle on the street corner / His mom would always beg him to quit, but he didn't wanna / As he got older he got even worse / Till a real dealer showed him the purpose of a hearse."

The acclaim lavished on *Mr. Scarface Is Back* established Scarface as the breakout member of the Geto Boys, resulting in tension within the group. In 1993 they released *Till Death Do Us Part*, with a new member, Big Mike, replacing a disgruntled Willie D. This was followed by *Makin' Trouble* (1994), *The Resurrection* (1996), and the last Geto Boys release to date, *Da Good Da Bad & Da Ugly* (1998). While none of these quite attained the critical or commercial success of *We Can't Be Stopped*, Scarface's solo career continued to thrive. In 1993 he followed up his debut with *The World Is Yours*, which departs from its predecessor by embracing the then-dominant G-funk sound, the laid-back, melodic production style pioneered by the LA-based rapper/producer Dr. Dre. *The World Is Yours* also introduces a note of introspection to Scarface's lyrics, notably in the single "Now I Feel Ya," a seven-and-a-half-minute chronicle of the lessons learned in his life. He continued in this vein a year later with the more modest *The Diary*, which featured a collaboration with Ice Cube. Collaborations with Dr. Dre and Tupac Shakur appeared on his fourth solo album, *Untouchable* (1997), which was followed by *My Homies* (1998) and *Last of a Dying Breed* (2000). While none of these albums achieved blockbuster success, they all sold respectably, simultaneously adding to Scarface's legendary status in the hip-hop community. In 2000 Def Jam Records acknowledged this status by appointing Scarface head of its new Atlanta office, Def Jam South. He quickly justified Def Jam's faith in him by signing Atlanta-based rapper Ludacris, who became one of the breakout successes of the early 2000s. In 2002 Def Jam South released Scarface's seventh solo album, *The Fix*, which earned positive reviews and brought him perhaps the greatest exposure of his career.

As a member of the Geto Boys and as a solo artist, Scarface spent the 1990s creating cinematic and provocatively graphic narratives of inner city crime and violence. Although his lyrics at times sacrificed subtlety for shock value, they increasingly uncovered the pain and vulnerability beneath "gangsta" posturing. Scarface's extensive and consistent body of work, along with his role as one of the original success stories of southern-based rap, marks him as one of the pioneers of 1990s hip-hop.

SELECTIVE DISCOGRAPHY: *Mr. Scarface Is Back* (Rap-A-Lot, 1991); *The World Is Yours* (Rap-A-Lot, 1993); *The Diary* (Rap-A-Lot, 1994); *Untouchable* (Rap-A-Lot, 1997); *My Homies* (Rap-A-Lot, 1998); *Last of a Dying Breed* (Rap-A-Lot, 2000); *The Fix* (Def Jam South, 2002); *Greatest Hits* (Rap-A-Lot, 2002). **With the Geto Boys:** *We Can't Be Stopped* (Rap-A-Lot, 1991); *The Resurrection* (Rap-A-Lot, 1996).

WEBSITES: www.defjamsouth.com.

MATT HIMES

DIANE SCHUUR

Born: Tacoma, Washington, 10 December 1953
Genre: Jazz
Best-selling album since 1990: *Heart to Heart* (1994)

Unofficially crowned "the new First Lady of Jazz," Diane Schuur has been a foremost voice in American pop and jazz since 1984. Mentored by jazz legend Stan Getz in the early stages of her career, Schuur is a major recording artist, two-time Grammy Award winner, and an inspiration to millions all over the world for her indomitable spirit.

Music became a part of Schuur's life at a very young age while growing up in Aubern, Washington, near Seattle. The only child of a police captain who enjoyed playing the piano and a mother who loved jazz, she was left completely blind by a hospital mishap shortly after birth. She was encouraged early on to sing and would imitate jazz greats Sara Vaughan and Dinah Washington, both of whom she is now compared to. Blessed with perfect pitch and self-taught on the piano from sitting next to her father as he played, Schuur was performing professionally in area clubs by the age of ten.

After high school, she continued professionally in music, developed a tremendous local following in the Seattle area, and completed a few modest recording efforts. In 1975 she garnered raves at the Monterey Jazz Festival when she performed with the band of *Tonight Show* drummer Ed Shaughnessy. She returned to Monterey in 1979 and astounded the audience after being beckoned to the stage by Dizzy Gillespie and finessing an impromptu version of *Amazing Grace*. Her spirited performance so impressed jazz legend Getz that he brought her along with him to perform at the White House for President Ronald Reagan and the First Lady Nancy Reagan. Schuur became a favorite of Nancy Reagan's, and on a subsequent White House performance she met GRP Records executive Larry Rosen, who promptly signed her to a recording contract. Schuur's first album, *Deedles* (1984), an eclectic mix of musical genres highlighting her four-octave range, astounded listeners. The word "Deedles" is a longtime favorite nickname of Schuur's, although her close friends have shortened it to "Deeds." Critics lauded her hornlike approach to singing, which is often compared to the way Ella Fitzgerald vocally attacks her material. In addition to the success of *Deedles*, her recurring appearances on *The Tonight Show* thrust Schuur further into the national spotlight.

Over the next thirteen years, Schuur recorded eleven albums for GRP Records and won Grammy Awards in 1987 and 1988 for Best Female Jazz Vocalist. The highlight of her recordings, at least from a jazz point of view, was her work with the Count Basie Orchestra in 1987. Her personal favorite was a well-received album *Heart to Heart* (1994). She enjoyed the opportunity to work with blues legend B.B. King, and the recording also cemented an already solid reputation as a performer proficient enough to triumph in a wide array of musical styles—pop, gospel, country, blues, and jazz. Jazz is considered her strength, and Schuur's dabbling in other musical styles has been met with the dismay of some jazz fans and critics.

However, those who managed Schuur's career in the late 1990s felt that GRP Record's jazz vision was too restrictive for her to attain the expansive, mainstream appeal that she deserved. Schuur always admired pop singers such as Judy Garland and Barbra Streisand, and she decided to aim for that kind of broad-based appeal. This led to her changing record labels, first to Atlantic for *Music Is My Life* (1999) and then to Concord Records for *Friends for Schuur* (2000), produced by the illustrious hit maker Phil Ramone. Both of these recordings, particularly *Friends for Schuur*, feature a generous portion of pop standards.

Friends for Schuur is a dynamic recording of Schuur singing duets and sharing song material with various close friends from the music business, including Herbie Hancock, Stephen Bishop, Dave Grusin, Stevie Wonder, Ray Charles, and Stan Getz, whose solo on "Easy Living" was digitally reintroduced through modern recording technology. (Getz died in 1991.) One of the album's highlights is a live song from a Kennedy Center performance by Schuur in which Victor Borge, Sean Connery, and Stevie Wonder were paid tribute. Schuur, with Herbie Hancock backing her on piano, flabbergasted Wonder by singing a slow tempo, show-stopping rendition of his hit "I Just Called to Say I Love You." Wonder was overwhelmed. Wonder's vocals were mixed as a tight duet later, and it is sometimes difficult to tell the two singers apart.

Schuur's smiling, open manner lends an easy atmosphere to live performances, almost as if she were singing in her living room. Sometimes she coaxes her husband, Les Crockett, onstage and proceeds to croon a love ballad for his benefit. This generosity of spirit combined with extraordinary vocal skills is a chief reason for her tours' worldwide popularity. Crockett, a retired aerospace engineer, and Schuur were married in 1996.

Both *Music Is My Life* and *Friends for Schuur* were well received and critically acclaimed recordings. In 2001 she returned to jazz with the recording *Swingin' for Schuur,* in which she is accompanied by the big-band swing sounds of Maynard Ferguson and his eleven-piece Big Bop Nouveau Band. Longtime admirers of each other's skills, they had been trying to carve out time to record together for years. The album features Schuur at her brassy best as she belts out jazz standards like "Love Letters" and "Deep Purple."

Schuur became the favorite of another presidential administration when she sang for President Bill Clinton and his wife at the White House in 1995. In 2000 the American Foundation for the Blind selected Schuur to receive the prestigious Helen Keller Personal Achievement Award. The award is given to an individual who acts as a role model or improves the quality of life for people who are blind or visually impaired.

Whether she is belting a pop tune or riffing on a jazz standard, Schuur's perfect tone, multioctave range, and unrestrained swing meld into a unique talent. However, almost every fan agrees it is Schuur's catchy optimism and zest for life that lend her music soul and lift it to an even higher level.

SELECTIVE DISCOGRAPHY: *Deedles* (GRP, 1984); *Schuur Thing* (GRP, 1985); *Diane Schuur and the Count Basie Orchestra* (GRP, 1987); *Talkin' Bout You* (GRP, 1988); *Collection* (GRP, 1988); *Pure Schuur* (GRP, 1991); *In Tribute* (GRP, 1992); *Love Songs* (GRP, 1993); *Heart to Heart* (GRP, 1994); *Love Walked In* (GRP, 1996); *Timeless* (GRP, 1996); *Blues for Schuur* (GRP, 1997); *The Best of Diane Schuur* (GRP, 1997); *Music Is My Life* (Atlantic, 1999); *Friends for Schuur* (Concord, 2000); *Swingin' for Schuur* (Concord, 2001).

DONALD LOWE

JOHN SCOFIELD

Born: Dayton, Ohio, 26 December 1951

Genre: Jazz, Fusion

Best-selling album since 1990: *A Go Go* (1998)

John Scofield is a pragmatist among jazz's electric guitarists. He is a multifaceted but artistically inclined musician who has increasingly focused on transforming popular elements of soul jazz, blues, New Orleans R&B, "jam band," and ambient styles into something recognizably his own. Simultaneously, he has retained the expansive sensibility of jazz, and he does not deny its complexities and abstractions.

Raised in Connecticut, a guitar enthusiast since his early teens, Scofield played in high school rock and blues bands and attended the Berklee School of Music in Boston. He entered the professional jazz world by performing and recording with established artists, including "cool school" musicians Chet Baker and Gerry Mulligan at Carnegie Hall in New York, and was soon freelancing on recordings by veteran Kansas City pianist Jay McShann and composer/bassist Charles Mingus. He also joined drummer Billy Cobham's fusion group. Beginning to record under his own name in 1977, Scofield demonstrated a confident mastery of a spectrum of modern jazz idioms, including a skill for composing quirky but hummable melodies and improvising imaginative variations on them in small, interactive combos.

In 1982 Scofield joined trumpeter Miles Davis's band. Compositions derived from his improvisations appeared on Davis's album *Decoy*, and Scofield wrote the title track of *You're Under Arrest*. He remained with Davis until 1985. Throughout that tenure, he continued to record his own albums, including *Electric Outlet* (1985), on which he overdubbed multiple parts.

In 1990 Scofield released *Time on My Hands*, his first album on Blue Note Records. Though he was already well known and had produced a catalog of well-received, commercially viable albums, this project, with bassist Charlie Haden, drummer Jack DeJohnette, and saxophonist Joe Lovano (who continued in his quartet), signaled the guitarist's arrival among the top tier of jazz leaders. His original compositions refer to the deeply rhythmic works of Mingus and the bluesy but melodically unpredictable songs of Ornette Coleman; they contain country music inflections, reflective passages, and humorous turns.

His subsequent recordings continue in those directions, and his earlier recordings, many reissued during the 1990s, foreshadow them. Scofield typically writes a sheaf of new material and works in small group settings, with special guests contributing to particular tracks. He collaborates with his foremost peers, guitarist Bill Frisell on *Grace Under Pressure* (1992) and guitarist Pat Metheny on *I Can See Your House from Here* (1994). On *Hand Jive* (1994), he delves into soul-jazz with master-of-the-style Eddie Harris and organist Larry Goldings.

On *Quiet*, his 1996 debut on Verve, Scofield plays acoustic guitar exclusively; tenor saxophonist Wayne

John Scofield [PATTI PERRET/BLUE NOTE RECORDS]

Shorter is his other principal soloist, and reeds and brass sections perform Scofield's extended yet subtly muted arrangements, which show a side of his sensibility he also drew on for saxophonist Joe Henderson's albums *So Near, So Far (Musings for Miles)* (1993), and *Porgy and Bess* (1997).

Scofield contributes significantly to pianist Herbie Hancock's *The New Standard* (1996), adapting rock and pop hits by Peter Gabriel, John Lennon and Paul McCartney, Prince, and Kurt Cobain to jazz explications. However, on his own *A Go Go* (1998), with jam band Medeski, Martin & Wood as the rhythm section, Scofield is even more successful in addressing what has proved to be his abiding interest: the use of sharp, sometimes distorted guitar figures to build coherent statements over syncopations redolent of Chicago blues, New Orleans rhythm and blues, and Motown hits.

His follow-up, *Bump* (2000)—with "enhanced CD" content, including a slide show and video interview—expands on similarly emphatic backbeat material, adding sound effects from samplers, extra drums, and percussion to his palette, employing musicians from the bands Deep Banana Blackout, Soul Coughing, and Sex Mob. Scofield turns to modern swing (and one free improvisation) with young lions Kenny Garrett (alto sax), Brad Mehldau (piano), and Christian McBride (bass) on *Works for Me* (2000), as if to reestablish his credentials with jazz purists. Another such step is his membership in ScoLoHoFo, a jazz superstar quartet with Joe Lovano, Dave Holland, and Al Foster.

On *Überjam* (2002) Scofield facetiously flirts with musical elements associated with late 1960s psychedelic rock. A liner note states "John Scofield wants his audience to know that (despite evocative tune titles) he has not used drugs and alcohol since 11 July 1998." This, as well as his music, suggests that whatever costume he dons, Scofield is essentially about catchy rock/blues/R&B-meet-jazz melodies—"hooks"—and late twentieth-century American vernacular rhythms.

SELECTIVE DISCOGRAPHY: *Time on My Hands* (Blue Note, 1990); *Meant to Be* (Blue Note, 1991); *Grace Under Pressure* (Blue Note, 1992); *What We Do* (Blue Note, 1993); *Hand Jive* (Blue Note, 1994); *Liquid Fire: The Best of John Scofield* (Rykodisk, 1994); *Groove Elation* (Blue Note, 1995); *Quiet* (Verve, 1996); *A Go Go* (Verve, 1998); *Works for Me* (Verve, 2000); *Bump* (Verve, 2000); *Überjam* (Verve 2002); *Up All Night* (Verve, 2003). With Herbie Hancock: *The New Standard* (Verve, 1996). **With Joe Henderson:** *The Gershwins' Porgy and Bess* (Verve 1997); *So Near, So Far (Musings for Miles)* (Verve, 1993). **With Pat Metheny:** *I Can See Your House from Here* (Blue Note, 1994). **With ScoLoHoFo:** *Oh!* (Blue Note, 2003).

WEBSITE: www.johnscofield.com/bio.html.

HOWARD MANDEL

JILL SCOTT

Born: Philadelphia, Pennsylvania, c. 1972

Genre: R&B

Best-selling album since 1990: *Who Is Jill Scott?: Words and Sounds, Vol. 1* (2000)

Hit songs since 1990: "Gettin' in the Way," "A Long Walk"

With an album that incorporates blues, jazz, modern R&B, poetry, and elements of hip-hop, Philadelphia street poet Jill Scott more than answered the question posed in the title of her 2000 debut, *Who Is Jill Scott?: Words and Sounds, Vol. 1.* The romantic, word-of-mouth album slowly caught fire and brought attention to the multitalented, honey-voiced vocalist, whose songwriting abilities had already earned her a Grammy Award before her debut hit the streets.

Born in Philadelphia in 1972, Jill Scott was an only child raised by her mother and grandmother. Subject to the abuse of her stepfather, Scott sought escape through writing, chronicling the vagaries of everyday life in her poetry, from the numbers in her school locker combination to run-ins with suspicious shopkeepers in her neighborhood. Scott was encouraged to keep writing her fly-on-the-wall observations by an eighth grade English teacher, who introduced her to the African-American poet Nikki Giovanni.

Scott majored in English at Temple University and continued writing her poetry and performing at the October Gallery coffee shop/art gallery, but soon found the drab confines of academia to be stifling to her creative drive and dropped out. Soon after, Scott formed a creative partnership with Philadelphia studio musician Scott Storch, with whom she wrote the song "You Got Me" for famed Philadelphia rap group the Roots. The song was featured on the Roots' 1999 album *Things Fall Apart*, with Scott's vocals replaced by singer Erykah Badu, who record label MCA thought would be a bigger, more commercial draw.

The song won a Grammy Award for Best Rap Performance in 1999 and, even though Scott felt burned by being replaced by Badu, the singer pressed forward, joining the Canadian cast of the Broadway musical "Rent" and plotting her own album. The Grammy acclaim brought her work writing songs for and with such R&B and hip-hop stars as Eric Benet, Will Smith, and Common.

The Rise of Neo-Soul and a Breakthrough Debut

By the late 1990s, Philadelphia had become a hub for a new generation of musicians who had picked up the mantle of the famed Philly International R&B label of the late 1960s and early 1970s, which had briefly made Philadelphia the apex of the funk/soul universe. A loose conglomeration of musicians calling themselves the "Soulquarians" (a combination of soul and Aquarians) began to create a fusion of jazz, soul, R&B, and hip-hop dubbed "neo-soul" by the media.

Along with the Roots and Badu, a member of the extended Soulquarians family was Jeff "Jazzy Jeff" Townes, who had come to fame in the 1980s with his partner, movie star and rapper Will "Fresh Prince" Smith. When Townes asked Scott to turn some music he had into a song, the singer returned several days later with the breakthrough hit from her debut, the jazz pop poem, "A Long Walk," which described Scott's first date with her fiancé-to-be. Ironically, on songs such as the sensual, loungey jazz track "Do You Remember," Scott's voice is a dead ringer for Badu's soulful delivery.

Those songs took their place on *Who Is Jill Scott?: Words and Sounds, Vol. 1* (2000), released in July by the

California-based smooth jazz label Hidden Beach, founded by former Motown executive Steve McKeever. With middling promotion, the eighteen-track album began to gain a street buzz and was picked up for distribution several months later by major label Epic Records, selling half a million copies by October 2000.

Fans were wooed by Scott's combination of sassy spoken word ("Exclusively") and such languorous R&B/gospel kiss-offs as "Gettin' in the Way," in which Scott forcefully, and mellifluously, warns another woman to back off of her man or face the consequences. The album went on to sell more than 1 million copies and score three Grammy nominations. Scott was named one of *People* magazine's "50 Most Beautiful People" in 2001.

Scott feted Aretha Franklin at VH1's Divas Live in April 2001 and, ironically, picked up an Album of the Year Award at the Soul Train Lady of Soul Awards in August after organizers mistakenly announced the winner as Badu. The singer was the opening act for rock star Sting in the spring of 2001—leaving the tour briefly with a lung infection—and released the two-CD set *Experience: Jill Scott 826+*, in November. The release features a live album with meandering jazz poems such as the twelve-minute "Love Rain (Suite)" and expanded, be-bopping versions of songs from her debut that find Scott in fine, brassy voice. The second disc contains ten new, loose-limbed studio recordings that critics said sound more like funky sketches for future songs than finished compositions.

After a one-year hiatus during which she took singing and music lessons and penned articles for *Oprah* and *Grace* magazines, Scott plotted a return in 2003 with a double album that integrated influences ranging from Qawwali devotional singing to opera and classical string sections.

In an age of pencil-thin R&B divas singing vapid, sexually charged songs written by someone else, full-figured Jill Scott was a refreshingly natural talent who not only wrote her own material but was also unafraid to tackle serious, thoughtful topics in her sung/spoken song poems. Despite comparisons to everyone from jazz singer Betty Carter to contemporary Erykah Badu, Scott brought a new vision and perspective to modern R&B.

SELECTIVE DISCOGRAPHY: *Who Is Jill Scott? Words and Sounds, Vol. 1* (Hidden Beach/Epic, 2000); *Experience: Jill Scott 826+* (Hidden Beach/Epic, 2001).

GIL KAUFMAN

SEAL

Born: Sealhenry Olumide Samuel; Paddington, London, England, 19 February 1963
Genre: Rock, R&B

Best-selling album since 1990: *Seal* (1994)

Hit songs since 1990: "Crazy," "Kiss from a Rose," "Prayer for the Dying"

Fusing techno dance rhythms with classic soul, Seal was one of the most commercially successful English R&B acts of the late 1990s.

Born to Brazilian and Nigerian parents, Seal grew up in England along with his five brothers. He graduated from school with an architectural degree and bounced around in odd jobs before joining an English funk band called Push. Push's tour itinerary took Seal as far as Japan; he later joined a blues band in Thailand and spent time in India as well.

Returning to England, Seal found the London club scene and radio waves dominated by the electronic beats and ambient sounds of techno music. Seal hooked up with techno producer Adamski and provided lyrics and vocals for Adamski's demo "Killer." Released to clubs and later to radio, "Killer" became a Top 15 hit in the United Kingdom and established Seal as an up-and-coming artist.

Sire Records signed Seal to a recording contract and released his self-titled debut album in 1991. The single "Crazy" was an immediate sensation. Though at heart a soulful song, "Crazy" sets Seal apart from traditional R&B artists with its pulsing back beat and detached, otherworldly vocal. The unique sound and memorable hook ("But we're never gonna survive unless we get a little crazy") made "Crazy" an international hit; the single reached the Top 15 in the United Kingdom and the Top 10 in the United States. Seal also became somewhat of a visual icon on MTV, as the singer's lanky six-foot-four-inch frame, dreadlocks, and distinctive facial scars from a childhood skin ailment made him an instantly recognizable figure, particularly cast against the stark background of the promotional video for "Crazy." The success of "Crazy" spurred sales of *Seal* to more than 3.5 million copies worldwide.

Seal's debut earned him the respect of critics as well as members of the rock elite. In 1993 he appeared on *Stone Free: A Tribute to Jimi Hendrix,* covering Hendrix's "Manic Depression" along with British guitar legend Jeff Beck. Seal also appeared as a vocalist on folk icon Joni Mitchell's album *Turbulent Indigo* (1995).

Seal's much-anticipated second album, also self-titled, was even more successful than its predecessor. At first, the album was a slow mover, with the single "Prayer for the Dying" barely denting the Top 40. "Prayer for the Dying" features Seal contemplating various forms of death ("Fearless people / Careless needle / Harsh words spoken / And lives are broken / Forceful ageing / Help me I'm fading / Heaven's waiting"); the song's morbid subject matter, coupled with the lack of a big chorus in the fashion of "Crazy," prevented "A Prayer for the Dying" from becoming the anticipated hit lead single. *Seal* (1994) did not take off until the track "Kiss from a Rose" appeared on the soundtrack to the film *Batman Forever* (1995). An ornate ballad with lush, classically styled strings, "Kiss from a Rose" features an impassioned Seal celebrating his romantic lover: "Baby, I compare you to a kiss from a rose on the grey / Ooh, the more I get of you, the stranger it feels yeah / Now that your rose is in bloom / A light hits the gloom on the grey." *Seal* (1994) sold 5 million copies on the strength of its hit single, which landed at number one on the pop charts and also spent twelve weeks atop the adult contemporary charts. Seal won critical plaudits for his work, earning Record of the Year, Song of the Year, and Best Pop Vocal Performance honors at the 1996 Grammy Awards.

Seal struck commercial gold again with a movie soundtrack when he covered Steve Miller's "Fly Like an Eagle" for the film *Space Jam* (1996). Seal's airy version of "Fly Like an Eagle," replete with electronic drum machines, was a Top 10 hit on the *Billboard* singles chart.

Seal released his third album in 1998. *Human Being* was a commercial disappointment, briefly appearing in the Top 20 on the album charts before quickly falling into obscurity. In the years following the release of *Human Being*, Seal kept a relatively low profile, appearing only as a guest vocalist on other artists' albums, including Santana's *Shaman* (2002).

Though his recorded output was meager by most standards, Seal nevertheless developed into one of the most groundbreaking artists of the 1990s, offering a unique and forward-looking spin on the time-honored R&B genre.

SELECTIVE DISCOGRAPHY: *Seal* (Sire, 1991); *Seal* (Sire, 1994); *Human Being* (Warner Bros., 1998). **Soundtracks:** *Batman Forever* (1995). **Soundtrack:** *Space Jam* (1996).

SCOTT TRIBBLE

JON SECADA

Born: Juan Secada; Havana, Cuba, 4 October 1962
Genre: Latin
Best-selling album since 1990: *Jon Secada* (1992)
Hit songs since 1990: "Just Another Day," "Mental Picture," "Es Por Tí"

A collaborator with Gloria Estefan, Secada stepped out on his own in the early 1990s and enjoyed a brief run as a pop heartthrob, presaging the subsequent "Latin explosion."

Secada's family immigrated to the United States in 1971, settling in Miami with hundreds of thousands of other Cuban exiles. Adjusting to his new country in the 1970s, Secada soaked up R&B influences from Stevie Wonder, Earth Wind and Fire, and Marvin Gaye. He also enjoyed the drama-infused pop-rock of Billy Joel and Elton John.

He earned a master's in jazz vocal performance from the University of Miami and in 1989 began working with Gloria Estefan as a songwriter and backup singer. He co-wrote six cuts for her *Into the Light* (1991), including number one hit "Coming Out of the Dark."

Emilio Estefan, Gloria's husband and manager, helped Secada get a record deal. His debut CD *Jon Secada* (1992) keeps the Latin influences subtle but does incorporate Afro-Cuban percussion into the fiery dance-floor cut "Do You Really Want Me." In general, he tends toward R&B-influenced adult contemporary, as on his first single, "Just Another Day." The song bounces along with a metallic shuffle beat as Secada mourns a lost love with full-blast vocals that evoke shades of Bill Medley. The album produced three other Top 40 singles, briefly making Secada one of the country's hottest pop stars. His second single, "Do You Believe in Us," is cut from the same musical cloth while featuring more optimistic lyrics. Secada emotes into near histrionics on the ballad "Angel," tailor-made for prom-night slow dancing, and offers New Age feel-good advice on "Free," a gospel-tinged cut. Meanwhile, he made a bid for Latin success with the Spanish album *Otro Día Más Sin Verte* (1992), which contains some Spanish versions of tracks from *Jon Secada* and some Spanish-only ballads. It won the Grammy for best Latin pop album in 1992.

His follow-up album, *Heart, Soul & A Voice* (1994), emphasizes Secada's R&B influences more, especially on the sultry midtempo "Whipped." However, the album's biggest hits proved to be a couple of adult contemporary tracks that echo the groove of "Just Another Day": "If You Go" and "Mental Picture." He released the Spanish companion *Si Te Vas* and followed that with Spanish-only release *Amor* (1995). The return to roots did him good because he sounds more comfortable crooning polished, string-filled Latin ballads than he does performing as a pop-R&B moppet. The album won a Grammy in 1995 for best Latin pop performance.

Perhaps taking a cue from the success of *Amor*, Secada continues with string-filled, classy balladry on the Spanish-language *Secada* (1997). Though his commercial prospects continued to fade, he wrote songs for the late-1990s breakouts Ricky Martin and Jennifer Lopez. In 2001 he co-wrote "El Último Adios," an all-star Latin benefit song for 9/11 victims.

By the early 2000s he was still recording occasionally, but even a 2003 duet with his old mentor Gloria Estefan ("Por Amor") produced only moderate impact on Latin radio. Secada's successes as a performer have been sporadic, but he's made a major behind-the-scenes impact since the late 1980s as a key player in Emilio Estefan's Miami hit factory.

SELECTIVE DISCOGRAPHY: *Jon Secada* (SBK, 1992); *Heart, Soul & A Voice* (SBK, 1994); *Amor* (EMI Latin, 1995); *Secada* (Capitol, 1997); *Better Part of Me* (Epic/550 Music, 2000); *Amanecer* (Sony, 2002).

RAMIRO BURR

SELENA

Born: Selena Quintanilla; Freeport, Texas, 16 April 1971; died Corpus Christi, Texas, 31 March 1995

Genre: Latin

Best-selling album since 1990: *Dreaming of You* (1995)

Hit songs since 1990: "Como la Flor," "Amor Prohibido," "I Could Fall in Love"

Selena's great talent was her ability to reinvent the basic Mexican cumbia rhythm, turning it into a keyboard-driven dance party. Her tejano/pop hits crackled with catchy hooks, sing-along choruses, the celebratory improvisations of salsa, and even the sweaty jump fever of reggae.

The cumbia, known for its staccato, midtempo beat, spread to Mexico beginning in the 1960s and soon became one of the most popular rhythms in regional Mexican and Tejano music. *Tejano* is Spanish for "from Texas" and refers to Mexican-Americans born in Texas. The music genre that bears its name uses polka and cumbia as the rhythmic base but borrows from many Mexican and American styles, including hip-hop, jazz, country, and mariachi.

Selena began her career at age eleven, when her father encouraged her, her sister Suzette, and her brother A.B. to form a band, Selena y los Dinos. By the time their album *Ven Conmigo* (1990) came out, the group, which by then called itself simply Selena, had evolved a rhythmic style that demonstrated its increasing ability to create catchy cumbias such as "Baila Esta Cumbia" and the title track. Selena began pouring more emotion and soul into her music. On the next album, *Entre a Mi Mundo* (1992), the band took a page from the sax-cumbia-meister Fito Olivares, producing the marvelous "La Carcacha," which was marked by what became the group's signature style: danceable tunes that moved the feet but also poked fun at life in the barrio. A.B. was improving as a songwriter, developing a penchant for power-pop, synth-driven cumbias.

On April 2, 1992, Selena married the band's guitarist, Chris Pérez, in Corpus Christi, Texas. The following year she won a Grammy for her *Selena Live* CD. In the spring of 1994, the album was still riding the charts when *Amor*

Spot Light | *Amor Prohibido*

Amor Prohibido, Selena's last complete studio album, showcases the singer and her team at their best. "Fotos y Recuerdos," a Spanish version of the Pretenders' "Back in the Chain Gang," is an inspired piece. That song—along with Selena's original "Bidi Bidi Bom Bom," a reggae-tinged tune—could have easily worked in European clubs because it is almost indistinguishable from the Euro-pop dance tunes on the radio. "No Me Queda Más," written by the Dinos keyboardist Ricky Vela, is another unforgettable work, a touching song about finding the strength to walk away from a romance. Selena fully conveys the pain of love and the tone of redemption.

Tejano music has traditionally been a singles-oriented genre, with more emphasis on creating a few catchy songs for radio and sticking to a yearly release schedule than attaining high concept. Nevertheless, *Amor Prohibido* features strong tracks like the hip-hop inspired "Techno Cumbia" and the torchy "Si Una Vez," an adventurous juxtaposition of cumbia beats with mariachi backing.

Amor Prohibido briefly charted on the *Billboard* 200 in the spring of 1994, becoming the first Tejano album to do so. After Selena's death, it rose all the way to number twenty-nine and sold more than 2 million copies, making it the best-selling Tejano album of the 1990s.

Prohibido was released. It was the band's crowning achievement, hinting at the pop potential of a band at its creative peak.

During 1994 Selena played to packed stadiums and festivals across the United States and Mexico. Commercially and artistically, she was indisputably the queen of Tejano music—no one else came close. Not only did she possess looks and dance moves that few others could match, but she also had a songwriting team—A.B., the backup vocalist Pete Astudillo, and the keyboardist Ricky Vela—that kept her supplied with top-notch original material.

On February 26, 1995, Selena performed for more than 61,000 fans at the Houston Stock Show and Rodeo.

Busy recording her English crossover debut, the band took a rare month off from touring. Then disaster struck. On March 31, 1995, less than three weeks shy of her twenty-fourth birthday, Selena was shot and killed by Yolanda Saldivar, the former president of her fan club, in a Corpus Christi motel. In a scene reminiscent of Elvis's funeral at Graceland, more than 30,000 fans filed past Selena's casket at the Bayfront Plaza Convention Center.

Four months after Selena's death, EMI Records released the crossover album *Dreaming of You*. The CD included three original English tracks and several previously released but newly rearranged hits. With the singles "I Could Fall in Love" and "Dreaming of You" garnering nationwide Top 40 airplay, the country got just a hint of what Selena would have accomplished had she lived.

In 1997, the Gregory Nava–directed biopic *Selena* hit theaters, starring Jennifer Lopez. The role foreshadowed Lopez's own stellar music career. At her concerts, Lopez pays tribute to the woman she portrayed, performing a touching Selena medley. Despite the tragic brevity of her career, Selena will be making an impact on Tejano music for decades to come as she inspires countless young Latinas to follow their artistic dreams.

SELECTIVE DISCOGRAPHY: *Mis Primeras Grabaciones* (Freddie, 1984); *Ven Conmigo* (EMI Latin, 1990); *Entre a Mi Mundo* (EMI Latin, 1992); *Amor Prohibido* (EMI Latin, 1994); *Dreaming of You* (EMI Latin, 1995).

RAMIRO BURR

SEMISONIC

Formed: 1995, Minneapolis, Minnesota

Members: Dan Wilson, guitar, lead vocals (born Guam, 20 May 1961); John Munson, vocals, guitar, bass (born St. Paul, Minnesota); Jacob Slichter, drums (born 5 April 1961).

Genre: Rock

Best-selling album since 1990: *Feeling Strangely Fine* (1998)

Hit songs since 1990: "Closing Time," "Secret Smile," "All about Chemistry"

Semisonic's moment of ascendancy in pop music in 1998 was brief, but the erudite outfit did contribute the enduring "Closing Time" to the pop canon.

Dan Wilson and John Munson first got together in Trip Shakespeare, a Minneapolis-based outfit with an eccentric pop sound conceived at Harvard University. Wilson, who had studied art in Harvard's graduate program,

joined the Trip Shakespeare lineup after its first album. After three subsequent albums with the band, Wilson recruited former classmate Jacob Slichter to join him and Munson in a new band called Semisonic. Semisonic released its first album, *Pleasure*, in 1995 and a full-length follow-up called *Great Divide* on MCA Records the following year.

Semisonic's clever songwriting and tight pop-rock sound initially made little headway with radio, but *Feeling Strangely Fine*, released in 1996, was a major success due to the wild popularity of the single "Closing Time." Buoyed by a simple, melodic piano and Wilson's plaintive vocal, "Closing Time" balances a wistful survey of a bar scene at the end of an evening ("So gather up your jackets, move it to the exits / I hope you have found a friend"), with the narrator's exuberance over finding his own match: "I know who I want to take me home." "Closing Time" also belies some of the band's intellectual roots, as audiences puzzle over lines like "Every new beginning comes from some other beginning's end." "Closing Time" remained at number one on *Billboard*'s modern rock charts for ten weeks and in the Pop Top 10 for fifteen weeks.

The follow-up single "Secret Smile," on the merits of its infectious hook ("Nobody knows it, but you've got a secret smile") and simple pop arrangement, was a hit, but it failed to capture the imagination of pop audiences in the way that its predecessor had. The same fate befell Semisonic's follow-up album, *All about Chemistry*, despite continued plaudits from critics for the band's clever pop sound.

Semisonic's highest profile gig since its "Closing Time" days came in 2001, when the band appeared on the Paul McCartney tribute album *Listen to What the Man Said*. The band paid tribute to the influential songwriting skills of the former Beatle by covering the classic "Jet."

SELECTIVE DISCOGRAPHY: *Great Divide* (MCA, 1996); *Feeling Strangely Fine* (MCA, 1998); *All about Chemistry* (MCA, 2001).

SCOTT TRIBBLE

BRIAN SETZER

Born: in New York, New York, 10 April 1959

Genre: Rock

Best-selling album since 1990: *The Dirty Boogie* (1998)

Hit songs since 1990: "Jump, Jive an' Wail"

A solid music education, respect for history, energetic singing, and technically proficient guitar picking helped Brian Setzer modernize, revitalize, and capture the nearly forgotten fire of

Brian Setzer [PAUL NATKIN/PHOTO RESERVE]

the venerable and influential American genres of rockabilly and swing.

Raised in Massapequa, New York, Setzer began learning guitar as a kid. By the time he was a teenager, he had absorbed his teacher's jazz lessons and loved coloring his assigned songs with jazzy modulations. Though he didn't know it at the time, his learning how to read and write music, as opposed to just playing by ear, would become a key advantage in his eclectic career.

With Slim Jim Phanton and Lee Rocker, Setzer assembled the rockabilly-revival Stray Cats in 1979. The group used classic Carl Perkins and Elvis Presley moves as influences, but added a little bit of Rust Belt lyrical menace to the mix. The group scored big with "Rock This Town" and "Stray Cat Strut" from *Built for Speed* (1982), and "She's Sexy + 17" from *Rant N' Rave with the Stray Cats* (1983). Setzer did most of the songwriting, and his quivering vocals seemed to arrive from a 1959 time warp. By 1984 Setzer thought his band mates had let success go to their heads. He quit and headed to Los Angeles to regroup.

His solo debut, *The Knife Feels Like Justice* (1986), finds Setzer groping for a solo identity. Produced by Don Gehman, the album follows the mid-1980s album-rock template of punched-up backbeats and jangly guitar. Set-

zer comes across as a minor-league Tom Petty or John Mellencamp. The music lacks Setzer's energetic stamp, and his vocals don't remind anyone of his Stray Cats days either. Gone is his rebellious sneer, supplanted by a more generic baritone. Interestingly, his move to Los Angeles seems to have awakened him to the Chicano movement, as "Maria" and "Aztec" promote Mexican conquest of the southwestern United States. While the title track was a middling rock-radio hit, many observers guessed that Setzer's best days were behind him.

The Stray Cats reunited for the indifferently received *Blast Off* (1989) and suffered an even worse flop with *Choo Choo Hot Fish* (1994). However, Setzer had another project in the works that led to a comeback—the Brian Setzer Orchestra. Fusing jazz, blues, and rockabilly with a meatier big-band backing, Setzer updated 1940s swing music and helped promote awareness of the genre, just as he'd done for 1950s rockabilly in the 1980s. *The Brian Setzer Orchestra* (1994) represents a bold move; few critics thought the public would care about a washed-up rocker digging even further into the nostalgia well. Another risk for Setzer was financial—he had gone more than ten years without a money-making hit, and first-class big bands are expensive. But though the album wasn't a blockbuster, it sold well enough to convince Setzer he was on to something. "Lady Luck" channels Sinatra with a swing tempo, baritone vocals, and the resigned lyrics "bartender, pour a double." He more overtly pays tribute to Sinatra on the jazz ballad "September Skies." Setzer nimbly shifts to Paul Shaffer–like jazz/rock with "Ball and Chain." The call-and-response "Sittin' on It All the Time" provides double-entendre humor over a squealing sax solo. Setzer doesn't use his Stray Cats voice, using a more dignified croon, and he finally shows he has important contributions to make outside the group.

Setzer sounds more like his Stray Cats self on *The Dirty Boogie* (1998), also recorded with the orchestra. Slinging his words instead of crooning them, Setzer leaves no doubt that he's reverted to his old singing style. More confident, he mugs with theatrical élan on the minor-key blues title track. The socially conscious poet of the mid-1980s has given way to the upscale hipster urging listeners to follow their wanderlust on the jazz/rock/swing "Let's Live It Up."

Still restless, Setzer formed a three-piece rock band in 2001, the '68 Comeback Special, whose name pays tribute to Elvis Presley's famous NBC concert. His group's *Ignition!* (2001) contains his usual explosive fire and shows off his excellent guitar playing. Setzer adopts an advanced-rockabilly style called flatpicking, whereby he plays the melody with his thumb and fingers and squeezes the pick in his palm.

Aside from the occasional misstep, Setzer has made a career out of creating his own trends instead of following others'. With his rebellious voice, amazing guitar playing, and knowledge of many styles, Setzer has given his fans a history lesson and a peek into the future.

SELECTIVE DISCOGRAPHY: *The Knife Feels Like Justice* (Razor & Tie, 1986); *The Brian Setzer Orchestra* (Hollywood, 1994); *The Dirty Boogie* (Interscope, 1998); *Ignition!* (Hollywood/Surf, 2001).

RAMIRO BURR

SHAGGY

Born: Orville Richard Burrell; Kingston, Jamaica, 22 October 1968

Genre: Rock, Reggae

Best-selling album since 1990: *Hot Shot* (2000)

Hit songs since 1990: "Boombastic," "It Wasn't Me," "Angel"

Shaggy is one of the best-selling dancehall artists in the world. Dancehall, a variant of reggae, rarely enjoys the U.S. sales of hip-hop and other forms of black music. Nevertheless, thanks to pop hooks and easily understood lyrics, Shaggy has attained superstar status. Shaggy's formula combines pop and R&B with sampling and interpolating popular songs.

Shaggy grew up in Jamaica, and his family moved to the Flatbush section of Brooklyn, New York, when he was sixteen years old. He earned his nickname in childhood, after the cartoon character and friend of Scooby Doo. As a teenager Shaggy took up DJing and singing. He recorded songs with an area producer, Shaun "Sting" Pizzonia. After high school Shaggy joined the U.S. Marines but remained committed to his craft, driving from North Carolina to New York to record music on the weekends. His independent releases "Mampie" and "Big Up" topped the reggae charts. His update of a 1960s reggae hit, "Oh Carolina," reached number one in England in 1993. Shaggy's success won him a contract with Virgin Records. Virgin released the album *Pure Pleasure* (1993), which contains "Oh Carolina." Songs like "Nice and Lovely" with the crooner Rayvon foreshadowed the melodic sound that came to dominate his biggest hits.

The follow-up, *Boombastic* (1995), and the title track were even more successful. Both the single and the album sold more than 1 million copies, and Shaggy's efforts were hailed by the establishment. *Boombastic* won the 1995 Best Reggae Album Grammy. Unlike his first two albums, Shaggy's third effort, *Midnite Lover* (1997), lacked a defining big hit, and MCA Records dropped him.

Re-signed by Virgin Records, Shaggy bolstered his fourth album with hit-friendly ingredients. The album *Hot Shot* (2000) boasts the production team Jimmy Jam and Terry Lewis, a duet with label mate Janet Jackson, and a sample of the Jacksons' "Shake Your Body Down to the Ground" on "Dance and Shout." The lead single "It Wasn't Me," featuring Rik Rok, is mischievous and raunchy. It was one of the most popular songs of 2000. "Angel," an update of the Juice Newton hit "Angel of the Morning," had broad appeal to country, reggae, R&B, and pop listeners. *Hot Shot* topped the *Billboard* pop chart for six weeks. It hit number one in fifteen other countries, and it went platinum six times in the United States.

Shaggy's follow-up, *Lucky Day* (2002), did not equal this success; with songs like the title track, "Strength of a Woman," the album's reverent, romantic themes diverged too far from the frisky fare of Shaggy fanatics.

Shaggy's career has been marked by as many international hits as all-out misses. Despite his erratic commercial trajectory, Shaggy's core strength remains intact:

He boldly mixes a variety of musical styles to stretch the boundaries of dancehall.

SELECTIVE DISCOGRAPHY: *Pure Pleasure* (Virgin, 1993); *Boombastic* (Virgin, 1995); *Midnite Love* (Virgin, 1997); *All Virgins* (Signet, 1999); *Hot Shot* (MCA, 2000); *Lucky Dray* (MCA, 2002).

DARA COOK

SHAKIRA

Born: Shakira Mebarak; Barranquilla, Colombia, 2 February 1977

Genre: Rock, Latin

Best-selling album since 1990: *Laundry Service* (2001)

Hit songs since 1990: "Estoy Aquí," "Ciega, Sordamuda," "Wherever, Whenever"

Talented, alluring, and authentic, the Colombian singer/songwriter Shakira became ubiquitous on MTV, on the radio, and on magazine covers after 2000. Though she was a child prodigy, Shakira still had to overcome record-label resistance, machismo, and culture shock to reach the ultimate crossover success with her multiplatinum English debut, *Laundry Service.*

Born to a father of Lebanese descent and a Colombian mother, Shakira grew up among two cultures whose influences were woven into her unique rock fusion. Shakira learned to appreciate the beauty of Colombian, Arabic, and Anglo-American music, from vallenato and cumbias to reggae and rock. A gifted early reader, she picked up on her father's love for writing. She also seemed to have an instinctive knack for belly dancing, which she attributes to "genetic memory."

She wrote her first song at the age of eight, "Tus Gafas Oscuras," about her father's sunglasses. At eleven she began winning regional and national talent contests. Shakira's first album, *Magia* (1991), is made up of original tunes she wrote between the ages of eight and thirteen, including "Tus Gafas Oscuras." However, that album and the 1993 follow-up, *Peligro,* sold poorly and were never released in the United States. Saying she feels embarrassed by their "immaturity," she has blocked their re-release.

In 1994–1995 Shakira appeared on the Colombian soap *El Oasis* but soon reaffirmed her real dream of becoming a singer/songwriter. Released in 1996, the album *Pies Descalzos* was a critical breakthrough, establishing her as a rising star. This release was a major risk because she had overruled label advice to set aside her love of rock in favor of something more stereotypically commercial like ballads or salsa. Shakira agonized over losing her record contract and returning to modeling. But the first single, "Estoy

Aquí," was a smash hit and was followed by four more Top 10 singles. She became the first international Colombian female rocker.

The title track of 1998 CD *Dónde Estan Los Ladrones* criticizes corruption in politics and the clergy. It was another risk because Colombia is the kidnapping capital of the world and labels don't like controversy. The CD also contains the intriguing "Ciega, Sordamuda," a rock-flamenco-mariachi fusion that was a radio and dance-club favorite.

In 1998, Shakira moved to Miami, signing a management deal with the Latin music mogul Emilio Estefan, who encouraged her to record in English. Shakira then took on her biggest challenge, the ultimate pop crossover. It was a tough task. She had to sing and write in a new language. Shakira's thirteen-track CD, *Laundry Service,* was released to great fanfare in November 2001, with the thundering "Wherever, Whenever," quickly climbing the Top 40. Her new manager, Freddy DeMann, the star maker who helmed the careers of Madonna and Michael Jackson, was making her as ubiquitous as Britney Spears and *NSYNC.

Although Shakira's undulating dance moves and revealing outfits made her one of Latin and pop music's biggest sex symbols, she created a strong bond with her female fans thanks to lyrics that tackle insecurities, body image, and jealousy. With a voice that can go from plaintive wails to gaspy, girlish whoops, she has drawn comparisons to Natalie Merchant, Alanis Morissette, and the Cranberries' Dolores O'Riordan.

SELECTIVE DISCOGRAPHY: *Magia* (Sony Colombia, 1991); *Pies Descalzos* (Sony Latin, 1996); *Dónde Están los Ladrones?* (Sony Latin, 1998); *MTV Unplugged* (Sony Latin, 2000); *Laundry Service* (Sony/Epic, 2001).

BIBLIOGRAPHY: X. Diego, *Shakira: Woman Full of Grace* (New York, 2001); E. Garcia-Ochoa, *Shakira: Nueva Diosa del Rock* (Bogotá, 2001).

WEBSITE: www.shakira.com.

RAMIRO BURR

DUNCAN SHEIK

Born: Montclair, New Jersey, 18 November 1969

Genre: Rock

Best-selling album since 1990: *Duncan Sheik* (1996)

Hit songs since 1990: "Barely Breathing," "Bite Your Tongue," "Wishful Thinking"

Duncan Sheik is best known for his breakthrough single "Barely Breathing," a surprise radio hit. Despite its decidedly downbeat subject matter—a bitter breakup—"Barely Breathing" is classic pop with a catchy, guitar-based melody. Sheik's sensitive lyrics, and his clean, rich baritone, which is imbued with a dreamy sadness, made him a poster boy for Sensitive Nineties Guy. The success of the single helped propel his self-titled debut on Atlantic Records to gold status by August 1997.

As a child, Sheik lived with his mother in New Jersey until they moved to Hilton Head, South Carolina. Sheik started to play the piano before the age of five. Later, as a teenager, he picked up guitar. Though Sheik was relatively unknown before his first single, he had played guitar with Lisa Loeb, a singer/songwriter who was a classmate of his at Brown University in the early 1990s.

After graduating from Brown with a degree in semiotics, Sheik moved to Los Angeles and shopped his demo tape around. Atlantic Records signed him, and released his self-titled debut in 1996. Critics called the album a stunning pop masterpiece. In his early songwriting, Sheik shows a penchant for rich orchestrations and clear guitar playing. Cellos and violins dot the songs, including the cinematic sweep of the opening track, "She Runs Away," in which he sings, "Happiness ain't ever how you think it should be so / She runs away." In the album's hit single, "Barely Breathing," the shoe is on the other foot as Sheik is the one who runs away from a troubled relationship: "Cause I am barely breathing / And I can't find the air / Don't know who I'm kidding / Imagining you care."

After the first album, Sheik left Los Angeles for New York, where he became acquainted with playwright and fellow Buddhist Steven Sater, who was scripting a play called *Umbrage*. Sater wrote the lyrics and asked Sheik to supply the music. The end result was *Phantom Moon*, a primarily acoustic and somewhat experimental effort that his record label released on a suitable imprint, Nonesuch Records, home to artists such as Laurie Anderson and Phillip Glass. Sheik had been playing the entirety of British folk singer Nick Drake's album *Pink Moon* in clubs in New York City, and the title, *Phantom Moon*, is in homage to Drake's album. The *New York Times* called him a "supersensitive, superspiritual troubadour" after its release.

Daylight (2002), his fourth album, is full of classic rock textures and layered guitars. With some distinctly different albums under his belt, all illustrating a predilection for strong pop composition, Sheik follows the whims of his inspiration, whether folk, instrumental, pop, or rock.

SELECTIVE DISCOGRAPHY: *Duncan Sheik* (Atlantic, 1996); *Humming* (Atlantic, 1998); *Phantom Moon* (Nonesuch, 2001); *Daylight* (Atlantic, 2002). **Soundtracks:** *Great Expectations* (Atlantic, 1998).

BIBLIOGRAPHY: D. Ikeda, with a foreword by D. Sheik, *The Way of Youth: Buddhist Common Sense for Handling Life's Questions* (Santa Monica, California, 2000).

WEBSITE: www.duncansheik.com.

CARRIE HAVRANEK

KENNY WAYNE SHEPHERD

Born: Shreveport, Louisiana, 12 June 1977
Genre: Blues
Best-selling album since 1990: *Live On* (1999)
Hit songs since 1990: "Blue on Black," "In 2 Deep"

Along with Jonny Lang and Mike Welch, Kenny Wayne Shepherd was part of a wave of teenage blues performers who achieved notable commercial success during the 1990s. Only eighteen years old when he released his first album, Shepherd was immediately hailed by critics as a worthy successor to Stevie Ray Vaughan, the influential blues guitarist and vocalist who was killed in a helicopter crash in 1990. Like Vaughan, Shepherd has cultivated the support of a young, rock-oriented fan base, thereby increasing popular exposure to blues music. An energetic, dexterous guitarist, Shepherd plays with a fire and maturity beyond his years. While some critics complain that his sound is all style and no substance, others applaud the life he infuses into a valuable idiom—the blues—that many feared would be lost with the passing of time.

Raised in Shreveport, Louisiana, Shepherd began playing guitar at the age of seven, inspired by the blues artists—in particular, legendary Chicago performer Muddy Waters—in his father's record collection. Shepherd's life changed soon after when his father, who worked in radio, took him to see Vaughan in concert. Watching Vaughan's performance from the top of an amplifier, Shepherd was so inspired that he immediately began practicing in his family's garage. At age thirteen, he was invited onstage to perform with blues singer Brian Lee during a family trip to New Orleans. The success of that appearance—Shepherd remained onstage for several hours—encouraged him to form his own band shortly thereafter.

Signing a deal with Giant Records, a subsidiary of the major label Warner Bros., Shepherd released his debut album, *Ledbetter Heights* (1995) when he was only eighteen. Sparked by Shepherd's youthful energy and drive, the album was applauded as a powerful homage to the style and spirit of Vaughan. "Born with a Broken Heart," one of the highlights, sports Shepherd's raging guitar solos, underscored by a throbbing bass and heavy drums. On "I'm Leaving You (Commit a Crime)," a classic blues song originated by legendary performer Howlin' Wolf, Shepherd spices his performance with blistering guitar runs. While acknowledging that Shepherd's style is imitative of Vaughan's, *Blues Access* magazine commended the "passion and sincerity with which he approaches his craft."

Trouble Is (1997), Shepherd's follow-up, largely follows the same format as its predecessor, yet displays an increased sense of artistic assurance. Inspired on the album by the furious electric guitar playing of late rock legend Jimi Hendrix, Shepherd, now twenty years old, displays his precocious mastery of rock-oriented blues on tracks such as "I Don't Live Today" and "Slow Ride." Featuring lead vocal duties by group member Noah Hunt, the album stands as an engaging continuance of Shepherd's modern blues style. In 1999 he released what many critics consider his finest album, *Live On*. Shepherd sounds most vital when working in front of an audience, and the album features compelling live versions of songs such as "Oh Well," first recorded by rock group Fleetwood Mac, and "In 2 Deep," which earned substantial airplay for Shepherd on rock stations.

While his style is heavily indebted to blues masters such as Vaughan, Shepherd is a unique, powerful artist in his own right. Characterized by writers as a prodigy due to his youth and startling talent, Shepherd can be credited with exposing a new generation of fans to blues music.

SELECTIVE DISCOGRAPHY: *Ledbetter Heights* (Warner Bros./Giant, 1995); *Trouble Is* (Warner Bros., 1997); *Live On* (Giant, 1999).

WEBSITE: www.kwsband.com.

DAVID FREELAND

HOWARD SHORE

Born: Toronto, Ontario, 18 October 1946
Genre: Soundtrack
Best-selling album since 1990: *Lord of the Rings: The Fellowship of the Ring* (2001)

Howard Shore is a film soundtrack composer, arranger, orchestrator, conductor, and music director whose specialty is the sound of other worlds, especially those that are dark or strange. Winner of an Academy Award for his score for

The Lord of the Rings: Fellowship of the Ring (2001), Shore has composed scores for the other two installments of that nearly nine-hour trilogy, *The Lord of the Rings: The Two Towers* (2002) and *The Lord of the Rings: The Return of the King* (2003); in February 2003 he conducted the London Philharmonic Orchestra, London Voices, and the London Oratory School Schola in two of six movements drawn from the entire work.

Shore is a supremely prolific movie-music maker; while working on *The Lord of the Rings*, he contributed a concert piece, "Brooklyn Heights," to the soundtrack of Martin Scorsese's *Gangs of New York* (2002) and prepared the score for *Spider* (2003), sustaining his three-decade-long collaboration with the Canadian director David Cronenberg.

Shore earned a degree from Boston's Berklee School of Music in the late 1960s and then returned to Canada, where he co-founded the thirteen-piece jazz-rock fusion band Lighthouse. As leader of that ensemble from 1969 through 1972, he played flute, saxophone, trumpet; vocalized; wrote songs and arrangements; and went on concert tours. Lighthouse won several Juno awards (Canadian Grammys). Shore was the first musical director of the television show *Saturday Night Live*, hired by SNL's Canadian director Lorne Michaels for a tenure that began in 1975 and that continued through his initial film project with Cronenberg, *The Brood* (1979). Since then he has concentrated on writing for movies, while composing chamber music for personal satisfaction (as such, it has not been heard or recorded). In 1993 he wrote the main title theme for Conan O'Brien's late-night television show.

At first, Shore worked on low-budget horror pictures, although Cronenberg's *Scanners* (1981), *Videodrome* (1983), and *The Fly* (1986) have other ambitions than simply to scare. Shore also scored Scorsese's Kafkaesque comedy about downtown New York, *After Hours* (1985). One of his most successful early soundtracks was for the sunny Tom Hanks vehicle *Big* (1988), but Shore returned to the dark genre for Cronenberg's *Dead Ringers* (1988), for which he won a Genie (Canadian Oscar) in 1989.

In the 1990s, Shore applied himself to a greater range of subjects, including higher-budget suspense films and thrillers (*The Silence of the Lambs* [1991]; *A Kiss Before Dying* [1991]; *Prelude to a Kiss* [1992]; *Single White Female* [1992]; *Sliver* [1993]; *The Client* [1994]; *Seven* [1995]; *Crash* [1996]; *Cop Land* [1997]; *The Game* [1997]; *The Cell* [2000]; *Panic Room* [2002]); off-beat comedies and satires (*Mrs. Doubtfire* [1993]; *Ed Wood* [1994]; *The Truth About Cats & Dogs* [1996]; *Striptease* [1996]; *That Thing You Do!* [1996]; *Analyze This* [1999]; *eXistenZ* [1999]; *Dogma* [1999]; *High Fidelity* [2000]); and the occasional drama (*M. Butterfly*

[1993]; *Philadelphia* [1993]; *Nobody's Fool* [1994]; *White Man's Burden* [1995]; *Gloria* [1999]; *The Yards* [2000]). Shore even scored *Looking for Richard* (1996), Al Pacino's nonfiction film of fragmentary performances of Shakespeare's *Richard III*.

Shore does not hew to any one style or strategy but allows each film to suggest its own appropriate, if sometimes odd, choices. For instance, in *Naked Lunch* (1991), Cronenberg's adaptation of the surreal novel by the beat writer William S. Burroughs, Shore had the avant-garde saxophonist Ornette Coleman solo in countermelody to a pre-recorded song by Thelonious Monk. Shore's score for Cronenberg's *Crash* (1996) employed multiple dissonant guitars, while his addition to *Philadelphia* was a sad yet comforting instrumental piece that closes the soundtrack album. His score for the first *Lord of the Rings* movie included vocals by the New Age singer Enya and mystical choral cues; he claimed the second of the three films contained 95 percent new music.

Shore is capable of working with world music, period genres, conventional symphonic forces, and electronic sounds. Far from taking the safe path of lulling the viewer/listener into a comfort zone, his work is unpredictable and often creates a feeling of excitement or surprise.

SELECTIVE DISCOGRAPHY: *Silence of the Lambs* (Hannibal, 1991); *Naked Lunch* (Milan, 1991); *Mrs. Doubtfire* (Arista, 1993); *M. Butterfly* (Varese Saraband, 1993); *Philadelphia* (Epic Soundtrax, 1993); *That Thing You Do!* (Sony Columbia, 1996); *Striptease* (EMI, 1996); *Crash* (Milan, 1996); *Looking for Richard* (Angel 1996); *Existenze* (RCA Victor, 1999); *High Fidelity* (Universal, 2000); *The Lord of the Rings: Fellowship of the Ring* (Warner Bros./Reprise 2001); *The Lord of the Rings: The Two Towers* (Warner Bros./Reprise, 2002); *The Lord of the Rings: Return of the King* (Warner Bros./Reprise 2003).

HOWARD MANDEL

WAYNE SHORTER

Born: Newark, New Jersey, 25 August 1933

Genre: Jazz, Fusion

Best-selling album since 1990: *Footprints Live!* (2002)

Hit songs since 1990: "Aung San Suu Kyi"

Tenor and soprano saxophonist, composer, and bandleader Wayne Shorter is enjoying a December bloom. Long considered an aficionados' darling, contributing significantly but with an unusual degree of self-effacement to high-profile pop and rock projects as well as at least three of the most renown ensembles in jazz, as he attains "elder statesman" status he has emerged as the front man of his own quartet, supported by exciting, much younger virtuosos.

A musical prodigy whose older brother Alan (died 1988) was a jazz trumpeter with a more marginal career, Shorter began his professional life in 1956 with a stint in pianist Horace Silver's band, before being drafted into the army, which he served by playing in musical units stationed in New Jersey. Following discharge, Shorter joined trumpeter Maynard Ferguson's big band, where he met pianist Joe Zawinul, with whom he founded Weather Report, the foremost electric jazz-fusion ensemble, in 1970.

Prior to Weather Report, though, Shorter established himself as a memorable composer in Art Blakey's Jazz Messengers (from 1959 to 1963), penning bluesy "hard-bop" themes that have earned status as standards in the mainstream jazz repertoire. Then he joined Miles Davis's innovative mid-1960s quintet with pianist Herbie Hancock, bassist Ron Carter, and drummer Tony Williams. During that band's transition from a relatively straight-ahead outfit to an iconoclastic, electrified ensemble, Shorter contributed pieces characterized by spare or fragmentary motifs, sometimes spinning through cycles or offset by silence.

During Davis's occasional down times, Shorter recorded a series of outstanding, mostly acoustic albums of his original compositions on the Blue Note label. His writing in that context investigates unusual harmonic relationships within common song formats. Throughout the 1960s Shorter also honed his saxophone sound, resulting in timbres lighter than those of John Coltrane or Sonny Rollins on tenor, and swooning and squealing on the soprano, which he first used in 1968. He won *Down Beat* magazine polls in the soprano saxophone category for thirteen consecutive years, beginning in 1969.

In Weather Report, Shorter's sax rode over Zawinul's multiple electric keyboards parts, aggressive trap drums, African-Caribbean-South American percussion, and the virtuosic electric bass of Jaco Pastorius. Even before he left the band in 1985 he pursued his own projects, collaborating with Brazilian singer Milton Nascimento on *Native Dancer* (1974), with the studio rock/pop duo Steely Dan on *Aja* (1976), with singer/songwriter Joni Mitchell, and with Latin-oriented rock guitarist Carlos Santana. Shorter and Santana co-led a band that toured internationally in the late 1980s and produced one album featuring them both.

Shorter shared a Grammy Award for Best Instrumental Composition (other than Jazz) for the track "Call Sheet Blues" (1987), which he co-created for the film

Round Midnight (1986), and in which he appeared. He released three albums during the late 1980s that intrigued musicians more than critics or the general public, as electric jazz had fallen out of favor. A Nirichen Buddhist since 1970, Shorter seemed unphased by the uncertain reception that his music met.

However, in the 1990s Shorter gained new momentum, winning Grammies for Best Instrumental Jazz Performance, Individual or Group in 1994 for his participation in *A Tribute to Miles* (1994); for Best Contemporary Jazz Performance, Instrumental in 1996 for *High Life* (1996), in which he played soprano sax against elaborate MIDI scores; for Best Instrumental Composition (Other Than Jazz) in 1997 for "Aung San Suu Kyi," dedicated to the Burmese human rights Nobel laureate, from a duet album (*1+1*, 1997) with Herbie Hancock; and for Best Jazz Instrumental Performance, Soloist in 1999 for "In Walked Wayne," on trombonist J. J. Johnson's album *Heroes* (1998).

In 2001 Shorter convened his first touring quartet ever, with pianist Danilo Perez, bassist John Patitucci, and drummer Brian Blade, all born after 1959. His first in-concert album, *Footprints Live!* (2002), topped many critics' Top 10 lists, won a 2003 Grammy nomination for Best Jazz Instrumental Album, and received rave reviews. Shorter's follow-up, *Alegría* (2003), was recorded in advance of the *Footprints Live!* tour. His first all-acoustic album since 1967, it features an orchestral array of percussion, brass, woodwinds, and strings as well as his young quartet. The program comprises a Celtic folk song, a piece by Brazilian composer Heitor Villa-Lobos, and revisions of some 1960s compositions, as well as the inimitable tension of Shorter's alternately shy and aggressive saxophone sound.

SELECTIVE DISCOGRAPHY: *High Life* (Verve, 1995); *1+1* (Verve, 1997); *Footprints Live!* (Verve, 2002); *Alegría* (Verve, 2003). **With Various Artists:** *A Tribute to Miles* (Qwest/Warner Bros., 1994); *Herbie Hancock, Gershwin's World* (Verve, 1998). **Soundtracks:** *Round Midnight* (Columbia, 1986); *The Fugitive Soundtrack* (Nonesuch, 1993); *Glengarry Glen Ross: Music from and Inspired by the Motion Picture* (Elektra, 1992).

WEBSITE: www.imnworld.com/shorter.html.

HOWARD MANDEL

PAUL SIMON

Born: Newark, New Jersey, 13 October 1941

Genre: Rock

Best-selling album since 1990: *The Rhythm of the Saints* (1990)

Paul Simon [PAUL NATKIN/PHOTO RESERVE]

Often remembered as the creative half of the singing duo Simon and Garfunkel, singer/songwriter Paul Simon is one of the most accomplished pop songwriters in American music history. Whether playful or poignant, Simon's songs are driven by agile, often sophisticated lyrics and engaging melodies. He has recovered from commercial and creative slumps by making incisive changes in his musical handiwork to remain at the forefront of the industry since the 1960s.

Priming Rhymin' Simon

Simon grew up in the Forest Hills section of Queens, New York, under the erudite auspices of a mother who was a schoolteacher and a college professor father with a doctorate in semantics. Louis Simon was also a jazz bassist and exposed a preteen Simon to the world of jazz; however, like many teenagers growing up in the 1950s, Simon soon became enthralled with the sound of rock and roll. In 1955 Simon and a boyhood friend from the neighborhood, Art Garfunkel, formed a singing duo called Tom and Jerry with Simon singing and playing guitar and Garfunkel accompanying vocally. The conservative political backdrop of the 1950s fueled the boys' idea to call the twosome Tom and Jerry, avoiding any possible stereotyping for their

Jewish names. They broke up when Garfunkel went away to college but recorded several singles together, including "Hey, Schoolgirl." Meanwhile, Simon went on to perform solo under the name Jerry Landis and scored some limited radio play with "Lone Teen Ranger."

Simon and Garfunkel re-formed in the early 1960s, this time under their own names, and recorded an album, *Wednesday Morning, 3 A.M.* (1964). The album fared poorly, the duo broke up, and Simon moved to England to work solo in the growing folk scene there. Back in the United States, however, a song from *Wednesday Morning, 3 A.M.*, "Sound of Silence," had been remixed and released as a single. It gained tremendous popularity, eventually reaching number one on the charts. Simon and Garfunkel quickly regrouped and recorded their next album, *Sounds of Silence* (1966), which included their surprise hit in addition to Simon's folk anthem, "I Am a Rock." Simon and Garfunkel recorded three more albums of Simon's songs until creative differences forced them apart in 1971 shortly after the release of *Bridge Over Troubled Water* (1970).

Going solo after such success with Garfunkel was perilous territory for Simon. Along with the two previously mentioned songs, their partnership had spawned radio classics including "Homeward Bound," "The Boxer," "The 59th Street Bridge Song," "Mrs. Robinson," and "Scarborough Fair/Canticle"—all written by Simon. The duo won five Grammy Awards, and their work was later acknowledged with an induction into the Rock and Roll Hall of Fame in 1990 and with a Lifetime Achievement Award at the 2003 Grammy Awards. Nevertheless, Simon's first solo album after the breakup, *Paul Simon* (1972), went platinum and started a string of successful releases and major hits throughout the 1970s.

Some of Simon's best-known hits include "Kodachrome," "Slip Slidin' Away," "Still Crazy After All These Years," "50 Ways to Leave Your Lover," and "Me and Julio Down by the Schoolyard" and earned him the tag "Rhymin' Simon." Along the way, he reunited with Garfunkel for special projects and appearances, most notably a concert in New York's Central Park that was released as an album. Afterward they agreed to re-form and cut a studio album but ended up disagreeing about Simon's material so it was scrapped. Most of those songs went into Simon's *Hearts and Bones* (1983), a spectacular album that inexplicably sold poorly. Simon had been experiencing a decline in sales since his ambitious *One-Trick Pony* (1980), which was a soundtrack to an autobiographical film that he scripted and starred in as an actor.

Exploring the World's Musical Terrain

Although no contemporary folk/pop artist in the post–Bob Dylan era was more successful at blending poetic lyrics with catchy music to produce hits, Simon still yearned for something creatively different. In addition, he felt a change in the musical atmosphere, a greater interest in ethnic, world music. Simon traveled to South Africa and soaked up varieties of the country's rhythmic music by working with many tribal musicians. Simon placed his lyrically powered songs within this framework to produce one of the greatest triumphs in contemporary music history, *Graceland* (1986). The album sold more than 10 million copies within two years, and critics across the board hailed it for its musical richness. *Graceland* earned Simon a Grammy Award for Album of the Year in 1987. However, the album also brought criticism from political groups who accused Simon of carpetbagging in the struggling third world milieu and for using their music to tell his stories. Nevertheless, Simon employed a similar strategy with his next album, *The Rhythm of the Saints* (1990). This time he traveled to Brazil, worked with local musicians there, and produced an album of his songs that again focused on ethnic rhythms and sounds. Although interest generated by *The Rhythm of the Saints* paled in comparison to *Graceland*, it still managed to sell 4 million copies and was a major success under any other definition of success.

In late summer of 1991, Simon, a resident of Manhattan's Upper West Side, performed (as he did with Garfunkel ten years previous) in a concert just a few blocks from his home in Central Park. The free event was attended by 750,000 people who peacefully watched Simon do selections from his deep catalog of hits. The concert was released later that year as *Paul Simon's Concert in the Park* (1991). Although Garfunkel was conspicuously absent from the Central Park concert, Simon teamed up with him in 1993 to perform at a variety of benefits and promote a three-CD box set retrospective of their music.

In another creative adventure, Simon began writing songs for a Broadway show concept that eventually materialized when the musical play *The Capeman* (1997) opened in New York at the Marquis Theatre in 1997. The play, based on a double homicide in Manhattan's Hells Kitchen district in 1959, opened up old wounds for relatives of the victims—many of whom reside within blocks of the Broadway theater district—as Simon's play cast the perpetrator in a sympathetic light. The show's songs were somewhat well received, as were the musical performances of the two leading men, Marc Anthony and Ruben Blades. However, *The Capeman* was marred by a poorly conceived story, terrible dialogue, and clumsy staging as Simon insisted that there be little movement or anything else to distract from his music. Only a swell of interest generated by the production's skewed view of history kept it running for as long as it did—sixty-eight performances—and it now lies in the record books as one of Broadway's biggest flops. An album of the show's songs, *Songs from the Capeman* (1997), performed by Simon, was released.

In 1999 Simon went on tour with a singer/songwriter of equal legend, Bob Dylan. They successfully toured throughout 1999 and into 2000, performing concerts that contained their own solo sets, which were followed by a forty-five-minute set of them playing together.

Simon received a Grammy Award nomination for his ninth solo album, *You're the One* (2000). The album was less conceptual than his work of the 1990s and harked back to the introspective and melancholic wit of his earlier work. Simon received his second induction into the Rock and Roll Hall of Fame in 2001, this time as a solo performer. He earned one of America's grandest tributes when he was honored at the 2003 Kennedy Center Honors.

Aside from being one of the most important songwriters of his time, Simon is also an enchanting performer with a rich voice, and his classically influenced folk guitar style is highly revered.

SELECTIVE DISCOGRAPHY: *Paul Simon* (Columbia, 1972); *There Goes Rhymin' Simon* (Columbia, 1973); *Still Crazy After All These Years* (Columbia, 1975); *Hearts and Bones* (Warner Bros., 1983); *Graceland* (Warner Bros., 1986); *The Rhythm of the Saints* (Warner Bros., 1990); *Paul Simon's Concert in the Park* (Warner Bros., 1991); *Songs from "The Capeman"* (Warner Bros., 1997); *You're the One* (Warner Bros., 2000). **With Simon and Garfunkel:** *Wednesday Morning, 3 A.M.* (Columbia, 1964); *Sounds of Silence* (Columbia, 1966); *Parsley, Sage, Rosemary and Thyme* (Columbia, 1966); *Bridge over Troubled Water* (Columbia, 1970); *The Concert in Central Park* (Warner Bros., 1982). **Soundtrack:** *One-Trick Pony* (WEA, 1980).

BIBLIOGRAPHY: J. Perone, *Paul Simon: A Bio-Bibliography, Vol. 78* (Westport, CT, 2000); L. Jackson, *Paul Simon: The Definitive Biography of the Legendary Singer/Songwriter* (New York, 2003).

DONALD LOWE

SIMPLE MINDS

Formed: 1978, Glasgow, Scotland

Members: Charlie Burchill, guitar (born Glasgow, Scotland, 27 November 1959); Jim Kerr, vocals (born Glasgow, Scotland, 9 July 1959). Former members: Derek Forbes, vocals (born Glasgow, Scotland, 22 June 1956); Malcolm Foster, bass (born Gosport, England, 13 January 1956); Mel Gaynor, drums (born London, England, 29 May 1959); Kenny Hyslop, drums (born Helensburgh, Scotland, 14 February 1951); Brian McGee, drums; Mick MacNeil, keyboards (born Glasgow, Scotland, 20 July 1958); Mark Taylor, keyboards, guitar (born Newcastle, England, 1956).

Genre: Rock, Pop

Best-selling album since 1990: *Good News from the Next World* (1995)

Hit songs since 1990: "She's a River"

Emerging from the art rock scene in the late 1970s, Simple Minds produced slick pop songs saturated with synthesizer textures and electric guitar punctuations. They contributed to the rise of European synthesizer-based pop in the mid-1980s, a movement characterized by such groups as Tears for Fears, Depeche Mode, and the Pet Shop Boys. Although their most popular song, "Don't You (Forget about Me)," was penned by unaffiliated songwriters, it introduced the group to an international audience. While undergoing numerous personnel changes, its principal songwriters, Jim Kerr and Charlie Burchill, have maintained the group's carefully crafted pop style.

Originally formed from the remnants of a short-lived punk band, Simple Minds revolved around the vocalist Kerr and guitarist Burchill. After several false starts the group began to coalesce with drummer Brian McGee, keyboardist Michael MacNeil, and bassist Derek Forbes. After recording an impressive demo, they were signed to Zoom Records and had a minor hit with the single "Life in a Day." Immediately rescinding this approach as derivative of David Bowie and Roxy Music, Simple Minds produced *Real to Real Cacophony* (1979), an experimental collection of songs that featured the jaunting and pulsating "I Travel."

Simple Minds were signed to Virgin Records in 1981 and quickly released *Sons and Fascination/Sister Feelings Call* with its attendant singles, "The American," "Love Song," and "Sweat in Bullet." The upbeat dance single, "Love Song," features a mix of sounds: A synthesizer reiterates a single note acting as an added percussion track, the electric guitar provides a sweeping array of distorted effects, and Kerr announces the taunting chorus, "Love song, love song, love song."

Simple Minds underwent several personnel changes and eventually recruited drummer Mel Gaynor during the recording of *New Gold Dream (81–82–83–84)* in 1982. This album featured a highly polished commercial sound with an emphasis on synthesizer textures, especially evident in the songs "Glittering Prize" and "Someone Somewhere (in Summertime)." Working with U2 producer Steve Lillywhite, Simple Minds scored a minor success with *Sparkle in the Rain* (1984). During the subsequent tour, Kerr announced his marriage to Chrissie Hynde of the Pretenders.

In 1985 Simple Minds began working on their next album with American producers Jimmy Iovine and Bob

Clearmountain. At the same time they were asked to perform the song, "Don't You (Forget About Me)," written by Keith Forsey and Steve Schiff for the upcoming film *The Breakfast Club* (1985). Simple Minds reluctantly recorded the song and were surprised when it rose to *Billboard*'s number one slot, becoming the group's first American success. *Once Upon a Time* (1985) contributed to their momentum and featured the hit singles "Alive and Kicking," "Sanctify Yourself," and the overtly political "Ghost Dancing."

As they gained popularity, Simple Minds reasserted their political awareness with specific songs and performances for Live Aid and Amnesty International. For the celebration of Nelson Mandela's seventieth birthday, the group wrote "Mandela Day," a simple and inviting melody accompanied by piano and guitar. Eventually they released this song along with "Belfast Child," a slow lament based on the traditional folk melody "She Moved through the Fair." This song reflected the political struggles of Northern Ireland and included the hopeful line, "One day we'll return here when the Belfast child sings again."

After the release of *Street Fighting Years* (1989), personnel changes reduced the group to a duo and Kerr's marriage to Hynde crumbled. Kerr and Burchill retreated to Amsterdam and their subsequent material deals with emotional and personal themes. The song "Let There Be Love" from *Real Life* (1991) exhibits this new approach with Kerr's stirring vocal performance. With the release of the compilation album *Glittering Prizes 81/92* (1992) the group took a short hiatus.

In 1993 Kerr and Burchill began working on *Good News from the Next World* (1995), shifting their focus to guitar-driven songs. "She's a River" begins with an ecstatic drum exclamation and an adamant electric guitar riff. The first verse is buoyed by a synthesizer bass and various guitar textures as Kerr proclaims, "I just found my new direction." Subtle harmonic changes gradually lead to the chorus, textures are added, and the song builds to an ecstatic end. After changing record labels, Simple Minds released *Neapolis* (1998), which featured the epic "Glitterball" and the colorfully brooding ballad "War Babies." An album of cover songs, *Neon Lights* (2001), paid tribute to Patti Smith, David Bowie, and other artists. With *Cry* (2002) the group reasserted their connection to pop technology by utilizing subtle electronica beats within thoughtful ballads, exemplified in the singles "Cry" and "One Step Closer."

Simple Minds produced well-crafted pop songs driven by synthesizer textures, guitar riffs, and a smooth vocal delivery. While they enjoyed international popularity in the 1980s, their subsequent releases have only appeared in the U.K. charts. Despite creative ventures in the 1990s

ranging from guitar-driven pop to light electronica, their popularity has slowly dwindled.

SELECTIVE DISCOGRAPHY: *Life in a Day* (Zoom, 1979); *Real to Real Cacophony* (Arista, 1980); *Empires and Dance* (Arista, 1980); *Sons and Fascination/Sister Feelings Call* (Virgin, 1981); *New Gold Dream (81–82–83–84)* (Virgin, 1982); *Celebration* (Arista, 1982); *Sparkle in the Rain* (Virgin, 1984); *Once Upon a Time* (Virgin, 1985); *Simple Minds Live: In the City of Light* (Virgin, 1987); *Street Fighting Years* (Virgin, 1989); *Real Life* (Virgin, 1991); *Glittering Prize* (Virgin, 1992); *Good News from the Next World* (Virgin, 1995); *Neapolis* (Chrysalis, 1998); *Neon Lights* (Red Ink, 2001); *The Best of Simple Minds* (Virgin, 2001); *Cry* (Eagle, 2002). **Soundtrack:** *The Breakfast Club* (A&M, 1985).

WEBSITE: www.simpleminds.com.

WYNN YAMAMI

SIMPLY RED

Formed: 1983, Manchester, U.K.

Members: Michael James "Mick" Hucknall, vocals (born Manchester, England, 8 June 1960); Gota Yashiki, drums (born Kyoto, Japan, 26 February 1962); Ian Kirkham, saxophone (born England); Dee Johnson, backing vocals. Former members: Tony Bowers, bass (born England, 31 October 1956); Chris Joyce, drums (born Manchester, England, 10 November 1957); Tim Kellett, trumpet, keyboards (born Knaresborough, England, 23 July 1964); Sylvan Richardson, guitar; Aziz Ibrahim, guitar (born Manchester, England); Heitor Teixeira Pereira, guitar (born Brazil); Shaun Ward, bass; Janette Sewell, backing vocals; Fritz McIntyre, keyboards (born Birmingham, England, 2 September 1958).

Genre: Rock

Best-selling album since 1990: *Stars* (1991)

Hit songs since 1990: "For Your Babies," "Fairground," "Say You Love Me"

Although Simply Red started life as a soul band in 1984, the act's front man Mick Hucknall quickly asserted his right to be the leader and decision-maker within the group. Over the subsequent decade and a half, a sizable parade of musicians came and went; Simply Red's lead vocalist, nicknamed Red after his striking mane of red hair, proved to be the man in control of the creative strategy and the hiring and firing policies that accompanied it. Yet it was some years before Hucknall confessed that Simply Red had always been his "solo career." It had clearly taken him quite a while to realize that his fellow musicians were merely the supporting act to his formidable singing talents.

Hucknall, the one-time lead singer with the Manchester punk band the Frantic Elevators, changed course in 1983 and decided to pursue a black sound that was soulful and R&B-tinged rather than one built on the more aggressive tendencies of new wave rock. He gathered a number of instrumentalists, most with Manchester links, to shape a soul combo that would initially present itself as a democratic sextet in which all members would have a say. Three of the musicians emerged from legendary city group the Durutti Column: the bassist Tony Bowers, the drummer Chris Joyce, and the keyboardist and brass player Tim Kellett. They were joined by the guitarist Sylvan Richardson and another keyboardist, Fritz McIntyre.

Notable Debut Album

Snapped up by Elektra, Simply Red issued a notable debut album, *Picture Book* (1985). While the first single, a cover of the Valentine Brothers R&B song "Money's Too Tight (to Mention)," made only a modest impression, it was the re-release of "Holding Back the Years," a Hucknall original, that propelled the group to the lofty heights of the U.K. and U.S. charts. In the United States the song became a surprise number one hit and helped secure platinum status for the album.

While the American audiences were familiar with the phenomenon of blue-eyed soul—white acts immersing themselves in R&B stylings, such as the Box Tops in the 1960s and Hall and Oates in the 1970s—it was not familiar to the English, and questions arose about Hucknall's authenticity. But the singer's distinctive and passionate vocal delivery was the perfect answer to those doubters.

Expectations were high for the second album, *Men and Women* (1987). Focusing on a classy range of covers—Bunny Wailer's "Love Fire," Cole Porter's "Ev'ry Time We Say Goodbye," and Sly Stone's "Let Me Have It All"—sales of the recording matched those of the debut album. Hucknall also linked up with the legendary Motown writer Lamont Dozier. By now the carousel was turning, and the band's personnel began to change. The vocalist Janette Sewell briefly came on board, and the guitarist Sylvan Richardson was replaced by Aziz Ibrahim and then by the Brazilian Heitor Teixeira Pereira, otherwise known as Heitor T.P.

Topping the U.S. Charts

With the third album, *A New Flame* (1989), Hucknall climbed to the top of the U.S. charts again with a version of Harold Melvin and the Blue Notes' Philly classic "If You Don't Know Me by Now," and global sales of the collection confirmed Simply Red as one of the leading purveyors of smooth, slick soul with a white gloss.

Yet the American honeymoon appeared to be over as the 1990s commenced. *Stars* (1991) enjoyed huge U.K. success—five singles, including "Something Got Me Started," and "For Your Babies" achieved solid chart placings in Britain—and more than 9 million copies were sold worldwide, but America was less taken with the set. Nonetheless, Hucknall confirmed that Simply Red was more than just a highly talented covers act; the album features all original material and reveals a range of styles, from hip-hop to house, augmenting the basic soul model.

By the time *Stars* was released, Tony Bowers and Chris Joyce had joined the exodus, with Shaun Ward coming in on bass, Gota Yashikion on drums, and Ian Kirkham on saxophone. Yet the revolving door continued to spin, and by the time of the release of *Life* (1995), the two rhythm players had also gone, with Hucknall, Heitor T.P., McIntryre, Kirkham, and backing singer Dee Johnson forming the remaining lineup. The album gave the band their first U.K. number one hit: "Fairground" hit the top in 1995. But the group's impetus in the United States had faded, despite its huge successes elsewhere.

Establishes Reggae Label

In 1996 Hucknall wrote "We're in This Together," the official theme song for the European soccer championships held that year in the U.K.; the band's *Greatest Hits* (1996) album was notable for a collaboration with the Fugees on Aretha Franklin's "Angel." A year later, he was back with a version of Gregory Isaac's reggae gem "Night Nurse," featuring Jamaican rhythm superstars, the drummer Sly Dunbar, and the bassist Robbie Shakespeare; the track reflected Hucknall's love of the Caribbean genre. Shortly afterward he established the label Blood & Fire, which aimed to promote vintage reggae tracks.

Blue (1998) saw Hucknall and company return to form with the exquisite "Say You Love Me," a U.K. Top 10 hit, but the album also saw a return to the earlier cover version approach, with the Hollies' "The Air That I Breathe" securing another high chart placing in Britain. *Love and the Russian Winter* (1999) was a more eclectic affair, tapping into club and drum and bass stylings, but the pleasing ballad "Your Eyes" became a U.K. hit in 2000. The impact on the United States was, however, minimal.

Mick Hucknall and Simply Red have explored areas generally denied to white English performers. Avoiding the more predictable gestures of rock, the band has drawn on a range of principally black styles—soul in the 1980s and reggae and dance in the 1990s. They have never quite built on the foundation of their early successes in the United States, however.

SELECTIVE DISCOGRAPHY: *Picture Book* (Elektra, 1985); *Men and Women* (Elektra, 1987); *A New Flame* (Elektra, 1989); *Stars* (EastWest, 1991); *Life* (EastWest, 1995); *Greatest Hits* (EastWest, 1996); *Blue* (EastWest, 1998); *Love and the Russian Winter* (EastWest 1999).

BIBLIOGRAPHY: M. Middles, *Red Mick: The Biography of Mick Hucknall of Simply Red* (London, 1993).

WEBSITE: www.simplyred.com.

SIMON WARNER

FRANK SINATRA

Born: Francis Albert Sinatra; Hoboken, New Jersey, 12 December 1915; died Los Angeles, California, 14 May 1998

Genre: Vocal

Best-selling album since 1990: *Duets* (1993)

Frank Sinatra defined the role of popular vocalist in the twentieth century, influencing nearly every singer who came after him, from pop artist Tony Bennett to country performer George Strait. The impact of Sinatra's drawn-out phrasing and lyrical interpretation was matched by the durability of his image. A combination of swinging hipster, tough guy, and vulnerable romantic, Sinatra's persona—loosened tie, slightly cocked hat, cigarette held introspectively—projected a cool sophistication that symbolized mid-century masculinity, strong but soul-searching. The power and versatility of his image allowed Sinatra to grow with his audience, progressing from teen pop idol in the early 1940s to high-flying man of the world in the 1950s to contemplative midlife sage in the 1960s and beyond. Acknowledging but never succumbing to newer music styles such as rock and roll, Sinatra carved out his own path during a career that lasted nearly sixty years.

Early Years

Slight and wiry during his youth, Sinatra grew up in Hoboken, New Jersey, the son of Italian-American working-class parents. Dropping out of high school in the mid-1930s to pursue his musical ambitions, he performed with a local vocal group and worked as a singing waiter. In 1939 Sinatra was discovered singing on the radio by bandleader and trumpeter Harry James, with whom he made his

first recordings that year. Beginning in 1940 Sinatra was the featured vocalist on a string of pop hits for trombonist Tommy Dorsey's band, but it was a dramatic performance with famed clarinetist Benny Goodman on New Year's Eve 1942 that secured his fame. Suddenly, Frank Sinatra was a pop phenomenon, receiving the same adulation that was showered on stars like Elvis Presley in the 1950s.

By the mid-1940s Sinatra had signed with Columbia Records, releasing hits such as the atmospheric "I'm a Fool to Want You" (1951). Recording with lush strings and a powerful vocal chorus, Sinatra built his performance with artful precision, displaying masterful phrasing and control of volume and tone. Influenced by great jazz and blues singers such as Billie Holiday, Sinatra was one of the first popular vocalists to sing long phrases in one breath. The result was a controlled, smooth, "legato" vocal sound that gave his singing a yearning emotional quality. Delving into the songbooks of great 1930s composers such as Cole Porter and Irving Berlin, Sinatra became one of popular music's most meaningful interpreters. While jazz singers such as Anita O'Day improvised the melody and lyrics, Sinatra for the most part stayed true to the song as written.

1950s and 1960s Masterworks

This quality became a hallmark of Sinatra's work after his move to Capitol Records in 1953. Coinciding with the development of the "long play" album, which sequenced over thirty minutes of music on a vinyl disc, Sinatra's Capitol tenure marked the peak refinement of his art. Working with gifted musical arrangers such as Nelson Riddle and Gordon Jenkins, Sinatra used the LP medium to construct song cycles unified by contours of sound and theme. Alternating swinging, up-tempo albums with ballad sets, Sinatra released classic works such as *In the Wee Small Hours of the Morning* (1955). Recorded shortly after his break-up with actress Ava Gardner, the album is remarkable for its display of feeling. On songs such as "I Get Along without You Very Well," "I See Your Face Before Me," and the poignant title cut, Sinatra achieves a depth and pathos rare in popular music, using his mellowed baritone to draw out subtleties within the lyrics.

Up-tempo releases of the Capitol period, such as *Come Fly with Me* (1958), are just as stirring, conveying a jaunty, carefree sense of rhythm and swing. At Capitol, Sinatra was simultaneously the "intercontinental" sophisticate and lovesick loner, both sides of his personality represented with maturity and taste. Moving to his own record label, Reprise, in 1961, Sinatra recorded another string of classic albums, in particular *September of My Years* (1965). On the title song, an introspective exploration of aging, Sinatra delivers an impeccably controlled performance, the slight tremor in his voice suggesting a well of emotion held in check by technique. The haunting strings, arranged by

Gordon Jenkins, follow Sinatra's every melodic curve, supporting his vocal with weight and resonance. In the 1970s and 1980s Sinatra recorded less frequently; still, he managed to release critically acclaimed albums such as *L.A. Is My Lady* (1984), produced by arranger Quincy Jones.

1990s Successes

By the 1990s Sinatra had lost much of his vocal range and elasticity, although his phrasing and timing remained intact. More a clever marketing scheme than a cohesive album, *Duets*, Sinatra's 1993 showcase of performances with other vocal stars, became the most successful album of his career, selling more than 2 million copies. The success of the album was due largely to publicity hype aimed at young urbanites entranced by Sinatra's cool hipster image. In actuality the songs on *Duets* were solo performances, with Sinatra recording his parts first. Next, the guest artists entered different studios and recorded around Sinatra's vocals. The separate tracks were then stitched together by producer Phil Ramone to give the illusion of duets. Despite a roster including Barbra Streisand, Aretha Franklin, and Liza Minnelli, *Duets* emerges solidly as Sinatra's album.

Critics noted that, with few exceptions, the guest performers sing the material with more embellishment than necessary, as if struggling to prove their worth alongside Sinatra. Attempts to create an air of casual improvisation, such as Franklin tacking on a spoken "See ya," after Sinatra's final "goodbye" on "What Now, My Love?" seem especially forced, considering the fabricated nature of the production. Streisand and Minnelli fare better than the other performers, perhaps because their work has always relied on heavy doses of artifice for its effectiveness. Unaware of the vocal pyrotechnics going on around him, Sinatra often sounds assured despite the deterioration of his voice. On the medley "All the Way / One for My Baby (and One More for the Road)," he even captures some of his old romantic wistfulness and vulnerability.

In 1994 Sinatra released a follow-up album, predictably titled *Duets II*. Although it features less of a high-profile cast, *Duets II* nonetheless sounds very similar to its predecessor. According to critics, the album's most impressive track is "Embraceable You," featuring the mellowed voice of legendary pop interpreter Lena Horne. With its feel of two vocal legends exchanging life experiences, "Embraceable You" works on the basis of sheer professionalism. "Come Fly with Me," a duet with Latin pop star Luis Miguel, is another high point. Possessing a bright, agile voice, Miguel follows the melodic path of the arrangement and pulls off the admirable feat of keeping up with Sinatra. On other tracks, performers such as flamboyant R&B diva Patti LaBelle clash with Sinatra's terse, subdued style. In 1995 Sinatra, afflicted with chronic health problems

and frequent hospitalizations, retired from performing. Three years later he died after suffering a heart attack at his home in Los Angeles.

While much has been written about Sinatra's turbulent private life—his purported connections with Mafia leaders such as Lucky Luciano and his stormy relationship with Ava Gardner—he is best remembered for his music, a body of work that stands alongside the greatest recordings of the twentieth century. Balancing technical precision with emotional honesty, Sinatra invented a new understanding of popular vocalizing. The effortless quality of his singing belied its inner complexity; many imitate Sinatra, but few succeed in conveying his warmth and assuredness of swing. Although his hit 1990s albums paled in comparison to his greatest work, they provide ample evidence of his enduring relevance and integrity.

SELECTIVE DISCOGRAPHY: *Swing and Dance with Frank Sinatra* (Columbia, 1944); *In the Wee Small Hours* (Capitol, 1955); *Songs for Swingin' Lovers* (Capitol, 1956); *Where Are You* (Capitol, 1957); *Come Fly with Me* (Capitol, 1958); *Only the Lonely* (Capitol, 1958); *Nice 'n' Easy* (Capitol, 1960); *September of My Years* (Reprise, 1965); *My Way* (Reprise, 1969); *L.A. Is My Lady* (Reprise, 1984); *Duets* (Capitol, 1993); *Duets II* (Capitol, 1994).

SELECTIVE FILMOGRAPHY: *Anchors Away* (1945); *It Happened in Brooklyn* (1947); *On the Town* (1949); *From Here to Eternity* (1953); *Guys and Dolls* (1955); *High Society* (1956); *Pal Joey* (1957); *A Hole in the Head* (1959); *Ocean's Eleven* (1960); *The Manchurian Candidate* (1962); *Come Blow Your Horn* (1963); *Von Ryan's Express* (1965); *The First Deadly Sin* (1980).

BIBLIOGRAPHY: K. Kelley *His Way: The Unauthorized Biography of Frank Sinatra* (New York, 1986); W. Friedwald, *Sinatra!: The Song Is You* (New York, 1995); C. Granata, *Sessions with Sinatra: Frank Sinatra and the Art of Recording* (Chicago, 1999).

WEBSITE: www.franksinatra.com.

DAVID FREELAND

SLEATER-KINNEY

Formed: 1994, Olympia, Washington

Members: Carrie Brownstein, vocals and guitars (born Seattle, Washington, 27 September 1974); Corin Tucker, vocals and guitar (born 9 November 1972 Seattle, Washington); Janet Weiss, drums, vocals (born 25 September 1965, Hollywood, California). Former members: Lora McFarlane, drums.

Genre: Rock

Best-selling album since 1990: *Dig Me Out* (1997)

Hit songs since 1990: "You're No Rock n Roll Fun," "Get Up," "All Hands on the Bad One," "One Beat"

The powerful feminist rock trio Sleater-Kinney, one of the most critically acclaimed bands to emerge in the 1990s, bridged the attitude and approach of punk with the tunefulness of contemporary rock. Sleater-Kinney came out of the Northwest independent rock scene that had gained momentum in cities like Seattle and Olympia, Washington, and Portland, Oregon. The band is a trio: two guitarists, Carrie Brownstein and Corin Tucker, who also sing, and the drummer Janet Weiss, who pitches in on backup vocals. Sleater-Kinney's music is smart, energetic, and intricately tuneful. It charts the psychological territory of women struggling to find an identity in a male-dominated world.

Feminism Plus Punk Rock Equals Riot Grrls

Named after a road in Olympia, Washington, Sleater-Kinney coalesced following the heyday of riot grrl subculture, which brought together the politics of feminism with the culture of punk rock. Brownstein, a Seattle-area native, met Tucker in 1992, when Tucker was one-half of the duo Heavens to Betsy. Brownstein, inspired by her new friend, formed her own band, Excuse 17. Tucker and Brownstein briefly dated and recorded their self-titled debut (1995) with Lola MacFarlane. Their current drummer Janet Weiss had played with her then-husband Sam Coomer in Qasi, a Seattle indie band; she even divided her time between the bands for a while after she joined Sleater-Kinney in 1996. The politically charged, visceral, self-titled debut on Chainsaw Records, a Washington independent label, began to earn the group a following. They became known for explosive live performances and bristling guitar work.

The three women of Sleater-Kinney form an unlikely powerhouse. With the propulsive drumming of Weiss as a backup, the bone-rattling caterwaul of Tucker and the comfortably warm voice of Brownstein vie to be heard. The guitar lines weave and bob and play off each other with an intensity matched by few guitar duos, male or female. Beneath the noise they are just a trio of two guitars and a drum.

From Subculture to Pop Culture

From their early days, including their second album, *Call the Doctor* (1996), the group impressed the local scene with their blisteringly raw guitar playing and shrill feminist polemics. They boasted a small, mostly local following. With the release of *Dig Me Out* (1997), their

Spot Light | *Dig Me Out*

With the release of their third album (and their debut on the respected independent rock label Kill Rock Stars), Sleater-Kinney made a name as a lyrically talented, intricately melodic, and politically charged punk-pop trio of women. Sustaining the rawness of their previous work, the album catapulted them into the spotlight, thanks to the adoring words of respected music critics such as Greil Marcus and Robert Christgau. Sleater-Kinney landed on the *Spin* 40 in April 1997. The recording is an assault to the senses right from the furious lead-off, title track. In her bone-chilling voice, Corin Tucker cries "Dig me out / Dig me in / Outta this mess / baby outta my head." "One More Hour" offers a superb example of the Tucker-Brownstein guitar technique, and "Words and Guitar" is a joyful and unforgiving celebration of classic rock and roll. *Dig Me Out* is the leanest Sleater-Kinney record. Almost every track maintains an arresting fever pitch.

best-selling album, Sleater-Kinney moved into the spotlight. Editors gave them magazine covers, and the group earned accolades as the most important new rock band of their time. They went from virtual obscurity to near fame—as famous as a band on an independent label with limited distribution powers could be. The album's stunning success resulted in their having to fight off offers from major labels. Sleater-Kinney defended their independence.

The follow-up, *The Hot Rock* (1999), utilizes the point-counterpoint technique of the guitar/singers and is a more polished effort. The guitars are no longer a bleating distortion but a crystalline squall. The lyrics treat the destructive aspects of fame. In "The End of You" Brownstein warns, "I'd rather fly / don't wanna get caught in this endless race," to which Tucker wails, "Tie me to the mast of this ship and of this band / Tie me to the greater things / The people that I love." The album appeared on many critics year-end ten-best lists. At this point, Sleater-Kinney was the biggest band that almost nobody, other than music critics and diehard indie rock fans, had heard of.

Riding on the momentum of the release, the band toured extensively and then brought out *All Hands on the Bad One* (2000). Their fifth collection is more playful but no less emotionally unyielding. The women continue to stretch themselves. Tucker, whose all-encompassing voice had previously been used as a force to be reckoned with, now takes on a smug, all-knowing tone; at times it is not always clear who is singing, as in "Youth Decay." Tucker also swings from self-confidence to a desperate wail in the chorus of "Milkshake n' Honey."

On stage Sleater-Kinney is an energizing band and their shows usually sell out. After *All Hands on the Bad One*, they took time off. They reconvened for the release of *One Beat* (2002) and continued to bring their clarion call to feminism and self-determinism to audiences across the United States.

SELECTIVE DISCOGRAPHY: *Sleater-Kinney* (Chainsaw, 1995); *Call the Doctor* (Chainsaw, 1996); *Dig Me Out* (Kill Rock Stars, 1997); *The Hot Rock* (Kill Rock Stars, 1999); *All Hands on the Bad One* (Kill Rock Stars, 2000); *One Beat* (Kill Rock Stars, 2002).

WEBSITE: www.killrockstars.com.

CARRIE HAVRANEK

SLICK RICK

Born: Ricky Walters; London, England, 14 January 1965

Genre: Rap

Best-selling album since 1990: *The Art of Storytelling* (1999)

Hit songs since 1990: "I Shouldn't Have Done It," "Mistakes of a Woman in Love with Other Men," "Sittin in My Car," "Street Talkin'"

Slick Rick is one of hip-hop's most respected and vital rappers. Best known for his humorous storytelling, Slick Rick raps with a lilting British accent, making him a one-of-a-kind voice. Lionized by artists like Snoop Dogg, Slick Rick is among hip-hop's most celebrated rappers.

Ricky Walters was born to Jamaican parents in the South Wimbledon district of London. Blinded in infancy in his right eye by broken glass, Walters began wearing an eye patch. When he was eleven years old, his family emigrated to the Bronx, New York, the birthplace of hip-hop. The energy of the Bronx changed the course of Walters's life. While attending the LaGuardia High School of Music & Art in Manhattan, Walters met rapper Dana Dane and adopted the rap name Slick Rick. The duo sported Kangol, a popular brand of English hats, and dubbed themselves the Kangol Crew. They sharpened their rap skills through impromptu rhyme competitions with rappers across New York City. The most famous contest occurred in the Bronx in 1984 against beatboxer and rapper Doug E. Fresh. (The event was dramatized by Slick

Rick, Dana Dane, and Doug E. Fresh in the 2002 film *Brown Sugar*.) As a result of the meeting, Slick Rick began performing with Doug E. Fresh and his Get Fresh Crew. Together they recorded the rap classics "La Di Da Di" and "The Show," produced by a young Teddy Riley.

Slick Rick secured a solo contract with the label Def Jam and showcased his storytelling prowess in his aptly titled debut, *The Great Adventures of Slick Rick* (1988). An instant classic, it is a collection of tales ranging from the cautionary "A Children's Story" and the romantic "Mona Lisa" to the misogynistic "Treat Her Like a Prostitute." With his signature trademarks, the always present Kangol, gold chains, and teeth, and his eye patch, Slick Rick had all the packaging of a genuine rap star. He teamed with R&B singer Al B. Sure! for a remix of "If I'm Not Your Lover," which almost topped the *Billboard* charts in 1989.

In 1990 Slick Rick was charged with shooting his cousin and another man, and he was arrested for attempted murder. Out on bail, he quickly recorded the album *The Ruler's Back* (1991). The danceable catchy beats of *Great Adventures*, largely provided by Public Enemy producer Hank Shocklee, are replaced by lackluster tracks from the less accomplished Vance Wright. The album sounds rushed, and Slick Rick's stories are not articulated as they are in his debut. Nevertheless, the danceable "I Shouldn't Have Done It" and the moody "Mistakes of a Woman in Love with Other Men" received favorable attention.

In 1993 a work-release program enabled Slick Rick to record *Behind Bars* (1994), which boasted the mild hit "Sittin in My Car." Unable to get the necessary promotion, neither *The Ruler's Back* nor *Behind Bars* sold well. Following his parole in 1995, Slick Rick was jailed again by the Immigration and Naturalization Service (INS) because he was not a U.S. citizen. In 1996 he won his appeal and his freedom.

During his incarceration, artists like Snoop Dogg kept Slick Rick's name alive in commercial hip-hop circles by crediting him as a major inspiration. Snoop Dogg even remade "La Di Da Di" on the song "Lodi Dadi" from his debut *Doggystyle* (1993). Younger rap fans embraced Slick Rick's return after his release from prison. His *The Art of Storytelling* (1999) features popular artists OutKast, Nas, Raekwon (of Wu-Tang Clan), and Snoop Dogg, as well as live versions of the seminal songs "The Show" and "La Di Da Di" with Doug E. Fresh. As the title indicates, the focus is on Slick Rick's core strength. He vividly rhymes about the early days of hip-hop on "Memories" and the trials of a personal relationship on "Why, Why, Why." The album claimed a gold plaque and glowing critical reviews.

Big name rap artists invited the veteran rapper to cameo on their albums, further cementing Slick Rick's reputation. He appeared on releases by Jay-Z, De La Soul, and Jermaine Dupri. In 2002 Slick Rick faced renewed legal troubles when he performed on a cruise ship. Upon returning to port in Miami, Florida, INS authorities seized the star, citing a federal law requiring the automatic deportation of foreign nationals who have served more than five years for a felony conviction. Slick Rick had passed that mark by twelve days. High-profile entertainment figures like Russell Simmons, Will Smith, and Chris Rock came to his support. In late 2002 a judge placed a temporary stay on the deportation. As of May 2003 Slick Rick remains in custody, awaiting a deportation decision.

Despite INS troubles, Slick Rick's stature as a rap icon remains unsullied. His narrative power is undisputed, and his storytelling skills in rap continue to inspire.

SELECTIVE DISCOGRAPHY: *The Great Adventures of Slick Rick* (Def Jam 1989); *The Ruler's Back* (Def Jam, 1991); *Behind Bars* (Def Jam, 1994); *The Art of Storytelling* (Def Jam, 1999).

DARA COOK

SLIPKNOT

Formed: 1995, Des Moines, Iowa

Members: Paul Grey, bass (born Los Angeles, California, 2 October 1974); Craig Jones, keyboards (born Des Moines, Iowa, 5 July 1972); Corey Taylor, vocals (born Des Moines, Iowa, 8 December 1976); Joey Jordison, drums (born Des Moines, Iowa, 26 April 1977); Sid Wilson, turntables (born Des Moines, Iowa, 3 March 1978); Chris Fehn, percussions (born Des Moines, Iowa, 24 February 1973); Shawn Crahan, percussions (born Des Moines, Iowa, 24 September 1971); Mick Thompson, guitar (born Des Moines, Iowa, 3 November 1976); Jim Root, guitar (born Des Moines, Iowa, 2 October 1974).

Genre: Rock

Best-selling album since 1990: *Slipknot* (1999)

Hit songs since 1990: "Liberate," "Spit It Out"

Intense, loud, and visceral, Slipknot burst onto the nu-metal scene with a hard-edged fusion that used the vernacular of Staind, Incubus, Nickelback, and Limp Bizkit. But beyond the howling vocals, floor-rumbling bass, and machine-gun drums, the band's chief calling card was their disturbing look, consisting of ghoulish masks, makeup, and generic overalls. No one used names onstage—their outfits bore only the numbers one through nine. It was macabre, but it had the desired effect: young boys were thrilled, and parents were appropriately shocked and stupefied.

Slipknot came together when the founding members, percussionist Shawn Calvins and Joey Jordison, assembled the initial roster of musicians to play local gigs. After a few minor changes the lineup settled with nine members,

an unusually high number for a rock band. "Everybody freaks out that there are nine guys in the band," Jordison told the *Los Angeles Times*. "I didn't want nine guys in the band; that's too many ******** people! But that's what it took to get the sound we want."

Initially, people scoffed at the idea that a metal band would launch in Des Moines, Iowa. But that very dismissiveness ignited the band's imagination and prompted the device of nameless stage visuals. But it was the band's intense firepower on their debut *Mate. Feed. Kill. Repeat.* (1996) that turned most adolescents' heads. Released on Halloween of 1996, the eight-song, fifty-minute CD demonstrated the budding group's penchant for distorted sound, extreme guitars, and complex song structures. The group's sonic signature came together on *Slipknot* (1999) as they spiced their sound with edgy turntable scratches and Korn's metallic burns. Slipknot's musical palette nonetheless leaned heavily towards death metal. Lyrically, songs like "Wait and Bleed," "Tattered and Torn," "Liberate," and "No Life" reflected metal's anger and rage—not that most of the songs' lyrics, recorded or performed live, were discernible.

Slipknot's metal fusion and comiclike outfits swiftly became popular. Their follow-up album, *Iowa* (2001), debuted at number one on the *Billboard* charts, which was ironic considering their antisocial look and angry lyrics. With the help of their producer, Ross Robinson, Slipknot cranked the thrash and death factor a notch higher on the album. On songs like "People = S***" and "New Abortion," guitars and drums are played at an industrial pace. All throughout the band convincingly evinces their darkness and mayhem credentials. Like other late-1990s nu-metalers, Slipknot's public visibility benefited from key spots on the Ozzfest tours. In their live shows Slipknot worked hard to make themselves the most aggressive, violent, and unrelentlessly brutal of the bunch. In lyrics like "I wanna slit your throat and f*** the wound," from "Disasterpiece," Slipknot provided an outlet for the expression of the contents of raging adolescent ids.

Harder than Korn or Nine Inch Nails and weirder than Marilyn Manson, Slipknot used excess in their music and message to provide a compelling experience for fans in the expanding nu-metal market of the late 1990s.

SELECTIVE DISCOGRAPHY: *Mate. Feed. Kill. Repeat.* (ismist, 1997); *Slipknot* (Roadrunner, 1999); *Iowa* (Roadrunner, 2001).

RAMIRO BURR

SMASH MOUTH

Formed: 1994, San Jose, California

Members: Greg Camp, guitars (born West Covina, California, 2 April 1967); Paul DeLisle, bass (born Exeter, Ontario,

13 June 1963); Steve Harwell, vocals (born Santa Clara, California, 9 January 1967); Michael Urbano, drums. Former member: Kevin Coleman, drums (born San Jose, California, 21 October 1965).

Genre: Rock

Best-selling album since 1990: *Astro Lounge* (1999)

Hit songs since 1990: "Walkin' on the Sun," "All Star," "Then the Morning Comes"

Tagged by many critics as a likely one-hit wonder, Smash Mouth instead evolved into one of the most successful mainstream pop rock acts of the late 1990s, consistently scoring hits with its party-flavored fusion of 1960s rock and 1980s punk.

Prior to 1994 Steve Harwell had been rapping in a San Jose band called F.O.S. ("Freedom of Speech"); F.O.S. drew inspiration from House of Pain, the early 1990s Caucasian rap group that enjoyed a crossover smash with "Jump Around." After House of Pain fell out of vogue, Harwell gave up on F.O.S. and instead began jamming with local drummer and longtime friend Kevin Coleman. Harwell and Coleman eventually hooked up with guitar player Kevin Camp and bass player Paul DeLisle; the quartet became known as Smash Mouth.

Smash Mouth subsequently recorded two demo tracks, which earned significant airplay at local radio station KOME in April 1996. That summer Smash Mouth played a KOME festival along with high-profile acts such as Beck and No Doubt. Interscope Records quickly scooped up the rising band and, in 1997, released Smash Mouth's debut album *Fush Yu Mang*. *Fush Yu Mang* owed much to the contemporary California punk sound of bands such as the Offspring, NOFX, Green Day, and Rancid, but it was the song "Walkin' on the Sun" that foreshadowed the formula that Smash Mouth would ultimately ride to the top of the charts. An ode to 1960s hippies, "Walkin' on the Sun" boasts a bright and decidedly retro instrumental sound, with splashy organs and fuzzy guitars reminiscent of 1960s garage and surf rock. Delivered in a half-sung, half-rapped style by Harwell, the song's lyrics eulogize 1960s idealism: "Twenty-five years ago they spoke out and they broke out / Of recession and oppression and together they toked / And they folked out with guitars around a bonfire / Just singin' and clappin' man what the hell happened." Smash Mouth's fusion of 1960s rock with the sensibilities of modern punk had major appeal, and "Walkin' on the Sun" became a number one modern rock hit.

Smash Mouth further refined its commercial formula with its cover of "Can't Get Enough of You Baby," featured on the soundtrack to the 1998 movie *Can't Hardly Wait*. "Can't Get Enough of You Baby" was a garage-rock classic made popular by ? and the Mysterians. Liberal in its use of retro organ flourishes and driven by Harwell's raspy vocals, Smash Mouth's "Can't Get Enough of You Baby" retains the party spirit of the original, while smoothing out the rough edges for commercial appeal.

Critics were skeptical that Smash Mouth could carry its successful formula across a second full-length album, but the band proved its doubters wrong with the even more successful follow-up, *Astro Lounge* (1999). The lead single "All Star" reached the top five on the singles charts. Propelled by Camp's snappy guitars and Harwell's unique quasi-rap delivery, "All Star" was omnipresent in the summer of 1999. The song's catchy chorus ("Hey now, you're an All Star, get your game on, go play") made it a favorite at sporting events, including Major League Baseball's All-Star Game, at which Smash Mouth performed in 1999. The follow-up single "Then the Morning Comes" had a darker vibe than previous Smash Mouth hits, but its infectious chorus ("The way that you walk / It's just the way that you talk like it ain't no thing / And every single day is just a fling") made the song a staple on radio as well as on MTV. On the strength of its two successful singles, *Astro Lounge* sold more than 3.5 million records.

For the second time between album releases, Smash Mouth struck gold with a movie soundtrack appearance; in 2001, the band appeared on the soundtrack for the DreamWorks film *Shrek*, covering the Monkees' "I'm a Believer." The song benefited not only from its inclusion on the soundtrack of the high-profile animated film featuring the voices of Mike Myers, Eddie Murphy, and Cameron Diaz, but also from its use as a musical number for the final scenes of the movie. Crooned by Eddie Murphy's donkey character in the film, "I'm a Believer" abounded with familiar Smash Mouth energy—a fitting end to the climax of the fairytale film. The movie as well as its unofficial theme song both became major hits. "I'm a Believer" also appeared on Smash Mouth's self-titled third album released in 2001.

Smash Mouth's repeated success with movie soundtracks scored the band further high-profile gigs, including the *Austin Powers in Goldmember* (2002) soundtrack, for which Smash Mouth offered up the new "Ain't No Mystery," recorded with the Tower of Power's famed horn section. Smash Mouth also appeared on *Disneymania* (2002), a collection of popular Disney soundtrack favorites reinterpreted by contemporary artists; Smash Mouth offered a funked-up version of "I Wanna Be Like You" from Disney's animated film *The Jungle Book* (1967).

Much to the consternation of its critics, Smash Mouth was anything but a one-hit wonder by the early 2000s, having cemented its place on mainstream radio with its retro-influenced sound and string of hits.

SELECTIVE DISCOGRAPHY: *Fush Yu Mang* (Interscope, 1997); *Astro Lounge* (Interscope, 1999);

Smash Mouth (Interscope, 2001). **Soundtracks:** *Shrek* (DreamWorks, 2001); *Austin Powers in Goldmember* (Warner Bros., 2002); *Disneymania* (Disney, 2002).

SCOTT TRIBBLE

SMASHING PUMPKINS

Formed: 1988, Chicago, Illinois; Disbanded 2000
Members: Jimmy Chamberlin, drums (born Joliet, Illinois, 10 June 1964; fired in 1996, rejoined in 1999); Billy Corgan, guitar/vocals (born Glendale Heights, Illinois, 17 March 1967); James Iha, guitar (born Elk Grove, Illinois, 6 March 1968); Melissa Auf Der Maur, bass (joined 1998; born Montreal, Quebec, 17 March 1972)). Former members: Matt Walker, drums (touring member 1996–1997; born Chicago, Illinois); D'Arcy Wretzky, bass (born South Haven, Michigan, 1 May 1968; left group 1998).
Genre: Rock
Best-selling album since 1990: *Mellon Collie and the Infinite Sadness* (1995)
Hit songs since 1990: "Cherub Rock," "Tonight Tonight," "Bullet with Butterfly Wings"

Like a rock and roll Icarus, Chicago's Smashing Pumpkins aimed high and flew daringly close to the sun during their decade-long ascent to the highest peaks of rock stardom. The brainchild of the restlessly creative singer/guitarist Billy Corgan, the group put Chicago on the rock and roll map in the early 1990s with a sound that paid homage to heavy metal, glam rock, folk, electronic music, and new wave. At the group's creative peak, albums such as the double-CD *Mellon Collie and the Infinite Sadness* (1995) took rock to dramatic new heights while spinning off such indelible alternative rock radio hits as "Tonight, Tonight" and "1979."

Origins

Billy Corgan, the son of a jazz guitarist, formed the Smashing Pumpkins in Chicago in 1988, playing at first with the guitarist James Iha as a duo with a drum machine. After a heated argument in a parking lot with D'Arcy Wretzky, Corgan asked the lithe bassist to join his group, rounded out by the drummer Jimmy Chamberlin. The band quickly won a following in their hometown with fierce live shows during which Wretzky would take her stoic stance alongside a wildly flailing Corgan, an impassive Iha, and the thundering, powerful Chamberlin.

Major-Label Breakthrough

After releasing the 1990 single "I Am One" on Chicago's Limited Potential label and "Tristessa" on Seat-

tle's Sub Pop Records, the band signed with Virgin Records, though they released their debut album, *Gish* (1991), on the smaller subsidiary Caroline to retain their underground, "indie" credibility.

Gish is a template for the angst-ridden grunge rock sound that came to define early 1990s rock and roll. Produced by Butch Vig—who soon thereafter produced Nirvana's breakthrough album, *Nevermind*—*Gish* is a blend of screaming psychedelic rock and mellow, folk-inflected songs, many of which rise and fall through several dynamic passages. Featuring Corgan's high, nasal voice, furious guitar solos and confessional lyrics, tracks such as "I Am One" and "Siva" are closer to the grandiose arena rock of the 1970s than Nirvana's more intense, shorter, punk-inspired songs.

In a sign of their persistent personal tensions, the former lovers Iha and Wretzky underwent a nasty breakup while touring to support *Gish*; Chamberlin began a dangerous addiction to drugs and alcohol at the same time as Corgan slipped into a dark depression. With the various personal clouds hanging over them, the group again entered the studio with Vig in 1992 to record their official major-label debut, *Siamese Dream* (1993). Corgan threw himself into the work, writing all but two of the songs alone and reportedly playing nearly every guitar and bass line as well, which helped fuel the impression that the band's other members were mere observers of Corgan's creative vision.

The album, which debuted on the *Billboard* charts at number ten, is a triumph of dark emotion and soaring rock and roll, with Corgan's lyrical torment and Jimi Hendrix-like flights of guitar fancy gelling into a lush, fully realized sound that is at once pompous and touchingly insecure. Corgan's image of a tortured, wounded angel comes to fruition on songs such as the driving, explosive hit single "Cherub Rock" and the majestic rock ballad "Today."

While many of the songs revel in chaotic swirls of feedback and barrages of guitar, they are also clearly carefully crafted, over-the-top pop morsels meant to appeal to radio listeners and take listeners on a proscribed journey. "Cherub Rock," "Disarm," and "Today" all became radio anthems.

Mellon Collie and the Infinite Sadness (1995) is the realization of Corgan's wildest musical fantasies. A two-disc set of songs that runs the gamut from string and piano-laden symphonic instrumentals ("Mellon Collie and the Infinite Sadness") to searing, scorched-earth heavy metal ("Jellybelly," "X.Y.U."), the album debuted at number one on the *Billboard* charts and was hailed as a masterpiece by many critics and fans. "Bullet with Butterfly Wings" won the 1996 Grammy for Best Hard Rock Performance.

Smashing Pumpkins. L-R: D'Arcy Wretzky, James Iha, Billy Corgan, and Jimmy Chamberlin [PAUL NATKIN/PHOTO RESERVE]

With production from Flood and Alan Moulder, both known for their work with the electronic rock band Nine Inch Nails, and a rich, orchestral sound, the album features bits of synthesizer-laden electronic songs that presaged the band's next musical transformation. The album sold 4 million copies in the United States and spawned such hits as the ballad "Tonight, Tonight," the fiery hard-rock song "Bullet with Butterfly Wings," and the bouncy "1979."

Drugs, Death, and Dissolution

The good times were short-lived, however. On July 12, 1996, the band's touring keyboardist, Jonathan Melvoin, was found dead of a heroin overdose in the hotel room in which he had shared the drug with Chamberlin. The drummer survived but was fired from the group and arrested for heroin possession. The band went on a two-month hiatus and reemerged in late August.

The first Pumpkins album recorded without Chamberlin, *Adore* (1998), produced by Corgan, was the band's first musical misstep. A dark series of down-tempo acoustic tracks, layered with electronic drums, electric guitars, and keyboards, the album was dismissed by most critics and the band's fans. Songs such as "Perfect" reveal the influence of such new wave pop groups as New Order, with a syncopated drum track and a chiming guitar sound. The rebuke was especially difficult for Corgan, who had written some of his most emotionally naked lyrics to date for the album, such as the hushed piano ballad dedicated to his mother, "For Martha," which features the lyrics "If you have to go don't say goodbye / If you have to go don't you cry." In November1999 the former Hole bassist Melissa Auf Der Maur replaced Wretzky, who quit the group after the release of *Adore*. Chamberlin returned to the group in mid-1999. To coincide with what Corgan announced would be the group's final tour, the band released the enigmatic rock opera *MACHINA: The Machines of God* (2000), which features a convoluted back story in which each band member plays the part of a fictional character in the band the Machines of God, after the fashion of David Bowie's *Ziggy Stardust*. A mixture of the majestic rock of *Mellon Collie* and the electronic keyboards and new wave influences of *Adore,* the album did not reach a wide audience.

When Virgin refused to release a second collection of songs, *MACHINA II: The Friends and Enemies of Modern Music,* the group offered it for free download on the Internet in September 2000. On December 2, the Smashing Pumpkins played their final show at the Metro in Chicago, the site of their first club show in 1988. Corgan reemerged a year later with a new band, Zwan, featuring Chamberlin on drums.

The Smashing Pumpkins tried it all during their decade-long assault on the senses: progressive rock, heavy metal, folk, electronic pop, and experimental rock. Billy Corgan's creative vision for the group helped make the Pumpkins one of the most revered, successful, and unpredictable groups of the alternative-rock era.

SELECTIVE DISCOGRAPHY: *Gish* (Caroline, 1991); *Lull* (Caroline, 1991); *Siamese Dream* (Virgin, 1993); *Pisces Iscariot* (Virgin, 1994); *Mellon Collie and the Infinite Sadness* (Virgin, 1995); *The Aeroplane Flies High* (Virgin, 1996); *Adore* (Virgin, 1998); *MACHINA: The Machines of God* (Virgin, 2000); *MACHINA II: The Friends and Enemies of Modern Music* (Constantinople, 2000); *Greatest Hits* (Virgin, 2001)

GIL KAUFMAN

ELLIOTT SMITH

Born: Steven Paul Smith; Omaha, Nebraska, 6 August 1969

Genre: Rock

Best-selling album since 1990: *XO* (1998)

Hit songs since 1990: "Miss Misery," "Sweet Adeline"

Elliott Smith, a Beatles-influenced singer/songwriter from Portland, Oregon, started playing guitar around age eleven. He was born in Omaha, Nebraska, but spent his childhood in Dallas, Texas, following his parents' divorce and his mother's remarriage when he was a toddler. Family troubles eventually forced him out at age fourteen, and he moved to Portland to live with his father. The Northwest turned out to be a fruitful location. In the 1990s, Seattle and Portland spawned a new rock sound called grunge, characterized by loud, angry guitars and a do-it-yourself, punk-rock ethic, made famous by the band Nirvana.

Smith moved back to Portland after graduating from Hampshire College in Amherst, Massachusetts, and formed a rock band called Heatmiser with college classmate Neil Gust. The band put out three albums, but Smith was also busy composing his own decidedly hushed and introspective songs. He sent nine songs, which he recorded at home, to the Portland-based label Cavity Search, hoping they would put out a single. Instead, they wanted to put out an entire album, which became his first solo release, *Roman Candle* (1994). Within a year, the groundbreaking, independent label Kill Rock Stars, based in Olympia, Washington, released his self-titled *Elliott Smith* (1995).

Smith's songwriting on *Elliott Smith* and *Either/Or* (1997) is characterized by its sparseness; many of the tunes feature only his acoustic guitar, with minimal drumming. Smith played most of the instruments and recorded the albums himself. His songs, replete with heartbreaking tales of bitter disappointments, social isolation, and too many nights of drinking, somehow sound sweet coming from his airy baritone and impassioned guitar. "Pictures of Me" suggests a psychic discomfort with his own growing popularity: "So sick and tired of all these pictures of me / Totally wrong / Completely wrong." Lyrics such as "Drink up one more time and I'll make you mine" ("Between the Bars,") typify his hopeless romanticism. Although he has been compared to the similarly troubled-sounding English folksinger Nick Drake, Smith is more interested in rock and roll. He was once quoted as saying he does not like being called a "singer/songwriter." Critics and fans of indie rock responded favorably to his solo efforts; they took to his keen sense of melody and his somber acoustic compositions.

Smith's commercial breakthrough came shortly after *Either/Or* was released. Filmmaker and fellow Portland resident Gus Van Sant Jr. asked Smith if he would contribute songs to an upcoming film. Smith submitted four songs from *Either/Or,* and composed a new one, "Miss Misery." Van Sant Jr's film *Good Will Hunting* (1998) became a surprise hit and earned Smith an Academy Award nomination for Best Original Song for "Miss Misery." The shy, introspective performer appeared on the Academy Awards telecast in an ill-fitting white suit and sang the nominated song while sitting on a stool. The soundtrack went on to sell more than 250,000 copies.

The exposure Smith garnered through *Good Will Hunting* and the Academy Award nomination forced him further into the spotlight. Major record labels expressed interest in him, and he signed with DreamWorks Records. For *XO,* his 1998 major-label debut, Smith again played nearly all the instruments himself, and again brought along Tom Rothrock and Rob Schnaf, with whom he had shared producing, recording, and mixing duties on *Either/Or.*

Grandiose in its scope, with soaring, lush arrangements ("Sweet Adeline"), explosive, guitar-drenched angry rock ("Amity") and a pair of ballads ("Waltz #1, Waltz #2"), *XO* proved Smith's previously untapped creative potential as both a composer and arranger. One could almost hear the big-label budget in every swooping string arrangement and multilayered, harmonized track of Smith's whisper-thin voice. His fondness for 1960s popular music is evident in "Baby Britain," with a guitar riff quotation from the Beatles' "Getting Better All the Time." The album's chilling, angelic, a cappella closing tune, "I Didn't Understand," recalls the Beach Boys. In 1999 *Spin* magazine named Elliott Smith its number two artist of the year and declared *XO* one of its top twenty albums of the year.

In 2000 Smith released *Figure 8*, his second album for DreamWorks, a sprawling, sixteen-track excursion that at times echoed the harder sounds of his Heatmiser days. Ultimately, though, *Figure 8* was both built on and slightly departed from previous releases. It is a sign of a growing musician unafraid to place a tearjerker ballad, "Everything Reminds Me of Her," next to an ethereal, string-laden song, "Everything Means Nothing to Me," only to mix in the cynical, aggressive "Stupidity Tries" a few tracks later. Smith recorded the album with the same producers from *XO*, Rothrock and Schnaf, at several studios, including the famous Abbey Road. Perhaps inspired by the location, *Figure 8* is characterized by a varied sonic palette and continuous flow, much like the Beatles' *Abbey Road*.

In 2002, two years after *Figure 8*, fans were still waiting for a follow-up release. Smith had reportedly worked out a deal with DreamWorks to produce the album independently. Tentatively titled *From the Basement on the Hill*, it promised to be a return to his do-it-yourself roots: He wrote, arranged, and produced it himself.

SELECTIVE DISCOGRAPHY: *Roman Candle* (Cavity Search, 1994); *Elliott Smith* (Kill Rock Stars, 1995); *Either/Or* (Kill Rock Stars, 1997); *XO* (DreamWorks, 1998); *Figure 8* (DreamWorks, 2000). **With Heatmiser:** *Dead Air* (Frontier, 1993); *Cop and Speeder* (Frontier, 1994); *Mic City Songs* (Caroline, 1996). **Soundtrack:** *Good Will Hunting* (Capitol/EMI, 1997).

WEBSITE: www.elliottsmith.net.

CARRIE HAVRANEK

PATTI SMITH

Born: Patricia Lee Smith; Chicago, Illinois, 30 December 1946

Genre: Rock

Best-selling album since 1990: *Land (1975–2002)* (2002)

Hit songs since 1990: "Summer Cannibals," "Strange Messengers"

While painting and poetry were her first obsessions, Patti Smith changed direction in the early 1970s to form an amplified band and record several albums of authentic rock and roll, blending furious, passionate but sometimes tender verse and grainy, grimy white R&B. In doing so she propelled poetry into the forefront of the pop experience for the first time since Bob Dylan had offered his own forays into Beat-inspired writing a decade earlier.

Ignited by the spark of New York's new wave, Smith became the high priestess of punk poetry, declaiming her views on life and love to a jagged rock soundtrack. In doing so, she became one of the most significant artists working at the edge of the avant-garde and popular culture. Yet her career since has been far from straightforward. At the beginning of the 1980s she took an extended break from the business of performing and recording, returning during the next decade to prove that her muse had not deserted her.

Born in Chicago, Smith moved with her family to Philadelphia, Pennsylvania, in 1950; they later relocated to New Jersey in 1955. After graduating from high school in 1964 she did factory work—an experience that fed into one of her earliest songs, "Piss Factory"—but then set out on a course to train as an art teacher.

Rimbaud, the Rolling Stones, and Manhattan's Musical Hotbed

Her painting was at the center of her creative activity at the time—she was inspired by the Paris-based painters at the turn of the twentieth century, Amedeo Modigliani and Chaim Soutine—but she also took close notice of the French poets like Arthur Rimbaud, who had lived in the French capital around the same time. She was also deeply affected by her early sightings of the Rolling Stones on American television.

Moving to New York in 1967, she began to develop an artistic network that sustained her for the next few years. She had a relationship with the photographer Robert Mapplethorpe, lived in the Chelsea Hotel (the famed hangout of artists on the margins), and at the end of the decade became a denizen of Max's Kansas City, a club where painters, including Andy Warhol, met. At the time, it was beginning to attract a crowd interested in rock music.

In 1969 Smith made her first public appearance before an audience when she took part in a play entitled *Femme Fatale*, a piece written and produced by members of the Warhol entourage. Linking with guitarist Lenny Kaye and keyboardist Richard Sohl, she became vocalist in a trio that performed her poetry with a rock backing. In 1974 they issued their first single—"Piss Factory" backed with a version of "Hey Joe"—and the following year, joined by Ivan Kral on bass and Jay Dee Daugherty on drums, Smith issued her acclaimed debut album, *Horses* (1975).

The album marries Smith's distinctive poetic voice on tracks like "Redondo Beach" and "Birdland" with new interpretations of 1960s classics like "Gloria" and "Land of a Thousand Dances." Produced by former Velvet Underground member John Cale, the record signalled the arrival of a major talent and, in its acerbic, aggressive manner, shaped in the musical hotbed of Manhattan, the recording was a fine example of the new energy and attitude infusing the rock revolution that was punk.

On the subsequent albums *Radio Ethiopia* (1976), *Easter* (1978), and *Wave* (1979), released in the name of the Patti Smith Group, she maintained her aural assault with "Babelogue" and "Rock 'n' Roll Nigger" distilling her uncompromising methods. She also reveals a more reflective side on "Because the Night," a co-composition with fellow rocker Bruce Springsteen that gave her a hit in the United States and the United Kingdom in 1978, and "Frederick," a tribute to Fred "Sonic" Smith, the musician she would marry in 1980.

That year she left New York with Fred Smith to relocate to Detroit, where she took an extended break from the rock and roll lifestyle, raising her two children during most of the 1980s. It was not until 1988 that she released her next album, *Dream of Life*, co-produced by Fred Smith, and with Sohl and Daugherty still on board. Critically well received, the record was not a commercial winner. Critics noted that Patti Smith's absence and the poor health of her husband, which affected live promotion of the piece, contributed to a disappointing public response.

Deaths of Friends and Her Husband

Yet this setback did not derail the Smith project entirely. Despite the loss of friends (Mapplethorpe in 1989) and collaborators (Sohl in 1990), she entered the new decade with an appearance at a major AIDS benefit in 1991 and contributed musically to the soundtrack to Wim Wenders's motion picture *Until the End of the World* (1991).

A book of short stories, *Wool Gathering*, was published in 1993 but in late 1994 she suffered the latest of a sequence of personal blows when her husband died of a heart attack. A tribute concert to her late partner was given in Ann Arbor, Michigan, in spring 1995 as Smith threw herself into a demanding tour schedule. During the summer she also made an unannounced contribution to the New York leg of the Lollapalooza tour. At the end of the year she opened for Bob Dylan at a number of East Coast tour dates.

Returning to the studio, she dedicated her 1996 album *Gone Again* to Fred. Affected by Dylan's recent *World Gone Wrong*, Smith's release echoed that acoustic melancholy. It includes a title track penned with her husband, and another song written with Fred, "Summer Cannibals," plus a Dylan song, "Wicked Messenger." Also featured is a piece written with Oliver Ray, a younger musician who had become part of the Smith band and who later became her lover.

Stipe Hooks up with European Trek

Although she did not tour the United States to showcase *Gone Again*, she did successfully take her band—including Lenny Kaye, Jay Dee Daugherty, and former Television front man Tom Verlaine—to Europe and was joined by R.E.M. vocalist and friend Michael Stipe, who photographed the tour for a book.

Peace & Noise (1997) followed and saw most of the compositional credits shared with Oliver Ray. It features a song called "Spell," which makes reference to work by the American poet Allen Ginsberg, a large influence on Smith, who died the same year the album was released.

Smith's own role as poet had not been shelved. Numerous appearances in this guise saw her read at an Albert Hall event in London in 1996 and in 1998 she participated in a benefit for Tibet, performing extracts from *Howl*, the key verse work by Ginsberg, and John Lennon's "Power to the People."

In 2000 the album *Gung Ho* was released. It offers a lengthy critique of the urban nightmare on "Strange Messengers," and draws comparisons to Blondie on the track "Gone Pie." But her new work lacks the resounding power of her earlier recordings and the arrival of *Land* (1975–2002), an outstanding compilation of her career output, only serves to emphasize this assessment. Over two compact discs, the collection captures the intensity of her oeuvre on album and in a live setting.

Determinedly eclectic, Smith has never been tied down by notions of pop stardom. Her existence has been shaped by an ability to move across the creative arts with facility, from painting to theater to spoken word. But without the doors that rock music opened to her, she would have been a significant artist who remained in the shadows of the mainstream. Rock afforded her a large, global audience. Through the upsurge of the new wave, and specifically the quality of her first album, Smith achieved a notable triumph. She managed to combine the potency of raw, direct verse with the muscular rhythms of rock and roll and showed that a woman could take an active part in a world previously dominated by men. As a result, she has been a role model for several waves of women since—from punks to riot grrrls.

SELECTIVE DISCOGRAPHY: *Horses* (Arista, 1975); *Radio Ethiopia* (Arista, 1976); *Easter* (Arista, 1978); *Wave* (Arista, 1979); *Dream of Life* (Arista, 1988); *Gone Again* (Arista, 1996); *Peace & Noise* (Arista, 1997); *Gung Ho* (Arista, 2000); *Land* (1975–2002) (Arista, 2002). **Soundtrack:** *Until the End of the World* (Warner Bros., 1991).

BIBLIOGRAPHY: V. Bockris, *Patti Smith* (London, 1998).

WEBSITE: www.Pattismithland.com.

SIMON WARNER

WILL SMITH

Born: Willard Christopher Smith; Philadelphia, Pennsylvania, 25 September 1968

Genre: Rap, R&B

Best-selling album since 1990: *Willennium* (1999)

Hit songs since 1990: "Gettin' Jiggy Wit' It," "Wild Wild West"

As the "Fresh Prince" half of the popular duo D.J. Jazzy Jeff and the Fresh Prince, Will Smith brought a refreshing comic sensibility to rap of the late 1980s. In contrast to tougher-sounding rap acts such as Public Enemy and N.W.A., Smith and his recording partner Jeff Townes specialized in lyrically "clean" raps that explore the humorous side of adolescence. Smith recorded his first solo album in 1997, after establishing a successful career as an actor in Hollywood films and on television. On hits such as "Gettin' Jiggy Wit' It" and "Wild Wild West," he continued to promote the wholesome image for which he had become known. While often dismissed as a lightweight by fans of hard-core "gangsta" rap, Smith creates danceable music with an unwavering sense of groove, his rapping style dexterous and assured. By the early 2000s, Smith's high-profile work in films had eclipsed his recording career, although he continued to release successful albums.

Years with D.J. Jazzy Jeff

Born and raised in West Philadelphia, Pennsylvania, Smith met up-and-coming disc jockey Townes while rapping at a party in 1986. Soon the pair began performing together, becoming audience favorites on the local Philadelphia rap scene. After the duo was offered a recording contract with Jive Records in 1987, Smith turned down a university scholarship at the prestigious Massachusetts Institute of Technology, deciding to make performing his full-time career. The next year, D.J. Jazzy Jeff and the Fresh Prince released their breakthrough album, *He's the D.J., I'm the Rapper* (1988). Featuring gentle, lighthearted hits such as "Parents Just Don't Understand" and "Nightmare on My Street," the album countered critics who denounced rap music as sexist and violent. In 1991 the duo released its biggest hit, "Summertime," a breezy, nostalgic evoca-tion of childhood summers in Philadelphia. Having begun his acting career the year before with a starring role in the hit television series *The Fresh Prince of Bel-Air*, Smith left the duo to focus on a burgeoning film career. After his performance as a charming con artist in the film *Six Degrees of Separation* (1993) received critical acclaim, Smith earned starring roles in the Hollywood hits *Bad Boys* (1995), *Independence Day* (1996), and *Men in Black* (1997).

Late 1990s Stardom

In 1997, having devoted the previous four years to acting, Smith released his debut solo album, *Big Willie Style*. Propelled by the funk-laden, rhythmic hit, "Getting' Jiggy Wit' It," the album advanced the audience-friendly style Smith had pioneered during his career with D.J. Jazzy Jeff. Bypassing the social commentary featured in the work of many of his rap and R&B contemporaries, Smith displays on *Big Willie Style* a simple desire to entertain. "Miami" qualifies as an infectious celebration of the Florida resort city, with lyrics repeated in English and Spanish, while "Candy" is an engaging duet with Larry Blackmon, leader of the 1980s funk band Cameo. While the album's tone is largely comic, "Just the Two of Us" is a sensitive and absorbing exploration of single fatherhood, dedicated to Smith's son with his first wife, actress Sheree Zampino: "If the world attacks, and you slide off track / Remember one fact, I got your back." Having divorced Zampino, Smith married actress Jada Pinkett in 1997.

In 1999, after starring in his first box-office failure, the western-adventure film *Wild Wild West*, Smith released a second solo album, *Willennium*. Borrowing the synthesizer riff from Stevie Wonder's 1976 song "I Wish," the hit "Wild Wild West" climbed to number one on the pop charts. Well constructed, with an intricate, danceable rhythm, the song represents Smith at his spirited best. "Will 2K" uses a sample from the Clash's 1982 hit "Rock the Casbah" to create a celebratory atmosphere, although some critics complained of the track's self-aggrandizing stance, a quality mirrored on the remainder of *Willennium*. Writing for noted Internet music magazine, *Pop Matters*, critic Cynthia Fuchs observes, "Nearly every track here extols the endless wonderfulness of being Will Smith." For all his self-important posturing, however, Smith exudes an affecting sweetness and likability, qualities that ensure his enduring appeal. As evidenced in a review of the album by influential English music magazine *Q*, even Smith's detractors note the easy accessibility of his music: "'Will 2K' even makes a Clash sample sound squeaky clean. Nevertheless, there's something beguiling about Smith's profanity-free style."

On the heels of his most acclaimed acting triumph, portraying boxing legend Muhammad Ali in the movie *Ali* (2001), Smith released *Born to Reign* in 2002.

Although it lacks the catchy, radio-friendly hits of its predecessors, the album contains the enjoyable "1,000 Kisses," featuring vocals by Pinkett. Incorporating elements of Luther Vandross's 1981 hit, "Never Too Much," the song re-cements Smith's friendly persona. In addition to showcasing the talents of Pinkett, Smith allows his young son Jaden to babble extensively on the track. "Cool, calculating stuff," writes the U.K. newspaper *The Guardian*, "but annoyingly enjoyable." Other reviews were less kind, falling back on the familiar criticism of Smith's music as bland and ineffectual. *Rolling Stone*, for example, describes the album as "a nice try from a nice guy." By this point in Smith's career, however, recording had become secondary to his status as one of Hollywood's top leading men.

Beginning his career in the late 1980s as part of the successful rap team D.J. Jazzy Jeff and the Fresh Prince, Will Smith earned critical and popular respect as a film actor before releasing his first solo album in 1997. Famed for his convivial dance songs, Smith won fans with his family-friendly style that downplayed the aggressiveness of much contemporary rap and hip-hop.

SELECTIVE DISCOGRAPHY: *Big Willie Style* (Columbia, 1997); *Willennium* (Columbia, 1999); *Born to Reign* (Columbia, 2002). **With D.J. Jazzy Jeff and the Fresh Prince:** *He's the D.J., I'm the Rapper* (Jive, 1988); *Homebase* (Jive, 1991).

SELECTIVE FILMOGRAPHY: *Six Degrees of Separation* (1993); *Bad Boys* (1995); *Independence Day* (1996); *Men in Black* (1997); *Ali* (2001); *Men in Black II* (2002).

WEBSITE: www.willsmith.com.

DAVID FREELAND

SNOOP (DOGGY) DOGG

Born: Calvin Broadus; Long Beach, California, 20 October 1972

Genre: Rap

Best-selling album since 1990: *Doggystyle* (1993)

Hit songs since 1990: "What's My Name," "Gin & Juice," "Still a 'G' Thing"

Boosted by his distinct, lazy drawl and a history of run-ins with the law, Snoop Dogg became one of the most successful rappers of the 1990s, the epitome of West Coast, gangsta-style rap and the G-funk style.

A Thug's Life

Raised in the tough neighborhoods of Long Beach, California, Calvin Broadus was nicknamed Snoop by his mother, Beverly Broadus, because of his resemblance to the cartoon character Snoopy. His father, Vernall Varnado, left the Broadus family not long after Snoop's birth. His absence strongly affected Snoop. Although his mother did what she could to help and to educate Snoop, he drifted in and out of trouble for most of his life. Shortly after his high school graduation, Snoop left school to join the Crips, a prominent Los Angeles gang. He sold crack cocaine and lived for a time in his car.

Snoop was arrested several times in the early 1990s for cocaine possession and spent time in jail. He seemed destined to live out his days as a small-time drug dealer. Snoop's life turned around, though, as he began recording raps with Warren G, the brother of producer and rapper Dr. Dre, on homemade cassette tapes. Eventually Warren G asked Dre to listen to Snoop's raps; Dre was so impressed with Snoop's style that the two were soon working together, first on the 1992 single "Deep Cover" for the movie with the same name. Dr. Dre then gave Snoop's raps a prominent place on Dre's *The Chronic* (1992), an album that established West Coast, gangsta rap as the dominant hip-hop sound of 1990s rap. This style of rap eschewed the overt politics of rap acts such as Public Enemy, depicting instead the grim realities of urban life to a beat that blended 1970s funk with electronic music. Critics have long praised Snoop's laconic drawls as the perfect counter to Dr. Dre's famous tightly wrapped, funk-inspired G-sound. Snoop himself has described his rap style as "an easy loping style of walking and talking and bumping." Snoop has said that when other rappers turn on the accelerator, he likes to let up "and get a little backstroke working." There is no doubt his early laid-back style is also a reflection of his legendary marijuana ("chronic") use, a habit he claims to have given up. What makes his voice most distinctive is its calm irreverence. Whether he is satirizing popular culture or detailing a violent incident in his raps, Snoop always sounds like a detached, sometimes threatening, sometimes affable, stoner.

Doggystyle: The Death Row Years

Snoop's solo recording career began with the highly anticipated release of *Doggystyle* (1992). The album, produced by Dr. Dre, was the first debut album to top *Billboard* charts the first week of its release. It remains one of the best selling rap records of the 1990s. *Doggystyle* was released on the Death Row label, then led by Suge Knight, a soon-to-be-infamous CEO credited with bringing gangster-style intimidation tactics to the music business. Two tracks from *Doggystyle*—"Gin & Juice" and "What's My Name?"—were released as singles, with the latter becoming the song most associated with Snoop's early persona. "What's My Name?" features an irresistible P-funk beat and textured vocals and raps that alternate between hilarious and threatening raps, and the chanting of Snoop (Doggy)

Dog's name. Like all of Snoop's best material, the tracks on *Doggystyle* do not hold up well under careful analysis—they are sexist, violent, and filthy—yet Dre's grinding beats and Snoop's loopy raps somehow disarm many listeners' reservations. Snoop's major contribution to gangsta rap is that he makes it fun.

At the moment of his great breakthrough, Snoop found himself in trouble with the law. On August 25, 1993, Snoop's bodyguard Malik shot Philip Woldemariam, a man Snoop claimed had been stalking and trying to kill him. Snoop was arrested and then tried as an accomplice to murder. He and gangsta rap were widely vilified in the popular press. When the film *Murder Was the Case* (1996), directed by Dre and featuring Snoop rapping in the title song and on two other tracks, was released, Snoop seemed to be capitalizing on his infamy, a charge he later denied. He was acquitted of all charges in 1996. During his trial, Snoop's friendship with rapper Tupac Shakur emerged. "Closer than a brother" is how Snoop described Tupac after the latter's murder in 1996. Although the two rappers grew up on different coasts and had distinct rap styles, their friendship and dual appearance in Tupac's video "2 of Americaz Most Wanted" (1996) fueled the rivalry between East and West Coast rappers and Tupac's feud with rappers Biggie Smalls and Puff Daddy (Sean Combs). Snoop and Tupac's cameo at the 1996 MTV Music Awards was one of Tupac's last public appearances. Since the murders of Tupac and, later, Biggie Smalls, Snoop has attempted to steer clear of rap's thug culture, though controversy continues to cling to him.

After Death Row; Snoop-a-Flies

In 1996 he released the self-produced album, *Tha Doggfather* and dropped "Doggy" from his name. *Tha Doggfather* is most notable because of the absence of Dr. Dre's production, though it treads ground familiar to fans of *Doggystyle*. *Tha Doggfather* was Snoop's last album for the Death Row label. Snoop went on to record two albums for the No Limit label—*Da Game Is to Be Sold, Not to Be Told* (1998) and *Top Dogg* (1999). Both albums were successes and great party albums but lacked the edge and focus of his early works. On *Tha Last Meal* (2000), Snoop reemerged as a major creative force in rap. He reunites with Dr. Dre, who produced three tracks on the record, returning Snoop to the best of his early sound. The album also features tracks produced by several emerging producers influenced by Dre, including Scott Stroch, Jelly Roll, and Meech Wells. "Set It Off" and "Snoop Dog (What's My Name, Pt. 2)" are among Snoop's best songs.

Tha Last Meal also marks the start of a new phase in Snoop's career. His 1999 autobiography, *Tha Doggfather,* written with Davin Seay, details Snoop's life in Long Beach, discusses his trials and friendships, and records his growing maturity as an artist and father of three young children. The book manages to capture Snoop's personality and gifts with language. Snoop's publication of his memoirs about his early years suggests that he was ready to leave his past behind. *Tha Last Meal* reveals that he is in control of his artistry and is able to work with an array of both veteran and new producers and rappers.

In 2002 and 2003 Snoop achieved mainstream stardom. He appeared regularly on late night television, even co-hosting the first week of ABC's *The Jimmy Kimmel Show*. Snoop also narrated an episode of the notorious "Girls Gone Wild" video series in 2002, the same year he made a cameo appearance in *A Very Merry Muppet Christmas Movie*. There are two Snoop Dogg action figure dolls (Snoopafly and Little Junior) and a line of Snoop Dogg-inspired clothing. Snoop has also founded Doggy Style Records, a label whose stable of talent includes Snoopafly, Mr. Kane, Latoiya Williams, E-White, and June Bugg.

Despite these seemingly mainstream entrepreneurial moves, Snoop maintains his thug image and appeal. *Paid Tha Cost to Be Da Boss* (2002) is one of Snoop's strongest recordings, featuring some of his oldest friends such as Warren G and Redman and new collaborators such as Pharrell, Lady of Rage, and RBX. Two of his best singles, "From Tha Chuuuch to Da Palace" and "Beautiful," punctuate a loosely organized collection that satirizes thug culture and *The Sopranos* television series. "Beautiful," with its sweet riffs and sentimental chorus, is Snoop's closest move to mainstream R&B, although his self-deprecatory raps add the right amount of irony. Other tracks on *Paid Tha Cost* include "Pimp Slapp'd," a verbal attack on former Death Row executive Suge Hill. The album went platinum within a year of its release.

Snoop made headlines again on April 11, 2003, when a gunman in a speeding car opened fire on his five-car motorcade in Los Angeles, injuring one of his eight bodyguards. Snoop, who was riding alone in a Cadillac, escaped unharmed.

One of the most prolific and recognizable figures in rap music, Snoop Dogg's *Paid Tha Cost* signals his ability to adapt his roots in gangsta rap with changing times. Snoop's famous mug, his sense of humor, and his laid-back raps help make him one of the twenty-first century's most important hip-hop artists.

SELECTIVE DISCOGRAPHY: *Doggystyle* (Death Row, 1993); *Tha Doggfather* (Death Row, 1996); *Da Game Is to Be Sold, Not to Be Told* (No Limit, 1998); *Dead Man Walkin'* (2000, D-3); *Tha Last Meal* (Priority, 2000); *Paid Tha Cost to Be Da Boss* (Priority/Doggy Style, 2002). **Soundtracks:** *Deep Cover with Dr. Dre* (Capitol, 1992); *Murder Was the Case* (Priority, 1994).

BIBLIOGRAPHY: S. Dogg and D. Seay, *Tha Doggfather: The Times, Trials, and Hardcore Truths of Snoop Dogg* (New York, 1999).

WEBSITE: www.snoopdogg.com.

SHAWN GILLEN

SON VOLT

Formed: 1994, New Orleans, Louisiana

Members: Dave Boquist, guitar, banjo, fiddle, lap steel, dobro; Jim Boquist, bass, vocals; Jay Farrar, vocals, guitar (born Belleville, Indiana, 26 December 1967); Mike Heidorn, drums.

Genre: Rock, Alternative Country

Best-selling album since 1990: *Trace* (1995)

Hit songs since 1990: "Drown"

Son Volt's melancholy alternative country music owes as much to the slash-and-burn sonics of punk as to the plain-spoken storytelling of country legends Johnny Cash and Hank Williams. Their songs veer from reverent ballads to ferocious rock, but it is their commitment to authenticity that truly sets them apart from the glossy country mainstream. Lead singer and songwriter Jay Farrar formed the band after splitting from alternative country pioneers Uncle Tupelo, and has continued to mine the subject matter of broken hearts, small-town desolation, and highway driving with grace and poignancy. Though subsequent albums did not garner similar acclaim, the band's album *Trace* (1995) stands as a touchstone of a distinctly American genre.

Childhood friends Farrar and Jeff Tweedy formed Uncle Tupelo while attending high school in rural Belleville, Illinois, in the mid-1980s. The band cultivated a fervent local following by matching the raucous guitars of underground rock to the broken hearts and rough lives subject matter of traditional country music. Their constant touring and rising popularity in the Midwest earned the band a recording contract with Rockville Records, which released the critically lauded *No Depression* in 1990. Though not the first band to blend country music and hard-edged rock, Uncle Tupelo stood apart due to the considerable talents of its songwriters. Farrar tackled fiery political tunes and traditional ballads, while Tweedy's work leaned toward the melodic love songs of country-rock singer Gram Parsons. After several years of nonstop recording and touring, tensions between the pair forced Farrar to leave the band following the tour for *Anodyne* (1993), their final album. Tweedy recruited the Tupelo touring band to form Wilco, and Farrar repaired to New Orleans to contemplate his next move.

After a few months of rest and writing, Farrar recruited a pair of musicians, multi-instrumentalist Dave Boquist and his brother, bassist Jim Boquist, from folk rocker Joe Henry's touring band to form Son Volt. Original Uncle Tupelo drummer Mike Heidorn rounded out the lineup, and the four-piece group began recording new songs in the fall of 1994 in Northfield, Minnesota, for producer Brian Paulson. Warner Bros. Records released the resulting album, *Trace*, in September 1995.

Trace showcases Farrar at the peak of his powers, writing and singing with a heartfelt intensity that easily matches his best work in Uncle Tupelo. The propulsive opening track, "Windfall," sets the tone for the record, with brightly strummed guitars, longing pedal steel and fiddle accompaniment, and a mission statement chorus of "may the wind take your troubles away / both feet on the floor, two hands on the wheel." The album plays as a travelogue through a cracked-pavement Americana of AM radio, dusty ghost towns, and forlorn hearts. Though musically spare and bleak in parts, the themes of change and movement imbue each song with the hope of revitalization, and better days ahead. Thus, the somber "Tear Stained Eye" sits comfortably beside the raging guitars of "Route," achieving a perfect balance of country earnestness and rock defiance. The album also notched a minor radio hit with the song "Drown," a tribute to the restorative powers of the road. With a rapidly expanding fan base, Son Volt seemed poised to rescue commercial country music from its long slide into mediocrity.

Their follow-up effort, *Straightaways* (1997), is a darker affair, and did not achieve the broad appeal of *Trace*. Critics noted that while the album preserves the Son Volt hallmarks of driving rock, well-played traditional balladry, and fine musical interplay, it lacks the liberating spirit of their debut. Some pointed out that several tracks sound like retreads of earlier material. Fans remained loyal, however, urged on by the atmospheric "Last Minute Shakedown," and the small-town anthem "No More Parades." *Wide Swing Tremelo* (1998) attempts to answer the critics of *Straightaways* with a handful of rousing, hard-rocking tunes, but then lapses back into less inspired territory.

Perhaps to remedy this situation, Farrar issued a solo album titled *Sebastapol* (2001), which successfully functions as a cobweb-clearing exercise. While not as overtly experimental as former Uncle Tupelo band mate Tweedy's work with Wilco, the songs feature a fresh mix of instruments that give Farrar's familiar musings a significant kick. The album proves that Farrar can write music that appeals beyond his dedicated fan base. Whether or not this innovation ever seeps into Son Volt, *Trace* ensures the band's place within the worlds of both country and rock.

SELECTIVE DISCOGRAPHY: *Trace* (Warner Bros., 1995); *Straightaways* (Warner Bros., 1997); *Wide Swing Tremolo* (Warner Bros., 1998).

WEBSITE: www.wbr.com/sonvolt.

SEAN CAMERON

STEPHEN SONDHEIM

Born: New York, New York, 22 March 1930
Genre: Musical Theater
Best-selling album since 1990: *Passion* (1994)

Getting his start as a lyricist in the late 1950s, Stephen Sondheim had by the 1970s become the most influential Broadway theater composer of his generation, changing the way in which the musical as an art form is understood and appreciated. Sondheim is the sole modern Broadway composer whose work withstands comparison to that of theatrical tunesmiths and lyricists of the past such as Richard Rodgers and Oscar Hammerstein II. Beyond the complexity and richness of his music, Sondheim's greatness lies in his daring pursuit of subject matter previously considered off-limits for Broadway musicals. Exploring themes of obsession, evil, the fragility of human relationships, and the dissociation and cynicism of modern life, Sondheim has pushed the musical form in new, startling directions. Yet his work evinces respect for Broadway's long tradition of escapism and fun; far from depressing, Sondheim's musicals often display a darkly humorous edge. Always more popular with critics than with mainstream audiences, who have tended to prefer more accessible, pop-oriented composers such as Andrew Lloyd Webber, Sondheim has remained active in the 1990s and 2000s, creating challenging new musicals, contributing to Hollywood film soundtracks, and influencing a new generation of theater composers.

Early Life and Success

Born to a wealthy New York manufacturing family of German-Jewish descent, Sondheim endured an unhappy childhood after his father left to live with a girlfriend. The scars from that experience—coming when Sondheim was only ten—along with the influence of a dominating mother, later found voice in his best-known work, particularly through themes of alienation and isolation. In his early teens Sondheim's life changed after his mother moved to Bucks County, Pennsylvania. Soon Sondheim had fallen under the creative influence of his new neighbor Hammerstein, then working on a show, *Oklahoma!* (1943), that proved to be a landmark of American musical theater. After graduating from Williams College, where he won the Hutchinson Prize for Music Composition, Sondheim studied with the renowned modern classical composer Milton Babbitt before getting hired to write lyrics for the Broadway musical *West Side Story* (1957). As a result of the show's great success, Sondheim was also recruited as a lyricist for *Gypsy* (1959). Based on the memoirs of famed stripper Gypsy Rose Lee, the musical was a commercial hit and an artistic triumph, paving the way for Sondheim's first success as both a composer and lyricist, *A Funny Thing Happened on the Way to the Forum* (1962). The show's lyrical intelligence and racy sense of humor proved that a successful Broadway musical could be both entertaining and challenging.

Peak Artistic Years

Working with the Broadway director Harold Prince, Sondheim embarked upon his greatest artistic period in the early 1970s, composing a series of groundbreaking musicals: *Company* (1970), *Follies* (1971), *A Little Night Music* (1973) and *Sweeney Todd* (1979). While *Company*, a modern look at love and relationships through the eyes of a thirty-five-year-old bachelor, brought a new degree of wit and sophistication to the Broadway stage, *Sweeney Todd* saw Sondheim's humor take on a dark, macabre edge—the musical told the story of a revenge-seeking barber who kills his customers. *A Little Night Music* contains one of Sondheim's best-known songs, "Send in the Clowns," a wistful distillation of romantic confusion that became a pop and jazz standard. During the 1980s Sondheim continued experimenting with form and structure: *Merrily We Roll Along* (1981), for example, moves backward in time, tracing the life of a composer from adulthood to youth. Unfortunately, such experiments did not endear Sondheim to the Broadway theatergoing public: *Merrily We Roll Along* ran for only sixteen performances

After presenting two highly regarded Broadway musicals, *Sunday in the Park with George* (1984) and *Into the Woods* (1987), Sondheim turned to the lower profile world of off-Broadway for *Assassins* (1990), one of his darkest, most compelling works. Produced by the noted New York theater company Playwrights Horizons, the musical surveys American assassinations through the ages. It features historical characters such as Abraham Lincoln's assassin, John Wilkes Booth, and John Hinckley, who in 1981 tried to kill President Ronald Reagan. In a deliberately perverse move, Sondheim presents "Unworthy of Your Love," a duet between Hinckley and President Gerald Ford's attempted assassin, Squeaky Fromme, as a cheerful, Top-40 style love ballad. Beyond its unusual subject matter, *Assassins* challenges audiences through its rejection of a linear plot; instead, its scenes are arranged according to thematic references. The famous Presidential march, "Hail to the Chief," is used throughout the musical as a means of linking characters and scenes; in Sondheim's typically ironic fashion, music familiarly associated with reverence becomes a commentary on political insecurity and death.

Challenging Audiences in the 1990s

Sondheim turned to high-profile film work in the 1990s, contributing songs for the Hollywood movies *Dick Tracy* (1990) and *The Birdcage* (1996). Nevertheless, he continued to explore anxious, dark themes with the Broadway musical, *Passion* (1994). The story of a sickly, unattractive woman obsessively in love with an Army soldier—himself involved with a married woman—*Passion* is a compelling study of desire and transformation. A modest hit that ran for six months, *Passion* was perhaps too challenging musically and thematically to achieve widespread success. During the remainder of the 1990s and early 2000s Sondheim largely focused on teaching, although his earlier work was celebrated in several Broadway revivals, including a 2002 production of *Into the Woods* that starred the pop singer and actress Vanessa Williams. After many delays and title changes, Sondheim's new musical, *Bounce*, was scheduled to open at Chicago's Goodman Theatre in the summer of 2003. *Bounce*, which reunites Sondheim with director Prince, is the story of Addison and Wilson Mizner, two brothers who led picaresque lives as con artists, entrepreneurs, and celebrities during the early twentieth century.

By the turn of the millennium, Sondheim was widely acknowledged as the most important living artist in musical theater, his work influencing younger composers such as Michael John LaChiusa, Adam Guettel, and Jason Robert Brown. Hailed for his daring, complex use of theme and structure, Sondheim raised the musical form to a new level of artistic ambition and achievement, stimulating audiences with his invention, humor, and intelligence.

SELECTIVE DISCOGRAPHY: **Original Broadway and off-Broadway cast recordings:** *West Side Story* (Columbia, 1957); *Gypsy* (Columbia, 1959); *A Funny Thing Happened on the Way to the Forum* (Angel, 1962); *Anyone Can Whistle* (Columbia, 1964); *Company* (Columbia, 1970); *Follies* (Angel, 1971); *A Little Night Music* (Columbia, 1973); *Sweeney Todd* (RCA Victor, 1979); *Sunday in the Park with George* (RCA Victor, 1984); *Into the Woods* (RCA Victor, 1987); *Assassins* (RCA Victor, 1991); *Passion* (Angel, 1994). **Film soundtracks:** *Music from and Inspired by the Film Dick Tracy* (Sire, 1990); *The Birdcage* (Edeltone, 1996).

BIBLIOGRAPHY: M. Secrest, *Sondheim: A Life* (New York: 1998).

WEBSITE: www.sondheim.com.

DAVID FREELAND

SONIC YOUTH

Formed: 1981, New York, New York

Members: Kim Gordon, bass, vocals (born Rochester, New York, 28 April 1953); Jim O'Rourke, multi-instrumentalist (born Chicago, Illinois, 1969); Thurston Moore, guitar, vocals (born Coral Gables, Florida, 25 July 1958); Lee Ranaldo, guitar, vocals (born Glen Cove, New York, 3 February 1956); Steve Shelley, drums (born Midland, Michigan, 23 June 1962). Former member: Bob Bert, drums.

Genre: Rock

Best-selling album since 1990: *Dirty* (1992)

Hit songs since 1990: "Kool Thing," "100%"

In the 1960s and 1970s New York City produced a number of experimental guitar groups that fused the primal power of rock with high-minded artistic exploration. Sonic Youth represents the last major band of this cycle, with their self-consciously modernistic take on guitar rock and deliberate reinvention of traditional sounds and song structures. The band formed amid the downtown New York avant-garde art scene and borrowed the aesthetics of performance art and free-form jazz to create a strange and dissonant sound that resonated throughout the rock underground. In the 1990s they were lauded as the godfathers of alternative rock and achieved a popularity that seemed unthinkable for such a willfully obscure and challenging band.

Underground Roots

The guitarist Thurston Moore formed Sonic Youth in 1981 with his bassist girlfriend Kim Gordon and a second guitarist, Lee Ranaldo. Gordon had been involved in the art world for some time, graduating with a degree in fine arts from the Otis College of Art and Design in the early 1970s. She later moved to New York and became active in the No Wave scene, an artistic movement that applied a postmodern rejection of traditional structures to popular art forms, including rock music. During this time she organized the "Noise Festival" in which Sonic Youth made their live debut. With the drummer Bob Bert the band recorded the albums *Confusion Is Sex* (1983) and *Bad Moon Rising* (1985), both frenzied and abrasive affairs that feature extended guitar meandering and eerie, poetic vocals. While unfocused and hardly easy listening, the albums were well received in the underground rock circles for their uncompromising experiments with feedback and noise.

Bert exited the band and was replaced by Steve Shelley, and the band released the albums *EVOL* (1986) and *Sister* (1987), which featured a tentative embrace of song structures in addition to atmospheric noise explorations. The band's great leap forward came with the release of *Daydream Nation* (1988), a stunning collection that perfects their mix of artful subversion and emotional texture. The songs on the album are stirring instead of distant, ranging from the tuneful immediacy of "Teenage Riot" to the hallucinatory "Eric's Trip." *Daydream Nation* proved that Sonic Youth was more than just clever noise and that their conceptual structures could convey meaning beyond themselves. The attention generated by the album lead to the band signing a contract with DGC records in 1990.

Kool Things

Goo (1990), their first album for DGC, proved that a band from the underground could retain their artistic integrity on a major label. While not a masterwork like *Daydream Nation*, the record finds the band employing a bigger production budget and tighter arrangements that result in a noisy, cathartic experience. "Kool Thing" proposes a link between the noise experiments of rock and rap with a guest vocal by Public Enemy's Chuck D. Gordon's breathy vocals intertwine with Chuck D's booming baritone for a sexy effect that is enhanced by the warped, competing guitars of Moore and Ranaldo. "Tunic" is a busy epic that imagines Karen Carpenter addressing her family from heaven, and "Dirty Boots" rocks with rare focus and intensity. Overall *Goo* is more muscular than the band's other albums, and rocks in a more conventional yet hardly commercial way.

The band further refined their sound on *Dirty* (1992), which was recorded after a European tour with their newly signed label mates Nirvana. The band hired Butch Vig, who also produced Nirvana's *Nevermind* (1991), to record the album, and the result was a similarly big, professional-sounding production. While viewed as a run at the mainstream, *Dirty* remains a challenging album, full of fractured epics like "Theresa's Sound World" and the political rants "Youth Against Fascism" and "Chapel Hill." Vig's signature style works best when it amplifies Sonic Youth's strengths, such as the teen-lust anthem "100%," whose straight-ahead structure is heightened by fits of squealing noise, and the tuneful explosions of "Wish Fulfillment. " There are also classic Sonic Youth moments of oddly tuned guitar terrorism, such as the frenetic "Purr." *Dirty* may be the band's most accessible work, but it is still lovably twisted.

The band worked with Vig again on *Experimental Jet Set, Trash, and No Star* (1994), their most sedate record to date. Though the record is hardly conventional, the band loses much of their signature feedback and distortion to create a quiet but eerie set of songs. The Gordon-sung "Bull in the Heather" is a pop treasure, and "Self Obsessed and Sexee" charts the life and loves of the city hipsters that the band loves to hate.

Sonic Youth returned a year later with *Washing Machine* (1995), which was hailed as a return to experimental form. While still working within traditional song structures, it exhibits the same ethereal grace as the best moments of *Daydream Nation*, especially on the gorgeous epic "The Diamond Sea." The same year the band headlined Lollapalooza, the annual summer tour of alternative rock's best and brightest, and funneled their profits into the construction of a studio and a record label, SYR Records.

The new studio allowed the band to pursue music at their own pace, and they released the results of this newfound freedom as a series of EPs, beginning with *SYR 1* in 1997. These tonal songs exhibit the same understanding of emotional shadings that made *Daydream Nation* and *Washing Machine* so compelling. The layers of feedback and distortion are traded for exploratory instrumentals, resulting in a work that is gentle and surprisingly tuneful. In 1998 the band recorded *A Thousand Leaves* for DGC. The album is crafted from the same loose sessions, making for the most cerebral work of their major-label career.

Sonic Youth fell into a creative funk on their next releases. First came *Goodbye 20th Century* (1999), a messy and self-indulgent collection of cover versions of classic avant-garde composers. They followed with *NYC Ghosts and Flowers* (2000), an equally frustrating tribute to the more bohemian New York City of past decades. Once again the songs are unfocused and lifeless, and critics wondered if the studio freedom that produced the wonderful *SYR* series had become too much of a good thing.

Back to the Streets

The band answered its critics with the marvelous *Murray Street* (2002), which featured a new member, Jim O'Rourke, a former member of Chicago postrock outfit Gastr del Sol; he produced *NYC Ghosts and Flowers* and *SYR 3* (1998) and was invited to join the band full-time in 2001. O'Rourke's primary contribution is the album's warm, open sound, which he also created for Wilco's masterpiece, *Yankee Hotel Foxtrot* (2001). This organic approach especially suits "The Empty Page," the leadoff track, Sonic Youth's most straightforward song in years. Once again the band finds the perfect balance between experimentation and the comforts of traditional song structure as evidenced in the rousing but gentle "Disconnection Notice" and "Rain on Tin." Even if it took them a while to iron out a workable sound, the collaboration between the band's core and its new member has paid off handsomely.

Sonic Youth doubtless follows a muse, that of the grimy streets of New York's artistic heyday. They have succeeded not only because of their commitment to inventiveness but also because of their humility and willingness to engage in self-criticism, qualities that have helped them to loom large over the rock scene.

SELECTIVE DISCOGRAPHY: *Confusion Is Sex* (Neutral, 1983); *Bad Moon Rising* (Blast First, 1985); *EVOL* (SST, 1986); *Sister* (SST, 1987); *Daydream Nation* (Blast First, 1988); *Goo* (DGC, 1990); *Dirty* (DGC, 1992); *Experimental Jet Set, Trash, and No Star* (DGC, 1994); *Washing Machine* (DGC, 1995); *SYR 1* (SYR,1997); *A Thousand Leaves* (DGC, 1997); *Goodbye 20th Century* (SYR, 1999); *NYC Ghosts and Flowers* (DGC, 2000); *Murray Street* (DGC, 2002).

WEBSITE: www.sonicyouth.com.

SEAN CAMERON

SOUL ASYLUM

Formed: 1981, Minneapolis, Minnesota

Members: Dave Pirner, vocals and guitar (born Green Bay, Wisconsin, 16 April 1964); Dan Murphy, guitars and vocals (born Duluth, Minnesota, 12 July 1962); Karl Mueller, bass and vocals (born Minneapolis, 27 July 1963); Grant Young, drums (born Iowa City, Iowa, 5 January 1964).

Genre: Rock

Best-selling album since 1990: *Grave Dancers Union* (1992)

Hit songs since 1990: "Runaway Train"

A hit album from the early 1990s announced the arrival of Midwest pop/punk quartet Soul Asylum. To longtime fans, the band already had a ten-year history with five albums. Holding onto loyalists while trying to please new fans became Soul Asylum's longstanding conflict in its heyday. Nevertheless, the band became known as one of the most exciting live acts in the decade and the epitome of the Midwestern punk band searching for, then coming to terms with, multiplatinum success.

The foursome were all in their late teens when they came together in Minneapolis under the name Loud Fast Rules. Singer Dave Pirner sat behind the drums but in a matter of years—after a name change and the addition of drummer Grant Young—he moved to the front playing guitar. Minneapolis was the heart of blue collar garage punk, music that became synonymous with the hometown bands the Replacements and Husker Du. Soul Asylum rose on the heels of those bands. Husker Du leader Bob Mould produced the band's 1984 debut *Say What You Will, Clarence . . . Karl Sold the Truck* and it was released on Twin/Tone, the Minneapolis label that had already launched the Replacements.

Soul Asylum's early sound was loud and sloppy melodic rock infused with punk energy and elements of country. Pirner emerged as the band's principal songwriter and, like the Replacements' Paul Westerberg, he fashioned the band's image as a group of blue collar losers with a hidden sensitive side. Soul Asylum spent much of the 1980s establishing itself on Twin/Tone. In 1988, the group released *Hang Time* on the major label A&M Records with which Twin/Tone had a distribution deal. Produced by Lenny Kaye, guitarist for New York art punk songwriter Patti Smith, it was the band's most mature album to date. The band's short tenure on A&M did not result in large enough sales, and when Columbia Records showed interest, the band was released from its contract.

Soul Asylum's Columbia debut, *Grave Dancers Union (1992)*, ended up selling over 1 million copies and earned the band a Top 10 hit song, "Runaway Train." The music was more midtempo and slick than its previous albums; after tabloids reported a romance between Pirner and Hollywood actress Winona Ryder longtime fans felt the band had forsaken its roots.

The two albums that followed did not reach the sales of *Grave Dancers Union*, but continued the band's new direction toward radio-friendly pop. In the 1990s members paused for solo projects. Murphy became a part of Golden Smog, a supergroup featuring participants of other rootsy Midwestern bands including Wilco and the Jayhawks. With Golden Smog, he toured on several occasions and recorded two albums, on which Pirner makes a vocal cameo. In late 2002 Pirner released his first-ever solo album, *Face and Names*. It is a response to living in New Orleans, his newly adopted home. In press interviews, he assured fans that Soul Asylum was still very much alive and healthy.

Even though its early reputation was as the stepchild of wily Twin Cities' punk outfits, the Replacements and Husker Du, Soul Asylum endured, selling over 4 million records and hitting a commercial stride in the early 1990s. Although many lamented the band's straying from its roots, Soul Asylum remained a popular live act that lived up to the spontaneous energy of punk.

SELECTIVE DISCOGRAPHY: *Say What You Will . . . Anything Can Happen* (Twin/Tone, 1984); *Say What You Will, Clarence . . . Karl Sold the Truck* (Twin/Tone, 1984); *While You Were Out* (Twin/Tone, 1984); *Made to Be Broken* (Twin/Tone, 1985); *Time's Incinerator* (Twin/Tone, 1986); *Clam Dip and Other Delights* (Twin/Tone, 1988); *Hang Time* (Arista/Twin/Tone, 1988); *Soul Asylum and the Horse They Rode In On* (Arista/Twin/Tone, 1990); *Grave Dancers Union* (Columbia, 1992); *Let Your Dim Light Shine* (Columbia, 1995); *Candy from a*

Stranger (Columbia, 1998); *Black Gold: The Best of Soul Asylum* (Columbia/Legacy, 2000).

WEBSITE: www.soulasylum.com.

MARK GUARINO

SOUNDGARDEN

Formed: 1984, Seattle, Washington; Disbanded 9 April 1997

Members: Matt Cameron, drums (born San Diego, California, 28 November 1962); Chris Cornell, vocals (born Seattle, Washington, 20 July 1964); Ben Shepherd, bass (born Okinawa, Japan, 20 September 1968); Kim Thayil, guitar (born Seattle, Washington, 4 September 1960). Former members: Scott Sundquist, drums; Hiro Yamamoto, bass (born 13 April 1961).

Genre: Rock

Best-selling album since 1990: *Superunknown* (1994)

Hit songs since 1990: "Outshined," "Black Hole Sun," "Fell On Black Days"

Seattle's grunge movement marked the crossroads of punk and classic rock, but Soundgarden set themselves apart by injecting heavy metal into that already-potent mix. With a sound that combined the sludgy riffs of Black Sabbath with the frenzied spirit of the Stooges, they attracted an audience that found Nirvana's sensitive soulbearing too abrasive and the posturing of pop-metal bands like Poison too silly. Their primary accomplishment lies in bringing heavy metal back to earth: by the late 1980s, the genre had descended into irrelevance with the proliferation of bubble-headed glam-rock outfits. Soundgarden's later work added a dose of psychedelia to the punk metal sound, resulting in a vivid and visceral series of albums that resonated with a loyal following.

The Dawn of Grunge

The roots of Soundgarden extend back to the dawn of the grunge era. Childhood friends Kim Thayil, Hiro Yamamoto, and Bruce Pavitt moved to Olympia, Washington, to attend college after graduating from high school in Illinois in 1981. Thayil and Yamamoto began playing in bands in the burgeoning Seattle underground rock scene, and Pavitt founded a fanzine (a local and independently produced magazine). The fanzine became Sub Pop, the record label that helped to initiate the grunge explosion. Yamamoto, a bassist, founded a band with his roommate, vocalist Chris Cornell, and the pair recruited Thayil to play guitar. They added Scott Sundquist on drums and chose the name Soundgarden. Over the next two years the band hit the Seattle club circuit and earned a devoted following; they eventually replaced Sundquist with Matt Cameron.

The band signed to Pavitt's newly formed label and released the EP *Screaming Life* in 1987. The cover photograph captures what became the archetypal grunge image: Cornell in midwail, his long hair falling wildly over his shoulders. The music on *Screaming Life* is similarly striking, driven by Thayil's swirling guitar chords and Cornell's grandiose, rock-god vocals. The plodding assault of "Hunted Down" and the tense "Tears to Forget" provide the clearest examples of their developing sound, with thudding guitars propelled by punk rock rhythms. The sound is at once familiar and strange, with the signature repetition of metal applied to the deliberately twisted song structures of underground rock. They jumped to the legendary punk label SST for their first full-length album, *Ultramega O.K.* (1988). The album finds the band becoming much more comfortable with their fusion of metal theatrics and punk fire, but the material tends to wallow in its own sludgy texture. What sets the album apart from *Screaming Life* is the psychedelic flavor of songs like "Flower" and "Head Injury" and Thayil's growing prowess as a muscular, inventive guitarist.

Soundgarden continued in the punk-metal vein on their major label debut *Louder Than Love* (1989). The cover photo of Cornell careening on stage harks back to the image that graces *Screaming Life*, but with more inspired energy, and the music follows suit. "Ugly Truth" opens the album with an aggressive guitar attack that provides appropriately grand accompaniment for Cornell's otherworldly howl. Cornell's vocal dynamics veer from high-pitched screech to a low, mournful croon, a range that lends the imposing music an emotional texture usually absent from metal. Cornell chants, "If you were mine to give / I might throw it away" over a barrage of Thayil's psychedelic notes. "Loud Love" and "Hands All Over" surge with Thayil's deep grooves, and "Gun" seethes with rare anger. Despite the band's increasing success and growing audience, Yamamoto left Soundgarden to return to school; he was replaced in early 1990 by Ben Shepherd.

Breaking Out of the Cage

Soundgarden's third album, *Badmotorfinger* (1991), proved to be a major creative leap forward, their breakthrough work. The album was released on the cusp of the grunge revolution, in which punk-influenced rock from Seattle surged in mainstream popularity; the band's association with the city brought them a great deal of media attention. *Grunge* became a catchall term for any guitar-based rock recorded by younger bands, and many groups bristled at the misleading label. The grunge hype, however, could not diminish the artistic strength of *Badmotorfinger*, a focused and confident set that stands among the best albums by the Seattle pack.

Badmotorfinger opens with "Rusty Cage," an intense, jittery rocker that announces the arrival of Soundgarden's evolving sound with the defiant chorus "I'm gonna break my rusty cage / And run!" Thayil's guitar commands attention as he strips away the sludge of his previous work and conjures a wiry and rhythmic approach that refocuses the band's music with a new energy. This dynamic, coupled with Cornell's bold vocals, sends songs like the darkly anxious "Jesus Christ Pose" into the stratosphere and makes for their most consistent and ambitious set of songs. Indeed, despite the growing commercial viability of grunge, *Badmotorfinger* represents Soundgarden's most arty and cerebral work, and the hard-hitting approach connected with an audience in need of new, heavier thrills. "Outshined," the band's first major single, crystallizes the frustrations of the "slacker generation" with its deathless lyrics ("I got up feeling so down") and catchy, rhythmic attack. "Room a Thousand Years Wide" is an atmospheric epic that reinvents the mysticism of Led Zeppelin for the postmodern age ("Listen, hear, he is inside / One who lives while others lie"), and the nervy "Drawing Flies" pulses with the intensity of the best punk rock. *Badmotorfinger* helped to define the public's perception of grunge, but it also placed Soundgarden outside of any simple categorization.

Soundgarden spent the next two years on tour, including a stint on Perry Farrell's well-timed Lollapalooza festival. In that summer of 1992 the band won more followers with their savage set, which included a reading of Body Count's controversial antipolice anthem "Cop Killer. "

Touring and the surprise success of *Temple of the Dog* (an album recorded with the members of Pearl Jam) led to a commercial blockbuster, Soundgarden's fourth album, *Superunknown* (1994). The album debuted at number one on the pop album charts and produced the hit singles "Spoonman" and "Black Hole Sun." *Superunknown* finds the band branching out even further into eclectic territory, abandoning metal almost entirely to perfect their union of postpunk and psychedelic pop. Freed from the blitzkrieg guitars of *Louder Than Love*, the record showcases Soundgarden at their most experimental and compelling. Thayil tones down his guitar to a skeletal riff for the aching "Fell on Black Days " and ratchets up for "The Day I Tried to Live." The album's key track, however, is the mind-bending "Black Hole Sun," a classic of neopsychedelia that matches rubbery guitars to morbid yet colorful lyrics ("Black hole sun / Won't you come / And wash away the rain?"). The album is a sprawling, nuanced work, featuring their most accomplished songwriting and their most vivid production techniques.

Soundgarden's next album, *Down on the Upside* (1996), was a less ambitious production than *Superunk-*

nown. Although stripped down, it hardly represents a return to their former sound. Instead, the band focuses on tight song craft, eschewing the sonic detail of their previous two records and letting the laser-sharp structures speak for themselves. The effect is dark and jarring, with an unadorned anger that, whether intentional or not, provides the logical endpoint of grunge. "Pretty Noose" features one of Cornell's most inspirational vocals, with angular guitar work by Thayil. "Ty Cobb" is the most spare and cutting song in their catalog, and "Blow Up the Outside World" provides a bleak, bare-knuckle update of their signature epic approach. *Down on the Upside* is a troubling work, crafted in the teeth of significant intraband tension; it sounds like a breakup in process. The band toured in support of the record and announced their split the following year.

In 1997, the band released *A-Sides,* a retrospective that included every single from their recording career. The set provides a clear view of their rise from protogrunge innovators to ambitious sonic explorers. Thayil contributed his signature guitar work to a number of obscure acts, Matt Cameron joined Pearl Jam, and Cornell embarked on a solo career. After issuing the largely ignored album *Euphoria Morning* in 1999, Cornell resurfaced as the front man of Audioslave, a band he formed with the former members of Rage Against the Machine.

Soundgarden will likely be remembered for the experimental neopsychedelia of *Badmotorfinger* and *Superunknown,* and for their stature as one of Seattle's big three (along with Nirvana and Pearl Jam, despite the bands' marked musical differences). Like the best bands of the grunge explosion, they transcended the constrictions of the genre to produce timeless music.

SELECTIVE DISCOGRAPHY: *Screaming Life* (Sub Pop, 1987); *Fopp* (Sub Pop, 1988); *Ultramega O.K.* (SST, 1988); *Louder than Love* (A&M, 1988); *Badmotorfinger* (A&M, 1991); *Superunknown* (A&M, 1994); *Down on the Upside* (A&M, 1996); *A-Sides* (A&M, 1997).

SEAN CAMERON

BRITNEY SPEARS

Born: Kentwood, Louisiana, 2 December 1981
Genre: Rock, Pop
Best-selling album since 1990: . . . *Baby One More Time* (1999)

Hit songs since 1990: ". . . Baby One More Time," "Oops! . . . I Did It Again," "I'm a Slave 4 U"

Britney Spears skyrocketed to stardom in the late 1990s with catchy pop tunes and a canny

Britney Spears [PAUL NATKIN/PHOTO RESERVE]

PR/media blitz. Her music videos displayed a frankly sexual demeanor, playing upon the duality of youthful innocence and sexual promiscuity. Controversial as this was, considering that Spears was sixteen years old at the time of her first hit, ". . . Baby One More Time," this erotic alchemy made her a superstar. She has appeared on the cover of *Rolling Stone* four times, performed at the MTV Video Music Awards, and starred in the movie *Crossroads* (2002). Although Spears attempted to break new musical ground in her third album, *Britney* (2001), working with new producers and co-writing several songs, many critics have dismissed her as a manufactured pop icon.

Early Ambition

Spears was raised in Louisiana by her mother, Lynne, an elementary-school teacher, and her father, Jamie, a building contractor. The second of three children, Spears showed an early interest in music and dance, and was soon appearing in local talent shows and choirs. She auditioned for The Disney Channel's *Mickey Mouse Club* at the age of eight but was too young to join the cast. However, she was encouraged to continue her training, and she spent the next three summers in New York studying the performing arts. Spears landed a role in the off-Broadway play

Ruthless, appeared in several commercials, and won as a contestant on *Star Search.* With this added experience, she was granted a spot in the *Mickey Mouse Club* and moved to Orlando, Florida, for two years. During this time she met Justin Timberlake and Joshua "JC" Chasez, also regulars on the show, who later joined the boy band *NSYNC.

Still a young teenager, Spears auditioned with Jive Records and was teamed with several songwriters and producers: Eric Foster White, who had previously worked with Whitney Houston, and the Swedish team of Max Martin and Rami, producers for the Backstreet Boys. Despite its various influences, Spears's first album . . . *Baby One More Time* (1999) was consistent in tone, style, and production, balanced with upbeat pop tunes and innocent ballads.

Eric Foster White contributed songs traversing different musical styles, from the frothy "Soda Pop" to the clever remake of "The Beat Goes On." The ballad "From the Bottom of My Broken Heart" was especially suitable for the young singer. Buoyed by a prominent acoustic guitar, lush synthesizer textures, and backup singers, Spears projected confidence in her vocal delivery. The line "You were my first love, you were my true love" projected the image of Spears as a young woman grappling with typical adolescent ordeals and endeared her to a generation of young fans. While White offered memorable ballads and a variety of stylistic challenges, Max Martin produced the formula for her success.

". . . Baby One More Time" presents a catchy pop beat, initiated by an acoustic piano and carried into the rhythm section. The melodic line emphasizes Spears's low vocal register and cleverly displays internal rhymes in the verse: "Show me how you want it to be. Tell me baby." The bridge reiterates the piano textures from the introduction, creating an atmospheric and intimate moment that builds to the final chorus. The forceful and provocative lyrics, "Hit me baby one more time," are accompanied by an unforgettable melodic oscillation, providing the hook for Spears's first big hit.

Like many of her pop predecessors, Spears aired her songs and honed her performing skills on a brief tour of shopping malls. After the release of her first single, ". . . Baby One More Time," in October 1998, Spears earned a spot as an opening act for *NYSNC's winter tour. Although the media spotlight was directed toward boy bands in the late 1990s (especially the Backstreet Boys, *NSYNC, and Hanson), the phenomenon of "girl power" was beginning to blossom. Building upon the success of the Spice Girls and their playful sensuality, Spears insured her iconic status with a video in which she danced through high school hallways, suggestively revealing her midriff in a Catholic-school uniform.

Spot Light

2000 MTV Video Music Awards

In support of her album, *Oops! . . . I Did It Again,* Britney Spears performed at the 2000 MTV Video Music Awards. Spears began her act sedately, singing her pop rendition of the Rolling Stones's "Satisfaction." Wearing a suit and tie costume, she appeared to be taking a dignified approach. With a quick gesture, Spears shocked the audience with an onstage costume change, tearing off her black suit to reveal a glittery skin-toned outfit. The music immediately shifted to "Oops! . . . I Did It Again," allowing Spears to proclaim, "I'm not that innocent."

This momentary façade of nudity reaffirmed and epitomized the image of Spears as a youthful provocateur who had capitulated to the commercial imperatives of a sex-driven music industry. Although Christina Aguilera adopted Spears's method of sexual exhibition, a host of other female performers consciously avoided this mode of frank display.

Spears has consistently juxtaposed these two identities—the innocent ingenue and the sexy provocateur—in her songs, videos, and numerous media publications. In 1999 she was featured on the cover of *Rolling Stone* in a decidedly revealing pose, lying on a bed with a black bikini top while grasping a stuffed animal and talking on the phone. This combination of teenage purity and sexuality worried many parents and, for the same reason, enraptured many fans.

Pop Phenomenon

By the end of her highly successful summer tour, Spears had become a pop phenomenon. She released three followup songs, "Sometimes," "From the Bottom of My Broken Heart," and "(You Drive Me) Crazy"; she garnered four awards at the 1999 MTV Europe Music Awards. During breaks from touring and promoting, Spears managed to record new songs for her second album. *Oops! . . . I Did It Again* (2000) largely features the work of Max Martin and Rami and repeats many of the song themes of the first album, from the everyday girl of "Don't Let Me Be the Last to Know" and "Dear Diary" to the self-assured young woman of "Oops! . . . I Did It Again" and "Stronger."

The title track proved to be the strongest hit from the album, although it barely crept into the *Billboard*'s Top 10. "Oops! . . . I Did It Again" was a pop proclamation of inadvertent sexual power. Spears declares, "I'm not that innocent" while repeatedly uttering "oops" in a coquettish manner. The song itself displayed typical pop textures in many ways similar to her first hit. Unique to this song is the bridge, which takes the form of a narrative sequence referring to the blockbuster movie *Titanic* (1997).

"Stronger" reveals her independent side with a strident beat, synthesized bass sounds, and slightly distorted vocal effects. The chorus states, "I'm stronger than yesterday" and leads into the verse with a melodic ascent and an emphasis on the word "stronger." This sentiment is repeated in the song "Don't Go Knockin' on My Door," which declares, "I don't need nobody, better off alone." Spears transforms the Rolling Stones' raucous anthem "Satisfaction" into a benign, finger-snapping song that is prefaced with a phone call dialogue between Spears and a friend. This unsuccessful cover invited harsh criticism from rock musicians and critics alike. "Don't Let Me Be the Last to Know" has a pleasant melody with an interesting harmonic progression, but the remainder of the songs were innocuous, hastily crafted, and numbingly formulaic.

Her third album, *Britney* (2001), reveals a different side of Spears. Rather than repeating herself, she teamed up with the producers N*E*R*D (formerly the Neptunes), who infused her album with dance-club textures and R&B grooves. In "I'm a Slave 4 U," Spears adopts a darker vocal tone with a repeated vocal slide on "slave." This approach is repeated in "Boys," with its overt references to Janet Jackson's "Nasty Boys" and "Control." These darker textures allowed Spears to adopt a self-assertive stance, singing "Let's turn this dance floor into our own little nasty world." Spears contributed to the songwriting process in "Lonely," "Anticipating," "Let Me Be," and "That's Where You Take Me." For the rest of the songs, Spears again relied upon Max Martin and Rami, who crafted "Overprotected," with its hip-hop-influenced bridge, and "Bombastic Love." Unfortunately, Martin and Rami produced yet another coming-of-age ballad for Spears in the insipid "I'm Not a Girl, Not Yet a Woman."

Although Spears attempted to break new musical ground in *Britney,* the album did not sell as well as its predecessors. Moreover, she had to contend with an anti-Britney movement that perceived her as a manufactured pop icon. Gossip columns ruthlessly charted her relationships with Justin Timberlake, Fred Durst of Limp Bizkit, and others, while new female stars challenged Spears's preeminence. Christina Aguilera stressed an R&B

aesthetic, Avril Lavigne produced music with a harder edge, and Pink stated outright in her single "Don't Let Me Get Me," "Sick of being compared to damn Britney Spears." Spears contributed to the music industry's renewed focus on female performers and songwriters. In meeting these personal and professional challenges, Spears sustained a booming and unflagging popularity.

SELECTIVE DISCOGRAPHY: . . . *Baby One More Time* (Jive, 1999); *Oops! . . . I Did It Again* (Jive, 2000); *Britney* (Jive, 2001).

SELECTIVE FILMOGRAPHY: *Crossroads* (2002).

BIBLIOGRAPHY: B. Spears, *Stages* (Chicago, 2002).

WEBSITES: www.britneyspears.com; www.britney.com.

WYNN YAMAMI

THE SPICE GIRLS

Formed: 1993, Maidenhead, Berkshire, England

Members: Victoria Beckham, vocals (born Victoria Adams, Essex, England, 7 April 1975); Mel B., vocals (born Melanie Brown, Leeds, England, 29 May 1975); Emma Bunton, vocals (born London, 21 January 1976); Mel C., vocals (born Melanie Chisolm, Liverpool, England, 12 January 1976). Former member: Geri Halliwell, vocals (born Watford, England, 7 August 1972).

Genre: Rock, Pop

Best-selling album since 1990: *Spice* (1996)

Hit songs since 1990: "Wannabe," "2 Become 1," "Spice Up Your Life"

The Spice Girls represent the first important manufactured girl group of the 1990s, drawn as they were from auditions prompted by a 1993 advertisement in the London-based theatrical weekly *The Stage*, which called for the creation of a hit female act. The group raised interesting questions about the role of women and the role of gender in pop music making. Until they emerged, the debate about the domination of popular music by male musicians and the marginalization of women had focused principally on rock. In addition, the Spice Girls briefly suggested that the golden days of British music might return. As mid-1990s British pop music promised to repeat some of the glories of the British Invasion of 1964 to 1966, when a Beatles-led assault stirred unprecedented interest in music from the United Kingdom, this all-singing, all-dancing quintet hit the jackpot with its debut single "Wannabe." The song not only hit the top spot in United Kingdom and in twenty-one other countries, but it was also the first time since 1964—when the Animals struck with "House of the Rising Sun"—that a debut single by a British act had topped American music charts.

Wannabes on the Rise

The brainchild of Simon Fuller, who had managed former Eurythmics lead singer Annie Lennox, the Spice Girls took root in 1993 when an advertisement sought young women to try out for a new group: "RU 18–23 with the ability to sing/dance? RU streetwise, outgoing, ambitious and dedicated?" The successful applicants set up home in Maidenhead, Kent, initially under the name of Touch. Geri Halliwell, Melanie Chisolm, Victoria Adams, and Melanie Brown formed the initial core but were joined later by Emma Bunton. After two years of hard rehearsal and relative obscurity, the group was signed by Richard Branson's Virgin Records in 1995. A combination of astute management and promotion and the selection of an outstanding first single, "Wannabe," saw the Spice Girls attain the number one place on U.K. music charts in July 1996. The record spent twenty-five weeks in the Top 75.

After the success of "Wannabe," fame came quickly and easily for the group. In March 1997 when the double A side (a pair of tracks released on the same disc which typically combine a sentimental ballad with an assertive rant) "Mama" / "Who Do You Think You Are" became their fourth number one in succession in the United Kingdom, the Spice Girls surpassed a record previously held by Gerry and the Pacemakers and Frankie Goes to Hollywood, whose debut trio of singles had topped the charts. In December 1997 they extended their sequence of British chart-toppers to six; only a number two placing for "Stop" in 1998 halted the run. By this time, the group had also caught America's imagination, as "Wannabe" became the most successful debut single in America by a British act.

The premise for the Spice Girls' success was a blend of potent pop songs—ranging from lush romantic pop to Motown pastiche, ersatz street rap to Latin extravaganza, all penned by a team of Sheffield-based writers and producers—and the most skillful of marketing strategies, which exploited a series of nicknames the five girls were given by British pop publication, *Top of the Pops*, early in their careers. Halliwell became Ginger Spice, a reference to her hair color; Chisolm, Sporty Spice, a comment on her athleticism; Emma, Baby Spice, a remark on her infant-like appearance; Adams, Posh Spice, referring to her aspirational and sartorial tendencies; and Brown, Scary Spice, a comment on her rugged and uncompromising nature. Their management established personality profiles for the five members, which became a key factor in selling the act globally. Fans around the world could speedily connect with the five distinct individuals whose traits were stressed in interviews, promotional images, and videos.

In a broader sense, the group became closely associated with the notion of the Halliwell-inspired term, "girl power," the sense that the Spice Girls stood for a new era of independence for young girls and young women. This slogan quickly proved to be little more than that, although the campaign did appear to bring ideas of sex and sexuality to even younger audiences, prompting, in part, the emergence of a new generation of liberated teen performers such as Britney Spears and Christina Aguilera.

At a time when traditional U.K. rock bands like Oasis and Blur were trying to ride the new Britpop wave in the United States, utilizing traditional means of touring and gigging, the Spice Girls' formula, which utilized the members' diverse personalities to win media attention, was more instantly effective. "Wannabe"'s huge international impact laid the ground for a string of subsequent singles that would also make a sizable impact, and within half a decade, the group had sold 35 million albums and 25 million singles worldwide. In the process, they employed another important selling device to spread the gospel: their 1998 release *Spiceworld: The Movie*. It carried echoes of an earlier pop age when Elvis Presley, the Beatles, and others became involved in a number of career-boosting, big-screen projects. The film paid homage to the 1960s format, marrying elements of the Beatles' *A Hard Day's Night* and the Monkees' television series.

Managerial Split and Solo Projects

But by 1998 the astonishing momentum that had fueled the Spice Girls to record-breaking achievement and success on stage and in movie theaters was beginning to ebb. Disagreements with manager Fuller led to a split—he went on to launch a new act, S Club 7, and an accompanying television show—and the announcement that the members would manage themselves. Not long after, Halliwell, the older, driving force behind much of what they did, revealed her intention to quit and go solo. Her two solo albums have spawned a string of hits including a debut number one in the United Kingdom, "Look at Me."

The subsequent years proved to be quieter but hardly uneventful. The period saw the four-piece group continue to record and perform, if intermittently. In 2000 their ninth U.K. number one hit with the R&B-influenced "Holler." Additionally, solo projects have been pursued by all group members. Chisolm's solo career has included collaborative work with Bryan Adams and the late Lisa "Left-Eye" Lopes on "Never Be the Same Again." Brown has worked alongside Missy Elliott on the single "I Want You Back" (1998). That same year she was briefly married to dancer Jimmy Gulzar and for a short time adopted the name Mel G.

Adams. Brown, the only Spice Girl not to achieve a solo number one, has nonetheless become in Britain the most famous member of all. Married to England's premier soccer player, David Beckham of Manchester United in 1999, she is now the one Spice Girl most likely to be found in the pages of celebrity and gossip magazines, rivaling the media attention that Princess Diana enjoyed at her height.

Although no official announcements were made about the actual demise of the act, the Spice Girls appeared, at best, to be a dormant group, but as a brand they retained the status and potential selling power they had earned during their greatest years. In early 2003, rumors of a possible return surfaced, but were speedily dismissed by Mel C. While their naïve, postfeminist manifesto seems to have been little more than a brilliant marketing tool, the ability of five young British women to take on the U.S. music scene and win some notable victories cannot be overlooked. They have inspired dozens of U.K. imitators from All Saints to the Sugarbabes and Atomic Kitten. The Spice Girls have shown that while they may have relied on a formula, there was also a business alchemy built on a team of skillful writers and producers and astute promotion that has been almost impossible to replicate.

SELECTIVE DISCOGRAPHY: *Spice* (Virgin, 1996); *Spiceworld* (Virgin, 1997); *Forever* (Virgin, 2000).

SIMON WARNER

BRUCE SPRINGSTEEN

Born: Freehold, New Jersey, 23 September 1949

Genre: Rock

Best-selling album since 1990: *The Rising* (2002)

Hit songs since 1990: "Streets of Philadelphia," "Secret Garden," "The Rising"

With a career that spans more than four decades, Bruce Springsteen remains one of America's most popular—and populist—rock songwriters and performers. The popularity of his working-class sensibility is reflected in the tens of millions of albums he has sold. Springsteen has maintained a connection to fans by evoking the struggles and dreams of average Americans through music known for both lyrical depth and a hard-rock backbeat. While early critics hailed him as a successor to Bob Dylan, the folk-rock auteur of the 1960s, Springsteen made evident his direct debt to Woody Guthrie, the folk music radical of the 1930s, and to rock originators such as Roy Orbison and Chuck Berry. Backed by the expansive E Street Band—whose core personnel has, for the most part, remained the same since

Bruce Springsteen [PAUL NATKIN/PHOTO RESERVE]

his club days in the early 1970s—Springsteen is known for marathon live shows in which he translates the private experiences of his songs into stadium-sized euphoria.

Early Career

One of two children, Springsteen was born into a middle-class family. He skipped college after high school and moved to New York City. After discovering he was too late for the legendary folk scene in the city's Greenwich Village district, he returned to New Jersey and settled in Asbury Park. The dying coastal town became the mythic backdrop of his songs. Springsteen returned to Greenwich Village to play acoustic solo gigs, but mostly he played with several club bands in Asbury Park before forming the E Street Band. He was eventually signed to Columbia Records by John Hammond Sr., the industry veteran who also discovered legends such as the jazz singer Billie Holiday, the swing jazz bandleader Count Basie, and Bob Dylan.

Greetings from Asbury Park, N.J. and *The Wild, the Innocent & the E Street Shuffle* indeed bore traces of Dylan, including wildly hallucinatory lyrics and story songs featuring misfit characters on the fringe.

Breakthrough

Although they received favorable reviews, both sold poorly. Springsteen's breakthrough came with *Born to Run* in 1975. The album features the immortal "Tenth Avenue Freeze-Out," along with seven other songs set within a sweeping sonic backdrop. Its production is similar to the "Wall of Sound" technique of the 1960s producer Phil Spector. Springsteen's epic-sounding album became a Top 10 hit, and Springsteen was praised for bringing back classic rock at a time when heavy metal and progressive art rock reigned.

Over the next few years Springsteen expanded his musical range, but only slightly. He recorded the lean and gritty rock album *Darkness on the Edge of Town* in 1978 and followed it up with the two-album set *The River*, which again presents Springsteen as a serious chronicler of working-class drama. But, if only to show off the E Street Band's ensemble sound, it features several bar band party jams.

In 1982 Springsteen countered his image as a rock band front man with *Nebraska*. Originally meant to be demos (they were recorded on a four-track cassette machine at his home), the rough recordings feature Springsteen by himself, singing first-person narratives set in rural America. The ten songs were compared to the work of the short-story writer Raymond Carver for their gothic themes and attention to detail.

Commercial Peak

Springsteen's commercial peak came with the 1984 album *Born in the U.S.A.*, which sold more than 20 million copies and led to a two-year-long stadium tour. Seven of its twelve songs were hit singles. The cover art features a picture of Springsteen's backside shot in front of an American flag; the title song recounts the agony of a Vietnam veteran who feels left behind by his country. The album's slick production and heavy synthesizers broadened Springsteen's pop appeal, but many long-time fans were dismayed: The music lacked the edge or tension found in Springsteen's previous recordings.

The title song and the album were interpreted by some as a pledge to a type of patriotic fervor represented by the "Morning in America" campaign, President Ronald Reagan's agenda to restore conservative values in the United States. Springsteen was asked by Reagan staff to endorse the president's 1984 reelection bid and to lend the song to the cause. When he refused, Reagan invoked Springsteen in his speeches anyway; Springsteen publicly expressed doubts that Reagan had listened to *Nebraska*, the set of songs thought to represent the dark side of the country's economy by giving voice to those on the bottom rungs of the ladder.

Springsteen spent the early 1990s trying to come to terms with the larger-than-life image spawned during the 1980s. In 1991 he married his backup singer, Patty Scialfa, after divorcing his first wife, the actress Julianne Phillips. The breakup of his first marriage is thought to be the driving force bind his *Tunnel of Love* (1987), which dwells on the dark underpinnings of relationships.

Exploring New Directions

Entering the decade and a new marriage, Springsteen looked for ways to realign his life in other ways as well. Much to his fans' surprise, he moved from New Jersey to posh Beverly Hills. He also fired the E Street Band, explaining he wanted to experiment with other musicians. In 1992 he released two albums, *Human Touch* and *Lucky Town*, both recorded by himself and studio musicians, including Scialfa and the E Street pianist Roy Bittan. The heavily textured *Human Touch* continued in the style of somber introspection laced with synthesizers that he showcased on *Tunnel of Love*. *Lucky Town* was a hardy collection of generic rockers. Most critics and fans balked, and the two albums are widely considered the least successful of his career. Springsteen did tour to support both records, but he went on the road with an entirely new band. The result of that period was the European release of an MTV *Unplugged* appearance he taped while on the road.

By this point, the alternative rock era was in full swing with new bands such as Nirvana, Alice in Chains, the Smashing Pumpkins, and Pearl Jam dominating the charts. For the first time in his career, Springsteen was a veteran artist unable to attract a new generation of fans. He transformed himself from a rock bandleader back into the singer/songwriter of *Nebraska*. In 1993 he released "The Streets of Philadelphia," a song written for the Tom Hanks film *Philadelphia* and sung from the perspective of a person suffering from AIDS. It resulted in an Oscar for best song and five Grammy awards.

The solitary spirit of the song was a natural bridge to his next album, *The Ghost of Tom Joad* (1995), a collection of personal and political narratives of the dispossessed named for a central character in *The Grapes of Wrath*, John Steinbeck's novel of the Great Depression.

After a solo tour Springsteen sought to reconnect himself to his glory days. He was inducted into the Rock and Roll Hall of Fame in 1999 and the same year reunited with the E Street Band for a triumphant tour that continued through 2000. Refusing to play only his greatest hits, Springsteen juggled the set list each night, adding in obscurities from his early albums, occasional covers, and a new song, "American Skin (41 Shots)." Written in response to the shooting death of a twenty-year-old West African immigrant, Amadou Diallo, by New York City police officers, the song sparked controversy as it challenged the image of Springsteen as a flag-waver for the status quo.

Around this time, Springsteen began to flood the market with products to capitalize on his newfound stature as a heritage artist. Along with a greatest hits CD in 1995, he released *Songs*, a coffee-table book of handwritten lyrics, *Tracks*, a four-CD boxed set of outtakes, and *Live in New York City*, a concert from his reunion tour.

By the time Springsteen stepped into the studio to record with the E Street Band for the first time since 1984, the terrorist attacks of September 11 had taken place. In 2002 Springsteen released the result of those sessions, *The Rising*. Although its accompanying media blitz informed the public it was written directly in response to September 11, the music was nuanced. The songs recapture the bar-band fraternity of the E Street Band. Unlike many jingoistic songs prevalent at the time, *The Rising* paused to examine subtle areas. The song "Worlds Apart" involves

<table><tr><td>

Spot Light | *The Ghost of Tom Joad*

Bruce Springsteen's dilemma in the 1990s was to find a way to reinvigorate his songwriter sensibilities after playing the rock megastar. The two albums with which he entered the decade—*Human Touch* and *Lucky Town*—were criticized for not taking risks and sounding like a rehashing of his mid-career commercial successes such as *The River.* That's why, when *The Ghost of Tom Joad* hit stores in 1995, it threw a curve to fans conditioned to expect more of the same. The album was far from commercial. A bookend to *Nebraska,* it features twelve quiet character songs that place the listener inside the marginal worlds of illegal immigrants, Vietnam vets, migrant workers, and prisoners trying to go straight. With a title character plucked from *The Grapes of Wrath*—John Steinbeck's 1939 novel of the plight of migrant workers during the Great Depression—and a somber spirit that evoked the songs of early American folk songwriter Woody Guthrie, Springsteen evokes an earlier era of folk-music storytelling, drawing attention to life on the fringes and infusing it with dignity. The album allowed Springsteen to try a different performing tactic. He set off on a solo tour, playing small theaters across the country. Onstage in front of quiet rooms, he transformed some of his early rock hits into quiet folk ballads. That included the song "Born in the U.S.A.," which he softened and transformed into a nightmarish blues song. *The Ghost of Tom Joad* also helped Springsteen connect to a younger generation. In 2000, on their album *Renegades,* the political rap/rock band Rage Against the Machine recorded a cover of the title song, turning the song into an intense rock anthem.

</td></tr></table>

former, and a complex political troubadour. It is his unflinching humanity that makes his music compelling.

SELECTIVE DISCOGRAPHY: *Greetings from Asbury Park, N.J.* (Columbia, 1973); *The Wild, the Innocent and the E Street Shuffle* (Columbia, 1973); *Born to Run* (Columbia, 1975); *Darkness on the Edge of Town* (Columbia, 1978); *The River* (Columbia, 1980); *Nebraska* (Columbia, 1982); *Born in the U.S.A.* (Columbia, 1984); *Live 1975–1985* (box set, Columbia, 1985); *Tunnel of Love* (Columbia, 1987); *Chimes of Freedom* (EP, Columbia, 1988); *Lucky Town* (Columbia, 1992); *Human Touch* (Columbia, 1992); *Greatest Hits* (Columbia, 1995); *The Ghost of Tom Joad* (Columbia, 1995); *MTV Plugged* (Columbia, 1997); *Tracks* (box set, Columbia, 1998); *Live in New York City* (Columbia, 2001); *The Rising* (Columbia, 2002).

WEBSITES: www.brucespringsteen.net; www.backstreets.com.

MARK GUARINO

SQUIRREL NUT ZIPPERS

Formed: 1993, Efland, North Carolina

Members: Jim Mathus, vocals, guitar, tenor banjo, trombone (born Clarksdale, Mississippi); Katherine Whalen, vocals, banjo, baritone ukelele (born Greenville, North Carolina, 24 April 1968); Tom Maxwell, vocals, guitar, baritone saxophone, clarinet, resonator (born, TK); Ken Mosher, guitar, alto and baritone saxophone, vocals (born St. Louis, Missouri); Chris Phillips, drums, percussion, backing vocals (born 19 June 1969); Don Raleigh, bass; Je Widenhouse, trumpet (joined band in August 1996).

Genre: Rock, Pop

Best-selling album since 1990: *Hot* (1997)

Hit songs since 1990: "Hell," "Put a Lid on It," "Suits Are Picking Up the Bill"

Named for the old-time candy, Squirrel Nut Zippers offered a blend of swing, blues, country, and jazz that became popular in the mid-1990s, around the same time as the swing revival. The Zippers' unusual, energetic music is reminiscent of the 1930s and 1940s. Their seven members are multi-instrumentalists who use old-time instruments such as banjo and ukelele to create a special sound.

Jim Mathus and Katherine Whalen, a married couple, formed Squirrel Nut Zippers in 1993 after leaving Chapel Hill, North Carolina, for the small town Efland, where they bought a farmhouse. They met the locals Don Raleigh, Chris Phillips, Ken Mosher, and Tom Maxwell.

the hardship between lovers of different religious traditions, and "Paradise" opens with the perspective of a suicide bomber. *The Rising* won a 2003 Grammy as the year's best rock album.

Bruce Springsteen is a lyricist of depth, an introspective singer/songwriter, a renowned arena rock per-

"Hell"

"Hell," by Squirrel Nut Zippers, was a surprise alternative-music hit from their breakthrough album *Hot* (1997). The song had the timing needed to take a band to the next level. The song is not a swing song and is more akin to a samba, and the subject matter of death and the afterlife is more aligned with classic blues music, yet "Hell" peaked at number thirteen on the *Billboard* Modern Rock tracks because of its association with swing music. The Zippers capitalized on the momentum of the sleeper indie film *Swingers* (1996), which introduced a new generation to the culture of swing music. The renewed interest extended to Generation Xers who enrolled in swing dance classes and developed a fascination with martinis and lounge music. After the Zippers hit it big with "Hell," other similar retro bands became popular, including Big Bad Voodoo Daddy, thanks to its placement on the successful *Swingers* soundtrack. Ironically, the Zippers are now associated with the swing-culture revival of the mid-to-late 1990s even though their music is far too eclectic to fit into that pigeonhole.

After a few months playing together, they made their debut in Chapel Hill and started to gather a strong following in the South. The alternative label Mammoth, based in North Carolina, signed them, and their second album, *Hot*, went platinum, thanks to the strength of the song "Hell." Their follow-up, *Perennial Favorites*, achieved gold status. The band's sound is typified by the samba-blues song "Hell." Rhythmically propelled by horns and zany, theatrical singing, it is a frightful tale of the afterlife.

Perennial Favorites (1998) carries on the same musical melange and yielded a hit with the slightly cynical swinger, "Suits Are Pickin' Up the Bill." In mid-1999 Tom Maxwell left the band to pursue other interests. In 2000, with the release of *Bedlam Ballroom*, it seemed that the band was verging on self-parody, and lackluster sales and a lukewarm critical reception suggested that the band's appeal was beginning to wane. Although Mathus and Whelan had both released solo albums by 2000, the climate of pop music had changed, with attention shifting to boy bands and teen-pop queens. *Bedlam Ballroom* barely

made an impact; its peak position on the *Billboard 200* album chart was 195.

Squirrel Nut Zippers rode their offbeat, eccentric wave through the mid- to late 1990s and emerged with a legion of fans and a platinum album.

SELECTIVE DISCOGRAPHY: *The Inevitable Squirrel Nut Zippers* (Mammoth, 1995); *Hot* (Mammoth, 1997); *Perennial Favorites* (Mammoth, 1999); *Bedlam Ballroom* (Mammoth, 2000).

WEBSITE: www.snzippers.com.

CARRIE HAVRANEK

ST. GERMAIN

Born: Ludovic Navarre; Boulogne-Billancourt, France
Genre: Electronica
Best-selling album since 1990: *Tourist* (2000)
Hit songs since 1990: "Rose Rouge," "Deep in It," "Montego Bay Spleen"

Noted composer, producer, and mix master Ludovic Navarre, known by his stage name St. Germain, became one of the leading names in the rising French electronic music scene of the late 1990s. His pioneering style mixed modern dance-music styles like house and electronica with jazz elements.

As a teenager, St. Germain loved sailing and windsurfing. St. Germain began experimenting with music mixing with a computer he received while recovering from an accident. From his early testing, St. Germain became a fanatic, slowly incorporating many of the influences he grew up with such as jazz and blues. St. Germain counts his influences as Fela Kuti, Miles Davis, Marvin Gaye, Lightning Hopkins, and Burning Spear, among others.

His early disc jockey work at private parties inspired DJs to mix and match elements of ambient blues, techno, jazz, dub, and house. In the early 1990s St. Germain worked under various aliases including Subsystem, Modus Vivendi, and Deepside, for a range of French imprints. He eventually teamed up with another Frenchman, DJ/producer Laurent Garnier, for whose label F Communications, St. Germain recorded his debut *Boulevard* (1996). It eventually sold more than 300,000 copies worldwide and was later named record of the year in England. The album fuses bluesy vocals, ambient hip-hop-flavored house beats, and live jazz. An influential work, it helped develop, alongside French artists such as Daft Punk and Air, the late-1990s French house scene.

It was also durable. In 2002 *Boulevard* peaked at number seventeen on *Billboard*'s Top Contemporary Jazz

St. Germain [BLUE NOTE RECORDS]

Albums chart and at number twenty-five on *Billboard*'s Top Electronic Albums chart. St. Germain's innovative and popular work brought him to the attention of the legendary American jazz label Blue Note, whose representatives signed St. Germain and released his follow-up *Tourist* (2000). St. Germain built upon his chief strengths, the seamless blending, mixing, looping, and sampling of dance rhythms by adding jazz musicians to solo over his rough-edged patchworks. These included keyboardist Alexandre Destrez, trumpeter Pascal Ohse, saxophonist-flutist Edouard Labor, and percussionist Edmondo Carneiro. St. Germain also incorporated vocal samplings and trance piano stylings. The main revelation though was the musical possibilities that came with wrapping electronica and house rhythms around a jazz ensemble. In tracks like "Rose Rouge" and "Montego Bay Spleen," one can hear snippets of funk, jazz, samba, old-style blues, gospel, soul, and Jamaican dub reggae. Despite the occasional meandering jams, the album is infused with smooth-bumping dance rhythms.

On his tours St. Germain used many of the same musicians to complement his work as live mixer and loop master. The album went gold in France, and *Rolling Stone* magazine named it one of the Top 50 albums of 2000. It also peaked at number one on *Billboard*'s Top Contemporary Jazz Albums chart in the United States. *Billboard* named St. Germain the Top Contemporary Jazz Artist in 2000 and *Tourist* was named Top Contemporary Jazz album of 2001. *From Detroit to St. Germain* (2001) was released by F Communications as a compilation of St. Germain's early work, B-sides, and outtakes.

Few artists have been able to experiment successfully with so many divergent music styles or generated as much fanfare. In record stores, St. Germain's albums have been filed under acid jazz, house, new age, and electronica sections.

SELECTIVE DISCOGRAPHY: *Boulevard* (F Communications, 1996); *Tourist* (Blue Note, 2000).

RAMIRO BURR

STAIND

Formed: 1995, Springfield, Massachusetts

Members: Johnny April, bass (born Enfield, Connecticut, 27 March 1965); Aaron Lewis, vocals, guitar (born Rutland, Vermont, 13 April 1972); Mike Mushok, guitar (born Manhassett, New York, 10 April 1970); Jon Wysocki, drums (born Northampton, Massachusetts, 17 January 1972).

Genre: Rock

Best-selling album since 1990: *Break the Cycle* (2001)

Hit songs since 1990: "Outside," "It's Been Awhile"

Staind was one of the most successful commercial hard rock acts of the late 1990s, winning over mainstream audiences with its dark, moody power ballads.

Comprised of Johnny April on bass, singer Aaron Lewis on guitar, Mike Mushok on guitar, and Jon Wysocki on drums, Staind played its first gig in February 1995. The band built a small but faithful following by aggressively touring throughout the Northeast. Staind's big break came when friends from the band Sugarmilk invited Staind to play with them and rising stars Limp Bizkit at the Webster Theater in Hartford, Connecticut, in October 1997. Staind's high-energy live show impressed Fred Durst of Limp Bizkit, who invited the band to record demo tracks for his production company. Later, with Durst's help, Staind signed a recording contract with Flip Records.

After Staind enjoyed a high-profile coming-out party on the Vans Warped Tour, Flip released the band's debut album, *Dysfunction*, in 1999. With a sound influenced heavily by early 1990s grunge kings Alice in Chains, songs such as "Mudshovel," "Home," and "Just Go" made significant inroads with MTV audiences. Staind's relentless touring in support of the album paid off, as *Dysfunction* sold more than 1 million copies.

Staind's ultimate commercial breakthrough came in a rather unconventional manner. In 1999 Staind toured with Limp Bizkit and other bands as part of the "Family Values Tour"; at one concert in Biloxi, Mississippi, Lewis, at Durst's urging, performed an unfinished song called "Outside." Alone on acoustic guitar with only Durst singing in harmony, Lewis debuted the brooding song, droningly delivering his damning lyrics: "I'm on the outside / I'm looking in / I can see through you / See your true colors / Inside you're ugly, ugly like me / I can see through you / See to the real you." MTV subsequently began airing a clip of the performance, and Staind entered into heavy rotation on the music television station, the ballad format appealing to audiences far beyond Staind's traditional aggressive, hard-rock circles.

Staind released its much-anticipated second album, *Break the Cycle*, in 2001; the album debuted at number one on the *Billboard* album charts. In addition to "Outside," *Break the Cycle* featured the hit single "It's Been Awhile." A bleak, midtempo ballad in the vein of "Outside," "It's Been Awhile" musically emphasizes Lewis's tortured vocals and acoustic guitar. Lyrically, Lewis turns his critical eye upon himself: "And it's been awhile since I could say that I wasn't addicted / And it's been awhile since I could say I loved myself as well." On the strength of "It's Been Awhile," *Break the Cycle* sold 3 million records.

For a band with its roots in hard rock and heavy metal, Staind ironically became commercial heavyweights on the merits of their affecting ballads.

SELECTIVE DISCOGRAPHY: *Dysfunction* (Flip/ Elektra, 1999); *Break the Cycle* (Flip/Elektra, 2001).

SCOTT TRIBBLE

STATIC-X

Formed: 1996, Los Angeles, California

Members: Tony Campos, bass; Tripp Eisen, guitar; Ken Jay, drums; Wayne Static, vocals. Former members: Koichi Fukuda, guitar.

Genre: Rap, Metal

Best-selling album since 1990: *Wisconsin Death Trip* (1999)

Hit songs since 1990: "Push It," "Bled for Days"

Fusing elements of new wave heavy metal bands Sepultera, White Zombie, and Ministry, Static-X became one of the leading nu-metal bands of the late 1990s. The group mixed electronic dance beats with metal fury to land a valued spot on the 1999 and 2000 Ozzfest tours.

Static-X began to coalesce as a group in Los Angeles in 1996. Vocalist Wayne Static had left his home in Michigan and teamed up in Chicago with drummer Ken Jay. After playing with local bands, the duo went to Los Angeles to start anew. There they enlisted Tony Campos on bass and Osaka, Japan, native Koichi Fukuda to handle original guitar and keyboards.

Touring relentlessly, they were eventually noticed by Warner Bros. label representatives who signed them in February 1998. The quartet's first album, *Wisconsin Death Trip* (1999), went gold quickly. Like other nu-metal bands, Static-X carved out a successful niche by fusing various musical elements for a fresh sound. *Wisconsin Death Trip* combined power chords, guttural vocals, aggressive electronics, and industrial techno drumbeats. Illustrative was the tune "Push It," which became a favorite among the nu-metal crowd.

But the main engine that drove the band's success was constant touring. A big step came when they landed a choice spot on the 1999 and 2000 Ozzfest tours, alongside other hot metal bands like Powerman 5000, Dope, and Chevelle. Headlined by groups like Fear Factory and Megadeth, the tours drew thousands. Also helping to raise their profile were Static-X's contributions to various film soundtracks, including *Scream 3* ("So Real") in 2000 and *Valentine* ("Love Dump") in 2001.

Static-X went a little more techno on their next album, *Machine* (2001). While similar in approach— furious beats, distorted guitars, and howling vocals— *Machine*'s barely distinguishable tunes are aided by electronic beats that provide some melodic sense to the thrashfest. Among the better tunes, "This Is Not" features hypnotic loops and electronic samples. "A Dios Alma Perdida" sounds like the soundtrack for a horror movie; in "Get to the Gone" a barely perceptible melody arises from the sonic fury. Those are the highlights. The rest of the tunes are indistinguishable in this morass of extreme, mechanical music that some critics alternately called "evil disco" and "transcore." Songs like "Permanence" and "Machine" deal with the predictability of society. But the band also has humor, as in the song " . . . In a Bag," which describes getting caught short a long way from a comfort station.

While constant touring helped the band's visibility, it came with a price. In early 2001 Fukuda opted out to spend more time with his family. He was replaced with former Dope guitarist Tripp Eisen. In the newly configured band's live shows, favorite songs included "Push It," "Bled for Days," "Love Dump," and "I'm with Stupid." A signature sight at the band's intense shows was Static's spiky, gravity-defying hairstyle (think Don King), an instant attention getter.

Static-X made its mark in the nu-metal world with its unique mixture of blazing guitar riffs and electronic techno programming. While some tunes sound the same, a distinguishing characteristic of their music was its sheer intensity and raw power. Hard metal rockers at heart, Static-X stood apart from similar metal bands through their willingness to experiment and pull in elements from other musical styles.

SELECTIVE DISCOGRAPHY: *Wisconsin Death Trip* (Warner Bros., 1999); *Machine Warner* (Warner Bros., 2001). **Soundtracks:** *Scream 3* (Wind-Up, 2000); *Valentine* (Warner Bros., 2001).

RAMIRO BURR

STEELY DAN

Formed: 1971, New York City

Members: Walter Becker, vocals and guitar (born Queens, New York, 20 February 1950); Donald Fagen, vocals and keyboards (born Passaic, New Jersey, 10 January 1948)

Genre: Rock

Best-selling album since 1990: *Two Against Nature* (2000)

Hit singles since 1990: "Cousin Dupree"

Steely Dan, Walter Becker's and Donald Fagen's thirty-year vehicle, first appeared at the crossroads of the 1960s and the 1970s, when pop's optimistic bloom had taken on a darker, more serious tone. The group's composers embodied that trend with admirable skill, wedding hummable tunes to probing lyrics that touched on the underbelly of the American urban dream. Their characters are outsiders from dime-store paperbacks—drifters, losers, barflies, forgotten jazz players—all evoked in immaculately turned musical arrangements.

Steely Dan's output hardly fits a conventional template. Their barbed wit recalls Frank Zappa at his more acerbic, yet their arrangements, constructed with legendary zeal, often owe much to the big-band tradition. New Yorkers transplanted to California, they began as long-haired composers when hippiedom was in vogue, yet they never subscribed to the utopian visions of the West Coast. Their home terrain appeared to be the subterranean jazz cellar of the 1950s, where saxophones interwove with beatnik verse. Despite these seemingly esoteric inspirations, Steely Dan has enjoyed hits on the pop charts and has been inducted into the Rock and Roll Hall of Fame.

From Writing to Performing

Becker and Fagen began as jobbing tunesmiths at the end of the 1960s, part of that fading tradition of songwriters who turned out work on demand for a producer, publisher, or artist who required it. As the 1970s dawned, their quirky approach to songwriting—they always sought an original twist in the words, tune, or tempo—saw them move toward writing material that they liked and wanted to record with a band of their own. It took a while to convince anyone that the Becker-Fagen credit had real credibility or commercial punch, but when they teamed with producer Gary Katz to make the album *Can't Buy a Thrill* (1972), the writers' belief in their own songs began to bear fruit; they linked with the guitarists Jeff "Skunk" Baxter and Denny Dias, the drummer Jim Hodder, and the vocalist David Palmer. But it was Fagen's singing tones that stood out on the set's two most memorable pieces, "Do It Again" and "Reelin' in the Years."

The group seemed capable of delivering potent pop melodies in a highly sophisticated setting. Their tunes had an instant accessibility that recalled the work of the wall-of-sound creator, Phil Spector, or the Beach Boys' resident genius, Brian Wilson; their arrangements had a sleek gloss born of the expertise of jazz session players. Unravelling the meaning behind the songs was a challenge from the start. Even "Do It Again," seemingly an infectious, Latin-flavored jamboree, hides an enigmatic message in its words, "In the mornin' you go gunnin'/ For the man who stole your water."

Productive Decade

The 1970s saw almost annual outings of new Steely Dan material. Notoriously reticent as touring musicians, Fagen and Becker saw their first batch of sidemen quickly drift away in search of live performance opportunities. Yet Baxter stayed long enough to deliver a sensational solo on "My Old School," a key moment on the second album, *Countdown to Ecstasy* (1973), before joining the Doobie Brothers. The album also included the sardonic "Show Biz Kids," in which an insistent, razor-sharp guitar riff accompanied a satire on the record business, including a self-reflective reference to "Steely Dan T-shirts".

Buoyed by the arrival of the singer Michael McDonald and the percussionist Jeff Pocaro, *Pretzel Logic* (1974) sustained Steely Dan's momentum. "Barrytown" is its sweetest track; "Parker's Band" shows swing affinities and pays homage to the jazz groups of the 1940s. "East St Louis Toodle-Loo," the band's only cover, brings a Duke Ellington classic to a rock audience.

The album *Katy Lied* (1975), despite the rolling thunder of the opening track "Black Friday," marked time as illness dogged Fagen's voice. But *The Royal Scam* (1976) features some notable gems: the soap opera sentiments of "Haitian Divorce," the slight but haunting enticements of "The Fez," and the Wild West saga of "Don't Take Me Alive": "I crossed my old man back in Oregon / Don't take me alive."

Yet it was *Aja* in 1977 that seemed to draw the best from the group's writing duo and producer Katz. The mysteriously named album featured extraordinarily stylish and sleek music. Now able to draw a stable of the very best session players—the saxophonist Wayne Shorter and the drummer Steve Gadd among them—Becker and Fagen fully indulged their musical vision: a rich mix of exquisite pop harmonies and virtuosic jazz playing. "Peg" and "Deacon Blues" proved to be masterpieces of melodic and lyrical construction.

Drifting Apart

The story appeared, however, to have run its course. Although the album *Gaucho* emerged in 1981, the circumstances surrounding its delivery were traumatic. Becker was mired in personal difficulties: drug problems, a fractured leg sustained in a road accident, and the suicide of his girlfriend. Steely Dan's dissolution ensued shortly after the release of the album. The split did not slow either man's productivity, however: Fagen recorded the acclaimed solo album *The Nightfly* (1982), and Becker eventually took the producer's chair for Rickie Lee Jones and the British group China Crisis.

During the 1990s Becker became active in the New York Rock and Soul Revue and appeared on their album *Live at the Beacon* (1992); in 1993 Fagen released his much-anticipated second solo outing, *Kamakiriad*, which drew on Becker's production talents and sparked speculation about a possible resurrection of Steely Dan. The album, a concept affair with sci-fi overtones, features eight interconnected works relating the story of a journey in a dream car set in the near future.

The following year Becker issued the underrated and self-deprecatingly named album *11 Tracks of Whack* (1994), a collection which hinted at some of Steely Dan's more melancholy moments and featured Fagen at the studio controls. Artistically, it even over-shadowed *Kamakiriad* with a string of edgy, bitter pieces like "Junkie Girl," "This Moody Bastard," and "Cringemaker." This positive rush of solo activity after more than a decade of collaborative silence prompted the duo to discuss the return of the band that had made them famous.

Reuniting on Tour

Initially, and uncharacteristically, Steely Dan stepped from the shadows as a live combo, touring in 1994 and reprising their extensive body of hits. To the widespread interest of critics and the delight of their patient fans, their 1995 album, *Alive in America*, captured some of the on-stage excitement that had been largely missing from the group's earlier history. But such developments suggested that new material might also be in the cards, and the group eventually lived up to expectations with the release of *Two Against Nature* (2000), produced this time not by Gary Katz but the two songwriters themselves.

With the typical irony Becker and Fagen chose a title that implied they had survived despite the onset of age, extended absence, and the ever-changing whims of the popular music landscape. Yet their 2002 recording was carved from the same stone that had made their 1970s output so distinctive—the jazz voicings of the chords, the displays of vocal and instrumental virtuosity, and a string of new, typically oblique melodies that hinted that they'd never really been away.

They seemed lighter at times, a little less world-weary and cynical. "What a Shame about Me" appears to be more tongue-in-cheek than wallowing misery, and "Cousin Dupree" is a charming comedy of family manners. But the somber, minor-key tunes "Almost Gothic" and "West of Hollywood" still see life through sepia-tinted glasses. *Two Against Nature* won both critical plaudits and a Grammy for Best Pop Album.

Steely Dan has managed to combine melodic invention and lyrical sophistication, delivering music in a diverse range of styles—rock and soul, jazz, and Latin—while still retaining a pop sensibility in some of the best American songwriting of the post–Elvis Presley era.

SELECTIVE DISCOGRAPHY: *Can't Buy a Thrill* (MCA, 1972); *Countdown to Ecstasy* (MCA, 1973) ; *Pretzel Logic* (MCA, 1974); *Katy Lied* (MCA, 1975); *The Royal Scam* (MCA, 1976); *Aja* (MCA, 1977); *Gaucho* (MCA 1980); *Two Against Nature* (Giant, 2000). **Solo, Donald Fagen:** *The Nightfly* (Warner Bros., 1982); *Kamakiriad* (Reprise, 1993); **Solo, Walter Becker:** E *11 Tracks of Whack* (Warner Bros., 1994).

BIBLIOGRAPHY: B. Sweet, *Steely Dan: Reelin' in the Years* (London, 2000).

WEBSITE: www.steelydan.com.

SIMON WARNER

STEREOLAB

Formed: 1991, South London, England

Members: Tim Gane, guitar, keyboards (born Barking, Essex, London, 12 July 1964); Simon Johns, bass; Laetitia (Seaya) Sadier, vocals, keyboards (born Paris, France, 6 May 1968); Andy Ramsay, drums, percussion, vocals. Former member: Mary Hansen, guitar, vocals (born Maryland, Queensborough, Australia, 1 November 1966; died London, England, 1 December 2002).

Genre: Electronica

Best-selling album since 1990: *Dots and Loops* (1997)

Hit songs since 1990: "Wow and Flutter," "Cybele's Reverie," "The Free Design"

Few bands manage to name themselves as fittingly as the British avant jazz-electronica-rock band Stereolab, which truly treats the process of making music as an experimental, carefully orchestrated process. Throughout the 1990s, the band released a handful of challenging art-rock albums that were critically appreciated. With cool, subdued vocals from French-born Laetitia Sadier, who alternates singing in French and English, they were the epitome of experimental, heavily produced, but always melodic electronic rock. Stereolab fuses the experimental and often futuristic looping and sampling that electronic music is known for with the improvisational tradition of jazz.

Stereolab formed in 1991 with primary songwriters Tim Gane on guitar and keyboards and girlfriend Sadier on vocals and keyboards. Their first two releases, *Switched On* (1992) and *Peng!* (1992), the latter of which was their official debut, earned them a devout following in the United Kingdom. Mary Hansen joined the band around this time as keyboardist as did Andy Ramsay, whose skillful, consistent drumming kept everything grounded. With the release of their first album together on a major label, *Mars Audiac Quintet* (1994), the first of many oddly titled albums, Stereolab emerged as an arty alternative rock band. At this point, Sean O'Hagan, who had been a full-time keyboardist with Stereolab, dropped down to part-time member to form his own group, the High Llamas. Stereolab has seen much ebb and flow in terms of personnel, but never to detrimental effects. *Mars Audiac Quintet* was well received and showed they were capable of writing a straightforward pop song. "Wow and Flutter" is driven by a catchy guitar riff and Sadier's cool singing of lines like "I thought IBM was born with the world / The U.S. flag would float forever." Other songs are far more esoteric and space age.

With their follow-up, *Emperor Tomato Ketchup* (1996), Stereolab started to hit their stride producing melodically engaging songs that could veer from jazz to hip-hop to electronic dance beats and back again. O'Hagan dropped back in for string arrangements. Their music influenced other bands from England, including trip hop acts Morcheeba and Portishead, though Stereolab pioneered the sound and most other groups fed from their energy. On *Emperor Tomato Ketchup*, Sadier sings mostly in French. Standout tracks include the string-tinged "Cybele's Reverie"; "Percolator" is a notable and effective display of the band's shuffling around time signatures.

Themes of Stereolab songs in English are loosely concerned with politics, existentialism, and personal freedom. There is a sense that the meaning must get lost in translation, as with "Spark Plug" from *Emperor Tomato Ketchup*, which features the lines "There is no sense in being interested in a child a group or in a society / There is no sense if one cannot see in them before anything else." In 1997 Stereolab continued the momentum with *Dots and Loops*, which brings in vibraphone, the warmth and fuzzy sound of Fender Rhodes' piano, and the welcome increase of songs in English, as in the lead-off track "Brakhage." The trumpet section on the French-sung "Miss Modular" adds a 1960s, Burt Bacharach feel, but the foreign language lyrics keep things somewhat obscure and inaccessible. The songs on *Dots and Loops* abandon the stiff structure of pop music and instead, like jazz compositions, opt for four-, five-, or seventeen-minute-long sonic extravaganzas, as in "Refractions in the Plastic Pulse." Stereolab shifts around playfully with time signatures in "Rainbo Conversation" and "Flower Called Nowhere."

Through the late 1990s, starting with *Dots and Loops*, Stereolab continued to release albums that solidified their reputation as an intellectual, jazz/electronica rock group, prone to noodling on a particular riff for minutes on end. This is especially evident in their 1999 *Cobra and Phases Play Voltage in the Milky Night* and in the dark, impressionistic *Sound-Dust* (2001). Sadly, in December 2002, Stereolab lost one of their longtime members, Mary Hansen, when she was knocked off her bicycle in London and died shortly thereafter.

Stereolab has built a formidable reputation with a unique style that combines jazz, electronic, and pop in an avant-garde sensibility.

SELECTIVE DISCOGRAPHY: *Mars Audiac Quintet* (Elektra, 1994); *Emperor Tomato Ketchup* (Elektra, 1996); *Dots and Loops* (Elektra, 1997); *Cobra and Phases Play Voltage in the Milky Night* (Elektra, 1999); *Sound-Dust* (Elektra, 2001).

CARRIE HAVRANEK

ISAAC STERN

Born: Kreminiecz, Russia, 21 July 1920; died New York, New York, 22 September 2001
Genre: Classical

One of the foremost violinists of his day, Isaac Stern was also one of the most influential and powerful figures in the classical music world. He is credited with having saved Carnegie Hall in the 1950s when it was threatened by developers. He helped promote the careers of numerous young colleagues, and he acted as a kind of international cultural ambassador, promoting various global causes.

Born in Russia in 1920, Stern emigrated to the United States with his family when he was ten months old. The family settled in San Francisco, where Stern began learning the violin at the age of eight, studying with Naoum Blinder and Louis Persinger. Stern gave his first solo recital at the age of thirteen, and at the age of sixteen made his professional debut with the San Francisco Symphony.

He made his New York debut at Town Hall in 1937 and his Carnegie Hall debut in 1943, by which time he was recognized as one of the foremost violinists of his generation. In the 1940s he performed extensively throughout the United States, but also traveled abroad to play for Allied troops in Greenland, Iceland, and the South Pacific.

He also toured Australia and Europe. In 1951 he made a historic tour of the Soviet Union.

Stern always had an interest in chamber music, and in 1961 joined with cellist Leonard Rose and pianist Eugene Istomin to form a piano trio. The trio performed until Rose's death in 1984. Stern's wide-ranging performing career brought him to most of the world's major concert halls, performing with the world's leading orchestras and with distinguished colleagues in more than 100 concerts a year.

In the late 1950s he became politically active when developers threatened to tear down Carnegie Hall and build an office tower. He organized a campaign to help save it and became its president—a post he held for forty years. In 1986 he oversaw the hall's extensive restoration, and in 1997 the main hall was renamed after him.

Stern was a founding member of the National Endowment for the Arts and founder of the Jerusalem Music Center. In 1974 he was named Commander of the French Ordre de la Couronne, was made a Fellow of Jerusalem and awarded the Commander's Cross by the Danish government and the Albert Schweitzer Music Award. He won a Kennedy Center Honor in 1984, and was named Musical America's Musician of the Year in 1986. He won a Grammy Lifetime Achievement Award in 1987, and an Emmy Award that year for a televised concert celebrating the reopening of Carnegie Hall after its restoration. In 1991 he was awarded the National Medal of the Arts, and in 1992 the Presidential Medal of Freedom.

In 1979 he made a historic trip to perform in China, and the film from that trip *From Mao to Mozart: Isaac Stern in China* won a 1981 Academy Award for Best Documentary Feature Full-Length Documentary. Other film projects include playing the role of violinist Eugene Ysaye in *Tonight We Sing* (1953), and playing in the soundtrack of the motion picture *Fiddler on the Roof* (1971). On television he was featured on *60 Minutes, Sesame Street, Live From Lincoln Center*, and numerous other shows, and was the subject of a biography on the Arts & Entertainment network in 1993, which was later released as a home video.

Stern made more than 100 recordings of more than 200 works. In 1985 he was named Sony's first "artist laureate" in recognition of his long association with the label. His repertoire was extensive, encompassing all of the standard violin solo, chamber, and concerto literature, and he was committed to performing contemporary music, premiering works by Leonard Bernstein, Krzysztof Penderecki, William Schuman, and George Rochberg.

In 1991 he went to Israel to perform during the Persian Gulf War. At a concert in Jerusalem, air raid sirens began to go off during the performance and the audience began donning gas masks, but Stern played on, completing the program. That year he also helped organize and perform in Carnegie Hall's hundredth anniversary concert, which was broadcast live on PBS.

Throughout his life Stern was a teacher, holding master classes around the world. He is credited with helping to launch the careers of such artists as Emmanuel Ax, Yo-Yo Ma, Itzhak Perlman, Pinchas Zukerman, Shlomo Mintz, and Yefim Bronfman.

Stern was an artist very much in the tradition of the old school. His playing was heartfelt and his musicianship was not bound by the latest musicological canons. In later years, though he still toured and performed frequently, much of his energy and attention was taken up with his various administrative and educational projects.

SELECTIVE DISCOGRAPHY: *Isaac Stern: A Life in Music* (Sony, 1995).

BIBLIOGRAPHY: C. Potok and I. Stern, *My First 79 Years: Isaac Stern* (New York, 1999).

WEBSITE: www.isaacstern.com.

DOUGLAS McLENNAN

ROD STEWART

Born: Roderick David Stewart; in Highgate, North London, England, 10 January 1945

Genre: Rock

Best-selling album since 1990: *Unplugged . . . and Seated* (1993)

Hit songs since 1990: "Rhythm of My Heart," "Have I Told You Lately," "Leave Virginia Alone"

Outstanding singing talent made Rod Stewart a major presence among contemporary rock singers; his charismatic appeal both on and off the stage made him a sex symbol. Stewart accomplished a successful transition from 1960s heavy rock into 1970s mainstream pop, although it came at some cost as he faced criticism for abandoning his talent to play too heavily on his heartthrob image. Nevertheless, in his later years Stewart found a more serious audience, fitting his very recognizable voice into a variety of adult-pop genres, including jazz standards.

From Hot Rod to Mod Rod

As the youngest child of five in a blue-collar London family, Stewart was a promising soccer player and nearly turned professional in the sport. Stewart also did a stint as a gravedigger while pursuing music with several local club bands. English blues legend Long John Baldry heard Stewart playing the harmonica in 1964 and asked him to join his band. He knocked around over the next two years

Rod Stewart [J-RECORDS-BIFF WARREN]

with Baldry's Steampacket, gaining a reputation as a talented rhythm and blues singer with a unique voice. In 1967, he and guitarist Ron Wood, who reluctantly switched to bass guitar, joined guitar virtuoso Jeff Beck to form the hard rock-based Jeff Beck Group. Beck's reputation was already huge, Stewart's was growing, and the same could be said for their egos. Stewart's vocals took a backseat to Beck's guitar playing, although the two albums they recorded, *Truth* (1968) and *Beck-Ola* (1969), are rock classics. The Jeff Beck Group gets credit for initiating rock's trend of pairing an energetic lead singer with a hot guitar player. While Beck recovered from a severe car accident in 1969, Stewart and Wood left the band to join Small Faces, whose name was shortened to Faces. They quickly earned a reputation as a working-class party rock band. Meanwhile, Stewart also embarked on a solo career, which he juggled while remaining in Faces. His third solo album, *Every Picture Tells a Story* (1971), contained the megahit, "Maggie May," and another hit, "I'm Losing You," and went to number one in both Britain and the United States. His next album, *Never a Dull Moment* (1972), contained another big hit, "You Wear It Well." Stewart had reached superstar status, but he stayed with Faces, recording five albums until he left them in 1976, by which time his solo career had overshadowed the band's.

Stewart's stage style is distinctive in its athletic and boundless energy. He weaves and bobs, electrifying audiences with a cocky strut, effusive handclaps, and a mischievous charm. He is one of an exclusive group of rock lead singers—Mick Jagger, Robert Plant, Roger Daltrey, Paul Rodgers, Steven Tyler, and the late Freddie Mercury among them—who combine visceral stage theatrics with throaty, expressive, yet tuneful vocals. Stewart's voice is bluesy and high with an inimitable raspy hoarseness. It is a consummate rock voice but also supports ballads such as "Maggie May" and "Tonight's the Night" as well as chart-topping pop/rock romps like "Hot Legs" and "Do Ya Think I'm Sexy."

After leaving Faces, Stewart also left England to escape the high taxes. He settled in Los Angeles, where his popularity grew, in part because of his jet-setting with movie stars and models. His next release, *A Night on the Town* (1976), went platinum, and his following release, *Foot Loose and Fancy Free* (1977), went triple platinum. These and subsequent albums put more emphasis on a pop sound and contained less of the blues/rock that earlier drew Stewart vast critical praise. He reached a celebrity zenith in 1979 with the brash, disco-influenced mega-hit, "Do Ya Think I'm Sexy" from *Blondes Have More Fun* (1978).

Proving the Critics Wrong

Singers who made their mark in the golden era of rock/blues from 1965 to 1975 faced dizzying music trend changes over the next fifteen years: punk rock and disco in the mid 1970s; New Wave shortly after; the heavy-metal explosion of the 1980s; and synthesized pop and hip-hop of the late 1980s. Those who survived, as Stewart did, either continually reinvented themselves and/or fused with one or several of these styles. Stewart entered the 1980s by emphasizing more pop and new-wave styles into his sound. The album *Tonight I'm Yours* (1981) sold well, but Stewart's next efforts were not as successful and prompted talk that Stewart was getting too old for the "Do Ya Think I'm Sexy" routine. By the middle 1980s he was mired in the first slump of his fruitful career. It revived in 1989 with his rendition of a Tom Waits song, "Downtown Train," which became a hit and brought Stewart his first Grammy Award nomination.

Stewart began the 1990s by releasing a career retrospective, *Storyteller, the Complete Anthology: 1964–1990* (1990). The fifty-song, four-CD set reminded both fans and skeptics that he had amassed a formidable body of work and that he was more than just a celebrity pop star. The album also seemed to focus him in a more mature, seasoned vein, and his career began to edge forward. His next release, *Vagabond Heart* (1991), left behind some of the excess trappings of the previous decade and displayed Stewart once again as a masterful song interpreter. The album features his version of Van Morrison's ballad "Have

I Told You Lately" and features guest work by Tina Turner on "It Takes Two."

In 1993, Stewart reunited with Ron Wood to take part in MTV's show *Unplugged*. The appropriately named album from the concert, *Unplugged . . . and Seated* (1993), was another boost for Stewart's career revival. It contains acoustic versions of Stewart's biggest hits as he and Wood sat on stools during the subdued concert setting; it was difficult, however, for the effervescent singer to remain seated through some of the numbers. His renditions of classics such as "Stay with Me," "Handbags and Gladrags," "Mandolin Wind," and his chestnut, "Maggie May," reminded anyone who may have forgotten that Stewart is an expressive song interpreter; the acoustic format allowed him to find even deeper meanings in his signature material. In addition, he and Wood appeared to have a rollicking good time, giving a scaled down glimpse of their camaraderie from their days in Faces. *Unplugged . . . and Seated* was both a critical and commercial success—triple platinum—and the year following its release Stewart was inducted into the Rock and Roll Hall of Fame.

Stewart maintained an affinity to balladry with his sweet sandpapery vocals on his next studio release, *Spanner in the Works* (1995). The album's title is a British expression whose meaning is akin to the American saying, "a fly in the ointment." It contains the hit single, "Leave Virginia Alone," which was written by Tom Petty. Stewart also added Tom Waits's song "Hang on St. Christopher," Bob Dylan's "Sweetheart Like You," and the powerfully sweeping "This" to the album's twelve songs. Stewart followed the album's release with a world concert tour and brought a twenty-two-piece orchestra in addition to his twelve-piece band.

In an effort to link today's new generation rock with his Faces-era sound, Stewart recorded *When We Were the New Boys* (1998). The album took his audience in a direction they had not seen for years as he dropped the twenty-two-piece orchestra and rekindled the electricity of his earlier days. However, he returned to the adult-pop that had given him so much success already with the release of *Human* (2001).

In his quest to keep fostering success with warmer, more accessible music, Stewart recorded *It Had to be You . . . The Great American Songbook* (2002), a collection of American standards from the 1930s and 1940s. Stewart had secretly admired and longed to sing this classic music since his "Do Ya Think I'm Sexy" days. Sales of the record have reached 3 million, and a sequel was planned for release in 2003.

Critics were tough on Stewart in the late 1970s for the alleged abandonment of his abundant skills as a song interpreter for blander commercial formats. Yet as other singers from his era keep trying to relight the flame of their early brilliance, Stewart seems content to let that go and mature gracefully. His talent has always been his ability to put a unique touch on any music that he sings.

SELECTIVE DISCOGRAPHY: *An Old Raincoat Won't Ever Let You Down*(Mercury, 1969); *Gasoline Alley* (Mercury, 1970) *Every Picture Tells a Story* (Mercury, 1971); *Never a Dull Moment* (Mercury, 1972); *Sing It Again, Rod* (Mercury, 1973); *Smiler* (Mercury, 1974); *Atlantic Crossing* (Warner Bros., 1975); *A Night on the Town* (Warner Bros., 1976); *Foot Loose & Fancy Free* (Warner Bros., 1977); *Blondes Have More Fun* (Warner Bros., 1978); *Tonight I'm Yours* (Warner Bros., 1981); *Camouflage* (Warner Bros., 1984); *Out of Order* (Warner Bros., 1988); *Storyteller, the Complete Anthology: 1964–1990* (Warner Bros., 1990); *Vagabond Heart* (Warner Bros., 1991); *Unplugged . . . and Seated* (Warner Bros., 1993); *Spanner in the Works* (Warner Bros., 1995); *When We Were the New Boys* (Warner Bros., 1998); *Human* (Atlantic, 2001); *It Had to Be You . . . The Great American Songbook* (J. Records, 2002). **With the Jeff Beck Group:** *Truth* (Epic, 1968); *Beck-ola* (Epic, 1969). **With Faces:** *The First Step* (Warner Bros., 1970); *A Nod Is as Good as a Wink . . . to a Blind Horse* (Warner Bros., 1971); *Ooh la La* (Warner Bros., 1973).

DONALD LOWE

STING

Born: Gordon Matthew Sumner; Newcastle-upon-Tyne, England, 2 October 1951

Genre: Rock

Best-selling album since 1990: *Brand New Day* (1999)

Hit songs since 1990: "If I Ever Lose My Faith in You," "Brand New Day"

Singer/songwriter/actor Sting was the singer, bassist, and primary creative force for the supertrio the Police prior to going solo in 1984. He transcended the band's initial punk rock leanings with infusions of jazz and reggae and attained megasuccess as a solo artist by building on that style. Forging out a solo career has also allowed Sting to focus on his acting aspirations, and he has made several noteworthy stage and film forays. Additionally, he stays active in human rights and environmental causes.

Police in a Sting Operation

Gordon Sumner earned the nickname Sting from an older jazz musician after the seventeen-year-old Sumner came to a club gig dressed in a bumble bee-styled yellow and black striped sweater. Sting grew up in the industrial town of Newcastle, England, and he used his disdain for both the town and his immediate family as motivation for a better life. A self-taught musician, he first gained professional musical experience by playing bass guitar in local jazz clubs. In 1971 he attended Warwick University and studied education. After graduation, Sting taught high school English, while also playing in a punk band called Last Exit. In 1976 he left teaching and ventured to London where he grouped with drummer Stewart Copeland and guitarist Andy Summers to form a jazz- and reggae-informed "new wave" band called the Police.

Sting gained notoriety when his high, glass-clear vocals rang out in their first hit, "Roxanne," which he wrote. His aching vocalization of the name "Roxanne"—the first word of the song—is definable as one of rock music's signature moments. The Police's debut album, *Outlandos d'Amour* (1979) (which contains "Roxanne"), and their subsequent four albums propelled the band into superstardom. At the very height of their success, Sting and his two Police band mates decided to go separate ways. With Sting singing and writing most of the material, the Police scored five Grammy Awards and a multitude of hits including the smash single, "Every Breath You Take." Each member of the group had already begun solo ventures by the time the Police played their last concert in 1986, a benefit for Amnesty International. In 2003 the trio finally regrouped when they performed at the band's induction ceremony into the Rock and Roll Hall of Fame. In the seventeen years between those gigs, Sting's solo career had blossomed, far surpassing the other two members of the Police.

A Beeline for Solo Stardom

Sting's first album as a solo artist was *Dream of the Blue Turtles* (1985) and it produced three hits: "If You Love Someone Set Them Free," "Fortress around Your Heart," and "Russians." The album features the talents of prominent New York jazz players, saxophonist Branford Marsalis, keyboardist Kenny Kirkland, and Omar Hakim on drums, and the material is a more erudite augmentation of the musical direction that the Police were heading. Sting recorded three more albums in the 1980s before slowing down at the decade's end to mourn his parents who had died within six months of each other. Earlier in his career, Sting had publicly chastised his family—much to the detriment of his relationship with them. Consequently, his unresolved feelings after the death of his parents, particularly with his father, triggered a severe case of writer's block that lasted nearly three years. His album *The Soul Cages* (1991) was a breakout from that dark period and he dedicated the album to his father. Sting's next album, *Ten Summoner's Tales* (1993), marked a return to his pen-

---

Spot Light | *All This Time*

Extraordinary circumstances surrounded Sting's first live album in fifteen years, *All This Time* (2001). Instead of recording from a concert venue, as is usually the case, Sting opted for an intimate setting in his Tuscany home among an invited audience of about 200 close friends and family. Sting and his band rehearsed for eight days in preparation. The album, a compilation of songs from Sting's twenty-five-year recording career, was set, not only for audio recording, but also to receive a live international webcast. The event was scheduled for the evening of September 11, 2001. That morning, as cameras and sound equipment were being set up, news that the United States had suffered a devastating terrorist attack reached the band and crew. After hours of angst and deliberation, it was decided that the performance would go forward; however, the webcast would feature just one song: "Fragile" from Sting's album, . . . *Nothing Like the Sun* (1987). Many of the songs took on new meaning that day, particularly "Fragile," which ends by repeating the line, "How fragile we are."

---

chant for complex time signatures and jazz-oriented rock. It contains the hit, "If I Ever Lose My Faith in You."

By this time, Sting's raspy tenor had become not only one of the leading voices of pop/rock, but also a voice for political and environmental issues, which many of his songs reflect. He and his wife, film director Trudi Styler, initiated the Rainforest Foundation in 1989 and raised money for the organization—which is committed to preserving the Brazilian rain forests—by hosting an annual star-filled concert in New York City. The 2002 concert at Carnegie Hall featured Elton John, James Taylor, Jeff Beck, Patti LaBelle, and many others. Sting and his wife dedicated the event to Herman Sandler, the other co-chair, who perished in his office at the World Trade Center in the previous year's terrorist attacks on September 11.

Sting scored a collaborative hit in 1993 with fellow rockers Rod Stewart and Bryan Adams with "All for Love" from the movie *The Three Musketeers*. The film industry embraced Sting as an actor early on in his musical career, and his chiseled features are frequently cast as the quiet, brooding type. Sting has acted in more than a dozen films including *Quadrophenia* (1979), *Dune* (1985), *The Bride* (1985), *Stormy Monday*, (1988), and *Lock Stock and Two Smoking Barrels* (1998). Additionally, he portrayed the serial-killing Macheath in Bertolt Brecht's *Threepenny Opera*, which opened on Broadway in 1989. Reviews were mixed and the show had a short run.

His next two studio albums, *Mercury Falling* (1996) and *Brand New Day* (1999), display Sting's ability as a composer to fearlessly meld a variety of styles—Latin rhythms, gospel, classical, and Celtic—to create his silver-tongued, literate adult pop sound. *Brand New Day* earned Sting his fifteenth and sixteenth Grammy Awards for Best Male Pop Vocal Performance and Best Pop Vocal Album. While some fans yearn for the edgier resonance of his days with the Police, Sting, the socially conscious solo artist, has transcended that success by maturing musically with the times. He has proved to be one of the most notable and intelligent songwriters to emerge from England's post-punk/new wave music scene, and is many critics' choice as contemporary music's best singer.

SELECTIVE DISCOGRAPHY: *The Dream of the Blue Turtles* (A&M, 1985); *Bring on the Night* (A&M, 1986); . . . *Nothing Like the Sun* (1987); *The Soul Cages* (A&M, 1991); *Ten Summoner's Tales* (A&M, 1993); *Mercury Falling* (A&M, 1996); *Brand New Day* (Interscope, 1999); *All This Time* (Universal, 2001). **With the Police:** *Regatta de Blanc* (A&M, 1979); *Zenyatta Mondatta* (A&M, 1980); *Ghost in the Machine* (A&M, 1981); *Synchronicity* (A&M, 1983).

SELECTIVE FILMOGRAPHY: *Quadrophenia* (1979); *Radio On* (1980); *Dune* (1984); *The Bride* (1985); *Plenty* (1985); *Bring on the Night* (1985); *Stormy Monday* (1988); *The Grotesque* (1997); *Lock, Stock and Two Smoking Barrels* (1998).

BIBLIOGRAPHY: C. Sandford, *Sting: Demolition Man* (New York, 1998); W. Clarkson, *Sting: The Secret Life of Gordon Sumner* (New York, 1999).

DONALD LOWE

STONE TEMPLE PILOTS

Formed: 1990, Los Angeles, California

Members: Dean DeLeo, guitar (born New Jersey, 23 August 1961); Robert DeLeo, bass (born New Jersey, 2 February 1966); Eric Kretz, drums (born Santa Cruz, California, 7 June 1966); Scott Weiland, vocals (born Santa Cruz, California, 27 October 1967).

Genre: Rock

Best-selling album since 1990: *Purple* (1994)

Hit songs since 1990s: "Plush," "Big Empty," "Sour Girl"

Stone Temple Pilots emerged as grunge commanded the hearts and minds of the mainstream, and they were often criticized as a second-tier unit in comparison to the original wave of Seattle-based bands. When the grunge fever cooled, however, it became clear that the band owed more to arena rock of the 1970s than the outsider sound of punk. As the 1990s progressed, the band incorporated elements of glam and pop into its heavily guitar-driven mix, and they won critical plaudits that evaded their earlier incarnation. Despite the highly publicized drug problems of their lead singer Scott Weiland, Stone Temple Pilots still mine the anything-goes spirit of rock with verve and style.

Success Type Thing

Scott Weiland and bassist Robert DeLeo met by chance at a punk concert in Los Angeles and discovered that they were dating the same woman. Despite this inauspicious beginning, the two began to write songs together. They recruited DeLeo's brother Dean to play guitar and Eric Kretz to play drums to form Mighty Joe Young, later renamed Stone Temple Pilots (the name was inspired by the logo of STP motor oil). The band moved south to San Diego to take advantage of a less crowded rock scene and eventually caught the eye of an agent from Atlantic Records. The band signed a contract and went to work on their debut album.

Core was released in 1992, just as grunge bands like Nirvana and Pearl Jam were reintroducing heavy guitar-based music to the American public. The album features immaculate production and tight, catchy songcraft, qualities that made it one of the most popular albums of the 1990s. Dean DeLeo's dense wall of guitars and Kretz's thudding percussion provide perfect accompaniment for Weiland's dark and muscular croon. The first single, "Sex Type Thing," made an instant impression on rock fans with its crushing rhythm and aggressive guitars, but it attracted the scorn of critics for its derivative sound. Pegged as a grunge clone, the band offered an amalgamation of classic and hard rock styles. "Plush," a jagged, confessional rock ballad, sent the album to the top of the charts the following year, as Weiland's searing vocal performance invited comparisons to the mournful wail of Pearl Jam's Eddie Vedder. The song is classic 1970s heavy metal, a self-important stomp that is nonetheless ideal for highway driving.

After a series of highly successful tours in which Weiland came into his own as a flashy and formidable front man, the band recorded their second album. *Purple* (1994) debuted at number one on the album charts, powered by the epic "Big Empty," which revisits the wall-of-guitars balladry of "Plush." The song is a transcendent arena-rock classic, heightened by a quiet verse/loud chorus structure and faux-profound lyrics ("Time to take her home / Her dizzy head is conscience laden"). Like the rest of the album, the song is pitch perfect, an unabashed grab for the mainstream rock crown. While their contemporaries shunned rock stardom, Stone Temple Pilots abandoned the modesty of grunge, recognizing the need for songs that above all rock. The band sounds looser and more inspired, playing with supreme confidence on rockers like the snaky "Vasoline" and the invigorating "Silvergun Superman." They scored another hit with "Interstate Love Song," an uncharacteristically light-hearted anthem marked by ringing guitars and lyrics of escape.

Artistic Triumph and Personal Turmoil

Soon after the release of *Purple*, Weiland developed a drug habit that resulted in his arrest and sentencing to a rehabilitation facility in 1995. Following his release, the band recorded and released their third album, *Tiny Music . . . Songs from the Vatican Gift Shop* (1996). The album adds elements of pop and psychedelia to their hard rock sound, resulting in an edgy and ambitious set of songs. "Tumble in the Rough" builds from a rubbery guitar riff to a powerful, rhythmic chorus. "Big Bang Baby" features a taut rhythm and gangly guitars that add depth to the band's heavy metal structures, and "Lady Picture Show" employs complex and catchy instrumentation that suggests the Beatles. *Tiny Music* proved Stone Temple Pilots to be a creative act; unfortunately, Weiland was admitted again to a drug rehabilitation facility shortly after its release, and the band canceled their summer tour.

With Weiland's future in question, the band recruited the singer Dave Coutts to form Talk Show; they released an album of the same name in 1997. Weiland released a solo album titled *12 Bar Blues* in 1998, but neither of the side projects garnered the commercial success of Stone Temple Pilots. The band reunited to record the remarkably focused *No. 4*, released in 1999. The album rocks just as hard as *Core*, but with the melodic sense of *Tiny Music*. The punishing opening track, "Down," is followed by the dynamic "Heaven & Hot Rods," in which a head-spinning riff morphs into a swirling psychedelic ending. The band notched a hit with "Sour Girl," a strange and melodic ballad that ranks among their best work. Weiland's voice is in fine form, expressive and emotional, able to cut through the expansive production to drive each song home. Once again, their tour plans were upset by Weiland's drug problems—

the singer was sentenced to a year in jail for charges stemming from a previous offense.

With a new commitment to sobriety, Weiland rejoined the band to record *Shangri-La Dee Da* (2001). The album continues in the same vein as *No. 4*, balancing gripping rockers with an ever-improving sense of melody and pop complexity. "Days of the Week" is one of the most engaging tracks in their catalog, with a jaunty guitar riff and a powerful vocal turn from Weiland. The blistering "Coma" benefits from hip-hop-inspired noise layered over their signature churning rhythm, and Weiland's versatile vocals add depth to the propulsive "Hollywood Bitch." The bittersweet ballad "Hello It's Late" is a tender account of fading love. *Shangri-La Dee Da* breaks no new ground but shows the band making well-crafted pop rock at a high level.

Once the most critically maligned band of the grunge era, Stone Temple Pilots evolved into a consistently engaging unit capable of producing compelling and cathartic commercial rock.

SELECTIVE DISCOGRAPHY: *Core* (1992, Atlantic); *Purple* (1994, Atlantic); *Tiny Music . . . Songs from the Vatican Gift Shop* (1996, Atlantic); *No. 4* (1999, Atlantic); *Shangri-La Dee Da* (2001, Atlantic).

WEBSITE: www.stonetemplepilots.com.

SEAN CAMERON

GEORGE STRAIT

Born: Poteet, Texas, 18 May 1952

Genre: Country

Best-selling album since 1990: *Carrying Your Love with Me* (1997)

Hit songs since 1990: "Easy Come, Easy Go," "Blue Clear Sky," "Round About Way"

An enduring presence in country music since the early 1980s, George Strait is a prolific, consistent performer whose work rarely strays from a "neo-traditional" country formula, using drums, fiddles, and steel guitar for instrumentation. Unlike contemporary performers such as Faith Hill and Garth Brooks, Strait has mostly avoided hard rock and pop elements in his music. Instead, he favors a more restrained sound that recalls the western swing and honky-tonk music of the mid-twentieth century. While Strait excels at up-tempo dance songs, he is also a convincing balladeer in the alternately smooth and gritty style of country legend Merle Haggard. Strait's personal image reflects his back-to-basics musical approach.

With his sharply creased jeans, oversized belt buckle, broad cowboy hat, and toothy grin, Strait comes off as a model of all-American masculinity, a hardy, durable figure whose sex appeal is based on romantic constancy and solidity.

Born into a Texas family that had raised cattle for nearly a century, Strait grew up on an expansive ranch where he learned the mechanics of farming at an early age. As a youth he also developed an interest in country music, inspired by the soulful, stripped-down barroom style of his idol Haggard. In 1971, having eloped with his high school sweetheart Norma, he dropped out of college and enlisted in the army, where he began performing in a country band while stationed in Hawaii. After returning to Texas in 1975 with Norma and his young daughter Jenifer, Strait studied agriculture at Southwest State University and formed his own country band, Ace in the Hole.

After several lean years of financial struggle, Strait decided to leave performing and accept a job at a ranch equipment company in Uvalde, Texas. Fortunately Norma, always confident in her husband's abilities, urged him to make one more try as a performer. The gambit paid off when Strait's recurring gig at the small Prairie Rose nightclub in San Marcos, Texas, led to a contract with MCA Records, one of the biggest labels in country music. Like many of his later recordings, Strait's first hit, "Unwound (1981)," honored the "western swing" style of country music popular in the 1930s and 1940s. Rooted in West Texas and Oklahoma, western swing was known for its lively, up-tempo jazz rhythm supported by instrumentation of steel guitar, piano, and twin harmonizing fiddles.

1980s: Stardom and Tragedy

In the early 1980s country music was reeling from two decades of the dominant "countrypolitan" style, which enveloped vocalists in beds of swirling strings and cooing background choruses. Strait was at the vanguard of a group of young performers seeking a return to a more basic instrumental approach, one in keeping with western swing and the rough-and-tumble honky-tonk sound of the 1950s. Of these 1980s "neo-traditionalists," whose ranks included Ricky Skaggs and Randy Travis, Strait emerged as the most consistently successful from a commercial perspective, scoring more than twenty-five country hits during the decade. Recording an album a year, Strait packed his releases with top-quality songs, well served by strong but subtle production values. *Does Fort Worth Ever Cross Your Mind* (1984) is a classic of his early period, a stirring collection of swing tunes and sensitive ballads. The album gathers the various strands of Strait's influences—swing, tough country, pop balladry—into a warm and cohesive effort. Sadly,

Strait's success was tempered by personal loss: His thirteen-year-old daughter was killed in a car accident while riding with friends in 1986. Already known for avoiding interviews, a devastated Strait didn't speak to the press for an entire year. Soon after the tragedy, he and Norma established the Jenifer Strait Memorial Foundation, which donates money to various children's charities each year.

Crossover Success in the 1990s

During the early 1990s Strait enjoyed crossover pop success, a result of his starring role in the film *Pure Country* (1992) and albums such as *Easy Come, Easy Go* (1993), which, due to its breezy, tuneful title track, scored on both the country and pop charts. *Easy Come, Easy Go* continues the winning format of Strait's 1980s releases, with spirited performances and restrained production. Critics remarked that the swinging first track, "Stay Out of My Arms," showcases Strait at his best, his expressive, slightly pinched voice conveying a down-home swagger and twang. Writers have noted that country balladry is characterized by emotional generosity, an emphasis on feeling over technique. In this respect, Strait's heart-tugging performance on the lovelorn "Just Look at Me" links him with legendary balladeers of previous generations, particularly his main influence, Merle Haggard. If Strait's pitch wavers slightly near the end of phrases, it's an inconsistency that brings out the emotional fragility of the song. Critics noted that his vocal quality is less ideally suited to the album's closing number, "We Must Be Loving Right," a sophisticated ballad reflecting Strait's admiration for Frank Sinatra. Unlike Sinatra, a singer who harnessed emotion within the larger framework of technique, Strait does not possess the vocal nuance or subtle control of dynamics for this type of laid-back material. As a result, reviewers observed that Strait sounds constrained by the sedateness of the arrangement. His ambitious but flawed performance illuminates a key difference between country and pop: A pop stylist rarely abandons technical control in the pursuit of emotion, but for a country singer this sacrifice is a fundamental key to communication, a way of digging into the soul of the material.

Such missteps notwithstanding, Strait's musical consistency in the 1990s prevented him from releasing a bad album, the quality of his work ranging from listenable to excellent. Nonetheless, *Blue Clear Sky* (1996) deserves special attention as one of his most heartfelt works, achieving a quiet power that recalls his best 1980s albums. While all tracks are strong, the highlight is "Rockin' in the Arms of Your Memory," a ballad that finds its special power through haunting imagery: "Been twenty years and counting, I'm drowning in your love a little more each day." Here Strait reveals himself as a first-rate storyteller, pulling listeners into his tale of loss while retaining a sense of ambiguity. It is unclear whether his sadness comes from a romantic break-up or death; the complexity of his interpretation allows for both possibilities. In contrast to the meat-and-potatoes realism of many country songs, "Rockin' in the Arms" leaves behind a lingering air of mystery. *Entertainment Weekly*, in its review of *Blue Clear Sky*, praised Strait's new maturity, asserting that the singer "finally sounds like he's living his lyrics."

Strait's later releases, including *George Strait* (2000), show signs of artistic decline while remaining solid albums. Songs like the mild-mannered "Go On" (2000), while catchy enough to hit the charts, suffer from blandness, crossing the line between consistency and predictability, critics noted. Still, Strait remained a formidable presence in post-2000 country music, preserving his rugged cowboy image and individualistic spirit. Honoring his personal history as a rancher and rodeo man, Strait sponsors a yearly competition in team roping, a variation on calf roping in which two cowboys converge on a steer simultaneously. He is one of the few successful country performers to live outside of Nashville, shunning city glamour for the tranquility of his Texas ranch, where he resides with Norma and son George Jr., nicknamed "Bubba." Comparing Strait's habits with those of the famously reclusive billionaire, the *Ottawa Sun* in 1998 called him "as mysterious as Howard Hughes." "I haven't done a lot of interviews in the past," Strait told a writer for the country.com website in 2000. "I don't mind [interviews] that much sometimes, but I do like my privacy also."

During the early 1980s Strait spurred popular interest in traditional country music, paving the way for later neo-traditionalists such as Alan Jackson and the Judds. As he matured, Strait grew into an expressive performer who captures the dramatic essence of his material. Most importantly, he has maintained a high level of popular success without losing his swinging, individualistic sound.

SELECTIVE DISCOGRAPHY: *Strait Country* (MCA, 1981); *Does Fort Worth Ever Cross Your Mind* (MCA, 1984); *Beyond the Blue Neon* (MCA, 1989); *Pure Country* (MCA, 1992); *Easy Come, Easy Go* (MCA, 1993); *Blue Clear Sky* (MCA, 1996); *George Strait* (MCA, 2000); *The Road Less Traveled* (MCA, 2001).

SELECTIVE FILMOGRAPHY: *Pure Country* (1992).

WEBSITE: www.georgestrait.com.

DAVID FREELAND

BARBRA STREISAND

Born: Brooklyn, New York, 24 April 1942
Genre: Vocal
Best-selling album since 1990: *Higher Ground* (1997)
Hit songs since 1990: "I Finally Found Someone," "Tell Him"

The quintessential American popular vocalist, Barbra Streisand has led a long and varied career that began during the early 1960s, when her youthful, dynamic presence on the Broadway stage propelled her to international stardom. Influenced by great twentieth-century pop singers such as Lee Wiley and Judy Garland, Streisand brought a no-holds-barred energy to her early performances, matching technique with an irrepressible desire to entertain. Her stamina and zest were channeled through a distinctive voice, widely regarded as one of the finest in popular music. Brassy and powerful, yet capable of softness at its edges, it was equally effective on tender ballads and brazen up-tempo tunes. As Streisand matured, her performances became more controlled and mannered, with some critics charging that her impeccable technical skills were obstructing genuine emotion. In the 1970s she increasingly turned her attention to Hollywood films, acting in—and later directing—a series of box office hits. Despite her broadening career focus, Streisand managed to release a series of intelligent, representative albums in the 1980s and 1990s.

Brooklyn Beginnings and Early Stardom

Raised in Brooklyn, New York, where as a child she attended the Beis-Yakov Hebrew school, Streisand set her sights on performing from an early age, singing regularly for her neighbors. Her father died when she was fifteen months old, creating in her what she would later describe as a lifelong feeling of abandonment. Graduating from high school in 1959, she moved to Manhattan and won a singing contest at the Lion, a gay bar in Greenwich Village. In 1961, having developed her reputation with steady nightclub work, she earned critical acclaim for her performance in the Broadway musical, *I Can Get It for You Wholesale*. Hailed by the press as a rising young star, she signed with Columbia Records and released *The Barbra Streisand Album* in early 1963, before reaching her twenty-first birthday. Streisand's fans often appraise the album as her finest work—one that she has, in many respects, failed to top. Capturing subtleties of mood with passion and humor, Streisand sings with a freedom absent from much of her later work. Her belting treatment of "Happy Days Are Here Again" is the album's masterpiece, with Streisand expressing both optimism and—reading against the grain of the lyrics—frantic desperation. In 1964 she starred in the hit Broadway musical *Funny Girl*, portraying famed comedienne Fanny Brice, a role that earned her an Academy Award when she reprised it for the 1968 film version.

Mixed Critical Success in the 1970s and 1980s

Throughout the 1970s and 1980s Streisand pursued a dual recording and acting career, with many of her hits, including "The Way We Were" (1974) and "Evergreen" (1977), coming from movies in which she starred. Within the entertainment industry, she had become known as a willful perfectionist who exerted control over all aspects of her films. This change in her persona was also noticeable in her recorded performances, which became steelier and more serious beginning in the 1970s. Never embracing rock music fully, she nonetheless flirted with rock-inflected pop on "My Heart Belongs to Me" (1977) and disco on "The Main Event" (1979). In a pattern shared by the followers of R&B legend Aretha Franklin, longtime fans continued to buy Streisand's albums while bemoaning her loss of spontaneity. In his 1990 book, *Jazz Singing*, noted critic Will Friedwald cited her as an example of "vocalists who have so much technique that they can use it as a way of shielding what they really feel from their audiences." Criticisms such as these aside, Streisand continued to issue powerful recordings such as *The Broadway Album* (1985), a stirring collection of songs by some of musical theater's top composers, including Stephen Sondheim. At the same time, she expanded possibilities for women in entertainment, becoming, with *Yentl* (1983), the first woman since the silent film era to direct, produce, write, and star in a Hollywood movie.

Ongoing Success in the 1990s and Beyond

While she spent much of the 1990s directing and starring in hit films such as *The Prince of Tides* (1991) and *The Mirror Has Two Faces* (1996), Streisand found time to record strong albums such as *Higher Ground* (1997). Exploring on the album her interest in spirituality and its manifestation within popular song, Streisand creates an often muted, reflective mood, which is rare within her recorded work. Although critics expressed disappointment in the watery strings provided by famed arrangers Marvin Hamlisch and David Foster, they also noted that Streisand sounds warmer and more relaxed than on her 1980s albums. Pairing two of the most frequently recorded "inspirational" songs in pop music, Streisand displays her classic vocal control on a medley of "I Believe" and "You'll Never Walk Alone," shifting meaning through subtle changes in dynamics. Backed with a gospel-infused organ and choir, Streisand sails vocally over a swelling, orchestrated modulation—perhaps the only singer in pop music with the skill and bravura to pull off such a calculatedly dramatic move. With its lyrics of self-empowerment, "A Lesson to Be Learned" reflects Streisand's personal philosophy: "The greatest lesson is loving yourself through it all." Acknowledging her influence on pop divas of the 1990s, Streisand duets with Celine Dion on the hit "Tell Him."

Reflecting her new sense of personal security and happiness, Streisand celebrated her 1998 marriage to actor James Brolin by releasing *A Love Like Ours* (1999), an album of romantic-themed songs. Her voice remaining strong at age fifty-seven, Streisand creates a lush, inviting atmosphere on tracks such as "I've Dreamed of You" and "Isn't It a Pity." Never fond of giving live performances, Streisand announced her farewell concerts in 1999, documenting one of them in the album, *Timeless: Live in Concert* (2000). Interspersing spoken reflections on her life with powerful versions of songs that have defined her career—"People," "Evergreen," "Happy Days Are Here Again"—she gives a vital, if somewhat measured, performance.

In 2002 Streisand released *Duets*, an album composed of previously recorded performances with pop singers such as Neil Diamond, Barry Gibb, and Celine Dion. Although the album also features several new songs, critics for the most part looked upon it unfavorably, citing Streisand's penchant for self-indulgence. In the Internet publication *All Music Guide*, writer William Ruhlmann observed dryly, "[Streisand's] unsuitability to the duet format is repeatedly evidenced, as she seems virtually incapable of shutting up when her partner is trying to take a solo." Fans have long proven a willingness to tolerate Streisand's excesses, however, and *Duets* succeeded in ranking on the Top 40 album charts. During this period, Streisand continued her long commitment to liberal activism, fundraising for the Democratic Party in 2000 and, the next year, speaking out against the nomination of conservative senator John Ashcroft for attorney general.

Regarded by critics and a loyal cadre of fans as one of the most remarkable voices in popular music, Streisand has enjoyed a wide-ranging career encompassing recording, acting, writing, and filmmaking. While many charge that her recorded output after the 1960s does not reflect her full artistic capabilities, Streisand in the 1990s continued to create music that, despite its flaws, honors her standing as a legendary performer.

SELECTIVE DISCOGRAPHY: *The Barbra Streisand Album* (Columbia, 1963); *People* (Columbia, 1964); *Stoney End* (Columbia, 1971); *The Way We Were* (Columbia, 1974); *Guilty* (Columbia, 1980); *The Broadway Album* (Columbia, 1985); *Back to Broadway* (Columbia, 1993); *The Concert* (Columbia, 1994); *Higher Ground* (Columbia, 1997); *A Love Like Ours* (Columbia, 1999); *Duets* (Sony, 2002).

SELECTIVE FILMOGRAPHY: *Funny Girl* (1968); *Hello, Dolly!* (1969); *The Owl and the Pussycat* (1970); *The Way We Were* (1973); *A Star Is Born* (1976); *Yentl* (1983); *Nuts* (1987); *The Prince of Tides* (1991); *The Mirror Has Two Faces* (1996).

WEBSITE: www.barbrastreisand.com.

DAVID FREELAND

THE STROKES

Formed: 1999, New York, New York

Members: Julian Casablancas, vocals (born New York City, 23 August 1978); Nikolai Fraiture, bass (born New York City, 13 November 1978); Albert Hammond Jr., guitar (born Los Angeles, 9 April 1979); Fabrizio Moretti, drums (born Rio de Janeiro, 2 June 1980); Nick Valensi, guitar (born New York City, 16 January 1981).

Genre: Rock

Best-selling album since 1990: *Is This It?* (2001)

Hit songs since 1990: "Hard to Explain," "Last Nite"

The Strokes. L-R: Nikolai Fraiture, Julian Casablancas, Fabrizio Moretti, Nick Valensi, Albert Hammond, Jr. [COLIN LANE/BIG HASSLE MEDIA]

Along with talent, hype has long been an essential component of rock and roll stardom. Few bands from the 1990s, however, were the subject of as much feverish expectation as New York's the Strokes. Anointed as the saviors of rock and roll by the British music press after releasing just three songs, the quintet's debut, *Is This It?* (2001), was greeted with waves of adulation for its compression of 1970s New York punk and 1980s arty new wave. While the album could not possibly have lived up to the buildup, the group was lumped in with the Vines and the Hives as part of the equally media-hyped "garage rock revival" of the new millennium.

Just one year after coming together in New York City in 1999, the Strokes were already being called the first significant rock band of the 2000s. The band had its origins in 1998, when singer Julian Casablancas (son of Elite modeling agency founder John Casablancas), drummer Fabrizio Moretti, and guitarist Nick Valensi began playing music together while attending the Manhattan private prep academy the Dwight School. Another prep school kid, bassist Nikolai Fraiture, soon joined, followed by a childhood friend of Casablancas from the Swiss boarding school L'Institut Le Rosey, guitarist Albert Hammond. The latter is the son of singer/songwriter Albert Hammond, author of the pop songs "It Never Rains in Southern California" and "To All the Girls I've Loved Before."

The band spent most of 1999 writing songs and rehearsing before making their live debut in September at the New York club the Spiral. The high-energy performance earned the nascent band a string of new bookings and a deal with the Rough Trade label, which released their three-song *The Modern Age* demo album in January 2001.

As a bidding war to sign the band was erupting in the United States—ultimately won by RCA Records—the EP was drawing rave reviews in the United Kingdom and multiple feature stories from the U.K. rock weekly *New Musical Express*; additionally, the single "Hard to Explain" debuted at number sixteen on the U.K. music charts. Restless to document their new songs, the band began recording their debut album before signing their record deal.

Band Drops Song in Wake of Terrorist Attacks

By the time *Is This It?* was released in late summer 2001 in the United Kingdom, the hype had reached deafening proportions. Every move made by the group became fodder for articles, including their original choice of album art, a suggestive photo of a woman's nude behind with a leather glove-clad hand resting on it. When U.K. retailers objected, the U.S. version—released in October—was changed to feature an abstract, lattice-like image.

More controversy followed, however. In the wake of the September 11, 2001, terrorist attacks on New York, band members were pressured to remove the song "New York City Cops," which features the line "New York city cops, they ain't too smart"; it was replaced by the song "When It Started." When the album was finally released, it was hailed by critics as a work of genius, synthesizing the street attitude and jagged guitar sounds of such important New York bands as the Velvet Underground and Television with the buoyant, pop-inspired sensibility of rock legends the Beatles and Buddy Holly.

With Casablancas's vocals sounding as if he is singing through a megaphone, songs such as "Hard to Explain" burn with a dark energy, propelled by Hammond's distorted, jazzy guitar riffs and Fraiture's steady, elongated bass lines. The combination of high society boys dressed in thrift store clothes playing a previous generation's music clicked with audiences, who more often than not ate up the spectacle of the disheveled, mop-topped Casablancas stumbling around the stage clutching a beer while yanking on his jean jacket lapels.

Casablancas plays the part of world-weary club kid to the hilt, penning lyrics about life as a disaffected twentysomething, summed up by the opening couplet to the title track. "Can't you see I'm trying, I don't even like it / I just lie to get to your apartment / Now I'm staying there just for a while / I can't think 'cause I'm just way too tired," he sings in a monotone over Hammond's spiky guitars, Moretti's steady, marching beat, and Fraiture's bouncy bass line.

The group debuted a handful of new songs during a fall 2002 U.S. tour and were named *Spin* magazine's Group of the Year for 2002. A second album was expected in 2003.

Despite a sound that added little original spin on the underground New York punk of the 1970s, the Strokes were hailed as the first great rock band of their generation. Ignoring the buzz, the band delivered on the promise in their live shows and released a debut album that features a classic combination of twentysomething ennui coupled with brash, rock and roll energy.

SELECTIVE DISCOGRAPHY: *Is This It?* (RCA, 2001).

WEBSITE: www.thestrokes.com.

GIL KAUFMAN

SUBLIME

Formed: 1988, Long Beach, California; Disbanded 1996

Members: Floyd "Bud" Gaugh IV, drums (born 2 October 1967); Bradley James Nowell, vocals, guitar (born 22 February 1986; died San Francisco, California, 25 May 1996); Eric Wilson, bass (born 21 February 1970).

Genre: Rap, Rock

Best-selling album since 1990: *Sublime* (1996)

Hit songs since 1990: "What I Got," "Santeria," "Wrong Way"

Few bands of the 1990s had a career arc that was as full of promise, excitement, and tragedy as that of Sublime. A fun-loving trio of friends who created a wholly original style of music that incorporated reggae, pop, classic rock, ska, hip-hop, and spoken word, Sublime had perfected their sound on hits such as "What It's Like" and "Wrong Way" on their self-titled third album (1996). Their celebration was short-lived, however, as lead singer and musical life force Brad Nowell died of a drug overdose two months before the album's release, silencing the band forever.

Sublime sprang to life in the surfing community of Long Beach in 1988, but their roots stretched back to the early 1980s. Drummer Bud Gaugh and bassist Eric Wilson grew up across an alley from each other and became fast friends. Wilson met singer Nowell in sixth grade, but the two did not begin making music together until 1988, when Nowell came home for a break two years into pursuing his finance degree at the University of California at Santa Cruz. Wilson, Gaugh, and Nowell began jamming and formed Sublime, but had difficulty getting gigs in local clubs due to their hard-to-pigeonhole musical style.

The trio gradually gained a following among the surfing/skateboarding crowd in the Long Beach area and caught the ear of Miguel Happoldt, who ran the label Skunk Records and agreed to release the band's debut, *40 Oz. to Freedom* (1992), recorded for $1,000. Sublime's debut is the musical equivalent of attention deficit disorder, randomly zigzagging from mellow reggae ("Smoke Two Joints") and echo-laden dub to drum machine-assisted psychedelic rock covers of the Grateful Dead ("Scarlet Begonias"), lightning fast punk ("New Thrash"), jazzy hip-hop rapping ("Waiting for my Ruca"), and plaintive Caribbean acoustic pop ("Badfish").

An Unexpected Break

The group got an unexpected break early in 1994, when the powerhouse Los Angeles alternative rock station KROQ began playing "Date Rape," a song about a sexual assault and revenge told over a bouncy reggae-influenced ska beat. Though the song drew fire for treating a sensitive subject lightheartedly, the album began selling briskly and the group's following grew.

They followed up with an album that took their sound experimentation even further, adding more elements of surf rock, rapping, bizarre spoken word passages, hardcore punk, and salsa. *Robbin' the Hood* (1994) also features "Saw Red," a ska pop duet with Gwen Stefani, singer of the then little-known southern California band No Doubt. With fellow punk bands the Offspring and Green Day having paved the way for the success of new California punk, Sublime were primed for a breakthrough, but even they could not have predicted what came next.

In 1995 they played the first annual traveling Warped skateboarding/punk festival, from which they were ejected for a week due to their drunken behavior and because their dog/mascot, a Dalmatian named Lou, bit one of the skaters. Though they often sang about drugs and smoking marijuana, Nowell was being drawn further into an addiction to heroin.

On the strength of their wild live shows and albums, MCA Records signed the group in 1995. Nowell's longtime girlfriend, Troy, gave birth to their son, Jakob, in June 1995.

Sessions Yield a *Sublime* Masterpiece; Tragedy Strikes

After sending Nowell to a rehab center to clean up, in early 1996 the label packed the trio off to Willie Nelson's studio in Pedernales, Texas, to record with Butthole Surfers guitarist Paul Leary, and later to Hollywood to work with producer David Kahne. Nowell was voraciously consuming drugs during the sessions, but his voice is smooth, confident, and clear on the album's songs.

Kahne and Leary were able to focus the band's energy on producing bright pop songs with reggae influences that were not as scattershot and wildly irreverent as their previous work, albeit without sacrificing the band's unique vision. The resulting album, *Sublime* (1996), is one of the decade's classics, producing one of the enduring alternative radio songs of all time, "What I Got." A reggae-rap song floated on an appealing, folky acoustic guitar line, turntable scratching and a steady beat, like many of the songs on *Sublime*, "What I Got" is a story about the band's everyday lives. "Lovin's what I got / It's within my reach / And the Sublime's style's still straight from Long Beach," Nowell sings in his sweet cigarette rasp on the chorus.

With an album everyone felt was going to be a sure-fire hit, the group hit the road for a tour. On May 25, 1996, one week after marrying Troy in a Hawaiian-themed Las Vegas wedding, Nowell was found dead of a heroin overdose in his San Francisco hotel room by band mate Wilson. Two months later, *Sublime* was released, and "What I Got" became an instant radio hit. By the time they'd realized their dreams, Sublime had broken up, with Gaugh and Wilson going on to front the nine-piece quasi Sublime tribute band, Long Beach Dub AllStars.

A string of releases followed, including a rarities collection (*Second-Hand Smoke*, 1997), a live album (*Stand By Your Van—Live in Concert*, 1998), and an acoustic album (*Bradley Nowell and Friends*, 1998).

Sublime were unlike any band who came before them, but, like too many of their peers, the band never got to bask in the glow of their stardom due to the drug-related death of their lead singer. Their fans, however, were left with three albums of stylish reggae rock that sounds as fresh today as it did when Nowell was alive.

SELECTIVE DISCOGRAPHY: *40 Oz. to Freedom* (Skunk, 1992); *Robbin' the Hood* (Skunk, 1994); *Sublime* (MCA/Gasoline Alley, 1996); *Second-Hand Smoke* (MCA/Gasoline Alley, 1997); *Stand By Your Van—Live in Concert* (MCA/Gasoline Alley, 1998); *Acoustic: Bradley Nowell and Friends* (MCA/Gasoline Alley, 1998).

GIL KAUFMAN

SUGAR RAY

Formed: 1992, Newport Beach, California

Members: Craig "DJ Homicide" Bullock, DJ (born 17 December 1972); Stan Frazier, drums (born 23 April 1969); Murphy Karges, bass (born 20 June 1968); Mark McGrath, vocals (born Hartford, Connecticut, 15 March 1970); Rodney Sheppard, guitar (born 25 November 1967).

Genre: Rock, Pop

Best-selling album since 1990: *14:59* (1999)

Hit songs since 1990: "Fly," "Every Morning"

Some musicians have so much confidence and ego that they seem destined from birth to be rock stars. The members of Sugar Ray have spent their entire career gaping in wonder at the repeat success of such breezy California pop hit singles as "Fly," "Every Morning," and "When It's Over." After abandoning their ill-conceived hard rock proclivities, the five-man band spent the 1990s surfing the wave of their success with good cheer, a healthy streak of self-deprecation, and a desire to write simple, cheerful pop rock songs.

If you listen to Sugar Ray's major label debut, *Lemonade and Brownies* (1995), you would be hard pressed to find the band that would return two years later with one of the most indelible pop hits of the late 1990s. Sugar Ray began life in 1992 as a Newport Beach, California, cover band called the Shrinky Dinx, whose specialty was songs by 1980s heavy metal/hard rock bands such as Judas Priest and Loverboy. The group's members bonded over the same love of reggae, ska, and 1980s new wave as such fellow Southern California up-and-comers as No Doubt and Sublime.

Singer Mark McGrath was a former truck driver, bassist Murphy Karges was a pizza chef, drummer Stan Frazier a paralegal, and guitarist Rodney Sheppard a telemarketer. Sheppard and Frazier had been in a local 1960s rock band called the Tories, which transformed into Sugar Ray when McGrath joined in 1992.

Forced to change their name to Sugar Ray—for boxer Sugar Ray Leonard— after Milton Bradley threatened a lawsuit over the Shrinky Dinx name, the band quickly developed a devoted fan base in Southern California and signed with Atlantic Records in 1994. In a nod to what the band members insist was dumb luck, the group scored the record deal when Atlantic Records president Doug Morris viewed a videotape of their song "Caboose," signing them without even hearing a full demo recording of their songs. With such sophomoric songs as "Like Me" and "Goldigger" in their repertoire, Sugar Ray set about recording their debut, *Lemonade and Brownies* (1995).

An Inauspicious Start

The album is a hackneyed mix of Red Hot Chili Peppers funk, heavy metal guitar anthems ("Mean Machine"), and nasal rapping. The group spent most of 1995 and 1996 touring in support of the album alongside rappers Cypress Hill and up-and-coming hard rockers Korn.

Though their second album, *Floored* (1997), features a similar mix of jokey hard rock, Beastie Boys–inspired nasal rapping, and sophomoric lyrics, it also contains a number of significant additions that would change the band's fortunes. Craig "DJ Homicide" Bullock joined the group prior to the album's recording, adding heft to their sound with his scratching and sampling and David Kahne signed on as their producer, beginning a creative collaboration that would bring the band unexpected fame and fortune.

With the help of Los Angeles rock station KROQ—the leading alternative rock station in the country—the song "Fly" began to gain attention for its light-hearted mix of Jamaican reggae, smooth California rock, and McGrath's scratchy, alluring croon. The song, with a guest rap from reggae star Super Cat, became a smash hit, pushing *Floored* to sales of more than 2 million and securing the group a more permanent place on the rock and roll pecking order.

Prior to the song's explosion, the group played on the third stage of the punk and skateboarding Warped Tour in the summer of 1997; by that fall they were headlining their first major American tour.

McGrath Becomes a Pin-up Star

At the same time, McGrath, with his movie star pout, perfectly coifed, spiked hair, and chiseled body, became a sex symbol, appearing on a string of teen magazine covers and being named one of America's sexiest men by *People* magazine in 1998.

Again banking on their low expectations, Sugar Ray's third album, *14:59* (1999), bore a title that alludes to Andy Warhol's famous maxim that in the future everyone would be famous for fifteen minutes; Sugar Ray believed they were about to use theirs up. With expert production from Kahne, the album proved that "Fly" was not a fluke, as it contained a string of gloriously easy-to-digest pop ditties and homages to 1980s new wave that made Sugar Ray even bigger stars.

Sheppard's guitar work takes on a more nimble, approachable tone on the album and critics noticed that McGrath finally gives up his more forceful, hard-edged vocals for tuneful, harmonious singing. Songs such as "Someday" and "Falls Apart" abandon the sophomoric humor and irony of the past for more adult concerns about relationships and romantic yearning. Flamenco pop song "Every Morning" combines a surfy guitar line, Beach Boys harmonies, turntable scratching, and McGrath's sincere

vocals for a surefire hit that displays the band's maturity and growth. "Couldn't understand how to work it out / Once again as predicted left my broken heart open / And you ripped it out," McGrath sings. The album sold more than 3 million copies.

Sugar Ray performed at the ill-fated Woodstock '99 concert during the summer and McGrath made a guest appearance on the popular NBC drama *E.R.* in the spring of 2000. A follow-up album, *Sugar Ray* (2001), though hailed as another creative leap forward in maturity and songcraft, failed to connect with fans with songs such as "Answer the Phone" and "When It's Over."

A period of dormancy followed, with the group beginning work on a new album in late 2002 with the help of Kahne and ultra-hot hip-hop production team the Neptunes. The album was due in mid-2003.

Over the course of a decade, Sugar Ray grew from an amateurish funk-metal band to a veteran pop group with a facility for crafting breezily infectious, slightly funky pop songs. Despite fears of being a one-hit wonder band, Sugar Ray persevered and matured with good humor and songs that provided the soundtracks to countless lazy summer days.

SELECTIVE DISCOGRAPHY: *Lemonade and Brownies* (Lava/Atlantic, 1995); *Floored* (Lava/Atlantic, 1997); *14:59* (Lava/Atlantic, 1999); *Sugar Ray* (Lava/Atlantic, 2001).

WEBSITE: www.sugarray.com.

GIL KAUFMAN

KEITH SWEAT

Born: Keith "Sabu" Crier; New York, New York, 22 July 1961

Genre: R&B

Best-selling album since 1990: *Keith Sweat* (1996)

Hit songs since 1990: "Make You Sweat," "I'll Give All My Love to You," "Twisted"

A rhythm and blues singer who has proved his influence over the course of a long and durable career, Keith Sweat is a pioneer of the sound known as "New Jack Swing." Bouncy, danceable, and exuberant, New Jack Swing was a key development in late 1980s R&B, paving the way for the brash hip-hop music of the 1990s. Known for his whining vocals, Sweat imparts a sensuous, urgent feel to both up-tempo songs and ballads. A factor in his success has been his foresight in choosing not to flood the market with album releases. Rather, he issues albums at intervals of two to three years, a tactic that allows him to maintain quality, consistency, and popularity.

Raised around the corner from the famed Apollo Theatre in Harlem, New York, Sweat began his career in the mid-1980s by submitting self-financed demo recordings to various record labels. An executive at Elektra Records heard one of these demos and offered him a recording contract in 1987. Late that year Sweat released his first and most influential album, *Make It Last Forever*. Boasting the thumping, insistent rhythms of the hit, "I Want Her," the album was a crucial bridge between the romantic R&B vocalizing of the 1970s and the aggressive hip-hop style that would predominate in the 1990s. Sweat's soulful rendition of "In the Rain," a song originally recorded by 1970s R&B group the Dramatics, suggested his admiration for the vocal traditions of the past, while "I Want Her" helped define the burgeoning New Jack Swing sound.

Sweat maintained his winning streak throughout the 1990s, delivering a solid follow-up to "I Want Her" with the driving hit, "Make You Sweat" (1990). *Keith Sweat* (1996) was a career peak; the success of its hit single "Twisted" propelled the album to the upper reaches of both the pop and R&B charts. Sweat's singing is distinctive and memorable, setting the trend for the nasal style favored by younger R&B artists such as Usher. The pleading quality of his voice gives his music a seductive undercurrent and erotic edge, although, unlike contemporaries such as D'Angelo and Next, Sweat rarely ventures into sexual explicitness. On *Keith Sweat*, he again displays his proficiency on dance tracks and slow love ballads, his assured phrasing adapting well to both formats. Although he failed to revisit the album's strong crossover success, Sweat continued to release quality recordings during the late 1990s and early 2000s, maintaining his professionalism and steady sense of groove. On *Rebirth* (2002), he proves that his voice is still strong, with the power to make a boasting track such as "100% All Man" believable. By this point in his career, Sweat had relocated to the R&B industry nexus of Atlanta, Georgia, where he established his own management agency and recording studio.

One of the few 1980s R&B performers who maintained a viable career into the 2000s, Sweat brandishes his unique, insistent voice on free-spirited dance music and intimate ballads, rarely deviating from his successful formula. Retaining a sense of youth and vitality into his forties, Sweat is acknowledged by fans as a father of hip-hop and a leader in contemporary R&B.

SELECTIVE DISCOGRAPHY: *Make It Last Forever* (Elektra, 1987); *I'll Give All My Love to You* (Elektra, 1990); *Keith Sweat* (Elektra, 1996); *Didn't See Me Coming* (Elektra, 2000); *Rebirth* (Elektra, 2002); *Keith Sweat Live* (Elektra, 2003).

DAVID FREELAND

MATTHEW SWEET

Born: Lincoln, Nebraska, 6 October 1964
Genre: Rock
Best-selling album since 1990: *Girlfriend* (1991)
Hit songs since 1990: "Girlfriend," "Ugly Truth," "Sick of Myself"

Matthew Sweet, pop singer, bass player, guitarist, and piano player, broke through with the highly-acclaimed album *Girlfriend* (1991), a tapestry of power pop radio-friendly ballads and brokenhearted love songs inspired by his crumbling first marriage.

Sweet was born and raised in Lincoln, Nebraska, where he worked in a music store and played in various New Wave cover bands during high school. He graduated in 1983 and moved to Athens, Georgia, for a brief spell before winding up in New York. After two unsuccessful albums on A&M Records, independent Zoo Records picked him up and released *Girlfriend* (1991), which would become a platinum-selling debut for their label. Nearly every song is a pop masterpiece, especially the classic rock and roll sound of the title cut. In "You Don't Love Me," Sweet creates a truly heartbreaking ballad, "'Cause you don't love me / You don't love me / You can't see how I matter in this world."

After the success of *Girlfriend*, Sweet delved into a darker period with *Altered Beast* (1993), a guitar-dense album that won him comparisons to Neil Young. It was not as commercially successful, but his fans stuck by him. Perhaps to combat the album's perceived somber qualities, Sweet cheekily named his next album *100% Fun* (1995), which landed in many critics' Top 10 lists and reached gold status.

Sweet's most noteworthy follow-up to *Girlfriend*, in terms of what he achieves in songwriting, scope, and production, is *In Reverse* (1999). It finds Sweet fully immersing his music in a 1960s "wall of sound" technique whereby a maximum, echo-laden sound is achieved through the synthesis of many instruments. Sweet has been involved in all aspects of his albums' productions. By the time he recorded *In Reverse*, he knew he wanted a large, all-encompassing, echoing effect, which was achieved by employing several people to play the same instrument part simultaneously. Sweet claims that he overdubbed a lot of the songs. Four of the songs were recorded in Los Angeles' Cello Studio, with a seventeen-piece band, including horns and theremin. "I Should Never Have Let You Know," complete with soaring harmonies, tack piano, and organ, best exemplifies Sweet's homage to the 1960s "wall of sound." Though *In Reverse* did not succeed commercially—it peaked at number 188 on the *Billboard* Top 200 chart—artistically it was a serious accomplishment.

The pop music of Sweet is bittersweet both in theme and sound. Few performers so creatively and compellingly fuse the influences of classic 1960s pop with a contemporary sensibility.

SELECTIVE DISCOGRAPHY: *Girlfriend* (Zoo, 1991); *Altered Beast* (Zoo, 1993); *100% Fun* (Zoo, 1995); *Blue Sky on Mars* (Zoo, 1997); *In Reverse* (Volcano, 1999); *Time Capsule: The Best of Matthew Sweet* (Volcano, 2000).

CARRIE HAVRANEK

SWV

Formed: 1990, New York, New York; Disbanded 1999

Members: Cheryl "Coko" Gamble, lead vocals (born Bronx, New York, 13 June 1974); Tamara "Taj" Johnson, vocals (born Bronx, 1974); Leanne "Lelee" Lyons, vocals (born Bronx, 1976)

Genre: R&B

Best-selling album since 1990: *It's About Time* (1992)

Hit songs since 1990: "I'm So into You," "Weak," "Right Here (Human Nature)"

SWV debuted in 1992 following a formula that had brought success to artists such as Jade, En Vogue, and TLC: old-fashioned, 1960s girl group-style harmonizing over the hip-hop infused R&B known as "New Jack Swing," with a playful sense of female empowerment. SWV's distinctive vocal talent and songwriting ability helped set them apart from the many so-called "New Jill Swing" groups flooding the market at the time. A string of Top 10 R&B singles, a number of which crossed over to the pop charts, made them one of the most successful R&B groups of the 1990s.

The members of SWV met while in high school in New York. Lead singer Coko is the daughter of gospel singer Tibba Gamble, who began grooming her daughter for a career in music from a young age. In 1990 the sixteen-year-old joined forces with two of her classmates, Leanne Lyons and Tamara Johnson, and the trio began performing at local talent shows under the name "Female Edition." In 1992 they attracted a manager, who changed their name to SWV, an acronym for "Sisters with Voices," and landed them a contract with RCA Records.

Their debut album, *It's About Time*, was released in the fall of 1992. It features SWV's deft harmonizing and lead singer Coko's impressive vocal range, which alternates between sweet and gritty. The album helped cement the group's down-to-earth, neighborhood-girl image. The first single, "Right Here," reached number thirteen on the R&B chart, but quickly fell off, and the album only sold a few hundred copies in its first few weeks. Sales picked up with the release of the next two singles. "I'm So into You," a ballad from the perspective of the "other woman," hit number two on the R&B chart and number six on the pop chart. Soon after, SWV scored a number one pop and R&B hit with "Weak," in which Coko's confident mastery as a singer contrasts with lyrical declarations of emotional helplessness: "Time after time after time I try to fight it. / Your love is so strong it keeps on holding on." "Weak" was quickly followed up with producer Teddy Riley's remix of *It's About Time*'s disappointing first single, "Right Here." Riley, widely credited with inventing New Jack Swing, blends the song with a sample of the 1983 hit "Human Nature" by Michael Jackson, whose falsetto moan serves as the hook. A classic of early 1990s "urban" R&B, "Right Here (Human Nature)" became another number one hit for SWV, and helped *It's About Time* to sell 5 million copies. It emerged as one of the best-selling albums of 1993, a year SWV ended with a Grammy nomination for Best New Artist.

In the spring of 1994 SWV released a remix album titled *Remixes*, which includes a collaboration with New York City rap collective the Wu-Tang Clan, then at the peak of their popularity. Their second album of new material, *New Beginning*, appeared in 1996. Although it yielded the number one R&B hit "You're the One," and sold well, it never equaled the success of *It's About Time*. Nor did their third album, the more hip-hop-oriented *Release Some Tension* (1997). In 1999 SWV broke up, citing personal differences and the desire to pursue solo careers. A greatest hits collection soon followed, along with Coko's solo album, *Hot Coko*.

Although neither the first nor most original of the girl groups to dominate R&B in the 1990s, SWV's tight harmonies and distinctive lead vocals made them stand out from many of their peers. While reaping commercial success, they also contributed a few songs that will endure as landmarks of 1990s R&B.

SELECTIVE DISCOGRAPHY: *It's About Time* (RCA, 1992); *Remixes* (RCA, 1994); *New Beginning* (RCA, 1996); *Release Some Tension* (RCA, 1997); *A Special Christmas* (RCA, 1997); *Greatest Hits* (RCA, 1999); *The Best of SWV* (RCA, 2001).

WEBSITE: www.swvonline.com.

MATT HIMES

SYSTEM OF A DOWN

Formed: 1995, Los Angeles, California

Members: John Dolmayan, drums (born Lebanon, 15 July 1974); Daron Malakian, guitar, vocals (born Glendale, California, 18 June 1975); Shavarsh "Shavo" Odadjian, bass (born Armenia, 22 April 1974); Serj Tankian, vocals (born Lebanon, November 1970).

Genre: Rock, Nu Metal

Best-selling album since 1990: *Toxicity* (2001)

Hit songs since 1990: "Chop Suey"

Serj Tankian of System of a Down [PAUL NATKIN/PHOTO RESERVE]

The Los Angeles-based hard rock band System of a Down began its ascent in the late 1990s when it appeared on festival stages with other popular nu-metal bands such as the Deftones, Korn, Slayer, and Slipnot. Although it shared a reverence for early metal originators like Black Sabbath, the band did not fit neatly into a specific category. The group's breakthrough album, *Toxicity* (2001), was praised for its originality. Instead of the screaming vocals, gothic doom, and dense sheets of guitars typical of mainstream metal, the album blended in Armenian folk music, unusual rhythms, and confrontational lyrics that explored spiritual and political themes. The band actively supported social justice and politically progressive causes. Because three of the four members are of Armenian descent, they became particularly vocal about shedding light on the genocide of their ancestors during World War I.

Vocalist Serj Tankian, guitarist Daron Malakian, and bassist Shavo Odadjian met while attending an Armenian-run high school in Hollywood. They began playing under the name Soil in 1993. Two years later they invited drummer John Dolmayan into the group, switched their name to System of a Down, and were soon building a buzz in the progressive heavy metal scene in southern California. At the time, metal bands were replacing their lead singers with rappers and adopting the culture of hip-hop. Hip-hop dominated the 1990s commercially with its anti-establishment stance that appealed to metal bands looking for streetwise credibility.

In the rap-rock explosion System of a Down was viewed as a band that succeeded in weaving rap into its music. Label mogul Rick Rubin, who produced both rap and metal artists like Public Enemy and Slayer, discovered the band. He signed them to his boutique label American, a subsidiary of Columbia Records, and produced the band's self-titled debut in 1998. Immediately, the band was launched on several high-profile summer festival tours like OzzFest, Family Values, and Summer Sanitarium.

But the band did not make its major breakthrough until 2001 with its second album, *Toxicity*, which debuted in the number one spot on the *Billboard* charts the week of the September 11 terrorist attacks. Co-produced by Rubin, it separated the band from its more formulaic rap-rock peers. The band incorporated pop melodies, jazz, Middle Eastern rhythms, tempo changes, whiplash rock riffs, and thought-provoking lyrics about war, prison overcrowding, spirituality, and totalitarianism. The song "Chop Suey" became an MTV hit and the band ended up headlining festivals including OzzFest. *Steal This Album!*, a collection of b-sides, followed the next year.

System of a Down used its newfound popularity to promote political causes. Tankian and Tom Morello, the guitarist for the political rap-rock band Rage Against the Machine, established axisofjustice.com, a website designed as a clearinghouse for social justice organizations. The group also became vocal proponents for recognizing the 1.5 million Armenians who were murdered or deported by Turkey during World War I. They supported a House Resolution in Congress sponsored by the Armenian National Committee of America that would have forced Turkey to accept official responsibility, which it has historically denied. "P.L.U.C.K. (Politically Lying, Unholy, Cowardly Killers)," a song from the band's first album that addresses the genocide, became a major staple in the band's live shows.

SELECTIVE DISCOGRAPHY: *System of a Down* (American/Columbia, 1998); *Toxicity* (American/Columbia, 2001); *Steal This Album!* (American/Columbia, 2002).

WEBSITES: www.systemofadown.com; www.axisofjustice.com.

MARK GUARINO

$$T \begin{array}{|l} t \\ \hline \mathbf{T} \end{array}$$

TAKE 6

Formed: 1985, Huntsville, Alabama

Members: Alvin Chea, bass (born San Francisco, California, 2 November 1967); Cedric Dent, baritone (born Detroit, Michigan, 24 September 1962); Joey Kibble, second tenor (born Buffalo, New York, 16 May 1971); Mark Kibble, first tenor (born Bronx, New York, 7 April 1964); Claude V. McKnight III, first tenor (born Brooklyn, New York, 2 October 1962); David Thomas, second tenor (born Brooklyn, New York, 23 October 1966). Former member: Mervyn E. Warren, second tenor (born 29 February 1964).

Genre: Jazz, Gospel, Doo-Wop

Best-selling album since 1990: *Join the Band* (1994)

Hit songs since 1990: "Spread Love," "Straighten Up and Fly Right"

Take 6 is an innovative and trend-setting male vocal group that has earned more Grammy Award nominations than any other gospel or soul vocal ensemble, and has racked up an unbroken string of gold- and platinum-selling albums since its debut in 1988. Although all its members are committed Christians and its songs all convey a religious message to some degree, the group's sound is as secular as it is spiritual, and its music is meant to be enjoyed by believers and nonbelievers alike.

Mark Kibble, a student at Oakwood College, a Seventh-day Adventist institution in Huntsville, Alabama, joined "The Gentlemen's Estate Quartet," a barbershop harmony group led by his childhood acquaintance, freshman Claude V. McKnight, upon hearing them rehearse in a dorm bathroom in 1980. Subsequently Kibble invited

Mervyn E. Warren, whom he knew from high school, into the group, which performed its unaccompanied gospel repertoire under the name "Alliance." When the ensemble's second tenor, baritone, and bass graduated from school and left town in 1985, they were replaced by Cedric Dent, David Thomas, and Alvin Chea. In 1987 the sextet was signed by Warner Bros., Nashville, and changed its name to Take 6.

Take 6's members have musical backgrounds, crossover tastes, and expansive ambitions. The Kibbles' father was minister of what Mark describes as "a very musical church." McKnight's grandfather, Fred Willis Sr., was a church choir director; and as a child McKnight attended his mother's rehearsals and learned to play trombone, which he says advanced his ear training. Chea has detailed his debt to jazz musicians such as Ron Carter for his "walking bass" vocal style.

Dent is a serious academic, who earned a Ph.D. in music theory from the University of Maryland in 1997. (He wrote his dissertation on the harmonic development of the black religious quartet singing tradition.) A frequent university guest lecturer, he hosted a Nashville Public Broadcasting Service (PBS) television station's music education series for children titled "Music to My Ears" in 1999, and has served as the music minister in several churches. Founding member Warren, since leaving Take 6 in 1991, has established himself as an independent music and film producer, working with such acclaimed musicians as Quincy Jones, Barbra Streisand, Smokey Robinson, and the Manhattan Transfer.

Rich voices, swinging arrangements, righteous lyrics, and overall exuberance earned *Take 6* (1988), the group's debut album, two Grammy Awards and Top 10 appearances on *Billboard* magazine's Contemporary Jazz and Contemporary Christian charts. These kudos put the group on the path to innumerable *Down Beat* magazine poll honors and Dove Awards from the Gospel Association. Take 6 sings original compositions and refreshed versions of traditional and standard spirituals such as "David and Goliath" and Thomas Dorsey's "If We Never Needed the Lord Before (We Sure Do Need Him Now)." They emphasize a warmly accessible, contemporary musicality—complete with finger-snapping, added percussion, and subtle electronic enhancements—rather than insistent preaching or folkloric purism. The group also brings out the spiritual side of soul songs such as Marvin Gaye's "How Sweet It Is to Be Loved by You" and Curtis Mayfield's "People Get Ready."

The group added instrumentation to its a cappella arrangements for one track on its third record, *So Much to Say* (1990), and also for *Join the Band* (1994), on which Ray Charles, Queen Latifah, Stevie Wonder, and Herbie Hancock guest star. *Brothers* (1996), produced by McKnight's brother Brian, a successful songwriter, has not even one a cappella track, which provoked concern from Take 6's core audience, but the group returned to the unaccompanied format on *So Cool,* varying arrangements to incorporate Ladysmith Black Mambazo–influenced South African choral singing as well as a quasi-big band track. *Beautiful World* (2002) was co-produced by Marcus Miller, the electric bassist who served as Miles Davis's producer during the mid-1980s; he, too, added select smooth jazz instrumentation to the ensemble's voices, without discernible harm. The faith-based entertainment of Take 6 clearly comforts audiences in times of stress; the band won a Grammy Award in 2002 for Best R&B Performance by a Duo or Group with Vocal for singing "Love's in Need of Love Today" with Stevie Wonder on the *America: A Tribute to Heroes* telecast in 2001.

Besides promoting Christianity and a cappella singing, Take 6 has had a significant and direct influence on secular pop singing groups such as the Backstreet Boys and *NSYNC and on a cappella soloist Bobby McFerrin.

SELECTIVE DISCOGRAPHY: *Take 6* (Reprise, 1988); *So Much 2 Say* (Warner Alliance, 1990); *He Is Christmas* (Reprise, 1991); *Join the Band* (Warner Alliance, 1994); *Brothers* (Reprise, 1996); *So Cool* (Warner Bros., 1998); *The Greatest Hits* (Reprise, 1999); *We Wish You a Merry Christmas* (Reprise, 1999); *Tonight: Live* (Reprise, 2000); *Beautiful World* (Warner Bros., 2002). **With Nnenna Freelon:** *Soulcall* (Concord, 2000).

HOWARD MANDEL

OLGA TAÑÓN

Born: Santurce, Puerto Rico, 13 April 1967
Genre: Latin
Best-selling album since 1990: *Te Acordarás de Mí* (1998)

The Puerto Rican diva Tañón has become the top female artist in merengue, a genre pioneered in the Dominican Republic. Her svelte good looks and R&B-informed singing helped make her tropical material palatable to Latin pop radio. Faster than its tropical counterparts cumbia and salsa, the merengue is a simple two-count rhythm often played in a minor key and accompanied by saxophone, trumpet, and, occasionally, the accordion.

The youngest of four children, Tañón began singing at eight with her church choir. She acted in school drama productions and competed in talent competitions, though she never won any of them. At the age of fifteen she began her professional career with the merengue group Las Nenas de Ringo y Jossie. After a brief stint with all-female merengue group Chantelle, she went solo in 1992.

Her first international hit was the merengue "Es Mentiroso" from *Siente el Amor* (1994). With fury and pain Tañón mocks an unfaithful partner's excuses and promises. For her 1995 follow-up, *Nuevos Senderos*, she called on the production talents of the Mexican singer/songwriter Marco Antonio Solis, who turned out a typically ballad-heavy effort. During the rest of the 1990s, Tañón alternated between pop and merengue releases.

As Tañón entered the new century, the distinctions between her merengue and pop CDs began to blur. *Yo Por Tí* (2001) adds soulful touches to her tropical canvas. The single "Como Olvidar," a number one hit on *Billboard*'s Hot Latin Tracks, was released in ballad and merengue versions, and Tañón works in some gospellike vocal inflections on the chorus. She even raps on "Me Gusta," playfully boasting about her talent and describing Mr. Right: "I'm looking for a guy . . . who sings like Marc Anthony, dances like Chayanne / and looks like Ricky Martin when he shakes his bon bon." Co-produced by Tañón and the pop-oriented producers Humberto Gática (Air Supply, La Ley) and Kike Santander (Cristian Castro, Jennifer Peña), *Yo Por Tí* maintains a danceable, polished groove that reflects Tañón's perfectionist nature. The album won the best merengue album Grammy in 2002, just one year after *Olga Viva, Viva Olga* accomplished the same feat.

The hard-working Tañón was already looking for material for her next album by the time *Yo Por Tí* was released. In November 2002 she returned with *Sobrevivir,* which features the number one *Billboard* Hot Latin Tracks hit "Así Es la Vida." She reteamed with Gática and Santander and tapped her longtime tropical-music collaborator Manuel Tejada. Dedicated "to all the women and men who struggle every day to survive," *Sobrevivir* features tasteful ballads and tropical-pop fusions. On the flamenco-flavored "Así Es la Vida," produced by Gática, Tañón tells a repentant ex that it's too late to come crawling back. An adult contemporary track, "A Partir de Hoy," features Spanish guitar and self-help lyrics like "I'm going to get rid of the custom of loving / he who mistreats me." Lush string arrangements and vocal experimentation combine to make *Sobrevivir* a musical step forward.

Tañón infused the male-dominated merengue genre with sisterhood, winning a largely female fan base through empowering lyrics that ranged from sympathetic pop psychology to righteous indignation. Not one to record blatantly autobiographical albums, Tañón says she prefers to sing about a variety of moods, regardless of what's going on in her notoriously topsy-turvy personal life. She and her first husband, Jesús Suarez, her former manager, divorced in 1994. In 1996 she married the professional baseball player Juan Gonzalez. They had one daughter, Gabriela Marie. After a turbulent relationship, the couple divorced, and Tañón married for a third time in 2002.

SELECTIVE DISCOGRAPHY: *Siente el Amor* (WEA Latina, 1994); *Nuevos Senderos* (WEA Latina, 1996); *Olga Viva, Viva Olga* (WEA Latina, 1999); *Yo por Tí* (Warner Music Latina, 2001); *Sobrevivir* (Warner Music Latina, 2002).

RAMIRO BURR

JAMES TAYLOR

Born: James Vernon Taylor; Boston, Massachusetts, 12 March 1948
Genre: Rock
Best-selling album since 1990: *Hourglass* (1997)
Hit songs since 1990: "Shed a Little Light," "Copperline"

James Taylor's career is as vibrant today as in the late 1960s, when a generation of young people identified with his image as a guitar-playing troubadour whose music mirrored their feelings. Taylor's brand of tuneful, personal songs and his honey-smooth singing style were major influences in the introduction of folk music to a mainstream audience. Widely esteemed for his affecting and often memorable melodies and lyrics, Taylor was called "a national treasure" by President Bill Clinton for his contributions to American culture.

Battling Drugs and Mental Illness with Music

Taylor's interest in music began at an early age while growing up in Chapel Hill, North Carolina. He was born the second of five children into a prominent Boston family that moved south after Taylor's father, Dr. Isaac Taylor, was offered the deanship at the University of North Carolina medical school. In 1963 Taylor's parents sent him to Milton Academy, a prep school outside of Boston where he began writing songs and meeting other musicians, most notably Danny "Kootch" Kortchmar, who later became a major contributor to and sideman on Taylor's recordings.

In 1964, his junior year, Taylor dropped out of high school to pursue music professionally. He moved to New York City and produced his first recordings with a short-lived band that he and Kortchmar formed called the Flying Machine. Although he recorded *James Taylor and the Original Flying Machine* in 1966, the album was not released until 1971, after he had achieved star status. This period of his life was also marked with hospital stays for serious depression. He eventually earned his high school diploma while seeking treatment during a ten-month stay at the McLean Psychiatric Hospital in Massachusetts in 1965.

Taylor fled the country for England in 1968 and shortly thereafter met Paul McCartney. He auditioned for the Beatles' record company, Apple Records, and, at McCartney's urging, Apple offered a recording contract. The resulting self-titled album, *James Taylor* (1968), was a success with critics, who lauded the agreeable melodies of songs like "Carolina in My Mind" and "Something in the Way She Moves." The album also features the eerily autobiographical songs "Something's Wrong," which deals with his heroin addiction, and "Knockin' Around the Zoo," a song about his stay in a mental institution. However, sales were slow, mostly because of the poorly managed record company's impending bankruptcy.

Taylor moved back to the United States, signed a record contract with Warner Bros. Records, and commenced a long string of musical triumphs with songs now firmly ensconced in American pop culture such as "Fire and Rain," "Sweet Baby James," "Walking Man," and "Shower the People." In 1971 *Time* magazine featured Taylor on its cover and touted him as the architect of the singer/songwriter era. That same year Taylor won his first Grammy for Best Male Vocal performer with his cover of Carole King's "You've Got a Friend."

Taylor has had tremendous success performing not only his own songs but also those of other major pop composers—for example, his enormously popular rendition of Holland, Dozier, and Holland's "How Sweet It Is (to Be Loved by You)," "Handyman" by Otis Blackwell and Jimmy Jones, and the Drifters' hit "Up on the Roof."

Throughout Taylor's rise to stardom, the singer was burdened by an addiction to heroin. His marriage in 1972 to singer Carly Simon, herself a major pop star, caught the imagination of the public. They scored a hit by combining talents on an Inez and Charlie Foxx pop standard

"Mockingbird." Their stormy union ended in divorce ten years later, but they remained friends and occasionally perform benefits together. They have two children, both of whom are singer/songwriters.

Despite his longevity in the music business, Taylor has not suffered a noticeable creative lull throughout his career. He continued to tour and recorded well-received albums throughout the 1970s and 1980s, such as *One Man Dog* (1972), *Flag* (1979), *Dad Loves His Work* (1985), and many others. He carried that success into the 1990s with his album *New Moon Shine* (1991). This album features a tribute to Martin Luther King Jr. titled "Shed a Little Light," and an anti-Gulf War song, "Slap Leather." His remake of the traditional "The Water Is Wide" expresses the intimacies of love and mutual respect. Taylor also turned once again to Sam Cooke's material and added some fun with "Everybody Loves to Cha Cha Cha."

Taylor resists writing his own story or assisting with biographies, claiming that the songs cover it adequately. (Two unauthorized biographies were published after 2000.) Hence he remains somewhat of a mystery to his fans, especially given his history of emotional trials and drug addiction. In the 1990s, however, he seemed to shake free of those demons.

Settling with Success

Three releases in the 1990s attempted to capture Taylor's much-revered live concert presence: *Live* (1993), the scaled-down *Best Live* (1994), and the video *Live at the Beacon Theater* (1998). Taylor's live shows attract a multi-generational fan base that delights in watching him perform. Tall and thin, Lincoln-like in aura, Taylor charms his audience with a self-effacing humor that is evident in his stories and patter between songs. His adroit folk styling on the guitar brings him tremendous praise among musicians.

The album *Hourglass* (1997) earned Taylor two Grammy Awards. It sold 70,000 copies in its first week and later went platinum. *Hourglass* features guest work from Stevie Wonder, who plays harmonica on "Little More Time with You;" Shawn Colvin, who sings on "Yellow and Rose;" and Sting, who sings backup on "Jump Up Behind Me." The album, which is a collection of songs on themes of hope and rebirth, features the talents of Yo-Yo Ma and Branford Marsalis as well.

Taylor has earned forty gold, platinum, and multi-platinum awards for his immense body of recorded work. His original *Greatest Hits* (1976) album has sold more than 10 million copies. In 1998 *Billboard* magazine awarded Taylor with the prestigious Century Award. He was inducted into both the Rock and Roll Hall of Fame and the Songwriter's Hall of Fame in 2000 and was awarded a Grammy in 2002 for Best Male Pop Vocal Performance

for "Don't Let Me Be Lonely Tonight," from Michael Brecker's *Nearness of You* collection; it was a song Taylor wrote in the 1970s.

In the early 2000s, Taylor rekindled an old relationship with Russ Titelman, who had produced his albums *Gorilla* (1975) and *In the Pocket* (1976), to create *October Road* (2002). Just as in his earlier trademark material, the songs on *October Road* are autobiographical and, according to Titelman, give wider play to the many textures of Taylor's guitar talents. Taylor's daughter Sally sings backup on "My Traveling Star" and "Buffalo Baby." *October Road* features accompaniment by legendary guitarist Ry Cooder and saxophonist Michael Brecker. Characteristically, Taylor adds a classic song into the mix, this time choosing to remake "Have Yourself a Merry Little Christmas" from the 1944 film *Meet Me in St. Louis*. By November 2002 *October Road* had sold more than 1 million copies. In November 2002 Taylor released a live DVD, *Pull Over*, which gives viewers a glimpse into the making of *October Road*, a complete concert of twenty-five songs, and a biography of the singer.

Having surmounted the burdens of depression and drug addiction, Taylor has endured as an artist, producing touching and graceful songs that have won the admiration of several generations of listeners.

SELECTIVE DISCOGRAPHY: *James Taylor* (EMI, 1968); *Sweet Baby James* (Warner Bros., 1970); *James Taylor and the Original Flying Machine* (Gadfly, 1971); *Sweet Baby James/Mud Slide Slim and the Blue Horizon* (Warner Bros., 1971); *One Man Dog* (Warner Bros., 1972); *Walking Man* (Warner Bros., 1974); *Gorilla* (Warner Bros., 1975); *In The Pocket* (Warner Bros., 1976); *Greatest Hits* (Warner Bros., 1976); *JT* (Columbia, 1977); *Flag* (Columbia, 1979); *Dad Loves His Work* (Columbia, 1981); *That's Why I'm Here* (Columbia, 1988); *New Moon Shine* (Columbia, 1991); *Live* (Columbia, 1993); *Best Live* (Columbia, 1994); *Hourglass* (Columbia, 1997); *Greatest Hits Volume 2* (Columbia, 2000); *October Road* (Columbia, 2002).

BIBLIOGRAPHY: I. Halperin, *Fire and Rain: The James Taylor Story* (New York, 2000); T. White, *James Taylor: Long Ago and Far Away* (London, 2001).

DONALD LOWE

LOS TEMERARIOS

Formed: 1982, Fresnillo, Zacatecas, Mexico

Members: Adolfo Ángel, keyboards, musical director (born Fresnillo, Zacatecas, Mexico, 1963); Gustavo Ángel, guitar, vocals (born Fresnillo, Zacatecas, Mexico, 1968); Fernando

Ángel, bass; Karlo Vidal, drums; Jonathan Amabiliz, percussion.

Genre: Latin

Best-selling album since 1990: *Cómo Te Recuerdo* (1998)

Hit songs since 1990: "Mi Vida Eres Tú," "Una Tarde Fue," "Como Tú"

At the turn of the twenty-first century, Los Temerarios found themselves kings of the hill in the regional Mexican subgenre known as *grupero*. The term refers to a band that plays ballads or tropical cumbias and does not give any member top billing.

Brothers Adolfo and Gustavo Ángel realized they wanted to go into music in the late 1970s, when their father rented a rehearsal room to local musicians. In 1982 they recruited their cousin, Fernando, to play bass. They recorded their first album for CBS Records in 1983. Their first hits, the ballads "Copa Rota" and "Por Ella Lloramos los Dos," foreshadowed the group's penchant for sentimentality and drama. The deep-pocketed label insisted on providing them with a producer, but even as greenhorns, Los Temerarios took charge of production and arrangements. Adolfo writes most of their material, drawing from personal experience.

However, their twangy norteño-grupero fusions did not meet sales expectations, and in 1987 the group signed with the Monterrey, Mexico, independent label Disa. While there the group adapted to a more urban, ballad-centered sound. Gustavo's voice had matured into a piercing tenor that was equal parts Art Garfunkel and George Michael. Decked out in sport coats and slacks, the group added a pop sheen to a genre stigmatized by some in Mexico as working-class.

Los Temerarios reached a creative peak with the album *Mi Vida Eres Tú* (1991), whose stirring title track juxtaposed mariachi trumpets with a stately, echoing beat. The cumbia track "Esa Mujer" became a staple at Mexican dance halls thanks to Fernando's staccato bass lines and Adolfo's ethereal synthesizers.

The album was the first under the Ángels' label, AFG Sigma Records, which eventually signed more than fifty artists but was locked in a hopeless battle for market share with the dominant player, FonoVisa. The Angels got out of the business side of things in 1996 when they sold AFG Sigma to FonoVisa. Their new label's promotional muscle helped make them Mexico's most popular *grupero* act by 1998.

As the 1990s ended, the group continued to evolve toward pop, using more acoustic guitar and piano and fewer drum machines. For the quintet's 2002 CD, *Una Lágrima No Basta*, Adolfo played a greater role, writing all the songs and singing or sharing lead vocals on four cuts. The title track,

Spot Light | *Cómo Te Recuerdo*

With the 1998 album *Cómo Te Recuerdo*, which was certified platinum by the Recording Industry Association of America for sales exceeding 1 million units, Los Temerarios became the best-selling act in *grupero* music.

Los Temerarios have always been more about a sound than poetic or deep lyrics, and *Cómo Te Recuerdo* represents the culmination of their layered, echoing production. The title track presents a gorgeous introduction complete with acoustic guitar, congas, and strings. Gustavo's honeyed tenor squeezes every last drop of conviction out of the heartbroken lyrics. "Bella Pero Mala" incorporates touches of piano and twangy guitar. The track also illustrates Adolfo's predilection for less-than-subtle lyrics about his personal life: "She fell in love with someone, and that someone left her alone, / all alone, and she came back," he proclaims with resignation. The album's design represented a quantum leap for the group, which left behind the low-budget packaging typical of the genre in favor of a twenty-four-page booklet. But it also took more than a worthy album to get them to the top of the *grupero* heap. The genre heavyweights Los Bukis and Bronco broke up in 1996 and 1997, respectively, clearing the way for Los Temerarios, whose fraternal bond has held them together for over two decades.

the album's first single, is a heartbreak-themed ballad with a doo-wop rhythm and calliope-sounding keyboard riffs. "Por Qué Será," a lovely power ballad, uses steel guitar to impart country shadings. "Comer a Besos" demonstrates the subtle but contagious grooves of the group's cumbias. Unfortunately, Adolfo, who sings like a smoother, blander Ringo Starr, takes an ill-advised turn as lead vocalist on the track. Adolfo also sings lead on another creative track, the flamenco "Gitana Baila." Although he is a talented tunesmith, his lyrics are more simplistic than those of his songwriting idols, Juan Gabriel and José Alfredo Jiménez.

Although Los Temerarios' tightrope walk between rootsy regional Mexican and sugary pop has sometimes alienated hardcore fans in both camps, their sugary melodies and inoffensive lyrics have helped them remain radio staples since the late 1980s.

SELECTIVE DISCOGRAPHY: *Mi Vida Eres Tú* (AFG Sigma, 1991); *Tu Última Canción* (AFG Sigma, 1993); *Camino del Amor* (FonoVisa, 1995); *Cómo Te Recuerdo* (FonoVisa, 1998); *En la Madrugada Se Fue* (FonoVisa, 2000); *Una Lágrima No Basta* (FonoVisa, 2002).

RAMIRO BURR

THE TEMPTATIONS

Formed: 1961, Detroit, Michigan

Members: Barrington Henderson, baritone vocals (born Washington, Pennsylvania, 10 June 1956); Harry McGilberry Jr., bass vocals; Ron Tyson, tenor vocals (born Monroe, North Carolina, 8 February 1948); Terry Weeks, tenor/baritone vocals (born 23 December 1962); Otis Williams, tenor vocals (born Texarkana, Texas, 30 October 1941). Selective former members: Dennis Edwards, baritone vocals (born Birmingham, Alabama, 3 February 1942); Melvin Franklin, bass vocals (born Birmingham, Alabama, 12 October 1942; died Los Angeles, California, 23 February 1995); Eddie Kendricks, tenor vocals (born Birmingham, Alabama, 17 December 1939; died Birmingham, Alabama, 5 October 1992); David Ruffin, tenor/baritone vocals (born Whynot, Mississippi, 18 January 1941; died Philadelphia, Pennsylvania, 1 June 1991); Paul Williams, baritone vocals (born Birmingham, Alabama, 2 July 1939; died Detroit, Michigan, 17 August 1973).

Genre: R&B

Best-selling album since 1990: *Phoenix Rising* (1998)

Hit songs since 1990: "Soul to Soul," "I'm Here"

As the most commercially successful male group at Detroit's famed Motown Records during the 1960s, the Temptations set a new standard for vocal artistry and stage presentation. Their intricate harmonies, dazzling choreography, and flashy costumes provided a model for virtually every male rhythm and blues group that followed them, from the early 1970s band the Jackson 5 to 1990s superstars Boyz II Men. Most remarkably, the Temptations retained their distinctive sound long after most of the original members had departed, keeping their style fresh into the 1990s and beyond.

Motown Stars

The Temptations were formed in Detroit in 1961, created from members of two separate vocal groups, the Primes and the Distants. Sparked by the high, ethereal tenor of Eddie Kendricks, and, after 1964, the gospel-

charged vocals of Mississippi-born David Ruffin, the Temptations' 1960s records were models of vocal refinement, enlivened by moments of calculated abandon. With the tight Motown studio band the Funk Brothers providing instrumental support, the group turned out a string of melodic, joyous hits that rank as some of the most memorable singles of the decade: "The Way You Do the Things You Do," "My Girl," "Ain't Too Proud to Beg," and "I Wish It Would Rain."

While famous for their youthful pop and R&B hits, the Temptations proved their versatility with the album *In a Mellow Mood* (1967), featuring older, "standard" tunes executed with graceful skill. In 1968 the troubled, unpredictable Ruffin was replaced by fiery vocalist Dennis Edwards, who led the group on hits featuring a grittier sound more in keeping with the toughness of late 1960s R&B: "Cloud Nine," "I Can't Get Next to You," and the moody, sinuous "Papa Was a Rollin' Stone." Although Kendricks left the group for a solo career in the early 1970s, the Temptations continued recording top-notch material into the 1980s, with hits such as the tuneful ballad, "Lady Soul" (1986). In 1989 the group was honored for its profound influence with an induction into the Rock and Roll Hall of Fame.

1990s Changes

The early 1990s were marked by loss: Ruffin, after decades of drug problems and financial insolvency, died from an overdose of crack cocaine in 1991, while former tenor Kendricks died of lung cancer the following year. After recording another album of standards, *For Lovers Only* (1995), the group suffered the passing of member Melvin Franklin, who collapsed from a brain seizure in 1995. Because of the many changes in personnel over the years, the lineup on the group's 1998 album, *Phoenix Rising*, and its fine follow-up, *Ear-Resistable* (2000), is substantially different from the "classic" Temptations of the 1960s and 1970s, with tenor Otis Williams acting as group leader, co-producer, and lone original member.

The most striking aspect of *Ear-Resistable* is its consistency with past efforts. By recruiting new members tenor/baritone Terry Weeks and bass Harry McGilberry, Williams preserved the rich harmony sound that made the group famous. At the same time, the album sounds wholly contemporary, featuring the seductive hit, "I'm Here," produced by 1990s R&B artist Joe. On the ballad "Proven and True," the high falsetto vocals of Ron Tyson interact with Barrington Henderson's rough baritone to create a mood of visceral excitement. The expert way in which the members exchange leads on the song, underscoring the melody with complex harmonies, is a testament to the group's ongoing integrity. Eschewing the sometimes off-key vocal approach of modern R&B artists such as Usher and Mary J. Blige, the Temptations honor their roots with performances that are full-bodied, aggressive, and exciting.

In 2001 the group released another album, *Awesome*, which makes for pleasant listening while lacking the distinctive fire of its predecessor. The subtly grooving "My Baby," however, captures the group's classic intensity through the powerful drive of Henderson's vocals, while "That's How Heartaches Are Made" is a charming, jazzy update of a 1963 hit by sultry R&B vocalist Baby Washington. In keeping with the group's fractious history, this successful period was not without its share of controversy. During the late 1990s former lead vocalist Edwards, his gravelly voice intact, toured nationally with an entirely different group of Temptations, an example of the confusion that often reigns when classic groups from the 1960s break up and divide into separate aggregations. After a prolonged court battle with Otis Williams, who holds the trademark to the name Temptations, Edwards was forced to perform as "The Temptations Review featuring Dennis Edwards."

The Temptations have overcome divisiveness, death, and changing trends in pop and R&B music to become one of the most durable acts in history, one of the few groups to experience hits in every decade since the 1960s. Through the seasoned leadership of Otis Williams, the group has remained contemporary without sacrificing the richness of their unique harmony sound.

SELECTIVE DISCOGRAPHY: *Meet the Temptations* (Gordy, 1964); *The Temptations Sing Smokey* (Gordy, 1965); *Temptin' Temptations* (Gordy, 1965); *In a Mellow Mood* (Gordy, 1967); *All Directions* (Gordy, 1972); *Truly for You* (Gordy, 1984); *For Lovers Only* (Motown, 1995); *Phoenix Rising* (Motown, 1998); *Ear-Resistable* (Interscope, 2000); *Awesome* (Universal, 2001).

BIBLIOGRAPHY: O. Williams with P. Romanowski, *Temptations* (New York, 1988).

WEBSITE: www.thetemptations.com.

DAVID FREELAND

BRYN TERFEL

Born: Bryn Terfel Jones; Pantglas, North Wales, 9 November 1965

Genre: Classical

Best-selling album since 1990: *Something Wonderful: Bryn Terfel Sings Rodgers and Hammerstein* (1996)

Bryn Terfel brought a superstar status to the bass-baritone voice in the 1990s that is usually reserved for the most high-profile tenors and

sopranos. Blessed with a gorgeous vocal instrument that can range from the most delicate and expressive introspection to outright musical thunder, Terfel possesses a charismatic stage arsenal that runs the gamut from reckless comedy and suave romance to intense and angst-filled drama. His wide repertoire includes plum opera roles, oratorios, lieder, the folksongs of his native Wales, operetta, and Broadway-style musical theatre. Terfel not only brings impeccable technique and superb musicianship to his material, but also manages to communicate the inner meaning of the words he is singing in a unique and personal manner that has an extraordinary effect on his audiences.

Growing up on a farm in a country where even chores are routinely accompanied by song, Terfel was taught vocal technique early on by a family friend, D. G. "Selyf" Jones, and began singing in local choruses and winning amateur singing contests in nearby villages. Singing was the only ambition that Terfel ever had, and in 1984 he moved to London to attend the Guildhall School of Music and Drama, where he studied with Arthur Reckless and Rudolf Piernay. Upon graduating in 1989 and winning the school's Best Singer Gold Medal, Terfel placed second to Dmitri Hvorostovsky in the Cardiff Competition, though he did take home the Lieder prize. He made his operatic debut in 1990 as Guglielmo in Mozart's *Cosi fan tutti* at the Welsh National Opera and sang the title role in Mozart's *The Marriage of Figaro* there as well. Those extraordinary successes had London's Covent Garden clamoring to have Terfel sing the title role in Mozart's *Don Giovanni*, but Terfel wisely chose to accept the small role of Masetto—and later Leporello—instead, allowing himself to develop before he would accept the title role.

Terfel's 1992 Salzburg Festival appearance as John the Baptist in Richard Strauss's *Salome* made Terfel an international sensation. That same year Terfel sang the Mahler Symphony No. 8 with James Levine and the Chicago Symphony Orchestra at the Ravinia Festival and made his American recital debut there the following evening, tossing off songs of Schubert and Schumann with such elegance, style, and meaning that those present could only marvel at how such talent and sophistication were possible in such a young singer. When Terfel sang his first Wagner role, the bit part of the thunder god Donner in *Das Rheingold*—the prologue to Wagner's four-opera *Der Ring des Nibelungen* cycle—at Lyric Opera of Chicago in 1993, audiences and critics alike were already clamoring for Terfel to sing the gargantuan role of Wotan, the ruler of the gods, and a central character of the *Ring* cycle. Terfel's much-anticipated and triumphant Metropolitan Opera debut was in 1994 as Figaro in *The Marriage of Figaro*, the role in which he had made his American operatic debut at the Santa Fe Opera two years earlier.

"Not yet" has become a Terfel mantra in an era in which most opera companies are only too happy to exploit young singers with large box office appeal by offering them roles that may be beyond their experience and endurance levels and that could wear out their voice before it has fully developed. Terfel has remained careful about what he would sing and when, continuing to sing supporting roles in operas that he knew he would sing leading roles in eventually as a way to further develop his long-term character portrayals. By the time Terfel began singing the title role of Verdi's *Falstaff* in 1999, for instance, he had already sung Ford under director Peter Stein at the Welsh National Opera and collected a notebook of ideas from Stein about the lead character that served him well when he sang the lead in his much-acclaimed first performances of the role in Australia and Chicago, and for the reopening of Covent Garden.

In addition to breathing new life into the opera world, Terfel also recorded a successful collection of Rodgers and Hammerstein songs called *Something Wonderful: Bryn Terfel Sings Rodgers and Hammerstein* (1996). That was followed by *If Ever I Would Leave You* (1998), a Lerner and Loewe songbook, and a collection of Broadway duets with soprano Renée Fleming, *Under the Stars* (2003). Not simply an opera singer who sings musical theater for crossover appeal, Terfel gave a chilling interpretation of the title role in Stephen Sondheim's *Sweeney Todd* at Lyric Opera of Chicago (2002), realizing a longtime ambition of the composer to have Terfel bring his musicianship and acting ability to the role. Terfel did not disappoint, and music critics, theater critics, and "serious" music and theater audiences alike were mesmerized by the powerful sonority, intensity, and dark humor that Terfel brought to his stunning portrayal of the "Demon Barber of Fleet Street."

That Terfel will continue to conquer the repertoire that he carefully chooses for himself seems a virtual certainty. Already a two-time Grammy Award winner who is selective about his recording projects, Terfel has indicated his desire to become the Wotan of the next generation, to take on Verdi and Puccini baritone roles, and to perform musical theater roles on Broadway.

SELECTIVE DISCOGRAPHY: R. Strauss, *Salome* (Deutsche Grammaphon, 1991); Delius, *Sea Drift, Songs of Farewell, Songs of Sunset* (Chandos, 1994); Mozart, *Le nozze di Figaro* (Deutsche Grammaphon, 1994); *An die Musik: Favorite Schubert Songs* (Deutsche Grammaphon, 1994); Lehár, *The Merry Widow* (Deutsche Grammaphon, 1995); *The Vagabond* (Deutsche Grammaphon, 1995); Wagner, *Lohengrin* (RCA, 1995); Schumann, *Scenes from Goethe's Faust* (Sony, 1995); *Opera Arias* (Deutsche Grammaphon, 1996); *Something Wonderful: Bryn Terfel Sings Rodgers and Hammerstein* (Decca, 1996); Mozart, *Idomeneo* (Deutsche Grammaphon, 1996); Beethoven, *Symphony No. 9* (Deutsche Grammaphon, 1996); *Handel Arias* (Decca, 1997); Mendelssohn, *Elijah* (Decca, 1997); Mozart, *Don Giovanni* (Decca, 1997); Berlioz, *La damnation de Faust* (Deutsche Grammaphon, 1998); Mozart, *Don Giovanni* (Deutsche Grammaphon, 1998); *If Ever I Would Leave You* (Deutsche Grammaphon, 1998); Stravinsky, *The Rake's Progress* (Deutsche Grammaphon, 1999); *in paradisum* (Deutsche Grammaphon, 1999); *We'll Keep a Welcome* (Decca, 2000); *Songs of My Welsh Home* (Marquis re-release, 2000); Schumann, *Schwanengesang* (Marquis re-release, 2000); Schumann, *Liederkreis, Op. 39, Romanzen and Balladen* (Deutsche Grammaphon); Verdi, *Falstaff* (Deutsche Grammaphon, 2001); *Wagner* (Deutsche Grammaphon, 2002). **With Cecilia Bartoli:** *Cecilia and Bryn* (Decca, 1999). **With Renée Fleming:** *Under the Stars* (Decca, 2003).

DENNIS POLKOW

THALÍA

Born: Thalía Ariadna Sodi; Mexico City, Mexico, 26 August 1971

Genre: Latin

Best-selling album since 1990: *Arrasando* (2000)

Hit songs since 1990: "Piel Morena," "Amor a la Mexicana," "Arrasando"

As a singer and actress of the late 1990s, Thalía produced disposable but catchy and well-produced singles for enjoyment at discos and parties. Even as a child Thalía knew she wanted to be a star, and she relentlessly pursued her goal. From 1986 to 1989, she belonged to Mexico's hottest teen-pop group, Timbiriche. She credited that job to years of experience with the more obscure kiddy group Din Din, which she joined in 1980. Thalía has said she always knew she would never be content to be just another face in a group, even one as popular as Timbiriche.

Thalía recorded her self-titled debut album in 1989. She registered moderate sales for that effort and her 1991 follow-up, *Mundo de Cristal*. Expressing her admiration for the Doors, she adopted a neo-flower-child image for her pop persona. Meanwhile, she played a plucky, optimistic poor girl in the legendary "María" trilogy of Mexican soap operas between 1992 and 1995: *María Mercedes, Marimar,* and *María la del Barrio*.

Her recording career reached A-list status with the 1995 album *En Extasis*, produced by Emilio Estefan. Featuring the single "Piel Morena" ("Brown Skin"), the album was a huge success, helping to turn Estefan's Miami studios into a Latin hit factory that is today compared to Motown. An expression of cultural pride that fuses booming bass with the folksy, midtempo Colombian rhythm known as Cumbia, "Piel Morena" showcases Estefan's pan-Latin sensibilities. It was Estefan who introduced the singer to Sony Music president Tommy Mottola in 1997 at a New York restaurant. Mottola and Thalía married in December 2000.

Thalía teamed with Estefan again on *Amor a la Mexicana* (1997). A rollicking pop-cumbia fusion that celebrates Mexico's love of "horses, boots and sombrero; tequila, tobacco and rum," the album was significant for appealing to a broad range of Mexicans in the notoriously class-conscious country. The final entry in the Estefan-produced trilogy, *Arrasando* (2000), contains her usual mix of tropical/dance ear candy and throwaway ballads.

Always noncommittal about the "crossover" to English attempted by Latin artists such as Enrique Iglesias, Paulina Rubio, and Shakira, Thalía did record a few songs in English for *Thalía* (2002). A new version of Alan Shacklock's "The Mexican," with Marc Anthony on backing vocals, received some Top 40 airplay, and she also pays tribute to the 1980s music of her teenage years with a campy cover of Dead or Alive's "You Spin Me Round (Like a Record)," sung in an affected British accent.

As Thalía entered her thirties, she kept up the youthful public persona she has cultivated throughout her career while attempting to negotiate the tricky transition into more "mature" music and acting roles.

SELECTIVE DISCOGRAPHY: *Love* (Universal, 1993); *En Extasis* (EMI Latin, 1995); *Amor a la Mexicana* (EMI Latin, 1997); *Arrasando* (EMI Latin, 2000); *Thalía* (EMI Latin, 2002).

RAMIRO BURR

THEY MIGHT BE GIANTS

Formed: 1982, Brooklyn, New York

Members: John Flansburgh, vocals (born Lincoln, Massachusetts, 6 May 1960); John Linnell, vocals, accordion (born Lincoln, Massachusetts, 12 June 1959).

Genre: Rock

Best-selling album since 1990: *Flood* (1990)

Hit songs since 1990: "Birdhouse in Your Soul," "Twisting," "The Statue Got Me High"

The funny, kooky duo They Might Be Giants are truly in a class all their own. Childhood friends, John Flansburgh and John Linnell—or "the Johns," as their fans and family refer to them—formed a band in their late teens, developing a style that stems from the greater recesses of their imaginations, and songs that often take funny, unexpected turns. Their live shows are legendary, and they have formed a career out of what could be described as "novelty music," with songs about such topics as a triangle man, a birdhouse in your soul, or a shoehorn. By the turn of the twenty-first century, the band had reached a new level of success: They had sold more than 3 million records, and won a Grammy Award for the theme song to the Fox network's zany family comedy, *Malcolm in the Middle*. Their success is surprising because they are an unorthodox band and unlikely rock stars.

The Formation of Giants

They Might Be Giants, whose name is derived from the 1971 movie starring George C. Scott and Joanne Woodward, was formed in Brooklyn, where the pair moved after college. The Johns grew up outside of Boston and attended elementary and high school together. Linnell, singer, accordionist, and keyboardist, did not start to seriously pursue music until a year or so after high school. Flansburgh, who attended a few different colleges and ultimately dropped out, taught himself guitar. In 1981 they moved to the same apartment building in Brooklyn and started writing songs using a drum machine and tape recorder. They managed to find some gigs in the East Village; their first show as They Might Be Giants took place in February 1983. They quickly developed a cultlike following through their shows, generated record label interest, and started something unique in the music business: Dial-a-Song. The duo recorded new songs on Flansburgh's answering machine as the outgoing message, so that fans could hear material and leave their own messages, too. By 1988 the band had written 300 songs and received on average 100 calls per day.

With goofy titles like "Put Your Hand Inside the Puppet Head" and "Youth Culture Killed My Dog" the material on their self-titled debut fared well. With twenty songs and two cheaply produced music videos, They Might Be Giants gained some steady play on MTV and college radio stations. Thanks to MTV, their debut began to sell about 1,000 copies per month. Luckily for them, They Might Be Giants formed at a time when quirky bands were all the rage. In 1988 they released their second album, *Lincoln*, which fared even better. The album contains oddball songs like the accordion-driven "Ana Ng," the silly ode to 1960s nostalgia "Purple Toupee," and "Shoehorn with Teeth," whose chorus proclaims "He wants a shoehorn / The kind with teeth / Cause he knows there's no such thing." Nonsensical lyrics aside, these songs are a great example of the catchy, cleverly arranged and humorously felt nature of the duo's music.

A *Flood* of Success

The pair's career took off with the release of *Flood* in 1990. *Flood* spawned several hits during the heyday of alternative rock, when radio stations would devote entire programming segments to the likes of such unusual, underground music. The song "Birdhouse in Your Soul" peaked at number three on the *Billboard* Modern Rock chart. It did not matter that the idea of a birdhouse in your soul was ridiculous; They Might Be Giants let the world know that they were serious about creating music replete with unexpected images. The album's second single, "Istanbul (Not Constantinople)," is a zany, danceable cover of the 1950s song of the same name. Other notable tracks include the reggae-tinged "Particle Man" and the semi-serious "Your Racist Friend." Though critics greeted *Flood* with mixed reviews, the album, which borrows from polka, rock, folk, reggae, and even television jingles, remains the group's best seller.

The Johns followed up the album with *Apollo 18* (1992), which they recorded with a full band for the first time. Although it did not fare as well commercially as *Flood*, it sealed their appeal to fans and continued the onward march of insanely titled music, with the odes "I Pallindrome I" and "My Evil Twin." Their follow-ups, *John Henry* (1994) and *Factory Showroom* (1996), were more or less ignored by the press but their popularity has never waned, due in part to the fact that their live shows are so enjoyable, replete with sing alongs and other gags that often involve audience participation.

Giants in Their Field

Toward the late 1990s, They Might Be Giants began to branch out into other media, releasing songs on their website for fans to download on their home computers. They wrote the mock-spy thriller song "Doctor Evil," reminiscent of James Bond films from the 1960s, for the Mike Myers film *Austin Powers: The Spy Who Shagged Me* (1999). They expanded into other territories, including children's music, for the joyful batch of songs on *No!* (2002).

They Might Be Giants began as a duo whose eclectic, everything-but-the-kitchen-sink approach was seemingly at odds with fame, fortune, and full-fledged rock stardom. By the time the band celebrated their twentieth anniversary together in the summer of 2002 with a live show in Central Park in New York City the zany, talented duo had truly become giants.

SELECTIVE DISCOGRAPHY: *They Might Be Giants* (Bar/None, 1986); *Lincoln* (Restless/Bar/None, 1988); *Flood* (Elektra, 1990); *Apollo 18* (Elektra, 1992); *John Henry* (Elektra, 1994); *Factory Showroom* (Elektra, 1996); *Severe Tire Damage* (Restless, 1998); *Mink Car* (Restless, 2001); *No!* (Idlewild/Rounder, 2001). **Soundtrack:** *Austin Powers: The Spy Who Shagged Me* (Warner Bros., 1999).

CARRIE HAVRANEK

THIRD EYE BLIND

Formed: 1995, San Francisco

Members: Brad Hargreaves, drums (born San Francisco, California, 30 July 1971); Stephan Jenkins, vocals, guitar (born Oakland, California, 27 September 1963); Tony Fredianelli, guitar (born Las Vegas, Nevada, 2 April 1970); Arion Salazar, bass (born Oakland, California, 9 August 1970). Former members: Adrian Burley, drums; Jason Slater, bass; Kevin Cadogan, guitar (born Oakland, California, 14 August 1970).

Genre: Rock

Best-selling album since 1990: *Third Eye Blind* (1997)

Hit songs since 1990: "Semi-Charmed Life," "Graduate," "How's It Going to Be"

With hit songs about drugs, abortion, and suicide, Third Eye Blind was one of the most unlikely success stories of the late 1990s. Led by the unique vision of singer Stephan Jenkins, albums such as the band's self-titled debut (1997) tackled serious subjects within disarmingly catchy pop arrangements.

Even though he was an unknown quantity in the music business, Stephan Jenkins began his career in the driver's seat. Upon graduating from the University of California at Berkeley in 1988 with an English degree, Jenkins began playing solo acoustic shows at San Francisco venues. After several years of going it alone, Jenkins attempted to put together a band, initially with little success. Not until Jenkins hooked up with former Fungo Mungo bassist Arion Salazar did Third Eye Blind begin to take shape. In 1995 Kevin Cadogan, a former student of renowned rock guitarist Joe Satriani, introduced himself to Jenkins at a show and was asked to join the group, along with one-time Counting Crows drummer Brad Hargreaves.

The group struggled to make a name for itself, even though Jenkins had already received praise for his production work on the Braids' 1996 hit rendition of "Bohemian Rhapsody," a rock operetta by the English band Queen. Thanks in part to a strong Bay Area following, Third Eye Blind's fourteen-song demo recording began to draw the attention of record labels. Jenkins managed to get the group an opening slot on Oasis's April 1996 show at the Bill Graham Civic Auditorium in San Francisco. The group was called back for an encore, an unusual honor for an opening act.

Shortly thereafter, the group signed with Elektra Records, which offered Jenkins the opportunity to produce the band's debut himself. The resulting album, *Third Eye Blind* (1997), spawned one of the most unlikely hit singles of the 1990s, a delightfully frothy pop song, "Semi-Charmed Life," which camouflages a series of dark images of illicit drug use and oral sex with a poppy, upbeat rhythm and Jenkins's carefree, sung/spoken vocals. "I want something else / To get me through this semi-charmed kind of life / I'm not listening when you say goodbye," Jenkins sings, his voice shooting into a falsetto at the end of the chorus, before breaking into a series of "doot, doot, doot" nonsense syllables. The song reached number one on *Billboard*'s Modern Rock charts and number four on the pop charts, and the album sold more than 4 million copies. Elektra's decision to allow Jenkins to produce the album proved prescient.

Several other hits followed in early 1998, including the rousing pop anthem "Graduate," the cello-assisted acoustic ballad "How's It Going to Be," and the pop folk ballad "Jumper," a bracing, wistful track about a gay friend committing suicide.

A two-year world tour ensued, including opening dates for U2 and the Rolling Stones. Prior to the release of their second album, *Blue* (1999), the band became embroiled in a censorship battle with their label, which requested that Jenkins remove the song "Slow Motion" from the album, citing the "current social climate" in the wake of that year's deadly shootings at Columbine High School in Littleton, Colorado. The song, written before the shootings, was intended to be a comment on the destructive gun culture of the United States. The lyrics in question included the lines "Miss Jones taught me English, but I think I just shot her son / 'Cause he owed me money, with a bullet in the chest / With a bullet in the chest he cannot run / Now he's bleeding in a vacant lot." The group included an instrumental version of the track on the album.

Again produced by Jenkins, the album adds more aggressive, 1970s rock-inspired electric guitars, a children's choir, and string sections to songs such as "Anything" and "10 Days Later." Despite its more elaborate take on the band's signature blend of risqué topics (abortion, violence against women, sex) and catchy, pop rock arrangements, *Blue* did not sell as well as its predecessor. Cadogan was fired from the group in January 2000 and later sued over songwriting royalties; the suit was amicably settled in 2002. The original guitarist, Tony Fredianelli, returned to replace Cadogan.

Proving that cleverly crafted, smart pop songs about serious subjects can be made into radio hits, Third Eye Blind made a smashing debut in 1997 thanks to Stephan Jenkins's vision and determination to do things his way.

SELECTIVE DISCOGRAPHY: *Third Eye Blind* (Elektra, 1997); *Blue* (Elektra, 1999); *Out of the Vein* (Elektra, 2003).

WEBSITE: www.3eb.com.

GIL KAUFMAN

RICHARD THOMPSON

Born: London, England, 3 April 1949

Genre: Rock, Folk

Best-selling album since 1990: *Watching the Dark: The History of Richard Thompson* (1993)

Hit songs since 1990: "I Feel So Good," "Hide It Away"

A founding member of the seminal 1960s British folk rock group Fairport Convention, Thompson traded on a personal folk rock style that won critics over but did not produce a mass following. Critics hailed Thompson, sometimes called the British Neil Young, for his brilliant guitar work and the lyrical richness of his extraordinary songwriting.

Thompson joined Fairport Convention in 1967, recording five studio albums including *Fairport Convention* (1968) and *What We Did on Our Holiday* (1968). But by 1971, Thompson, feeling his songwriting was ill-suited for the group, opted out to pursue a solo career. His first solo album *Henry the Human Fly* (1972) was released on the Hannibal label and sold poorly. Over the next twenty-five years, Thompson produced thirty-odd albums, almost equally divided between solo work and various collaborations.

One of his early landmark albums, *I Want to See the Bright Lights Tonight* (1974), is a collaboration with his first wife, singer Linda Peters. Her powerful and passionate vocals are perfectly suited for Thompon's dark compositions. In tunes like "Has He Got a Friend for Me" and "The Little Beggar Girl," somber lyrics of solitude and longing are counterbalanced by blissful and memorable rhythms. "Down Where the Drunkards Roll" is a sympathetic description of the drunk's life, written by a man who never drank alcohol.

The Thompsons would produce five more critically acclaimed, but marginally selling, albums, including *Pour Down Like Silver* (1975), which is highlighted by the tune "Dimming of the Day." A familiar "please-come-back-I'm-nothing-without-you" lament, the tune is elevated by Linda's emotive vocals.

After a brief recording hiatus while the couple joined a communal Muslim sect, the Thompsons recorded their last collaboration in *Shoot out the Lights* (1982). Since the album was recorded while the couple worked through a divorce, many critics assumed its songs chronicled their rocky separation. Actually, they had been written two years earlier for another project that was eventually discarded. While marital discord, death, and stormy relationships had always been part of Thompson's thematic repertoire, there is conspicuous, perhaps creative, tension in these songs. In the end, the couple's separation added poignancy to the proceedings. Highlights include "Wall of Death," a thrilling, guitar-fueled rush about the irony of feeling "the nearest to being alive" while riding "on the wall of death one last time." The title track refers to the injustice and sadness felt by many when Soviet troops went into Afghanistan. Ultimately, Linda's sweet but husky vocals contrasted with Richard's dark lyrics and ringing guitar work to produce unforgettable music.

Richard Thompson's solo career resumed with *Hand of Kindness* (1983). With titles like "Tear-Stained Letter" and "A Poisoned Heart and a Twisted Memory," critics speculated the songs were more grievances from a spurned lover. But Thompson was already happily remarried. While Thompson's strength lay in dark tales, he was not immune to simple joyful tunes like the Cajun-flavored "Two Left Feet," in which the narrator, atop infectious rhythms, rebukes a partner for below-par dancing.

In an interview with the London daily the *Independent*, Thompson defended his often gloomy lyrics. "There's something very appealing about sad music. It is a way of dealing with sadness, rather than wallowing in it, and a way of sharing it. As a songwriter, through looking into yourself and having courage, you can express the unexpressed. You can say things that need to be said, but that people don't always say. You can hold them up to an audience and say, 'look, this is inside everyone, this is a common experience, let's have a look at it in the comfort of our living room armchairs, or in the comfort of our theatre seats'—and it's a pleasant way of dealing with this, let's deal with it as entertainment."

Thompson teamed up with producer Mitchell Froom on *Amnesia* (1988), a decidedly more upbeat album. On the urgent "Jerusalem on the Jukebox," Thompson criticizes television evangelists, while on the mellow "Can't Win," he describes the futility of growing up. But Thompson did not forget his morose side, and chose to include the dark "I Still Dream" and "Waltzing's for Dreamers," which features the haunting lyrics: "One step for aching / Two steps for breaking / Waltzing's for dreamers and losers in love."

Thompson peaked again on *Rumor and Sign* (1991), a more lyrically upbeat and polished work featuring eloquent treatments of romantic misadventure. The follow-up, *Mirror Blue* (1994), shines with brilliant, though

melancholy, songs like "King of Bohemia" and "Beeswing." The latter is a moving account of love lost on the road not taken.

You? Me? Us? (1996) is a nineteen-track double disc, again produced by Froom. Uneven, it still displays Thompson's strengths, including his deep baritone, dark wit, and piercing guitar. Over a thirty-year career, Thompson carved out his spot in folk rock music with a body of work that reveals him as a pensive songwriter/philosopher and an excellent guitarist.

SELECTIVE DISCOGRAPHY: *I Want to See the Bright Lights Tonight* (Hannibal, 1974); *Pour Down Like Silver* (Hannibal, 1975); *Shoot Out the Lights* (Hannibal, 1982); *Hand of Kindness* (Hannibal, 1983); *Amnesia* (Capitol, 1988); *Watching the Dark: The History of Richard Thompson* (Rykodisc/Hannibal, 1993); *Mirror Blue* (Capitol, 1994).

RAMIRO BURR

3 DOORS DOWN

Formed: 1996, Escatawpa, Mississippi

Members: Daniel Adair, drums (born Vancouver, 19 February 1975); Brad Arnold, lead vocals, drums (born Escatawpa, Missisippi, 27 September 1978); Todd Harrell, bass (born Escatawpa, Mississippi, 13 February 1972); Chris Henderson, guitar (born Escatawpa, Mississippi, 30 April 1971); Matt Roberts, guitar (Escatawpa, Mississippi, 10 January 1978). Former member: Richard Liles, drums (born Kiln, Mississippi, 25 February 1973).

Genre: Rock

Best-selling album since 1990: *The Better Life* (2000)

Hit songs since 1990: "Kryptonite," "When I'm Gone"

3 Doors Down, exemplars of postgrunge or alternative rock, emerged from the small town of Escatawpa, Mississippi, in the mid-1990s. The group developed a loyal fan base and was eventually signed to Universal Records after a showcase performance at the renowned rock club CBGB's in New York City. Their first hit, "Kryptonite," received tremendous airplay and was largely responsible for the success of their debut album, *The Better Life* (2000). After lengthy tours, 3 Doors Down returned to Mississippi and wrote the songs for their next album, *Away from the Sun* (2002).

The group began as a power trio consisting of Brad Arnold, Matt Roberts, and Todd Harrell. Arnold was the driving force in this early lineup, working simultaneously as the singer, drummer, and sole lyricist. Soon guitarist Chris Henderson was added to the group, and in this incar-

3 Doors Down. L-R: Todd Harrell, Brad Arnold, Chris Henderson, Matt Roberts [FRANK OCKENFELS/UNIVERSAL MUSIC]

nation 3 Doors Down quickly established itself as a solid rock band entrenched in the alternative rock textures of the 1990s. After signing with Universal Records and recording their first album, drummer Richard Liles was added to the lineup, allowing Arnold to function as the front man.

"Kryptonite" was released in the summer of 2000 and peaked at *Billboard*'s number three slot. Initiated by an electric guitar and snare-drum riff reminiscent of U2's "Sunday Bloody Sunday," the song gradually builds throughout the first and second verses. At the chorus distorted power chords are introduced as Arnold sings, "If I go crazy then will you still call me Superman." Aside from a subdued guitar solo, the formal structure is largely based on repetition, with the simple addition of a single verse.

Their subsequent single, "Duck and Run," is propelled by a metal riff shared by the bass and electric guitars. The first chorus is abbreviated, immediately sliding back into the verse and functioning as a premonition of the full chorus. Phrases are shared between sections, producing an audible continuity: "I'm already here" ends the full chorus and initiates the transition to the guitar solo. "I won't turn around" is transformed into "I won't duck and run," allowing for the full exposition of the chorus and the bridge.

This formal simplicity allowed for radio-friendly hits, but also produced a single dimension of sound. In this way, *The Better Life* is hindered by wholly predictable songs and dismal rock clichés. Their second album, *Away from the*

Sun (2002), reveals a more contemplative approach, emphasizing themes of loneliness and frustration. It sold reasonably well, going platinum and peaking at *Billboard*'s number eight. The first single release, "When I'm Gone," is an anthem of supplication: "Hold me when I'm scared, and love me when I'm gone." Other tracks reiterate this general feeling of powerlessness, from the well-crafted "Away from the Sun" to the banal "Ticket to Heaven."

In the early 2000s, 3 Doors Down reinvigorated the alternative rock scene by creating popular radio hits with an edge. However, the economy of musical material that allowed for such hits also hindered their development. Although the group has produced several exceptional songs, their music is still largely indistinguishable from that of other alternative rock bands such as matchbox twenty, Creed, and Nickelback.

SELECTIVE DISCOGRAPHY: *The Better Life* (Universal, 2000); *Away from the Sun* (Universal, 2002).

WEBSITE: www.3doorsdown.com.

WYNN YAMAMI

311

Formed: 1990, Omaha, Nebraska

Members: Nick Hexum, vocals, guitar (born Madison, Wisconsin, 12 April 1970); Douglas Vincent "S. A." Martinez, vocals (born Omaha, Nebraska, 29 October 1970); Tim Mahoney, guitar (born Omaha, Nebraska, 17 November 1970); Chad Sexton, drums (born Lexington, Kentucky, 7 September 1970); Aaron Charles "P-Nut" Wills, bass (born Indianapolis, Indiana, 5 June 1974).

Genre: Rock

Best-selling album since 1990: *311* (1995)

Hit songs since 1990: "All Mixed Up," "Down," "Transistor"

311 followed in the footsteps of the Beastie Boys and Red Hot Chili Peppers in bringing rap/rock to mainstream airwaves. While incorporating hip-hop, reggae, and dance-hall music into its hard-rock attack, the group retained a Midwestern lyrical sensibility that appealed to college audiences.

The group's name comes from the Omaha police code for indecent exposure—the group's original guitarist, Jim Watson, was once arrested for skinny dipping. However, the cryptic name came back to haunt them later, when some gossips started the rumor that it was code for "KKK" (*k* is the eleventh letter of the alphabet). The band worked quickly to quash the rumor and disavow any connection to racism.

After becoming a local favorite, the group relocated to Los Angeles in 1991, signing with Capricorn Records.

Though the group faced the financial hardships common to unknown rockers, the members fully expected to break big sooner or later. They spent their early years in the shadow of the angst-ridden grunge movement. With positive lyrics and danceable rhythms, 311 represented the antithesis of that genre.

Their major-label debut album, *Music* (1993), with its rap-rock fusions, set the tone for their subsequent work, but it features more of a funk vibe than later efforts. P-Nut, who had taken formal bass lessons for four years, shines with his finger-popping riffs. The album produced 311's first minor hit, "Do You Right," which made number twenty-seven on *Billboard*'s Modern Rock Tracks. A wistful song about holding on to important moments, it exemplifies the group's belief in positive lyrics. However, the album also demonstrates the group's capacity for polemic protest. In line with their middle-class background, they attack not inner-city problems but environmental degradation on "F*** That Bull****." Never interested in adopting a petulant pose, the group released "clean" versions of all its 1990s albums.

311 added reggae to their palette for their follow-up album, *Grassroots* (1994), but it is on *311* (1995) that they finally reach the culmination of their pastiche of chainsaw heavy-metal riffs, chilled-out tropical rhythms, and Hexum's laid-back, regular-guy vocals. The group also overcame any residual resistance to rap-rock from alternative radio. The ultimate frat-boy album of the period, *311* spent seventy-two weeks on the *Billboard* 200 thanks to the monster hit singles "Down" and "All Mixed Up."

Hubris caught up with 311 on the album *Transistor* (1997), which is overlong and meandering at seventy-four minutes and twenty-one tracks. Though it debuted at number four, giving 311 its highest album ranking ever, it only lasted thirty-three weeks on the Top 20. The album did, however, produce two alt-rock hits: the title track, a psychedelic dance-hall-metal fusion, and "Beautiful Disaster," an ominous antidrug salvo.

Soundsystem (1999), produced by the studio wizard Hugh Padgham, marks a return to form, featuring rhythmic shifts that are unpredictable but unforced. Despite the sunny, tropical vibe, "Eons" and "Large in the Margin" contain lyrics that betray Hexum's "lack of direction and self-doubt," as he put it.

More than a decade after moving to Los Angeles, 311 continued with the same five members and in 2002 released *From Chaos*. By then many groups like Incubus and No Doubt were nimbly fusing rock with hip-hop, and 311's trademark party vibe seemed to have lost its trendsetter status. Nevertheless, 311 created an influential blend of Caribbean, hip-hop, and rock fusions that other popular groups continue to refine.

SELECTIVE DISCOGRAPHY: *Music* (Capricorn, 1993); *Grassroots* (Capricorn, 1994); *311* (Capricorn, 1995); *Transistor* (Capricorn, 1997); *From Chaos* (Volcano, 2001).

RAMIRO BURR

THE THREE TENORS

Formed: 1990, Rome, Italy

Members: Jose Carreras (born Barcelona, Spain, 5 December 1946); Plácido Domingo (born Madrid, Spain, 21 January 1941); Luciano Pavarotti (born Modena, Italy, 12 October 1935).

Genre: Classical

The Three Tenors—Jose Carreras, Luciano Pavarotti, and Plácido Domingo—are the biggest-selling classical music act of all time. Although classical artists usually perform in concert halls, the Tenors sold out a succession of stadium shows around the world throughout the 1990s. The Tenors have sold more than 20 million recordings of their concerts and have been seen on television by billions of viewers. Their recordings dominated the classical recording charts for much of the 1990s.

Soccer fans all, the tenors first got together for a concert celebrating the 1990 World Cup in Rome. Considered the world's leading tenors at the time, the three had considerable star appeal individually that multiplied by an order of magnitude when they joined forces. They performed together for the first time at the ancient Roman ruins of the Baths of Caracalla before an audience of 6,000 (100,000 fans had tried to buy tickets). The concert—featuring a huge orchestra of 200 conducted by Zubin Mehta—was televised throughout the world and became an immediate sensation. The concert recording sold 11 million copies, and the video became a staple of public television pledge drives, selling millions more.

The three singers had donated all their earnings from the concert to charities—Domingo to earthquake relief in Mexico, Carreras to cancer research (he had recently been treated for leukemia in Seattle), and Pavarotti to medical care in Italy—but were astonished by how much money the event generated. So in 1994 they came together again for another concert in Dodger Stadium at the World Cup in Los Angeles. Tickets sold for hundreds of dollars apiece, and the stadium was filled with 60,000 fans, among them hundreds of Hollywood celebrities. The concert was carried live on TV (hosted by violinist Itzhak Perlman) and watched by more than 1 billion viewers worldwide.

Now the tenors, each of whom had busy careers in his own right, began playing stadiums around the world—in

Spot Light | The Three Tenors at the Baths of Caracalla

There have been many "concerts of the century." Most are just hype. But the night when tenors Luciano Pavarotti, Plácido Domingo, and Jose Carreras first got together in the ancient Roman ruins of the Baths of Caracalla—July 7, 1990—deserves due consideration for the title. Of course the concert was hype. Was it the best concert ever? Of course not. Did it even bring the three best tenors in the world together, as it claimed? Probably not. But as an "event," an extraordinary occasion bigger than the music being sung, it was a complete and utter success. Everything about it was super-sized: three enormous egos; an orchestra of 200; 100,000 fans trying to buy tickets (6,000 got in); and a television audience numbering in the hundreds of millions. A recording of the proceedings sold 11 million copies—more than any classical recording in history. And millions more videos were sold. The concert launched the Three Tenors franchise, which changed the way classical music is marketed. Over the next decade the three singers were seen and heard by billions of fans.

Tokyo, at Wembley Stadium in London, Giants Stadium in New York, Olympic Stadium in Munich, Skydome in Toronto—earning millions of dollars for these appearances.

In 1998, with another World Cup, the Tenors performed under the Eiffel Tower in Paris with l'Orchestre de Paris conducted by James Levine, this time drawing more than 100,000 fans to the free concert and a worldwide television audience of 2 billion viewers in seventy-five countries. Over the next five years, the trio slowed the pace of stadium appearances to a couple per year, performing in the Forbidden City in Beijing, Las Vegas, Sao Paulo, Seoul, Vienna, and Japan.

The Three Tenors have been a phenomenon of shrewd marketing. Promoter Tibor Rudas helped create story, spectacle, and occasion to sell the concerts more as multimedia happenings than as musical events. Outings were packaged more in the style of rock concerts—with massive stages, giant video screens, and special lighting—than classical music concerts. The first concert was billed as a welcome back for Carreras, who had battled cancer

and was trying to restart his career. Then the story line focused on who was the best singer of the three.

There is no concert literature for three tenors, and programs resembled a kind of friendly musical slugfest in which each singer took turns belting out a popular aria or pop song. The repertoire was familiar, and the three sang in half a dozen languages, adding to the international appeal. Special arrangements of popular tunes were made so the tenors could sing together, and onstage the three kibitzed and engaged in good-natured rivalry.

They alternated singing one another's favorite tunes—*Nessun Dorma, La donna è mobile, O Sole Mio, Grenada, Tonight* (from *West Side Story*)—pretending to try to outdo one another. At their best, Pavarotti, Domingo, and Carreras were high-spirited, gracious stars enjoying one another and the enormous crowds.

The Three Tenors concerts received mixed critical notices. Amplified and piped out to tens of thousands in the audience, the voices sounded processed and manufactured. In time, the good-natured play between the singers onstage sometimes seemed forced or indifferent, and lack of rehearsal and preparation made some of the concerts seem slapdash. Critics engaging in which-tenor-is-best games also could not fail to notice that Carreras's voice had not recovered fully from cancer treatments; his voice could not match those of his partners.

Nevertheless, the Three Tenors were such a crossover sensation that the classical music world worked overtime trying to understand the secrets to their success; the trio spawned numerous imitators, and the "Three Tenors Phenomenon" spawned a new era of slick mass-marketing and crossover stratagems in the financially strapped world of classical music.

SELECTIVE DISCOGRAPHY: *Carrera—Domingo—Pavarotti: The Three Tenors in Concert* (London, 1990); *The Three Tenors In Concert: 1994* (Atlantic, 1994); *The Best of the Three Tenors* (Universal, 2002).

WEBSITE: www.threetenors.com.

DOUGLAS MCLENNAN

LOS TIGRES DEL NORTE

Formed: 1968, Rosa Morada, Sinaloa, Mexico

Members: Jorge Hernández, bandleader, vocals, accordion (born Rosa Morada, Sinaloa, Mexico, 7 August 1949); Eduardo Hernández, accordion, saxophone, bajo sexto, vocals; Hernan Hernández, bass, vocals; Luis Hernández, bajo sexto, vocals; Oscar Lara, drums; Lupe Olivo, saxophone.

Genre: Latin

Best-selling album since 1990: *Jefe de Jefes* (1997)

Hit songs since 1990: "Pacas de a Kilo," "El Circo," "De Paisano a Paisano"

Combining meaty social conscience with chart-topping popularity, Los Tigres del Norte are the best-selling group in the history of norteño ("of the north"), a folk-based rural Mexican genre. As its name implies, it was born in northern Mexico, influenced by the introduction of the accordion, the waltz, and the polka by German and Czech railroad engineers. Los Tigres were founded by the four Hernández brothers—Jorge, Raúl, Eduardo, and Hernan—plus cousin Oscar Lara. In 1968 the group received a temporary visa to perform in California prisons with other Latino artists. At the border an immigration inspector called the young musicians "little tigers," and the group adopted *tigres* as its moniker. The visa ran out, but Los Tigres found work easier to come by in California and put down roots in San Jose. The members eventually became permanent residents of the United States but kept their Mexican citizenship.

Los Tigres became widely known thanks to their 1972 megahit corrido, "Contrabando y Traición." Mexican corridos are story ballads, and their tradition dates back to the nineteenth century. "Contrabando y Traición" was an early "narco-corrido," a story-song about the drug trade. The song's success began a tidal wave of similarly themed corridos that continues to the present day.

During the 1980s, the group began producing political corridos such as "La Jaula de Oro," which deals with the 1986 immigration amnesty. In 1988 Los Tigres won a Grammy for the album *Gracias! América sin Fronteras*, which called for open borders. Although Los Tigres do not write their own material, they work closely with a stable of songwriters, including Teodoro Bello, Enrique Franco, and Enrique Valencia, who are in sync with the group's philosophy and sometimes provide made-to-order songs.

In April 2000, the group set up the Los Tigres del Norte foundation to preserve Mexican and Mexican-American folk music traditions. The first grant, $500,000, was awarded to UCLA's Chicano Research Center, with whom Los Tigres participated in a 1998 workshop. The money was used to digitize 32,000 corrido recordings from 1904 to 1954, from music historian Chris Strachwitz's personal collection.

Los Tigres' 2001 CD, *Uniendo Fronteras*, spent three weeks at number one on the *Billboard* Latin Albums chart and spun off several singles: "Mi Fantasia," "De Rama En Rama," "Somos Mas Americanos," and "Recuerdos Que Duelen." But the song that generated the most controversy

---

Spot Light | *De Paisano a Paisano*

De Paisano a Paisano (2000) marked the culmination of Los Tigres' transformation from entertainers into social commentators/activists. Instead of the usual straight-ahead cover photo depicting the band, the cover art depicts a mural by the Los Angeles artist Paul Botello, showing the "futuristic life of historical figures who have had a lot to do with our race," in the words of Jorge Hernández. The title track first single, a fierce ranchera written by Enrique Valencia, expresses an immigrant's desire to be buried in Mexico. Being buried in America, he said, "would be like dying twice." "They've made war on us, patrolling the border," Hernández sings ominously. On "A Quien Corresponda," Hernández condemns border-area ranchers in Arizona, who make citizens' arrests of illegal immigrants. The album signaled a rare coming together of Los Tigres' first-generation immigrant politics and Chicano activism.

---

was "Crónica de un Cambio." Recorded a few months after Vicente Fox's inauguration as president of Mexico, the song details problems he inherited from previous governments and asks when change is coming. However, "Crónica" was not released to Mexican radio until July 2002, a circumstance that led to its misconstrual as a criticism of Fox's administration. Fearful of offending the federal government, a major advertiser in Mexico, most stations avoided the song.

The group was hit by another partial Mexican radio ban later that year for the narco-corrido "La Reina del Sur," the title track of their 2002 album. Considering that many norteño groups record far more explicit material, some wonder if Los Tigres are simply convenient scapegoats because of their visibility and their willingness to criticize the Mexican government.

SELECTIVE DISCOGRAPHY: *Gracias . . . América sin Fronteras* (FonoVisa, 1987); *El Ejemplo* (FonoVisa, 1995); *Jefe de Jefes* (FonoVisa, 1997); *De Paisano a Paisano* (FonoVisa, 2000); *La Reina del Sur* (FonoVisa, 2002).

RAMIRO BURR

TIMBALAND

Born: Tim Mosley; Virginia Beach, Virginia, 10 March 1971

Genre: Rap

Best-selling album since 1990: *Welcome to Our World* (1997)

Hit songs since 1990: "Up Jumps Da Boogie," "Here We Come"

In the late 1990s the influence of producer/artist Timbaland in the R&B/hip-hop world knew few boundaries. His bounces-and-beats sound pervaded many of the top hits by such artists as the late Aaliyah, Ginuwine, Boyz II Men, Nas, Jay-Z, and Missy "Misdemeanor" Elliott. Like the influential mid-1980s producers Jimmy Jam and Terry Lewis (Janet Jackson), Timbaland created a new rap blueprint that used stuttered beats to set the rhythm and add power to rap's pop hooks. The new sound was so attractive and exciting that it helped transform modern rap into a lively and relevant part of American culture.

Timbaland began his career working in Da Bassment, a loose-knit group of producers, writers, and MCs who worked in the background behind Jodeci. He later formed a duo with the rapper Magoo in Norfolk, Virginia. The two had met as teenagers in the early 1990s and had begun to write songs for several artists, including Ginuwine and Missy Elliott. Timbaland's genius for creating infectious rhythms was first showcased in Missy Elliott's influential CD *Supa Dupa Fly* (1997), which bristles with electric beats, futuristic atmospherics, and dancehall flavors. The CD features guests Busta Rhymes, Lil' Kim, Da Brat, and Aaliyah. Timbaland and Magoo produced their first single, "Up Jumps Da' Boogie," in the fall of 1997. Featuring Missy Elliott and Aaliyah, the single peaked at number twelve on the *Billboard* Hot 100. Timbaland and Magoo included the single on their platinum-selling debut album, *Welcome to Our World* (1997). With its eighteen tracks, the CD showcases Timbaland's knack for fusing catchy beats and minor sampling for a distinctive sound.

While waiting to work on his solo CD, Timbaland kept producing, writing, and remixing for other artists. Timbaland's *Tim's Bio: Life from Da Bassment* (1998) pays tribute to early funk and, radically, samples the themes from *Spider-man* and *I Dream of Jeannie*; it features a stellar list of guests including Nas, Jay-Z, Mad Skillz, Aaliyah, and others. The album resonates with skittering beats, call-and-respond raps, and fresh, fun rhythms. Timbaland's strength is his fearless sense of experimentation in the studio. His hits, his own and the ones he wrote for others, make him a much sought-after and much-copied producer.

Legal problems delayed his follow-up, *Indecent Proposal* (2001), by almost a year. It provides a new sonic template that stretches the possibilities of commercial rap. Freely mixing and matching 1970s funk, disco, and soul with bits of jazz and ambient grooves, Timbaland continued with his trademark envelope pushing. "Indian Carpet" is fueled by futuristic beats, while other tunes feature snippets of Asian, Arab, and Indian music. The mellow, reflective ballad "I'm Music" features Aaliyah (her last recording) with the singer/songwriter Beck. Other guests include Snoop Dogg, Twista, Jay-Z, Ludacris, Bubba Spar, and Magoo.

Timbaland's talent for creating memorable grooves comes from his understanding that new, original, but contagious beats fuel the catchy power of tunes. Using these skills, Timbaland has elevated his game and along the way he has helped expand rap's commercial potency in the new millennium.

SELECTIVE DISCOGRAPHY: *Welcome to Our World* (Blackground, 1997); *Tim's Bio* (Blackground, 1998); *Indecent Proposal: Life from Da Bassment* (Blackground, 2001).

RAMIRO BURR

TLC

Formed: 1991, Atlanta, Georgia

Members: Lisa "Left Eye" Lopes, vocals (born Philadelphia, Pennsylvania, 27 May 1971; died Jutiapa, Honduras, 25 April 2002); Rozonda "Chilli" Thomas, vocals (born Atlanta, Georgia, 27 February 1971); Tionne "T-Boz" Watkins, vocals (born Des Moines, Iowa, 26 April 1970).

Genre: R&B

Best-selling album since 1990: *CrazySexyCool* (1994)

Hit songs since 1990: "Ain't 2 Proud 2 Beg," "Waterfalls," "No Scrubs"

Female trio TLC formed in 1991, when the hip-hop-oriented R&B known as "New Jack Swing" was at its height. Strong hooks, flamboyant clothes, and an unapologetic embrace of female sexuality helped them break through to immediate pop success, which they maintained throughout the decade while evolving into more mature artists. On their way to becoming the biggest-selling female group in history, they spawned successful imitators such as SWV and Destiny's Child and made headlines with a host of financial, legal, and personal problems. After the death of Lisa "Left Eye" Lopes in 2002, the remaining members announced that they would never again tour under the name TLC, without officially dissolving the group or ruling out the possibility of releasing new albums.

TLC. Front to back: Chilli, Lisa, and T-Boz [PAUL NATKIN/PHOTO RESERVE]

Tionne "T-Boz" Watkins and Lisa "Left Eye" Lopes met in Atlanta, Georgia, as members of an all-female R&B group. In 1991 they decided to go their own way and soon met Rozonda "Chilli" Thomas, with whom they formed TLC. They shortly landed a manager, 1980s R&B singer Pebbles, and began working with local producer Dallas Austin. Pebbles brought TLC to the attention of her then-husband, Antonio "L.A." Reid, and his partner, successful producer/singer Kenneth "Babyface" Edmonds. Reid and Edmonds signed TLC to their LaFace label, which released their debut album, *Oooooooohhh . . . On the TLC Tip*, in early 1992.

Oooooooohhh . . . On the TLC Tip favors the typical New Jack production of the time, leaning toward up-tempo dance songs that intermingle T-Boz's husky croon, Chilli's smoother, more melodic singing, and Left Eye's growling raps. The first single, "Ain't 2 Proud 2 Beg," employs a hip-hop groove and a call-and-response chorus to present a bouncy yet aggressive celebration of the female libido: "Yo if I need it in the morning or the middle of the night / I ain't 2 proud 2 beg." The accompanying video established the trio's young and sassy image, showing off their exuberant dancing and colorful, oversized outfits, which Left Eye memorably accessorized with a condom-turned-

eye patch. "Ain't 2 Proud 2 Beg" became a Top 10 pop hit, and was followed by the equally successful singles "Baby Baby Baby" and "What About Your Friends," eventually driving sales of the album to 4 million.

In the two years before releasing their follow-up album, TLC maintained their public profile with "Get It Up," a hit single from the soundtrack to the 1993 movie *Poetic Justice*, starring pop singer Janet Jackson. Less favorable publicity came in June 1994, when Left Eye was arrested in Atlanta for burning down the house she shared with her then-boyfriend, Atlanta Falcons wide receiver Andre Rison. As part of her defense, Left Eye made public Rison's alleged physical abuse and admitted to a drinking problem, agreeing to enter rehab to avoid jail time. A few months later TLC released their second album, *CrazySexyCool*.

Growing Up

CrazySexyCool represents a significant departure for TLC, toning down the rowdy playfulness of their debut and adopting a more sophisticated, mature approach. The group moves away from the heavily rap-influenced sound characterizing *Oooooooohhh . . . On the TLC Tip* in favor of smooth R&B tracks emphasizing T-Boz's sultry lead vocals and Chilli's harmonizing. The result is an elegant fusion of hip-hop and classic soul that makes *CrazySexy-Cool* one of the defining albums of 1990s "urban" pop. *CrazySexyCool* was a commercial breakthrough as well. The lead single, "Creep," a jazzy, assured endorsement of the benefits of occasional infidelity, became a number one pop hit. The album's next single, "Red Light Special," also topped the charts, as did "Waterfalls," which uses muted horns and T-Boz's melancholy vocals to plead for an end to self-destructive behavior in the inner city. The groundbreaking video for the latter, which employs cutting-edge special effects to emphasize the track's underlying message of compassion, won the group four MTV Video Music Awards in September 1995. *CrazySexyCool* became the second biggest selling album of 1995. It eventually went eleven times platinum, making TLC the biggest selling female group of all time.

It was at the height of this success that TLC faced a public financial crisis. A recurrence of T-Boz's sickle-cell anemia forced the group to cut short a tour in support of *CrazySexyCool*, costing them millions of dollars in potential revenue. In July 1995 the trio filed for bankruptcy, blaming debts in connection with Left Eye's arson charges and their less-than-fair share of royalties from sales of *CrazySexyCool*. This latter complaint eventually led them to part ways with their manager, Pebbles, who by then had undergone a bitter divorce from L.A. Reid. TLC's problems had little effect on the continuing success of *CrazySexyCool*. In February 1996 it won a Grammy Award for Best R&B Album, with "Creep" winning Best R&B Performance by a Duo or Group with Vocal.

TLC largely spent the next year and a half away from the spotlight, sorting out their finances and planning their next album. In June 1997 Chilli and Austin had a son. At the same time, TLC announced that Austin would not be reprising his producer duties on the upcoming album, citing a dispute over his fees. By the end of the year, however, Austin was back on board for his third consecutive TLC album. *FanMail* was released in February 1999, more than four years after its predecessor.

FanMail finds TLC largely revisiting the territory charted by *CrazySexyCool*, this time employing a wide variety of producers in addition to Austin. The result, while not groundbreaking, is nonetheless solid, and the album enjoyed substantial critical and commercial success. The first single, "No Scrubs," distinguishes itself from previous TLC hits by featuring Chilli on lead vocals. She deftly uses her gentle, feminine voice to introduce a sassy warning to would-be suitors without the funds to back up their posturing: "If you don't have a car and you're walking / Oh yes, son, I'm talking to you." "No Scrubs" spent a few weeks at number one, and hit enough of a nerve that it inspired an answer song from New York City rap trio Sporty Thievz, "No Pigeons." The album spawned two more Top 10 hits with "Unpretty" and "Dear Lie," and went on to sell 6 million copies. In September 1999 "No Scrubs" won an MTV Video Music Award for Best Group Video.

Strife and Sorrow

As TLC was enjoying renewed success with *FanMail*, tensions between Left Eye and the other two members were threatening to tear the group apart. In an infamous interview with the magazine *Entertainment Weekly* in November 1999, T-Boz and Chilli accused Left Eye of distancing herself from the group, while Left Eye criticized her bandmates' business acumen and challenged them to a competition in which each would release a solo album. TLC managed to settle their differences enough to perform that February at the 2000 Grammys, where they earned a Best R&B Performance by a Duo or Group for "No Scrubs" and a Best R&B Album for *FanMail*.

On April 25, 2002, Left Eye was killed in a car accident while on vacation in Honduras. At the time of her death, TLC had begun recording their fourth album, *3D*. A mourning Chilli and T-Boz completed the album and released it in November 2002, subsequently announcing that it would be their last as TLC.

By skillfully applying three distinct vocal talents to top-notch production and consistently provocative songwriting, TLC dominated urban music for virtually the entire 1990s. In the process of winning unprecedented

commercial success, they helped define the hip-hop-flavored soul that characterized the decade. The sudden death of member Lisa "Left Eye" Lopes left TLC's future uncertain, just when the group was showing promising signs of further growth.

SELECTIVE DISCOGRAPHY: *Ooooooohhh . . . On the TLC Tip* (LaFace, 1992); *CrazySexyCool* (LaFace, 1994); *Fanmail* (LaFace, 1999); *Greatest Hits* (LaFace, 2001); *3D* (LaFace, 2002). **Soundtrack:** *Poetic Justice* (Sony, 1993).

BIBLIOGRAPHY: N. E. Krulik, *Lisa Lopes: The Life of a Supernova* (New York, 2002).

WEBSITE: www.laface.com/#tlc.

MATT HIMES

TOO $HORT

Born: Todd Anthony Shaw; Los Angeles, California, 28 April 1966

Genre: Rap

Best-selling album since 1990: *Cocktails* (1995)

Hit songs since 1990: "Get in Where You Fit In"

Too $hort emerged as an early West Coast rap icon in a hip-hop environment dominated by East Coast music. With his thick western drawl, Too $hort spins vivid tales of lawlessness that impart an authenticity that made him a founder of gangsta rap and an essential figure in rap music.

Born middle class to two accountants in the South Central neighborhood of Los Angeles, California, Todd Shaw moved with his family to the northern California city of Oakland at age fourteen. Influenced by books about pimping by authors Iceberg Slim and Donald Goines, Shaw began rapping about these topics. His five-foot-two-inch frame earned him the stage name Too $hort. He began producing and selling his own songs, and he attracted the attention of an independent record label, 75 Girls, which signed him to a contract. The deal resulted in three albums that increased his local Oakland profile. Ever the entrepreneur, Too $hort formed his own label, Dangerous Music, and in 1986 released the full-length album *Born to Mack*, which became a San Francisco Bay–area smash. Shortly thereafter, a major label, Jive Records, which had rap acts D.J. Jazzy Jeff and the Fresh Prince and Boogie Down Productions on its roster, signed Too $hort and re-released *Born to Mack* with national distribution in 1988.

Too $hort's style of rapping is an unabashed early version of gangsta rap. His subject matter centers around pimping, prostitution, and other street hustles. America perceived *Born to Mack* as a window into a shrouded lifestyle and purchased more than 500,000 copies of the album. His second Jive effort, *Life Is . . . Too $hort* (1988), doubled those sales figures.

After 1990, Too $hort's career changed direction. At age twenty-four, he was involved in a head-on car collision that resulted in the death of the other driver. He began to include at least one cautionary tale in his subsequent albums, punctuating the outlaw reveries. Though he enjoyed a string of strong-selling albums after *Mack*, Too $hort's West Coast voice was no longer unique on the national scene in the mid-1990s. In 1992, the Los Angeles–based Dr. Dre released the classic album *The Chronic* and his Long Beach, California, protegé Snoop (Doggy) Dogg entered the market with the multiplatinum *Doggystyle* in 1993. Furthermore, the media branded the often-violent, misogynist releases by Dr. Dre, Snoop (Doggy) Dogg, and their immediate hip-hop associates as "gangsta rap" and omitted Too $hort from this negative, albeit highly marketable category. In seeming response, Too $hort decided to retire in 1996, but managed to record a song with Notorious B.I.G., "The World Is Filled . . .," for B.I.G.'s album *Life after Death* (1997).

In the mid- to late 1990s, the rap landscape became increasingly materialistic, largely driven by Sean "Puffy" Combs's Bad Boy Records, and gangsta rap faded into the background. Into this environment Too $hort briefly came out of retirement to record the song "A Week Ago" with Jay-Z for Jay-Z's *Billboard* number one album *Vol. 2: Hard Knock Life* (1998). In 1999, Too $hort made a comeback with the album *Can't Stay Away*. Rarely one to collaborate with other artists in the 1980s and early 1990s, here Too $hort builds upon his recordings with Notorious B.I.G. and Jay-Z and includes songs with Combs, Atlanta rapper/producer Jermaine Dupri, and Jay-Z. The album entered the *Billboard* charts in the Top 10.

After 2000, Too $hort began some markedly different projects, perhaps to counteract the disappointing sales of *Chase the Cat* (2001) and *What's My Favorite Word?* (2002), his first efforts to sell under 500,000 copies since he signed to Jive Records. In 2001, Too $hort and another Bay area rap superstar E-40 announced plans to record a joint album. In 2002, Too $hort produced "Get in Where You Fit In," the first in a series of pornographic films bearing the titles of his songs. Also that year, he recorded an X-rated response record to the feminine anthem "My Neck, My Back" by Khia called "My D*ck, My Sack." Too $hort expressed a desire to create a "one hundred percent positive album," announcing to MTV News in 2002 that while he would still rhyme about pimps and prostitutes, "I'm not going to speak on it in any other way than a positive way."

No matter the direction Too $hort chooses to take, his importance in hip-hop remains secure. He was one of the first artists bold enough to record graphic songs about the underworld and to maintain a vision throughout his career.

SELECTIVE DISCOGRAPHY: *Don't Stop Rappin'* (75 Girls, 1983); *Players* (75 Girls, 1984); *Born to Mack* (Dangerous Music, 1986); *Life Is . . . Too $hort* (Jive, 1988); *Short Dog's in the House* (Jive, 1990); *Shorty the Pimp* (Jive, 1992); *Get in Where You Fit In* (Jive, 1993); *Cocktails* (Jive, 1995); *Gettin' It (Album Number Ten)* (Jive, 1996); *Can't Stay Away* (Jive, 1999); *You Nasty* (Jive, 2000); *Chase the Cat* (Jive, 2001); *What's My Favorite Word?* (Jive, 2002); *It's About Time* (75 Girls, 2003).

DARA COOK

TOOL

Formed: 1990, Los Angeles, California

Members: Danny Carey, drums (born Paolo, Kansas, 10 May 1961); Justin Chancellor, bass (born London, England, 19 November 1971); Adam Jones, guitar (born Libertyville, Illinois, 15 January 1965); Maynard James Keenan, vocals (born Ravenna, Ohio, 17 April 1964).

Genre: Rock

Best-selling album since 1990: *Aenima* (1996)

Hit songs since 1990: "Sober," "H.," "Parabola"

Tool's rumbling, complex hard rock and dark, disturbing imagery have earned it a cult following. The group also enjoys widespread alt-rock appeal thanks to Keenan's intense tenor and Jones's chainsaw guitar rumblings. Made up of three midwestern Americans and an Englishman (Chancellor), the group released its debut EP, *Opiate* (1992), while building a following on the Los Angeles scene. Enjoying regional success, the group earned a spot on the 1993 Lollapalooza tour and released the full-length *Undertow*.

A memorable marriage of music and video made Tool's first single, "Sober," a radio and MTV staple. Displaying a sense of dynamics often missing from novice rockers, the band starts the song with soft, foreboding guitar and bass while Keenan sings in semi-croon mode. But he and the group blast into a cathartic, sing-along chorus whose drama is accentuated by self-loathing lyrics spiced with religious imagery. Jones's stop-motion animation video, featuring cutely macabre figurines, also makes an impression. Their second single, "Prison Sex," which made number thirty-two on *Billboard*'s Mainstream Rock Tracks airplay chart, is one of the most explicit songs to have ever received mainstream radio play; the title neatly sums up the lyrical content. While *Undertow*'s vaguely Satanic artwork and dark themes appealed to death-metal followers, the album's instrumental expertise and experimentation with odd time signatures attracted art-rock fans who otherwise had little to cheer about in the early 1990s. As Tool's fame grew, so did their reputation for being distant from fans.

As a band that had achieved success fairly early in its career, Tool still had room to improve, and their sophomore set, *Aenima* (1996), shows a group whose playing has grown tighter and more challenging. "Stinkfist" is a cynical take on an instant-gratification world that burns with hyped-up, hard-rock aggression. The album's signature song is the title track, "Aenima," which enlists a doo-wop beat in service of a grinding, apocalyptic anthem. With misanthropic, gallows humor, Keenan tells everyone from "gun-toting hip gangster wannabes" to "insecure actresses" that the end is near, so "learn to swim." The song won a Grammy for best metal performance.

Tool co-headlined Lollapalooza 1997 with Korn, but business disputes kept the group away from the recording studio. Keenan used the downtime to form A Perfect Circle, which scored a Top 10 album and three radio hits with its debut release, *Mer de Noms*.

Lateralus (2001) broke the silence, debuting at number one, beating out albums by R.E.M. and Weezer that were released the same week. The album takes Tool into more esoteric territory, complete with sound effects and extended song suites. "Schism," a symbolism-filled song about the difficulty of interpersonal communication, won the group its second Grammy for best metal performance.

Tool has avoided being pigeonholed and has maintained its reputation for innovation with philosophical, satirical lyrics, impressive musicality, and headbanger-friendly crunch.

SELECTIVE DISCOGRAPHY: *Undertow* (Zoo, 1993); *Aenima* (Ignition, 1996); *Lateralus* (Ignition, 2001).

RAMIRO BURR

ALI "FARKA" TOURÉ

Born: Ali Ibrahim Touré; Gourmararusse, Mali, 1939
Genre: World
Best-selling album since 1990: *Talking Timbuktu* (1994)

Ali Farka Touré is a virtuoso guitarist and vocalist from the West African nation of Mali who performs a distinctively African-inspired style of blues that has captured an international audience of listeners. Despite having performed for nearly four decades, Touré's prominence in the West has largely been a phenomenon of the 1990s.

Touré was the tenth child born to his mother in the remote Timbuktu region of Mali, and the first to survive. That staying power earned him the nickname "Farka" (the Songhay word for "donkey"), since he was considered stubborn enough to survive. As a child, Touré taught himself to sing and play African folk songs using traditional rural instruments such as the gurkel, a single-stringed instrument made out of a gourd, and the njarka, a single-stringed violinlike instrument made of wood. At the age of seventeen, Touré heard a performance by Guinea National Ballet director and guitarist Ketita Fodeba that changed his life. He was so moved by the expressive qualities and harmonic capabilities of the guitar that he obtained one and taught himself to play it using the same techniques that he had used to play the gurkel and the njarka.

Touré's encounter with American blues via John Lee Hooker in the late 1960s was also a powerful experience, though he was surprised that Hooker was not as at home and familiar with Touré's native music of Mali as Touré was with Hooker's blues world. Touré began playing and singing his own brand of blues that combined African rhythms, pedal points, repetitions, and antiphons with Mississippi Delta blues–style improvisations and melancholy. Touré's first albums were released in France in the mid-1970s and were made from tapes he had made and sent off himself. The success of these—from which Touré never received a dime—prompted a French tour in which Touré backed up Hooker. In order to have access to studio facilities, Touré trained and then worked as a sound engineer for Radio Mali, allowing him to record and broadcast his own music on the side. When he had saved enough money to buy his own rice and fruit farm on the edge of the Sahara Desert along the Niger River and near his boyhood village of Niafunké, he moved there in 1980 and became a farmer.

Since 1989 Touré has recorded and occasionally even toured in the West, with mixed results. Already in his mid-fifties, he seemed poised for the major career that was so long overdue when his rather commercial collaboration with Ry Cooder, *Talking Timbuktu* (1994), won a Grammy Award and was subsequently supported by a world tour. But Touré found the whole Western notion of music as "entertainment" at odds with his performance style; and being cut off from the land, life, and beauty of the homeland that he realized was truly the source of his music, he became homesick and returned to his farm in Mali. Seemingly oblivious to the money and stardom that had been just within his grasp, Touré was content to play simply to appease his livestock and help nurture the growth of his crops.

It would be five years before Touré would be heard from again, with his album *Niafunké* (1999). Even that only came about because his London-based manager and record producer Nick Gold was willing to trek a mobile studio along with hundreds of feet of cable and a generator all the way from the Mali capital of Bamako to Niafunké. It is that remote village in northern Mali that continues to inspire and inform Touré's unique musical vision, which successfully seeks to minimize the distance between the Niger and the Mississippi.

SELECTIVE DISCOGRAPHY: *Ali Farka Touré* (Mango/Island, 1989); *African Blues* (Shanachie, 1990); *The River* (Mango/Island, 1990); *The Source* (Hannibal/Rykodisc, re-release 1993); *La Drogue* (Sonodisc, 1994); *Radio Mali* (Nonesuch/Elektra re-release, 1999); *Niafunké* (Hannibal/Rykodisc, 1999). **With Ry Cooder:** *Talking Timbuktu* (Hannibal/Rykodisc, 1994). **Soundtracks:** *Equinox* (Varese, 1993); *Addicted to Love* (TYT, 1997); *Besieged* (Milan, 1999); *Wonders of the African World* (Warner Bros., 1999).

DENNIS POLKOW

PETE TOWNSHEND

Born: Peter Dennis Blandford Townshend; London, England, 19 May 1945

Genre: Rock

Best-selling album since 1990: *The Best of Pete Townshend: Coolwalkingsmoothtalkingstraightsmokingfirestoking* (1996)

Pete Townshend is one of the most revered songwriters in rock and a founding member of the Who, a classic rock band. He created the rock opera, which combines the storytelling skills of Broadway musicals with contemporary rock music. As much as Townshend is known as a conceptualist who is responsible for dozens of endurable hit songs, he is also an influential rock guitarist. With the Who he created the type of guitar thunder and violent stage behavior most would associate with the punk rock of the 1970s. The tremendous energy Townshend threw into his playing complemented his songwriting, which celebrated the power of individuality and the importance of spiritual wholeness in the face of adversity. The Who formally broke up in 1982, prompting Townshend to launch a full-time solo career. In the 1990s he looked back at his large body of work and repackaged it for a new audience.

Beginnings

In 1965 Townshend wrote the Who's three defining hit singles: "I Can't Explain," "Anyway, Anyhow, Any-

where," and "My Generation." In packages of just three minutes, they announced the arrival of a new wave of teenage rebellion, one that was self-assured and intense. Townshend was anointed as the spokesperson of his generation and was a hit with the "Mods," a British youth movement that embraced modern trends in music, fashion, and attitude. The Who capsulated this energy into their chaotic live shows. After Townshend happened to destroy a guitar in frustration, guitar-smashing quickly became an awaited climax of Who shows.

Townshend used the Who as a vehicle to address an array of serious subjects in his songwriting. He began writing longer songs that incorporated classical and baroque structures and themes. In 1969 he released *Tommy*, a double-album rock opera that told the story of a boy who goes deaf, dumb, and blind due to a childhood trauma and ends up a messianic idol. *Tommy* was a smash hit and paved the way for *Quadrophenia* (1973), an epic rock opera about the harrowing life of a Mod youth. During this period Townshend worked on a third rock opera about virtual reality called *Lifehouse* but could not finish it. The remaining songs ended up becoming *Who's Next* (1971), the Who's best-known album, which brought in synthesizers and dramatic guitar hooks.

At the height of the Who's success, Townshend began studying with the Eastern mystic Meher Baba, who inspired him to write gentler and more personally introspective songs. The first result of Baba's teachings was Townshend's debut solo album, *Who Came First* (1971). He followed it up years later with *Rough Mix* (1977), a breezy and intimate collaboration with folk songwriter and fellow Meher follower Ronnie Laine.

The Who suffered a major setback with the death of drummer Keith Moon in 1978. Although drummer Kenny Jones was recruited to fill Moon's spot and two more albums were released, the band played its farewell tour in 1982.

After the Who

In the meantime, Townshend was already actively engaged in a solo career. His most successful and most critically praised non-Who album is *Empty Glass* (1980). Featuring his first solo hit, "Let My Love Open the Door," the album is deeply introspective and hints at his struggles with alcohol and drugs. Without the swaggering vocal power of the Who's lead singer Roger Daltrey, Townshend was free to explore his metaphysical side, with several songs hinting at bisexuality. *All the Best Cowboys Have Chinese Eyes* (1982) deals with the malaise of stardom and the quest for salvation.

After that creative endeavor, Townshend retreated from making albums about his own personal demons and, once again, moved toward more conceptual music. *White*

City (1985) is subtitled *A Novel*. It accompanied a short film he wrote about life in a West London public housing complex. He followed up with an elaborate album, *The Iron Man* (1989). Based on a children's story by the English poet Ted Hughes, it features songs sung by guest vocalists including Daltrey, blues legend John Lee Hooker, and jazz diva Nina Simone. It sold poorly.

Even so, the album prompted a Who reunion tour the same year, in what would become a routine occurrence throughout the 1990s. The reunited group (later featuring Zak Starkey, son of Beatles drummer Ringo Starr, on drums) would play greatest hits shows to mixed reviews over the years. *Psychoderelict* (1993) remains Townshend's last solo album as of 2003. Another semi-autobiographical look at the trappings of celebrity, it tells the story of Ray High, a rock musician on the comeback who is fighting alcoholism and the disdain of a rock journalist bent on destroying him. Interspersed with spoken dramatic segments, the music includes instrumental passages that pay tribute to Meher Baba as well as self-deprecating rock songs ("Let's Get Pretentious") mocking the cult of fame. It yielded the minor hit single, "English Boy." For the most part, *Psychoderelict* confused Townshend's audience and failed to break into the Top 100. The album was accompanied by a tour that featured multimedia visuals and actors who performed between songs.

Tommy and Beyond

Townshend's energies during the 1990s focused on the past. He broke ground on Broadway with a restaging of *Tommy* in 1993. Although it had already been a film and a concert tour, its Broadway incarnation exceeded expectations. It was a box office blockbuster. Featuring a cast of unknown musical theater singers and dancers, it received mixed reviews with some critics accusing Townshend of shamelessly exploiting his past for the sake of nostalgia and a quick buck. Nevertheless, *The Who's Tommy* (its new title) received five Tony Awards in 1993 and toured the world. The same year Townshend staged *The Iron Man* in London. He later regrouped the Who in 1996 to resurrect *Quadrophenia*. The band embarked on a tour to perform the rock opera in its entirety. By this point, his guitar playing had diminished due to ear damage and he stuck mainly to playing rhythm, not lead. Townshend also finally got around to completing *Lifehouse*, the musical project he had abandoned nearly thirty years earlier. He adapted it into a radio play for the BBC in 1999 and the next year released *The Lifehouse Chronicles* (2000), a six-CD set of songs and spoken word that he released on his own Eel Pie label.

In January 2003 Scotland Yard arrested Townshend under suspicion of possessing child pornography. Townshend admitted he had visited child porn websites but maintained it was only for research for an autobiography he was writing that explored sexual abuse in his childhood. He was later released and never charged.

Townshend is one of rock's most complex figures. He broke out of the conventional pop song mold and created the rock opera. With the Who, he delivered classic rock anthems, yet when he retreated to his solo work, he freely explored a sensitive and philosophical side.

SELECTIVE DISCOGRAPHY: *Who Came First* (Decca, 1972); *Rough Mix* (Decca, 1977); *Empty Glass* (Atco, 1980); *All the Best Cowboys Have Chinese Eyes* (Atco, 1982); *White City—A Novel* (Atco, 1985); *Pete Townshend's Deep End Live!* (Atco, 1986); *The Iron Man* (Atco, 1989); *Psychoderelict* (Atlantic, 1993); *The Best of Pete Townshend: Coolwalkingsmoothtalkingstraightsmokingfirestoking* (Atlantic, 1996); *The Lifehouse Chronicles* (Eel Pie, 2000). **With the Who:** *The Who Sings My Generation* (Decca, 1965); *Tommy* (Decca, 1969); *Live at Leeds* (Decca, 1970); *Quadrophenia* (MCA, 1973); *Who Are You* (MCA, 1978).

WEBSITE: www.petetownshend.com.

MARK GUARINO

TRAIN

Formed: 1994, San Francisco, California

Members: Charlie Colin, bass (born 1976); Rob Hotchkiss, guitar (born Japan, 1960); Patrick Monahan, vocals (born Erie, Pennsylvania, 1969); Jimmy Stafford, guitar (born Morris, Illinois, 1964); Scott Underwood, drums (born Saratoga Springs, New York, 2 January 1971).

Genre: Rock

Best-selling album since 1990: *Drops of Jupiter* (2001)

Hit songs since 1990: "Meet Virginia," "Drops of Jupiter," "She's on Fire"

On the basis of two hugely successful singles, "Meet Virginia" and "Drops of Jupiter," Train became one of the more successful mainstream rock acts of the late 1990s, bringing a down-home, roots-based flavor to the genre.

Train has its origins in a chance meeting between singer Patrick Monahan and a Los Angeles band called the Apostles. Monahan had moved from his native Erie, Pennsylvania, to Los Angeles in the hopes of launching a musical career. In 1993, while in Los Angeles, Monahan became acquainted with the Apostles, which featured Rob Hotchkiss and Jimmy Stafford on guitar. When the Apostles broke up, Monahan and Hotchkiss formed a musical duo, performing acoustically in area coffeehouses.

Train. L-R: Jimmy Stafford, Rob Hotchkiss, Scott Underwood, Patrick Monahan, Charlie Colin [PAUL NATKIN/PHOTO RESERVE]

The pair ultimately expanded their lineup to include Stafford as well as drummer Scott Underwood and bass player Charlie Colin; the new band dubbed itself Train and relocated to San Francisco.

Columbia Records expressed interest in the fledgling band, but opted to farm the group out to Aware Records, a smaller label on which the band could hone its craft. After signing with Aware, Train cut its teeth on the road, touring with high-profile acts such as Counting Crows, Blues Traveler, and Barenaked Ladies. In 1998 Aware Records released Train's self-titled debut album. The single "Meet Virginia" was a surprise hit. Its lyrics celebrate a woman who marches to the beat of her own drummer: "She doesn't own a dress / Her hair is always a mess / If

you catch her stealin', she won't confess / She's beautiful." Musically, "Meet Virginia" bounces along jauntily to country-style guitars—an anomaly for mainstream radio. Nevertheless, the song reached the Top 10 on the *Billboard* singles charts and helped Train sell 1 million copies of its debut album.

As a result of its initial success, Train faced increased expectations. Columbia Records raised the bar higher when it elevated Train to its international label for the release of *Drops of Jupiter* (2001). The title track is reminiscent of the sound of 1970s arena-rock power ballads, featuring a lush string-based arrangement in conjunction with sprightly keyboards, all the while retaining the band's rollicking roots-rock style. The music builds to a crescendo for the anthem-like chorus: "Tell me did you sail across the sun / Did you make it to the Milky Way to see the lights all faded / And that heaven is overrated." "Drops of Jupiter" was the fourth best-selling single on the *Billboard* charts for 2001 and pushed sales of the album past 3 million copies. The song won a Grammy Award for Best Rock Song. Following in the footsteps of the Wallflowers and matchbox twenty, Train brought classic rock sounds back to the pop charts.

SELECTIVE DISCOGRAPHY: *Train* (Aware, 1998); *Drops of Jupiter* (Columbia, 2001).

SCOTT TRIBBLE

RANDY TRAVIS

Born: Randy Traywick; Marshville, North Carolina, 4 May 1959

Genre: Country

Best-selling album since 1990: *Heroes and Friends* (1990)

Hit songs since 1990: "Hard Rock Bottom of Your Heart," "Forever Together," "Whisper My Name"

During the late 1980s and early 1990s Randy Travis was one of country music's most commercially successful singers, writing and recording hits that, with their sparse instrumentation, recalled the "classic country" sound of the 1960s. Critics and fans agree that Travis imbues his songs with honesty and sincerity, radiating a down-home goodness that rarely cloys. His most remarkable asset, however, is his voice: Rich and creamy, ranging from a lustrous bass to a keening baritone, it is distinctive and recognizable. Unlike contemporary country singers such as George Strait and Alan Jackson, who possess strong if not brilliant voices, Travis's voice bears an inbred emotional pull, a special vocal catch that stamps each of his recordings with charm and personality.

Travis's humble, self-effacing public personality belies the roughness of his early life in rural North Carolina. His father, a country music fan, encouraged Randy and his brother Ricky to play guitar at an early age. Although the two performed locally as the Traywick Brothers, Travis spent the larger portion of his youth dealing with an array of legal misdemeanors. Fueled by alcohol and drugs, he was convicted of carrying a concealed weapon in 1975 and of breaking and entering twice in 1976. During the mid-1970s he moved to the nearby city of Charlotte, North Carolina, where he began performing at a club, Country City U.S.A. The club's owner, Lib

Hatcher, was so impressed with Travis's voice and talents that she became his manager, leaving her husband and moving with Travis to Nashville in 1982. Together the pair, who married in 1991, slowly made inroads into the country music industry.

1980s Neo-traditionalist

During the early 1980s country music still bore the effects of the "countrypolitan" sound of the 1970s, a style that often buried singers in pop-oriented, string-laden arrangements. In this ornate musical climate, Travis's stripped-down performance style was rejected by several record labels as sounding too country. Eventually Hatcher arranged for Travis to be signed to Warner Bros. Records, for whom he released his debut album, *Storms of Life*, in 1986. Along with the contemporaneous work of Strait and others, *Storms of Life* heralded a back-to-basics approach in country, employing traditional instruments such as steel pedal guitar. Drawing strength from its refreshing, pared-down sound and Travis's compelling voice, the album sold 3 million copies.

Travis soon embarked on a string of hits that embodied old-fashioned ideals of romantic constancy and humility while retaining a winning sense of humor. On hits such as the catchy "Forever and Ever, Amen" (1987) he conveys an infectious, easygoing charm: "As long as old men sit and talk about the weather . . . I'm gonna love you forever and ever." Travis's affable demeanor and good looks enhanced his popularity; tall and lanky, he radiated a boyish quality that contrasted with the gravelly maturity of his voice.

1990s Maturity

Travis's hit-making streak slowed down somewhat in the early 1990s, superseded by the work of artists such as Garth Brooks, who found success by incorporating hard rock elements into his music. Still, Travis hit the country charts with regularity, recording fine albums that display his vocal richness. Rarely does Travis's voice rise to more than a mild push; in fact, critics observe that if his singing has a weakness it is that it sometimes sounds overly mellow or sleepy. On "That's Where I Draw the Line," a song from *This Is Me* (1994), he gives an indication of how much he holds in reserve by belting the line, "I won't let you break my mind," with full vocal power. Coming suddenly during an otherwise restrained performance, it is cited by critics as a moment that demands attention. Tasteful and intelligent, Travis uses his upper range sparingly, as a means of giving the lyrics special emphasis.

On one of his finest albums, *Full Circle* (1996), he demonstrates how his art lies in subtleties of vocal shading and texture. "Future Mister Me," a self-penned ballad featuring a great country theme—Travis comes face to face with his ex-wife's fiancée—is punctuated by his dips into a smoky bass register, almost spectral in its quiet intensity. Midway through the song Travis shifts the narrative focus to the ex-wife, attesting that, "if I can see you're in good hands / maybe I can make it without you." The line, arresting in its selflessness, reveals the humanitarian core lying beneath Travis's art, saving even the most timeworn material from sounding clichéd.

In 2000, after a gradual religious conversion inspired by his wife, Travis released *Inspirational Journey*, an album of contemporary gospel songs. While it addresses themes of sin and salvation, the album is similar in sound to Travis's secular work, sparsely produced and instrumentally restrained. Vocally Travis sounds invigorated, however, imparting to "Doctor Jesus" an aching quality that evinces genuine emotion. On the engaging, spirited "Feet on the Rock," he opens with a spoken intro bearing the charisma of an old-time country preacher, then quickly shifts the song into an up-tempo swing number. With its rocking, good-time feel, *Inspirational Journey* proves that, even when aiming for a higher purpose, gospel music can appeal to the body as well as the soul. In 2002 Travis released a follow-up gospel album, *Rise and Shine*.

Travis stands as one of the few modern country singers to approach the vocal artistry of 1960s legends such as George Jones, a singer with whom he shares a similar aching vocal quality. In the late 1980s Travis found success through eschewing pop influences for a return to country's roots, then lost his commercial footing as the industry shifted back to pop in the 1990s. Through it all he has retained his distinctive, oak-mellowed voice, continuing to record music that is tasteful and inspiring.

SELECTIVE DISCOGRAPHY: *Storms of Life* (Warner Bros., 1986); *Old 8x10* (Warner Bros, 1988); *Heroes and Friends* (Warner Bros., 1990); *This Is Me* (Warner Bros., 1994); *Full Circle* (Warner Bros., 1996); *Inspirational Journey* (Warner Bros., 2000); *Rise and Shine* (Warner Bros., 2002).

DAVID FREELAND

GLORIA TREVI

Born: Gloria de los Angeles Treviño; Monterrey, Mexico, 15 February 1968

Genre: Latin

Best-selling album since 1990: *Tu Ángel de la Guardia* (1991)

Hit songs since 1990: "Dr. Psiquiatra," "Pelo Suelto," "Papa sin Catsup"

The story of one of Mexico's most promising 1990s rockers had, by the end of the decade, turned into a horror-show of accusations, rumors, and alleged crimes. At the age of thirteen, Trevi trekked to Mexico City to pursue an acting career. There she met some Monterrey friends, one of whom hooked her up with the manager Sergio Andrade, who was forming an all-female pop quintet called Boquitas Pintadas. She joined as a vocalist and keyboardist in 1985. She went solo in 1990, retaining Andrade as her manager. Personable and open when the cameras were off, she projected a wild, rebellious image for public consumption.

Her debut album, *Qué Hago Aquí?* (1990), features the hits "Dr. Psiquiatra" and "El Último Beso," a cover of J. Frank Wilson and the Cavaliers' "Last Kiss." She adopted a growling vocal style influenced by Janis Joplin and reminiscent of another up-and-coming Mexican rocker, Alejandra Guzman. But unlike Guzman, Trevi wrote much of her material.

Her follow-up album, *Tu Ángel de la Guardia* (1991), contains the anthem "Pelo Suelto" ("Undone Hair"). The song is a metaphor for taking a casual attitude toward conservative social norms in other aspects of life—figuratively letting one's hair down. That year she released a calendar full of risqué shots that sold over 300,000 copies. Never before had such a blatantly sexual celebrity made such an impact on Mexican popular culture.

In 1994 Trevi released *Más Turbada Que Nunca*. The album contains the bluesy hit "Papa sin Catsup," which is accompanied by a feminist video portraying Trevi as an abused housewife who finally gets her revenge. By then, however, her career was heading downhill. In 1998 the parents of a seventeen-year-old girl in Mexico accused Andrade of luring their daughter into his orbit with promises of fame and then fathering a child with her. Wanted by Mexican authorities, Trevi and Andrade dropped out of sight. In October 1999 their baby daughter was born in Brazil. The infant was reported to have died of unknown causes at the age of one month and two days. Andrade, Trevi, and her choreographer were arrested in January 2000 in Rio de Janeiro. Andrade and Trevi waited in a Brazilian jail while the extradition process inched forward. Trevi gave birth to a son in prison in 2002. No one was able to confirm the father's identity, although Trevi said it was a prison guard whom she would not name. Brazil finally extradited Trevi to Mexico in early 2003. Trevi had the potential to influence youth culture and sexual politics in Mexico the way Madonna has in the United States; her story is a cautionary tale about the pitfalls of stardom and the illusions it inspires in young and impressionable fans.

SELECTIVE DISCOGRAPHY: *Tu Ángel de la Guardia* (BMG, 1991); *Me Siento Tan Sola* (BMG, 1992);

Más Turbada Que Nunca (BMG, 1994); *Si Me Llevas Contigo* (BMG, 1995).

RAMIRO BURR

A TRIBE CALLED QUEST

Formed: 1988, Queens, New York; Disbanded 1998, New York, New York

Members: Ali Shaheed Muhammed (born Brooklyn, New York, 11 August 1970); Phife Dawg (Malik Taylor; born Brooklyn, New York, 20 April 1970); Q-Tip (Jonathan Davis; born Brooklyn, New York, 10 April 1970).

Genre: Hip-Hop

Best-selling album since 1990: *Low End Theory* (1991)

Hit songs since 1990: "Can I Kick It?" "Check the Rhime," "Award Tour"

Along with the Digable Planets and Gang Starr, New York's A Tribe Called Quest pioneered the use of jazz in hip-hop music during the early 1990s. After years of James Brown–influenced funk production, critics and audiences alike welcomed a change in sound. However, A Tribe Called Quest did more than simply sample jazz melodies and rhythms. They, better than most, understood how the aesthetics of jazz could be used to transform hip-hop's sound and culture.

The trio of rappers—Q-Tip, Phife Dawg, and DJ Ali Shaheed Muhammed—first came to public notice with *People's Instinctive Travels and Paths of Rhythm* (1990). Like other members of their collective, the Native Tongues Family (De La Soul, Jungle Brothers, Queen Latifah), the group members dressed in neo-African fashion and rapped with equal parts humor and social consciousness. Their aesthetic was colorful and playful, an expressive, sunny artistry that stood in contrast to the darker, harder edge of rappers like Kool G Rap in New York or N.W.A. in Los Angeles. Their album borrows liberally from across the musical spectrum, including the moodiness of rocker Lou Reed (for their call-and-response club hit "Can I Kick It?"), the bounciness of the funkateers Brothers Johnson (for their single "I Left My Wallet in El Segundo"), and the complexities of the obscure saxophonist Billy Brooks (for the French-filled "Luck of Lucien"). Creatively, the group displayed a musical breadth not previously seen in hip-hop.

With their second album, *Low End Theory* (1991), the group refocused and refined their sound. Hip-hop might have sampled jazz before *Low End Theory*, but A Tribe Called Quest's sophomore effort was one of the first that a jazz afficionado could truly appreciate. Rather than stack a heavy wall of noise, Tribe strips everything down to the bare bones: a rhythm section of bass lines and drums and minimalist melodic arrangements of jazz loops and soul samples. From the catchy, midtempo bounce of "Check the Rhime" to the energetic rush of "Scenario," the album remains one of hip-hop's best produced efforts. Q-Tip and Phife Dawg's lyrics are more complex on this album as they tackle a range of issues. From critiquing unscrupulous record execs and gossiping groupies to eulogizing fallen rappers, *Low End Theory* captures the ethos of "beats, rhymes, and life," in the words of one of their later album titles.

Tribe's follow-up album, *Midnight Marauders* (1993), builds on all the elements that made its predecessor so memorable. Their sublime samples plumb deeper, and their lyrics are more clever: This album captures the group at the height of their abilities. The sound they produce is impressively sophisticated—every element is meticulously engineered with songs like "We Can Get Down" and "Oh My God" blending elements from several songs to create a cohesive whole out of spare musical parts. Songs like "God Lives Through" and "Steve Biko (Stir It Up)" also reflect the group's spirituality and forward-looking perspective. *Midnight Marauders* represents one of the last hurrahs of commercially embraced optimism in rap music before artists like the Wu-Tang Clan and Notorious B.I.G. dramatically darkened hip-hop's worldview.

The group's last two albums before disbanding in 1998—*Beats, Rhymes, and Life* (1996) and *The Love Movement* (1998)—attempt to follow the same path as their predecessors but with mixed results. At a time when hip-hop had become harder and grittier, some saw Tribe as too soft to stay contemporary, but the real liability was their change in musical style. On *Beats, Rhymes, and Life*, Tribe began to work with Detroit producer Jay Dee, whose penchant for filtering his samples—making everything softer, more muddled—alienated previous fans who liked Tribe for the clarity and sharpness their songs traditionally offered. By the time *The Love Movement* was released, Tribe was treated as has-beens, lumbering musical dinosaurs who had been overtaken by a new species of hip-hop.

A Tribe Called Quest may not have survived the end of the 1990s, yet they largely embodied and defined hip-hop's loftier ideals in the first half of the decade. The group's progressive outlook and impressive musical versatility made them popular not only with hip-hop fans but also with jazz devotees and rockers.

SELECTIVE DISCOGRAPHY: *Low End Theory* (Jive/Zomba, 1991); *Midnight Marauders* (Jive/Zomba, 1993).

OLIVER WANG

TRAVIS TRITT

Born: James Travis Tritt; Marietta, Georgia, 9 February 1963

Genre: Country

Best-selling album since 1990: *It's All About to Change* (1991)

Hit songs since 1990: "Anymore," "Can I Trust You with My Heart," "Foolish Pride"

A performer whose gritty style owes a heavy debt to rock music, Travis Tritt was one of the most popular new country artists of the 1990s. Unlike other male country singers of the era, Tritt resisted the popular "hunk in a cowboy hat" trend by leaving his head uncovered and cultivating a rugged "outlaw" image that recalled 1960s and 1970s performers such as Waylon Jennings. Compared to smooth 1990s country stars such as John Michael Montgomery and Brad Paisley, Tritt's singing is grainy and tough, his muscular voice suggesting a strong blues influence. As a writer, Tritt has displayed an ability to evoke time-honored country themes of loneliness and heartbreak, integrating them into an electrified modern setting. Tritt's unrepentant style caused him to fall out of favor during the late 1990s, an era marked by increasing slickness in mainstream country. By 2000, however, he had rebounded with a new label affiliation and a ballad hit, "Best of Intentions," that emphasizes country's new pop sensibility.

Learning guitar at age eight and writing his first song at fourteen, Tritt set his sights on a music career while still a child, although his practical-minded parents discouraged his artistic ambitions. His childhood musical influences included country stars such as Jennings, as well as rock groups Lynyrd Skynyrd and the Eagles. Enduring two marriages and divorces by the time he was twenty-two, Tritt supported himself by working on a loading dock and later for an air conditioning company, all the while performing in clubs in his native Georgia. In 1982 he made a demo recording for a small studio, whose owner, Danny Davenport, was also a talent scout for Warner Bros. Records. Over the next several years Tritt refined and sharpened his unique rock-based country sound and, with Davenport's help, signed with Warner Bros. in 1989. Tritt's debut album, *Country Club* (1990), is a well-rounded effort that ranges from the rocking "Put Some Drive in Your Country" to the tender ballad "Help Me Hold On," Tritt's first number one country hit. On the album's title track, Tritt establishes his rowdy, down-home image: "I drive an old Ford pickup truck / I do my drinking from a Dixie Cup."

In 1991 Tritt released his breakthrough album, *It's All About to Change*, featuring his second number one country hit, the warm love ballad "Anymore." Proving his versatility, Tritt performs the up-tempo rocker, "Bible Belt," and old-fashioned heartache ballads such as "Nothing

Short of Dying," with equal conviction, while displaying flashes of sardonic humor on the tongue-in-cheek "Here's a Quarter (Call Someone Who Cares)." Capturing the gravelly intensity of great country singers of the past such as George Jones, Tritt delivers the song with an exaggeratedly callous edge. "Here's a Quarter" became a favorite at Tritt's flashy live concerts, often spurring audience members to throw quarters on stage. Both *T-r-o-u-b-l-e* (1992) and *Ten Feet Tall and Bulletproof* (1994) continue Tritt's winning formula; the albums were accompanied by slick videos that recast him as a sexy, leather-clad rocker. In 1996 Tritt released one of his finest albums, *The Restless Kind*, a restrained, stripped-down sound supplied by noted rock producer Don Was. The album's hit, "More Than You'll Ever Know," inspired by Tritt's third wife, Theresa Nelson, is notable for its warmth and honesty: "I know living with me ain't always easy / I dam up emotions some men just let flow."

By 1998 Tritt was no longer hitting the upper reaches of the charts with frequency, his rough-and-tumble sound having been supplanted by gentler country vocalists such as Kenny Chesney. Although he never fell off the charts completely, Tritt was becoming a casualty of country's late 1990s crossover sound, which adopted the heavily orchestrated qualities and nice-guy lyrical messages of pop music. By 2000 he had left Warner Bros. and signed with Columbia, releasing *Down the Road I Go* (2000) and scoring his first number one country hit in six years, "Best of Intentions." His voice still strong and assured, Tritt imbues the gentle ballad with sincerity and tenderness. While the remainder of the album is less pop-oriented, sporting a rock sound that recalls the spirit of his early work, it successfully repositions him within the top rank of country singers. Another fine album, *Strong Enough*, followed in 2002. On the album's opener, "You Can't Count Me Out," Tritt revels in his new popularity: "I'm back in the saddle, doing better than a body should . . . you can't count me out yet."

One of the most rock-oriented of 1990s country performers, Travis Tritt won fans with his bold, spirited sound and fine voice. Never content with following the latest country trends, Tritt diminished in popularity near the end of the 1990s, but regained his commercial strength in 2000, balancing his rock instincts with country's new pop-styled sensibility.

SELECTIVE DISCOGRAPHY: *Country Club* (Warner Bros., 1990); *It's All About to Change* (Warner Bros., 1991); *T-r-o-u-b-l-e* (Warner Bros., 1992); *Ten Feet Tall and Bulletproof* (Warner Bros., 1994); *The Restless Kind* (Warner Bros., 1996); *Down the Road I Go* (Columbia, 2000); *Strong Enough* (Columbia, 2002).

WEBSITE: www.travis-tritt.com.

DAVID FREELAND

TINA TURNER

Born: Annie Mae Bullock; Nutbush, Tennessee, 26 November 1938

Genre: R&B

Best-selling album since 1990: *What's Love Got to Do with It* (1993)

Hit songs since 1990: "I Don't Wanna Fight," "Missing You"

A legendary performer who overcame many hardships on her way to the top, Tina Turner has been singing rhythm and blues professionally since the 1950s. Admirers credit her longevity to personal courage, unbounded energy, and, most of all, great talent. Turner's voice is famous for its distinctive husky quality. Her basic vocal approach has changed little over the years: Often she begins a song using the deep, gravelly end of her voice, then slowly increases volume before breaking forth with a high-pitched scream. Her high-voltage style reflects the turbulence that has often characterized her life.

From "A Fool in Love" to Stardom

As a child growing up in rural Nutbush, Tennessee, Annie Mae Bullock picked cotton and dreamed of becoming a nurse. Her plans changed, however, when rhythm and blues singer Ike Turner discovered her at age eighteen, married her, and changed her name to Tina Turner. As Ike and Tina Turner, the couple led one of the most energetic, dynamic acts in rhythm and blues. Their success lasted from the 1960s well into the 1970s with hits such as "A Fool in Love" (1960) and "Proud Mary" (1971). Famous for her wild antics onstage, Turner would dance, writhe, scream, and engage in blatantly sexual dialogue with her husband. Although they cultivated the image of a happy couple, behind the scenes it was a different story. Turner later alleged that Ike took drugs and beat her repeatedly during these years, telling television journalist Mike Wallace in 1996, "I have had, basically, my face bashed in." Finally leaving Ike in 1976, Turner converted to Buddhism and began focusing on a solo career. At first she struggled in low-paying lounges and clubs, but the hard work paid off in 1984 when her *Private Dancer* album became a multimillion seller on the basis of catchy hits such as "What's Love Got to Do with It" and "Let's Stay Together." At age forty-five, Turner had finally achieved mega-stardom, crossing over to the pop market through recordings that emphasized rock and roll glamour over R&B grit. Along with her music she updated her image, popularizing fishnet stockings and blonde fright wigs with a look many female entertainers copied. In 1986 she pub-lished her autobiography, *I, Tina: My Life Story*, which deals candidly with her years of abuse and the Buddhist chanting practices that changed her life.

Pop Survivor

By the beginning of the 1990s Turner was famous worldwide, with the financial freedom to perform and record when she chose. She settled into a luxurious home in the south of France with her partner, German record executive Erwin Bach, and found a level of personal happiness that had eluded her during her years with Ike. In 1993 *I, Tina* was made into a film titled *What's Love Got to Do with It*, starring actress Angela Bassett. For the film's soundtrack, Turner recorded new versions of songs that had distinguished her career, including the autobiographical "Nutbush City Limits" and "Proud Mary." The album is a showcase for Turner's range and versatility, presenting a compendium of rhythm and blues music styles from the 1960s to the 1990s. On "Rock Me Baby," she growls and shouts, displaying her skills as a tough blues singer. "Darlin' You Know I Love You" is a raucous number in which Turner recreates the swaggering type of R&B popular in the 1950s and early 1960s, while "Disco Inferno" recalls the dance music of the 1970s. On the album's contemporary hit, "I Don't Wanna Fight," Turner sings from deep personal experience, giving listeners an indication of just how far she has come: "Hanging on to the past / It only stands in our way. . . . It's time for letting go."

In the late 1990s Turner continued to perform exhausting, kinetic live shows that would have been a physical challenge for performers half her age. Reviewing a 2000 performance, the *Toronto Sun* enthused, "Half of the time at a Turner concert is spent just marveling at her still gorgeous physical state—her legs, her body, her face, her energy, her presence, her vocal power." In 2000 Turner released *Twenty Four Seven*, an album enlisting the services of contemporary producers Mark Taylor and Brian Rawling, both of whom oversaw the production of fellow diva Cher's multimillion-selling *Believe* album in 1998. *Twenty Four Seven* features the same electronic production sound as *Believe*, but is distinguished by Turner's undiminished vocal range and prowess. She sounds tough and unsparing on "Absolutely Nothing's Changed," a powerful tale of survival. "I'm bruised but I ain't broken," she sings matter-of-factly, using her rough-hewn voice to deliver a testament to personal strength and conviction. The title track has a driving rock feel that recalls some of her best work from the 1980s, according to many critics. While the smooth production on the album keeps the music at the same emotional level, Turner transcends it through her dynamism and professionalism. Whether whispering hoarsely or shouting at the top of her range, she never misplaces a note or loses control of pitch. In September 2000, Turner announced plans to retire from live performing. "This time, I know it's a closure," she told Mike Wallace, "I can feel it." Reflecting on her past adversity and present contentment, she observed, "It's almost like the war is over. It's all finished."

Turner began performing during an era when old-fashioned showmanship and vocal talent were prized attributes for rhythm and blues performers. During the decades that followed she never lost those qualities, continuing to infuse her work with spirit and zest some forty years after entering the business. In the process she set a standard of endurance that continues to inspire younger artists.

SELECTIVE DISCOGRAPHY: *Private Dancer* (Capitol, 1984); *Break Every Rule* (Capitol, 1986); *Wildest Dreams* (Virgin, 1996); *Twenty Four Seven* (Virgin, 2000). **Soundtrack:** *What's Love Got to Do with It* (Virgin, 1993).

BIBLIOGRAPHY: T. Turner, *I, Tina: My Life Story* (New York, 1986).

WEBSITE: www.tina-turner.com.

DAVID FREELAND

SHANIA TWAIN

Born: Eileen Regina Edwards; Windsor, Ontario, 28 August 1965

Genre: Country

Best-selling album since 1990: *Come on Over* (1997)

Hit songs since 1990: "You're Still the One," "Man! I Feel Like a Woman!," "That Don't Impress Me Much"

Born in Windsor, Ontario, Shania Twain grew up in rural Timmons, roughly 500 miles north of Toronto. She lived with her mother Sharon and stepfather, an Ojibway Indian named Jerry Twain, as well as with her three younger siblings. The petite Twain aided her parents in providing for the family, spending summers working with her stepfather on a reforestation crew in the Canadian bush.

Early Attraction to Music

Twain was drawn to music at an early age, learning to play guitar and writing songs before she was a teenager. Twain's parents recognized and encouraged the youngster's talents, shuttling her to community events, senior citizens' homes, and local television studios—wherever her parents could book her a gig.

Twain's parents died in a tragic car crash when she was twenty-one, and Twain was forced to support herself and her younger siblings. She made ends meet by performing at the Deerhurst Resort in Ontario, where, in addition to singing, Twain also had the opportunity to learn theatrical performance. Once her younger siblings were old enough to support themselves, Twain set off on her own, even shedding her birth name in favor of "Shania," an Ojibway word meaning "I'm on my way." Twain recorded a demo tape of original music and attracted the attention of various record labels. Mercury Nashville signed her to a recording contract and, in 1993, released Twain's self-titled debut album. Though Twain had been signed on the basis of her original material, *Shania Twain* features only one composition by the artist herself; the album was a minor hit.

Though Mercury Nashville was apparently skeptical of Twain's compositional ability, she found an ardent supporter in noted producer Robert John "Mutt" Lange. Lange had an impressive pedigree in the rock world, having worked with artists such as AC/DC, Def Leppard, Foreigner, and Bryan Adams. The pair began collaborating and fell in love in the process, marrying six months after meeting.

Crossover Success

The Woman in Me, Twain's second album, appeared in 1995 and became a major smash. Though many country purists found fault with Lange's bombastic rock-styled production, the lead single, "Whose Bed Have Your Boots Been Under?," reached number eleven on the country singles charts. Conservative Nashville elements also found fault with the song's promotional video, in which Twain prances around in sexy, revealing apparel, singing the rousing chorus: "Whose bed have your boots been under? / And whose heart did you steal I wonder? / This time did it feel like thunder, baby? / Whose bed have your boots been under?"

The follow-up single "Any Man of Mine" was an even bigger hit for Twain. Again fusing country themes and instruments with rock drums and heavy, layered chorus vocals, "Any Man of Mine" topped the country charts and further established Twain as a leading artist. On the strength of its two smash singles, *The Woman in Me* sold 9 million copies.

Twain's next album, *Come on Over*, was even more successful than its predecessor. The lead single, "You're Still the One," climbed all the way to number two on the pop charts and was followed by four more Top 40 hits. The song "Man! I Feel Like a Woman" typifies the Twain-Lange formula for crossover success. With piping synthesized horns and crunching guitars, "Man! I Feel Like a Woman" bursts with rock attitude, while Twain's spunky lyrics and ever-so-slight vocal twang belie her country roots. The song, which cosmetics company Revlon adopted as its anthem, also fires back at critics who spent more time analyzing Twain's midriff-baring clothes than they did her music: "Oh, oh, oh, go totally crazy—forget I'm a lady / Men's

Spot Light | Come on Over

Shania Twain was one of the pivotal figures in the country crossover phenomenon of the 1990s. Well before Twain reached her commercial pinnacle, Garth Brooks had parlayed his rock influences to reach mainstream audiences in a manner that no country artist had previously achieved. His 1990 album *No Fences* sold a record-shattering 13 million copies, while *Ropin' the Wind* (1991) became the first country album to debut at the top of the pop charts. While Brooks made country's presence known on the pop album charts, mainstream radio continued to avoid country-flavored tunes. Twain shattered that boundary in 1997 with a barrage of singles from her album *Come on Over*. Though Twain's singles were perhaps more pop than country, they all bore the unmistakable stamp of the Nashville sound, be it through fiddles, steel guitars, or the occasional vocal twang. Top 40 radio stations seized upon Twain's cosmopolitan brand of country and placed "You've Got a Way," "That Don't Impress Me Much," "You're Still the One," "From This Moment On," and "Man! I Feel Like a Woman!" in heavy rotation alongside more traditional pop fare from acts such as Madonna, Enrique Iglesias, and Hanson. Twain's chart success opened pop radio to other country artists, including Faith Hill, LeAnn Rimes, and the Dixie Chicks.

disc of the same songs mixed in a pop/rock style; and a third international disc with a Latin-Asian production. *Up!* reached the top of *Billboard*'s country and pop charts and features the hit single "I'm Gonna Getcha Good!"

Twain's crossover success engendered a radio revolution in the late 1990s; as a result of her phenomenal success, pop audiences came to embrace an array of country artists and increased the genre's popularity.

SELECTIVE DISCOGRAPHY: *Shania Twain* (Mercury, 1993); *The Woman in Me* (Mercury, 1995); *Come on Over* (Mercury, 1997); *Up!* (Mercury, 2002).

SCOTT TRIBBLE

2PAC

Born: Lesane Parish Crooks, changed to Tupac Amaru Shakur; Brooklyn, New York, 16 June 1971; died Las Vegas, Nevada, 13 September 1996

Genre: Rap

Best-selling album since 1990: *All Eyez on Me* (1996)

Tupac Shakur was perhaps the definitive rap star of the 1990s. His controversial life and music made him hip-hop's first international icon. Unlike other rap stars who talk about the thug life without having lived it, Shakur had a history of legal troubles and time served in prison, which gave him a credibility his peers could not match. His tough lyrics, misogyny, and thug lifestyle were matched with a more sensitive persona, leading him to dedicate songs to his mother and the poor. Shakur was an acclaimed actor who appeared in some of the most well-received films about black urban life of the 1990s. His murder in 1996 further increased his notoriety, turning him into a pop martyr along the lines of Nirvana singer Kurt Cobain and 1960s rock icons Jimi Hendrix and Jim Morrison.

Shakur was born in Brooklyn, New York, the son of two members of the Black Panther Party. His mother was pregnant with Shakur while serving time in a New York prison. Raised primarily by his mother, Shakur grew up in poverty, moving between radical and sometimes criminal circles. From an early age, he showed an interest in the arts, earning a place as a teen in the Baltimore School of the Arts. His family moved to California when he was seventeen and settled in Marin City. Much has been made of Shakur's subsequent years hustling on the streets of Oakland as a formative learning experience. Reassessments of Shakur's education in Baltimore, Maryland, and California, however, have revealed the depth of his formal influences. He was an avid reader who would later quote

shirts, short skirts / Oh, oh, oh, really go wild—yeah, doin' it in style."

At the height of the album's success, Twain released *Come on Over: The International Version* (1999), which features several pop radio remixes of her hit songs. In addition to selling more copies than any previous country album, *Come on Over* became the best-selling female solo album in history and the fifth-best selling album of all time.

After *Come on Over* ran its course, Twain retreated with Lange to Switzerland, where the pair raised their newborn son outside the media spotlight. Twain returned to the music world in 2002 with the album *Up!* She acknowledged her massive crossover appeal by releasing three versions of the album: one disc of country mixes; a second

Tupac "2Pac" Shakur [MITCHELL GERBER/CORBIS]

Machiavelli and other intellectuals in raps about his experiences on the streets.

His first hip-hop gig was with Oakland-based Digital Underground as a dancer and roadie. His short-lived stint with the group ended with the release of his first album, *2Pacalypse Now* (1991). The recording gained notice for its explicit lyrics but failed to launch Shakur into stardom. Songs about street life such as "Crooked Ass Nigga" fit the profile of typical West Coast gangsta style rap. A few tracks, notably the single "Brenda's Got a Baby," reveal Shakur's gifts as a social critic and storyteller. *2Pacalypse Now* attracted the notice of then U.S. vice president Dan Quayle, who attacked the album's explicit lyrics during the failed reelection bid of President George H.W. Bush.

Shakur's success as an actor propelled his rap career. His acclaimed performance in Ernest Dickerson's *Juice* (1992) led to a role in John Singleton's *Poetic Justice* (1993) alongside pop music icon Janet Jackson. The films appeared shortly after the release of Shakur's second album, *Strictly 4 My N.I.G.G.A.Z.* (1993). The album contains Shakur's first crossover hits "I Get Around" and "Keep Ya Head Up,"

and went platinum months after its release. Despite the accessibility of the album's hits, most of the record portrays the violent world Shakur defined as "thug life" (a phrase he had tattooed across his knuckles). Some of Shakur's critics and friends have commented that if Shakur had lived he would have matured into rap's first poetic spokesperson, but, as with the material on the album, he preferred reveling in his thug persona.

More than any rap artist of the decade, Shakur lived the troubled life his lyrics portrayed. In 1992 he was arrested after a six-year-old boy was killed by a stray bullet as Shakur and two other men fought. The suit was later settled out of court. In October 1993 he was arrested for shooting two off-duty police officers in Atlanta, Georgia. The case was later dismissed, but Shakur was arrested a month later in New York City. Already on bail for an outstanding charge of hitting a woman who wanted his autograph, he was charged and later convicted of sexual abuse of a young woman in a Manhattan hotel. Sentenced to one and one-half to four years in prison, he served eight months.

While he served time for sexual abuse, *Me Against the World* (1995), his third album, entered the charts at number one. The album captures almost all aspects of Shakur's sometimes contradictory stances. The single "Dear Mama," a loving tribute to motherhood, won him both acclaim and sympathy from critics and listeners. Tracks such as "F*** the World" maintain his darker side and kept his critics wary.

The day after his sentence was announced Shakur was almost murdered in the lobby of a New York City recording studio, apparently by muggers. From prison, Shakur accused the Notorious B.I.G. (alternately known as Biggie Smalls), Sean "Puff Daddy" Combs, Andre Harrell, and one of his own friends, Randy "Stretch" Walker, of planning a murder plot against him. Whether there was ever such a plot remains unknown, but the accusation fueled already growing tensions between East and West Coast rap artists. The tensions between these groups—most notably the Notorious B.I.G. and Combs representing the East Coast, and Shakur, Suge Knight, and Snoop (Doggy) Dogg representing the West—was based more on standing and personality than on music. The rivalry mimicked gang rivalries and thug aggression in urban America, made all the players notorious and famous, and attracted the attention of numerous critics.

Shakur was paroled from prison after Knight, the president of Death Row Records, posted a $1.4 million bail for Shakur's release. Shakur then started working with Death Row Records, whose stable of artists included Dr. Dre and Snoop (Doggy) Dogg. Shakur's first release with Death Row, *All Eyez on Me* (1996), a double album, debuted at number one and went platinum shortly thereafter. The album is a showcase of Shakur's talents as well as an excellent sampling of rap producers such as Dr. Dre, Roger Troutman, Dat Nigga Daz, and DJ Pooh. "California Love," produced by Dre and Troutman, was a smash hit: It not only contains Dre's famous G-funk sound, but it also captures Shakur's rougher edges and penchant for sentimental tributes. "How Do You Want It," another single from the album, reached number one on the pop and R&B charts.

All Eyez on Me contains songs that refer to Shakur's stay in prison, his rivalry with East Coast rappers, and his love/hate relationship with women. The infamous "Hit 'Em Up" epitomizes the uglier side of *All Eyez on Me*. In the song, Shakur brags that he has sexual relations with the Notorious B.I.G.'s spouse, singer Faith Evans. The album also reveals Shakur's morbid musings about his death on tracks such as "Heaven Ain't Hard to Find."

Although there were rumors that Shakur was considering leaving rap and thug culture behind to pursue an acting career, he never had the chance. Accusations that he was involved in the murder of Walker, one year to the day after Shakur was shot, plagued him. On September 7, 1996, Shakur was shot while driving with Knight in Las Vegas, Nevada. The two had attended the Mike Tyson–Bruce Seldon fight at the MGM Grand Hotel earlier in the evening and had been involved in a scuffle. Knight would later serve time for the fight, but no connection was ever made between it and the later shooting. Shakur survived for almost a week, before dying on September 13.

No one has ever been charged with Shakur's murder. Rumors about the reasons for the murder swirled for years after his death. Some people believe Shakur was shot by associates of the man he scuffled with at the MGM Grand. Others believe he was the victim of an execution-style murder orchestrated by the Notorious B.I.G., who himself would be shot and killed six months later. Another popular rumor is that Knight was displeased with Shakur's alleged decision to leave Death Row Records and quit the music business. There were also persistent rumors that Shakur was still alive.

In the years following his death, Shakur became a global hip-hop icon. His now-famous face appears on T-shirts, pennants, flags, and street mosaics as a martyr for rap and the underclass alongside the likes of historical figures Dr. Martin Luther King Jr., Malcolm X, and Che Guevara. Posthumous releases appeared almost immediately and struggles over rights to his large catalog of unreleased raps made their way to the courts. *The Don Killuminati: The 7 Day Theory* (1996) was released under his alias Makaveli. It contains two memorable tracks, the now prophetic "To Live and Die in L.A." and "Toss It Up."

Compilations, some laced with new material, followed *The Don Killuminati*. *Greatest Hits* (1998), a two-disc set,

Spot Light | 2Pac Lives

Within days of his death in Las Vegas, Nevada, stories and Internet rumors proclaimed that Tupac Shakur was, in fact, still alive and had staged his death. Anyone wishing to find evidence that he lived need only listen to his raps about his death and ability to survive, believers claimed. Predictions Shakur made about his own death on songs such as "Until the End of Time" were strung together by other theorists with statements he made in interviews and to friends that he wished to leave the rap scene behind. Shakur's remains were cremated a day after his death, sparking rumors that there never would be a dead body to confirm the death. Conspiracy theorists posited that Suge Knight had a hand in the staging of Shakur's "murder" because he knew the death would bring his Death Row record label profits. Knight drove the car Shakur was murdered in and was only grazed by a spray of bullets that riddled Shakur. The fact that police never resolved the shooting, the only likely suspect was later killed, and key players still refuse to speak to police only serves to further suspicions. The legend that Shakur survived the shooting places him alongside other popular musicians like Elvis Presley whose deaths are shrouded in similar myths. In the African-American community, rumors that Shakur is alive have turned him into a ghetto saint who survived his enemies and the callous social conditions that shaped his psyche and those of his generation.

contains his signature tracks and is the best of the Shakur collection. Although the tracks are not arranged in chronological order, the set still captures Shakur's thug persona and his more generous and tender moments.

Shakur's contribution to rap music and African-American culture has generated a number of books, scholarly articles, and conference papers. However Shakur is remembered by critics and cultural historians, his place in hip-hop culture remains secure. For millions of people his life epitomized the plight of young black males in the United States. His tough boyish looks and his lucid angry raps place him in the company of legends like Elvis Presley, Jim Morrison, and Kurt Cobain.

SELECTIVE DISCOGRAPHY: *2Pacalypse Now* (Interscope, 1991); *Strictly 4 My N.I.G.G.A.Z.* (Interscope, 1993); *Me Against the World* (Interscope, 1995); *All Eyez on Me* (Death Row, 1996); *The Don Killuminati: The 7 Day Theory* (Death Row, 1996); *R U Still Down? (Remember Me)* (Amaru/Jive, 1997); *In His Own Words* (Mecca, 1998); *Greatest Hits* (Interscope, 1998); *Until the End of Time* (Interscope, 2001).

BIBLIOGRAPHY: H. Farkos, *Tupac Shakur (They Died Too Young)* (New York, 1998); Q. Jones, *Tupac Shakur, 1971–1996* (New York, 1998); E. M. Dyson, *Holler if You Can Hear Me* (New York, 2001).

WEBSITE: www.2paclegacy.com.

SHAWN GILLEN

U | u
  | U

U2

Formed: 1978, Dublin, Ireland

Members: Bono, vocals (Paul Hewson, born Dublin, Ireland, 10 May 1960); David "the Edge" Evans, guitar (born Barking, England, 8 August 1961); Adam Clayton, bass (born Oxford, England, 13 March 1960); Larry Mullen Jr., drums (born Dublin, Ireland, 31 October 1961).

Genre: Rock

Best-selling album since 1990: *Achtung Baby* (1991)

Hit songs since 1990: "Beautiful Day," "Mysterious Ways," "One"

U2 is one of the most popular rock bands in the world. Since its early roots as an Irish punk band with strong Christian overtones, U2 has evolved into a stadium rock band that consistently advocates social justice and world harmony. Unlike most bands that dissipate after only a few years, U2 has managed to avoid any personnel changes for more than twenty years and has consistently achieved commercial success. The four core members—singer Bono, guitarist the Edge, bassist Adam Clayton, and drummer Larry Mullen Jr.—present a unified front in every new chapter of the band's history. After ending the 1980s with a commercial smash album, *The Joshua Tree* (1987), the band entered the 1990s on a decidedly different path. Subsequent albums experiment with several styles including electronic dance music and exotic world rhythms. U2 also embarked on high-concept multimedia tours designed to lampoon consumer culture. By the end of the decade the band returned to its rock roots with the successful comeback album *All That You Can't Leave Behind* (2000). The band went on a stripped-down world tour that unwittingly coincided with the terrorist attacks of September 11, 2001. Before long, U2 was transformed into a musical ambassador for world healing as its tour was revamped to empathize with the mourning and confusion.

Beginnings

The band came together when all four members attended the same high school in Dublin. From the start, half the band adopted nicknames. Singer Paul Hewson became "Bono Vox" (Latin for "great voice") which was later shortened to Bono. Guitarist Dave Evans called himself "the Edge." Group members released a few singles on their own and built a large following in Ireland, attracting the attention of local businessman Paul McGuinness, who signed on as U2's manager. He brought the band to Island Records in 1980. U2's first two albums, *Boy* (1980) and *October* (1981), are swept with romantic fury and Christian overtones, countering the nihilism of punk rock and the synthesizer pop of the early MTV days. U2 quickly created a reputation as an intensely passionate live band and soon was headlining U.S. clubs. The band's third album, *War* (1983), opened more doors in the United States. For the first time, the band addressed specific political issues in its music. The album's biggest single, "Sunday Bloody Sunday," mourned the fourteen people killed by British soldiers in the Bloody Sunday massacre in 1972 in Derry, Ireland. Bono wrapped himself in a white flag symbolizing peace each time he sang the song, which became a pinnacle of U2's live shows.

A turning point for U2 came after viewing an exhibit at the Peace Museum in Chicago. Titled "The Unforgettable Fire," it featured folk art by survivors of the atomic bomb in Hiroshima, Japan, in 1945. Bono agreed to sponsor a tour of the exhibit—as well as a second one on the life of civil rights leader Martin Luther King Jr.—to Dublin. Deciding to move in a more ambient direction for its next venture, the band hired producer Brian Eno, the pioneering composer known for creating minimal and dreamy atmospheric music. He brought along newcomer Daniel Lanois, who had had success creating instrumental experiments with Eno in the studio. Both ended up co-producing *The Unforgettable Fire* (1984), and they would become the group's most cherished musical collaborators in later years. Inspired by the two exhibits in Chicago, the album is draped in a mournful sound. It marries murky atmospheres with compelling tunes. The song "Pride (In the Name of Love)" is a tribute to King. The album moved U2 into arenas. At Live Aid, an all-day benefit concert for Ethiopian famine relief in 1985, the group's set became the highlight.

The Joshua Tree (1987) followed, and thrust the band into international stardom. Although the production mirrored *The Unforgettable Fire* (Eno and Lanois again were at the helm), the new album was stocked with many more radio-friendly songs. *The Joshua Tree* defines U2's signature sound: the Edge's experimental tunings and chopping riffs, Clayton's sensual bass lines, Mullen's pummeling drums, and Bono's emotional singing. Critics consider the lyrics among Bono's best. Using the desert as a metaphor for spiritual salvation and also moral devastation, the album explores questions of faith, redemption, political oppression, and social injustice. It won a Grammy Award for Album of the Year; and U2 embarked on a worldwide tour that was documented on film. The tour's accompanying album, *Rattle and Hum* (1988), features live songs and originals written in American musical styles like rockabilly, gospel, and blues, along with cameos by stars like B.B. King and Bob Dylan.

Reinvention

U2 entered the 1990s at a crossroads. Sitting on top of the world posed a unique challenge: How do you avoid becoming a parody of yourself? The band sought to remake its image through musical experiments and high concept tours that walked the line between alienating its audience and exposing them to new ideas.

Recorded partly in Berlin, *Achtung Baby* (1991) borrows the heavy electronic sound and apocalyptic attitude of industrial rock; it incorporates hip-hop flavored dance beats and electronic noise in the guitars. The dark textures set the band free. No longer caged in by having to make epic social statements, U2 now sounds sexy and loose. The rhythmic songs explore romance, jealousy, and desire. Critics and fans welcomed the change, especially because it yielded so many intoxicating hit singles.

The next year, U2 began the "Zoo TV" tour, a multimedia extravaganza. Intended to comment on identity, rock star celebrity, and the allure of mass media, the stage design called for onstage television monitors, live broadcast transmissions from around the world, and hand-held video cameras. The band members dressed in outfits borrowed from the gender-bending world of 1970s glam rock. Bono performed as characters "MacPhisto," "The Fly," and "Mirrorball Man" in an attempt to mock stardom's dark side.

The tour lasted two years and during a break, the band recorded *Zooropa* (1993), which incorporates blaring synthesizers, heavy beats, funky riffs, and lyrics that reflect the ironic detachment of jaded consumerism. It was U2's least successful album. But it opened the way for *Pop* and its accompanying world tour. Patterned after the work of the British electronic bands the Chemical Brothers, Massive Attack, and Prodigy, *Pop* is U2's biggest departure in style. "Discotheque," the kick-off single, is pure dance club music. Although it has some conventional songs like "Staring at the Sun," most of the music features electronic jams and lyrics drenched in kitsch.

The "PopMart" tour followed. Designed to lampoon consumerism, the tour's set featured a thirty-five-foot-high mirrorball lemon, a 100-foot-high yellow arch (reportedly patterned after the golden-arched logo of McDonald's), and a 100-foot-long toothpick stuck into a giant olive. Although it was the second highest grossing tour of 1997, the tour did not sell out and it left many fans confused. Critics argued the band had lost its way.

In the late 1990s Bono became a visible world crusader for AIDS relief in Africa and for debt relief for all Third World nations. He made speeches at world summits and met with U.S. president Bill Clinton, British prime minister Tony Blair, and Pope John Paul II. He raised awareness by traveling to Africa with U.S. Treasury Secretary Paul O'Neill in 2002 and later by touring the U.S. Midwest, meeting with community groups and newspaper editorial boards.

U2 returned to its roots in 2000. *All That You Can't Leave Behind* is a stripped-down rock record that recalls the band's heyday of more than a decade earlier. It earned a Grammy for Album of the Year.

Despite some sharp stylistic turns, U2 has remained popular throughout its career. Its many blockbuster albums and hit singles have supported its lead singer's social activism. Musically, it has refused to rest on its lau-

Spot Light | All That You Can't Leave Behind

U2 spent the 1990s trying not to be the U2 of the 1980s. That meant drifting away from guitar rock romanticism and toward the harsh beats and nightclub glamour of electronic music. In three different albums, the band pushed that sound as far it would go. The natural step was to go backward. *All That You Can't Leave Behind* (2000) won praise for its emphasis on the basics: tuneful melodies, soulful lyrics, and catchy hooks. Brian Eno and Daniel Lanois— the co-producers responsible for the band's best-loved albums—returned. After the terrorist attacks of September 11, 2001, the album unwittingly turned into a soundtrack for the times. "New York" became a tribute to the city, "Stuck in a Moment You Can't Get Out Of" and "Walk On" pleas for healing, and "Peace on Earth" a hymn for the future. U2 redesigned its tour to pay tribute to the lives lost. Appearing before a global audience during the Super Bowl XXXVI halftime, U2 scrolled the names of the September 11 victims on a screen during the song "Where the Streets Have No Name."

rels. U2 has explored new sounds while staying true to its rock roots.

SELECTIVE DISCOGRAPHY: *Boy* (Island, 1980); *October* (Island, 1981); *War* (Island, 1983); *Under a Blood Red Sky* (Island, 1983); *The Unforgettable Fire* (Island, 1984); *Wide Awake in America* EP (Island, 1985); *The Joshua Tree* (Island, 1987); *Rattle and Hum* (Island, 1988); *Achtung Baby* (Island, 1991); *Zooropa* (Island, 1993); *Pop* (Island, 1997); *The Best of 1980–1990* (Island, 1998); *All That You Can't Leave Behind* (Island, 2000); *The Best of 1990–2000 and B-Sides* (Island, 2002).

WEBSITE: www.u2.com.

MARK GUARINO

UB40

Formed: 1978, Birmingham, England

Members: Astro, vocals, trumpet (born Terence Williams; Birmingham, England, 24 June 1957); James Brown, drums (born Birmingham, England, 21 November 1957); Ali Campbell, vocals, guitar (born Birmingham, England, 15 February 1959); Robin Campbell, guitar, vocals (born Birmingham, England, 25 December 1954); Earl Falconer, bass (born Birmingham, England, 23 January 1957); Norman Hassan, percussion (born Birmingham, England, 26 January 1958); Brian Travers, saxophone (born Birmingham, England, 7 February 1959); Mickey Virtue, keyboards (born Birmingham, England, 19 January 1957).

Genre: Rock, Reggae

Best-selling album since 1990: *Promises and Lies* (1993)

Hit songs since 1990: "Can't Help Falling in Love (with You)," "Here I Am (Come and Take Me)," "The Way You Do the Things You Do"

UB40 were the unlikely proselytizers who brought reggae to an international audience. Born from the same musical and social ferment that spawned British punk and ska, UB40 popularized reggae through their cover versions of "Red Red Wine," "I Got You Babe," and "Can't Help Falling in Love (with You)." Sporting full horn and rhythm sections, this multiracial group tackled numerous social and political issues, from local unemployment and Third World poverty to the imprisonment of Nelson Mandela and the dangers of nuclear war.

Named after the British unemployment form, UB40 slowly gained an audience around their hometown of Birmingham, England. While not firmly aligned with British ska or two-tone, they voiced similar commentaries on social ills and frustrations. The group was formed around the brothers Robin and Ali Campbell and was multiracial in its makeup. Local reggae toaster Astro joined the group for the recording of "Food for Thought" and soon became a full-time member.

After touring with the Pretenders, the group formed their own label and released *Present Arms in Dub* (1981), which features the song "One in Ten," a biting commentary on British unemployment. In 1983 they produced their tribute album *Labour of Love*, which includes a cover version of Neil Diamond's "Red Red Wine." Moderately successful at first, the song climbed to *Billboard*'s number one spot after their performance at the Nelson Mandela concert in 1988. *Baggariddim* (1985), an experimental album using local disc jockeys, includes the hit song "Don't Break My Heart" and the cover version of "I Got You Babe," with Chrissie Hynde of the Pretenders. After extensive international touring the group returned with *Labour of Love II* (1989), their second tribute album, which features the Temptations' "The Way You Do the Things You Do."

In 1993 UB40 enjoyed tremendous success with their album *Promises and Lies*, which rose to number one in the

United Kingdom and number six in the United States. Their version of Elvis Presley's "Can't Help Falling in Love (with You)" reached *Billboard*'s number one position. After the song is introduced by soft keyboard textures, Ali Campbell sings his first phrase in an earnest and caressing manner. After a dramatic drum entrance and horn buildup, Campbell returns with the first verse over a jaunty bass ostinato. During the choruses the backup singers surround the melody with horns providing tight punctuation. UB40's second single, "Higher Ground," peaked at U.K. number two and was followed by "Bring Me Your Cup" and "C'est La Vie."

After court litigation over the authorship of "Don't Break My Heart," UB40 returned to the recording studio. Reaffirming their commitment to reggae musicians, they recorded the collaborative albums *UB40 Present the Dancehall Album* (1998) and *UB40 Present the Father of Reggae* (2002).

While UB40 began their career by focusing on social issues, they gained widespread popularity through their musical covers, most especially "Red Red Wine" and "Can't Help Falling in Love (with You)." Unlikely as it may seem, this British band disseminated reggae to an international audience. At the same time, UB40 assisted many young stars and collaborated with elder reggae musicians.

SELECTIVE DISCOGRAPHY: *Signing Off* (Graduate, 1980); *Present Arms in Dub* (DEP, 1981); *UB44* (DEP, 1982); *Live* (DEP, 1982); *Labour of Love* (DEP, 1983); *Geffery Morgan* (DEP, 1984); *Baggariddim* (DEP, 1985); *Rat in the Kitchen* (DEP, 1986); *CCCP: Live in Moscow* (DEP, 1987); *UB40* (DEP, 1988); *Labour of Love II* (DEP, 1989); *Promises and Lies* (DEP, 1993); *Guns in the Ghetto* (Virgin, 1997); *UB40 Present the Dancehall Album* (Virgin, 1998); *Labour of Love III* (Virgin, 1999); *Cover Up* (Virgin, 2001); *UB40 Present the Fathers of Reggae* (Virgin, 2002).

WEBSITE: www.ub40-dep.com.

WYNN YAMAMI

UNCLE KRACKER

Born: Matthew Lynford Shafer; Detroit, Michigan, 6 June 1974

Genre: Rock

Best-selling album since 1990: *Double Wide* (2000)

Hit songs since 1990: "Follow Me," "Yeah, Yeah, Yeah"

Ever since there have been rock bands, there have been side projects. Lead singers, guitarists, bassists, even drummers have launched their own solo careers over the years, but Matthew Shafer,

Matt "Uncle Kracker" Shafer [AP/WIDE WORLD PHOTOS]

known as Uncle Kracker, was one of the first disc jockeys (DJs) in a rock band to spin off a solo career that spawned a hit album. Kracker's solo debut, *Double Wide* (2000), melds country and classic rock, hip-hop and folk for a fresh sound that made the Detroit native a star alongside his boss, Kid Rock.

The careers of Kracker and Rock have been intertwined since their youth. Kracker began writing songs at age eleven, cementing his creative partnership with Rock at age thirteen, after the two met at Daytona's, a popular Clawson, Michigan, bar where Rock was taking part in an all-ages DJ contest. Rock was competing against Kracker's brother in the contest, but the two became fast friends, sharing a love for classic soul, hip-hop, southern rock, and country music. Kracker joined Rock's band, Twisted Brown Trucker, in 1990 and, despite not knowing how to work the turntables, he contributed to Rock's albums as his DJ and co-songwriter, beginning with Rock's 1991 debut, *Grits Sandwiches for Breakfast*.

Thanks to his high-profile work on Rock's multimillion-selling breakthrough album, *Devil without a Cause* (1998), and with audiences primed to hear a mix of folky rock and rapping thanks to former House of Pain leader Everlast's smash "What It's Like" (1998), the stage was set in 2000 for Kracker to go it alone on his solo debut, *Double Wide*. Rock gave Kracker an opportunity to perform during his 2000 tour dates, giving his audiences a taste of his DJ's style.

Double Wide, produced by Rock, was the first album on Rock's Top Dog imprint not to feature his name above the title. (Kracker was forced to add "Uncle" to his name prior to the album's release due to a conflict with a 1970s rock band of the same name.) It was recorded over the course of a year in the back of Rock's tour bus and features eight tracks co-written by the old friends.

Double Wide bears all the hallmarks of the pair's musical influences: Motown soul, country outlaws such as George Jones, the southern rock of Lynyrd Skynyrd, and mellow rapping built around strong pop choruses. Fellow Twisted Brown Trucker members Jimmie Bones (keyboards), Kenny Olson (guitar), Jason Krause (guitar), and Stefanie Eulinberg (drums) all contribute to the album, as does Rock, rapping on the country blues rapping ode to Detroit, "Heaven" ("If heaven ain't a lot like Detroit / I don't want to go"). In a nod to Kracker's influences, the song samples the 1982 Hank Williams Jr. track "If Heaven Ain't a Lot Like Dixie" (1982).

Success Comes Slowly, but Surely

Given the context in which they were conceived, it is not surprising that the Bob Seger–inspired classic rock song "You Can't Take Me" and the swamp boogie funk of "Better Days" contain litanies detailing the harshness of life on the road, recited in Kracker's trademark gravelly, soulful voice. Like Rock's *Devil without a Cause, Double Wide* was not an immediate best-seller. Despite the ubiquity of Rock's name in the music press, Kracker's album languished for more than eight months before the acoustic folk-rap song "Follow Me" began to catch fire and drive the album's sales. In the fall of 2001, Kracker appeared as a guest on the popular *Drew Carey Show* sitcom and lent his voice to the animated film *Osmosis Jones*. His songs also appeared on the soundtracks to the films *Shanghai Noon* (2000) and *Mission: Impossible 2* (2000).

After contributing to Rock's album *Cocky* (2001), Kracker worked on his own second solo album, *No Stranger to Shame* (2002). Stepping further outside the shadow of Rock, *No Stranger to Shame* was co-produced and co-written by Kracker and longtime collaborator Mike Bradford. The album again indulges in Kracker's love of classic early 1980s hip-hop ("Keep It Comin'") and 1970s soul ("Drift Away"), but more often than not finds Kracker crooning country soul songs in a Memphis-via-Detroit drawl. "Drift Away" features a cameo from soft rocker Dobie Gray, on whose 1973 song it is based.

Though their rapping cadence and delivery on fast tracks is similar, Kracker distinguishes himself from his benefactor Rock on his midtempo songs by incorporating elements of Creedence Clearwater Revival–inspired swamp blues ("Thunderhead Hawkins"), psychedelic rock ("Baby Don't Cry"), and brassy Motown soul ("I Do"). The album did not fare as well commercially as Kracker's debut, however.

Uncle Kracker achieved the rare feat of establishing his own identity outside the outsized shadow of his patron, rap-rocker Kid Rock. Matching Rock's bluster with a humble, blue-collar aesthetic, Kracker produced a pair of soulful solo albums that introduced rap fans to everything from southern rock to country blues.

SELECTIVE DISCOGRAPHY: *Double Wide* (Top Dog/Lava/Atlantic, 2000); *No Stranger to Shame* (Top Dog/Lava/Atlantic, 2002). **Soundtracks:** *Shanghai Noon* (Varese, 2000); *Mission: Impossible 2* (Hollywood, 2000).

WEBSITE: www.unclekracker.com.

GIL KAUFMAN

USHER

Born: Usher Raymond; Chattanooga, Tennessee, 14 October 1978

Genre: R&B, Pop

Best-selling album since 1990: *My Way* (1997)

Hit songs since 1990: "You Make Me Wanna," "Nice and Slow," "U Remind Me"

During the 1990s teenage star Usher represented the good-time, ebullient side of rhythm and blues music, alternately fun-spirited and seductive. Unlike artists such as Maxwell and Erykah Badu, who aim their music at an older audience via a back-to-the-roots sound recalling 1970s R&B, Usher looks and sounds entirely contemporary, reveling in high-tech production and flashy stage effects. A limber, effortless dancer, Usher truly comes to life in live performance and videos, where his nimble dance moves and sexy but sweet personality can be witnessed in person. His high-voltage style of showmanship is so impressive that even a rather modest singing ability—his nasal voice is frequently off-key—has not hampered his rise to stardom.

Beginnings

Usher spent his early years in the mid-sized Tennessee city of Chattanooga, where he sang in his mother's church choir and entered local talent shows. His father left the family shortly after his birth. When Usher was twelve his mother, always confident in her son's abilities, moved her family to Atlanta, Georgia, a larger city with a substantial music scene. After winning a competition on the television talent program *Star Search*, Usher auditioned successfully for producer Antonio "L.A." Reid, then seeking artists for his burgeoning LaFace label, a joint venture with producer Kenneth "Babyface" Edmonds. The singer's debut album, *Usher,* was released on LaFace in 1994 and features the midtempo dance hit, "Think of You." The song was bolstered with top-quality production by famed hip-hop artist Sean "Puffy" Combs, who gives Usher the kind of dense, grooving beat he supplied on contemporaneous work with singer Mary J. Blige. While strong, the material on *Usher* was perhaps not distinctive enough to bring the singer widespread fame, and Usher devoted the next several years to finishing high school and perfecting a sly, deeper vocal delivery. In interviews he began to exude more of his personality, smiling and answering questions with a sweet but rakish southern charm.

Stardom

Usher's second album, *My Way* (1997), established his stardom on the basis of the number one R&B hit, "You Make Me Wanna." The song, sporting a sinuous groove supplied by young producer Jermaine Dupri, capitalizes on the singer's new persona: sexy but vulnerable, seductive without being aggressive. Although Usher sings about desertion—in the song he falls in love with his girlfriend's best friend—he cultivates sympathy in his listeners through his abiding sense of conscience. Older, more hardened hip-hop performers might move on to the new liaison with callous detachment, but Usher is beset with anxiety. "I love her but I'm falling for you," he sings with pinched sincerity, confessing that, "I never meant to hurt her but I gotta let her go." Even when hurting the woman who loves him, he emerges as sensitive and likable. Addressing Usher's sexually aware but tender image, rock critic Robert Christgau described him as "the sweetest non-virgin a mama could ask [for]." Usher's physical appearance only highlighted his teen idol appeal: Lithe and muscular, often appearing in videos stripped to the waist, he emerged as a love man for the 1990s, the natural successor to smooth-voiced soul singers of the 1970s such as Al Green and Teddy Pendergrass. If Usher's voice sounds less assured than those of his predecessors, he makes up for it with the precision and grace of his dancing. His concerts, in which he performs multiple handstands and back-flips, are showcases for his dazzling athleticism.

By the late 1990s Usher was showing signs of growing up, moving beyond his teenage fan base with forays into film and television acting. Discussing his versatility with the *E!* television network in 1998 he professed his desire to be "the ultimate entertainer." Ironically, while contemporaries such as Maxwell display a greater historical awareness of the musical aspect of R&B, Usher perhaps better reflects the true spirit of the idiom. Recalling the fleet-footed technique and show-stopping antics of 1950s singers such as Jackie Wilson, as well as 1980s superstar Michael Jackson, Usher reinforces R&B's original standing as good-time party music—music to make people forget their troubles. While performers such as Badu infuse their work with socially conscious messages, Usher strives above all to entertain.

Although acting activities kept him away from the recording studio during the late 1990s, he returned with another hit album, *8701,* in 2001. Benefiting from an infectious synthesizer riff and thumping bass line, the single "U Remind Me" became his most successful outing to date, reaching the number one slot on the pop and R&B charts. One of the album's most enjoyable tracks is "U-Turn," in which Usher, employing "how-to" lyrics, updates the kind of high-spirited dance records popular during the 1960s: "Put your hands up, bend your knees / Bounce around in a circle, get down with me." While some of its material is uneven, *8701* evinces signs of a new vocal maturity. Usher's voice continues to lack power, especially in his thin upper range, but he has learned to harness it more effectively. At the end of "U Remind Me," for example, he adds variety by playing with his phrasing and timing instead of stretching for high notes. On the album's ballads Usher draws upon his familiar theme of sex combined with healthy doses of romance, promising his lover to "work it" from "11 to 6 in the morning," while offering enticements such as "a bed of rose petals."

Drawing upon old-fashioned show-biz pizzazz, Usher entertains fans through flamboyant displays of physical agility. As an artist he takes the basic qualities inherent within R&B for decades—danceable rhythm, catchy melody, convivial feeling—and updates them with his naughty but nice personal style. Beyond his charisma and effervescent music, Usher's appeal lies in a persona that tempers sensuality with sweetness and charm.

SELECTIVE DISCOGRAPHY: *Usher* (LaFace, 1994); *My Way* (LaFace, 1997); *Live* (LaFace, 1999); *8701* (Arista, 2001).

WEBSITE: www.usherworld.com.

DAVID FREELAND

$$V \left|\begin{array}{c} v \\ \hline v \end{array}\right.\!\!\!\text{—}$$

VAN HALEN

Formed: 1974, Pasadena, California

Members: Michael Anthony, bass (born Chicago, Illinois, 20 June 1954); Alex Van Halen, drums (born Nijmegan, Netherlands, 8 June 1950); Eddie Van Halen, guitar (born Nijmegan, Netherlands, 26 January 1955). Former members: Gary Cherone, lead vocals (born Malden, Massachusetts, 26 July 1961); Sammy Hagar, lead vocals (born Monterey, California, 13 October 1947); David Lee Roth, lead vocals (born Bloomington, Indiana, 10 October 1955).

Genre: Rock

Best-selling album since 1990: *For Unlawful Carnal Knowledge* (1991)

Hit songs since 1990: "Right Now," "Poundcake"

Since 1990 Van Halen has spent more time in the gossip pages than on the album charts. The band began the decade at their commercial height, but a series of drastic missteps found them at a career low just a few years later. Despite their personal problems and frenzied lead-vocalist changes, Van Halen remained the premiere American party rock band, buoyed as ever by Eddie Van Halen's showy guitar technique and escapist songwriting.

The Van Halen brothers, Eddie and Alex, began playing music together while growing up in Pasadena, California. The sons of a Dutch musician, the boys received classical music training throughout their childhood. After discovering rock and roll, Alex took up guitar and Eddie learned to play the drums. They soon switched instruments and, after forming the band Mammoth, Eddie developed into a guitar virtuoso, creating a signature stock of sound effects and tricks (including "tapping," in which the fingers on the strumming hand bang out a flurry of notes on the neck of the guitar) that eventually became de rigeur for heavy metal guitarists. While playing in the Southern California circuit, they recruited David Lee Roth as their singer and Michael Anthony to play bass. They changed their name to Van Halen in 1974 and soon became the most popular band in the Los Angeles area, with a reputation built on Eddie's guitar playing and Roth's outlandish showmanship. The band released their first album, *Van Halen*, in 1978, and it promptly went platinum. Less ponderous than the heavy metal of the era, their pop hooks and playful performances made an instant impact on the mainstream. The band released an album every year until their masterwork *1984* (1984), which includes the party staples "Jump," "Panama," and "Hot for Teacher."

By the mid-1980s, tensions between Roth and Eddie Van Halen sent the singer packing and on to a solo career. The band recruited the arena rock journeyman Sammy Hagar as lead vocalist, which began a more earnest but no less successful chapter for the band. Fans and critics initially balked at the news, but the results were surprisingly solid—Hagar brought a credible party persona as well as a penchant for straight-ahead balladry that satisfied the core audience and broadened the band's mainstream appeal. *5150* (1986) and *OU812* (1988) sold millions and produced a number of hit ballads. *For Unlawful Carnal Knowledge* (1991) saw the band pumping out anthems with renewed energy and scoring a best-selling single with the uplifting "Right Now." The songs on the album are arena-ready, with big choruses driven by Eddie's blinding guitar work and Hagar's warm heavy metal wail. The 1991–1992

705

tour was a rousing success. The band ripped through their catalog with energy and conviction. The tour was documented and released on album and home video under the title *Van Halen Live: Right Here, Right Now* (1993).

The band reconvened to record *Balance* in 1995, but new tensions between Eddie and Hagar made for less focused work. Eddie, fresh out of an alcohol rehabilitation program, tired of Hagar's hard-partying ways, and the tour was less successful than its predecessor. A year later the band began to prepare a greatest hits compilation against Hagar's wishes and even recorded two new songs with David Lee Roth. It has never been revealed whether Hagar then left the band or was fired. The original Van Halen lineup appeared in public for the first time in twelve years on the MTV Video Awards in September 1996 to overwhelming applause. Days later, the band issued a statement claiming that Roth had not been rehired as singer and that they were searching for a new vocalist.

The band eventually enlisted Gary Cherone from the band Extreme and recorded *Van Halen III* (1998), a winking nod to their rotating vocalist situation. The lineup change gave the music a sharp edge—the single "Without You" in particular sounds fresh and forceful. But many tracks feel awkward, mainly because of Eddie's sincere attempts at expanding the band's musical scope with new rhythms and topical lyrics. The audience was not won over. The album and subsequent tour faltered, and Cherone was released from his duties in 1999.

All signs pointed to another reunion with Roth, who confirmed unofficially that he had been recording new material with the band. News that Eddie Van Halen had been battling cancer halted the momentum. In 2001 the band left the Warner Bros. label and admitted that they were still without a singer. Eddie emailed the band's official website in May 2002 reporting that his doctors had given him a clean bill of health, but the band's future was still uncertain. While many fans hope for a successful reunion with Roth, Van Halen has proved that they can retool their music to fit a new lead singer. The rock solid musicianship of its core members keeps the band relevant, and the lead vocalist slot remains one of the most coveted in rock music.

SELECTIVE DISCOGRAPHY: *Van Halen* (Warner Bros., 1978); *Van Halen II* (Warner Bros., 1979); *Women and Children First* (Warner Bros., 1980); *Fair Warning* (Warner Bros., 1981); *Diver Down* (Warner Bros., 1982); *1984* (Warner Bros., 1984); *5150* (Warner Bros., 1986); *OU812* (Warner Bros., 1988); *For Unlawful Carnal Knowledge* (Warner Bros., 1991); *Van Halen Live: Right Here, Right Now* (Warner Bros., 1993); *Balance* (Warner Bros., 1995); *The Best of Van Halen, Vol. 1* (Warner Bros., 1996); *Van Halen III* (Warner Bros., 1997).

WEBSITE: www.van-halen.com.

SEAN CAMERON

LOS VAN VAN

Formed: 4 December 1969, Havana, Cuba

Members: Juan Formell, guitar, bass, composer, bandleader (born Havana, Cuba, 8 February 1942); Cesar "Pupy" Pedroso, piano; Roberto "Cucurucho" Carlos, piano; Jose Luis "Changuito" Quintana, congas, timbales; Samuell Formell, drums; Boris Luna, synthesizer; Angel Bonne, Pedro Calvo, Mayito Rivera, Roberto "Guayacan" Hernández, Yeni Valdes (first woman member), Abel "Lele" Rosales, vocals.

Genre: World

Best-selling album since 1990: *Llego . . . Van Van ("Van Van Is Here")* (1999)

Hit songs since 1990: "El Negro Está Cocinando," "¡Que Sorpresa! (Voy a Publicar Tu Foto)"

Havana-born Juan Formell studied music as a child with his father, an honored music educator, and the bassists Orestes Urfe and Orestes López "Cachao," among others. The Mexican Trio Los Panchos, singer Benny Moré, and trumpeter Chapottin were the favorite entertainers of his youth. At age sixteen he embarked on a career as a bar-hopping troubadour, but his efforts were interrupted by his conscription as a bassist into Fidel Castro's National Police Band in 1959, the year of the Cuban revolution.

To perform for state functions Formell had to quickly master a broad repertoire of traditional Cuban songs and rhythms such as the mambo, bolero, rumba, son, and danzon. While in the police band, Formell also had his first exposure to radio broadcasts from Miami, which opened up new worlds of American R&B, jazz, rock and roll, and country music. Through this musical education on the fly, he prepared himself to lead one of the most enduring hot dance bands of the past four decades.

Returning to civilian life in a Havana liberated from the rule of Batista, he became a journeyman in the then-dispirited world of the Cuban dance hall. Formell assimilated and adapted everything he heard, scoring a dance hit with "El Martes" while serving as musical director for Elio Reve's courtly flutes-and-violins charanga Orquesta Reve. He introduced rock chord progressions, electric guitars, and bass lines to the "country son" reveries of Reve's ensemble and promoted the sound as "El Changui '68."

In 1969 Formell left Revé to establish Los Van Van—"the go-go's!" or "go, go!"—with an even more aggressive approach to his musical heritage. Formell called his new jazz-inflected sound "songo." The sound added three trombones to two violins, two flutes, string bass, and piano, along with a seductive trio of male vocalists singing Formell's own witty lyrics, all piled atop layers of expertly synchronized polyrhythms.

Los Van Van was a vehicle for Formell's songo tracks throughout the 1970s. In the 1980s he announced his "buey cansado" sound, incorporating electric keyboards, synthesizers, and drum machines into already dense, churning instrumentation. This stylistic development of Formell's was eagerly embraced by audiences and record buyers—except in the United States, which enforces restrictions on cultural exchange and commercial activities with Cuba.

Such sanctions have not hindered Formell, Los Van Van, or other Cuban musicians from realizing world-class musical standards or achieving ambitions similar to those of the best bands. Professional Cuban bands (officially employed by the state) vie to top each other as did swing bands during the Depression years in the United States. In the late 1980s the rise of NG Banda, which introduced a looser, funkier "timba" as its own "new sound," pressed Formell to continually reinvent Los Van Van. He has evidently accomplished that feat and composes essential timba anthems while leading Los Van Van in acclaimed timba albums.

Juan Formell y Los Van Van remains a star attraction at music festivals and fiestas worldwide. They suffered personnel attrition with the departure of Changuito in 1992, Cesar "Pupi" Pedroso in 2000, and Pedro Calvo in 2001, each to form his own band. But Formell has attracted equally gifted musicians as replacements, so that Van Van maintains a reputation for finding and launching new talents.

Los Van Van boasts a discography of twenty recordings and more than 150 original songs, some of which have been covered by Rubén Blades, Harry Belafonte, Ray Barreto, and El Gran Combo de Puerto Ríco. The albums that have been released in the United States have been highly acclaimed. *Llego . . . Los Van Van* (1999) won a 1999 Grammy Award for Best Salsa Performance. Los Van Van are invariably included in anthologies surveying popular Cuban music since 1969, and the band's tour schedule rivals that of any comparable top-tier ensemble. Los Van Van has traveled throughout South, Central, and Caribbean America as well as to Asia, Europe, the United States, and the former Soviet Union.

SELECTIVE DISCOGRAPHY: *Songo* (Mango, 1988); *Dancing Wet* (World Pacific, 1993); *Azucar* (Xenophile, 1995); *Ay, Dios ¡Ampárame!* (Caribe, 1995); *Lo Ultimo En Vivo* (Qbadisc, 1996); *Con La Salsa Formell* (Cubacan, 1997); *Best of Los Van Van* (Milan, 1997); *La Colección Cubana* (Music Club,

1998); *Llego Van Van* (Atlantic/Calie 1999); *Coleccion, Vol. 7* (Egrem, 2002); *Live in America* (AJ, 2003).

HOWARD MANDEL

LUTHER VANDROSS

Born: New York, New York, 20 April 1951
Genre: R&B
Best-selling album since 1990: *Power of Love* (1991)
Hit songs since 1990: "Power of Love/Love Power," "Endless Love," "Your Secret Love"

Since the early 1980s Luther Vandross has established himself as one of the most successful, durable performers in rhythm and blues. Known for his supple tenor voice, Vandross favors romantic love ballads with clear, easily recognizable melodies, while his lyrics explore themes of devotion, longing, and heartbreak. In this respect, his music shares more in common with rhythm and blues songs of the 1960s and 1970s than with the more sexually explicit sounds of younger performers such as D'Angelo and Sisqó. Nonetheless, Vandross has maintained his popularity with mainstream audiences by keeping in touch with changing trends while at the same time holding on to his core musical values. Vandross has also gained respect for his work with other artists, writing and producing songs for singers such as Aretha Franklin and Whitney Houston.

Early Years

Raised on New York's Lower East Side, Vandross grew up listening to early 1960s pop music, as well as gospel songs. He received his first break in early 1975, when his composition "Everybody Rejoice" was featured in the Broadway musical, *The Wiz*, based on the popular film *The Wizard of Oz* (1939). That same year, he contributed vocals to rock singer David Bowie's *Young Americans* album, cowriting "Fascination" with Bowie. By the end of the decade, he had performed extensively as a jingle and background singer and recorded the album *Luther* (1976) with his own band.

In 1981 he was given a recording contract with Epic Records and released his first solo album, *Never Too Much*. For the remainder of the decade he racked up a sizable number of rhythm and blues hits, including "Never Too Much," "It's Over Now," and "Any Love." His albums, which he produced, wrote, and arranged himself, became showcases for his creativity and rich musical imagination. The hit "Wait for Love" perfectly illustrates the Vandross

Luther Vandross [PAUL NATKIN/PHOTO RESERVE]

approach. Working against a lush, rhythmic arrangement, with a powerful female chorus providing dramatic tension, Vandross slowly builds intensity through subtle changes in the volume and timing of his vocals. By the end, he is improvising freely, playing with the words in a manner that draws out the song's emotion.

On the strength of his singles and albums, Vandross developed a loyal, largely female, fan base. However, he had yet to achieve full-fledged pop stardom by the late 1980s. Perhaps his music was too rhythm-and-blues-oriented, although a factor more likely to have prevented his crossing over to a pop audience was the laid-back, conservative image he projected both in music and in his personal life. In an era dominated by performers such as Michael Jackson, Prince, and Madonna, all of whom made audacious statements in their fashion and music, Vandross seemed slightly old-fashioned. Neither glamorous nor trend setting, he was instead characterized by consistency.

Pop Success

In 1989, Vandross's years of commitment finally paid off when "Here and Now," another romantic ballad, stormed into the Pop Top 10. "Here and Now" has a slicker, more polished sound than his previous hits, making it more accessible for mainstream radio audiences. The song won a Grammy Award for Best R&B Vocal Performance in 1990 and transformed Vandross into a pop star. The next

year, he hit his commercial and artistic peak with *Power of Love*, an album many critics regard as his finest. In his notes to a reissue of the album in 2001, *Billboard* magazine writer Matthew S. Robinson called it "one of [Vandross's] most fulfilling meditations on the search for love." The album's first single, "Power of Love/Love Power," became Vandross's biggest pop hit and carried him to a new level of popularity. With its bouncy rhythm, upbeat lyrics, and infectious melody, the song proved extremely influential, pointing to the hip-hop style of the 1990s while staying rooted in the smooth vocalizing of the past. A soaring vocal choir gives the song an inspirational quality that hearkens back to Vandross's childhood love of gospel music. The rest of the album is a cohesive blend of seductive up-tempo tunes and atmospheric ballads, all sung with emotion and tenderness. Both the album and the "Love Power/Power of Love" single won Grammy Awards in 1991. In 1992 Vandross scored another big hit with "The Best Things in Life Are Free," a duet with Janet Jackson from the film *Mo' Money* (1992).

In 1994 Vandross released a version of the 1981 Diana Ross/Lionel Richie hit "Endless Love" with fellow super-star Mariah Carey. The new "Endless Love" was so successful that it led to an album, *Songs* (1994), in which Vandross interprets material initially made famous by other performers. The album was a commercial hit, although some longtime fans complained that Vandross was aiming too heavily for the mainstream pop market. Nonetheless Vandross remained at the top of his game, earning his fourth Grammy in 1996 for the hit "Your Secret Love." The success of the song, taken from his album of the same name, proved that at age forty-five Vandross had no intention of slowing down. Always good-natured and diplomatic, he succeeded in keeping his personal life out of the press, although he openly discussed his battles with diabetes, food, and weight gain.

New Directions

After *Your Secret Love*, Vandross ended his long association with Epic Records, a relationship sometimes marked by conflict. In 1992, for example, he had filed suit against Epic's parent company, Sony Entertainment, citing a portion of the California Labor Code that stipulates a seven-year limit for personal service contracts. Speaking to the *Amsterdam News* in 1998, Vandross hinted that he had been frustrated by Epic's inability to give him a number one pop hit, a goal which he claimed "was never aimed for and prioritized as important" at the label. That year he moved to Virgin Records and released *I Know*, a solid album that was accepted warmly by both critics and fans. Due to inadequate publicity, however, it failed to garner any substantial hits.

In 2001 Vandross signed with J-Records, a new label headed by music industry veteran Clive Davis, and he released a self-titled album that brought him fully back into the contemporary spotlight. The album differs from most previous Vandross efforts in that it employs the skills of outside producers and songwriters, among them proven hit-makers Kenneth "Babyface" Edmonds, Warryn Campbell, and Shep Crawford. Vandross's image was updated as well: Having lost 125 pounds prior to the album's release, he now sported a sleek new wardrobe of designer clothes. In many ways, however, *Luther Vandross* stays true to the qualities that made the singer a star. Although he did not write it, the album's hit ballad, "I'd Rather," closely resembles his compositions from the 1980s and 1990s. The melody is lilting and catchy, while the lyrics embody values of romantic dedication: "I'd rather have bad times with you, than good times with someone else / I'd rather be beside you in a storm, than safe and warm by myself." On the heels of the album's release Vandross resumed his rigorous live touring schedule, performing extensively in the United States and Europe during 2001 and 2002. In April 2003 Vandross suffered a debilitating stroke in his New York apartment. Although he had yet to regain full consciousness, his record company released a new album, *Dance with My Father*, in June.

While other singers came and went during the 1980s and 1990s, Vandross remained near the top. His longevity is the combined result of tremendous talent, a solid commitment to creating great music, and an understanding that good love songs will always be in style.

SELECTIVE DISCOGRAPHY: *Never Too Much* (Epic, 1981); *The Night I Fell in Love* (Epic, 1985); *Give Me the Reason* (Epic, 1986); *Any Love* (Epic, 1988); *The Best of Love* (Epic, 1989); *Power of Love* (Epic, 1991); *Never Let Me Go* (Epic, 1993); *Songs* (Epic, 1994); *This Is Christmas* (Epic, 1995); *Your Secret Love* (Epic, 1996); *I Know* (Virgin, 1998); *Luther Vandross* (J-Records, 2001).

WEBSITE: www.luthervandross.com.

DAVID FREELAND

VANILLA ICE

Born: Robert Van Winkle; Miami Lakes, Florida, 31 October 1968

Genre: Rap

Best-selling album since 1990: *To the Extreme* (1990)

Hit songs since 1990: "Ice Ice Baby," "Play That Funky Music"

In the late 1980s Miami-born and Dallas-raised Robert Van Winkle emerged from obscurity with his hit "Ice Ice Baby" (1990). One of hip-hop's first "great white hopes," his success on the pop charts and his meteoric rise later compromised his credibility in the hip-hop community.

"Ice Ice Baby"—which originated as a B-side of his debut single, "Play That Funky Music" (1990)—was a surprise runaway hit throughout the South. Re-released by SBK records, Ice's single rose rapidly on the charts. Built on his cool delivery and an obvious sample of David Bowie and Queen's "Under Pressure" (for which he was later sued), the single spent sixteen weeks at number one and helped his debut album, *To the Extreme*, sell more than 7 million copies. Though the Beastie Boys had already established a fledgling place for white rappers in the mid-1980s, what made Ice unique was his apparent street credibility as a troubled youth who had dabbled with gang life as a teen.

Despite his play for class authenticity, Ice's soft raps and unimpressive beats were savaged by hip-hop's hardcore fan base. Critics accused him of repackaging an African-American musical style for safe consumption by suburban white audiences, the same sort of number that Elvis Presley had done on R&B four decades prior. Worse yet, accusations swirled that Ice's hardscrabble childhood had been a fabrication. This last point was a contentious one, with Ice insisting he had experienced the trials of a fatherless household and a childhood spent in the streets of Miami and Dallas.

Although Ice's sketchy background did not lead directly to his downfall, it contributed to the overexposure that led to the demise of the great white hype. In early 1991 Ice released *Extremely Live*, an obvious ploy to capitalize on his sudden fame with a hastily arranged set of live hits. That year he also appeared in two films, first in a cameo role in *Teenage Mutant Ninja Turtles II: The Secret of the Ooze* (to which he contributed the soundtrack cut, "Ninja Rap") and then in his own star vehicle, *Cool as Ice*. By the time *Cool as Ice* debuted, it was clear that Ice's moment had passed; the soundtrack barely cracked the charts.

Rather than fading into obscurity, Ice spent the remainder of the 1990s trying unsuccessfully to reinvent himself, first as a loping, marijuana-obsessed rapper in the image of Cypress Hill, later as a hardcore gangsta, and still later as a rap-rock specialist fusing heavy metal's sonic aggression with his own angst-riddled lyricism. As the pop ambassador marshalling hip-hop's early-1990s rise through the commercial charts, Ice was a ubiquitous if ephemeral presence. By the late 1990s his career was spoken of mainly in the past tense when it was mentioned at all.

SELECTIVE DISCOGRAPHY: *Hooked* (Ichiban, 1990); *To the Extreme* (SBK, 1990); *Extremely Live* (SBK, 1991); *Cool as Ice* (SBK, 1991); *Mind Blowin'* (SBK, 1994); *Hard to Swallow* (Republic, 1998); *Bipolar* (Liquid, 2001).

HUA HSU

SUZANNE VEGA

Born: Santa Monica, California, 11 July 1959
Genre: Folk
Best-selling album since 1990: *Solitude Standing* (1987)
Hit songs since 1990: "Tom's Diner," "99.9 F," "Caramel"

Suzanne Vega made her mark in pop music with her sad, evocative song about child abuse, the thoughtful 1987 hit "Luka." A folk-influenced singer/songwriter with a hushed voice, aloof persona, and propensity toward veiled, distanced examinations of emotions and relationships, she developed a devoted following in the late 1980s that continued through the 1990s. Her success helped pave the way for a score of female singer/songwriters, folk-influenced and otherwise, including Sinead O'Connor, Tracy Chapman, Michelle Shocked, and Shawn Colvin.

Vega grew up in Spanish Harlem in New York after her mother, a jazz guitarist, moved there following a divorce from Suzanne's father when Suzanne was two years old; she later remarried the Puerto Rican novelist Ed Vega. Vega found solace in folk music and taught herself to play the guitar at age eleven. She developed a following in the New York City folk circuit, and after three years of rejections, including two by A&M Records, her managers finally convinced A&M to sign her. Her self-titled debut had quick success both in England and the United States, selling 200,000 copies.

After overcoming a bout of writer's block, she produced a second album, *Solitude Standing* (1987). Vega had an accidental hit when British dance band DNA took Vega's a capella song "Tom's Diner," set it against a thumping bass and dance beat, and called it "Oh Suzanne." When she discovered the piracy, Vega allowed for the single's official release under its original title, and it became a hit in the United States and the United Kingdom.

Her experience with "Tom's Diner" seemed to contribute to the direction of her subsequent two albums, *99.9 F* (1992) and *Nine Objects of Desire* (1996). For these albums she collaborated with the experimental producer Mitchell Froom, whom she married in 1995 and with whom she had a daughter, Ruby, in 1994. The production of *Nine Objects of Desire* brings a smoother, fuller sound to her compositions, though some critics felt that Froom's production ruined Vega's songwriting on the album. His production brings Vega's voice forward, allowing for an unusually funky vibe to permeate the recording and creating a sound that is more aligned with pop than folk music. From the waltzy "Honeymoon Suite," set in a Paris hotel room that offers an intimate window into marital bliss, to the first-person tale of a call girl, "Stockings," each

tune is a short story. The bossa nova–flavored "Caramel" was a moderate hit for Vega. It begins with her crooning, "It won't do / To dream of caramel / To think of cinnamon and long for you," starting off a smart, subtle food-as-love-metaphor, tinged with touches of trumpets and a clarinet that carries itself through the course of the song.

Following her painful divorce from Froom in 1998, Vega released *Songs in Red and Gray*, one of her most critically hailed albums. It is less fussy and more low-key; in many ways it is a return to the introspective, acoustically oriented compositions of her earlier and more commercially successful albums. Vega wrote the songs on the album and performed them at the revered Songwriters Exchange, a Monday night songwriting workshop at the Cornelia Street Café in New York City's Greenwich Village. The album's delicately stirring arrangements are an apt accompaniment to Vega's cool vocals and her characteristically dark but hopeful story-songs.

SELECTIVE DISCOGRAPHY: *Solitude Standing* (A&M, 1987); *99.9 F* (A&M, 1992); *Nine Objects of Desire* (A&M, 1992); *Songs in Red and Gray* (A&M, 2001).

BIBLIOGRAPHY: S. Vega, *The Passionate Eye: The Collected Writing of Suzanne Vega* (New York, 1999).

CARRIE HAVRANEK

CAETANO VELOSO

Born: Caetano Emanuel Vianna Telles Veloso; Santo Amaro da Purificacao, Bahia, Brazil, 7 August 1942
Genre: World
Best-selling album since 1990: *Tropicalista 2* (1993)

Brazilian singer/songwriter Caetano Veloso is a creative musical force with few peers. He is a prolific artist who projects palpable intimacy with a tender voice over acoustic guitar. He demonstrates structural mastery in his soundtracks for Academy Award-nominated films. Veloso has a signature sound—nuanced vocals that may comment on politics or romantic love—but he seldom repeats himself.

Having followed his sister, the singer Maria Bethania, to Rio de Janiero from their home in eastern Brazil in the early 1960s, Veloso won song competitions with lyrics he wrote for her and was contracted by the international recording giant, Philips. He was already in awe of bossa nova composer/performer Joao Gilberto, and he had met fellow musician Gilberto Gil while studying philosophy at the Federal University of Bahia.

With Gil, Gal Costa (Veloso's collaborator on his debut album, *Domingo* [1967]), Tom Zé, and other like-minded musicians, writers, painters, and filmmakers, Veloso established the tropicalia movement, politicizing Brazilian popular media in the manner of the Beatles, Jefferson Airplane, Bob Dylan, Jimi Hendrix, and others of the era. The movement ran afoul of the Brazilian military dictatorship that seized power in a coup in 1968; Veloso and Gil, the movement's chief proponents, were jailed for two months and placed under house arrest for four more for "disrespecting the national anthem and the Brazilian flag." After defiantly performing together, they chose voluntary exile in England and were not allowed to return to Brazil until 1972.

Upon their return tropicalia was thriving along with their reputations; Brazilian artists had been recording Veloso's and Gil's songs all along. Veloso worked to expand his frame of reference; he is credited for being the first Brazilian to use reggae elements in the rock tune "Nine Out of Ten" (1972). By the 1990s Veloso considered no music off limits or unusable. His album *Noites de Norte* (2001) embraces raucous electric guitar, gentle acoustic guitars, strings, percussion (including "knife and plate"), brass, and reeds; he sings mostly in Portuguese but also in English when the whim strikes.

Throughout the 1970s and 1980s Veloso stretched in many directions, teaming with Gil, Costa, and Bethania for an album, tour and film; publishing his articles, poems, and lyrics in a book, *Alegria, Alegria* (1977); and touring Africa, France, Israel, and, in 1983, the United States, where he won over influential New York critics and began to build a devoted American audience, even though all his albums were hard-to-find, expensive imports. He maintained popularity at home, co-hosting "Chico e Caetano," a television talk and variety show, with singer/songwriter Chico Barque in 1986.

Caetano Veloso (1987), his first U.S. release, introduces songs from his twenty-year repertoire, sung with only his own guitar accompaniment. *Estrangeiro* (1989) couches his mostly Portuguese vocals in spiky "downtown" electric tracks, as does *Circulado* (1991); both are produced by Arto Lindsay, a "fake jazz" singer/guitarist who was raised in Brazil and produces sophisticated MPB-style records of his own. *Tropicalia 2* (1993), Veloso's duet album with Gilberto Gil, celebrates twenty-five years of Tropicalia and their thirty-year friendship. The release, which further enhanced their critical and public standing in the United States, features a cover of Hendrix's "Wait Until Tomorrow." *Circulado ao Vivo* (1997) contains Veloso's renditions of Michael Jackson's "Black and White" and Dylan's "Jokerman." Its release launched his extensive American tour in 1997.

Livro (1998), released concurrently with the publication in Brazil of Veloso's well-received historical memoir, *Tropical Truth: A Story of Music and Revolution in Brazil*,

won a 1999 Grammy for best world music album. Simultaneously, Veloso became involved in film-related projects: soundtracks for *Tieta* (1997), *O Quatrilho* (1997), the Carlos Diegues film *Orfeu* (2000), *Ommagio à Federico e Giulietta* ("homage to the films of Federico Fellini and Giulietta Masina") (1998), and the song "Cucurrucucu Paloma," which he performed at the Academy Awards in New York City in 2003, written for the soundtrack of Pedro Almodóvar's *Talk to Her* (2002).

Noites do Norte ("Nights of the north") (2001), a meditation on race and slavery in Brazil's pursuit of national identity, is one of Veloso's most serious thematic works and won a Latin Grammy Award in 2001. *Live in Bahia* (2002), a 2-CD set, attended the publication in English of *Tropical Truth*. Boxed-set retrospectives and collections of Veloso's recordings of the 1960s, 1970s, and early 1980s proliferate. However, Veloso shows no sign of resting on his laurels, and there is every indication that he will continue to explore Brazil's cultural legacy, while adding to it with inspired creations of his own.

SELECTIVE DISCOGRAPHY: *Caetano Veloso* (Nonesuch, 1987); *Circuladô* (Nonesuch, 1991); *Caetano Veloso—Personalidade Series* (Verve, 1993); *Tropicália 2* (Nonesuch, 1993); *O Quatrilho* (Blue Jackel, 1996); *Circulado Ao Vivo* (Polygram, 1997); *Livro* (Elektra/Asylum, 1998); *Ommagiò à Federico e Giulietta* (Elektra/Asylum, 1998); *Orfeu* (Nonesuch, 1999); *Cinema Caetano* (Universal, 2000); *Noites do Norte* (Nonesuch, 2001); *Live in Bahia* (Nonesuch, 2002).

BIBLIOGRAPHY: C. Veloso, *Tropical Truth: A Story of Music and Revolution in Brazil* (New York, 2002); C. McGowan, *The Brazilian Sound: Samba, Bossa Nova, and the Popular Music of Brazil* (Philadelphia, 1991).

WEBSITE: www.thebraziliansound.com/caetano.htm.

HOWARD MANDEL

THE VERVE

Formed: 1989, Wigan, Lancashire, England; Disbanded 1999

Members: Richard Ashcroft, vocals, guitar (born Billinge, Wigan, Lancashire, England, 11 September 1971); Simon Jones, bass (born Liverpool, Merseyside, England, 29 July 1972); Nick McCabe, guitar (born St. Helens, Lancashire, England, 14 July 1972); Peter Salisbury, drums (born Bath, Avon, England, c. 24 September 1971).

Genre: Rock

Best-selling album since 1990: *Urban Hymns* (1997)

Hit songs since 1990: "Bittersweet Symphony," "Lucky Man," "Sonnet"

The British band the Verve spent a good portion of the early 1990s relatively unknown internationally but fairly popular in their native U.K. Their hit "Bittersweet Symphony" from their album *Urban Hymns* (1997) is an anthemic, swooping, mid-tempo pop song with a full orchestra that ended up in a Nike ad.

The Verve formed in 1989 in the northern England town of Wigan. Lead singer Richard Ashcroft, whose full lips and rock-star swagger have often earned him comparisons to the Rolling Stones' Mick Jagger, was joined by guitarist Nick McCabe, bassist Simon Jones, and drummer Peter Salisbury. Their first few albums received much critical acclaim but barely registered on the sales charts. Their 1995 album, *A Northern Soul*, reputedly recorded under the influence of the drug Ecstasy, features a swooping, psychedelic explosion of guitars. After the album's release Ashcroft left the band, only to reassemble it a few weeks later. Prior to the release of *A Northern Soul*, the band had had its troubles, including a lawsuit from the major jazz label Verve, which forced the band to change its name to the Verve, and bad-boy rock-star behavior: Salisbury was arrested for damaging a Kansas City hotel room, and Ashcroft was hospitalized for dehydration.

The band split up after *A Northern Soul* but got back together to release their breakthrough LP, *Urban Hymns* (1997). The success of the single "Bittersweet Symphony," which borrows a sampled loop from the Rolling Stones song "The Last Time," boosted the album to the twenty-third position on the *Billboard* Top 200 chart, with that track reaching number four on the *Billboard* Modern Rock chart. Its placement in a Nike advertisement guaranteed that anyone who spent time watching television would hear the song.

Urban Hymns is filled with love songs such as "Lucky Man" and "Sonnet" that belie the rancor among band members that preceded its release. With its plainspoken, unapologetic lyrics—"Yes there's love if you want it / Don't sound like no sonnet / My love"—and its emotional climax, "Sonnet" helped lend a romantic graciousness to the band's image. Confessional lyrics in "The Drugs Don't Work" added to the softening. Ashcroft reveals, "Now the drugs don't work / they just make you worse / but I know I'll see your face again."

Despite the band's problems, *Urban Hymns* remains a classic modern-rock album of the late 1990s. With its sweeping strings and hypnotic, psychedelic guitar loops, *Urban Hymns* became one of the fastest-selling British albums of all time and garnered the band three awards, including Best British band, at the 1998 BRIT awards. Sadly, the Verve never gave themselves an opportunity to top that success. In April 1999 the band announced it was calling it quits and Richard Ashcroft embarked upon a solo career.

SELECTIVE DISCOGRAPHY: *A Northern Soul* (Vernon Yard/Virgin, 1995); *Urban Hymns* (Virgin, 1997).

BIBLIOGRAPHY: M. Clarke, *The Verve: Crazed Highs and Horrible Lows* (London, 1998); S. Egan, *Verve: Starsail* (London, 1999).

CARRIE HAVRANEK

VIENNA BOYS CHOIR

Formed: 1498, Vienna, Austria

Genre: Classical

Formed on the order of Holy Roman Emperor Maximilian I in 1498 to sing at his court, the Vienna Boys Choir (Wiener Sängerknaben) is one of the world's oldest performing arts institutions. The choir's rigorous training, clear sound, and technical prowess are renowned, and through its annual international tours, the Vienna Boys have become cultural ambassadors for Austria.

The choir has a long and colorful history stretching back more than five hundred years. It has produced numerous first-class vocalists, violinists, and pianists who helped shape Vienna as one of Europe's musical capitals. Joseph Haydn sang with the court choir in the eighteenth century, Franz Schubert wrote some of his first compositions for the choir in the nineteenth century, and numerous composers, including Senfl, Fux, Salieri, Haydn, and Bruckner, wrote music for it.

When the Habsburg dynasty collapsed in 1918 at the end of World War I—and with it most court institutions—it looked like the choir might disappear. But it was refounded in 1924 by Joseph Schnitt, who believed that the boarding school method of training choristers was the only way to keep alive the famous Viennese musical tradition.

Until the 1920s the choir had performed only at the court. Its refounding marks the beginning of the choir's modern history of touring and a system of musical education that brought it to the attention of the world. By the end of the 1930s the choir had performed all over the world. Since 1932 it has made more than fifty tours of America.

The Vienna Boys Choir is actually a group of more than 100 members between the ages of ten and fourteen, divided up into choirs of 24 members each. Two choirs make annual tours, presenting some 300 annual performances for more than 500,000 fans. Tours generally last about three months each. The other two choirs stay in Vienna studying. Members live in the historic Augarten Palace, studying academic subjects in the morning and music in the afternoon.

The Vienna Boys Choir has made dozens of recordings, cutting across numerous styles and genres of classical and popular music. The group has worked and recorded with some of the twentieth century's best conductors, including Leonard Bernstein, Herbert von Karajan, and Sir George Solti. It has performed for world leaders, and appeared frequently on television. The choir has also contributed to a number of film soundtracks, including *Primal Fear* (1996) and *The 13th Floor* (1999). Despite all its international activity, the choir still sings weekly mass at Vienna's Hofburg Chapel, as it has done since 1498.

By the early 1990s the Vienna Boys Choir had become something of a "tourist trap," performing more than it should to earn money for its operations. Musical standards and training had slipped since the 1970s, its training methods were out-of-date, and the choir had lost its recording contract.

But the choir took steps to revitalize itself, modernizing its curriculum, cutting down on the number of performances, and expanding its repertoire. It has embarked on multimedia projects, found new collaborators, and participated in the creation of children's operas, and has worked to update its image for the twenty-first century.

SELECTIVE DISCOGRAPHY: *The Best of the Vienna Boys Choir* (Delta, 2000).

BIBLIOGRAPHY: F. Endler, *Vienna Choir Boys* (Vienna, 1987); K. Lorenz, *A History of the Vienna Boys's Choir* (Sussex, England, 1998).

WEBSITE: www.wsk.at/english/main.asp.

DOUGLAS MCLENNAN

VIENNA PHILHARMONIC ORCHESTRA

Formed: 1842, Vienna, Austria

Genre: Classical

The Vienna Philharmonic Orchestra (Wiener Philharmoniker) is unlike any other major orchestra. It is run more as a society or club than a modern musical business. In an era when globalization means that players, conductors, and soloists come from virtually anywhere in the world and thus few orchestras have a geographically distinct sound, the Vienna retains a style all its own. It sounds like no other orchestra, and its musical traditions are directly linked to the core of the classical orchestral repertory.

Until the Philharmonic was founded in 1842, Vienna did not have a full-time professional orchestra. That means that in the time of Joseph Haydn, Wolfgang Amadeus Mozart, and Ludwig van Beethoven—all of whom worked in the city—there was no regular professional orchestra;

players were assembled for concerts on an ad hoc basis. But it also means that there was a strong musical tradition upon which to build one strong enough to endure to the twenty-first century.

The structure of the Philharmonic is unusual. Its musician members, who are elected to management roles, run the orchestra. The players vote on major decisions. The Philharmonic also serves as orchestra for the Vienna State Opera (Vienna Staatsoper), and before a player can become a full member of the Philharmonic, he or she must serve in the opera orchestra for three years. Unlike most orchestras, the Philharmonic is not state-supported; it is an independent, self-governing institution.

The orchestra is one of the most prestigious in Europe, and has worked closely with composers such as Richard Wagner, Franz Liszt, Richard Strauss, Johannes Brahms, Anton Bruckner, and Giuseppe Verdi. Some of the most prominent conductors in the history of music have served as its conductors, among them Hans Richter (1875–1882 and 1883–1898), Gustav Mahler (1898–1901), Felix von Weingartner (1908–1927), and Wilhelm Furtwangler (1927–1930).

Despite its stellar conductor roster, however, in 1933 the orchestra took the unusual step of deciding to go without a permanent conductor, and it has employed guest conductors ever since. Prominent among these have been Arturo Toscanini, Leonard Bernstein, Karl Bohm, Herbert von Karajan, Otto Klemperer, Eugene Ormandy, George Szell, Bruno Walter, Carlo Maria Giulini, Georg Solti, Claudio Abbado, and James Levine.

The Philharmonic sound is unique because the orchestra largely retains ideals of performance adopted at the beginning of the nineteenth century. Partly this reflects a philosophical approach to tradition, but it is also the result of the orchestra's instruments. In other orchestras, instruments continued to evolve over time. But Vienna still uses versions of the brass, woodwinds, and percussion in use at the time of its founding, and they are mechanically different from modern instruments; they produce different sounds than modern instruments.

The orchestra has recorded extensively, and its historical collection of recorded performances of the core classical literature is highly prized. The orchestra's home is one of the great concert halls in the world, the Musikverein. The Vienna tours widely, and participates annually in Europe's most important music festivals. The orchestra's famous New Year's Eve concerts are televised worldwide to an audience of millions.

The 1990s were a time of reevaluation for the Philharmonic. The orchestra had always been an all-male preserve, which it justified with the argument that ethnic and gender uniformity leads to aesthetic superiority. But there was increasing pressure to admit women players and, after allowing women to perform with the orchestra beginning in the mid-1990s, it finally appointed an official woman member in 2002.

Importantly, in the 1990s the orchestra's nationalist traditions took some hits, with some critics challenging the orchestra's legendary musicianship. While many of the orchestra's fans appreciate the Vienna's traditional approach, some reviewers encountering the orchestra abroad have been critical of what they interpret as a style that has become increasingly ingrown. The orchestra still attracts top players, but its pay scale has slipped below top American orchestras, and the pool of players trained to perform on the Viennese instruments is small. While still considered one of the world's top orchestras, the Vienna has chosen to be a museum of German School tradition rather than an evolving modern organization.

SELECTIVE DISCOGRAPHY: *Masters of Classical Music (Vol. 1–10)* (Delta, 1990); *Strauss: The Best of Vienna* (Polygram, 1999).

WEBSITE: www.wienerphilharmoniker.at.

DOUGLAS MCLENNAN

CARLOS VIVES

Born: Carlos Alberto Vives Restrepo; Santa Marta, Colombia, 7 August 1961

Genre: Latin

Best-selling album since 1990: *Clásicos de la Provincia* (1993)

Hit songs since 1990: "La Gota Fría," "Fruta Fresca," "Déjame Entrar"

Carlos Vives helped spark a resurgence of the vallenato, a traditional Colombian Atlantic coast rhythm, by fusing it with refreshing strains of rock and reggae. A former Spanish-language soap opera star, he has also won fans with his raspy baritone vocals and movie-star good looks.

Vives began his artistic career as an actor in Puerto Rican and Colombian telenovelas; his music followed the pop/ballad mold. His recording debut was the album *Carlos Vives por Fuera por Dentro* (1986), which was more rock than anything else. But in 1990 he changed direction when he was selected to play vallenato troubadour Rafael Escalone in the Colombian soap *Escalone*.

Vives formed his own band, La Provincia, and debuted his vallenato-rock fusion on *Clásicos de la Provincia* (1993). Highlighted by the Andean-flavored hit single "La Gota Fría," the album proved to be a critical and commercial success, selling 1.5 million units worldwide and putting vallenato on the map all over Latin America. It was a triumph that surprised even Vives, who later said he was only trying to raise awareness of the music within Colombia.

Vives's reinvention of the vallenato has enlivened the genre across Latin America, influencing artists from Gloria Estefan to the countless regional Mexican groups that have put "Colombiano" or "Vallenato" in their names since the mid-1990s. Traditional vallenato—the Colombia folk rhythm with African, indigenous, and European influences—has always featured plaintive vocals; warm, reedy, three-row button accordions; *guacharacas* (cane scrapers); and *cajas vallenatas* (bongolike drums) in its basic cumbia repertoire. Vives supplemented the sound with rock instruments like the drum kit and guitar. Despite the departure from the original folksy form, Vives has won over most purists by including top vallenato musicians like the accordionist Egidio Cuadrado and the flutist Mayte Montero in his band. He also gives long-overdue recognition to the composers of classic vallenatos through his well-received cover versions.

Vives has, however, endured his share of criticism—some Colombian intellectuals and folk musicians see him as an opportunist who has made money off his country's Afro-Colombian musical traditions by presenting it with a "marketable" white face. Vives scoffs at such criticism, saying his country's music is for all Colombians, regardless of skin color.

In 1995 Vives returned with *La Tierra del Olvido*. In 1997 he released *Tengo Fe*, which yielded the hit "Que Diera" but was his weakest-selling album of the decade. He made a strong comeback with *El Amor de Mi Tierra* (1999), co-produced with Emilio Estefan. It turned down the accordion a notch, emphasizing a thundering Afro-Latin rhythm section, especially on the hit single "Fruta Fresca." Vives composed nine of the twelve tracks. In a nod to tradition, he updated José Barros's beloved cumbia oldie "La Piragua."

Perhaps finally aware of his impact on Latin music, Vives adopted a broader vision for *Déjame Entrar* (2001), recorded at Estefan's Miami studios. "Amor Latino," a danceable tune about ethnic pride, adds Latin jazz piano to the mix. The club-dance track "Carito" is a sweet, self-deprecating ode to an American English teacher on whom Vives had a crush as a fifteen-year-old. The title track, a quintessential Vives fusion of vallenato and rock released as the album's first single, won the best tropical performance Grammy in 2002.

Vives's success has done much to legitimize the idea that fusing rock with regional folklore can be commercially and musically relevant; the new Colombian artists Juanes and Cabas are but a few of the rock-en-Español acts who are in his debt.

SELECTIVE DISCOGRAPHY: *Clásicos de la Provincia* (EMI Latin, 1993); *La Tierra del Olvido* (EMI Latin, 1995); *El Amor de Mi Tierra* (EMI Latin, 1999); *Déjame Entrar* (EMI Latin, 2001).

RAMIRO BURR

W $\dfrac{\text{w}}{\text{w}}$

LOUDON WAINWRIGHT III

Born: Chapel Hill, North Carolina, 5 September 1946

Genre: Folk

Best-selling album since 1990: *History* (1992)

Loudon Wainwright III is a witty singer/songwriter whose three-plus decades of insightful music serve as a diary for the world and of his own interesting life. Spawned from a generation overflowing with musicians who carted a guitar and a message, Wainwright survived early stardom and career malaise to hit his mark as an important voice in contemporary music.

Born the oldest child of four into an affluent East Coast family, Wainwright grew up in Bedford, New York, a tony suburb of New York City. His father, Loudon S. Wainwright Jr., was a prominent columnist and editor of *Life* magazine and a direct descendant of Peter Stuyvesant, the last governor of the Dutch colony New Amsterdam (later New York). His upscale background and its trappings became song fodder for Wainwright. He learned to play guitar as a teenager, began writing songs, and adopted folksinger Bob Dylan as his hero after seeing the star perform at the Newport Folk Festival in 1962. When Wainwright released his first album, *Loudon Wainwright III*, critics raved and quickly compared him to Dylan. Wainwright scored a hit with the novelty song, "Dead Skunk," in 1972, but his career never reached the high initially anticipated. Yet, he scored Grammy Award nominations for *I'm Alright* (1985) and *More Love Songs* (1986) and by the 1990s Wainwright had melded his songwriting, act-ing, comic presence, and gift for social satire into a comfortable artistic voice and a solid career.

In 1992 he released the highly acclaimed *History*, an autobiographical collection of songs, performed with his usual aplomb, that deal with relationships between him and members of his family. He also gives a sarcastic nod to a time when critics compared every promising guitar-playing singer/songwriter to Dylan. The song, "Talkin' New Bob Dylan" suggests that all of the artists once christened "the new Bob Dylan" gather for a 12-step rehabilitation meeting.

Wainwright's songs are story songs, usually honest biographical sketches with a twist or a parody of some social condition that he finds personally interesting. A favorite on National Public Radio, Wainwright wrote a series of songs for the station that lampooned events and people like Y2K, the O. J. Simpson trial, skater Tonya Harding, former North Carolina senator Jesse Helms, and former president Bill Clinton. Many of these songs ended up on a collection titled, *Social Studies* (1999). Wainwright also hosted his own television show, *Loudon and Co.*, on England's BBC in 1994. Critics note his concert performances are characteristically bombastic, featuring amusing, sometimes confrontational, repartee with his audience. He sticks out his tongue, makes funny faces when he sings, and kicks with his leg for extra emphasis. The most significant ingredient of a Wainwright song is its lyrics and he sings them in a clear tenor voice while adroitly accompanying himself on guitar.

Wainwright's acting skills have served him well through the years and throughout 2001 he portrayed the nosy father of a college student as a regular on the Fox

Rufus Wainwright

Loudon Wainwright III [DEBORAH FEINGOLD/RED HOUSE RECORDS]

Wainwright's songs and style have not changed much through the years, but the times have. His musical stories reflect those times through the fabric of Wainwright's own life. Though criticized occasionally for writing songs that so quickly become dated, ultimately Wainwright is one of those rare musical artists whose music may earn a valued sense of timelessness.

SELECTIVE DISCOGRAPHY: *Loudon Wainwright III* (Atlantic, 1970); *Album II* (Atlantic, 1971); *Album III* (CBS, 1972); *Attempted Mustache* (CBS, 1973); *Unrequited* (CBS, 1975); *T-Shirt* (Arista, 1976); *Final Exam* (Arista, 1978); *A Live One* (Rounder, 1979); *Fame and Wealth* (Demon, 1983); *I'm Alright* (Demon, 1985); *More Love Songs* (Demon, 1986); *Therapy* (Silvertone, 1989); *History* (Virgin, 1992); *Career Moves* (Virgin, 1993); *Grown Man* (Virgin, 1996); *Little Ship* (Virgin, 1997); *Social Studies* (Hannibal, 1999); *Last Man on Earth* (Red House, 2001). **Soundtracks:** *28 Days* (Varese, 2000).

DONALD LOWE

RUFUS WAINWRIGHT

Born: Montreal, Quebec, 22 July 1974
Genre: Rock
Best-selling album since 1990: *Poses* (2001)
Hit songs since 1990: "April Fools," "Cigarettes and Chocolate Milk"

Being the progeny of famous songwriting parents is not easy, but singer and pianist Rufus Wainwright managed to carve his own niche in the pop music landscape toward the latter half of the 1990s. With a winsome quality, a flair for melodrama, and an affinity for the rhymes and musical styles of older artists, such as Cole Porter and other Broadway standard–writing greats, Wainwright is a throwback to another era. His songs are timeless, dramatic, and often find their protagonist, who is never male or female (Wainwright is openly gay), heartbroken and/or teetering on the edge of self-destruction.

Wainwright is the offspring of politically minded folk troubadour Loudon Wainwright III, and Canadian folksinger Kate McGarrigle. His father split up with McGarrigle (who writes and sings with her sister Anna) when Rufus was four. Rufus grew up with his mom in Montreal, and started playing piano at age six. By the time he was a preteen, he joined the family act, billed as the McGarrigle Sisters and Family, and toured Europe and the United States.

Wainwright attended a boarding school in upstate New York and then McGill University in Montreal for a

network sitcom, *Undeclared.* Prior to that, he played a guitar-strumming rehab patient in the comedy film *28 Days* (2000). The soundtrack for the film contains four of his songs. Wainwright has been in several off-Broadway plays in addition to the films *The Slugger's Wife* (1985) and *Jack-knife* (1989). In 1975 he combined his music and acting to play a singing surgeon for three episodes on the award-winning hit television series *Mash.*

Wainwright released another collection of personal songs on *Last Man on Earth* (2001). The album, despite its expected infusion of humor and irony, contains achingly lovely songs dealing with his mother's death, such as "Missing You," or the passing of both of his parents in "Homeless." Even the bluegrass-styled "I'm Not Gonna Cry" reveals an older, contemplative artist opening up his heart and soul for all to see. Another interesting song is "Surviving Twin," which exposes his rivalry with his father's success. Ironically, Wainwright's son, Rufus Wainwright, is a singer/songwriter sensation who, like his father, drew great critical praise for his first professional efforts. Wainwright's daughter, Martha, is also a recording artist.

while, but ultimately dropped out to start writing and pursuing a music career more seriously. His background helped him get his foot in the door—his mom passed along a tape of his to family friend, producer Pierre Marchand. It wound up in the hands of Lenny Waronker, who signed him to DreamWorks Records in 1996 and paired him with producer Jon Brion. The end result, after recording over fifty songs, is his self-titled debut. *Rufus Wainwright* (1998) is full of sweeping string arrangements and dashed hopes. The album's single, "April Fools," seems to typify Wainwright's cynical romanticism: "You will believe in love / and all that it's supposed to be / But just until the fish start to smell / And you're struck down by a hammer."

Shortly after his eponymous debut, the accolades came pouring in. *Rolling Stone* named him Best New Artist, and *Rufus Wainwright* earned Top 10 album of the year honors from the *New York Times*, *Entertainment Weekly*, *The New Yorker*, and the *Los Angeles Times*.

Wainwright toured extensively, appeared in magazines and a holiday Gap commercial, and released his sophomore effort, *Poses*, in 2001. An ambitious follow-up, *Poses* is cinematic in scope—each song's subject could have been a different character in a musical or film. Wainwright describes it as "a play with a cast of intriguing characters, and my voice is the star of the play." Writing in *Newsweek*, Lorraine Ali said, "*Poses* gracefully and painfully documents the world of the romantic megalomaniac . . . . If old-style Broadway musicals—think Cole Porter meets the biting irony of Oscar Wilde—ever made a resurgence in popular culture, Rufus Wainwright would be the perfect fit to pen the music." Her keen assessment succinctly summarizes Wainwright's abilities and proclivities as an unusual male singer of the late 1990s.

SELECTIVE DISCOGRAPHY: *Rufus Wainwright* (DreamWorks, 1998); *Poses* (DreamWorks, 2001).

CARRIE HAVRANEK

TOM WAITS

Born: Pomona, California, 7 December 1949
Genre: Rock Folk, Jazz
Best-selling album since 1990: *Mule Variations* (1999)

Singer/songwriter Tom Waits, troubadour of the disenfranchised, pours his fascination with the seedy side of life into his music. His earlier work combines beat generation poetry with a folky, lounge-styled jazz and his later music flirts artfully with the grotesque as he experiments with visceral rhythmic schemes, orchestral journeying, and deformed vocals. One of America's most remarkable artists, Waits performs in the persona of his

songs' characters, and it is rumored that he l[ives] like them as well. Waits's songs are wi[dely] recorded by others and his musical forays ext[end] into theater and film. Along the way, he for[ged] a successful acting career.

Waits was born in a taxicab. His parents were teach[ers] ers and the family lived nomadically all over Californ[ia.] Waits loved music early on and would spend hours tun[n]ing into whatever he could find on his homebuilt radi[o.] In addition, he devoured the works of Jack Kerouac an[d] other Beat generation writers. Eventually he dropped ou[t] of school and worked various dead-end jobs before mov[]ing to Los Angeles. There he attracted underground fame with his cigarette-dangling, drink-in-hand performance style. Waits also lived a lifestyle not unlike the characters in his songs, dressing in wrinkly suits, living in fleabag hotels, and frequenting after-hours bars. Even after finding success, Waits continued to reside in Los Angeles' Tropicana Motel, by no means a luxury hotel, but famous for harboring other denizens of the underground performing scene such as friend and fellow vagabond, singer Rickie Lee Jones.

His debut album, *Closing Time* (1973), displays his unique brand of smoky, blues-tinged jazz and his bizarre vocal quality suggests a sluggish impersonation of jazz legend Louis Armstrong. In some songs Waits speaks his lyrics in a funky ramble. Ambitiously recording throughout the 1970s and 1980s, Waits earned accolades for his songwriting, which contains heavy doses of wit and cynicism. Other artists began recording Waits's songs: The Eagles covered "Ol' 55," Bruce Springsteen had a huge hit with "Jersey Girl," Bette Midler had success with "Shiver Me Timbers," and Rod Stewart managed a career comeback with "Downtown Train."

Waits's style changed from poetic, jazzy ballads into uncharted musical territory with *Swordfishtrombones* (1983). The album features abnormal time signatures and jarring instrumentation, and Waits transforms his voice into a gruesome grind. He also made use of homemade or found instruments such as glass and scrap metal. *Swordfishtrombones* was the first release of a trilogy with *Rain Dogs* (1985) and *Frank's Wild Years* (1987). His wife, Kathleen Brennen, a noted script editor and frequent collaborator, helped Waits turn the latter into a musical stage play produced at Chicago's Steppenwolf Theater. Additionally, the 1980s kept him busy with acting roles in several films, including *The Cotton Club* (1984), *Down by Law* (1986), and *Iron Weed* (1987).

Waits won a Grammy Award for Best Alternative Music Performance with *Bone Machine* (1992). The album features raw, primal sounds and was his first studio album since 1987. Waits's vocal work reached new extremes, with Waits seemingly clearing his throat and spitting the songs'

lyrics. As in *Swordfishtrombones*, his music is innovative and spare. The subject matter is darker than that of any previous creative attempts and many of the album's songs, in particular "Earth Died Screaming," "All Stripped Down," and "Dirt in the Ground," reveal a preoccupation with death and one's fate after death.

In 1991 Waits released a soundtrack to the film *Night on Earth*, directed by Jim Jarmusch, and the following year he released an album of compositions for an operetta that opened in Hamburg, Germany, *The Black Rider* (1993). The operetta was directed by Robert Wilson and its text was penned by legendary Beat poet William Burroughs. The seventy-nine-year-old Burroughs even sang on some of the operetta's soundtrack. (Burroughs died in 1997.) Waits's musical contribution on *The Black Rider* recalls the torch songs of Kurt Weill mixed with melodies and sounds one might hear when strolling through a traveling carnival. The operetta toured successfully in Europe, but failed in New York after a short run at the Brooklyn Academy of Music. However, most critics praised Waits's music.

Waits waited nearly seven years before releasing his next non-soundtrack studio album, *Mule Variations* (1999), which turned out to be his most successful album commercially. Its sixteen songs are a rousing musical junkyard containing a mix of his 1970s sound and the exploratory style of his recent past with a little more blues tossed in. The album won a 1999 Grammy Award for Best Contemporary Folk Album.

He followed with the simultaneous releases of *Alice* (2002) and *Blood Money* (2002), both works inspired by his increased interest in the theater. *Alice* is a stoic collection of songs from an opera that he wrote in 1992 and *Blood Money* is a song narrative based on the play *Woyzeck*.

Eighty major artists have recorded songs from Waits's nineteen albums. He has composed music for five stage plays and eleven films. Additionally, Waits has acted in eighteen films. To those who try to dissect his personal life, he remains a mystery, for he is a master at subterfuge and politely diverting questions with conversational tangents. Heralded as one of music's most talented artists, Waits uncompromisingly marches to his own enigmatic beat.

SELECTIVE DISCOGRAPHY: *Closing Time* (Elektra, 1973); *The Heart of Saturday Night* (Elektra, 1974); *Nighthawks at the Diner* (Elektra, 1975); *Small Change* (Elektra, 1976); *Blue Valentine* (Elektra, 1978); *Swordfishtrombones* (Island, 1983); *Rain Dogs* (Island, 1985); *Frank's Wild Years* (Island, 1987); *Bone Machine* (Island, 1992); *Mule Variations* (Epitaph, 1999); *Alice* (Epitaph, 2002); *Blood Money* (Epitaph, 2002). **Soundtracks:** *One from the Heart* (CBS, 1982); *Night on Earth* (Island, 1992); *The Black Rider* (Island, 1993).

SELECTIVE FILMOGRAPHY: *The Cotton Club* (1984); *Down by Law* (1986); *Iron Weed* (1987); *The Two Jakes* (1990); *At Play in the Fields of the Lord* (1991); *Queen's Logic* (1991); *Bram Stoker's Dracula* (1992); *Short Cuts* (1993); *Mystery Man* (1999).

BIBLIOGRAPHY: J. S. Jacobs, *Wild Years: The Music and Myth of Tom Waits* (Toronto, 2000).

DONALD LOWE

THE WALLFLOWERS

Formed: 1990, Los Angeles, California

Members: Mario Calire, drums (born Buffalo, New York, 25 June 1974); Jakob Dylan, lead vocals, guitar (born New York, New York, 9 December 1969); Rami Jaffee, organ (born Los Angeles, California, 11 March 1969); Greg Richling, bass (born Los Angeles, California, 31 August 1970). Former members: Barrie Maguire, bass (born Philadelphia, Pennsylvania); Tobi Miller, guitar; Michael Ward, guitar (born 21 February 1967); Peter Yanowitz, drums (born Chicago, Illinois, 13 September 1967).

Genre: Rock

Best-selling album since 1990: *Bringing Down the Horse* (1996)

Hit songs since 1990: "6th Avenue Heartache," "One Headlight," "The Difference"

In the late 1990s, at a time when seminal American rock acts such as Bruce Springsteen and Tom Petty were largely absent from popular radio, the Wallflowers helped keep the classic-rock sound alive with its album *Bringing Down the Horse*.

The Wallflowers were the brainchild of Jakob Dylan, the son of folk-rock luminary Bob Dylan. In 1990 Dylan formed the Wallflowers, along with guitarist Tobi Miller, keyboard player Rami Jaffee, bassist Barrie Maguire, and drummer Peter Yanowitz. The Wallflowers signed to Virgin Records and released their self-titled debut album in 1992. The album did not sell well, and Virgin dropped the band from its label.

Dylan subsequently reconfigured the Wallflowers, retaining only Jaffe, and replacing the other members with guitarist Michael Ward, bassist Greg Richling, and drummer Mario Calire. Interscope Records picked up this new version of the Wallflowers and released the band's second album *Bringing Down the Horse* in 1996. On *Bringing Down the Horse*, Dylan settles into a comfortable compositional voice. Dylan's songs owe much to his father's evocative and literate style, as well as to his father's spiritual heir, Bruce Springsteen. The band retained its classic-rock feel, with clean, driving guitars and swirling organs to the fore, but the new lineup brought an excitement and freshness to the music.

The Wallflowers' new music resounded with listeners. The lead single "6th Avenue Heartache," a classic tale of love-gone-bad with a memorable chorus ("And that same black line that was drawn on you was drawn on me / And now it's drawn me in, 6th Avenue heartache"), established the band on popular radio. The follow-up, "One Headlight," was an even bigger hit, reaching the *Billboard* Top 10. "One Headlight," a dark, driving tune about the death of a friend, raised the eyebrows of some critics, who questioned Dylan's lyrical chops ("Man, I ain't changed, but I know I ain't the same"). But the song's dramatic sound, punctuated by Ward's swirling slide guitar and coupled with its fist-pumping chorus ("We can drive it home with one headlight"), was undeniable and propelled the Wallflowers to stardom.

Songs such as "One Headlight" and its follow-up "The Difference" filled a void in contemporary radio. The rock style of the Wallflowers had been the dominant sound of popular radio for decades, but it had largely been outmoded by grunge and the increased use of pop's electronic sounds. The Wallflowers picked up the rock mantle with *Bringing Down the Horse* and brought the sound back to popular radio.

Four years passed before the Wallflowers released their next album, *Breach* (2000). Aside from the minor hit "Sleepwalker," the album failed to dent the pop charts, and critics assailed the album as lackluster. *Red Letter Days*, released in 2002, encountered the same fate. Ward departed prior to the album's release; the band filled in with various session guitarists.

Whatever its final legacy, the Wallflowers' landmark album *Bringing Down the Horse* did much to keep alive the traditions of classic rock for a new generation of radio listeners.

SELECTIVE DISCOGRAPHY: *The Wallflowers* (Virgin, 1992); *Bringing Down the Horse* (Interscope, 1996); *Breach* (Interscope, 2000); *Red Letter Days* (Interscope, 2002).

SCOTT TRIBBLE

WEEZER

Formed: 1992, Los Angeles, California

Members: Brian Bell, guitar, vocals (born Knoxville, Tennessee, 9 December 1968); Rivers Cuomo, vocals, guitar (born Yogaville, Connecticut, 13 June 1970); Scott Shriner, bass, vocals (born Toledo, Ohio, 11 July 1971); Patrick Wilson, drums (born Buffalo, New York, 1 February 1969). Former members: Jason Cropper, guitar, vocals (born Oakland, California, 1970); Matt Sharp, bass, vocals (born Arlington, Virginia, 20 September 1969); Mikey Welsh, bass, vocals (born Syracuse, New York, 20 April 1971).

Genre: Rock

Best-selling album since 1990: *Weezer* (1994)

Hit songs since 1990: "Buddy Holly," "Undone—The Sweater Song," "Hash Pipe"

Seldom has a rock band made as much of a virtue of being uncool as Weezer has. Unabashedly uncool, the quartet, led by enigmatic, bespectacled singer/guitarist Rivers Cuomo, not only revel in their awkwardness, but also sell millions of albums with cheerful, hook-heavy power pop anthems such as "Hash Pipe" and "Dope Nose," with sometimes dark, risqué lyrics. Despite an unhip look and a retro 1970s sound that was stridently out of step with the hard rock and fluffy teen pop of the decade, Weezer became huge alternative radio stars and built a cult audience that hung on Cuomo's every word.

Weezer was formed in early 1992 in Los Angeles by Connecticut-raised Cuomo, a former member of several high school heavy metal bands, guitarist Jason Cropper, drummer Pat Wilson, and bassist Matt Sharp. After sixteen months of playing local clubs, the group drew the attention of Geffen Records, which signed them and packed the group off to New York to record their debut with former Cars singer Ric Ocasek. Cropper split with the group halfway into the recording of *Weezer* (1994) and was replaced by Carnival Art guitarist Brian Bell.

Released in May 1994, during the height of the noisy, bleak grunge rock period, *Weezer* yielded an immediate hit song in the oddball pop track "Undone—The Sweater Song." Over a lazily strummed guitar and lethargic drums, a pair of friends discuss their plans for the night before Cuomo's strident, deadpan vocals break in with the oblique chorus, "If you want to destroy my sweater / Hold this thread as I walk away / Watch me unravel, I'll soon be naked."

With short two- and three-minute songs, *Weezer* opts for economy over showy virtuosity, with few guitar solos, pleasant three-part harmonies, and joyous power pop guitar chords, sometimes mixed with the arena bombast of 1970s makeup rockers KISS. On the hit "Buddy Holly," a wistful new wave rocker that mixes the mindless, cheerful choruses of 1950s and 1960s pop with 1990s hip-hop slang and vintage early 1980s synthesizers, Weezer creates a template for its success: knowingly uncool music delivered with a smart, winking postmodern irony. The album's sales were boosted by equally ironic, arty videos, especially for "Buddy Holly," in which acclaimed film director Spike Jonze fused the group into the set of the popular 1970s sitcom *Happy Days*.

The album sold more than 2 million copies, but was followed by a period of inactivity. The unpredictable

Cuomo enrolled in Harvard University, Sharp and Wilson worked on the debut from their side band, the Rentals, and Bell recorded an album with his side project, the Space Twins. When Weezer emerged with the dark, self-produced *Pinkerton* in September 1996, fans were taken aback.

Pinkerton Almost Destroys Band on Way to Cult Classic Status

With crunchier, angrier guitars, keening keyboards, and at times yelping, screaming vocals, *Pinkerton* songs such as "Tired of Sex" and "Getchoo" reek of desperation and depression. Cuomo verily spits his lyrics above the cheerless din of slashing guitars, singing songs about heartbreak in which the veil of irony is pulled back to reveal someone who has clearly undergone an emotional trauma. Though he had been the main songwriting force in the band since its inception, the album marks the point at which Cuomo became the primary musical force in the group as well.

Even on songs such as the surfy punk track "Why Bother?," which retains the band's signature three-part harmonies and pop choruses, the pain is palpable ("Why bother, it's gonna hurt me / It's gonna kill when you desert me"). While it sold respectably over time, the album was not as commercially successful as its predecessor and was later repudiated by Cuomo, who said it was too revealing and embarrassing.

Though, for the most part, Cuomo shunned playing the album's songs and seemed uncomfortable even discussing it, *Pinkerton* became something of a cult classic, helping to launch a whole generation of late 1990s bands such as Dashboard Confessional and Saves the Day. Those groups were tagged as "emo," short for emotional, and were notable for their naked honesty and pop punk sensibility. Sharp left the group following the album's release to concentrate on the Rentals and was replaced by former Juliana Hatfield band bassist Mikey Welsh.

A long period of inactivity followed, with Rivers returning to Harvard and playing a series of solo shows in Boston with Welsh during 1998, Bell releasing a Space Twins album, and Wilson and Welsh touring with the Special Goodness. Despite meeting up several times in Los Angeles in 1998 to attempt recording sessions, Cuomo's heart was clearly not in it. The singer again drew into his shell, painting the walls and ceiling of a rented Los Angeles apartment black, disconnecting the phone, and shunning all human contact for months at a time.

To their shock, when Weezer began a series of shows under assumed names in the spring of 2000 and later booked themselves onto the punk/skate multi-act Warped Tour festival and into some clubs, the response was rabid . . . and the fans were young. The club tour was a sell-out and was followed by another sold-out tour of larger venues, many of them filled with teens who had discovered the group in the post-*Pinkerton* period.

The band reunited with Ocasek to record their second self-titled album (known as the "green album" due to its cover's color) in late 2000. It yielded a huge alternative radio hit with a bizarre story of a drug-smoking homosexual male transvestite prostitute, "Hash Pipe," notable for its churning, crime-jazz guitar riff and Cuomo's keening falsetto singing. After eschewing comical, flashy videos for their last album, the band returned with another classic clip for the song, this time featuring corpulent sumo wrestlers butting heads.

Despite having written more than 100 new songs, the brief (twenty-eight-minute) ten-track album is a triumph of pop smarts and economy, returning to the bright ("Don't Let Go"), hand-clapping ("Photograph"), poppy sound of the band's debut. During a summer 2001 tour, Welsh checked himself into a mental hospital and was permanently replaced by former Broken bassist Scott Shriner.

After posting dozens of in-process tracks on their website, the group quickly recorded another album, the self-produced *Maladroit* (2002). In an unpredictable career, it was yet another left turn, as it, seemingly without irony, slathers their pop hooks with bombastic guitar solos and chunky riffs that pay homage to the flashy heavy metal bands of the mid-1970s and late 1980s.

Weezer proved that the cool kids do not always get all the breaks. With a genius facility for pop hooks, a twisted imagination, and a career plan only he could understand, Cuomo wrote some of the most indelible pop hits of the 1990s. Along the way, he inspired a whole generation of emo rockers (Dashboard Confessional, Saves the Day, New Found Glory) to put their hearts on their punk-pop sleeves.

SELECTIVE DISCOGRAPHY: *Weezer* (DGC, 1994); *Pinkerton* (Geffen, 1996); *Weezer* (*Green Album*) (Geffen, 2001); *Maladroit* (Geffen/Interscope, 2002).

WEBSITE: www.weezer.com.

GIL KAUFMAN

GILLIAN WELCH

Born: New York, New York, 2 October 1967
Genre: Country, Folk
Best-selling album since 1990: *Revival* (1996)

Gillian Welch earned praise from several corners as she brought a sound and style from another era into the present. Claimed by bluegrass, country, alternative rock, and folk circles,

Welch has carved out her own nook-and-cranny with understated songs that evoke strong images as she sings in her haunting lilt.

Hearing Welch (whose first name is pronounced with a hard "g") sing, it is somewhat of a revelation to learn that she did not grow up in the back hills of Appalachia but rather in West Los Angeles, the child of parents who wrote music as a team for *The Carol Burnett Show*. Her parents were her first musical influences and often led the family through sing-alongs of Richard Rodgers and Lorenz Hart and Irving Berlin standards, in addition to various pop music songs of the time. Welch was playing acoustic guitar and singing folk and pop rock by the time she was ten and learned firsthand about songwriting by watching her parents do their work. While attending the University of California at Santa Cruz to study photography, Welch began playing in a local band. She had developed an affinity for bluegrass, and was particularly fascinated by the rawness of the Stanley Brothers and the Delmore Brothers. Theirs was a high, lonesome sound that could be described as a pre-bluegrass or roots music, containing a blend of country music and the traditional songs brought over by the first European settlers in Appalachia.

After graduating from college, Welch decided to approach music professionally. During the late 1980s she switched coasts to attend Boston's reputable Berklee School of Music where she studied songwriting. In Boston, she began performing in local coffeehouses and clubs, developing her unique acoustic traditionalist sound that hearkens back to the late 1880s. Right before leaving the jazz-inclined Berklee, Welch met guitarist David Rawlings, and discovered in him a kindred spirit for the old-time country music of Johnny Cash and Merle Haggard and the tight two-part harmonies of traditional bluegrass. The duo began performing and honing their skills on the road. Welch wrote most of the material, played guitar, and sang, while Rawlings sang harmony and filled in on acoustic lead guitar.

The duo settled in Nashville, where producer T Bone Burnett—who had produced such major stars as Los Lobos, Counting Crows, and Elvis Costello—saw them play at the Station Inn and proposed that they make a record together. With Burnett producing, Welch's stark, primitive sound was captured on her first album, *Revival* (1996). The album's opening track, "Orphan Girl," sets the stage with a song about a kinless child looking hopefully into the afterlife for a reunion with family members. "Annabelle" also carries the spiritual theme of a hard life becoming easier in heaven. Another song, "Pass You By," is a rock-beating grinder about a favorite car that she and Rawlings used to tour in, and "Tear My Stillhouse Down" is a yarn about a moonshiner's dying request. The songs echo a time long past and spin yearning tales of every-

Gillian Welch [MARC SELIGER/ACONY RECORDS AND BIG HASSLE MEDIA]

day people with the heartbreaking honesty of early bluegrass or depression-era music. Welch's music has strong country and folk influences but the arrangements and guitar styling of Rawlings, who at one point played in punk rock bands, skews the songs in their own unique direction. Aspects of punk rock are present in Welch's songs, not at all in the music, but rather in the rawness of the feeling.

Revival scored a Grammy Award nomination for Contemporary Folk, although Welch initially blanched at the "folk" label, preferring not to be pigeonholed. However, upon learning that Johnny Cash and Bob Dylan had both been labeled contemporary folk artists, she felt assured. With Burnett once again in the producer's role, they released her second album, *Hell Among the Yearlings* (1998). While *Revival* features the musical assistance of some of Nashville's finest artists such as guitarist James Burton, bassist Roy Huskey, and percussionists Jim Keltner and Buddy Harmon, this second album features only Huskey accompanying Rawlings and Welch. However, the esteemed bassist died unexpectedly and *Hell Among the Yearlings* became a true duet album. Welch plays either guitar or banjo to accompany her voice, while Rawlings adds the harmony and guitar fill-ins to create a batch of songs that give off an air of timelessness. This album goes deep into what is described as traditional music or music of the early Appalachian people, and it was recorded with the most basic engineering to preserve a more natural sound.

Always in pursuit of that "old-timey" sound, Welch and Rawlings searched Nashville for a studio in which to record their third album. They happened upon a relic of a room, a tourist attraction, located on Nashville's Music Row, called RCA Studio B, or as Nashville insiders call it, the house that Chet Atkins built. Studio B was a functional studio between the years of 1957 and 1977 and it is where Elvis Presley, the Everly Brothers, and many other stars from those eras recorded. Welch decided it was the perfect setting to record *Time (The Revelator)* (2001). Featured on the album is a tribute song to Welch's bluegrass favorites, the Stanley Brothers, titled "I Want To Sing That Rock and Roll." *Time (The Revelator)* was also Welch's first release on her own record label, Acony Records. The Acony Bell is a persevering flower that is usually the first to bloom in the spring.

Welch, with Rawlings, continued to tour extensively through Europe and the United States into the 2000s. She is a featured performer as part of a trio with Alison Krauss and Emmylou Harris on the soundtrack to the film *O Brother, Where Art Thou?* (2000) and has numerous other soundtrack credits. Welch has performed along with many other stars at the concerts sponsored by the Vietnam Veterans of America Foundation for a Landmine Free World.

Due to her urban California upbringing, more than one suspicious eye was cast in Welch's direction as she reproduced a clannish style of music that many felt belonged only in the hands of a select few. However, her music has gained the respect of old-time bluegrass critics and even hard-core enthusiasts of the raw sounds of Appalachia.

SELECTIVE DISCOGRAPHY: *Revival* (Almo Sounds, 1996); *Hell among the Yearlings* (Almo Sounds, 1998); *Time (The Revelator)* (Acony, 2001). **Soundtracks:** *The Horse Whisperer* (MCA, 1998); *Hope Floats* (RCA, 1998); *O Brother, Where Art Thou?* (Universal, 2000); *Songcatcher* (Vanguard, 2001).

DONALD LOWE

PAUL WESTERBERG

Born: Minneapolis, Minnesota, 31 December 1960
Genre: Rock, Punk
Best-selling album since 1990: *14 Songs* (1993)
Hit songs since 1990: "Dyslexic Heart"

Paul Westerberg endures as one of the most beloved singer/songwriters in rock. He is the founding member of the Replacements, a rock band from Minneapolis whose self-destructive behavior, anti-commercial attitude, and raw sound never earned them mainstream success, but helped build their legend long after they broke up. Westerberg's songs voice the boredom, alienation, and heartache of suburban teenagers stuck in the rut of Middle America during the Reagan years, much like the songs of the rhythm and blues singer Chuck Berry did in the Eisenhower era of the 1950s. In the Replacements, Westerberg grew from initially writing primal punk anthems to ultimately incorporating blues, folk, and country, all dosed with working-class defiance and back alley humor. He later developed into more of a pop craftsman. Critics generally agree the five solo albums that followed his career in the Replacements are more stripped down and somber. Westerberg wound up an elder statesman for the countless singer/songwriters he later influenced. He also became a touchstone for the pure rebellious spirit that is the foundation of rock music.

Westerberg was born the son of a Minneapolis Cadillac salesman. He received his first guitar at age fourteen and soon started learning the three-chord rock of first generation punk bands from the 1970s like the Sex Pistols, the Ramones, and the New York Dolls. A short time after, he formed the Replacements with drummer Chris Mars, guitarist Bob Stinson, and bassist Tommy Stinson. The band's debut, *Sorry Ma, Forgot to Take Out the Trash* (1981), was a straightforward hardcore punk record. In time, however, the band would record *Let It Be* (1984), an album that became a cult classic due to its focused songwriting, dynamic mix of styles (folk, blues, honkytonk country), and insurgent bite. By then, the band was nearly mythical for live shows that were either brilliantly executed or woefully sloppy, and usually both. They became the antithesis of the slick commercial rock on MTV that dominated the 1980s. Famously disdainful of marketplace expectations, the band initially refused to make videos. Instead, they railed against the new media in song ("Seen Your Video" includes the sneering lyric, "seen your video / that phony rock & roll / we don't wanna know") and, consequently, in a video ("Bastards of Young") that features just a solitary shot of a home stereo.

Once the band signed, in 1985, to the major label Sire, a division of Warner Bros., their music became more pop-oriented with some songs even featuring string and horns. At the same time, Westerberg grew into a more eloquent lyricist. Although some band members played on the band's swan song, *All Shook Down* (1990)—Bob Stinson had been fired and replaced by guitarist Slim Dunlap—it was mostly a Westerberg solo project featuring hired studio musicians.

The band's official breakup took place on July 4, 1991, onstage and midshow in Chicago's Grant Park.

The band's demise presented Westerberg with an opportunity to reinvent himself. "It's a fresh start," he said in an interview. "It's not like I'm walking away from a goldmine. I'm walking away from a band that went down the toilet. In essence, I'm starting over because no one knows who Paul Westerberg is."

Westerberg became a formal solo artist the next year with two songs on the soundtrack to the Cameron Crowe film *Singles* (1992). Soon afterward, he released his first solo album, *14 Songs* (1993). The very title was seen as a declaration that he now preferred to focus on the craftsmanship of writing songs rather than using music to quell personal demons. The album frustrated die-hard Replacements fans, who lamented the absence of any punk fury. Westerberg's debut collection was melodic, hook-driven pop with lyrics that were mostly relationship-oriented.

He continued to stray from his punk roots with later, more introspective albums. During this period, Westerberg admitted in interviews that he suffered from clinical depression as well as from problems with alcohol. He was also hit hard by the death of Bob Stinson, who died of a drug overdose in 1995. His next two albums—*Eventually* (1996) and *Suicaine Gratifaction* (1998)—were also quiet. They ended up poor sellers and received mixed reviews. The latter album was released the same year his son was born, after which Westerberg stopped touring altogether.

Little was heard from Westerberg over the following few years. Then came the album *Stereo* (2002), whose packaging includes a hidden second disc titled *Mono* (2002), credited simply to Grandpaboy. Westerberg first used the pseudonym on a limited run of the five-song EP *Soundproof/Monolyth* (1997) on a tiny Boston label run by a friend. It was rushed out as a lark to see if he could recapture the Replacements' original ragged sound and irreverent humor. It immediately won acclaim from critics who hailed his return to his earlier roots and fans clamored to see if that would lead to a long-awaited tour.

The new double album sparked a rebirth in Westerberg's career. It was released on Vagrant Records, a West Coast label with mostly young punk bands on its roster. In that environment, Westerberg was introduced to the younger generation as an acclaimed veteran of the punk rock era while at the same time he reconnected to his longtime audience. Recorded alone in his basement, both records were designed to showcase his past history and present direction. *Stereo* is a set of somber solo guitar songs while the songs on *Mono* are in full band glory in the vein of the Replacements—except this time it is Westerberg playing all the instruments. Lyrically, he makes a conscious effort to connect to his past. Just as "Bastards of Young" calls his generation to arms against bowing to the status quo, seventeen years later his new song "We May Be the Ones" is a quieter follow-up gauging how they had fared against complacency.

Because he had not toured in six years, Westerberg reemerged by playing a handful of in-store dates at Virgin Megastores around the country in 2002. Each stop was before capacity crowds and the mini-shows re-energized his enthusiasm for performing live. He ended up embarking on a full solo tour, for which he received his best reviews in years. Like *Stereo* and *Mono*, the shows captured the flavor of his Replacements days. While he could bring audiences to a dead silence, he also ably played the role of the aloof rock veteran, inviting members of the crowd onstage and taking requests—but only with the stipulation that he might need help remembering the lyrics.

Westerberg lives in Minneapolis with his wife and son. In interviews, he says he is content to keep recording and performing solo but has kept the door open to a Replacements reunion with bassist Tommy Stinson, who became a member of the pop metal band Guns n' Roses in the late 1990s.

SELECTIVE DISCOGRAPHY: *14 Songs* (Sire/Reprise, 1993); *Eventually* (Reprise, 1996); *Grandpaboy EP* (Soundproof/Monolyth, 1997); *Suicaine Gratifaction* (Capitol, 1998); *Stereo/Mono* (Vagrant, 2002). **With the Replacements:** *Sorry Ma, Forgot to Take Out the Trash* (Twin/Tone, 1981); *The Replacements Stink* EP (Twin/Tone, 1982); *Hootenanny* (Twin/Tone, 1983); *Let It Be* (Twin/Tone, 1984); *Tim* (Sire, 1985); *Pleased to Meet Me* (Sire, 1987); *Don't Tell a Soul* (Sire, 1989), *All Shook Down* (Sire, 1990); *All For Nothing/Nothing for All* (Sire, 1997). **Soundtracks:** *Singles* (Sony/Columbia, 1992); *Music from Melrose Place* (Warner Bros., 1994); *Tank Girl* (Elektra, 1995); *Tommy Boy* (Warner Bros., 1995); *Friends* (Warner Bros., 1995); *I Am Sam* (V2, 2002).

MARK GUARINO

THE WHITE STRIPES

Formed: 1997, Detroit, Michigan

Members: Jack White, guitar/vocals (born John Anthony Gillis, Detroit, Michigan, 9 July 1975); Meg White (born Megan Martha White, Grosse Pointe Park, Michigan, 10 December 1974).

Genre: Rock

Best-selling album since 1990: *White Blood Cells* (2001)

Hit songs since 1990: "Fell in Love with a Girl," "Dead Leaves and the Dirty Ground"

With just a guitar, drums, and a stripped-down rock sound, the Detroit duo the White

Spot
Light | *White Blood Cells*

The White Stripes' third album, *White Blood Cells* (2001), was hailed as a masterpiece and tagged as the shot that started the garage-rock revolution of the new millennium. Garage rock, an umbrella term for the short, energetic, often distorted songs created by backyard rock bands in the mid- and late 1960s, had been around for decades, but in early 2000 and 2001 the mainstream media finally caught on to some of the genre's leading lights. Seizing on the White Stripes for their combination of gritty blues, personal eccentricities, and striking color-coordinated style, the press lumped the pair in with a number of disparate bands. Among them were Australia's the Vines (more pop and grungy rock than the Stripes), New York's the Strokes (also a bit refined to be considered garage), and Sweden's the Hives (who channeled a jittery version of the Rolling Stones via 1970s punk).

Stripes unwittingly launched the garage-rock revival of the new millennium. The media-baiting duo became music industry darlings with their third album of gritty urban blues, *White Blood Cells* (2001).

Formed on Bastille Day in 1997, the White Stripes had all the markings of an art project gone punk rock. Guitarist/singer Jack White and drummer Meg White decided early on that their conceptual band would dress only in white and red and that they would not fill out the lineup with the third traditional rock element, a bass guitar. Drawing from a range of influences, including folk and country blues, 1960s British pop, and punk rock, the pair made their debut with the 1997 single "Let's Shake Hands," released on Detroit's Italy Records imprint. A second single, "Lafayette Blues," was released on Italy and was followed by their self-titled full-length debut album, which combines distorted Detroit punk and thundering Led Zeppelin–like blues with Jack White's high-pitched, slightly nasal vocals riding the crest of the noisy wave.

Songs such as "Stop Breaking Down" take the rural country blues of the South and plug them into the energy and urgency of late-1970s punk rock. The duo show their love of both blues and folk with a pair of covers: Robert Johnson's "Stop Breaking Down Blues" and Bob Dylan's "One More Cup of Coffee." With Meg White's bash-and-clatter drumming and Jack White's reverb-soaked slide guitar, the lack of a bass is scarcely noticeable.

The band's second album, *De Stijl* (The Style) (2000), was warmly embraced by American and British critics. Adding piano, harmonica, and electric violin to the mix, the album relies on the same combination of primal, rattling drumbeats and oddly tuned guitars. With a touch of the absurd, the album ping-pongs from the sugary pop of "You're Pretty Good Looking (for a Girl)" to the gritty slide blues of "Little Bird" to the player piano-driven "Apple Blossom," part Broadway show tune and part Neil Young blues. The album also features a cover of "Death Letter," by the blues legend Son House, and "Your Southern Can Is Mine," by the blues man Blind Willie McTell, to whom the album is dedicated.

The duo prefer to keep their private lives a mystery aside from the claim that they are siblings—an intentional falsehood that was exposed when the mainstream media dug up a marriage license that proved that the two were married in September 1996 and divorced in 2000.

Their next album, *White Blood Cells* (2001), was recorded in Memphis. This was the album that earned the band mainstream attention and helped to launch the garage-rock revival of 2001. It is the most refined version of the group's sound, with a hit single ("Fell in Love with a Girl") that is both mindlessly poppy and speedily punk. The accompanying video, in which the acclaimed director Michel Gondry cast the duo in animated Lego blocks, won three MTV 2002 Video Music Awards.

Jack White's lyrics, always on the elegantly simple side, were even more artful in *White Blood Cells*, as in the spare blues song "I'm Finding It Harder to Be a Gentleman." In his strained alto White sings, "Well I never said I wouldn't / Throw my jacket in the mud for you." The pair recorded their fourth album, *Elephant*, in London in two weeks in mid-2002; it was released in April 2003.

Just as the fifteen minutes was winding down on such teen pop acts as the Backstreet Boys and Britney Spears, in stepped Detroit's White Stripes to unleash a fresh burst of energy on a moribund, overly manicured music scene. With a style predicated on passion over fashion and jagged blues over slick pop, Jack and Meg White helped revive the blues for a new generation of punk-rock-loving fans.

SELECTIVE DISCOGRAPHY: *The White Stripes* (Sympathy for the Record Industry, 1999); *De Stijl* (Sympathy for the Record Industry, 2000); *White Blood Cells* (Sympathy for the Record Industry/V2, 2001); *Elephant* (V2, 2003).

GIL KAUFMAN

WHITE ZOMBIE

Formed: 1985, New York, New York

Members: Robert "Rob Zombie" Cummings, vocals (born Haverhill, Massachusetts, 13 January 1966); Jay "J." Yuenger, guitar (born Chicago, Illinois, 26 December 1967); Sean Yseult, bass (born Shauna Reynolds; Raleigh, North Carolina, 6 June 1966); John Tempesta, drums.

Genre: Rock

Best-selling album since 1990: *Astro Creep: 2000—Songs of Love, Destruction, and Other Synthetic Delusions of the Electric Head* (2000)

Hit songs since 1990: "Thunder Kiss '65," "Black Sunshine," "More Human Than Human"

In a decade that ushered in no-frills, acoustic-framed alt-rock, White Zombie took the theatrical, colorful road-less-traveled. Spending lots of time watching TV and reading comic books, Rob Cummings (who later renamed himself Rob Zombie) was something of a social outcast growing up in small-town New England. In his late teens he moved to New York City, where he found fellow travelers who shared his love for the tacky and vulgar side of Americana, and he formed a band that began to play locally. He also started a romantic relationship with a female bassist, Yseult, but their professional relationship proved more enduring.

White Zombie released the EP *Psycho Head Blowout* (1987) independently and followed that with debut album *Soul Crusher* (1988). Zombie was still going by the slightly cheesy pseudonym Rob Straker. The band got the attention of the legendary New York bassist/producer Bill Laswell, who signed them to his Caroline Records and released *Make Them Die Slowly* (1989). After five years of slogging it out in the tough New York scene, the band was deemed ready for prime time by Geffen Records.

Their debut on Geffen, *La Sexorcisto: Devil Music Vol. 1* (1992), was produced by Andy Wallace, who went on to become one of the most in-demand mixing engineers of the decade. He helped the band combine its monster-truck metal riffs with a rollicking groove. However, the album received little notice until the "Thunder Kiss '65" video got a "cool" recommendation from MTV's *Beavis and Butt-head* cartoon show. Zombie's dreadlocks, twangy rap singing, and fusion of metal with up-tempo R&B grooves set the band in stark contrast to the grunge movement. The lyrics evoke decadence and devil worship, though in a cheekier way than such metal predecessors as Black Sabbath and Dio.

White Zombie reached its high point with *Astro Creep: 2000—Songs of Love, Destruction, and Other Syn-thetic Delusions of the Electric Head* (1995). On the album, the band hones its amalgam of hard rock, industrial rock, and hip-hop. Their first single, "More Human Than Human," starts with stuttering synthesizers and Zombie's rabble-rousing "yeeeah" shout and subsequently explodes into a rafter-rattling blast of crunching guitars and hip-shaking beats. "Super-Charger Heaven" sustains the group's penchant for tongue-in-cheek Satanism and rolls along like a revved-up version of Tom Petty's "Running Down a Dream." Acknowledging their dance-music influences, White Zombie released a remix album, *Supersexy Swingin' Sounds* (1996), and covered KC and the Sunshine Band's "I'm Your Boogie Man" for *The Crow: City of Angels* (1996) soundtrack.

The band found themselves in a situation resembling the plot of the film *Footloose* in 1996 when the Johnson City, Tennessee, city council denied the band permission to perform at a city-owned venue. Some cried censorship, while others questioned whether lyrics like "Cupid brought a gun, he gonna blow the f**ker" (from "Electric Head Pt. 2") conformed to community standards in a small southern city.

Zombie went solo in 1998, claiming the other members were not into his trashy concept anymore. His former band mates vigorously denied the accusation, saying Zombie simply bailed out on them. Regardless, Zombie does indulge his macabre side more on his solo debut, *Hellbilly Deluxe*. He sings, "dig through the ditches / burn through the witches" on his first single, "Dragula," which conforms to his trademark template of electric beats and chainsaw guitars. "Living Dead Girl" uses a Nine Inch Nails–inspired industrial rhythm and comes with a video that pays homage to silent horror films. In fact, NIN members Charlie Clouser and Chris Vrenna did production work on *American Made Music to Strip By* (1999), another remix set.

White Zombie's concerts resembled carnival sideshows, with their ghoulish makeup, pyrotechnics, and images from old horror movies. Old-timers saw shades of Alice Cooper. For *The Sinister Urge* (2001), Zombie makes a few minor adjustments, aiming for pop accessibility on "Never Gonna Stop" and cooling down the tempo on "Land of 1000 Corpses." The single "Dead Girl Superstar" uses scratches and samples. But mainly he sticks to the cyber-groove-metal formula that has pleased his fans.

White Zombie and Rob Zombie brought rhythm, irony, and decadent fun to hard rock. Not ones to make stylistic leaps or reinvent themselves, they found a niche market of like-minded fans and gave them plenty of good, dirty fun.

SELECTIVE DISCOGRAPHY: *La Sexorcisto: Devil Music Vol. 1* (Geffen, 1992); *Astro Creep: 2000—Songs of Love, Destruction, and Other Synthetic*

Delusions of the Electric Head (Geffen, 1995); *Hell-billy Deluxe* (Geffen, 1998); *The Sinister Urge* (Universal, 2001).

RAMIRO BURR

THE WHO

Formed: 1964, London, England

Members: Pete Townshend, guitar, vocals (born London, England, 19 May 1945); Roger Daltrey, lead vocals (born London, 1 March 1944). Former members: Kenney Jones, drums (born London, 16 September 1948); Keith Moon, drums (born 23 August 1947; died London, 7 September 1978); John Entwistle, bass (born London, 9 October 1944; died Las Vegas, Nevada, 27 June 2002).

Genre: Rock

Best-selling album since 1990: *Thirty Years of Maximum R&B* (1994)

The Who's golden age was over by 1980; by then the British band had consolidated enough of a reputation as a live act and had produced sufficient material to ensure an upper berth in the pantheon of rock performers. Along the way, the group's history was peppered by the same tragedies that scarred many of the leading groups that came to prominence in the 1960s.

Addiction and death (two original members of the four-piece band have passed on) have marked a story that has been sustained, in the last two decades, primarily through touring. Yet the magnificent body of recorded material, which flowed principally from the musical pen of guitarist Pete Townshend from 1964 to the end of the 1970s, confirms the Who's glittering standing in the gallery of greats. Their potent blend of raw rock and roll, white R&B, and incisive lyrical commentary coupled with their awesome power as a live outfit left a deep imprint on their fans and generations of young bands who followed.

Origins

The product of London's nascent rock scene of the early 1960s, the band first emerged as the High Numbers and was linked to the ferment of the mod subculture: fashion-conscious young men and women who dressed with a sharp elegance and subscribed to the sounds of the British blues revival and American soul. In 1964 the High Numbers issued a single, "I'm the Face," the B-side of which was "Zoot Suit." The single's failure led the group to hire two new co-managers, Kit Lambert and Chris Stamp. The group's name was changed to the Who, and a residency at London's famous R&B venue the Marquee quickly followed.

In a stunning burst of energy, the Who then released a sequence of singles that left a deep impression on the British pop charts: "I Can't Explain," "Anyway Anyhow Anywhere," and "My Generation"; the last was speedily adopted as an anthem of fast-living adolescents. "People try to put us down / Just because we get around" sings Daltrey, reflecting on a new confidence and optimism infusing British youth culture. But it was Townshend's line, "Things they do look awful cold / Hope I die before I get old," that distilled the spirit of this youthful assault and reflects perceptively on the notion of a generation gap between adults and the young.

The energy and aggression of their shows were soon legendary, and the smashing of their instruments onstage became a notorious aspect of their live appearances. This element of the Who's persona, embodied particularly in the excessive behavior of drummer Keith Moon when on tour, helped to form the band's mystique.

By 1966 Townshend's songwriting abilities had been further showcased in tracks like "Substitute" and "I'm a Boy." Yet there were unusual aspects to their progress—they did not manage to ride the early British Invasion wave that allowed the Beatles, Rolling Stones, and others to make headway in the United States.

Tommy and After

The spring of 1967 brought the group belated transatlantic recognition as their live gigs in New York won applause. Their appearance that same summer at the Monterey Festival in California, the first-ever open-air rock event, stole the show. In the fall, "I Can See for Miles" gave them a hit in both England and the United States. In the spring of 1969, the larger vision that Townshend had already hinted at was unveiled when "Pinball Wizard" trailed the arrival of *Tommy*, a double-album odyssey, inspired by a short story by the British journalist Nik Cohn, that related the experiences of a deaf, dumb, and blind boy with a penchant for playing pinball. As the first single famously announces, "But I ain't seen nothing like it in any amusement hall / That deaf, dumb and blind kid sure plays a mean pinball."

The band's status as perhaps the premier live act of the period was confirmed some months later when the Who took the stage at the Woodstock Festival in August 1969 and proceeded to deliver a memorable, powerful set. Yet their insistence that they be paid in cash before going on stage at the event, the high tide of the hippie subculture, left almost as great an impact as their performance. The tour album *Live at Leeds* (1970) captures some of their live electricity, and the song "Won't Get Fooled Again" (1971) stunningly voices the political frustrations of the previous decade.

In the early 1970s *Tommy* began to take on a life of its own. In 1972 it became a stage musical, one of the first rock operas, and 1974 saw the release of the movie version, directed by Ken Russell and featuring Elton John, Tina Turner, and a number of other notable stars.

With *Quadrophenia* (1973) the Who's creative conveyor belt kept rolling. Another double album with a strong conceptual thread, the piece looked back to the mid-1960s, when the fashion-conscious mods, fans of the Who, clashed with their rivals the rockers, followers of earlier rock and roll. Although the collection spawned some single successes, like "5.15," the focus of the band was drifting as a series of solo projects took group members in different directions.

Dissolving and Re-forming

In 1978 Keith Moon died of an overdose of a drug that he was taking to battle his alcoholism; it was an unsurprising conclusion to a life that had been lived to the extreme. By the beginning of 1979, former Faces drummer Kenney Jones had been drafted to replace him. The early 1980s saw the band tread water in many ways, and by 1983 the group announced its dissolution. But the Who re-formed to play at Live Aid, the transatlantic live event that featured dozens of rock and pop acts in a benefit concert for African hunger charities. A decision to return to touring in 1989 proved that the split had been far from final.

Townshend's prodigious appetite for work resulted in a fine solo album, *Empty Glass*, in 1980. He also became involved with the literary publishing house Faber in an advisory capacity—they had already published his short stories; in 1989 he collaborated with the British poet laureate, Ted Hughes, in creating a musical version of Hughes's children's story *The Iron Man*.

Inducted into the Rock and Roll Hall of Fame in 1990, the Who have continued to play and tour intermittently. Townshend issued a further concept work in 1993 with *Psychoderelict*, a musical piece interspersed with dialogue, and that same year *Tommy* enjoyed a successful Broadway incarnation. Daltrey's fiftieth birthday celebration in 1994 brought a galaxy of stars, including Lou Reed and Eddie Vedder, to Carnegie Hall.

In 1996 *Quadrophenia* was mounted in a well-received revival in London's Hyde Park, but the group's ensuing tours seemed to rely too heavily on the legacy of the past and made less impact. In the wake of the terrorist attacks of September 11, 2001, the band was present at the New York benefit concert for victims of those events.

In June 2002 the original lineup suffered a further major blow when John Entwistle died of a heart attack on the eve of another U.S. tour amid news that Townshend, Daltrey, and Entwistle were working on their first new material in more than twenty years. Although the tour still proceeded as a tribute to the man they nicknamed the Ox, with Pino Palladino on bass and Zak Starkey on drums, the Who could not escape dark headlines.

At the start of 2003, Townshend, whose solo profile had been relatively low for some time, was propelled into the media glare once more with his arrest for having allegedly accessed an Internet site devoted to child pornography. Townshend asserted that he had been researching a project on the nature of child abuse.

The Who, like the Rolling Stones, produced a collection of albums and singles in their first decade that sustained their reputation long after the peak of their creative output had passed. Their outstanding sequence of early singles prefaced their more sustained, keynote works, *Tommy* and *Quadrophenia*. Yet those acclaimed concept albums, which enjoyed life as stage shows and movies, have become almost a burden to their principal creator.

Townshend, a proven master of the three-minute single by the end of the 1960s, has spent most of his professional life since striving to make bigger statements. In so doing he has attracted criticism for the very scale of his ambition, often from those nostalgic commentators who still remember him fondly as the young mod with an extraordinary capability for devising one-off pop classics.

SELECTIVE DISCOGRAPHY: *My Generation* (MCA, 1965); *A Quick One (Happy Jack)* (MCA, 1966); *The Who Sell Out* (MCA, 1967); *Magic Bus* (MCA, 1968); *Tommy* (MCA, 1969); *Live at Leeds* (MCA, 1970); *Who's Next* (MCA, 1971); *Meaty Beaty Big and Bouncy* (MCA, 1971); *Quadrophenia* (MCA, 1973); *The Who by Numbers* (MCA, 1975); *Who Are You* (MCA, 1978); *Thirty Years of Maximum R&B* (MCA, 1994).

BIBLIOGRAPHY: A. Neill and M. Kent, *Anyway, Anyhow, Anywhere: The Complete Chronicle of the Who, 1958–1978* (London, 2002); L. D. Smith, *Pete Townshend: The Minstrel's Dilemma* (London, 1999).

WEBSITES: www.thewho.net; www.petetownshend.co.uk; www.bbc.co.uk/aboutmusic/profiles/who.shtml.

SIMON WARNER

WILCO

Formed: 1994, Chicago, Illinois

Members: Leroy Bach, guitar, keyboards (born Chicago, Illinois, 21 August 1964); Glenn Kotche, drums (born Chicago, Illinois, 31 December 1970); John Stirratt, bass (born New Orleans, Louisiana, 26 November 1967); Jeff Tweedy, lead vocals, guitar (born Belleville, Illinois, 25 August 1967). Former members: Jay Bennett, guitar, piano, vocals (born 15 November 1963), Ken Coomer, drums (born 5 November 1960); Max Johnston, mandolin, dobro, banjo.

Genre: Rock

Best-selling album since 1990: *Yankee Hotel Foxtrot* (2002)

Hit songs since 1990: "Heavy Metal Drummer," "California Stars"

Following the demise of beloved country-influenced rock band Uncle Tupelo in 1994, Jeff Tweedy and his band Wilco emerged as what critics called one of the most inventive, emotionally resonant American bands of the 1990s and 2000s.

Tweedy formed Wilco in 1994 with several ex-members of Uncle Tupelo, among them drummer Ken Coomer, bassist John Stirratt, and multi-instrumentalist Max Johnston. The group's debut, *A.M.*, followed closely in the footsteps of the Uncle Tupelo style, which blended country music accents with rock, folk, and punk rock into a widely emulated modern country rock sound dubbed "no depression" after the name of Uncle Tupelo's 1990 debut album. However, with the addition of guitarist Jay Bennett in 1995, Wilco embarked on a new path that would lead them far from the nouveau country rock movement.

The two-album set *Being There* (1996), which won critical acclaim but was commercially unsuccessful, is the work of a band that was not simply stepping away from its previous sound. Like the Beatles in the late 1960s, who traded their simple pop ditties for complex, lushly arranged rock symphonies, Wilco completely reinvented its approach by abandoning, for the most part, its country sound and focusing on a broader palette of musical influences. Gone is the twangy sensibility of *A.M.* and in its place are baroque psychedelic dirges ("Sunken Treasure"), theatrical orchestral flourishes, and bubblegum-pop love songs such as "I Got You (At the End of the Century)" and the lovelorn "Red-Eyed and Blue."

Songs such as "Misunderstood," which features the lyrics, "There's a fortune inside your head / All you touch turns to lead / You think you might just crawl back in bed / The fortune inside your head," firmly established the hoarse-voiced Tweedy as a songwriter with a rich emotional range and an earthy, poetic style in the vein of one of the most important American folk artists of the early twentieth century, Woody Guthrie. Author of the quintessentially American anthem "This Land Is Your Land," Guthrie penned countless political and union songs such as "Dust Bowl Blues" and "Tom Joad" in the 1940s, setting the stage for the folk revival of the late 1950s/early 1960s which birthed such modern legends as folksinger Bob Dylan.

Wilco. L-R: Leroy Bach, Glenn Kotche, Jeff Tweedy, John Stirratt [PAUL NATKIN/PHOTO RESERVE]

In 1998 Wilco was invited by English singer/songwriter Billy Bragg to collaborate on a project that added music to previously unreleased Woody Guthrie lyrics. The resulting album, *Mermaid Avenue*, which was fraught with behind-the-scenes creative tension between Bragg and Tweedy, was nevertheless a commercial and artistic triumph. In reimagining Guthrie's songs as everything from rock to soul, it reveals a previously underappreciated tender side of the folk icon in songs such as the acoustic ballad "California Stars" and the rollicking "Hoodoo Voodoo"; a sequel, *Mermaid Avenue, Vol. II*, was released in 2000.

In between the *Mermaid Avenue* sets, Wilco released its most ambitious album to date, *Summerteeth* (1999). Though many of the songs are built on traditional pop structures, the emotionally wrenching tales about true love, infidelity, and fighting loneliness are frequently spiked with beeping, sonar-like keyboard figures, a ghostly banjo, and studio-manipulated sound effects. Tweedy's music had, by now, shed nearly all of its twangy edge for the heady, unorthodox feel of songs such as "She's a Jar." The emotional centerpiece of the album incorporates the keyboard-produced sounds of melancholy strings, train whistle harmonicas, and lyrics that mix love and longing in a dark manner ("Are there really ones like these / the ones I dream / float like leaves / and freeze to spread skeleton wings / I passed through before I knew you"). Rather than paying homage to the country rock of Gram Parsons, Tweedy seemed more interested in following in the footsteps of Beach Boys' studio wizard Brian Wilson and his "Teenage Symphonies to God." While the maverick arrangements were seen by some as the hallmark of a talented pop songwriter shooting himself in the foot by trying to be overly avant-garde, the unique touches furthered Tweedy's reputation as a wildly gifted songwriter unwilling to compromise his art for pop stardom.

With Artistic Triumph Comes Career Uncertainty

That independent streak would be sorely tested after the delivery of the group's widely regarded masterwork, *Yankee Hotel Foxtrot* (2002). If previous albums took liberties with traditional song structures, the band's fourth effort threw out the book entirely. Songs dissolve into washes of radio static, peals of ringing bells, arrhythmic piano runs, and disjointed rhythms, while the album's opening song, "I Am Trying to Break Your Heart," leads with one of the most intriguing lyrics of Tweedy's career, "I am an American aquarium drinker / I assassin down the avenue." Frustrated with Tweedy's reluctance to re-record any of the album's quirky, complex songs, Wilco was dropped by its longtime record label, Reprise Records, in 2001. The squabble with the label was chronicled in filmmaker Sam Jones's documentary "I Am Trying To Break Your Heart" (2002), which gave a fly-on-the-wall perspective of the artistic battle. Drummer Ken Coomer departed the band around this time and was soon followed by multi-instrumentalist Jay Bennett. Chicago drummer Glenn Kotche replaced Coomer, while guitarist/keyboardist Leroy Bach replaced Bennett.

Left with a finished album and no record label to release it, Wilco posted the unreleased music on their website in late 2001. Though Tweedy had performed some of the songs during a solo acoustic tour in the winter of 2001, the website finally allowed fans to hear the collection on which the band takes their experimentation, with tape manipulation and abstract noise, to new levels while again retaining their command of pop smarts. The nostalgic, straightforward pop rock songs "Heavy Metal Drummer" and "Kamera" show the band's ability to play it straight, complete with three-part harmonies and recognizable pop song structures, though neither is what one might call conventional. Both serve as something of a musical palate cleanser for the more esoteric efforts on the album. "Radio Cure" hums with acoustic guitars that scrape and buzz over a ghostly, heartbeat drum figure until the sounds of helicopters and a haunting counter rhythm on vibraphone overtake the song midway through. When "Ashes of American Flags" breaks down halfway through its acoustic lament under a bizarre wash of white noise, Tweedy is able to steer it back on course before the song collapses in a heap of hissing feedback and warped tape. In *Yankee Hotel Foxtrot*, Tweedy created a work that was the antidote to the manufactured pop of the day, one brimming with subtle musical flourishes and complex lyrics which reward repeated listens.

Wilco eventually persuaded Reprise to give the album back to them free and clear; they then signed a deal with Nonesuch, a label also owned by media conglomerate Warner Bros. Longtime manager Tony Margherita was frequently quoted as saying that Warner Bros. paid Wilco twice for an album they did not want. When it was finally released, *Yankee Hotel Foxtrot* was hailed by everyone from the *New York Times* to *Rolling Stone* magazine as a masterwork by one of America's most talented bands. During an era when the music business was focused on hit singles over artistic advancement, Tweedy and Wilco survived turnover and turmoil to emerge with music that challenged as it matured.

SELECTIVE DISCOGRAPHY: A.M. (1995); *Being There* (1996); *Mermaid Avenue* (1998); *Summerteeth* (1999); *Mermaid Avenue, Vol. II* (2000); *Yankee Hotel Foxtrot* (2002).

SELECTIVE FILMOGRAPHY: *I Am Trying to Break Your Heart* (2002).

GIL KAUFMAN

FRANK WILDHORN

Born: New York, New York, 29 November 1959

Genre: Musical Theater

Best-selling album since 1990: *Jekyll and Hyde: Original Broadway Cast Recording* (1997)

Hit songs since 1990: "This Is the Moment," "Where Do Broken Hearts Go," "You Are My Home"

One of the few composers to have had three Broadway shows running simultaneously, Frank Wildhorn derives much of his notoriety from the hit-and-miss world of New York's Broadway theater. However, his pop music has been recorded by a lengthy list of top musical artists and his classical compositions are performed all over the world. Wildhorn's gift for churning out melodic, catchy songs has clashed at times with the artistic notions of Broadway theater's critics and elitists.

Although he had no formal musical training, Wildhorn started composing music on the family organ. His passion for and skill in composing developed while writing and playing for rhythm and blues, jazz, and rock bands during his teenage years after his family had moved from

Queens, New York, to Hollywood, Florida, when he was fourteen. Following high school, Wildhorn attended Miami University but transferred after a year to the University of Southern California (USC) where he studied history and philosophy. He also moonlighted in the Los Angeles area as a musician in clubs and studios. Inspired after watching *West Side Story* and *Jesus Christ Superstar* on television in 1979, Wildhorn composed a musical loosely based on *Jesus Christ Superstar* titled *Christopher*. Later that year, he persuaded USC's drama department to stage *Christopher* as a main stage production. Although the play was considered unpolished and has never been produced again, it impressed Chrysalis Records enough to offer Wildhorn a song-publishing deal. This began an impressive songwriting career of over 250 published songs that have sold over 50 million records. A diverse list of artists have recorded Wildhorn's songs including Whitney Houston, Kenny Rogers, Sammy Davis Jr., Natalie Cole, Travis Tritt, Hootie and the Blowfish, Blues Traveler, and Dr. John. However, a strong fascination for musical theater remained.

In 1990 Wildhorn's musical, *Jekyll and Hyde*, received its first production at the Alley Theater in Houston. Wildhorn also released the show's songs in an album, *Jekyll and Hyde* (1990). Several of the songs received pop airplay, particularly "This Is the Moment", which was performed by Jennifer Holiday at President Bill Clinton's 1996 inauguration in addition to many other national events. After several years of rewrites, *Jekyll and Hyde* opened on Broadway at the Plymouth Theater in 1997. Critics were harsh, writing that the show was campy and the score was too bland, but theatergoers, drawn to the likable music and the play's raw, gothic feel, kept up a steady attendance. *Jekyll and Hyde* ran for 1,543 performances before closing on January 5, 2001. The original Broadway cast album from the show was released in 1997. One of the female stars of the show, the singer Linda Eder, met Wildhorn in 1987 when she auditioned for an earlier version of *Jekyll and Hyde*. They married in 1998 and have a son together in addition to another son from Wildhorn's first marriage. Wildhorn has written and produced several recordings for Eder.

In 1998 another Wildhorn musical, *The Scarlet Pimpernel*, opened on Broadway at the Minskoff Theater. Most critics panned this production as well, noting that the music was weak. These notions exasperated Wildhorn and he made public his ire regarding the state of Broadway theater, which in his opinion was a myopic world that only included a select few. However, just as with his first Broadway effort, the public still came despite the critics. *Pimpernel* has the odd distinction of closing and re-opening on Broadway only a year later with a new cast, this time at the Neil Simon Theater. Combined, the two *Pimpernel* productions ran 772 performances before closing. The

original cast album was released in 1998 and features stunning work by Broadway veteran Terrence Mann on engaging numbers such as "Falcon in the Dive" and "Where's the Girl?"

When Wildhorn's *The Civil War* opened on Broadway at the St. James Theater in 1999 it earned him the distinction of having three shows running on Broadway at the same time. The show was a series of songs that gave voice to actual diaries and documents from the time of the Civil War. *The Civil War*'s Broadway run lasted only two months as Wildhorn's music was lambasted for being better suited to radio and not appropriate for Broadway. Wildhorn released a recording of the show's songs on an album called *The Civil War: Nashville Sessions*, which features an array of country and pop singing stars. There is also a Broadway cast version of the musical available. A successful United States tour of *The Civil War* played for two years after the show closed on Broadway.

A self-described workaholic, Wildhorn is usually creating different projects simultaneously, often in collaboration or with the intent of producing a vehicle for his wife. In 2003 he was working on the musical productions *Camille Claudel*, *Dracula*, and *Havana*.

Wildhorn's inability to gain acceptance within the inner circles of Broadway theater seems to have little effect on the composer's enthusiasm for writing and creating shows for the theater. Throughout his career, Wildhorn has been able to generate music that draws listeners and fellow artists to his work.

SELECTIVE DISCOGRAPHY: *Jekyll and Hyde: Concept Recording* (BMI/RCA Victor, 1990); *The Scarlet Pimpernel: Concept Recording* (EMI Angel, 1992); *Jekyll and Hyde: The Complete Work* (Atlantic, 1994); *Jekyll and Hyde: Original Broadway Cast* (Atlantic, 1997); *The Scarlet Pimpernel: Original Broadway Cast* (Atlantic, 1998); *The Civil War: Nashville Sessions* (Atlantic, 1998); *The Scarlet Pimpernel: Encore!* (Atlantic, 1999); *The Civil War: The Complete Work* (Atlantic, 1999).

DONALD LOWE

DAR WILLIAMS

Born: Mount Kisco, New York, April 19, 1967

Genre: Folk

Best-selling album since 1990: *The Green World* (2000)

Hit songs since 1990: "When I Was a Boy," "As Cool As I Am," "What Do You Hear in These Sounds"

Singer/songwriter Dar Williams is known for her honesty, social consciousness, and sense of

Dar Williams [KEN SCHLES/RAZOR & TIE]

standout song, "When I Was a Boy," in which Williams imagines how her life might be different if she were a boy, and she tempers her imaginings with humor and sensitivity. The album itself has sold over 100,000 copies, an admirable feat for an independent label. The ensuing *Mortal City* (1996) produced the typically quirky Dar Williams tunes "As Cool as I Am" and "The Christians and the Pagans." By the time *End of the Summer* (1997) came out, Williams had boosted her songwriting with a strong back-up band. This third album was responsible for bringing Williams to a broader audience, as it was well received by critics and loved by fans.

For her fourth album, *The Green World* (2000), Williams switched to a different producer, Rob Hyman, noted for his work with rock singer Joan Osborne. Some folk purists objected to its shimmery, rock-and-roll vibe. Its title is perfect for a collection of songs about personal growth ("After All") and civil disobedience ("I Had No Right"), and matches the levity of the humorous but assertive "I Won't Be Your Yoko Ono."

The Beauty of the Rain, released in 2003, features guest appearances from John Medeski of the jazz-funk trio Medeski, Martin & Wood, and John Popper from the blues-rock band Blues Traveler. These appearances are a notable achievement for a singer/songwriter who spent a good portion of the early 1990s touring the coffee house circuit in relative obscurity.

SELECTIVE DISCOGRAPHY: *The Honesty Room* (self-released, 1993; reissued by Razor & Tie, 1995); *Mortal City* (Razor & Tie, 1996); *End of the Summer* (Razor & Tie, 1997); *The Green World* (Razor & Tie, 2000); *Out There Live* (Razor & Tie, 2001). **With Cry Cry Cry:** *Cry Cry Cry* (Razor & Tie, 1998).

CARRIE HAVRANEK

JOHN WILLIAMS

Born: New York, New York, 8 February 1932
Genre: Soundtrack, Classical
Best-selling album since 1990: *Schindler's List* (MCA, 1993)

One of the most in-demand film composers of the last quarter of the twentieth century, John Williams reinvigorated orchestral movie music, composing scores for more than 80 films and winning 5 Academy Awards, 17 Grammy Awards, 3 Golden Globe Awards, 2 Emmy Awards, and 5 BAFTA Awards from the British Academy of Film and Television Arts. He is the

humor, all of which permeate her folk-influenced songs. Williams has a gift for weaving complex tales over memorable melodies. Her preoccupations include the environment, relationships, and religion; sometimes these themes even dovetail within the same song. Throughout the 1990s Williams toured continuously, starting off in coffeehouses and folk festivals and finally landing in larger concert halls, often to standing-room-only crowds full of devoted fans, who affectionately refer to themselves as "Dar heads."

Williams was raised in the well-heeled town of Chappaqua, New York, the daughter of medical writer and editor Gray Williams and Marian Ferry, a Planned Parenthood activist. She began learning the guitar around age nine, and wrote her first song by age eleven. Williams grew up in a progressive environment; her parents were educated at Yale and Vassar, and she attended Wesleyan University in Connecticut from which she graduated with a degree in theater and religion. In 1990 she moved to Boston to start her theater career; she also began voice lessons. Eventually, she abandoned acting and moved to the artsy town of Northampton, Massachusetts.

In 1993 Williams released her debut, *The Honesty Room,* on her own label, Burning Fields Music; it was then picked up by folk-friendly label Razor & Tie. Williams's imaginative, poignant style is evidenced on the album's

composer of memorable theme music for television networks and special events such as the Olympics. He is a conductor, famous for his work leading the Boston Pops Orchestra. And he is a composer of music for the concert hall.

Williams was born in Queens, New York, a borough of New York City, and moved with his family to Los Angeles, California, in 1948. He studied composition with prominent composer Mario Castelnuovo-Tedesco and attended the University of California at Los Angeles. After a stint in the U.S. Air Force, Williams returned to New York in 1954, studying piano at the Juilliard School with Rosina Lhevinne, who was one of the most important piano teachers of her time. He played jazz piano in clubs and on recordings in New York, before moving back to Los Angeles where he began his career in the entertainment industry.

A Start in Hollywood

Landing in the Hollywood studios, he worked with studio orchestras and composers, composing and arranging music for numerous television shows in the 1960s. Among the shows on which he worked were *M-Squad*, *Wagon Train*, *Chrysler Theatre*, *Lost in Space*, *Gilligan's Island*, and *Land of the Giants*. He won two Emmys for NBC productions of *Heidi* (1968–1969) and *Jane Eyre* (1971–1972).

Williams's first screen credit as a movie composer was *Because They're Young* (1960). Quickly gaining a reputation as a composer/arranger he was much in demand because of his ability to write in multiple styles. He worked on numerous studio-assigned projects in the 1960s, including *Gidget Goes to Rome* (1963), *None but the Brave* (1965), *How to Steal a Million* (1966), *The Plainsman* (1966), and *Goodbye, Mr. Chips* (1969). In 1972 Williams won his first Academy Award for his adaptation of the score for *Fiddler on the Roof* (1971).

In 1974 he met the young director Steven Spielberg, then twenty-eight years old (Williams was forty-two years old) and one of the great director/composer relationships in movie history was born. Spielberg asked Williams to score his new movie *The Sugarland Express*, which was released later that year.

In the 1970s Williams established himself as the leading composer/arranger for film, working on some of the biggest movies of the decade. Among them were *The Poseidon Adventure* (1972), *Pete 'n' Tillie* (1972), *The Paper Chase* (1973), *Earthquake* (1974), *The Towering Inferno* (1974), *The Eiger Sanction* (1975), *Jaws* (1975) (for which he won his second Academy Award and a Golden Globe), *Star Wars* (1977) (for which he won a third Academy Award, three Grammys, and a second

Golden Globe), *Close Encounters of the Third Kind* (1977) (for which he won two Grammys), and *Superman* (1978). The recording of the soundtrack for *Star Wars* with the London Symphony became the best-selling soundtrack of all time.

Reinvigorating the Orchestral Score for Movies

With his scores of the 1970s, Williams revitalized orchestral movie music, which had increasingly turned away from the orchestral sound in the decade before. Williams is a traditionalist, but in the best sense of the word, coupling fresh ideas with a highly developed sense of craft. Moreover, his collaborations with Spielberg (*Jaws*, *Close Encounters*) and George Lucas (*Star Wars*) helped reestablish the power of a well-conceived musical score to contribute to the success of a movie. His collaborations with Spielberg were so tight that the music was often a primary element and a major influence on how Spielberg shot his films rather than an afterthought.

In 1980 Williams's career added a new branch when he was appointed music director of the Boston Pops Orchestra, succeeding Arthur Fiedler. Williams was a brilliant choice for the Pops, and he expanded the orchestra's repertoire. The orchestra gave him an instrument with which to perform and record, and his rich movie scores became staples of the orchestral pops repertoire. He continued to lead the Pops until 1993, and has guest conducted numerous other symphony orchestras.

Williams's movie career did not slow down throughout the 1980s, during which he produced some of his biggest film scores: *The Empire Strikes Back* (1980), *Raiders of the Lost Ark* (1981), *E.T.: The Extra-Terrestrial* (1982, winning Williams his fourth Academy Award), *Return of the Jedi* (1983), *Indiana Jones and the Temple of Doom* (1984), *The Witches of Eastwick* (1987), *Empire of the Sun* (1987), *The Accidental Tourist* (1988), *Indiana Jones and the Last Crusade* (1989), and *Born on the Fourth of July* (1989).

Movie projects in the 1990s included *Schindler's List* (1993), another Spielberg film, for which Williams won his fifth Academy Award. Other projects included *Stanley and Iris* (1990), *Presumed Innocent* (1990), *Home Alone* (1990), *Hook* (1991), *JFK* (1991), *Far and Away* (1992), *Home Alone 2: Lost in New York* (1992), *Jurassic Park* (1993), *Sabrina* (1995), *Nixon* (1995), *Sleepers* (1996), *Rosewood* (1997), *The Lost World* (1997), *Seven Years in Tibet* (1997), *Amistad* (1997), *Saving Private Ryan* (1998), *Stepmom* (1998), *The Phantom Menace* (1999), *Angela's Ashes* (1999), *The Patriot* (2000), *A.I.* (2001), *Harry Potter and the Sorcerer's Stone* (2001), *Attack of the Clones* (2002), *Minority Report* (2002), and *Harry Potter and the Chamber of Secrets* (2002).

Along with his movie and conducting career, Williams is known for his concert compositions and theme music. He has composed a well-regarded symphony, a cello concerto (1994) premiered by Yo-Yo Ma, and concertos for bassoon, trumpet, flute, violin, clarinet, and tuba. He has composed theme music for NBC News, and themes for the 1984, 1988, and 1996 Summer Olympic Games.

Hollywood has a long tradition of hiring serious composers to produce its music. Williams is a traditional, serious composer who knows how to sell a good tune, has an intimate understanding of his craft, and has the ability to adapt and collaborate in an art form that requires many chefs. He has an old-style romantic ear for melody and works in a harmonic language that is familiar but not hackneyed. He knows how to evoke emotion but avoids being maudlin, and his sense for the grand sweep of an orchestra is in the finest tradition of the golden age of movies. He has been fortunate to build relationships with some of the best directors of his day, directors who understand the power of music in a successful movie.

SELECTIVE DISCOGRAPHY: *By Request: The Best of John Williams and the Boston Pops Orchestra* (Polygram, 1990); *Star Wars Trilogy: The Original Soundtrack Anthology* (Arista, 1993); *John Williams: Greatest Hits, 1969–1999* (Sony, 1999).

WEBSITE: www.johnwilliams.org.

DOUGLAS MCLENNAN

LUCINDA WILLIAMS

Born: Lake Charles, Louisiana, 26 January, 1953

Genre: Country, Blues Rock

Best-selling album since 1990: *Car Wheels on a Gravel Road* (1998)

Hit songs since 1990: "Still I Long for Your Kiss," "Car Wheels on a Gravel Road," "Get Right with God"

Perfectionist, impressionist, and unmistakably southern, Lucinda Williams is a singer/songwriter whose most commercially and critically acclaimed work, *Car Wheels on a Gravel Road* (1998), came after spending two decades in the music business. Williams is known in music circles for being stubbornly principled; she is so painstakingly precise in her approach to the entire process, from the inception of a song to an album's final mixing, that years often go by in between albums. Williams struggled for most of the early part of her career not only to develop her particular voice but also to find a record label that respected her as an individual and not as a marketing tool. *Car Wheels* earned her scores of kudos, ending up on many music publications' year-end lists and winning three Grammy Awards, in dis-

Lucinda Williams [PAUL NATKIN/PHOTO RESERVE]

parate but not totally unrelated categories—Best Country Song, Best Contemporary Folk Album, and Best Female Rock Vocal. Williams is uncompromising and skilled, and writes songs that feel like the rough-hewn but well-written diary of a restless wanderer with a feisty spirit.

A Born Wanderer

Williams was raised throughout the South by Miller Williams, her English literature professor father. They moved from one college town to another, with stops in Mexico City and Santiago, Chile. Her mother, Lucille, a musician, was a great influence as well, though her parents' divorce at age eleven put Lucinda in her father's custody. Early in life she earned an appreciation for the blues and rock, showing a particular affinity for the guitar by age twelve and an enthusiasm for Bob Dylan's *Highway 61 Revisited*. Later she got into blues greats including Robert Johnson. By the time she was twenty-one, she had moved to Austin, Texas, and was part of a scene of singers and songwriters that included Patti Griffin and Lyle Lovett.

After moving to Texas in her early twenties and spending a good deal of time playing her own material and a mix of traditional blues and folk in clubs and bars, she landed a deal with Folkways Records. In 1979 the independent label released her debut record, *Ramblin' on My Mind*. Her career did not really take off until she moved to Los Angeles, California, but she was again stymied by a development deal with CBS Records in the mid-1980s that ended abruptly and with little explanation. Finally, in the late 1980s, after earning the respect of her peers, who helped her gain exposure by letting her sing on their albums, Williams released a couple of albums that landed her a little closer to rock: *Lucinda Williams* (1988) and *Sweet Old World* (1992). The latter includes a cover of a Nick Drake song, illustrating her kinship with beautiful, intricate melodies that are emotionally compelling and distilled to their essence.

From the late 1980s to early 1990s, Williams appeared on tribute albums for Merle Haggard and Victoria Williams, and Mary Chapin Carpenter scored a hit with Williams's song "Passionate Kisses." She got lucky again when "Still I Long for Your Kiss," a song she contributed to the soundtrack of the immensely successful Robert Redford film *The Horse Whisperer* (1997), became a hit, the same year she released her Grammy Award–winning album *Car Wheels on a Gravel Road*.

A Perfectionist at Heart

Both *Sweet Old World* (1993) and *Car Wheels on a Gravel Road* lingered for three years in production before Williams was satisfied; such attention to detail ensured that the end result was nothing short of perfection, which critics were quick to point out after both releases. Her restless, nomadic nature prevails throughout the aptly titled *Car Wheels*, especially on the title track. The refrain simply repeats the name of the song, but the imagery in the verses provides a snapshot of her childhood. Other highlights of the album include "2 Kool 2 Be 4-gotten" an homage to one of her musical heroes, Robert Johnson. On "Can't Let Go," Williams takes the lusty, slide-guitar shuffle penned by Randy Weeks to new heights. Her wrecked, wrought voice sings, "I'm broken down / Like a train wreck / It's over / I know / And I can't let go." Atop a bed of jangly guitars, woeful, wailing slide guitars, and mandolins, Williams's voice dips, wavers, and breaks off at all the right emotional moments, simultaneously conveying innocence and experience. *Car Wheels*, which mixes blues with folk, rock, and country music, features guest appearances by a stellar roster of well-regarded folk-blues musicians, including Emmylou Harris ("Greenville"), Jim Lauderdale ("Lake Charles," "I Lost It"), Buddy Miller, and Steve Earle.

After endless touring, Williams took only a few years before releasing the critically hailed *Essence* (2001). The title track is the emotional centerpiece of the album, which conveys a more subdued side of Williams, although contemplations on religion ("Get Right with God") are present. But *Essence*, critics were quick to point out, did not compare to *Car Wheels*; there are no foot-stomping, kick-up-some-dust rockers because the album's emotional core is far more unadorned and intimate.

In Spring 2003 Williams released the raw, rocking, sultry blues-rock album *World without Tears*, another stunning example of her meticulously detailed lyrics and blistering honesty, especially evident on the midtempo, smoldering tune "Righteously" and the straightforward, Rolling Stones–influenced "Real Live Bleeding Fingers and Broken Guitar Strings." Williams even dabbles with spoken word on "American Dream," and the title track is a thoughtful, hopeful ballad with an eye toward the future.

Williams's signature style is literate narration, which remains a constant on all her albums. From the dusty, blues-rock travelogue of longing, desire, and confusion on *Car Wheels*, to the honest, unadorned structure of *Essence*, to the rock of *World without Tears*, Lucinda Williams displays a unique blend of rock, blues, country, and folk.

SELECTIVE DISCOGRAPHY: *Lucinda Williams* (Rough Trade, 1988); *Sweet Old World* (Chameleon, 1992); *Car Wheels on a Gravel Road* (Mercury, 1998); *Essence* (Lost Highway, 2001); *World without Tears* (Lost Highway, 2003). **Soundtrack:** *The Horse Whisperer: Songs from and Inspired by the Motion Picture* (MCA, 1998).

CARRIE HAVRANEK

ROBBIE WILLIAMS

Born: Robert Peter Williams; Stoke-on-Trent, England, 13 February 1974)

Genre: Rock, Pop

Best-selling album since 1990: *Escapology* (2002)

Hit songs since 1990: "Angels," "Millennium," "Feel"

When Robbie Williams auditioned for the British boy band Take That in 1990, no one imagined that he would later emerge as one of the biggest pop celebrities in British history. Take That, a band equivalent to the 1980s American pop band New Kids on the Block, broke all sales records set by the Beatles. Of the five members in Take That, Williams stood out as the defiant and rebellious boy who could not fail to attract a British media addicted to lads showing off.

In 1995 Williams was reportedly fired from Take That. Despite a large fan following, Williams was not considered a likely candidate for a solo career because of his seemingly dissolute private life and his less-than-stellar vocal abilities. Yet five years later he had become England's most celebrated pop star, with sales of some 20 million albums.

Williams's first attempt with a solo single came in June 1996, when he did a cover of George Michael's "Freedom." This surprisingly good performance and arrangement peaked at number two in the British charts. In 1997 the singles "Old Before I Die," "Lazy Days," and "South of the Border" preceded Williams's first album, *Life thru a Lens*, which was released by Chrysalis. The album is a blend of catchy pop/rock songs and beautifully crafted ballads that are made endearing by Williams's delivery. Throughout the album, there are conscious musical references to other British artists, such as Elton John and the group Oasis. Although it sold slowly in the beginning, the British critics were cautiously optimistic. Eventually the album made it to number one in the U.K. This marked Williams's first success and allowed him to publicly demonstrate his scorn for Take That, who by this time had just broken up.

The main turning point of Robbie Williams's career came with the release of his single "Angels" in December 1997; it was co-written with Guy Chambers, a former member of World Party and Lemon Trees who had emerged during the 1990s as one of the most praised songwriters in the U.K. Williams instantly won over British audiences and was nominated for two Brit Awards for the category of best newcomer and best single for "Old Before I Die." In March 1998 the single "Let Me Entertain You" was released while the song "Angels" was still in the charts. By June 1998 he was playing sold-out concerts, most notably a show at London's Forum that was broadcast on pay-per-view. Following a spate of gigs and a major appearance at the legendary Glastonbury festival, his song "Millennium" was released in the U.K. in September 1998. With a theme borrowed from John Barry's score for the James Bond film "You Only Live Twice," this song became Williams's first solo number one single.

The album *I've Been Expecting You* was released the following month and immediately registered huge sales. It debuted at number one and remained in the top seventy-five for seventy-seven consecutive weeks. November 1998 saw the release of the song "No Regrets," with backing vocals by the Pet Shop Boys' Neil Tennant and Neil Hannon of the Divine Comedy.

By 1999 Williams was a superstar in Britain, with six nominations for the Brit Awards and awards for Best British Male Solo Artist, Best Single (for "Angels"), and Best Video (for "Millennium"). During 1999 he leveraged his celebrity to support several political causes such as the group Jubilee 2000, which sought cancellation of the Third World's $11 billion debt to advanced countries. Later in the year he took part in the Wembley Stadium segment of the NetAid concert that aimed to combat world hunger. During this year his single "Strong" peaked at number four in the charts. In 1999 Williams was runner-up to Elvis Presley for the title of Best Male Artist in a "Music of the Millennium" poll organized by HMV and Channel 4. By November Williams had completed a tour of the United States, where "Angels" was released as a single; in the same month a compilation of highlights from his two U.K. albums, *The Ego Has Landed,* was certified gold in the United States.

During 2000 Williams's success continued to soar as he received a spate of music awards. His first single in 2000, "Rock DJ," debuted at number one, selling almost 200,000 copies in its first week, the highest weekly total for any single in U.K. history. The video of this song was censored by BBC's "Top of the Pops" because it features Williams stripping off his clothes and then, by special effects, his flesh. Not surprisingly, this video won an MTV Video Music Award for best special effects in 2001, the same year the album *Swing While You're Winning* was released.

In 2002 Williams signed the biggest recording deal in British history with EMI for $125 million, only weeks before the release of his album *Escapology*, which became the best-selling album in the world. Finally, after years of struggling to break into the American market, it seemed that he had made it with this album. *Escapology* signals a newfound maturity, featuring songs geared to a more adult public. Songs such as "Feel" and "Love Somebody" are two of the ballads he performs with sincerity and deeply felt passion. The styles on the album are diverse, encompassing gospel, soul, pop, and middle-of-the-road rock. Notwithstanding the media's lurid preoccupation with Robbie Williams's personal life, his public popularity has yet to descend from the stratosphere.

SELECTIVE DISCOGRAPHY: *Life thru a Lens* (Chrysalis, 1997); *Angels* (Chrysalis, 1998); *I've Been Expecting You* (Chrysalis, 1998); *The Ego Has Landed* (Emd/Capitol, 1999); *Sing When You're Winning* (Chrysalis, 2000); *Swing When You're Winning* (Chrysalis, 2000); *Escapology* (Chrysalis, 2002).

BIBLIOGRAPHY: P. Lester, *Robbie Williams: The Illustrated Story* (London, 1998); R.Williams and M. McCrum, *Robbie Williams: Somebody Someday* (London, 2001).

STAN HAWKINS

VANESSA WILLIAMS

Born: Millwood, New York, 18 March 1963
Genre: R&B, Pop

Best-selling album since 1990: *The Comfort Zone* (1991)

Hit songs since 1990: "Save the Best for Last," "Running Back to You"

Few pop singers have triumphed over scandal more successfully than Vanessa Williams. In 1984, when the publication of a nude photo layout resulted in her forced resignation as the first African-American Miss America, few would have predicted that Williams would go on to become one of the most popular recording artists of the 1990s. Blessed with a supple, attractive voice, Williams brought class and elegance to 1990s pop with songs such as "Save the Best for Last." By the end of the decade, she had proven herself a gifted all-around entertainer, finding success on Broadway and in Hollywood movies.

Williams's life was steeped in music from an early age. Both of her parents were music teachers, and as a teenager growing up in a small suburb of New York City she performed in local musical theater on a steady basis. In 1981 she won a scholarship to study theater arts at Syracuse University and, soon after, began entering beauty pageants. In 1984 Williams made history as the first African-American woman to be crowned Miss America. Unfortunately, she abdicated the throne after nude photographs of her were published in *Penthouse* magazine. The lesbian theme of the photos, taken long before she won the pageant, further stirred the controversy. Never lacking confidence, Williams moved past the experience, working with her publicist husband Ramon Hervey to establish a singing career. By 1988 she had signed with Mercury Records' Wing subsidiary and released her first album, *The Right Stuff*. The album contains the hit single "Dreamin'," a mellow song that highlights the creamy contours of her voice.

In 1991 Williams released a follow-up album, *The Comfort Zone*, and became a pop star on the basis of its smash hit, "Save the Best for Last." The song's opening lines were a ubiquitous presence on radio stations worldwide: "Sometimes the snow comes down in June / Sometimes the sun goes round the moon." Fitting in perfectly with the laid-back, adult contemporary style prevalent in early 1990s pop, the song was more restrained than the music of Whitney Houston or Mariah Carey, but it benefited from a catchy melody and heavily orchestrated arrangement. A number one pop hit, "Save the Best for Last" pushed sales of *The Comfort Zone* album over the 2 million mark. The song qualified as plush, if unchallenging, pop music, but elsewhere on the album Williams proved she could handle tougher, up-tempo rhythm-and-blues songs with ease. Of particular note is Williams's version of "Work to Do," a song originally recorded by the R&B group the Isley Brothers in 1972. If lines such as "you

might as well get used to me coming home a little late" sound callous in the original version, Williams transforms them into a proud assertion of female independence.

Williams's intelligence as an artist was solidified on her next release, *The Sweetest Days* (1994). Overall *The Sweetest Days* is a more ambitious, well-rounded album than Williams's previous releases. "Betcha Never," written by the top producer Kenneth "Babyface" Edmonds, is a seductive R&B song that highlights the appealing lower part of Williams's vocal range. With its surging midtempo rhythm and acoustic guitar part, the song is similar in style and spirit to Babyface's contemporaneous work with singer Toni Braxton. "The Way That You Love" is an assertive, smooth dance number, while the jazzy "Ellamental" offers tribute to the legendary vocalist Ella Fitzgerald. One of the album's standout tracks is "Higher Ground," a gentle, inspirational ballad that bears the influence of country and folk music through its plaintive guitar and minimalist production. The lyrics reflect Williams's own personal journey and triumph: "I have walked too long in darkness . . . Blindly clutching fists of diamonds / That I found were only stones." Williams imbues the song with passion and dignity, proving her skills as an interpretive stylist of depth.

By this time Williams was branching into other areas of the entertainment industry with successful results. In 1994 she took over for the Broadway star Chita Rivera in the hit musical *Kiss of the Spider Woman*. Her performance as a glamorous movie star radiated vitality and a genuine command of stagecraft. Williams, drawing on her early musical theater training, adapted to the rigors of performing eight shows a week with no vocal strain. In 1996 she received her first major role in Hollywood, co-starring with Arnold Schwarzenegger in the action film *Eraser*. Although she released another album, *Next*, in 1997, she focused primarily on acting in the years that followed, appearing in the films *Soul Food* (1997), *Dance with Me* (1998), and *Shaft* (2000). In 2002 she returned to Broadway in the musical *Into the Woods*, a performance that inspired *New York Post* critic Clive Barnes to proclaim her "a born Broadway star." By now Williams was divorced from Ramon Hervey and had married Los Angeles Lakers basketball player Rick Fox, with whom she had a child, her fourth, in 2000.

With her classic beauty and ample singing talent, Vanessa Williams proved she had the skill and courage to overcome setbacks that would have discouraged lesser performers. As a recording artist she combined a solid pop sensibility with the intelligence of a vocal stylist, recording pleasant-sounding hits alongside material that was both personal and challenging.

SELECTIVE DISCOGRAPHY: *The Right Stuff* (Wing, 1988); *The Comfort Zone* (Wing, 1991); *The Sweet-*

est Days (Wing, 1995); *Star Bright* (Mercury, 1996); *Next* (Mercury, 1997).

SELECTIVE FILMOGRAPHY: *Eraser* (1996); *Soul Food* (1997); *Dance with Me* (1998); *Shaft* (2000).

DAVID FREELAND

CASSANDRA WILSON

Genre: Jazz

Best-selling album since 1990: *New Moon Daughter* (1996)

Hit songs since 1990: "Tupelo Honey," "Blue Light 'Til Dawn," "The Weight"

A moody vocalist with a stylistic range encompassing jazz, blues, soul, and rock, Cassandra Wilson built a reputation in the 1990s as an astute interpreter of lyrics, a challenging but rewarding artist who informs all she sings with a deep jazz sensibility. Possessing a grainy, textured voice, Wilson wraps her supple chords around songs as disparate as rock singer Van Morrison's "Tupelo Honey" and the self-penned call for slave reparations, "Justice." Relying on subtle shifts of mood, Wilson sings with a slow, burning introspection that rarely gets out of control. The mood she creates on her recordings is so rich that it sometimes seems she is hiding behind it, using sonic luxuriance as a means of avoiding genuine emotion. It would be a mistake, however, to interpret her restraint as a lack of involvement; a close listen to her music reveals an artist of spirit and integrity.

Born and raised in the Mississippi city of Jackson, Wilson spent her childhood soaking up a diverse array of musical influences. At a young age she sang with her mother and grandmother in church, although she was more attracted to the jazz and pop records collected by her father, a skilled bassist and cellist who once performed with R&B great Ray Charles. After receiving a college degree in communications, Wilson moved to New Orleans and settled into a day job while performing music on the side. Relocating to New York in the early 1980s, she started performing with talented young musicians such as saxophonist Steve Coleman. Although Wilson's late 1980s recordings for the small JMT label brought her critical praise, it was not until her move to Blue Note Records in 1993 that she received popular attention.

Critics hailed Wilson's first album for Blue Note, *Blue Light 'Til Dawn* (1993), as an entirely new kind of jazz record, one equally influenced by pop, blues, folk, and clas-

Cassandra Wilson [PAT MOLNAR/BLUE NOTE RECORDS 2001]

sic jazz styles. With its bold covers of songs such as soul singer Ann Peebles's "I Can't Stand the Rain," the album appeals to mainstream listeners not accustomed to buying a jazz recording. What critics and fans found most arresting, however, was the album's atmospheric sound, created through the use of gentle percussion, acoustic guitar, and unusual devices such as the imitation of rustling grass. Mysterious and evocative, the album conjures a magical universe that Wilson's warm, brocaded voice inhabits with a command of mood. On the title track, featuring complex key changes led by a keening steel guitar, Wilson sings with an eerie otherworldliness, sounding like a woman summoning supernatural powers. The spectral low tones Wilson employs on "Tell Me You'll Wait for Me" unmask the warmth and passion hidden beneath her carefully assembled, quiet veneer.

Wilson released a similar-sounding album, *New Moon Daughter,* in 1996 and gained even greater attention for her highly personal versions of pop songs such as "Last Train to Clarksville," a 1960s hit by the Monkees. Despite her interest in pop Wilson does not neglect more traditional musical forms; on her passionate version of blues performer Son House's "Death Letter" she offers glimpses of the fire raging beneath her cool facade. By the late 1990s Wilson was widely acclaimed as a master artist, and in 2001 she was named "America's best singer" by *Time* magazine. Despite Wilson's renown, her sedate vocal style had its detractors. In 2002 the *New York Times* criticized her voice as lacking emotional depth: "Because it's more sumptuous than a voice has any right to be, it wavers perilously between seductiveness and self-parody."

Still, the passion and idiosyncrasy with which Wilson pursued her recording projects seemed to belie such an analysis. Refusing to follow an easy commercial path, Wilson in 1999 released an intelligent tribute to legendary jazz trumpeter Miles Davis, and in 2001 traveled to the Mississippi Delta, the place of her birth and an area steeped in musical history, to record an album of blues-inspired music. The result, *Belly of the Sun* (2002), features the talents of great but neglected Mississippi musicians such as octogenarian pianist "Boogaloo" Ames. Recording in an old train station, Wilson and her band achieve a tight, cohesive sound, equal parts funk and smoothness. Her version of the Band's "The Weight" sounds laden with the soul-weariness of a long journey, while the stirring "Justice" imparts a social awareness rarely encountered in current pop and jazz music.

Through her talent and courageous musical exploration, Cassandra Wilson has fashioned one of the most successful careers in contemporary jazz. While her tastes are markedly eclectic, Wilson informs all of her material with a tone of reverence and hushed passion. Challenging musical boundaries, she has redefined the role of the jazz vocalist in the twenty-first century.

SELECTIVE DISCOGRAPHY: *Blue Light 'Til Dawn* (Blue Note, 1993); *New Moon Daughter* (Blue Note, 1996); *Traveling Miles* (Blue Note, 1999); *Belly of the Sun* (Blue Note, 2002).

WEBSITE: www.cassandrawilson.com.

DAVID FREELAND

GEORGE WINSTON

Born: Hart, Michigan, 1949

Genre: New Age

Best-selling album since 1990: *Summer* (1991)

George Winston caught the ears of music listeners in the early 1980s with his gripping, impressionistic piano instrumentals; by the turn of the century he had emerged as a major star in the field of New Age music. Although he spent some formative time in Florida and Mississippi, most of his youth was spent on the sparsely populated plains of eastern Montana. The distinct, sometimes harsh seasonal changes and the open landscape of Montana have served as musical inspirations for Winston throughout his career.

Winston's interest in creating music began after high school in 1967. Inspired by many types of music and a diverse list of artists such as the stride pianist Thomas "Fats" Waller, Ray Charles, Booker T and the MGs, the Ventures, and the legendary rock group the Doors, Winston started playing the organ and electric piano. In 1971, influenced further by Waller's stride piano style, he took up the acoustic piano. Winston recorded his first album, *Ballads and Blues* (1972), a year later. In the years that followed, Winston continued developing a piano style fashioned from a combination of stride piano, R&B, and classics that he describes as "rural folk-piano." His music features aching melodies that paint images and auras inspired by the natural vistas of Montana. His album *October* (1980) was unusually successful for this music genre and led to the release of *December* (1982). That album sold more than 4 million copies and helped to solidify Winston's reputation as a commercial composer of sweeping piano mood works.

After the release of his next album, *Winter into Spring* (1982), also a brisk seller, Winston took some time off from recording solo albums to take other musical journeys. One of those was contributing, along with a roster of other Windham Hill artists such as Mark O'Connor and David Grisman, to Charles Gross's gorgeous soundtrack for the film *Country* (1984). Winston played four solo piano pieces in addition to ensemble work on the soundtrack, which evoked an Iowa farm setting. He also accompanied Meryl Streep's narration in a children's video, *The Velveteen Rabbit*, in 1984. Winston went on to play piano, guitar, and harmonica for three more children's projects: *This Is America, Charlie Brown: The Birth of the Constitution* (1988), *Sadako and the Paper Cranes* (1995), and *The Pumpkin Circle* (1997).

Winston returned in 1991 to release another piano solo album, *Summer* (1991), which immediately sold more than 1 million copies. Like the previous seasonal releases, each song's title—"Garden," "Fragrant Fields," "Early Morning Range," and "Goodbye Montana"—hints at the subject while the impressionistic melody lets the listener's imagination fill in the rest of the ambience. Winston is not only a fine composer but also a masterful interpreter of others' music, and *Summer* contains his rendering of songs by Randy Newman ("Living without You"), Carmine Coppola ("The Black Stallion"), and Pete Seeger ("Living in the Country").

Winston realized a musical dream when he released *Linus and Lucy: The Music of Vince Guaraldi* (1996). An ardent fan of the famed jazz pianist—who had created the music for the television specials based on Charles Schultz's *Peanuts* characters—Winston was eager to lend his interpretations to Guaraldi's music. The result was an archive of familiar *Peanuts* jingles mixed in with some of Guaraldi's best-known songs such as "Cast Your Fate to the Wind" and "Treat Street."

Winston also paid tribute to the 1960s rock group the Doors by adding his solo piano interpretations to their music in his album *Night Divides the Day: The Music of the Doors* (2002). He takes an ethereal path through "Riders on the Storm," honky-tonks "Love Me Two Times," and lets his nine-foot concert Steinway weave in and out of the melody on "Light My Fire."

In between those two projects Winston sandwiched a return to contemporary instrumental music and nature with *Plains* (1999). This expressive musical journey across the flatlands of eastern Montana contains Sarah McLachlan's "Angel" and Chet Atkins's "Waltz for the Lonely" along with Winston's own compositions such as "Cloudburst," "The Swan," and "Plains (Eastern Montana Blues)." He also includes songs that reveal his infatuation with the beauty of Hawaii, such as "No Ke Ano Ahi Ahi" and other Hawaiian folk songs. Since 1974 a Hawaiian music form called slack guitar has fascinated Winston. A finger-picking style of various tunings played by Hawaiian cowboys in the 1830s, slack guitar preceded the steel guitar by nearly sixty years. Winston's private recording label, Dancing Cat Records, has been dedicated to recording the current slack guitar artists and has released thirty-two albums, with many more to follow. Winston has also mastered this playing style, and he performs it in concert and on some of his recordings.

The events of September 11, 2001, prompted Winston to record a memorial album of six songs called *Remembrance: A Memorial Benefit* (2001). He dedicated all profits from this recording to assist families affected by the loss of loved ones from the tragedy. The touching album features not only his piano work but also several guitar solos and a poignant bagpipe-style harmonica performance.

Winston continues to tour, typically performing more than 100 dates per year in the United States, Europe, and Asia. His piano instrumentals have redefined New Age music. In the forefront of a music genre populated largely by obscure artists, George Winston remains a giant commercial success.

SELECTIVE DISCOGRAPHY: *Ballads and Blues* (Dancing Cat, 1972); *Autumn* (Windham Hill, 1980); *Winter into Spring* (Windham Hill, 1982); *December* (Windham Hill, 1982); *Summer* (Windham Hill, 1991); *Forest* (Windham Hill, 1994); *Linus and Lucy: The Music of Vince Guaraldi* (Windham Hill, 1996); *Plains* (Windham Hill, 1999); *Remembrance: A Memorial Benefit* (Windham Hill, 2001); *Night Divides the Day: The Music of the Doors* (Windham Hill, 2002).

DONALD LOWE

LEE ANN WOMACK

Born: Jacksonville, Texas, 19 August 1966

Genre: Country, Pop

Best-selling album since 1990: *I Hope You Dance* (2000)

Hit songs since 1990: "I Hope You Dance," "I'll Think of a Reason Later"

Possessing a bell-clear soprano voice that recalls legendary country/pop singer Dolly Parton, Lee Ann Womack brought a refreshing air of ingenuousness to country music in the 1990s. Like many modern country artists, Womack is comfortable performing in a wide range of styles, from tough 1950s-styled honky-tonk to sophisticated 1970s "countrypolitan." Moving from rocking up-tempo numbers to string-laden love ballads, often within the course of the same album, Womack shows deep respect for tradition while remaining mindful of the slick, polished prerequisites of contemporary country. Although her hit "career song" of 2000, "I Hope You Dance," threatens to define her in the same way that country star Tammy Wynette was forever linked with the 1968 hit, "Stand By Your Man," Womack possesses the talent and ingenuity to overcome this limitation. Her post-2000 work, however, has pointed to artistic confusion stemming from the pressures of following up such a massive hit.

Womack spent her early years in Jacksonville, Texas, where her disc jockey father exposed her to a broad range of country music. As a child she would visit her father in his studio, often helping him choose which records to play. Enrolling in South Plains Junior College in Levelland, Texas, she studied country and bluegrass music, in one of the first academic programs of its kind. Like fellow 1990s artist Brad Paisley, Womack transferred to Belmont University, located in the country music hub of Nashville, Tennessee. In Nashville, she interned at MCA Records, one of the country's leading labels, and, by 1995, began penning songs for stars such as Bill Anderson. Eventually, she was signed by MCA's Decca imprint and in 1997 released her self-titled debut album. From the opening track, the fiddle-soaked heartache ballad, "Never Again, Again," Womack impresses with her mature phrasing and appealing resemblance to Parton. Elsewhere on the album, such as on the rock-influenced "A Man with 18 Wheels," Womack displays the ability to shift toward tougher material without losing her unique vocal identity.

Womack's follow-up album, *Some Things I Know* (1998), evinces an even deeper appreciation for country's timeless reliance on emotion and heartache. While not released as a single, "The Man Who Made My Mama

"I Hope You Dance"

In 1999 Nashville songwriter Tia Sillers was recovering from a messy divorce, attempting to sort out her life by vacationing on a Florida beach. "As I was leaving the beach," she told *Songwriter Universe* magazine, "I remember thinking that things weren't really so bad . . . that's when I came up with the line, 'I hope you still feel small when you stand beside the ocean.'" The line became a centerpiece of the song, "I Hope You Dance," co-written with songwriter Mark Sanders. After completing a demo version, Sillers and Sanders presented the song to Mark Wright, producer for rising country star Lee Ann Womack. Hearing its inspirational lyrics, written as a message of self-respect from parent to child, Womack decided to record the song, thinking of her two young children. When released in 2000, "I Hope You Dance" proved extremely influential, enhancing country's mainstream profile by crossing over to the pop charts and earning a Grammy Award for Best Country Song. While lyrics such as, "I hope you never fear those mountains in the distance," suggest a reliance on easy platitudes, the song is balanced by country group Sons of the Desert, whose backup chorus of "who wants to look back on their years and wonder where those years have gone" invests the song with a humbling awareness of life's disappointments. The recording's most impressive element, however, is Womack herself, who conveys the perfect combination of strength and tenderness.

Cry," is a highlight of Womack's career, a personal and moving account of an absentee father who suddenly reappears: "All I know about you is how to live without you." Singing against an arrangement that surges with gushing strings and cooing vocal choruses, Womack has rarely sounded so committed to the "countrypolitan" style of 1970s country, yet her self-assured perspective remains wholly contemporary. Despite the strengths of *Some Things I Know*, Womack's biggest commercial success lay just around the corner, with the 2000 release of *I Hope You Dance*.

Now a country and pop star, Womack returned in 2002 with *Something Worth Leaving Behind*. Capitalizing on the sexy image of hit country artists such as Shania Twain, the album cover features Womack dressed in a provocative outfit with teased blonde hair. The music inside sounds just as heavily styled, with scattershot production ranging from the breezy pop of "When You Gonna Run to Me" to the hard rock–edged "I Need You." Although the latter song, sparked by the daring line, "I need something like morphine, only better," finds Womack singing with new force in the manner of rock singer Sheryl Crow, critics observe that the album as a whole feels disjointed, too calculated to generate much warmth.

Womack was one of the most likable personalities to emerge in 1990s country music. Beyond her lilting voice, Womack's appeal lies in her ability to pull together a range of past country styles, treating each with respect and sensitivity. Although this approach failed in the wake of her big hit, "I Hope You Dance," Womack clearly possesses the talent to maintain her rank as a singer of intelligence and passion.

SELECTIVE DISCOGRAPHY: *Lee Ann Womack* (Decca Nashville, 1997); *Some Things I Know* (Decca Nashville, 1998); *I Hope You Dance* (MCA Nashville, 2000); *Something Worth Leaving Behind* (MCA Nashville, 2002); *The Season for Romance* (MCA Nashville, 2002).

WEBSITE: www.leeannwomack.com.

DAVID FREELAND

STEVIE WONDER

Born: Steveland Hardaway Judkins, Saginaw, Michigan, 13 May 1950
Genre: R&B, Pop
Best-selling album since 1990: *Jungle Fever* (1991)
Hit songs since 1990: "Gotta Have You," "These Three Words," "Fun Day"

Although the music of Stevie Wonder spans five decades and many different styles, it is unified by his far-reaching artistic vision. Wonder helped to pioneer the role of the visionary pop musician who oversees each aspect of the recording process, from songwriting to instrumentation to final production. His slightly nasal vocal style, with its sudden flights into his upper register, has influenced scores of younger rhythm-and-blues performers, from Michael Jackson to Usher. With each passing decade Wonder has continued experimenting, keeping his sound fresh while staying true to his roots.

Born in Saginaw, Michigan, and raised in the music-rich city of Detroit, Wonder has been blind since birth, the result of an accident in his incubator as a newborn. Encouraged by his doting mother Lula, Wonder was a musical prodigy by the age of nine, proficient on piano, drums, and harmonica. At age twelve he had his first rhythm-and-blues hit on Detroit-based Motown Records, "Fingertips" (1963), a driving song that highlights his harmonica playing. Wonder went on to have many hits on Motown's Tamla subsidiary as the 1960s progressed, recording in a wide array of styles, from tough rhythm and blues to sophisticated pop ballads arranged with strings.

In the 1970s Wonder took stronger control of his music and career, releasing a series of innovative, deeply personal albums that touched on themes of racism, inner-city despair, and spirituality. *Talking Book* (1972) and *Innervisions* (1973) are classics of this period, albums in which Wonder made pioneering strides with a new musical instrument, the synthesizer. For all his concern with social issues, Wonder also created some of the funkiest grooves of the 1970s on hits such as "Superstition" and "Boogie On, Reggae Woman." After *Hotter Than July* (1980), a joyous album featuring the celebratory single, "Master Blaster (Jammin')," Wonder's output grew less artistically consistent. Singles like "Part-Time Lover" (1985), although radio-friendly, were too reliant on simple melodic hooks to be artistically satisfying.

Wonder regained solid artistic footing with *Jungle Fever* (1991), a soundtrack album for a film by director Spike Lee about interracial dating. The sweet-sounding ballad "These Three Words" stressed the importance of human relationships. On lines such as "the ones you say you cherish every day / can instantly be taken away," Wonder evinces an awareness of mortality that, in its seriousness of purpose, distinguishes it from the simpler, lighthearted work of 1980s and 1990s balladeers such as Lionel Richie. The easygoing, jazzy rhythm of "Fun Day" points to one of Wonder's major artistic strengths: assimilating other musical genres—classical, jazz, gospel—into his work. Similarly, on the sophisticated ballad "Make Sure You're Sure," Wonder improvises with his vocal phrasing in the manner of a jazz singer. The haunting string arrangement only adds to the song's classy appeal. "Queen of the Black," in which Wonder belts out the lyrics at the top of his range, spotlights his undiminished vocal prowess. On the biting title track, "Jungle Fever," he takes on the prejudice faced by an interracial couple: "she can't love me, I can't love her / Cause they say we're the wrong color."

Wonder's only other studio album of the 1990s, *Conversation Peace* (1995), was another satisfying work, again informed by his encompassing vision. Over the decades Wonder has successfully adapted to changing styles in rhythm and blues music, and on *Conversation Peace* he

incorporates jumpy hip-hop rhythms without any sign of artistic strain. The album's finest moment, "Cold Chill," ranks with the most creative music of Wonder's career. Featuring a choppy female chorus arranged to sound like twittering birds, "Cold Chill" is more than a funky hip-hop track, it is an aural experience in which sound amplifies the imagery of the lyrics: "there's a cold chill on a summer night." In his review of the album, the rock critic Robert Christgau reflected upon Wonder's ability to construct total soundscapes within his songs: "Overlaying track after track in his studio, he's a font of melody, a wellspring of rhythm, a major modern composer."

Speaking to *Grammy* magazine in 1997, Wonder discussed the artistic process behind his work: "You just have to go through different experiences. . . . When I hear about a plane crash I'm there in the plane. . . . I'm imagining how it felt going down, I'm imagining what was going through the mind, I'm imagining all the different tears." Wonder's capacity for human empathy brings a social dimension to his songs, several of which have been used as vehicles for change. His 1980 recording, "Happy Birthday," was a tribute to legendary civil rights leader Martin Luther King Jr.; Wonder's lobbying helped lead to the official recognition of King's birthday as a national holiday. On the title track to *Conversation Peace*, Wonder again advocates social awareness and activism: "We shouldn't act as if we don't hear nor see / Like the holocaust of 6 million Jews and / A hundred and fifty million blacks during slavery." During the 1980s and 1990s Wonder lent his support to causes including the antiapartheid struggle, AIDS awareness, handgun control, and the fight against world hunger. In 1999 he received the prestigious Kennedy Center Honors, cementing his reputation as an American institution.

Stevie Wonder's influence can be felt in the work of younger artists such as Prince and Maxwell, performers who took Wonder's lead and exerted artistic control over the production of their music. He was one of the first artists to expand the traditional love-song themes of rhythm and blues to include social commentary and personal reflection, singing of love and justice in his clear, distinctively high-pitched voice. In the 1990s he dug deeper into the grooves he had created in the seventies, inserting contemporary elements into his music without losing its relevance or integrity.

SELECTIVE DISCOGRAPHY: *The Jazz Soul of Little Stevie* (Tamla, 1962); *I Was Made to Love Her* (Tamla, 1967); *Music of My Mind* (Tamla, 1972); *Talking Book* (Tamla, 1972); *Innervisions* (Tamla, 1973); *Songs in the Key of Life* (Tamla, 1976); *Hotter Than July* (Tamla, 1980); *Jungle Fever* (Motown, 1991); *Conversation Peace* (Motown, 1995).

WEBSITE: www.stevie-wonder.com.

DAVID FREELAND

WORLD PARTY

Formed: 1986, London, England

Members: Karl Wallinger, guitar, piano, vocals (born Prestatyn, Wales, 19 October 1957). Former members: Chris Sharrock, drums (born 1965); John Turnbull, guitar (born Newcastle-upon-Tyne, England, 27 August 1950); Dave Catlin-Birch, guitar, bass; Jeff Trott, guitar (born San Francisco, California); Chris Whitten, drums; Martyn Swain, bass.

Genre: Rock

Best-selling album since 1990: *Goodbye Jumbo* (1990)

Hit songs since 1990: "Way Down Now," "Put the Message in the Box"

Even when sporting a full complement of musicians, World Party was essentially a one-man band; at its center was Karl Wallinger, whose obsession with 1960s pop music engendered a few minor, retro-influenced hits in the early 1990s.

As a youngster growing up in Wales during the 1960s, Wallinger developed an affinity for the music of the Beatles, the Turtles, and the Box Tops, as well as for the American sound of Motown. In 1976 Wallinger made his musical debut with a band called Quasimodo, which later evolved into the Alarm. In 1984, after a period in London during which he played in a funk band and served as musical director for theater productions, Wallinger joined the Waterboys, a big-sounding U.K. rock outfit. After two critically acclaimed albums with the Waterboys, Wallinger, seeking more creative freedom, left the band to form World Party. World Party was, in fact, a Wallinger solo project; on World Party's 1987 debut, *Private Revolution*, Wallinger produced, sang, and played every instrument. The album draws heavily on Wallinger's pop influences and includes a cover of Bob Dylan's "All I Really Want to Do." The track "Ship of Fools" became a Top 40 hit in the United States.

Three years later, Wallinger expanded the World Party lineup and released *Goodbye Jumbo*, which features more of a full-band sound and enjoyed even more radio success. The lead single, "Way Down Now," a minor alternative-radio hit, showcases the expanded band's muscle; as Martyn Swain's bass and Chris Whitten's drums propel the chugging groove, Wallinger conjures up a 1960s spirit with the trippy catch phrase "I'm way down now." "Way Down Now" features an overt musical nod to 1960s pop-rock, with the end chorus of "ooh-oohs" bearing remarkable similarity to those from the Rolling Stones' classic "Sympathy for the Devil." The second single, "Put the Message in the Box," also harked back to 1960s-era pop, with its light, breezy feel as well as its simple, hippie-style message: "Put the message in the box / Put the box into the car / Drive the car around the world / Until you get heard." The poppy vibe of *Goodbye Jumbo* belies the ominous tone of Wallinger's lyrics, which frequently deal with global issues such as environmental abuse.

Wallinger continued to record sporadically with various musicians as World Party throughout the 1990s while also serving as musical director for the 1994 film *Reality Bites*. World Party's later albums did not yield any hits for the band, but the British sensation Robbie Williams was successful with a cover of "She's the One" from World Party's 1997 album *Egyptology*.

World Party never enjoyed mainstream appeal, but, with enduring songs such as "Way Down Now" and "Message in the Box," Wallinger's band did contribute to the preservation of 1960s pop-rock traditions within contemporary music.

SELECTIVE DISCOGRAPHY: *Private Revolution* (Papillon, 1987); *Goodbye Jumbo* (Papillon, 1990); *Bang!* (Papillon, 1993); *Egyptology* (Papillon, 1997); *Dumbing Up* (Papillon, 2000).

SCOTT TRIBBLE

WU-TANG CLAN

Formed: 1992, New York, New York

Members: GZA/Genius, vocals (Gary Grice); Ghostface Killah, vocals (Dennis Coles; born 9 May 1970); Inspectah Deck, vocals (Jason Hunter); Method Man, vocals (Clifford Smith; born 1 April 1971); Ol' Dirty Bastard, vocals (Russell Jones; born Brooklyn, New York, 9 May 1970); Raekwon, vocals (Corey Woods; born 12 January 1968); RZA/Prince Rakeem, vocals, producer (Robert Diggs; born 5 July 1969).

Genre: Hip-Hop

Hit songs since 1990: "Protect Ya Neck," "C.R.E.A.M."

Hip-hop had seen large confederations of artists prior to the Wu-Tang Clan, most famously the Native Tongues Family, which included the Jungle Brothers, De La Soul, and A Tribe Called Quest, as well as the Juice Crew, assembled by producer Marley Marl and including Biz Markie, Big Daddy Kane, and Kool G Rap. However, the talent-stocked Wu-Tang Clan were unlike any alliance that came before them, able to work as effectively en masse as they were on any individual level. Both as a larger unit and as solo artists, the Clan produced more commercially and critically acclaimed albums in the 1990s than any other comparable group.

The Clan's two main leaders—producer RZA and rapper Genius, also known as GZA—were both recording artists prior to the formation of Wu-Tang Clan. The Genius previously had a quiet career on the Cold Chillin' label, boasting one modest hit in 1990 with "Pass the Bone." The RZA was previously known as Prince Raheem and had been signed to Tommy Boy. From there, these two collected talent from around New York, especially the pair's home neighborhood of Staten Island. Given the size of the clan and the differing contributions of its members, it is difficult to delineate exactly who was in the group but the main team included Raekwon, Ghostface Killah, Method Man, Inspectah Deck, and Ol' Dirty Bastard, all of whom would go on, in unprecedented fashion, to release solo albums.

The Wu-Tang Clan's debut, *Enter the Wu-Tang (36 Chambers)* (1993), is largely a group affair. Only Method Man's self-titled song gives exclusive attention to any one member. On the album's other songs, including their first single, "Protect Ya Neck," rhyme duties are split between different configurations of Clan rappers, all of whom have their particular styles and strengths but overall seem equally matched in ability. Their chemistry as a group is explicit on songs like "7th Chamber" and "Can in Da Front," where Wu-Tang Clan builds a lyrical phalanx as each member inspires the performance of the other.

The Wu-Tang sound—derived from their lyrical styles as well as RZA's moody, grimy production—was rough, dark, and stark, a notable contrast to the lustrous sound of Dr. Dre's "G Funk" style, Teddy Riley's pop-influenced New Jack Swing, and the jazzy aesthetics of A Tribe Called Quest. They mirrored this ruggedness in their rhymes with the forcefulness of their delivery and the street perspective of their writing. Though many of the songs on *Enter the Wu-Tang (36 Chambers)* are built around braggadocio,

songs like "C.R.E.A.M." and "Can It Be All So Simple?" are inspired by the realities of life within underclass projects and on urban street corners. These deromanticized perspectives on death, crime, and violence only enhanced the group's stature for rap fans looking for grittier reality-based narratives and attitudes.

Following *Enter the Wu-Tang (36 Chambers)*, many of the Clan members worked on their own solo albums, including the GZA, Method Man, Ol' Dirty Bastard, and Raekwon. The Clan reassembled to release a double-album, *Wu-Tang Forever* (1997), whose immense, twenty-plus song length spoke as much to the group's ego as to their abilities. Though it has some impressive offerings, especially "Triumph," an informal sequel to "Protect Ya Neck," the album's sheer length allows for none of the efficiency of *Enter the Wu-Tang (36 Chambers)*. Wu-Tang Clan once again waited several years to release their next group album, *The W* (2000), though they quickly followed with *Iron Flag* (2001) a year later. Both albums have their share of strong material, but within the three years between *Wu-Tang Forever* and *The W*, hip-hop had undergone another sea change toward a more polished, pop sound (largely inspired by Sean "Puffy" Combs) that had made their gritty aesthetic less appealing. Though they seemed invincible in the mid-1990s, by the beginning of the new decade, the reign of the Clan seemed over though individual members such as Method Man and Ghostface Killah continued to thrive.

SELECTIVE DISCOGRAPHY: *Enter the Wu-Tang (36 Chambers)* (Loud/RCA, 1993).

OLIVER WANG

X | X
      x

XSCAPE

Formed: 1990, College Park, Georgia; Disbanded 1998

Members: Kandi Burruss (born Atlanta, Georgia, 17 May 1976); Tameka Cottle (born Atlanta, Georgia, 14 July 1975); LaTocha Scott (born Atlanta, Georgia, 2 October 1973); Tamika Scott (born 19 November 1974).

Genre: R&B

Best-selling album since 1990: *Hummin' Comin' at 'Cha* (1993)

Hit songs since 1990: "Just Kickin' It," "Understanding," "Who Can I Run To?"

A female vocal group whose tight, aggressive harmonies pointed to the influence of gospel music, Xscape was a consistent presence on R&B charts of the 1990s, exploring sexuality while avoiding the more explicit stance of contemporaneous groups such as TLC. Like En Vogue and, later, Destiny's Child, Xscape was part of a wave of 1990s groups whose records embodied female confidence and assurance. On songs such as "Just Kickin' It" and "My Little Secret," the group projected a relaxed, if unsentimental, stance on the dynamics of male-female relationships. Although the group's chart success continued through its third album in 1998, Xscape decided to unofficially disband that year, giving each member time to work on solo projects.

Xscape formed through the influence of sisters LaTocha "Juicy" and Tamika "Meatball" Scott, whose father, the Rev. Randolf Scott, groomed them as profes-

sional gospel singers from an early age. Attending Tri-City High School in the Atlanta suburb of College Park, Georgia, the sisters joined forces with classmates Kandi Burruss and Tameka "Tiny" Cottle and began performing together as a quartet. Xscape's big break occurred in 1991, after performing at a birthday party for young R&B producer Jermaine Dupri. Dupri quickly signed the group to his So So Def label, overseeing production duties on its first album, *Hummin' Comin' at 'Cha* (1993). A sturdy collection of tough, hip-hop-inspired beats embellished by the women's gospel-infused vocals, the album scored high on the R&B charts on the basis of the seductive hit, "Just Kickin' It." While "Just Kickin' It" helped establish Xscape's hard-edged persona, the group revealed an appealing softer side on the album's second hit, "Understanding." A gentle ballad built around a slow beat and gospel-tinged organ, "Understanding" finds the singers harmonizing and trading lead vocals with an assured sense of collaboration.

In 1995 the group released *Off the Hook,* a follow-up album that bears a distinct stylistic resemblance to its predecessor. While "Feels So Good" recalls the seductive groove of "Just Kickin' It," "Who Can I Run To?" is a slick ballad energized by the women's smooth, forceful vocals. The group's third album, *Traces of My Lipstick* (1998), maintains its successful R&B formula on the hit "My Little Secret," while incorporating a lush pop feel with ballads such as "The Arms of the One Who Loves You." Penned by top 1990s songwriter Dianne Warren, the latter song had rich orchestration and a distinctive melody that helped give the group its last R&B and pop hit. Riding the crest of its popularity, Xscape dissolved at the end of 1998, its members going on to pursue various solo projects. Burruss became one of the most successful R&B songwriters of the late 1990s and early 2000s, penning assertive hits such as "No Scrubs" for TLC, while Tamika Scott, for many years an ordained minister, recorded her first gospel album.

Xscape brought an appealing combination of seductiveness and sass to 1990s R&B. The group's strong gospel background lent its vocals an impassioned feel, while the ongoing influence of producer Jermaine Dupri ensured a steady, engaging groove on three highly successful albums.

SELECTIVE DISCOGRAPHY: *Hummin' Comin' at 'Cha* (So So Def/Columbia, 1993); *Off the Hook* (So So Def/Columbia, 1995); *Traces of My Lipstick* (So So Def/Columbia, 1998).

DAVID FREELAND

XTC

Formed: 1976, Swindon, Wiltshire, England

Members: Colin Moulding, bass, vocals (born Swindon, Wiltshire, England, 17 August 1955); Andy Partridge, vocals and guitar (born Swindon, Wiltshire, England, 11 November 1953). Former members: Barry Andrews, keyboards (born West Norwood, London, England, 12 September 1956); Terry Chambers, drums (born Swindon, Wiltshire, England, 16 July 1955); David Gregory, guitar, keyboards (born Swindon, Wiltshire, England, 21 September 1952).

Genre: Rock

Best-selling album since 1990: *English Settlement* (1982)

Hit songs since 1990: "Mayor of Simpleton," "Ballad of Peter Pumpkinhead," "I'm the Man Who Murdered Love"

The quirky and idiosyncratic critics' darling XTC is a band that owes much of its inspiration to fellow Brits, the Beatles, and the 1960s American sensation the Beach Boys. Combine a heavy dose of irony, political skepticism, and the band's own uniquely British humor and you have the appeal of XTC. Intellectual without being too heady and boring, playful without resorting to inane or goofy tactics, XTC is a quintessentially British pop band that found itself recording several unusual albums through the 1990s, most notably the two-volume set, *Apple Venus* (1999).

Andy Partridge started off in 1972 as Star Park and added Colin Moulding, Terry Chambers, and Dave Cartner to become Helium Kidz. This line-up was short-lived. Cartner dropped out and keyboardist Johnny Perkins passed through. Shortly after XTC signed to Virgin Records, keyboardist Barry Andrews joined them. In many ways XTC is an atypical rock band, from its intellectual leanings, to its social reticence, to the high and, at times, nasal vocals of Partridge. Their brand of high-mindedness and sharply drawn observation is generally best received in their native country. The melodic single "Senses Working Over Time," from *English Settlement* (1981), scored them a Top 5 hit in England in 1981. XTC did not debut an album in the United States until *Drums and Wires* (1979), after making a successful start of their career in the United Kingdom.

Shortly into their career, XTC discovered how ill-suited they were for the trappings of the music business when Partridge suffered an onstage collapse in the early 1980s. Because of this experience, Partridge declared that XTC would only be a studio band and would never perform live again, much to the chagrin of fans.

After catching the attention of British radio with "Senses Working Over Time," XTC released *Skylarking* (1986). A nearly epic collection of quirky story-songs that seamlessly flow from track to track a la the Beatles' album *Abbey Road*, *Skylarking* is a delightful listen from start to finish. The logical transition moves the listener from the imaginative "Ballet for a Rainy Day" to the chamber pop of the sad love song "1000 Umbrellas" to the appropriately sunny "Season Cycle." It is a tapestry of carefully orchestrated pop songs, produced by 1970s progressive rocker Todd Rundgren. The album also features the spiritually inquiring "Dear God," which begins innocently enough and climaxes in an angry, wordy fury. It is one of the band's best-known songs.

Although *Skylarking* did not exactly tear up the charts, it did please critics and diehard fans. With the somewhat psychedelic and sprawling *Oranges and Lemons* (1989) the band made more of an impression on American listeners. The album spawned a hit with the witty, self-deprecating "Mayor of Simpleton," which hit number fifteen on *Billboard's* Mainstream Rock Tracks. It also fared well in England. Their next release, *Nonsuch* (1992), succeeds where *Oranges and Lemons* fails. It is a cohesive paean to both the Beach Boys' album *Pet Sounds* and the Beatles' *Revolver* in its intricacies, guitar work, and lush sound.

After a seven-year absence, marked by music business woes and Moulding and Partridge declaring a "strike" against their former label, the band, consisting at this point of only the pair, scored a deal with TVT Records. They headed to the studio, and by the late 1990s they had released two sophisticated albums, the orchestral-pop *Apple Venus* (1999) and *Wasp Star* (*Apple Venus, Volume Two*) (2000), which together serve as a two-volume testament to their pop prowess. The seamless quality of *Skylarking* is in full-force on these albums but it is more beautifully and dramatically realized with lyrics that are expansive in their scope and reach.

Apple Venus starts off with the rich, symphonic syncopation of "River of Orchids," and slips into the galloping, whimsical ode "I'd Like That," in which Partridge sings "I'd laugh so much my face would crack in two / And you could fix it with your kissing glue." The album continues at a varying, though never too dizzying pace. *Wasp Star* features a catchy, self-deprecating, smart admission in "I'm the Man Who Murdered Love." The pair of albums, released a couple of years apart, were critically hailed and landed on many Top 10 lists. Because the sessions that created these two albums were so productive for the band, they released outtakes and demos from *Apple Venus* on *Homespun* later in 1999.

SELECTIVE DISCOGRAPHY: *English Settlement* (Virgin, 1982); *Skylarking* (Virgin, 1986); *Oranges and Lemons* (Geffen, 1989); *Nonsuch* (Geffen, 1992); *Apple Venus* (TVT, 1999); *Wasp Star (Apple Venus, Volume 2)* (TVT Records, 2000).

BIBLIOGRAPHY: N. Farmer, *XTC: Song Stories: The Exclusive Authorized Story Behind the Music* (New York, 1998).

CARRIE HAVRANEK

Y

YANNI

Born: Yanni Chryssomallis; Kalamata, Greece, 14 November 1954

Genre: New Age

Best-selling album since 1990: *Yanni Live at the Acropolis* (1994)

Hit songs since 1990: "Keys to Imagination," "Aria," "The Rain Must Fall"

One of the most prolific and high-profile contemporary instrumental New Age artists of the 1990s, keyboardist and composer Yanni spent the decade parlaying a growing cult following into international superstardom. His accessible, pop-influenced compositions, exhaustive touring, and a number of spectacularly produced live concert events expanded his fan base dramatically and helped him sell millions of records.

Born Yanni Chryssomallis in the small Greek village of Kalamata, Yanni began playing piano as a child. After a promising stint in his adolescence as a record-breaking member of the Greek National Swim Team, Yanni headed to the United States to attend the University of Minnesota. After graduating with a degree in psychology in 1976, Yanni began playing keyboards for the local rock band Chameleon, which developed enough of a following to tour regionally and release two albums independently. During this time, Yanni was also experimenting with his own keyboard compositions. In 1980 he independently released his first solo album, *Optimystique*. *Optimystique*'s grandiose and dynamic synthesized keyboard music,

spiced with drums, harp, and strings, distinguished Yanni from the more serene and static instrumental music put out by some of his New Age contemporaries. The album gradually sold well enough to attract the attention of New Age label Private Music, which signed Yanni and released a number of his albums in the 1980s, beginning with *Keys to Imagination* (1986). As his recording career developed, Yanni moved to Los Angeles, California, where he found work scoring films and television shows.

Yanni began the 1990s with somewhat of a breakthrough. While he had always sought to wrest an orchestra-like richness and bravura from synthesizers, in 1990 he performed live with the Dallas Symphony Orchestra. The resulting concert album sold well and raised his profile significantly. Over the next three years Yanni released the albums *In Celebration of Life* (1991), *Dare to Dream* (1992), and *In My Time* (1993)—the latter two of which scored Grammy Award nominations—all the while touring extensively. He won further notice when British Airways featured "Aria," a single from *Dare to Dream*, in a television commercial. In September 1993 Yanni again teamed with an orchestra—this time the London Philharmonic—to stage a concert at the historic Acropolis in his native Greece. Like the undeniably dramatic setting, the orchestral accompaniment deftly complemented Yanni's music, at times adding power and bombast, at others lightly underscoring its catchy melodies. The televised concert became a favorite on the Public Broadcasting Service, and an album culled from the concert, *Live at the Acropolis*, went on to sell millions of copies.

Emboldened by the Acropolis concert's huge success, Yanni mounted an even more ambitious undertaking: to be the first Western artist to perform at India's Taj Mahal and at China's Forbidden City. Requiring millions of dollars and massive organizational efforts, the concerts were a resounding success and were collected in the album, *Tribute* (1997). Although grounded in Yanni's keyboard and orchestral strings, *Tribute* reflects its Eastern settings by introducing ample non-Western elements, from gypsy violin and African chanting to bamboo saxophone. *Tribute* went on to sell millions of copies, further enhancing Yanni's popularity. Yanni spent the remainder of the 1990s releasing albums and touring at a steady clip. In mid-2003 he released an autobiography, *Yanni in Words*.

Bringing a rock star's sense of spectacle and grandiosity to a genre often derided as bland "elevator" music, Yanni spent the 1990s expanding the already extensive appeal of his sweeping and unabashedly romantic keyboard-based compositions. A number of high-profile, widely televised concerts in exotic locales helped him become one of the most popular and successful recording artists and performers of the decade.

SELECTIVE DISCOGRAPHY: *Keys to Imagination* (Private Music, 1986); *Chameleon Days* (Private Music, 1988); *In Celebration of Life* (Private Music, 1991); *Dare to Dream* (Private Music, 1992); *Yanni Live at the Acropolis* (Private Music, 1994); *I Love You Perfect* (Private Music, 1995); *In the Mirror* (Private Music, 1997); *Tribute* (Virgin, 1997); *Winter Light* (Private Music, 1999).

BIBLIOGRAPHY: Yanni with D. Rensin, *Yanni in Words* (New York, 2003).

WEBSITE: www.yanni.com.

MATT HIMES

GABRIEL YARED

Born: Beirut, Lebanon, 7 October 1949
Genre: Soundtrack
Best-selling album since 1990: *The English Patient* (1996)

Gabriel Yared is a composer whose identity seems to elude geographic, ethnic, or time-specific classifications, but rather is associated with a spectrum of moods between the poles of ennui and eroticism. Growing up in Beirut, Lebanon, Yared recalls his "only pleasure was to go to the church opposite [his home] to play the organ." That instrument, installed in 1930 in the Church of Saint-François, has exerted profound influence over the twentieth-century music of Beirut, and Yared claims to have been taught by Bertrand Robillard, a church organist who taught Lebanese composers Toufic Succar, Boghos Gelalian, and the Rahbani brothers.

Yared was a law student for three years at Université Saint-Joseph but dropped out to move to Brazil and work with singers Elis Regina and Ivan Lins. Upon settling in Paris in 1972, he audited classes at L'Ecole Normale du Musique, and the next year commenced a career as a freelance composer, writing for dance, advertisements, and television shows, as well as for singers such as Charles Aznavour and Johnny Hollyday.

Yared's first film soundtrack to gain significant attention was for Jean-Luc Godard's *Sauve Qui Peut la Vie* (*Every Man for Himself*; 1980). Following that, he worked principally on French films, winning Cesars (French Academy Awards) for the noir saxophone themes of *Betty Blue* (1986) and the score for the film of Marguerite Duras's novel *The Lover* (1992).

Yared's first major American film assignment was for director Robert Altman's *Beyond Therapy* (1987), and he worked with Altman again on *Theo and Vincent* (1990), about the Van Gogh brothers. But his poignant, dreamy, and suspenseful score for Anthony Minghella's Academy Award–winning *The English Patient* (1996) was his international breakthrough. Besides winning an Academy Award for Best Original Dramatic Score, Yared was named winner of the Anthony Asquith Award for Achievement in Film Music (from the British Academy of Film and Television Arts); the Golden Globe Award for Best Original Score, Motion Picture; and the Grammy Award for Best Instrumental Composition Written for a Motion Picture or for Television.

At Minghella's suggestion, Yared recruited Hungarian vocalist Márta Sebastyan from the folk group Muszikas for *The English Patient*, a prescient idea that stamped the film with a sonic character and boosted the ensemble's fame and audience. He dotted the movie—set during the last year of World War II in a makeshift medical clinic in rural Italy, populated by North American, Sikh, British, and North African characters—with nostalgic tracks by Fred Astaire, Benny Goodman, and Ella Fitzgerald, as well as the "Aria from the Goldberg Variations" for the character who claims it as her favorite music. Yared's writing for the Academy of St. Martin-in-the-Fields is remarkably detailed, and though many soundtrack albums boast that they provide stand-alone listening experiences, *The English Patient* is one that delivers on that claim.

Subsequently, Yared scored Minghella's *The Talented Mr. Ripley* (1999), a baroque thriller about a sociopath (based on a series of novels by Patricia Highsmith), the romantic comedy *Chocolat* (2000), and *Possession* (2002), a literary romance based on a novel by A. S. Byatt. As a dividend of his success (or evidence of his smart choices of employers), many of the albums Yared worked on in the 1970s are being reissued in the twenty-first century. His sensitivity to tasks at hand is evident in these disparate productions, which suggests he has much more to offer the field of movie soundtracks.

SELECTIVE DISCOGRAPHY: *The Lover* (Varese Sarabande, 1992); *The English Patient* (Fantasy, 1996); *Eden* (Angel, 1999); *The Talented Mr. Ripley* (Sony Classical, 1999); *Chocolat* (Sony Classical, 2000); *Possession* (RCA, 2002); *Messages Personnels* (EMI International, 2003).

HOWARD MANDEL

TRISHA YEARWOOD

Born: Monticello, Georgia, 19 September 1964

Genre: Country, Pop

Best-selling album since 1990: *Inside Out* (2001)

Hit songs since 1990: "She's in Love with the Boy," "Walkaway Joe," "Xxx's and Ooo's (An American Girl)"

Boasting a pure, effortless voice that adapts well to any type of material, Trisha Yearwood was one of the leading female performers in 1990s country. Like fellow country star Reba McEntire, Yearwood chooses songs that portray a diverse cast of female characters, from the rebellious daughter of "She's in Love with the Boy" and "Walkaway Joe" to the sad ex-lover of "Like We Never Had a Broken Heart." Regardless of style, Yearwood unfailingly projects honesty, sincerity, and directness. Her unabated presence on the 1990s country charts was due to the quality and consistency of her albums, comprised of songs by top Nashville songwriters such as Matraca Berg. While lacking the soul-baring grit of country legends such as Tammy Wynette and Loretta Lynn, Yearwood makes up for it with her flawless intonation, wide vocal range, and versatility. As the 1990s progressed Yearwood's records gradually became more pop-oriented without losing their charm and personality.

The daughter of a successful banker, Yearwood grew up on a large farm in Georgia. As a child she admired the music of rock pioneer Elvis Presley, as well as 1970s pop vocalist Linda Ronstadt. Attending Nashville's Belmont University in the mid-1980s, Yearwood studied music administration and performed an internship with the small MTM record label. Settling in Nashville full time in 1987, she worked as a background and demo singer, making friends with emerging country artists such as Garth Brooks, who encouraged her to pursue a professional career. Making good on his promise to help Yearwood in any way he could, Brooks used her as a background vocalist on his self-titled debut album in 1989.

Early 1990s Success

In 1990 producer Garth Fundis spotted Yearwood singing at a local bar and helped her sign with country music giant MCA. Yearwood hit commercial pay dirt with her first single, the exuberant "She's in Love with the Boy." One of the most infectious country hits of the early 1990s, the song established Yearwood's confident recording persona, mindful of country tradition yet unafraid to experiment with the bright accessibility of pop. A light-hearted tale of two young lovers facing parental opposition, "She's in Love with the Boy" bounces along on a sturdy rhythmic bed, its danceable groove punctuated by the catchy lyrics: "Her daddy says, he ain't worth a lick / When it comes to brains he got the short end of the stick." The song is a centerpiece of Yearwood's self-titled debut album, which ranges from wistful ballads such as "Like We Never Had a Broken Heart" to the up-tempo rocker, "That's What I Like about You."

Proving her dramatic range, Yearwood shifted focus on her next big hit, "Walkaway Joe" (1992). Again, the song features a young female protagonist who spurns parental advice to run off with her lover. This time, however, the parents are right: "Just a little while into Abilene / He pulls into a station and he robs it clean / She's waiting in the car / Underneath the Texaco star." In contrast to the cheery "She's in Love," "Walkaway Joe" bears an unadorned sadness that suggests the influence of folk music. Proving her skills as a sensitive, intelligent interpreter, Yearwood conveys a wide-eyed openness that mirrors her character's naïveté. The girlish innocence inherent in her performance makes it easy to sympathize with the young woman's plight. In addition to "Walkaway Joe," Yearwood's second album, *Hearts in Armor*, features the tough, bluesy "Wrong Side of Memphis," as well as the guitar-driven "You Say You Will." While Yearwood often holds her voice in check on ballads, with the up-tempo "You Say You Will" she reveals substantial power, belting the lyrics using the top part of her range. Singing the final, "but you never do," she plays with the words, bending them in a manner that recalls down-home country and blues vocalizing of the 1950s.

Pop Directions

As country music became slicker in the mid 1990s, aligning with the smooth, clean sound of pop, Yearwood updated her approach, singing with a directness that bore few traces of country twang. Regardless of approach, Yearwood's albums displayed consistently fine songs, such as "Xxx's and Ooo's (An American Girl)," a highlight of *Thinkin' about You* (1995). An example of the new female independence that characterized country music in the 1990s, "Xxx's and Ooo's" is a catchy, tuneful account of a girl on the verge of womanhood, unconcerned with traditional pressures of femininity: "She's gonna make it in her daddy's world." On the Matraca Berg–penned "Everybody Knows," from the 1996 album of the same name, Yearwood reveals a playful sense of humor, singing, "I don't want a shrink / Don't even want a drink / Give me some chocolate and a magazine."

By 2000 Yearwood was continuing to record strong, personable songs such as "Real Live Woman," from her 2000 album of the same title. Despite her success and fame, Yearwood possesses the sensitivity to make lines such as "I work nine to five, and I can't relate to millionaire" believable. In 2001 she released *Inside Out*, a typically confident, diverse effort. "I Would've Loved You Anyway," driven by a strong, rock-styled electric guitar, finds Yearwood singing with undiminished assurance, while "When We Were Still in Love" ranks as one of her most impassioned performances. Singing against a sparse background of piano and strings, Yearwood captures a sense of loss and regret, imbuing the final line, "love is gone," with quiet sadness.

With her flexible, precise voice and talent for intelligent song selection, Yearwood remained a consistently strong presence in country music during the 1990s and early 2000s, staying afloat by adapting to country's increasing reliance on the breeziness of pop music. A skilled actress, Yearwood creates vivid portrayals of a host of female characters, bringing to her songs a dramatic sense of truthfulness.

SELECTIVE DISCOGRAPHY: *Trisha Yearwood* (MCA, 1991); *Hearts in Armor* (MCA, 1992); *Everybody Knows* (MCA, 1996); *Real Live Woman* (MCA, 2000); *Inside Out* (MCA, 2001).

WEBSITE: www.trishayearwood.com

DAVID FREELAND

YO LA TENGO

Formed: 1984, Hoboken, New Jersey

Members: Georgia Hubley, drums, vocals; Ira Kaplan, guitar, vocals; Mike Lewis, bass; James McNew, bass, vocals; Dave Schramm, guitar

Genre: Rock

Best-selling album since 1990: *And Then Nothing Turned Itself Inside-Out* (2000)

Hit songs since 1990: "From a Motel Six," "Tom Courtenay," "Sugarcube"

Yo La Tengo is composed of enthusiastic rock fans. But rather than shamelessly ape the styles of their favorite bands, they have translated their reverence for the genre into a unique and transcendent sound. A married couple, Ira Kaplan and Georgia Hubley, formed the band in the mid-1980s during Kaplan's tenure as a rock journalist. They released a series of stylistically sprawling albums, eventually hitting their stride in the early 1990s after adding a permanent bassist, James McNew. On the albums *May I Sing with Me* (1992) and *Painful* (1993), they perfected a dreamy style of songcraft marked by tender, breathy vocals and Kaplan's frenzied bursts of guitar noise. This engaging sound earned them a reputation with fans and critics as one of America's finest independent rock bands.

Guitarist Kaplan and drummer Hubley began to play music together in the basement of Maxwell's, a legendary venue in Hoboken, New Jersey, in 1984. A true rock and roll obsessive, Kaplan wrote articles for *Spin* magazine and worked as a sound man at Maxwell's. The pair focused on playing covers, learning the songs of their favorite bands, obscure or otherwise, from throughout the rock era. In a further display of fandom, they named the band Yo La Tengo (Spanish for "I got it!"), a reference to the former New York Mets outfielder Richie Ashburn, who would shout the phrase while diving for fly balls.

After recruiting guitarist Dave Schramm and bassist Mike Lewis, the band recorded and released *Ride the Tiger* (1986), a quiet affair that displays their love of British Invasion pop and American folk music. While featuring Kaplan's gift for melody and Hubley's bracing vocals, the album only hints at the more experimental and potent direction of their later work. Schramm and Lewis left the band shortly after the release of the record, and Kaplan and Hubley worked with a rotating cast of musicians for the next several years. *New Wave Hot Dogs* (1987) and *President Yo La Tengo* (1989) found Kaplan embracing a noisy but refined style of guitar playing that was aggressive but still impressively tuneful, whereas Hubley evolved into a solid and commanding drummer. The band began to play with extremes, with songs like the droning "Barnaby, Hardly Working" and "The Evil That Men Do" exploring the power of matching shocking noise with near silence.

Yo La Tengo opened the 1990s with *Fakebook* (1990), a folky album recorded with Schramm. Mostly comprised of covers, the record functions as a tour through their favorite songs, marked by the pristine beauty of "Yellow Sarong" and "Speeding Motorcycle." The album strips away the electric noise of their previous two releases, revealing the increasingly gorgeous combination of Kaplan's deadpan singing and Hubley's ethereal vocals, which became just as important to the band's sonic design as their unique instrumentation.

May I Sing with Me (1992) proved to be the pivotal Yo La Tengo album, returning to the electric textures of *President Yo La Tengo* with invigorating results. Bassist James

Yo La Tengo. L-R: Ira Kaplan, James McNew, Georgia Hubley [PAUL NATKIN/PHOTO RESERVE]

McNew joined the band prior to recording, solidifying the band's rhythm section and adding expressive background vocals. The collection exhibits their knack for balancing catchy, uptempo rockers ("Upside Down") with blistering soundscapes ("Mushroom Cloud of Hiss"). With vivid sounds and soothing textures, *May I Sing with Me* provided the first clear look at the Yo La Tengo to come.

Painful (1993) was the band's first true masterpiece, a startling collection of strangely beautiful songs that pushed the limits of sonic texture and experimentation. The album is influenced by the U.K.-based shoegazer sound, in which layers of guitar noise are used to create slow, dreamy compositions. Specifically, Kaplan employs jagged, barbed guitar lines in the context of gentle pop melodies to forge a soothing, expansive sound. The album opens with the slowly awakening "Big Day Coming," which is revisited later in the album as a crushing, keyboard-driven anthem. Simple rockers like "From a Motel Six" are launched straight into the sky by Kaplan's propulsive guitar, but the band also recognizes the power of holding back completely, such as on the whispered romantic ballad "Nowhere Near."

Electr-O-Pura (1995) continues the sonic strides of *Painful,* but with more forays into stylistic eclecticism. The nervy drone of "Decora" and the epic "Blue Line Swinger" provide sonic thrills, but the band also grips the soul with the mournful country-tinged "Pablo and Andrea" and the incandescent "Don't Say a Word." Each song on the album is completely different, the only common feature being the band's mastery of creating patterns of sound. Thus, the shimmering pop of "Tom Courtenay" and the spastic rock of "Straight Down to the Bitter End" feel natural together. The band's vision fosters a wide array of possibilities.

The band continued to reach in all directions on *I Can Hear the Heart Beating as One* (1997). The band is all over the map, tackling giddy rockers ("Sugarcube"), psychedelic noise workouts ("Deeper into Movies"), bossa nova ("Center of Gravity"), and classic pop ("My Little Corner of the World"). Subtlety is key, as evidenced by the organic drone of "Autumn Sweater," which plays like a darkly romantic mystery ("We could slip away / Oh wouldn't that be better? / Leave with nothing to say / And you in your autumn sweater"). The sound is deep and cinematic, culminating in "We're an American Band," an awe-inspiring track with Kaplan and Hubley singing languorously over a gentle wave of guitars that build to a perfect swirling storm.

The calm moments that mark *Heart* take over completely on *And Then Nothing Turned Itself Inside-Out* (2000), the band's most enigmatic work. Each track on the album uses subtle, layered instrumentation to create an ambient mood. The opening track, "Everyday," employs the Yo La Tengo hallmarks of droning keyboards, guitar noise, and ethereal vocals to create an otherworldly dirge. The album is also intensely romantic, a testament to not only Kaplan and Hubley's enduring marriage but also their unceasing love of rock music. "Our Way to Fall" and "You Can Have It All" are dense love songs for the new century that address the complexity of relationships and revel in their possibilities. They show their sense of humor on the nimble samba "Let's Save Tony Orlando's House" and employ guitar fuzz on the catchy, comfortable rocker "Cherry Chapstick."

Yo La Tengo titled their 1998 collection of B-sides and outtakes *Genius + Love = Yo La Tengo*. The title might seem arrogant, but it is a pithy description of how the band operates. They possess the good taste of connoisseurs but also understand that the best rock possesses a warmth and spirit that can only come from the soul. This combination of smarts and passion makes their music unforgettable and indispensable.

SELECTIVE DISCOGRAPHY: *Ride the Tiger* (Matador, 1986); *New Wave Hot Dogs* (Coyote, 1987); *President Yo La Tengo* (Coyote, 1989); *Fakebook* (Bar/None, 1990); *May I Sing with Me* (Alias, 1992); *Painful* (Matador, 1993); *Electr-O-Pura* (Matador, 1995); *I Can Hear the Heart Beating as One* (Matador, 1997); *Genius + Love = Yo La Tengo* (Matador, 1998); *And Then Nothing Turned Itself Inside-Out* (Matador, 2000).

WEBSITE: www.yolatengo.com.

SEAN CAMERON

DWIGHT YOAKAM

Born: Pikeville, Kentucky, 23 October 1956

Genre: Country

Best-selling album since 1990: *This Time* (1993)

Hit songs since 1990: "A Thousand Miles from Nowhere," "Fast as You"

One of the first country "neo-traditionalists," Dwight Yoakam helped return the music to its roots during the 1980s and 1990s, popularizing a stripped-down sound built upon guitar, drums, and fiddles. Modeling his style after the twangy, guitar-based "Bakersfield Sound" created in the 1950s and 1960s by country performers Merle Haggard and Buck Owens, Yoakam retained his traditional approach even as country music became slicker and more pop-oriented in the mid- to late 1990s. For this reason, Yoakam did not become a country superstar, despite enjoying periodic success on the country charts. Instead, he found his core popularity among rock fans, an audience more appreciative of the somewhat ironic stance Yoakam brought to his music. Unlike fellow neo-traditionalist Randy Travis, who became one of the top-selling country performers of the 1980s and 1990s, Yoakam sometimes seems to be commenting upon his music from a distance, despite the reverence with which he performs it. By the late 1990s, his hip style had brought him success and acclaim as an actor in Hollywood films.

Born in the coal-mining town of Pikeville, Kentucky, but raised in Cincinnati, Ohio, Yoakam began playing guitar at the age of six. As a youth he acted in local plays while developing a fondness for the country artists in his mother's record collection. After a stint at Ohio State University, where he majored in philosophy, Yoakam moved to Nashville to pursue a career as a performer. There, he met Pete Anderson, a guitarist who would later produce most of his recordings. The pair moved to Los Angeles, where they found steady work performing on the punk rock circuit of the late 1970s. With the help of an insurance check meant to fix Yoakam's car, they released a professional-sounding six-track album, *Guitars, Cadillacs, Etc., Etc.* (1984), which received substantial airplay on college radio stations. In 1986 Yoakam signed with a major label, Reprise, which re-released his first album, adding four songs. Hailed by critics as a stimulating, honest recasting of traditional country themes, the album became a commercial success, reaching the number one position on the country charts. Two follow-ups, *Hillbilly Deluxe* (1987) and *Buenos Noches from a Lonely Room* (1988), fared equally well, with the latter spawning Yoakam's first number one hit, "Streets of Bakersfield," a potent duet with his musical idol, Owens.

During the 1990s Yoakam altered his basic musical approach little, although he refined and developed his sound. Critics argue that *If There Was a Way* (1990) is one of his strongest albums, highlighted by the aching ballad, "The Heart That You Own." Recalling the classic performances of Haggard, the song displays Yoakam's ability to write memorable lyrics with strong themes: "I pay rent on a run-down place / There ain't no view but there's lots of space / in my heart, the heart that you own." Throughout the performance, Yoakam's singing is gentle and restrained, although his voice lacks the rich timbre of his forebears Haggard and Owens.

In 1993 Yoakam released the noteworthy *This Time*, an album in which his traditional ideas and themes fully coalesce. "Home for Sale" takes on an elegiac tone through the addition of a soulful Hammond B-3 organ, while the title track uncannily captures the sound and feel of a classic 1960s "honky-tonk" ballad, with lean guitar, tinkling piano, and drums, creating a delayed, shuffling rhythm. Yoakam's nasal vocal quality approximates Owens's singing without fully capturing the soul Owens brought to his work. Unparalleled as a craftsperson, Yoakam often sounds detached from the emotional core of his music—a quality that gives him more in common with rock than with the sentiment and pathos of country.

After *This Time,* Yoakam's success on the country charts became more sporadic, with none of his post-1994 singles reaching the Top 10. By the mid- to late 1990s the neo-traditionalist phase in country had passed, supplanted by the slick pop approach of artists such as Shania Twain and John Michael Montgomery. Oblivious to this change, Yoakam continued to perform in his roots-based style, releasing strong albums such as *A Long Way Home* (1998) and *Tomorrow's Sounds Today* (2000), the latter of which features additional collaborations with Owens. By this time, Yoakam had also earned recognition for his acting work, having appeared in the films *Red Rock West* (1992) and, most notably, *Sling Blade* (1996). Unmarried, he shared high-profile romances with film actresses Sharon Stone and Bridget Fonda.

Unique among country artists in his refusal to follow trends, Yoakam has maintained his rebellious image, honoring musical traditions of the past at the risk of losing mainstream radio exposure. In the process, he has revitalized country in a manner that recalls the renegade style and personality of his musical heroes.

SELECTIVE DISCOGRAPHY: *Guitars, Cadillacs, Etc., Etc.* (Reprise, 1986); *Hillbilly Deluxe* (Reprise, 1987); *If There Was a Way* (Reprise, 1990); *This Time* (Reprise, 1993); *Gone* (Reprise, 1995); *A Long Way Home* (Reprise, 1998); *Tomorrow's Sounds Today* (Warner Bros., 2000).

SELECTIVE FILMOGRAPHY: *Red Rock West* (1992); *Sling Blade* (1996); *The Newton Boys* (1998); *Panic Room* (2002).

WEBSITE: www.dwightyoakam.com.

DAVID FREELAND

NEIL YOUNG

Born: Toronto, Ontario, 12 November 1945
Genre: Rock
Best-selling album since 1990: *Harvest Moon* (1992)

One of contemporary music's most enduring artists and songwriters, Neil Young remains as much a part of today's scene as he was of the burgeoning electric folk/rock era of the late 1960s, from which he emerged. His diverse musical vocabulary and inclination for drastic genre change is anchored by an identifiably edgy and emotional voice that is strikingly high-pitched. Through five decades Young has woven music that continues to surprise and in some cases confound listeners and critics. His impressive body of work includes country, blues, rock-a-billy, grunge rock, rhythm and blues, movie soundtracks, and the signature lyrical folk style from which many of his most acclaimed songs have emerged.

Young was raised in Toronto, Ontario, before moving to Winnipeg, Saskatchewan, with his mother when he was fourteen following her divorce from his father, Scott Young, a Toronto journalist. His interest in music was already in full swing, and he assembled several bands made up mostly of schoolmates. The last of these, the Squires, began playing professional dates throughout central Canada over the next two years until the band dissolved in June 1965.

Young journeyed to New York, where he located Stephen Stills and was introduced to Richie Furay. After an opportunity fell through to play guitar for a rhythm-and-blues band called the Mynah Birds, which featured Rick James on vocals, Young left for Los Angeles. Stills and Furay persuaded him to join a new band called Buffalo Springfield, made up of various refugees from the 1960s pop music scene. Young immediately became a central creative force within the band, and Buffalo Springfield released five albums over the next three years. Despite the band's success, Young yearned for a different musical path and sought out his fellow Canadian artist and friend Joni Mitchell, who put him in touch with her manager. He soon negotiated a deal with Reprise Records for a solo album, and the result, titled *Neil Young* (1968), began to confer superstar status on a reluctant artist.

Young's career peaked with the platinum-selling *Harvest* (1972). This sweet, poignant recording contains what many consider to be his signature songs. Hits off the album include "Heart of Gold" and "Old Man." Young followed *Harvest* with a series of musical departures that challenged his audience with continual reinvention. One example was an eerie soundtrack for a rarely seen film titled *Journey Through the Past* (1972) and another was the dark world of death and drugs Young explored on the haunting *Tonight's the Night* (1975). During the 1980s Young's output, often viewed as erratic, confused and alienated many of his fans. Each album called forth a radically different aesthetic: he was a country balladeer with a band called the International Harvesters and a techno-buzz rocker on *Trans* (1983); he turned to rock-a-billy with the Shocking

Pinks on *Everybody's Rockin* (1983) and to a pure country sound with turns from Waylon Jennings and Willie Nelson on *Old Ways* (1985); the slick bluesman on *This Note's for You* (1988) yielded to the hard-rock wielding axe-man on *Ragged Glory* (1990) and then to the pied piper of a much younger grunge-rock sound in *Weld* (1991) and *Arc* (1991).

Wedged between his first solo efforts and *Harvest* was another considerable musical kinship, begun when Young was asked to join the talented trio of David Crosby, Stephen Stills, and Graham Nash in 1969. Originally recruited to be a support member of the band, he held out for a more substantial partnership, and the trio agreed to form a quartet named Crosby, Stills, Nash, and Young. Although their time together was stormy and short, about two years, CSN&Y compiled a list of popular songs and enjoyed tremendous popularity as the group's essence mirrored the country's political turmoil. Many songs, such as "Ohio," "Woodstock," "Find the Cost of Freedom," and "Almost Cut My Hair" stand as 1960s anthems to this day. CSN&Y reunited briefly for a 1988 release of the album *American Dream* and the subsequent tour, but Young's participation was small, and he left the tour midway. In 1999 CSN&Y assembled yet again and have since enjoyed a renewed success on two tours.

Although Young's years after 1990 still carry his trademark unpredictability, his popularity is more robust than ever. He returned to the tuneful folk of earlier fame by finally releasing *Harvest Moon* (1992), a sequel to *Harvest*. In his usual contrary fashion, Young began performing the songs for *Harvest Moon* in concert well before the album was released. More than twenty years removed from some of his classic material, Young would often tire of audience members' impatience with the new material, lamenting that the old songs were distracting listeners from letting him do what he's always done—introduce new songs. He prevailed, and *Harvest Moon* was a giant success, his best-selling album in thirteen years. The songs reflect a shift toward writing more about areas of life that are closer to his home and heart.

Like the sharp changes in his music, Young's political views, usually identified with grassroots efforts, have sometimes flabbergasted his fans. For instance, in 1984 he once expressed his support for Ronald Reagan, the Republican presidential candidate. On the other hand Young revived a sixties impulse in the late 1980s as he fervently took sides against corporations for using classic contemporary music to advertise products. His R&B offering, "This Note's for You," a takeoff on Budweiser advertising phraseology, was made into a music video to emphasize his antisponsorship point. Ironically—and prophetically—it was banned by MTV out of fear that it would offend their corporate sponsors.

Young also returned to movie-soundtrack work by contributing the title song to the film *Philadelphia*. He

Spot Light | Farm Aid

In 1985 Neil Young, along with his fellow musicians Willie Nelson and John Mellencamp, responded to the adversity of the family farm and the rural way of life by organizing a series of concerts to raise money. Called Farm Aid, these concerts have brought together hundreds of artists who have donated their musical talents to the effort. Farm Aid has raised more than $15 million and distributed the money to more than 100 farming organizations and agencies that serve rural communities. The organization's primary impetus was to keep farmers on their land. However, it also channels funds for long-term solutions to other challenges faced in rural America by promoting outreach and education to increase the farm community's ability to react to a changing world. The message has been the same for seventeen years: By supporting family farmers, Americans eat healthier food, challenge the domination of agribusiness, and stave off urban sprawl.

accompanied himself on piano and sang the song's lamenting melody live at the 1995 Academy Awards broadcast. In 1996 he arranged the movie soundtrack for Jim Jarmusch's film *Dead Man*.

But it was *Sleeps with Angels* (1994) that helped Young turn another important corner. This eclectic batch of songs offers a career retrospective of sorts with bits and pieces of Young's musical stylings through the years on one album. Its huge success was an indication that listeners were beginning to release Young from preconceptions based on his earlier work and appreciate him for his wider artistic scope.

Young collaborated with the grunge band Pearl Jam in the making of *Mirror Ball* (1995) and shared the stage with them and other alternative rock acts on various tours. Attired for decades in a costume of boots, jeans, and flannel shirts, he has been appropriately dubbed "the father of grunge." He performed his cynical "Rockin in the Free World" with Pearl Jam on the night he was inducted into the Rock and Roll Hall of Fame in 1995.

He delighted critics again with *Broken Arrow* (1996), and released a fierce live rock recording, *Year of the Horse*

(1997). The personal *Silver and Gold* (2000) was a pliable musical offering that harked back to his Buffalo Springfield days. *Are You Passionate?* (2002) garnered praise for its soft, moving tones and slight Motown feel. Featured on *Are You Passionate?* is "Let's Roll," Young's tribute to the passengers on United Flight 93, one of the commercial airliners that was hijacked during the events of the September 11, 2001, terrorist attacks. The song's title is a reference to the phrase "Let's roll" that was uttered into a cell phone by one of the male passengers prior to his and other passengers' overtaking the hijackers, preventing them from crashing the plane into the Washington, D.C., area; the doomed flight went down in the rural Pennsylvania countryside. Young used the song's proceeds to assist families of the plane's passengers, none of whom survived.

Young has always been keenly attuned to social issues. He is a founding member of Farm Aid, an organization dedicated to rural causes to which he has lent abundant time. Another important association for Young is the Bridge School founded by his wife, Pegi Young. The Bridge School, located in the San Francisco Bay area, specializes in caring for and educating children with severe speech and physical impairments. Young has been raising money for the school since 1986 by mounting charity concerts and enlisting fellow musicians to do the same. One of his children, Ben, attends the school.

Throughout Young's career his personal life has lacked the notoriety of most of his rock-and-roll comrades. What he has achieved in fame has been the direct result of his music and not trashed hotel rooms and other binges of excess. His songs are a combination of personal memoir, emotionally driven images, and social commentary. Young's musical mosaic reflects the passion of an artist in a relentless endeavor to puzzle out the magnitude of life.

SELECTIVE DISCOGRAPHY: *Neil Young* (Reprise, 1968); *Everybody Knows This Is Nowhere* (Reprise, 1969); *After the Goldrush* (Reprise 1970); *Harvest* (Reprise, 1972); *Time Fades Away* (Reprise, 1973); *On the Beach* (Reprise, 1974); *Tonight's the Night* (Reprise, 1975); *Zuma* (Reprise, 1976); *Long May You Run* (Reprise, 1976); *American Stars 'N Bars* (Reprise, 1977); *Comes a Time* (Reprise, 1978); *Rust Never Sleeps* (Reprise, 1979); *Live Rust* (Reprise, 1979); *Hawks and Doves* (Reprise, 1980); *Re-ac-tor* (Reprise 1981); *Trans* (Geffen 1983); *Everybody's Rockin'* (Geffen, 1983); *Old Ways* (Geffen, 1985); *Landing on Water* (Geffen, 1986); *This Note's for You* (Geffen, 1988); *Freedom* (Reprise, 1989); *Ragged Glory* (Reprise, 1990); *Weld* (Reprise, 1991); *Arc* (Reprise, 1991); *Harvest Moon* (Reprise, 1992); *Unplugged* (Reprise, 1993); *Sleeps with Angels* (Reprise, 1994); *Mirror Ball* (Reprise, 1995); *Broken Arrow* (Reprise, 1996); *Silver and Gold* (Reprise, 2000); *Are You Passionate?* (Reprise, 2002).

BIBLIOGRAPHY: S. Young and P. Buck (ed.), *Neil and Me* (Ontario, 1997); J. McDonough, *Shakey: Neil Young's Biography* (London, 2002); S. Simmons, *Neil Young: Reflections in Broken Glass* (Edinburgh, 2002).

DONALD LOWE

$$Z \left|\begin{matrix} z \\ z \end{matrix}\right.$$

ZAP MAMA

Formed: 1990, Zaire

Members: Marie Daulne, vocals, compositions, and arrangements (born 1964, Zaire); Cecilia Kankonda; Celine 'T Hooft; Sabine Kabongo; Sylvie Nawasadio; Fancon Nuyens; Maris Cavenaile, vocals; Jean-Louis Daulne, human beat box; David Weemaels, percussion.

Genre: World

Best-selling album since 1990: *Adventures in Afropea 1* (1993)

Marie Daulne's life is an adventure story. Her father, a white Belgian, was killed in Zaire during the revolution of 1964, and her Bantu mother, who was pregnant, escaped attack in the forests, protected by a neighboring tribe of pygmies. Daulne grew up in Europe, assuming a Belgian/Walloon identity and nurturing a fondness for Stevie Wonder and Roberta Flack. She decided to return to Zaire to immerse herself in her Zairean/Bantu background upon hearing a record of pygmy music when she was twenty. As a result, she re-energized female vocal music in the West.

Daulne embarked on a concentrated study of Central African pygmies' onomatopoetic and syllabic techniques before returning to Belgium to initiate Zap Mama with remarkably fresh arrangements of original songs and music adapted from Zulu, Rwandan, Syrian, Central African, and Spanish sources. Zap Mama's debut album, *Adventures in Afropea 1* (1993), supported by a summer tour in which they opened for 10,000 Maniacs, established the singing group among the international music cognoscenti. *Billboard* magazine named them one of the top twenty world-music bands of the year. They performed at the WOMAD (World of Music Art and Dance) festival, at the North Sea Jazz Festival in the Hague, in Berlin, and in New York City.

Besides their beguiling sounds, Zap Mama members' exotic looks, complete with stylish adaptations of ethnic costumes, made them irresistible to media outlets and advertising agencies hungry for salable images. *Adventures in Afropea 1* was released in the United States on Luaka Bop, the Warner Bros. imprint run by David Byrne of Talking Heads fame, and so arrived on the market with considerable hipster endorsement. Byrne reportedly won the rights to the album in competitive bidding against Sting and Peter Gabriel, among others.

Sabsylma (1994), Zap Mama's sophomore effort, was nominated for a Grammy, and although Kabongo and Nawasadio returned to sing along with the newcomer Sally Nyolo, the project proved that Zap Mama is Daulne's outlet rather than any sort of collaborative enterprise. That year Daulne gave birth to her daughter Kesia and took time off from performing. During her hiatus, she negotiated an international distribution contract with Virgin Records.

It is to Daulne's credit that Zap Mama sustained its artistic credibility and the audience's respect through its next two albums—*7* (1997) and *A Ma Zone* ("In My Zone") (1999)—despite Zap Mama's surprising licensing deals and product endorsements (Coca Cola, Nokia) and an unabashed shift from acoustic world music ensemble to polished high-tech pop with dance-club imperatives. The common element is Marie Daulne, who still uses backup singers but none from the original Zap Mama. On *A Ma Zone* Daulne features a number of guest musicians—Manu Dibango, the Roots, Speech from Arrested Development, Spearhead's Michael Franti, and DJ U-Roy—but she remains firmly the focus of the recording.

Daulne is gifted with a compelling voice. Her sonic stylings range from closely harmonized chants to tightly timed hocket episodes (during which a melody is assembled from notes voiced in quick sequence by successive singers), imaginatively varied SABT charts, advanced use of samples, and "found sound." Zap Mama has also ventured some distance from its Pygmy foundation; Daulne still highlights vocal acrobatics of Pygmy derivation but roams the Mediterranean, Caribbean, South Pacific, and other likely ports of call for sounds that attract her ear. Some of her choices are surprising, but they are usually on the money: Zap Mama's contribution to the soundtrack of *Mission: Impossible 2* is a version of "Iko Iko," the often-recorded chant of New Orleans Mardi Gras Indians that likely goes back to the Louisiana Purchase and Congo Square.

If Walloon and Bantu are an unusual ancestral mix, Daulne has combined them to often magical effect. *Ancestry in Progress*, Daulne's first album under her own name, reflects her deepening commitment to self-fulfillment; her attraction to the neo-soul, Philadelphia funk, and punk-roots scene; and her move from Belgium to New York City. Her guest artists on that album include Erykah Badu, ?uestlove, Common, Talib Kweli, Bilal, and Bahamadia.

Zap Mama's future rests on whether Marie Dualne continues to present herself as a soloist or prefers to maintain an ensemble identity.

SELECTIVE DISCOGRAPHY: *Adventures in Afropea, Vol. 1* (Warner Bros./Luaka Bop, 1993); *Sabsylma* (Luaka Bop, 1994); *7* (Warner Bros./Luaka Bop, 1997); *A Ma Zone* (Luaka Bop, 2000); *Mission: Impossible 2 Original Soundtrack* (Universal International, 2001).

WEBSITE: houbi.com/belpop/groups/zapmama.htm.

HOWARD MANDEL

JOE ZAWINUL

Born: Josef Erich Zawinul; Vienna, Austria, 7 July 1932
Genre: Jazz, Fusion, Afro-Pop, World
Best-selling album since 1990: *Faces & Places* (2002)

Joe Zawinul is not conventionally associated with either the Viennese school of composers of the eighteenth and nineteenth centuries (Joseph Haydn, Wolfgang Amadeus Mozart, and Ludwig van Beethoven) or that of the early twentieth century (Arnold Schoenberg, Alban Berg, and Anton Webern)—yet he is a verifiable Viennese composer. Zawinul was born in Vienna, Austria, raised during the country's economic depression, affected by World War II and its dislocations, and drawn to jazz during America's postwar occupation of Germany. Emerging musically in late 1950s and 1960s America, Zawinul attained prominence as a founding member of the band Weather Report, and as writer of such electric jazz-rock fusion staples as "Boogie Woogie Waltz." Since the 1990s his music has increasingly reflected rhythms and harmonies from Africa, Asia, South America, and Eastern Europe, transformed through his electric keyboards and synthesizers.

Zawinul picked up the accordion as a child, practicing it backward and upside down to scramble its key and button sequences for greater independence of his hands. In his teens, he enrolled in the Vienna Conservatory to study classical piano and composition. Influenced by British-born pianist George Shearing and self-taught, exuberant Erroll Garner, Zawinul worked with Austrian saxophonist Hans Koller in 1952, then led his own trio in France and Germany. He was befriended by Austrian classical pianist Friedrich Gulda, with whom he made his recording debut playing four-hand in 1953.

Winning a scholarship to Berklee College of Music in 1958, Zawinul came to the United States but left school after one week to join trumpeter Maynard Ferguson's band, into which he helped induct saxophonist Wayne Shorter. While employed by Ferguson, Zawinul also met jazz great Miles Davis, who in the late 1960s solicited compositions from Zawinul that he performed for the rest of his life.

Zawinul accompanied soul-jazz singer Dinah Washington (in 1959–1961) prior to being hired by the Cannonball Adderley Quintet, one of jazz's few simultaneously successful and progressive bands. Zawinul wrote several songs for Adderley's book, employing a Wurlitzer electric piano he found in a recording studio hall on his biggest Adderley band hit, the gospel-derived "Mercy, Mercy, Mercy." Zawinul also accompanied mainstream musicians, including saxophonist Ben Webster, in traditional jazz piano style.

Though Zawinul recorded several times with Miles Davis (starting with *In a Silent Way*, to which he contributed the title track), he was never formally a member of Davis's band. He did, however, steal Davis's tenor saxophonist Shorter in December 1970 to establish Weather Report, an audacious ensemble that incorporated unfettered use of new electronic instruments and open-structured collective jazz improvisation along with

African, Caribbean, and Brazilian percussion, bowed bass solos, and boldly declarative melodies. Under Zawinul's increasing direction, and especially with the addition of electric bassist Jaco Pastorius in 1976, Weather Report grew to emphasize grooves over unanchored electronic sound fields. Its best-known song, "Birdland" (1977), was covered by Maynard Ferguson's brass-heavy band and the vocal quartet Manhattan Transfer, among others.

When Shorter left Weather Report in 1985, Zawinul operated as a one-man band, overdubbing solo, rhythm, and chordal tracks in his home studio for *Dialects* (1986). The sound he continued to purvey with young musicians in his new band, Zawinul Syndicate, over a series of albums (including *Lost Tribes*, 1992) was similar to Weather Report's, though electric guitarists took on lead lines, and Zawinul emulated Shorter's soprano saxophone timbres and phraseology on his Korg Pepe wind synthesizer. He is master of techniques allowing overdubbed tracks to breathe, bubble, and swing.

Zawinul encourages a one-world political viewpoint, mingling musicians, as well as music, from around the world. He produced Mali vocalist Salif Keita's Grammy Award–nominated *Amen* (1991), adding an electric gloss without obscuring the music's indigenous authenticity, and employing Shorter and guitarist Carlos Santana as guest artists. Keita sang on Zawinul's *My People* (1996), along with a Siberian throat singer, Anatolian percussionist Arto Tuncboyaciyan, Venezuelan Thania Sanchez, the Turkish Burhan Ocal, Cameroonian Richard Bona, and background vocalists from Peru, Guinea, and the Ivory Coast.

Zawinul reflects on his European heritage, too, especially in his symphonic work, *Stories of the Danube* (1996), which he orchestrated for his keyboards and processed vocals, plus guitar, oud, percussion, and drums, all accompanying the Czech State Philharmonic Orchestra Brno, conducted by Caspar Richter. The seven-movement, sixty-three-minute work follows the river's meander from spring-head to sea, with reference to diverse historical eras and a fully orchestrated rendition of his "Unknown Soldier" from Weather Report's *I Sing the Body Electric* (1972). As Weather Report's reissues and previously unreleased material came out in 2003, coupled with Zawinul's touring and participation in major festivals worldwide and his release of new albums on his own ESC Records label (including the Grammy-nominated *Faces and Places* [2002]), the sweep and unflagging energy of his career gained hold on new generations of jazz, world, and electronic musicians globally.

SELECTIVE DISCOGRAPHY: *The Rise and Fall of the Third Stream* (Vortex, 1965); *Zawinul* (Atlantic, 1970); *Dialects* (Columbia, 1986); *My People* (Escapade Music, 1992); *Stories of the Danube* (Polygram, 1995); *World Tour* (Zebra, 1998); *Faces and Places* (ESC, 2002). **With the Cannonball Adderley Quintet:** *Mercy, Mercy, Mercy! Live at "The Club"* (Capitol Jazz, 1995). **With Miles Davis:** *The Complete Bitches Brew Sessions* (Columbia Legacy, 1998); *The Complete In a Silent Way Sessions* (Columbia Legacy, 2001). **With Weather Report:** *Weather Report* (Columbia, 1971); *I Sing the Body Electric* (Columbia, 1972); *Sweetnighter* (Columbia, 1973); *Heavy Weather* (Columbia, 1977); *Live and Unreleased* (Columbia Legacy, 2003).

HOWARD MANDEL

WARREN ZEVON

Born: Chicago, Illinois, 24 January 1947; died Los Angeles, 7 September 2003
Genre: Rock
Best-selling album since 1990: *Life'll Kill Ya* (2000)

Singer/songwriter Warren Zevon's cynical wit, fascination with the macabre, and propensity for creating oddball characters all seep into his lyrically weighted, often satiric music. Zevon's *Excitable Boy* (1976) is one of rock music's most acclaimed albums and many of his songs have become hits for other artists. Zevon's ability to find irony in the saddest places was reflected in the way he came to terms with his own grave health issues.

Although Zevon was born in Chicago, his childhood was spent shuttling between California and Arizona because his father was a professional gambler. Before they were divorced, his parents settled for a time in Los Angeles where Zevon studied classical piano. He left home at age sixteen and moved to New York City to be part of the burgeoning 1960s Greenwich Village folk scene, but eventually found his way back to southern California a few years later. There he befriended and worked with many of the luminaries of that emerging folk rock scene, such as Linda Ronstadt, Jackson Browne, and members of the Eagles. He had sporadic success as a songwriter for the Turtles and April Stevens and finally recorded his first album, *Zevon: Wanted—Dead or Alive* (1969). The album went unnoticed by record buyers, although one song—"She Quit Me"— was used in the film *Midnight Cowboy* (1969).

After the album's failure, Zevon then went into survival mode as a jingle writer for commercials, a music director for the rock vocal duo the Everly Brothers, and a pianist in Spain at a touristy club before getting back to Los Angeles and signing a songwriting contract with recording giant David Geffen. This led to another shot at recording and he released *Warren Zevon* (1976). The album endeared Zevon to the critics and featured several songs that went

Warren Zevon [PAUL NATKIN/PHOTO RESERVE]

on to be recorded by other artists, including "Poor, Poor Pitiful Me" and "Hasten Down the Wind," both of which became more prominent after Linda Ronstadt recorded them. The success of *Warren Zevon* began a cult following for Zevon and his next album, *Excitable Boy* (1978), put him at the forefront of the music industry. *Excitable Boy* is a timeless work reflective of Zevon's attention to the grittier aspects of life. It stunned critics and listeners. The songs mix solemn fact and sublime fiction to create intelligent and striking satires. Zevon paints an apocalyptic picture of violence in a revenge tale about a betrayed fortune hunter in "Roland the Headless Thompson Gunner." His offhand horror spoof, "Werewolves of London," became Zevon's biggest hit. "Lawyers, Guns, and Money" humorously chronicles the cries for help from a spoiled rich kid during some decadent Third World travels and the title song combines a happy-go-lucky melody with a staggeringly disturbing story about a boy's violent nature.

Zevon's subsequent recordings continued to fare well with ardent fans, but they never gave him the commercial success that seemed promised after *Excitable Boy.* Alcoholism and its recovery blocked his progress in the early 1980s along with the decade's changing musical tide, which, curiously, turned against songs with lyrical wit. Zevon, in addition to other strong songwriters including Loudon Wainwright III, John Prine, and Randy Newman, all suffered a drop in popularity during the 1980s. In addition, Zevon's recordings of that decade lacked his trade-

mark bite and he did not return to that vein until *Mr. Bad Example* (1991), which contains the hilarious, "Things to Do in Denver When You're Dead."

More than any other artist, Zevon sang songs about death and related topics. His albums' logo is a grinning skull. He titled his forty-four-song anthology release *I'll Sleep When I'm Dead* (1996). Some critics liken Zevon to the graphic crime novelists who spare no detail about violence in their books and Zevon counted authors Stephen King, Hunter Thompson, and Carl Hiaasen as close friends and occasional song collaborators. In 2000 he received high critical praise for his album *Life'll Kill Ya* (2000) and the same for his follow-up release, *My Ride's Here* (2002).

Zevon was a multitalented musician who generally alternated between guitar and piano in concert. He had a droll, straightforward singing style that seemed to announce the words as opposed to melodically singing them. But when called for, as in bittersweet songs such as "Accidentally Like a Martyr," his voice could be full of emotional power.

In August 2002 Zevon was diagnosed with inoperable lung and liver cancer. The news did not blunt his humor or his recording career; he went right to work on *My Dirty Life and Times.* Zevon stated that the album (which had not been released as of May 2003) is a goodbye to a wide-ranging list of friends. *My Dirty Life and Times* features many of his past collaborators, including Bruce Springsteen, Bob Dylan, Jackson Browne, Don Henley, Billy Bob Thornton, Tom Petty, and Emmylou Harris. He died September 7, 2003.

Zevon wrote songs with the detail and zest of an investigative journalist. His body of work is produced not only from personal circumstances, but also as a comment about the world around him. It will serve as a journal of the times that Zevon lived.

SELECTIVE DISCOGRAPHY: *Wanted—Dead or Alive* (Imperial, 1969); *Warren Zevon* (Asylum, 1976); *Excitable Boy* (Asylum, 1978); *Bad Luck Streak in Dancing School* (Asylum, 1980); *Stand in the Fire* (Asylum, 1980); *The Envoy* (Asylum, 1982); *Sentimental Hygiene* (Virgin, 1987); *Transverse City* (Virgin, 1989); *Mr. Bad Example* (Warner Bros., 1991); *Learning to Flinch* (Warner Bros., 1993); *Mutineer* (Warner Bros., 1995); *Life'll Kill Ya* (Artemis, 2000); *My Ride's Here* (Artemis, 2002).

DONALD LOWE

JOHN ZORN

Born: New York, New York, 2 September 1953

Genre: Avant-Garde Contemporary Composition, Jazz, Punk

Best-selling album since 1990: *The Circle Maker* (1998)

It is reductive and inaccurate to describe John Zorn as a jazz musician, although one of his major musical activities since 1992 has been improvising on alto saxophone with hard-swinging combos such as the quartet Masada, for which he has written more than 200 songs loosely based on traditional Jewish motifs and scales. Zorn also has recorded albums of music by such jazz figures as Ornette Coleman and Sonny Clark, and worked with indisputable jazzers including organist Big John Patton, drummer Milford Graves, and bassist William Parker.

Though Zorn draws from jazz, he goes beyond it, taking it further than it has generally been defined, and operates completely outside it. As a composing improviser, he is a prolific creator of unusually structured, improvisational "game" pieces in which musicians play by rules dictating the duration of their contributions and the specific instrumental makeup of episodes within the pieces, employing their personal vocabularies to fill in the blanks rather than playing notes preordained in scores.

Zorn also writes through-composed (completely notated) works for orchestras and chamber ensembles, some of which have been used as soundtracks for independent films. He radically reconceives music by composers such as Ennio Morricone, Serge Gainsborough, Carl Stalling, and Burt Bacharach. He encourages works by a circle including guitarists/composers Elliott Sharp and Marc Ribot, pianists/composers Anthony Coleman and Wayne Horvitz, and dramatizing vocalist Shelly Hirsch, and curates music performances at New York venues including the Knitting Factory and Tonic. Zorn promotes "radical Jewish culture," producing albums by artists who address that banner, and releases other provocative albums by musicians from Europe and Japan as well as New York's edgy Lower East Side, financed by his own commissions and fees.

Zorn had childhood lessons in piano, flute, guitar, and composition (from age ten), but he is essentially self-taught. He has turned himself into an extraordinarily broad musicologist by delving deeply into twentieth-century popular, folk, and concert genres, including doo-wop, music for cartoons, surf-rock, field recordings from preindustrial societies, and compositions by iconoclasts including Igor Stravinsky, Charles Ives, Karlheinz Stockhausen, Harry Partch, John Cage, and Mauricio Kagel (his predecessor as a games composer). Attending Webster College in St. Louis, Missouri, Zorn was introduced to the avant-garde jazz collectives Black Artists Group and Association for the Advancement of Creative Musicians by alto saxophonist Oliver Lake, one of his teachers, and took up saxophone at age twenty.

In 1974, after eighteen months of traveling on the U.S. West Coast staging solo saxophone concerts, Zorn returned to New York City and began collaborating with a coterie of renegade musicians in small, often informal venues. Although this circle was steeped in jazz and classical traditions, its members addressed conventional materials with shattering energy and deconstructionist approaches. Zorn developed solo concerts using his instruments disassembled, with duck calls, whistles, and other odd noisemakers. He recorded *Lacrosse* (1978), his first game piece, on his Parachute label, and followed it with others in the idiom, culminating in *Cobra* (1991), which in 1995 was performed once a month by various casts of players at the jazz locale, the Knitting Factory, a venue catering to new and experimental musics.

Since the 1980s Zorn has recorded in an impressive array of contexts, including solo (*The Classic Guide to Strategy*, 1985), in improvisational trios (News for Lulu) and quintets (Naked City), and in ensembles performing his pieces comprising separate fragments of music written on file cards, shuffled for a given rendition's sequence (*Godard/Spillane*, 1988). On annual sojourns to Japan, he helped spark punk rock and free improvisation scenes. Much of his music is characterized by quick juxtapositions of dynamically and timbrally diverse sounds, fracturing linear processes and typical narrative arcs. He has also explored sonic densities, extremely concise and expanded durations, musical comedy, and violence. Since the late 1990s he has embarked on a campaign to recover ownership of all his recordings, repurchasing his rights to masters first released by the Elektra and Nonesuch labels.

In 1992 Zorn was invited to stage an evening-length presentation at a weeklong international festival of innovators in Munich, Germany. After a series of sets by New York bands comprised overwhelmingly of Jewish musicians, Zorn performed "Krystallnacht," named after the Nazi hooligan rampage that initiated open warfare on Jews in Germany in 1938. The concert hall's lights were turned off and its doors locked for the duration of the piece, which included the taped sounds of cattle cars rolling on railroad tracks.

This event marked the initiation of Zorn's "radical Jewish culture" movement, which has resulted in more than 300 recordings by Jewish and non-Jewish musicians considering religious and ethnic topics from a variety of viewpoints. It is no slight to Zorn's own vast catalog of original compositions and recorded improvisations to suggest that his support of other peoples' music on his own label Tzadik ("charity" or "good works" in Hebrew) is his most significant contribution to music since 1990.

SELECTIVE DISCOGRAPHY: *Naked City* (Elektra/Nonesuch, 1990); *More News for Lulu* (Hat Hut, 1992); *Masada: Alef* (DIW/Disk Union, 1994); *Kristallnacht* (Tzadik, 1995); *Naked City: Black Box* (Tzadik, 1997); *The Parachute Years, 1977–1980* (Tzadik, 1997); *New Traditions in East Asian Bar Bands* (Tzadik, 1997); *The Circle Maker* (Tzadik, 1998); *Godard/Spillane* (Tzadik, 1999); *The String Quartets* (Tzadik, 1999); *Masada: Live in Jerusalem 1994* (Tzadik, 1999); *Cobra* (Hatology re-release, 2002); *Filmworks XI, 2002, Volume One: Secret Lives* (Tzadik, 2002). **With Big John Patton:** *Minor Swing* (DIW/Disk Union, 1995).

HOWARD MANDEL

ZZ TOP

Formed: 1970, Houston, Texas

Members: William F. Gibbons, guitar, vocals (born Houston, Texas, 12 December 1949); Joe Michael (Dusty) Hill, bass, vocals (born, Dallas, Texas, 15 May 1949); Frank Beard, percussion (born Frankston, Texas, 11 June 1949).

Genre: Rock, Blues

Best-selling album since 1990: *Rhythmeen* (1996)

The trio ZZ Top is a little band with a big sound. With the same members since the band's inception in 1970, ZZ Top remains a constant in an industry fraught with change. They have broken concert attendance records, sold millions of albums, and played a presidential inaugural ball; yet the blues-rocking ZZ Top remains today what it has always been: a Texas good-time band with a sense of humor.

Texas Roots

ZZ Top formed in Houston, Texas, after guitarist and vocalist Billy Gibbons, bassist Dusty Hill, and drummer Frank Beard—all refugees from other Texas bands—decided to meet for a jam session in February 1970. The trio's first session together was a tremendous success, and they began to tour Texas, building a loyal following and gaining a reputation as a spirited boogie band that, on the strength of Gibbon's solid guitar work, could also play some serious blues.

After ZZ Top had gained some national exposure with "Francine," from their second album, *Rio Grande Mud* (1972), the Rolling Stones asked them to open for them on their 1972 tour. ZZ Top followed that successful tour with the release of *Tres Hombres* (1973), which contained their first hit, "La Grange." Based on a trademark blues riff sometimes credited to John Lee Hooker's "Boogie

Chillen" but also found in a variety of blues standards, "La Grange" is arguably ZZ Top's most identifiable song.

Wherever they played, the trio seemed to embody the image of a rowdy Texas bar band. By the time they released their next album, the half-studio, half-live *Fandango* (1975), ZZ Top was filling sports stadiums and other large concert venues with adoring fans who could not get enough of their raucous shows. In 1976 they shared the stage with long-horned steers, bison, coyotes, and rattlesnakes as they embellished their concerts with a stronger sense of Texas. That tour, which promoted their new release, *Tejas* (1976), broke concert attendance records previously held by the Beatles.

ZZ Top scored another hit with the droll "Tush," from *Fandango*, yet another in a long stream of riffed-up basic blues. "Tush" also remains one of the band's signature songs. Its primary message, "I ain't askin' for much . . . just looking for some tush," is emblematic of the playful lyrics found in much of their music. Many of their song messages are expressed simply by their impetuous titles: "She's Got Legs," "Cheap Sunglasses," "Tube Steak Boogie," and "Jesus Just Left Chicago."

Although there has always been a glut of southern boogie bands, ZZ Top manages to rise above the pack. One of the reasons for their success is that accompanying the "don't take us too seriously" message is a rhythmically strong bottom beat and the thick, dirty guitar funk of Gibbons, one of the world's top blues guitarists. Every song contains an opportunity for him to solo, and he finds remarkable variety within the sameness of the blues structure that ZZ Top's music generally employs.

ZZ Top's success stems not only from talent but also from some clever marketing. Recognizing the potential in the growing MTV video marketplace of the early 1980s, ZZ Top used music videos to brand themselves as fun-loving, pleasure-seeking hipster icons. Each member of the band went public with a look of exceptionally long beards, Stetson hats, crisp suits, and black sunglasses. Their MTV videos were replete with over-the-top gorgeous women whose limited acting duties were focused on their lavish attentions to the band. However, unlike other rock or rap videos, the content of ZZ Top's videos seemed to convey a nonthreatening attitude toward their female subjects. They left the impression that the band simply enjoyed the girls' company and sent them off with a peck on the cheek.

Adding emphasis to ZZ Top's laissez-faire attitude was the manner in which they approached the performance of their music, seemingly playing their instruments with bemused nonchalance. This further enhanced an image of cool and helped endear them to millions of fans worldwide. ZZ Top concerts continued to fill arenas and break financial records into the new millennium.

Returning to Roots

The band entered the 1990s in a quandary. Portrayed in popular videos throughout the 1980s as a lovable cartoon of a rock band, they had begun questing for a more serious image by sporadically experimenting with various electronics such as drum machines, Moog synthesizers, and sequencers. The release of *Recycler* (1990) marked a firm return to the music of ZZ Top's boogie rock/blues beginnings. It is where they have remained. One song, from *Recycler*, "My Head's in Mississippi," pays homage to blues legend Muddy Waters. This tribute was part of a continuing effort by ZZ Top to keep Waters's music alive and to acquaint a wider audience with the roots of blues. The previous year they had visited the Mississippi childhood home of the great blues legend and obtained a plank of wood from the cabin in which Waters once lived. Gibbons arranged for it to be fashioned into a guitar that was later displayed in various cities across the country. The proceeds of that traveling exhibit were distributed to the Delta Blues Museum in Clarksdale, Mississippi.

Throughout the 1990s ZZ Top remained a huge concert draw; their albums *Antenna* (1994) and *Rhythmeen* (1996) sold well. In 1998 they were inducted into the Music Hall of Fame. ZZ Top celebrated their thirtieth anniversary with the much-anticipated release of *XXX* (1999). The album is an honest return to their early work and, like *Fandango,* is part live, part studio. One of the four live songs is a bluesy version of Elvis Presley's "Teddy Bear," a tribute to the king of rock and roll, who influenced the lives of all three ZZ Top members. Of the eight studio songs, only "Fearless Boogie" was released as a single for radio play. The album's tour was canceled midstream in the summer of 2000 after the discovery that the band's bassist was suffering from Hepatitis C and needed to rest. The band took a hiatus until Hill recovered, and then they began a series of short tours. One of those was a European tour to fulfill a commitment to fans and promoters after the *XXX* tour had been canceled. In late 2002 ZZ Top was recording a soon-to-be-released album through RCA Records and planning the album's promotion with a world tour starting sometime in 2003.

ZZ Top is a remarkably consistent group whose straightforward music and lighthearted attitude have exemplified good-time rock and roll for more than thirty years. While they have managed to stay popular through innovative marketing strategies, their musicianship should not be undervalued. ZZ Top is a top-notch and well-respected blues band.

SELECTIVE DISCOGRAPHY: *First Album* (London, 1970); *Rio Grande Mud* (London, 1972); *Tres Hombres* (London, 1973); *Fandango* (London, 1975); *Tejas* (London, 1976); *The Best of ZZ Top* (London, 1979); *Deguello* (Warner Bros., 1979); *El Loco* (Warner Bros., 1981); *Eliminator* (Warner Bros., 1983); *Afterburner* (Warner Bros., 1985); *Recycler* (Warner Bros., 1990); *Antenna* (RCA, 1994); *One Foot in the Blues* (RCA, 1994); *Rhythmeen* (RCA, 1996); *XXX* (RCA, 1999).

DONALD LOWE

Appendix

GRUNGE: A BRIEF HISTORY OF A HARD ROCK GENRE

New popular music never evolves in a vacuum, and the hard rock genre that emerged in the late 1980s, dubbed "grunge" by the music media, was no exception. Its development reflected the turbulent social and economic times. Grunge became as much an aesthetic and cultural movement as it was a musical genre. It grew out of the heavy metal and punk rock of the 1970s and early 1980s, a do-it-yourself spirit, and the influence of underground magazine publishing. Icons such as Kurt Cobain, lead singer of Nirvana, gave voice to a generation of young music fans faced with bleak economic prospects, broken homes, and uncertain futures. Cobain summed up his numb detachment and that of many of his peers with a line from Nirvana's signature hit, "Smells Like Teen Spirit": "Here we are now, entertain us."

Grunge evolved outside the traditional music business, forging an identity through the close-knit nature of many of its early bands. Soon the mainstream caught on, leading to a number of copycat groups and fashions that seemed both to embarrass the first wave of grunge acts and speed the music's demise. As quickly as the genre rose, it fell prey to the dilution of its strong, initially uncalculating message and the deaths of several prominent singers, either by suicide or drug overdose. Before being supplanted by a surge of clean-living, apple-cheeked teen pop singers in the mid- to late 1990s, grunge created a new generation of rock idols. It spawned a feminist offshoot that empowered female rock musicians; it changed rock radio; and it made possible a handful of highly influen-

tial albums that continue to inspire new generations of hard rock musicians.

Before It Had a Name

Like folk, disco, and punk before it, grunge was a cultural as well as a musical phenomenon. A rough marriage of heavy metal, agitated punk, and new wave styles, the music grew out of the Pacific Northwest in the late 1980s and early 1990s. Performed almost exclusively by white young men and women in their early to mid-twenties, grunge was the music of a disaffected generation, many of whom grew up in the early 1970s during a boom in the U.S. divorce rate. Like their peers who were leaving college at the dawn of the first Bush administration in 1989, many of the musicians who formed the early grunge groups faced a tough economic recession. Jobs were scarce and popular radio was filled with the sounds of teen groups such as New Kids on the Block, bland heavy metal bands such as Poison, and, later, M.C. Hammer, the cartoonish pop rapper. The music created by bands such as the Melvins and Nirvana was, almost without exception, unremittingly dark, questioning, and aggressive, full of anger, sarcasm, and disillusionment.

At the same time, underground youth culture boomed, thanks to the desktop publishing revolution. Desktop publishing allowed young artists to create cheap, photocopied magazines (dubbed zines), which expounded on their obsessions, favorite music, and local art scenes. Stocked mostly in independent bookstores, zines helped to spread the word on the burgeoning underground rock movement.

Before it was called "grunge"—a term coined by the music media to describe its often muddy sound—the music that defined the genre was seen as the latest evolution of punk-inspired hard rock. Grunge's clamorous sound consisted of ominous, distorted guitar chords over booming drums and passionately screamed lyrics; it was partly a reaction against Los Angeles' preening, teased-hair heavy metal scene at the end of the 1980s and beginning of the 1990s, which included bands such as Mötley Crüe and Warrant. It was also a homage to the thundering classic rock of groups like Led Zeppelin. Grunge evoked a healthy appreciation for the chaos and abandon of punk rock, as expressed by artists like Iggy Pop, along with the dissonant noise of post-punk bands such as the Pixies and Wire. The post-punk sensibility took the aggressively amateurish and nihilistic punk sound and deconstructed it with artfully created noise and more thoughtful, if disjointed, lyrics. While many grunge bands had a keen appreciation for the melodies of the Beatles, they also thirsted for the cathartic release of punk, which is why so many classic grunge songs present a perfect mix of dissonance and tunefulness.

In Seattle, the city that came to define the genre at its outset, the sartorial style adopted by many of the bands represented a rejection of the put-together, upwardly mobile class of Young Urban Professionals ("Yuppies"). Torn jeans, cut into shorts and layered over thermal full-length underwear, long, unwashed hair, a goatee, and a worn T-shirt became the unofficial uniform of early Seattle grunge groups like Green River and Skin Yard. One possible explanation for the haggard look was that many of the groups had little money to spend on clothes so they preferred to shop at local thrift stores.

Seattle had long been a hub of noisome rock music. It is the birthplace of Jimi Hendrix, the legendary guitarist-singer-composer, and the home of 1960s garage rock bands, including the Sonics and the Kingsmen (of "Louie Louie" fame). But it was not until the mid-1980s that a new musical movement began to take place. The Seattle music scene had fallen into the doldrums in the decade before with rock shows driven to underground basement venues thanks to the city's repressive liquor laws and harassment by the police. At these clandestine shows a movement was born, with many future band leaders and record label founders sweating and slamming into each other in mosh pits to the furious sounds of the music. By 1984, the small scene was centered around clubs such as the Central Tavern, the Rainbow Tavern, and the Vogue, where several nights a week many of the same people gathered to listen to local bands. One of the first acknowledged releases in the genre was by the U-Men, whose 1985 mini-album, *Stop Spinning*, was released on Homestead Records. They, along with Seattle bands Malfunkshun, Soundgarden, Skin Yard, Green River, and the Melvins, appeared on a 1986 compilation album entitled *Deep Six*, an album that helped

define the grunge sound: a thick, aggressive mix of heavy metal guitars, punk attitude, and gothic darkness.

While the region's bands were releasing their first albums, a trio of non-musicians critical to the growth of the scene also made their mark. They consisted of two entrepreneurs, Bruce Pavitt and Jonathan Poneman, founders of Sub Pop Records, and a photographer, Charles Peterson, whose blurry, black-and-white snapshots became the abiding imagery of the early grunge years. Together, this trio helped to shape the look and sound of grunge. Pavitt had self-published a magazine called *Sub Pop* while living in Olympia, Washington, in the mid-1980s. In 1986, he released an album called *Sub Pop 100*, which featured notable national bands Sonic Youth and Big Black, as well as the Wipers, based in Portland, Oregon. Pavitt teamed up with fellow music aficionado Jonathan Poneman and released the debut mini-album by Green River, *Dry as a Bone,* in July 1987. It was followed by the debut single and mini-album from Soundgarden. The Sub Pop founders insisted on a consistent look for all of their releases, which is why Peterson's iconic photos—which matched the music note for note with grainy, brutish energy—graced the covers of nearly all of the label's early albums.

Also influential was record producer Jack Endino, who brought out early albums from Sub Pop stars Mudhoney, Screaming Trees, Soundgarden, TAD, Green River, and Nirvana. Like Peterson's photos, Endino's low-budget, gritty recording method made albums such as Mudhoney's *Superfuzz Bigmuff* and Nirvana's 1989 debut, *Bleach,* resonate with a low-fidelity, sludgy, snarling sound that communicated the urgency of the music with little adornment. A less gritty side of the scene consisted of groups such as Mother Love Bone. Featuring two future members of Pearl Jam, Mother Love Bone reveled in glam rack, the flashy, trashy 1970s aesthetic that mixed loud, primal rock with glittery outfits and theatrically applied makeup. Sadly, like several of grunge's best acts, Mother Love Bone failed to live up to its potential because of the death of its singer, Andrew Wood, from a heroin overdose in March 1990 just as the group was slated to begin a national tour.

Having established a look and a sound for the Northwest regional bands, Pavitt and Poneman set about spreading the gospel of grunge, releasing songs and albums by Los Angeles' L7 and Hole, Minneapolis' Babes in Toyland, Cincinnati's Afghan Whigs, and Denver's the Fluid. The Seattle scene, as yet undiscovered by the world at large, grew and became more vibrant. Frequently, musicians played in several different bands and engaged in sometimes irreverent, often explosive onstage antics, many of them captured by Peterson in legendary photos. Artists outside Seattle began to take notice as well, helping to spread the word about Seattle's bands overseas. Though one act,

Soundgarden, had already jumped ship and signed a major label deal in 1988 with A&M Records, it was in 1989 that grunge gained international attention. Poneman and Pavitt flew in journalists from leading English music magazines *New Musical Express* and *Melody Maker* to watch their bands and soak up the Seattle atmosphere. The gambit worked. The writers returned home and wrote gushing articles about the town's homegrown acts.

The crowds at shows began to swell and talent scouts increasingly flocked to Seattle to sign groups such as Alice in Chains, the Posies, Pearl Jam, and Screaming Trees to major label contracts. In a sign of grunge artists' close ties, Jeff Ament, Stone Gossard, Mike McCready, and Eddie Vedder of Pearl Jam teamed up with Matt Cameron and Chris Cornell of Soundgarden to form the supergroup Temple of the Dog. Pearl Jam, one of the acts that soon ascended to worldwide fame, finished its debut, *Ten*, in one month, in April 1991. But it was the band Nirvana that took grunge to the pinnacle of worldwide acclaim. After the September 1991 release of its second album, the groundbreaking *Nevermind*, Seattle, and grunge, would never be the same.

Grunge Hits the Mainstream . . . and the Mall

A high school pep rally turns sinister as tattooed cheerleaders shake their pom-poms and unruly students begin to riot—this is a scene from the video *Smells Like Teen Spirit* by Nirvana. It is four minutes of controlled anarchy that, for some, perfectly summed up the rage and frustration of an entire generation. The song, with its nonsense chorus of "A mulatto, an albino, a mosquito, my libido," followed by a shout of "Yeah!" and buoyed by Nirvana's patented song structure, a mix of sedate verses and explosive, loud choruses, became a mantra of sorts. *Nevermind* combines the aggressive grunge sound with Beatles-esque pop craftsmanship. Yet it did not begin by topping the charts; it actually entered the *Billboard* 200 at number 144 in September. By January 1992 the album had ascended to the number one spot, literally knocking the old guard from the top spot, in the guise of Michael Jackson. Its success served to vindicate a post-Baby Boomer generation dogged in the media as the apathetic, spoiled, and rootless "Generation X."

For several years, word of bands such as Nirvana had circulated on college campuses and in independent bookstores courtesy of self-published zines such as *Maximum Rocknroll* and *Chemical Imbalance*, which often chronicled music not heard on mainstream radio. The album's triumph signaled the national debut of a sound that came to dominate record sales and the airwaves for several years. It also paved the way for "Generation X" to seize the media spotlight with events such as Lollapalooza, the traveling, multiartist festival, which mixed rock, rap, and heavy metal,

and eventually brought the subcultural practices of piercing and tattooing to suburban teens.

Radio stations such as Seattle's KNDD ("The End") began playing more local music and a new format emerged, called alternative rock radio. The format grew out of 1980s "college radio," which mixed mainstream and less-well-known music by punk and independent bands, mostly on lower-wattage university bandwidths. With the power of corporate radio behind it, as well as the embrace of Music Television (MTV)—which saw in grubbily handsome Nirvana singer Kurt Cobain a rock star in the making—grunge was able to support a much larger platform. Having charismatic, long-haired, tortured souls as singers worked for a pair of other Seattle bands, too. Pearl Jam's Eddie Vedder relished the role of the Everyman, singing gravelly odes to teenage confusion and angst such as "Jeremy," and appearing on the cover of *Time* magazine in 1993. Soundgarden's lithe Chris Cornell wailed falsetto heavy metal anthems that mixed poetic vulnerability and raw power.

Cobain, with his sky blue eyes, dirty blonde hair, and vulnerable image, became the poster boy for grunge. The product of a broken home and a difficult childhood, Cobain married Courtney Love, quarrelsome singer of the female grunge band Hole, in February 1992, forming the most formidable power couple of rock. Though together for only a few years, the couple—she the attention-grabbing loudmouth, he the shy, fragile introvert—made headlines, such as when a *Vanity Fair* article reported that Love had abused hard drugs while pregnant with their only child, Frances Bean.

In film, fashion, and the press, grunge became a sensation. With albums by Nirvana, Pearl Jam, and Alice in Chains selling briskly, *Singles*, a breezy date movie about twenty-something friends living in the same apartment complex in Seattle, appeared in the summer of 1992. Directed by Cameron Crowe, it featured both credited and uncredited cameos by several members of Pearl Jam, Alice in Chains, and Soundgarden. Poorly reviewed and dismissed as an oversimplification of the city's music scene, nevertheless *Singles* illustrated that grunge had entered the mainstream. The bedraggled look that arose out of poverty and thrift store necessity soon hit the runways of Paris. *Vogue* magazine ran a 1992 "Grunge and Glory" fashion spread featuring $500 to $1,000 outfits by designers Calvin Klein and Ralph Lauren, and Marc Jacobs created his own line of grunge fashions. Flannel shirts, ripped jean shorts over thermal underwear, and Doc Marten boots became the look of choice for suburban teens and college kids alike.

In November 1992 Sub Pop receptionist Megan Jasper had a good laugh at the expense of the *New York Times*, when a reporter from the *Times* called to check on a lexicon of grunge originally printed in the British magazine,

Sky. The receptionist provided an extemporaneous list of meaningless jargon that the reporter took as gospel. Hence, the phrases "swinging on the flippety-flop" (hanging out), "wack slacks" (old ripped jeans), and "lamestain" (an uncool person) made their way into the newspaper's "Lexicon of Grunge: Breaking the Code."

Despite the worldwide embrace of grunge music, tragedy continued to dog the burgeoning movement when 22-year-old Seven Year Bitch guitarist Stefanie Sargent choked on her vomit and died after ingesting alcohol and heroin in June 1992. A year later, Mia Zapata, vocalist for popular grunge band the Gits, was raped and murdered in an alley behind a bar in Seattle; her killer was caught a decade later. Easy access to heroin in Seattle partly explained the abundance of drug casualties and addicts among the grunge bands, and the music's dim sound seemed to complement rock and roll's fascination with eternal youth, death, violence, and the use of drugs to escape from reality. The lyrics to the first three songs on *Nevermind* prominently mention guns; Alice in Chains's *Dirt* (1992) is filled with songs about heroin, such as "Sickman," "Junkhead," and "God Smack."

As with most entertainment movements that reach the mainstream, the grunge phenomenon was quickly co-opted by major media companies. By 1993, record stores and radio airwaves were flooded with a second wave of newly signed grunge bands such as Australia's youthful Silverchair, England's Bush, and the United States' Radish, Candlebox, Collective Soul, Verve Pipe, Filter, and Stone Temple Pilots, all of which met with varying degrees of commercial success. Most of these groups did not reach the level of success of Nirvana and Pearl Jam, and served mostly to dilute the genre's sound by offering up a patented mix of loud and quiet dynamics, often without any new artistic contributions.

Parallel to the rise of grunge was an offshoot movement dubbed "Riot Grrrl," which filled the gender gap in a mostly male alternative rock music scene. Spearheaded by bands such as L7, Bratmobile, the Gits, Dickless, Seven Year Bitch, Hole, and the Fastbacks, the music was no less aggressive than that of their male compatriots, but often suffused with a post-feminist rage at society's treatment of women. Shattering the traditional myth of beauty and music stardom, singers such as Kathleen Hanna of Bikini Kill and Courtney Love of Hole donned ripped and soiled baby doll dresses, wore smeared lipstick, and scrawled in marker empowering messages on their arms espousing support of abortion rights and denigrating rape. In the past, female pop and rock singers had been packaged either as comely sex objects or serious artistes; bands such as L7 put a combat boot in the face of this industry with such fearsome anthems as "Shove," "Fast and Frightening," and "Pretend We're Dead." The message that female musicians were strong and invested with authority resonated with their fans, who often adopted similar outfits and were inspired to pick up instruments and start their own bands.

A Precipitous Rise, a Mighty Fall

Just two years after breaking into the mainstream, grunge was big business, with Nirvana, Pearl Jam, Alice in Chains, and Soundgarden selling millions of albums and playing to tens of thousands of fans. However, tragedy was not far behind. April 8, 1994, became a black day in grunge history, when an electrician came to check on the security system at Cobain's house and found the singer dead of a self-inflicted gunshot wound to the face. Cobain, who had taken a large dose of heroin before his suicide, left a rambling note in which he quoted a lyric from one of his heroes, Neil Young: "it's better to burn out than to fade away." Bands such as Pearl Jam, Soundgarden, and Alice in Chains continued to release successful albums following Cobain's death, but the genre never again achieved the success it had enjoyed from 1990 to 1994. By 1995, Pearl Jam had voluntarily pulled back from the spotlight after their overwhelming initial success, refusing to make music videos or do many press interviews, and Alice in Chains was in limbo due to singer Layne Staley's debilitating heroin addiction and subsequent death from an overdose in April 2002.

Just six years after its rise, grunge was erased from the pop music charts by bubblegum pop groups such as Hanson and the Backstreet Boys and by a new generation of hard rock bands, dubbed "nu-metal." Nu-metal groups such as Godsmack (named after an Alice in Chains song), Linkin Park, Deftones, Puddle of Mudd, and Creed employed the angst of the grunge sound, but often augmented it with the turntable scratching of a DJ or more mainstream, classic rock edge.

The heyday of the grunge rock movement was short, but its influence was still felt in 2003, in everything from the contemporary emotional hard rock on the charts to the willingness of advertisers to market "alternative" culture products to teens and twenty-somethings. Cobain has joined Jimi Hendrix, Jim Morrison, and John Lennon among the pantheon of rock legends who died young, and the visceral music of Nirvana continues to resonate on radio and with fans.

In the minds of casual listeners, grunge was a fad much like disco or punk. But for devoted fans who came of age during the grunge years, the music was an ecstatic form of release during uncertain times, and it served as a reminder that the American underground music scene was alive and thriving outside the confines of what some critics considered a staid and predictable mainstream.

GIL KAUFMAN

RAP'S EMERGENCE INTO THE MAINSTREAM

Since 1990 rap music—once heard exclusively in a few African-American, Caribbean, and Latino neighborhoods in New York City—has steadily evolved into a dominant form of American popular music. At first a somewhat watered-down, mass-market version of rap appeared; but by the middle of the 1990s, as audiences became familiar with the genre, a more authentic style moved into the mainstream.

Traditional hip-hop culture in New York City consisted of four basic "elements": deejaying, emceeing, dancing, and graffiti writing. Deejaying refers to the use of two turntables to create new musical arrangements from existing records. Emceeing—also called rapping—is the recitation of rhythmic poetry. Hip-hop dancing includes locking (a bouncy, funk-oriented style), popping (a style that utilizes "robotic" movements), and b-boying (often called "breakdancing" in the mass media). Graffiti, from the Italian *graffio*, a "scratch," refers to handwriting or images on the surfaces of public areas, including buildings, printed advertising, subways, and trains. The elevation of emceeing as the hip-hop element with the most marketable potential occurred in the early 1980s following the release of the hit single "Rappers' Delight" by the Sugarhill Gang (1979), which unexpectedly sold eight million copies. The early 1980s also witnessed a hip-hop dance craze in movies such as *Breakin'* (1984) and *Beat Street* (1984), but the public soon tired of what was considered a commercial fad.

By the mid-1980s, many major labels began to produce recordings featuring emceeing, which was often accompanied by live instruments rather than a deejay. Because rapping was the most prominent aspect of these recordings, the whole genre soon became known as rap. As a result of its association with commercial recording, the term "rap music" has tended to denote shallowness relative to other forms of hip-hop music and culture. In fact, whereas "rap" in its broadest sense refers to any musical expression of hip-hop culture that utilizes emceeing, purists often use the term pejoratively to refer to forms of hip-hop music they consider to be unduly concerned with mainstream tastes.

Rap's commercial breakthrough may be traced to 1986 when the widely respected hip-hop group Run-D.M.C. enjoyed huge success with a version of Aerosmith's 1975 rock classic "Walk This Way" performed as an ensemble with the original artists. The song's popularity and the video's heavy rotation on the Music Television network (MTV) made rap accessible to rock's core fans. That same year a trio of white emcees, the Beastie Boys, released *Licensed to Ill* (1987), the first rap album to hit number one on the *Billboard* 200 album charts. The album's teen-rebellion fantasy "(You Gotta) Fight for Your Right (To Party!)," and its accompanying video, supported rap's long march into the suburbs. At the same time, hip-hop underwent a creative explosion. The rise of sampling (or digital sound manipulation), the increasing complexity of emcee rhyme schemes and rhythmic patterns, and the broad new range of subject matter in rap lyrics ushered in what hip-hop critics often refer to as the "Golden Age" of the late 1980s. These changes signaled an openness to new forms of expression in rap. One of the highest compliments that could be given at the time was to say that a song was "fresh," meaning innovative and energetic. The introduction in 1988 of "Yo! MTV Raps," a daily outlet for rap videos on rock-oriented MTV, encouraged these developments.

In the 1990s two different approaches by hip-hop artists drove rap's transition into the mainstream. One approach, "pop rap," aimed to appeal to a broad popular audience. The other approach, which may be called "popular underground rap," or rap music designed for a small, core audience, somehow managed to capture a broad pop market despite its refusal to follow pop trends. As many Americans familiarized themselves with the conventions of hip-hop, the pop rap approach became increasingly unnecessary and popular underground rap became the vogue.

Pop Rap

Pop rap was created by the same urban communities that produced other forms of hip-hop. It was tailored especially for listeners with little first-hand knowledge of hip-hop or African-American or Latino culture. Pop rap songs tended to have a number of characteristic traits. First, the language of the songs was designed to be understood by outsiders. When slang was used, it functioned more as a novelty than as a way to exclude the uninitiated. Terms that might be unfamiliar were often explained within the song's lyrics. Similarly, the subject matter tended to focus on issues common to all Americans, rather than those unique to urban communities. Artists' images also tended to be socially and politically non-threatening.

Pop rap songs aimed for danceability and catchy "hooks," or short melodic phrases that would attract radio listeners. This effect was partially achieved through the recycling of well-known pop songs from earlier eras; the strategy provided both instant familiarity and market-tested appeal: "We know it can be a hit, because it already was one." Pop rap tended to be radio-friendly on a pragmatic level: The songs were released by major record companies that employed large publicity departments and whose business relationships with radio stations, television shows, and other promotional venues facilitated access into the mainstream.

In 1989 the album *Loc-ed After Dark* by Tone-Loc (Anthony Smith) rode the success of its singles "Wild Thing" and "Funky Cold Medina" to become number one on the *Billboard* 200 album charts. In keeping with the pop rap format, the lyrics decode the use of the slang in both songs; both songs are based on melodies taken from rock (the former from Van Halen's "Jamie's Cryin'" and the latter from Free's "All Right Now" and KISS's "Christine Sixteen"). Rap's status as a distinct mainstream genre was confirmed in 1988 when the National Academy of Recording Arts and Sciences (NARAS) established a new category for its Grammy Awards: Best Rap Performance. (The award went to Jazzy Jeff and the Fresh Prince.) By 1995 there were three Grammy awards in the rap category: Best Solo Performance, Best Group Performance, and Best Rap Album.

The most important artist in the pop rap genre in the 1990s was Oakland's M.C. Hammer (Stanley Burrell). Tellingly, in 1991, he dropped the "M.C." from his name to minimize his connection to hip-hop, which he saw as a barrier to wide commercial appeal. Using an elaborate stage show that emphasized dancing and flashy clothing, Hammer drew upon an older tradition of crowd-pleasing African-American entertainment, as exemplified by legendary artists such as James Brown and Sammy Davis, Jr. In one video, Hammer appears before James Brown, who is seated on a royal throne, to ask for his blessing as an artist. In an era when hip-hop became anti-commercial and Black Nationalist—the phrase "no sell out" was a common refrain—Hammer's eagerness to entertain did not endear him to hip-hop's core audience.

Hammer's song "U Can't Touch This" exemplifies the pop rap category. Based on the melody of Rick James's 1981 R&B classic "Superfreak," the song's lyrics consisted primarily of dozens of repetitions of the title, bracketed by a few short stanzas concerning Hammer's excellence as an entertainer. In 1990, the single was awarded the Grammy for Best R&B Song, as well as the first Grammy ever awarded for Best Rap Solo Performance. Hammer was also one of the first MCs to diversify his brand and to supplement his musical income with other forms of merchandising, including toys and a short-lived Saturday morning cartoon-show, *Hammerman* (1991).

Vanilla Ice (Robert Van Winkle) was widely viewed as a white version of Hammer, and he did little to dispel the perception; his rhyme style and stage show were openly imitative of Hammer. Vanilla Ice's Teutonic good looks and dancing ability made him a pop star, in the mold of earlier generations of so-called "teen idols," such as Fabian and David Cassidy. Although the hip-hop community roundly dismissed him, he was arguably the first entertainer to be both an emcee and an object of white middle-class teen fantasy, a mantle soon to be taken up by many others. Vanilla Ice's music adhered closely to the pop rap pattern. His 1990 pop hit "Ice Ice Baby" is based on the 1982 pop hit "Under Pressure," recorded by Queen with David Bowie. Upbeat and danceable, the song demanded little of listeners and ultimately reached number one on *Billboard*'s Hot 100 and Hot Rap Singles charts.

Following the success of Hammer and Vanilla Ice, Atlanta-based producer Jermaine Dupri theorized that teen rap fans might be particularly receptive to rappers who were themselves teens. With this in mind he recruited two thirteen-year-old rappers named Chris Kelly and Chris Smith and molded them into a duo called Kriss Kross. Dupri carefully built an image for the two that continuously reinforced the group's name. One of the emcees was dubbed "Mac Daddy," the other "Daddy Mac." Dupri insisted that they wear their clothes backwards for public appearances. In 1992, they released the single "Jump," which sampled the 1970 hit "I Want You Back" by the Jackson 5. It reached number one on *Billboard*'s Hot 100 and Hot Rap Singles charts, and propelled the album, *Totally Krossed Out* (1992), to number one on both the *Billboard* 200 chart and the Top R&B/Hip-Hop Album chart.

It is worth noting that, although hip-hop was firmly associated with New York, Hammer came from Oakland, Vanilla Ice from Florida, and Kriss Kross from Atlanta. Their outsider status may help explain why they were viewed with suspicion by New York hip-hoppers, who were widely considered the de facto arbiters of taste for the culture. Not being part of the New York community, these artists felt less pressure to conform to its mandates. While this may have hurt their credibility with hip-hop's core, it allowed them to pursue a broad audience. In the mid-1990s, even New York produced its own breed of pop rap artists. New York's attempts to appeal to a broad national (and increasingly international) audience were presented, however, not as "selling out" but as "entrepreneurship."

The reconfiguration of pop rap as a business opportunity for urban youth was not merely a rationalization; the new generation of hip-hop artists learned from the hard lessons of their forebears: Hammer filed for bankruptcy in 1996; Vanilla Ice went nearly bankrupt; and Kriss Kross realized only a small percentage of the profits from their music. In the ensuing years, rap artists put at least as much energy into their business models as their music. In fact, rather than camouflage their business savvy behind flowery talk of "art"—as an earlier generation might have done—the new breed of artists made the drive for financial success an integral part of their appeal.

Sean Combs, though not the first hip-hop artist to display strong business instincts, was the first to make it a key part of his artistic image. Following the tradition of Motown Records, Combs established a musical brand identity that fans could trust to fulfill their expectations. His innovation was to promote not the brand, but his own savvy and initiative in having created it in the first place. Combs began his meteoric rise after dropping out of Howard University to become an intern at Uptown Records in 1990. Three years later he started his own label, Bad Boy Records, and soon he established his public identity as a corporate executive, record producer, and musical artist, freely mixing the three roles. By 1994 Sean Combs (known as "Puffy," "Puff Daddy," and later as "P. Diddy") had his first hits with Craig Mack's *Project: Funk da World* (1994) and the Notorious B.I.G.'s (aka Biggie Smalls) *Ready to Die* (1994), both of which he appeared on as a guest performer. An intense, street-oriented rhyme style combined with well-known soul, pop, and disco hits of the 1970s and early 1980s characterized the music that Bad Boy produced. In addition to its radio appeal, the easy danceability of Bad Boy product made it a natural for play in nightclubs. Combs's ability to exploit nightclub play as a promotional opportunity exerted a decisive influence on the hip-hop industry in the mid-1990s. It allowed the nightclubs and their disc jockeys to wield the power to popularize hip-hop songs. As a result of these strategies, Sean Combs was already a major star before he released his first album *No Way Out* (1997).

By combining the raw lyrics of Biggie Smalls and others with his own pop rap inclinations, Sean Combs maintained credibility with both audiences—the core hip-hop base and the pop mainstream. In the process, he introduced the pop audience to an uncensored view of life on the street while simultaneously reminding hardcore fans of the importance of nightclubs and dancing. In so doing, he made pop rap obsolete, and he opened the door to other strategies for mainstream acceptance, such as popular underground rap.

Popular Underground Rap

Critics and historians do not agree on a commonly accepted term for the hip-hop music that achieved mainstream popularity without overtly catering to mainstream tastes. This is largely because most underground practitioners did not distinguish themselves from other hip-hop artists. In fact, more often it was the behavior of the audience that helped to characterize popular underground rap. Hip-hop artists suddenly emerged in the mainstream because of deep cross-cultural sympathy or, more commonly, the superficial allure of their exoticism. Such widespread appeal often hurt the artists' credibility with their original fan base, forcing them to choose between mutually exclusive audiences. The various strategies artists used

to negotiate this situation (chasing mainstream appeal, rejecting mainstream overtures, attempting to reconcile their two constituencies) helped to define the rise of underground rap in the late 1990s.

In the early 1990s two popular underground rap artists appealed to mainstream audiences in part by openly celebrating drug use, an outlaw recreational activity that cut across lines of race and class. Both Dr. Dre, a solo artist formerly of N.W.A., and Cypress Hill, one of the first widely popular Latino hip-hop groups, were Los Angeles-based champions of marijuana. Cypress Hill was a quintessential street group—their lyrics celebrated violence and drug use and little else. Often their lyrics taunt outsiders for being unable to comprehend the violent realities of their lives, as in the refrain to their first single "How I Could Just Kill a Man" (1992): "Here is something you can't understand—how I could just kill a man." And yet the very fact that the lyric is addressed to outsiders suggests that, on some level, they were keeping this broader audience in mind. Moreover, their staunch advocacy of marijuana, the use of psychedelic art and lettering in their album packaging, along with their slow tempos and acid rock guitar samples, quickly endeared them to bohemian college students across the United States. As with most popular underground artists, general popularity led to questions from within hip-hop about their intentions, most of which were never fully resolved.

Dr. Dre—apparently unintentionally—also exploited the exotic appeal of Los Angeles street culture in his album, *The Chronic* (1992). The album title, a slang term for marijuana, established the mainstream appeal of Gangsta Funk as a distinctively Los Angeles style of rap. Gangsta Funk, or G-Funk, assembles blocks of synthesizer-based funk from the late 1970s and early 1980s, such as Parliament-Funkadelic and Zapp, over a slow, bass-heavy beat that is made to be played at high volume on elaborate car stereo systems. Vocals on *The Chronic*—many of which were performed by Snoop (Doggy) Dogg—have a relaxed, almost Southern feel that adds to the sense of menace created by the often gang-oriented lyrics. (Snoop Dogg was associated with the Crip set; label head Suge Knight was associated with the rival Bloods.) For listeners from a variety of social backgrounds, Dr. Dre served up an intoxicating combination: mellow music for driving, along with intrigue provided by intense lyrics.

The juxtaposition of rap's intensity with more relaxed musical forms was exploited in other areas as well, particularly in R&B music in the mid-1990s. In the early 1990s, Ron G, a New York underground mixtape deejay, achieved popularity with a series of so-called "blends" tapes, in which he layered the vocals of popular R&B songs over hard-edged beats from well-known rap songs, thereby creating a hybrid sound that gave an extra punch and street appeal to R&B.

Soon R&B artists began to adopt the style for their original recordings, often adding guest rappers to emphasize a hip-hop orientation. Because many of the R&B singers were female and most of the emcees were male, the opportunity for the romantic duet presented itself—always an appealing prospect for mainstream consumers. The establishment of a "Best Rap/Sung Collaboration" Grammy category in 2001 confirmed the approach's widespread success.

Meanwhile, the value of entrepreneurship—and its ability to soften the edges between underground and commercial hip-hop—crystallized in New York City.

In Staten Island, New York, a group of no less than eight emcees, the Wu-Tang Clan, began a remarkable rise from underground favorites to mainstream stars with the album *Enter the Wu-Tang (36 Chambers)* (1993). Wu-Tang Clan's music retained the characteristics of New York underground hip-hop, even as their business model swept them into the upper echelons of the record industry. Although the group as a whole was signed to Loud/RCA, each individual emcee was under contract to a different record company. Because they often made guest appearances on each other's albums, this meant that in practice Wu-Tang Clan had signed to multiple record labels at the same time, a position that gave them great leverage when it came time to negotiate.

Wu-Tang Clan was one of the first rap groups to sport a corporate logo—a stylized "W" that appeared on all of their projects. The logo immediately identified the Clan to consumers, and the group soon diversified its money-making pursuits. They established their own clothing line ("Wu-Wear," available in shopping malls across the United States), and they endorsed a series of re-releases of 1980s Hong Kong Kung Fu movies. Diversification and business acumen became part of Wu-Tang Clan's image. In 2003 the comedian Dave Chappelle even joked that Wu-Tang might soon open a corporate consulting firm called "Wu-Tang Financial."

Master P (Percy Miller) and his No Limit Records came out of New Orleans in the mid-1990s with a similar strategy: a strong brand identity, communal spirit, and a chief executive officer who was the record label's best-known rapper. No Limit Records also became known for making its own low-budget feature films, which starred artists on the label and which were often released directly to video. Films included *I'm Bout It* (1997), *Da Game of Life* (1998), and *Hot Boyz* (1999). *Forbes* magazine's list of "America's 40 Richest Under 40" indicated Master P had earned $56.5 million in 1998.

By the late 1990s, the entrepreneurial method found its ultimate practitioner in Jay-Z (Shawn Carter). Jay-Z's career approach is perhaps best expressed in a line from his 2001 song "U Don't Know": "I sell ice in the winter / I sell fire in hell / I am a hustler baby / I'll sell water to a well." The persona of the hustler, the one who does anything necessary to get ahead economically, suited rap perfectly in the late 1990s. In its refusal to accept poverty, it appealed to the economically disadvantaged; in its embrace of an essentially American Protestant work ethic, it appealed to the middle classes. At the same time, it seemed to justify the artists' material excesses and posited that ostentatious displays of wealth would serve as an inspiration to all. With a partner, Damon Dash, Jay-Z founded his own record company, Roc-A-Fella, and soon expanded into the marketing of clothing (Roca Wear) and low-budget film projects. By mixing often-humorous tales of life on the street with a chief executive officer's sense of business, Jay-Z exploited the strategies of both Biggie Smalls and Sean Combs.

In the mid-1990s, popular underground rap also became increasingly self-conscious and emotionally expressive. By far the most influential figure in this trend was Tupac Shakur. The son of activists in the Black Panther party, a militant organization founded in Oakland, California, in the 1960s, Tupac Amaru Shakur was raised in the Bronx and Baltimore, then as a teen moved to Oakland, where he began to socialize with criminals and revolutionaries. The conflict between activism and exploitation—between responsibility and indulgence—became the major thread of his music. Beginning with the album *2Pacalypse Now* (1991), Tupac made intensely personal hip-hop. Though he clearly operated within the great tradition of African-American history and culture, his lyrics addressed the kinds of struggles and regrets that could be understood by listeners of different backgrounds. He proved that ultra-personal revelations cut across boundaries and allowed a diverse audience to empathize with the artist, rather than to admire the artist from afar. After his death from gunshot wounds in 1996 (his assailant was never identified), Tupac became a larger-than-life figure, memorialized around the world.

By the time of Tupac's death, hip-hop rap had become pervasive in American culture. Its mainstream popularity produced a generation of youth who had been surrounded by the music for their entire lives, even if they knew little about the communities from which it had originated. Eminem (Marshall Mathers), a highly respected white MC from Detroit, was well positioned to take advantage of this state of affairs. His technical proficiency opened doors for him—many critics consider Eminem one of hip-hop's all-time best MC's; while his outrageous sense of humor and troubled persona made him popular with a generation of suburban teens. Like others of this era, he quickly established his own record company (Shady Records, named after his alter ego Slim Shady), and he began a career as a film actor. His debut, *Eight Mile*, a semi-autobiographical film directed by Curtis Hanson, was released to wide acclaim in 2002.

Since the late 1980s, hip-hop has undergone a series of transformations as it gained an essential place in the mainstream. Emerging out of a small, local music scene, it became a national mass-market pop phenomenon. It raised staggering financial opportunities for its most successful practitioners, and it made deep emotional connections with its fans. By the early 2000s its influence, in music, television, and fashion, was felt across the whole spectrum of American and international popular culture.

JOE SCHLOSS

THE TRANSFORMATION OF COMMERCIAL RADIO

Despite the rise in the 1990s of new music distribution technologies such as the Internet, mainstream radio exposure was still widely acknowledged as the chief determinant of an artist or band's success, spurring CD sales and fostering public demand for live performances and tours. While the dominance of commercial radio remained largely unchallenged, its behind-the-scenes structure changed dramatically in the 1990s as a result of technological advances, corporate ownership, and new marketing strategies. This reorientation affected the sound of radio's output, with most stations adopting a streamlined format that emphasized comfort and predictability while allotting extra time for advertisements. Many radio listeners were unaware of these changes, but artists, record companies, and music lovers often charged that the more diverse and individualized voices in rock, pop, R&B, and country music were being excluded. By the early 2000s, new products and services began to provide listeners with alternatives to mainstream radio as a music source.

Changes in the 1990s: New Technology and Corporate Programming

During rock music's early years—the 1950s and 1960s—the radio disc jockey held a substantial degree of power, determining which records to spotlight through heavy airplay—records that, in turn, became "hits." The DJ's importance began to decline in the 1970s, with the rise of FM radio and music "formats"—hard rock, Top 40, easy listening, and others—that created a more homogeneous sound from market to market. By the 1990s, the role of the DJ had diminished even further. "Voicetracking," a computerized process in which an announcer pre-records a program that is then sent digitally to stations in multiple markets, allowed station owners to cut costs by employing fewer DJs. While this practice is more common in smaller cities, it has also been employed in larger markets such as Atlanta. A 2002 article in the Atlanta Journal-Constitution describes how DJ Tony Lini tapes his local radio show in advance from Dallas, where he also records three other programs heard across the country. DJs such as Lini perform these services for the extra income, studying pronunciation guides to local terms in order to camouflage their lack of insider knowledge. Although critics charge that this process gives radio a sterile, synthesized feel and hinders the ability of stations to cover breaking local news and events, corporate executives defend it as a means of offering the best talent to a greater portion of the listening public. In a 2002 interview with Network magazine, a Clear Channel CEO explained, "the reason behind voicetracking is to put better content in more places."

The advance of computerized voicetracking in the 1990s was abetted by the Telecommunications Act of 1996, which deregulated the radio industry by removing national limits on station ownership and giving large companies the freedom to buy multiple stations within a market. By 2001, corporations such as Viacom and Clear Channel operated 60 percent of radio stations within the largest 100 cities in the country. Clear Channel owned 1,200 stations nationwide, or one of every nine stations across the United States. In Pittsburgh, for example, Clear Channel and Infinity (a subsidiary of Viacom) owned more than half of the city's commercial stations. In addition to creating an environment in which corporations could implement voicetracking on a widespread basis, this new consolidation also led to changes in radio programming.

Prior to the mid-1990s, program directors were widely viewed as the most powerful figures at a station, shaping its musical personality by determining which songs made the "playlist"—the set of songs placed in regular rotation by the station. With the new corporate ownership, program directors began to receive their playlists from regional managers in charge of several markets. The goal of this system was to develop pre-determined "templates" that could be applied to a number of stations. A veteran program director described the new climate to the Pittsburgh Post-Gazette in 2002: "Either the PD is constrained or he's taking orders from too many people higher up in the company, or both." By the end of the 1990s, stations with the same format sounded nearly identical from market to market. For example, the 1998 success of Los Angeles-based station KCMG with "Jammin' Oldies"—a format that combines R&B classics with disco and funk from the 1970s—led to the institution by the station's owner, Clear Channel, of dozens of similar "Jammin' Oldies" stations across the U.S. Corporations also sought to "brand" station names and call letters into the public's consciousness. As of 2003, for example, there were 48 stations nationwide bearing the name "KISS-FM."

Corporate executives develop programming strategy through the use of market research techniques such as telephone surveys and focus groups. After the data is gathered, it is fed into a computer that in turn creates a playlist of songs. Commercial radio playlists are usually short—youth-oriented, "Contemporary Hit Radio" or "Urban" stations often keep less than 40 songs in regular rotation—and new songs are added cautiously. As Eric Boehlert asserted in 2001 on the website Salon.com, "With today's tightly controlled playlists, any new song is a risk that can cause listeners to switch to a channel with an older or more comforting hit." Corporate playlists have had a notable effect on more niche-oriented music forms such as country. By the late 1990s, older, less marketable country artists such as George Jones and Dolly Parton no longer received significant mainstream airplay. In an editorial for the *Tennessean* in 2003, economist William Wade railed against rigid country playlists, linking them with a declining economy in Nashville, the longtime hub of the country music industry. Alluding to the young, sleek artists promoted by current country radio, he wrote, "If you are Faith [Hill] or Shania [Twain] or a very few others, corporate radio is your friend . . . for the lion's share of Nashville artists, though, the few program directors controlling playlists that govern airplay across the nation are the castle wall."

Radio corporations and the marketing companies that work for them have been quick to defend contemporary playlists, contending that the public is being given what it wants to hear. Corporate executives have further argued that the range of radio formats available to listeners has actually increased since the early 1990s, encompassing new variations such as "urban" for rap and hip-hop and "new adult contemporary" for jazz-inflected pop music. On the other hand, a 2002 study by the artist advocacy group Future of Music Coalition found that, while contemporary radio sports a larger number of formats, those formats are playing similar lists of songs. Musicians and small record company owners cited the report as proof that corporate consolidation has led to unfavorable trends in radio programming. Jodie Renk, general manager of a prominent market research firm, countered the criticism in a 2002 interview for the *Los Angeles Times*: "The big gap in the logic is that the authors [of the report] don't believe radio stations care about what consumers do . . . stations spend hundreds of thousands of dollars a year finding out what their listeners care about."

Concomitant with the rise in the 1990s of automated disc jockeys and regulated playlists was an increase in the airtime allotted for commercials. For years the radio industry standard was 12 minutes of commercials per hour; by the early 2000s it had jumped to as high as 20 minutes per hour. This increase was aided by the development in spring 1999 of a new digital program named "Cash," which creates extra space for commercials by shortening the pauses between words, thereby speeding up an announcer's speech. By 2000 Cash was being employed at 50 stations nationwide, with advertisers complaining that their messages were being diluted through listener saturation. In an interview with the *New York Times* in 2000, the vice president of a New York-based advertising agency bemoaned the increase in commercial time: "The clutter has gotten out of control." While station owners contended that the alterations were too imperceptible for most listeners to notice, the development of Cash technology only added fuel to the argument that radio had lost much of its spontaneity and personality.

Artist Responses

By the early 2000s, a number of recording artists were publicly criticizing the heavily formatted and programmed state of mainstream radio. Speaking to the *Chicago Tribune* in 2002, rock performer Tom Petty complained, "You can't say rock radio is the center of the rock universe anymore." Asserting that radio no longer meets the needs of music fans, he added, "A lot of my audience, and the rock audience in general, has given up on radio." Charges such as these had intensified by 2003, when Congress began to reassess the 1996 Telecommunications Act and debate current media ownership regulations. In June, the Federal Communications Commission voted in the corporations' favor, further loosening the rules that limit media ownership. The new laws allow a company to own up to three television stations, eight radio stations, and a daily newspaper within the same market. In a testimonial before the Senate in January, rock singer Don Henley argued that radio had devolved into an environment where "everybody gets the same McDonald's hamburger," adding that, "from an artist point of view, I think it has really harmed music . . . because of the millions of dollars it costs to get a record on the radio."

Henley is alluding to the music industry practice of "payola," in which radio stations are paid by record companies for playing specific songs. Although payola is technically illegal, for decades the industry has subverted the law through the use of third-party independent promoters, or "indies," who broker the payments, often billing them as "promotional" expenses. Critics of corporate consolidation have charged that ownership deregulation has served to more deeply entrench payola through the solidification of alliances between radio corporations and promotions companies. In the process, record labels have been forced to pay higher fees to ensure their artists receive airplay. In 2002 an article in the *Chicago Tribune* suggested that this system has curbed radio diversity: "Chance-taking is rarely found in commercial radio anymore, in part because the cost of promoting new or unknown acts to radio stations has become prohibitive for all but the largest record labels."

In addition to criticizing payola, artists such as Henley have complained that the corporate orientation of radio hinders them from speaking out on public issues. Although corporations cannot be said to have a single, definable political identity, many listeners, artists, and advocacy groups have detected an air of political conservatism in mainstream radio, noting how companies such as Clear Channel have offered financial support to the Republican Party. In early 2003, after the Dixie Chicks' lead vocalist, Natalie Maines, made public comments criticizing President Bush's plans for a US-led invasion of Iraq, Clear Channel stations were among the first to proclaim themselves "Chicks-free" (although no official corporate ban on the group's music was issued). An article in the Madison, Wisconsin, *Capital Times* also noted how, since the start of war preparations, station playlists had begun to favor jingoistic-themed songs such as Toby Keith's "Courtesy of the Red, White, and Blue," which lashes out at purported sources of terrorism in the Middle East. Following the Dixie Chicks fracas, even Madonna—for years one of the most outspoken recording artists—pulled the antiwar video for her single, "American Life."

In response to what they perceived as the constraining force of mainstream radio, and the music industry in general, certain artists in the early 2000s began to rely upon new outlets such as the Internet to distribute their music to the public. Many of these performers were already well established, with years of major-label releases and radio hits to their credit. In a 2003 *New York Times* article covering rock artist Natalie Merchant's decision to release an album independently, music lawyer Jay Rosenthal attested, "the only reason to go to the major labels is to get . . . . If you don't need to get on the radio, and you've got a name, go out there and go for yourself." In the same article, Merchant explained her move: "I didn't want to subject the music to that kind of corporate boardroom and radio censorship. Why subject myself and the work that I do to that kind of environment when it really doesn't matter any more?" Other artists who have bypassed the commercial radio distribution system include pop and R&B star Prince and rock performer Aimee Mann.

New Options for Consumers

Artist websites offering CD purchases and downloads were part of a wave of new music choices for fans in the early 2000s. Increasingly, listeners have turned to Internet radio stations, which promise a diverse array of music without the lengthy commercials of mainstream stations. Speaking to the *Chicago Tribune* in 2002, the owner of an Internet station outlined its consumer appeal: "We're telling people if they're tired of hearing [teen-pop band] *NSYNC played 10 times a day, come to our station, we'll play something cool, something they don't hear everywhere else." At the same time, satellite radio began to promise listeners up to 100 stations with a range of music options and few advertisements. In a *New York Times* arti-

cle in 2003, a satellite radio owner explained its benefits: "I have very eclectic tastes in music, and a lot of it is not the stuff you can hear on regular radio . . . [satellite radio is] like having almost an unlimited CD library and you just hit a button for whatever mood you happen to be in at a particular time."

In June 2003, an Associated Press article announced an even newer option: "My Music Choice," a television cable channel that allows listeners to program their own radio shows, with advertisements placed on the television screen rather than between songs. "The new service will allow viewers to create their own channels according to taste," the article explains. "A listener can program 10 percent bluegrass, 20 percent rap and 50 percent metal, if they want—or any other permutation." The operating ethic within the new satellite and cable music industry is one of customer convenience and flexibility, as described by Music Choice's programmer: "People want what they want when they want it . . . every company is trying to develop products that make [customers] feel like they have control."

Radio after 2000

Despite the development of new services such as Music Choice, mainstream radio continued to dominate the commercial music landscape of the early 2000s, primarily because of the strong distribution ties between record companies and radio corporations. Record labels rely upon radio stations for the dissemination of product, and a longstanding system of third-party payola is in place to safeguard the relationship. Further, as corporate executives argue, the majority of radio listeners seek comfort through songs with which they are familiar. For example, the popularity in the 2000s of stations playing 1980s pop and rock music speaks to the nostalgic impulses of listeners in their early thirties—a prime demographic target of commercial radio. At the same time, an increasing number of artists and music fans have sidestepped radio's influence through a combination of independent promotion and modern technology. While ongoing media deregulation has arguably made commercial radio more homogeneous in sound, these initiatives provide music fans with a wider array of alternatives.

DAVID FREELAND

THE MUSIC INDUSTRY: ECONOMICS, MARKETING, AND NEW ARTIST DEVELOPMENT

After World War II the development of full-frequency-range disc recording and the high-fidelity long-playing record (LP) triggered the accelerated growth of the record industry. A series of technical innovations followed: stereo tapes (1954); the compact acoustic-suspension loudspeaker (1955); stereo LP records (1958); stereo FM radio (1962); and, in the 1960s, the widespread use of multitrack recording. Annual U.S. recording sales grew from $200 million in the early 1950s to almost $15 billion in 1998. To meet public demand, U.S. record companies created and promoted career artists through a process called artist development.

The process is as follows: Young and presumably talented artists with the potential to become stars are signed contractually by major record companies (also called labels) or music publishers. The development process allows the artist to receive modest compensation and financial backing to cover the cost of recording original master tapes. In theory the record label permits an artist to make a few albums (and in some cases singles) with the goal of reaching monetary success and notoriety by the third album. From the perspective of the artist, it is on-the-job training; from the perspective of the company it is analogous to the research and development process undertaken by manufacturers. (A manufacturer dedicates funds and personnel to invent and develop future products. Not all of the prospective products make it into production. Those most likely to succeed after testing and market research are developed further; less promising "products" are discontinued.) By the beginning of the 1990s artist development was all but abandoned by the major record companies and left to smaller independent producers and firms. Less interested in artist development, the major companies on the whole moved into "corporate development."

In the late 1980s six major record companies dominated the U.S. music industry—Warner, Sony, BMG, MCA, PolyGram, and EMI. Responding to staggering potential profits in a boom economy, the major companies (and their corporate parents) began to purchase smaller companies at an aggressive pace with the aim of consolidating assets and market shares into larger business units. In the early 1990s the six major groups consolidated to five—BMG, EMI, AOL/Time-Warner, Sony, and Universal. In 2002 BMG completely acquired Jive/Zomba, the largest independent. Additional effort was made by BMG, AOL/Time Warner, and EMI to consolidate the industry to four groups. The aim was to make the business of producing and selling music as profitable as possible. By 2003, however, the industry was well down the road of the worst economic slump in its history. The retail record market was undermined and sales were slowing. Some critics pointed out that the major record companies had moved far away from the artist development model that had been their original calling, and, blinded by arrogance, had permitted problems to go unchecked until the entire industry was threatened with collapse.

Critics suggest that the record industry is no longer good at what it does. They argue that too many albums get made—including too many bad albums—which are then marketed with insufficient funds. In 2001 approximately 6,500 records were released in the United States; approximately 350 were certified gold or platinum. Assuming the gold or platinum designation indicates a measure of success, only two percent of records released were successful. Critics argued this was not a viable development model.

Furthermore, in the 1980s and 1990s new home entertainment media threatened the unique dominance enjoyed by recorded music. The interactive video game craze drove customer dollars toward these games—and away from recorded music. Gradually, as video games emerged as an entertainment powerhouse, the music majors were forced to acknowledge their impact on the market.

Corporate Aggregation Versus Entrepreneurial Development

In the years when the record industry was a collection of entrepreneurial, independently owned companies without corporate lines of credit, entrepreneurs built their businesses a dollar at a time by selling one record at a time. The boom years of the 1990s created a financial climate that made it attractive to generate profits by buying and selling whole record companies rather than by running one successfully. The valuation theory evolved that one percent of market share was worth a billion U.S. dollars in sales value (i.e., a record company with a ten percent market share was worth ten billion dollars). Companies focused on consolidation, market share, valuation, and corporate economics, not on running their core businesses well.

The business model required that compatible business units make for efficiency, in terms of management and overhead. Once aggregated and streamlined, the theory holds that more revenue with a smaller relative attribution to overhead creates greater net profit. Ultimately, the aggregated business units are sold on the open market at "enterprise value." Essentially, enterprise value means that the whole is greater, or at least worth more, than the sum of the parts. Yet historically in the music industry accelerated aggregation has not yielded the desired reduction in overhead or an increase in profitability or market share. What record industry analysts observed in the early 2000s is a drying up of enterprise value, at least at the major label level. For example, if the corporation Vivendi/Universal has a thirty percent market share, can one hope to find a buyer of its assets for thirty billion dollars? No, to the contrary, critics argued it appeared that major labels or their corporate parents would have to start selling off assets to raise stock prices (and to cut jobs in the process). Yet in 2003 the corporate heads at major labels continued to insist on aggregation as the solution to their problems.

As record companies were absorbed and consolidated the industry began to change. Many of the original entrepreneurs took their payouts and left. Eventually, the special nature of each of these companies was plowed over in favor of a more uniform and more consistent corporate culture. David Geffen, long known for his skills and acumen as a talent finder, producer, and record company executive, sold Geffen Records and in a single stroke turned his winnings into a billion-dollar fortune—from Geffen to MCA and from MCA to Matsushita. Industry observers noted that corporate efficiency experts started to manage music businesses strictly by the numbers, not by the heart, frequently overlooking the special and intangible assets of the companies they controlled. Employees who managed to survive mergers and layoffs were frequently rewarded with increasingly lucrative long-term, "pay or play" contracts (a common business practice in the record and entertainment business, but rarer in other areas of commerce). As senior executives found security in their large corporate contracts and equally large severance packages, the need to make money ceased to become a daily incentive. Corporate employee thinking (even at the highest executive levels) displaced American entrepreneurial thinking. Losses were subsidized by multinational corporate entities and written off, and the executives responsible for bringing in profits and minimizing losses thrived. Yet in 2003 the industry faced the difficult prospect of cutting prices and losing more revenue, all of which further highlighted disfiguring expenditures.

Some financial analysts suggested that, rather than aggregating, music companies should consider selling assets or copyrights as a way of re-energizing a sagging industry. This industry, they argued, is in the business of monetizing music, not collecting copyrights. Similarly, record companies are not just in the business of selling records or collecting artists; their business is to monetize masters. When a real estate company builds a portfolio of properties, office buildings, for instance, it manages the portfolio in ways directed by the market. If it owns a particular building that has amortized its costs and produced annual profits and if there is a need for cash to fund an emerging market with great "leverage" (i.e., the ability to earn high multiples of the investment), the older property's cash flow is discounted for future value. Once the property is sold, the cash is reinvested in the business to create more profit opportunities in the new market. Similarly, a record label may sell a particular catalog and successfully reinvest the profits to create many more profitable catalogs.

Doing Business, Badly

The basic business model used by all major record companies since 1990 created a misalignment of interests—with respect to the development and exploitation of an artist's trade name or "brand." In the traditional model, an investor values a business or property and sets goals for the entrepreneur to accomplish in order to remain employed, to reach bonus thresholds, and to advance. The entrepreneur runs the business. The investor usually has one or more seats on the board of directors and, as long as the entrepreneur does well, everyone is happy.

In the record industry, the label "invests" money in recording artists; once the money has been repaid at what works out to be an extraordinarily high rate of interest, the label continues to own the product, including the business, the rights to the music, and the rights to the trade name and brand. This is true in artist agreements, joint ventures, and label deals. Typically, in an artist recording agreement, the record company acquires exclusive rights to the artist's trademarks and images in connection with the sale, exploitation, and promotion of the artist's recordings. The artist retains rights in the trademarks for purposes of live touring, merchandising, and product endorsements (which are sometimes restricted by the terms of the recording agreement). Thus, the brand simultaneously is serving two masters whose long-term and short-term financial agendas are not the same. The misalignment of interests promotes the dysfunctional, often adversarial nature of artist/label relations.

Furthermore, as entertainment media multiplied, record companies sat by idly and watched others compete for entertainment dollars. The same companies continued to raise prices (to sustain their enormous overhead); they sold an increasingly antiquated product and refused either to update the product or to lower prices in an effort to remain competitive. In 2003 record labels were baked into a business model that did not work because it depended on a $19.99 list price for a tired, two-dimensional, twenty-year-old technology.

Before corporate development eclipsed artist development, old timers in the industry used to make statements like "It's about the music" or "It's gotta rock." In the old days, labels generally signed musicians and bands because someone at an executive level was passionate about the music. In the era of corporate aggregation, music companies chase records those in charge have not heard, and they sign artists based solely on research profiles. In the 1980s in New York City, it was not uncommon to be at a showcase for a band and to witness Artist & Repertoire representatives (A&R reps) from various companies discuss splitting taxis to get to the next showcase on the day's agenda. Many experienced A&R executives thought that signing talent based on other A&R reps' reactions was an odd way of doing business. But people in the industry came to accept the practice and did no more than laugh at the jokes frequently made at their expense.

By 2003, it became common practice for major record labels to pursue artists and music they never heard because their interest was based exclusively on secondhand proprietary service data. For example, Mediabase, a proprietary, for-profit service division of the corporation Clear Channel, offers record data. The data is based on a particular record's audience as measured by its radio play and the number of "spins" it receives. Soundscan, a proprietary service that tracks the sales of CDs to consumers through point-of-sale technology, and BDS, a proprietary service offered by *Billboard*, and a competitor of MediaBase, offer similar data readings. Of course, companies use such research creatively in different ways, but at least one label has relied heavily on data from research almost to the point of excluding creative factors. No one has demonstrated that the major labels have increased their odds of success using the research-driven A&R practice. This is not to say that numbers-driven research cannot help measure an artist's value. But can it be the driving force in what record executives used to refer to as a "creative decision"? Once active agents in the artist-development process, large companies have settled into the role of acquiring musicians established at a regional level by independent producers and small labels. Rather than look for the band that can be cut and polished into a diamond-selling artist, label research focuses almost exclusively on finding the act with a demo of fully produced hit songs in order to make a quick financial killing with a million-selling album. If the return is not immediate, not only can the band find itself without a record deal, the A&R representative may be out of a job.

In 1999 the Recording Industry Association of America (RIAA) established the diamond award— multi-platinum records selling in excess of 10 million units in the United States per release. Though partially a result of the overhead-intensive record business, the diamond award was created to acknowledge the sales of the "super albums" made by superstars. Although there were some scattered diamond-selling records before 1990—Pink Floyd's *Dark Side of the Moon,* Meatloaf's *Bat out of Hell,* the Eagles' *Hotel California*—most diamond albums were made in the late 1980s and 1990s, proving that "big talent" can still build huge audiences. Celine Dion had three releases in the 1990s that exceeded 20 million copies sold; the Fugees sold 13 million copies of *The Score*; Eminem and Linkin Park each sold 10 million copies. Still, without artist development—the process of nurturing an artist while allowing the artist to build an audience—diamond albums are basically winning lottery tickets. Because of enormous overheads and impractical marketing expenses, record companies are forced increasingly to rely on blockbuster releases to make a profit. But in the economic downturn of the early 2000s, the industry predicted few future upcoming super albums.

Consumer Disenfranchisement

In the early 2000s young people, the primary consumers of music, were technologically sophisticated, and they expected an entertainment experience to be an enriched experience; yet the essential music product, the record or CD, remained a simple, old-fashioned entity. At a $19.99 list price, twenty-year-old technology competed with the latest generation of PlayStation2 and XBOX games that are multi-dimensional 3-D, 5.1 surround sound, virtual reality—all for $29.99.

Furthermore, the Internet served to underscore the widening cultural gap between the attitudes of the music industry and the largest block of its core consumers. Even after consumers, especially young consumers, told the record labels that they wanted to get music in a peer-to-peer format, labels refused to entertain the idea. As a result, industry people lost credibility with their consumers, who became unwilling to hear what the record industry had to say about its own products. Consumers, and many recording artists, publicly vilified the majors. They turned to the Internet to remove the record labels from the process of making, acquiring, and sharing music. Peer-to-peer use represented to many consumers the ability to communicate about music without the mediation of a reactionary industry.

Ironically, Apple Computers, long recognized for its innovations in business and design practices, provided the record industry a lesson in digital music consumption. In the spring of 2003, Apple introduced I-Tunes, the content service that accompanies its hugely popular I-POD MP3 player. I-Tunes provides single song and complete album digital downloads, which flow directly from the user's Internet-connected computer to an I-POD, in the reasonably secure MPEG4 format. The process is simple and effective. Without the costs of physical goods manufacturing and delivery, the I-Tunes format is an efficient sale of product. Apple had hoped to sell $1 million worth of music in the service's first month of operation; even though Apple's selection of music at I-Tunes represented only a portion of CDs available in the marketplace, the company reached the goal in seven days. While not a peer-to-peer format, I-Tunes proved that if a company offers good music at a fair price in a desired format, customers not only will listen to the sales pitches, they will make the purchase.

In the 1970s, during the heyday of the recording business when the only access to music was via radio, records, and theatrical performances, records were one of the key entertainment items purchased by teens and adolescents. The virtual monopolies enjoyed by the record companies allowed them to price products at whatever level the market would allow. In the 2000s these conditions no longer prevailed. Other forms of entertainment, enhanced media, and the Internet competed for the limited number of consumer dollars. In 2003 young consumers bought backpacks, watches, and MP3 players; they owned cell phones, pagers, and high-end sneakers. They became cutting-edge consumers, particularly savvy about how to spend their allowances or earned money. Yet record companies continued to price and market in ignorance of teen and adolescent spending patterns. The price of CDs remained high, the quality low, and young consumers refused to be "hyped" into buying products they did not want. Record companies failed to treat their primarily youthful audience as the sophisticated, mature consumers they had become.

Piracy, the Internet, and Market Segmentation

In the summer of 2002, Forrester Research released a report examining competitiveness in the record industry and the downturn in the U.S. economy. It identified piracy as a red herring and suggested market segmentation as one of the culprits in the downturn of CD sales. Piracy is a constant in the music industry as it is in other industries. In the clothing business, for example, piracy is known as "shrinkage," the percentage of merchandise always expected to disappear without being bought. Aware of the problem, clothing retailers generally operate under the principle that, as long as shrinkage is less than a fixed percentage of the business, trying to eliminate it completely is a waste of time. Retailers acknowledge the loss and work to minimize it, if and when the problem grows beyond their profit margin.

Of course, the music industry is different because of the nature of its product. As the Internet emerged, the public naturally wanted to find meaningful uses for it. For various reasons, including technical considerations of available bandwidth, music became one of the Internet's early uses. However, as the potential of digitally delivered files became obvious, and as the young consumers wanted access to online music in downloadable form, the labels switched off the servers. At first the ostensible reason was security—an industrywide system was not yet in place. Related to security were issues of format as technology companies became involved and began to jockey for position: Liquid Audio versus Windows Media versus Real G2 format. Consumers were confused and frustrated; most importantly, they were not getting what they wanted.

Decision makers in the music industry feared releasing the digital genie (once on the Internet, unencrypted digital media cannot be secured), but again, some critics argued, the industry insulted and underestimated its customers. Ignoring the problem, the record industry refused to acknowledge that one young consumer might succeed in uploading music from a legitimately acquired CD to the Internet and the digital "genie" would never again be subject to corporate control. The bottom line was that record companies did not understand what their bottom line would be. They did not know what to charge and could not agree on a non-proprietary format, so instead of forging the new digital frontier in search of markets that might be gained the way entrepreneurs of the past might have done, the decision makers were motivated by the fear of what might be lost. Ignoring the probability of someone uploading a file to the Internet did not make the problem disappear. This is exactly what happened with peer-to-peer file-sharing and, most famously, with Napster.

In 1998, a computer science student from Northeastern University named Shawn Fanning began developing a file-transferring system wherein he used MP3 files as formats to hold music. MP3 is a shorter name for MPEG-1 Layer III, a technology first developed in Germany in 1987. These audio formats eliminate any unnecessary data in the standard digital design called WAV. The end-result of that process is an MP3 file, which easily transfers across the Internet. Simply put, the MP3 technology, in conjunction with Fanning's additional innovation, enabled computer users to download songs directly from the Internet. More importantly and unlike any other attempts to copy music on cassette tapes, MP3 technology does not denigrate the quality of the sound. On June 1, 1999, Fanning's company, Napster, was up and running. Napster itself did not stock the actual music on their site to download; rather it allowed visitors access to their site-free software, which connected them to other users' music files and enabled them to download music of their own choosing. Fanning made a profit by charging advertisers to place ads on Napster.

Shawn Fanning's peer-to-peer technology enabled young consumers from all over the world to share their musical collections with all the other young consumers from all over the world without the permission or intervention of the record business. Responding to these breathtaking developments in music distribution the RIAA filed copyright infringement suits and forced Napster to shut down operations. Additionally, in 2002, the RIAA along with a number of record labels served a subpoena on the communications company Verizon, seeking the identity of a Verizon customer who allegedly downloaded illegal music content. The RIAA did not disclose the reason for its subpoena and Verizon resisted cooperating. In the spring of 2003, Verizon was directed by court order to comply with the subpoena. Also, the RIAA prosecuted several college students in connection with allegations of online piracy. Notably, the students maintained their innocence but settled their cases with the RIAA because, they complained, they were victims of record company paranoia and could not afford to defend themselves against the huge corporations in the music industry.

In 2003 the music industry's course was the aggressive prosecution of its potential customers rather than the aggressive work of serving its consumer needs. What started out as a business that created music for the consumer became a business that sought to protect its commerce by prosecuting its consumers. By being reactionary instead of progressive, the major music companies missed the chance to co-opt peer-to-peer as a discovery tool par excellence. Peer-to-peer trading simply provides the discovery mechanism, while sites like Napster (before it was sued out of existence) and Kazaa provide the location. It should have surprised no one that when young consumers find a disc they like, they will go out and buy it.

At the end of 2003 the Internet's single greatest impact on the recording industry was not piracy, but market segmentation. File-sharing systems, chat rooms, and websites led to the emergence of parallel channels across which to discover and transmit music. These platforms enabled consumers to find or "discover" music based on peer recommendations or numbers of downloads. The result was that more and smaller subgroups of consumers with common tastes began to create, in effect, multiple variations of the existing formats we presently reference. What we used to refer to as rock and roll has become EMO, Agro, Speed Metal, Death Metal, Southern Rock, Pop Rock, Back-Pack, and so on.

Segmentation is at the core of the degradation of the major labels' businesses. Selling smaller quantities of records with less per-record expense and lower fixed overhead is a practice in which the major labels do not engage because there are unable to do so. Radio as a marketing tool is too expensive. Playing the independent promotion game no longer works. (It is not cost-effective for major labels to pay money to independent consultants who assist and coordinate radio airplay for particular records.) Second, like the labels themselves, radio stations are not serving the segmented market. Commercial radio is designed for broad-based mass-market appeal and is directed at the lowest common denominator, which is the antithesis of marketing to a segmented audience. So although listeners may hear music for free on the radio in their cars or in the workplace, they may not spend money to buy the records—because they are not especially interested in them. The result of industry trends may mean a more even distribution of the market. A viable and important emerging market—or more accurately a revitalized, previously abandoned market—exists for records selling anywhere from ten thousand to several hundred thousand units. This becomes one of the pillars on which the future of the music business will rest.

Having said all of this, it is worth noting that in July 2003 the Associated Press (AP) reported production of pirated recordings accounted for one-third of all CDs sold around the globe. "The estimated value of pirated recordings in 2002 hit $4.6 billion, and included some 1.1 billion CDs, according to the International Federation of the Phonographic Industry (IFPI), which represents 1,500 record companies in 70 countries." The IFPI press release announced enforcement efforts on ten major producers of pirated recordings in Brazil, China, Mexico, Paraguay, Poland, Russia, Spain, Taiwan, Thailand, and Ukraine.

Long-Term and Short-Term Effects of the Internet

In 2003 the conflict between the Internet music communities and the U.S. record business was well publicized. Predicting the conflict's long-term outcome is impossible because so many factors are in flux—including hardware, software, and the systems of delivery. Certainly, however, the Internet has the potential to shift power from the infrastructure-owning distributors to literally everyone else, leveling the playing field in one of the primary areas that kept the major record companies secure, which is control of the means of distribution. The Internet makes it easy and cost-effective for a small seller operating from a single location with low overhead to reach small numbers of buyers globally, and to make a profit. The Internet contributes to market segmentation, but in a way it allows for a new kind of consolidation. A likely effect may be that smaller companies emerge to handle back-office functions, marketing, promotion, and publicity (e.g. label management), with distribution largely handled through the Internet.

The return to the discovery of music is another exciting aspect of the Internet. One "cool" trait of music in the 1960s and 1970s was the process of discovering it through friends and family, on the radio, in teen or fan magazines, or at live concerts. The "Wild West," do-it-yourself nature of the Internet provides similarly exciting opportunities to find new music, whether by receiving a friend's MP3, participating in a chat room, listening to an alternative radio music station, or visiting a website. Many critics have pointed out that in the final analysis, the Internet is not the enemy of the music industry. As new business models and practices are developed to reconfigure the way music companies do business, the Internet will play an integral role, all the while empowering entrepreneurs. At the same time it will provide new paths for the development of the artists who make the music in the first place.

BIBLIOGRAPHY: F. Dannen, *Hit Men: Power Brokers and Fast Money Inside the Music Business*. New York: Alfred A Knopf, 1991; P. Eaton, "Tommy Mottola Faces the Music." *New York* (March 3, 2003); W. Knoedelseder, *Stiffed: A True Story of MCA, the Music Business, and the Mafia*. New York: Harper/Collins, 1993; B. Haring, *Off the Charts: Ruthless Days and Reckless Nights Inside the Music*

Industry. New York: Birch Lane Press, 1995; D.S. Passman, *All You Need to Know about the Music Business.* New York: Simon & Schuster, 2000.

HELPFUL RELATED BUSINESS PRIMERS: J.W. Bartlett, *Fundamentals of Venture Capital.* Lanham, MD: Madison Books, 1999; W. Poundstone, *Prisoner's Dilemma.* New York: Doubleday: 1992 [a nontechnical analysis of applied game theory and the work of John von Neumann].

MICHAEL SELVERNE

[This essay, revised in July 2003, is based on a speech delivered at the executive retreat of R.E.D. Entertainment in Tarrytown, New York, on October 24, 2002.]

Glossary

AIRPLAY: A song's transmission on the radio. "More airplay" means a song plays over the radio with greater regularity.

ALBUM: A vinyl disc containing approximately fifteen to thirty minutes of music on each side. Prior to the CD, albums were the primary means of music storage.

ARIA: (Italian, air). In opera, an extended musical solo.

ASCAP: American Society of Composers, Authors, and Publishers. A professional association of nearly 150,000 composers, songwriters, lyricists, and music publishers whose primary function is to protect members' rights and to secure royalty payments.

B-SIDE: The song on the second side of a single ("the flip-side"), usually the second choice after a single is picked for release to airplay. The first choice, the one most likely to achieve commercial success, appears on Side A. For example, the Beatles single of July 1964 features two songs: "A Hard Day's Night" on Side A and "I Should Have Known Better" on Side B.

BEL CANTO: (Italian, beautiful singing or beautiful songs). As a vocal performance style, the bel canto accentuates beauty of tone, brilliance of execution, and lyricism above dramatic content. Developed in Italy in the eighteenth century, it is most closely associated with the repertoire of the nineteenth-century Italian composers Vincenzo Bellini and Gaetano Donizetti, in contrast to the declamatory singing style made notable by the German composer Richard Wagner.

BILLBOARD: The magazine of record for the U.S. music recording industry. In addition to feature stories on musicians, it offers album reviews and published record sales statistics. It also charts the popularity of songs and albums on both a weekly and yearly basis.

BOOTLEG: Unauthorized recording of a live performance. Bootleg recordings are often marketed through underground means; however, some exist merely as bootleggers' keepsakes.

BRIT AWARD: The most prestigious music award in the United Kingdom of Great Britain and Northern Ireland. First presented in 1992.

CD: Compact disc. A laser-read data storage device on which audio, video, and textual material can be stored. An improved technology, it uses a reduced-sized vinyl disc to hold up to about eighty minutes of music. The technology was first developed in 1979 by the Philips Company of the Netherlands and introduced into the U.S. market in 1983. By 1990 over one billion CDs were sold annually. Since 1990, CDs greatly surpassed albums and cassette tapes as the primary means for storing recorded music.

CHART: As a verb form, signifies that a musical artist has an album or a single popular enough in sales and/or in radio airplay to be listed on one of the music charts, such as the Top 10 or Top 40.

CHARTS: As a plural noun, signifies within the music industry any of several listings that rate songs and albums in terms of their sales and/or radio airplay popularity over a certain period.

COMMERCIAL: Music that appeals to the masses. Also, a style reflecting what is popular at a given time. A commercial artist is one whose music or style is popular to the mass listening audience at a given time.

COVER: To perform or record a song previously made prominent by someone else. "Cover bands" are more associated with clubs and dance halls and generally strive to make the song sound like the original artistic rendition. However, when established artists "cover" a song often they style it with their own distinct interpretation. For example, the Rolling Stones' debut single in 1962 was a cover of Chuck Berry's "Come On." "The Way You Look Tonight," by Jerome Kern and Dorothy Fields, originally written for the film *Swing Time* (1936), was first performed by Fred Astaire. The song has been covered by artists including Tony Bennett (1958), Frank Sinatra (1964), and Rod Stewart (2002).

CROSSOVER: The transition of an artist from a compartmentalized "niche" status into the mainstream of popular recognition. It may signify, too, an artist's development into a definitive new style, as in "to crossover from rock to jazz" or "to crossover from rap to R&B."

DEEJAYING: In hip-hop music, the use of two turntables to create new musical arrangements from existing recordings.

DIAMOND: A sales distinction established by the RIAA (Recording Industry Association of America) to signify record (CD, album, and cassette) sales of over ten million.

DISCOGRAPHY: A listing of a body of recorded work by an artist or band.

DIVA: (Italian, divine woman or goddess; the masculine form is *divo*). Originally meant to signify a leading female opera singer to whom, in the words of Nicolas Slonimsky, the description *prima donna assoluta* (absolute first lady) seemed inadequate. The term in post-1990s pop culture has come to characterize almost any major female singer. More specifically, the post-1990s version of diva is often linked with female pop singers who have either prolific vocal skills or striking, dynamic personalities of a self-involved inclination.

DJ: Disc jockey. A radio host who introduces, announces, or comments on songs before and after they play over the radio. The term is derived from a time when DJs actually placed the vinyl discs—often of their own choosing—on a turntable and let them be heard by the public. In the post-1990s era, almost all radio stations pre-program their music on tape and the DJ no longer manually has to "put the song on," nor does the DJ generally have a hand in choosing which songs receive airplay.

DVD: Digital video disc. Capable of carrying five times the data as a standard CD. It was introduced into the U.S. retail commercial market in 1997.

EP: Extended play. A term used to describe recordings that are too long for singles and too short for albums. EPs are often considered "mini-albums," containing between five and eight songs.

EMCEEING: In hip-hop music, the recitation of rhythmic poetry; also calling rapping.

GRAMMY: The most prestigious music award in the United States. Presented annually since 1959 by the National Academy of Recording Arts and Sciences, today the Recording Academy.

GOLD: A sales distinction established by the RIAA (Recording Industry Association of America) to signify record (CD, album, and cassette) sales of over 500,000.

LP: Long-playing record; another term for album. First introduced in 1948 by Columbia Records, it plays back at a speed of 33 1/3 revolutions per minute (rpm) and has closely spaced grooves known as microgrooves. The stereo LP appeared in 1958.

MAINSTREAM: Refers to the most popular songs, sounds, or artists within a particular musical genre.

MP3: An audio compression into a digital file that can be transferred across the Internet.

MTV: Music Television. A broadcast network that serves as the media hub for the U.S. pop music industry. MTV began by airing music videos in August 1981, effectively elevating them into a performance art of their own. Michael Jackson's videos for the songs on his album *Thriller* (1982), featuring outstanding choreography, camera movement, and special effects, revolutionized the music video.

OVERDUB: Recording over something that had been recorded previously. The overdub either replaces the previous sound or adds to it.

PLATINUM: A sales distinction established by the RIAA (Recording Industry Association of America) to signify record (CD, album, and cassette) sales of over one million.

R&B: Short form of "rhythm and blues." The term originated as a substitute for "race records," the industry classification for commercial music made by African-American musicians for African-American audiences. It evolved to designate the distinct styles of music created by black inner-city musicians since World War II.

REMIX: To consider all or some of the musical components involved in a recording (for example, instruments, percussion, and vocals) and to change the final product by giving less or more prominence to various chosen components.

ROCK AND ROLL HALL OF FAME: Established by the Rock and Roll Hall of Fame Foundation, which formed in 1983 to recognize significant achievement in the history of rock music. The annual induction ceremony began in 1985. Artists become eligible for induction twenty-five years after the release of their first record. The Rock and Roll Hall of Fame and Museum, designed by architect I. M. Pei, opened in 1995, in Cleveland, Ohio.

SAMPLING: The process by which a piece of music is incorporated digitally into a larger musical work. Sampling is often associated with hip-hop music, in which songs frequently contain snippets, or "samples," of older recordings. Many hip-hop songs of the early 1990s, for example, sampled rhythmic grooves from 1970s hits by R&B star James Brown. By the early 2000s, sampling had also become a common feature of mainstream pop recordings.

SINGLE: A single song or track. A song from an album released to radio stations for airplay, primarily for promotional reasons, and chosen by the record company or the artist. Some singles with sleeve covers in a 45 rpm (revolutions per minute) format used to be released directly into the market, independent of an album. For example, in the period 1965–1970, the Beatles released a number of singles, including "Hello, Goodbye" and "Lady Madonna."

STADIUM TOUR: Derived from concerts held in sports stadiums; the term now refers to any large venue concert where attendance is in the realm of 20,000 to 120,000 spectators, or more.

STANDARD: A term arbitrarily placed on a popular song that stands out or represents the musical era of its time. "Rock Around the Clock" is considered a 1950s rock standard, while "Turn the Beat Around" is recognized as a 1970s disco standard. Sometimes interchangeable with the word "classic."

TRACK: A recorded song. Originally derived as a reference to the track or grooves in a vinyl album that store a song, "track" presently refers to any individual song from an album, CD, cassette tape, DVD, or video.

TOP 10: Within the music industry, a chart usually associated with the ten most popular albums per genre; it is compiled on a yearly basis.

TOP 40: A chart of the forty most popular songs per genre; compiled on a weekly basis.

VINYL: A reference to an album; the plastic material used in making the disc.

Genre Index

Use this index to find artists under the broad category of music with which they are most strongly associated.

ROCK/POP

AC/DC
Ace of Base
Adams, Bryan
Adams, Ryan
Aerosmith
Aguilera, Christina
Alice in Chains
Allman Brothers Band, The
Amos, Tori
Anthrax
Apple, Fiona
Backstreet Boys
Bad Religion
Barenaked Ladies
Beatles, The
Beautiful South, The
Beck
Beck, Jeff
Bee Gees, The
Belle and Sebastian
Belly
Björk
Black Crowes, The
Blind Melon
Blink-182
Blues Traveler
Blur
Bolton, Michael
Bon Jovi
Bowie, David
Bragg, Billy
Breeders, The
Buckley, Jeff
Buffett, Jimmy
Built to Spill

Burnett, T Bone
Bush
Byrne, David
Cake
Carey, Mariah
Cave, Nick and the Bad Seeds
Chapman, Steven Curtis
Chapman, Tracy
Cher
Clapton, Eric
Coldplay
Cole, Paula
Collective Soul
Collins, Phil
Corrs, The
Costello, Elvis
Counting Crows
Cowboy Junkies
Cracker
Cranberries, The
Creed
Crow, Sheryl
Cure, The
Dave Matthews Band
David, Craig
Days of the New
Def Leppard
Depeche Mode
Diamond, Neil
Dido
Dion, Celine
Duran Duran
Dylan, Bob
Eagles, The
Etheridge, Melissa
Everclear
Everlast
Extreme
Fabian, Lara
Faith No More

Finn, Neil
Flaming Lips, The
Fleetwood Mac
Fogerty, John
Folds, Ben
Foo Fighters
Fuel
Fugazi
Gabriel, Peter
Garbage
Gin Blossoms
Godsmack
Goo Goo Dolls, The
Grant, Amy
Grateful Dead, The
Gray, David
Green Day
Guided By Voices
Guns N' Roses
Hanson
Harper, Ben
Harrison, George
Harvey, PJ
Henley, Don
Hiatt, John
Hole
Hootie & the Blowfish
Incubus
INXS
Isaak, Chris
Jackson, Michael
Jamiroquai
Jane's Addiction
Jayhawks, The
Jewel
Joel, Billy
John, Elton
Jones, Norah
Jones, Rickie Lee
Jurassic 5

Carpenter, Mary Chapin
Carter, Deana
Cash, Johnny
Chesney, Kenny
Chesnutt, Mark
Dixie Chicks
Earle, Steve
Gill, Vince
Gilmore, Jimmie Dale
Griffith, Nanci
Harris, Emmylou
Hill, Faith
Jackson, Alan
Jones, George
Judd, Wynonna
Keith, Toby
Krauss, Alison
Lonestar
Lovett, Lyle
Lynne, Shelby
Mavericks, The
McBride, Martina
McClinton, Delbert
McEntire, Reba
McGraw, Tim
Messina, Jo Dee
Montgomery, John Michael
Nelson, Willie
Paisley, Brad
Parton, Dolly
Raye, Collin
Rimes, LeAnn
Strait, George
Travis, Randy
Tritt, Travis
Twain, Shania
Welch, Gillian
Williams, Lucinda
Womack, Lee Ann
Yearwood, Trisha
Yoakam, Dwight

ELECTRONICA
Air
Chemical Brothers, The
Daft Punk
Everything but the Girl
Oakenfold, Paul
Prodigy, The
St. Germain
Stereolab

FOLK
Brooke, Jonatha
Brown, Greg
Cockburn, Bruce
Cohen, Leonard
Colvin, Shawn
DiFranco, Ani
Indigo Girls
Prine, John
Vega, Suzanne
Wainwright, Loudon III
Williams, Dar

JAZZ
Benson, George
Brecker, Michael
Connick, Harry Jr.
Davis, Miles
DeJohnette, Jack
Frisell, Bill
Haden, Charlie
Hancock, Herbie
Jarrett, Keith
Kenny G
Krall, Diana
Marsalis, Branford
Marsalis, Wynton
McFerrin, Bobby
McLaughlin, John
Medeski, Martin & Wood
Metheny, Pat
Redman, Joshua
Reeves, Dianne
Rippingtons, The
Ritenour, Lee
Rollins, Sonny
Schuur, Diane
Scofield, John
Shorter, Wayne
Take 6
Wilson, Cassandra
Zawinul, Joe
Zorn, John

LATIN
Anthony, Marc
Cruz, Celia
Estefan, Gloria
Fernández, Vicente
Gabriel, Juan
Grupo Límite
Iglesias, Enrique
Intocable
Lopez, Jennifer
Maná
Martin, Ricky
Miguel, Luis
Secada, Jon
Selena
Tañón, Olga
Temerarios, Los
Thalí
Tigres del Norte, Los
Trevi, Gloria
Vives, Carlos

MUSICAL THEATER
Ahrens and Flaherty
Finn, William
Kander and Ebb
Larson, Jonathan
Lloyd Webber, Andrew
Sondheim, Stephen
Wildhorn, Frank

NEW AGE
Brickman, Jim
Enya
Liebert, Ottmar

McKennitt, Loreena
Winston, George
Yanni

RAP/HIP-HOP
Arrested Development
Ashanti
Beastie Boys
Bone Thugs-N-Harmony
Bounty Killer
Busta Rhymes
Cam'ron
Combs, Sean
Common
Coolio
Cypress Hill
De La Soul
DMX
Dr. Dre
Dru Hill
Elliott, Missy
Eminem
Eve
Fatboy Slim
50 Cent
Gang Starr
Geto Boys, The
Heavy D
Ice Cube
Ja Rule
Jay-Z
Juvenile
KRS-One
Lil' Kim
LL Cool J
LOX, The
Ludacris
M.C. Hammer
Ma$e
Master P
Mystikal
Nas
Nelly
Notorious B.I.G., The
Ol' Dirty Bastard
Organized Noize
OutKast
Public Enemy
Rakim
Roots, The
Run-D.M.C.
Salt-N-Pepa
Scarface
Slick Rick
Smith, Will
Snoop (Doggy) Dogg
Timbaland
Too $hort
Tribe Called Quest, A
2Pac
Vanilla Ice
Wu-Tang Clan

RHYTHM AND BLUES (R&B)
Aaliyah

Index

"Ain't No Woman," 1:330
"Ain't Nobody Here but Us Chickens," 1:362
"Ain't Nuthin' but a G Thang," 1:190, 1:191
"Ain't Too Proud to Beg," 2:670
Air, **1:14–1:15**, 1:168, 2:642
Air Force One (film), 1:264
"The Air That I Breathe," 1:376, 1:397, 2:613
"Airportman," 2:557
Air-traffic controller strike, 1:201
Aja (Steely Dan), 2:608, 2:645
Akai Electric Wind Instrument, 1:92
Akhnaten (Philip Glass), 1:261
Akil, 1:345
Akingbola, Sola, 1:326
Al B. Sure!, 2:617
Alabama, **1:15–1:16**
Aladdin (film), 2:444
Aladdin Sane (David Bowie), 1:84
Alafia, 1:360
Alagia, John, 2:425
Alanis (Alanis Morissette), 2:462
The Alarm, 2:742
Alba, Rebecca de, 2:418
Albarn, Damon, 1:72, 2:497
Albert, Nate, 2:453
Albini, Steve, 1:108, 1:291
Albinism, 1:351
Album of the Year (Faith No More), 1:222
Alcanzar Una Estrella II (film), 2:417
Alcohol. *See also* Drugs
    Eric Clapton, 1:134–1:135
    George Jones, 1:341
    Godsmack, 1:264
    Robert Pollard, 1:278
    Ronald McKernan "Pigpen," 1:269
Alegria, Alegria (book: Caetano Veloso), 2:711
Aletti, Vince, 1:304
Alexakis, Art, 1:214
Alexander, Dave, 2:541
Alexander, Lee, 1:341
Alfa label, 2:575
Alfanno, Omar, 1:23
Alfie (film), 2:580
Algeria, 2:406
Ali, Lorraine, 2:717
Ali (film), 2:625
Alias, Don, 1:173, 1:177
Alice (Tom Waits), 2:718
Alice in Chains, **1:16–1:19,** 1:160
    Pearl Jam compared to, 2:522
    Staind influenced by, 2:643
Aliens (film), 1:302
"Alison," 1:153
"Alive," 2:522
Alive (KISS), 1:363
"Alive Alone," 1:125
"Alive and Kicking," 2:612
Alive in America (Steely Dan), 2:645
"All about Chemistry," 2:602
All about Chemistry (Semisonic), 2:602
All about Love (Steven Curtis Chapman), 1:123
"All Apologies," 2:485, 2:488

"All Around the World," 2:497
"All at Once," 2:562
"All Dressed Up (with Nowhere to Go)," 2:431
All Eyez on Me (Monica), 2:461
All Eyez on Me (Tupac Shakur), 2:695, 2:696
"All for Love," 1:5, 2:651
All for You (Diana Krall), 1:367
All for You (Janet Jackson), 1:322
"All Hands on the Bad One," 2:616
All Hands on the Bad One (Sleater-Kinney), 2:616, 2:617
"All I Could Do Was Cry," 1:326
"All I Have," 1:393
All I Need to Know (Kenny Chesney), 1:128
"All I Really Want to Do," 2:742
"All I Wanna Do," 1:12, 1:161
All I Want (Tim McGraw), 2:434
"All I Want for Christmas Is You," 1:116
"All in a Day," 1:151
"All Mixed Up," 2:677, 2:678
"All My Loving," 1:50
"All Night," 1:177
"All Night Long," 1:213
"All Night Long (All Night)," 2:572
"All or Nothing," 1:127
All Out Records, 2:420
All Rise (Wynton Marsalis), 2:416
All Shook Down (Replacements), 2:722
"All Souls' Night," 2:435
"All Star," 2:619
"All Stripped Down," 2:718
"All That Heaven Will Allow," 2:423
All That I Can (Collin Raye), 2:566
"All That I Can Say," 1:67
All That Jazz: The Best of Ute Lemper, 1:378
All That Matters (Michael Bolton), 1:75
"All That She Wants," 1:4
All That You Can't Leave Behind (U2), 2:699, 2:700, 2:701
"All That's Got to Go," 1:194
All the Best Cowboys Have Chinese Eyes (Pete Townshend), 2:686
"All the Love in the World," 1:151
"All the Small Things," 1:69, 1:70
"All the Things We've Never Done," 2:426
"All the Way," 1:159, 1:356
"All the Way Live (Now)," 1:150
"All the Young Dudes," 1:85
"All Things Must Pass," 1:290
All This Time (Sting), 2:651
All This Useless Beauty (Elvis Costello), 1:154
All Time Greatest Hits (Lynyrd Skynyrd), 1:399
All You Can Eat (k.d. lang), 1:376
Allegria (Gipsy Kings), 1:260
Allen, Geri, 1:284, 1:315
Allen, Jimmy, 2:549
Allen, Rick, 1:176
Allen, Tony, 1:22

"Allentown," 1:336
Alliance, 2:665
"Allison," 2:538
Allison, Luther, 1:375
Allison, Rick, 1:221
Allman, Duane (Howard), 1:19, 1:134, 1:399
Allman, Gregg (Lenoir), 1:19, 1:20, 1:71
The Allman Brothers Band, **1:19–1:21**
    Lynyrd Skynyrd influenced by, 1:399, 1:400
    Melissa Etheridge influenced by, 1:211
Ally McBeal (television program), 1:94, 2:528
Alma Caribena: Caribbean Soul (Gloria Estefan), 1:211
Almodóvar, Pedro, 2:711
Almost Blue (Elvis Costello), 1:153
"Almost Cut My Hair," 2:756
Almost Famous (film), 1:200
"Almost Goodbye," 1:129
Almost Goodbye (Mark Chesnutt), 1:129
"Almost Gothic," 2:646
"Alone," 1:57, 1:288, 1:335
Alone and Acoustic (Buddy Guy and Junior Wells), 1:280
"Alone I Break," 1:366
"Alone in This World," 1:213
Alpha Band, 1:107
"Alpha Beta Parking Lot," 1:114
"Alright," 1:293, 1:322
Altered Beast (Matthew Sweet), 2:661
"Altered Boy," 1:105
Alternative country, 1:89, 2:442, 2:628
Alternative rock, 1:113, 2:493. *See also* Lollapalooza festival
    3 Doors Down, 2:676, 2:677
    Beastie Boys, 1:47–1:49
    Belly, 1:58–1:59
    Blur, 1:72
    the Breeders, 1:93
    Bruce Springsteen at variance with, 2:640
    Cowboy Junkies, 1:156
    the Cure, 1:164
    Days of the New, 1:174
    Depeche Mode, 1:179
    the Flaming Lips, 1:230, 1:231
    Fuel, 1:242, 1:243
    the Goo Goo Dolls, 1:265
    Green Day, 1:275
    Jane's Addiction, 1:327
    Medeski, Martin & Wood, 2:440
    Morrissey, 2:466
    Nine Inch Nails, 2:484
    Nirvana, 2:487
    No Doubt, 2:489
    Pearl Jam, 2:522
    Pixies, 2:538
    Sam Phillips, 2:532
    Sonic Youth, 2:630
    Tool, 2:684
    Weezer, 2:719
    World Party, 2:742